W9-DFH-722

St. Louis Community College

Florissant Valley Library
St. Louis Community College
3400 Pershall Road
Ferguson, MO 63135-1408
314-513-4514

WITHDRAWN

The Enchanted Screen

"Jack Zipes takes us beyond Disney and DreamWorks to the many films that draw on fairy-tale sorcery for their cinematic power. With fierce analytic energy, encyclopedic inclusiveness, and imaginative verve, he enlivens an expansive history that reaches back to Georges Méliès's enchantments and ends with the complex grotesqueries of *Pan's Labyrinth* and *Little Otik*."

—Maria Tatar, Harvard University

"*The Enchanted Screen* is a labor of love and a major work of scholarship, encyclopedic in reach and rich in sustained and detailed thinking. The 'unknown history' of fairy-tale film is lucky to have found such a skilled and dedicated narrator."

—Stephen Benson, University of East Anglia Norwich

The Enchanted Screen: The Unknown History of Fairy-Tale Films offers readers a long overdue, comprehensive look at the rich history of fairy tales and their influence on film, complete with the inclusion of an extensive filmography compiled by the author. With this book, Jack Zipes not only looks at the extensive, illustrious life of fairy tales and cinema, but he also reminds us that, decades before Walt Disney made his mark on the genre, fairy tales were central to the birth of cinema as a medium, as they offered cheap, copyright-free material that could easily engage audiences not only through their familiarity but also through their dazzling special effects.

Since the story of fairy tales on film stretches far beyond Disney, this book discusses a broad range of films silent, English and non-English, animated, live-action, puppetry, woodcut, montage (Jim Henson), cartoon, and digital. Zipes thus gives his readers an in-depth look into the special relationship between fairy tales and cinema, and guides us through this vast array of films by tracing the adaptations of major fairy tales like "Little Red Riding Hood," "Cinderella," "Snow White," "Peter Pan," and many more, from their earliest cinematic appearances to today.

Full of insight into some of our most beloved films and stories, and boldly illustrated with numerous film stills, *The Enchanted Screen* is essential reading for film buffs and fans of the fairy tale alike.

Jack Zipes is Professor Emeritus of German and Comparative Literature at the University of Minnesota. An acclaimed translator and scholar of children's literature and culture, his most recent books include *Relentless Progress: The Reconfiguration of Children's Literature, Fairy Tales, and Storytelling; The Collected Sicilian Folk and Fairy Tales of Giuseppe Pitrè; Why Fairy Tales Stick; Hans Christian Andersen: The Misunderstood Storyteller; Beautiful Angiola;* and *The Robber with the Witch's Head*, all published by Routledge.

The Enchanted Screen

The Unknown History of
Fairy-Tale Films

Jack Zipes

 Routledge
Taylor & Francis Group

NEW YORK AND LONDON

First published 2011
by Routledge
270 Madison Avenue, New York, NY 10016

Simultaneously published in the UK
by Routledge
2 Park Square, Milton Park, Abingdon, Oxon OX14 4RN

Routledge is an imprint of the Taylor & Francis Group, an informa business

© 2011 Taylor & Francis

The right of Jack Zipes to be identified as author of this work has been asserted by him in accordance with sections 77 and 78 of the Copyright, Designs and Patents Act 1988.

Typeset in Minion
by Keystroke, Station Road, Codsall, Wolverhampton

All rights reserved. No part of this book may be reprinted or reproduced or utilized in any form or by any electronic, mechanical, or other means, now known or hereafter invented, including photocopying and recording, or in any information storage or retrieval system, without permission in writing from the publishers.

Trademark Notice: Product or corporate names may be trademarks or registered trademarks, and are used only for identification and explanation without intent to infringe.

Library of Congress Cataloging in Publication Data
Zipes, Jack, 1937–
The enchanted screen : the unknown history of fairy-tale films / Jack Zipes.
p. cm.
Includes bibliographical references.
Includes filmography.
1. Fairy tales in motion pictures. 2. Fairy tales—Film adaptations. I. Title.
PN1995.9.F34Z57 2011
791.43'6559—dc22
2010042961

ISBN13: 978–0–415–99062–2 (hbk)
ISBN13: 978–0–415–99061–5 (pbk)
ISBN13: 978–0–203–92749–6 (ebk)

It is rare to have great scholars who are also great friends, and so I want to dedicate this book to Cristina Bacchilega, Don Haase, and Marina Warner, who have supported my efforts over the years and kept the critical fairy-tale spirit alive in extraordinary ways.

Table of Contents

List of Figures

Preface

Narrative informs all films. The question is, what kind of narrative and how? One of the best-kept secrets in the study of the cinema concerns the neglect of the influential role that the fairy-tale narrative has played in informing most of the films ever made—and it continues to do so. Yet, very few scholars in cinema studies have acknowledged this role.

For some strange reason, film critics and theorists have paid very little attention to the fairy tale and, more specifically, to the fairy-tale film. In fact, the leading encyclopedias and companions of film do not even cite it as a genre or grant it an entry. In America, there are only two major studies of the fairy-tale film, *Folklore/Cinema: Popular Film as Vernacular Culture* (2007), edited by Sharon Sherman and Mikel Koven, and *Fairy Tale Film and Cinematic Folklore* (2010), edited by Pauline Greenhill and Sidney Eve Matrix; one in the UK, *Cinema and the Realms of Enchantment* (1993) by Marina Warner; one in France, *Contes et légendes à l'écran* (2005), edited by Carole Aurouet; and two in Germany, *77 Märchenfilme* (1990), edited by Eberhard Berger and Joachim Giera, and *WunderWelten: Märchen im Film* (2004) by Fabienne Liptay.[1] The American books were produced by folklorists and literary critics, not by experts in film studies. Of course, there are numerous essays and reviews about fairy-tale films, and many, if not too many, books and articles about the Disney fairy-tale films. It is as if the fairy-tale film as genre had been invented by Walt Disney and as if the Disney films were the most significant in the field up through the twenty-first century. Nothing could be further from the truth.

My book is intended not simply to question notions of the Disney predominance in the field of fairy-tale films, but more important, I shall pay attention, long overdue, to the vast international production of fairy-tale films since the 1890s and provide a guide to a fantastic world of unknown films and their connection to one another. To be sure, this book is a critical introduction to fairy-tale films with a distinct ideological bias. It is the way I have always written—to argue critically for alternative views in culture and, in this case, to uncover cinematic gems in the enormous genre of the fairy tale. Without our realizing it, most fairy-tale films have deep roots in oral and literary tales and re-create them with great imaginative and artistic power. They have enriched the genre of the fairy tale and illuminated alternative ways of storytelling and living.

I have divided my book into three sections. The first comprises five chapters concerned with the historical origins of the fairy-tale film, questions of adaptation and appropriation, the rise of the Disney fairy-tale, and the significance of cartoons and feature-length animated films. The second section has seven chapters that explore the vast number of films based on classical fairy tales such as "Snow White," "Little Red Riding Hood," "Bluebeard," "Cinderella," "Hansel and Gretel," "Tom Thumb," "The Pied Piper," "Donkey Skin," "The Juniper Tree," "Beauty and the Beast," "The Frog Prince," and a number of Hans Christian Andersen stories. Filmmakers have themselves become storytellers and have changed and employed all sorts of fairy tales to establish specific and general discourses of films that are in dialogue with one another and with their source texts. It is fascinating to view how various filmmakers from all over the world have appropriated and re-created popular tales to address private and public concerns. These "unreal" films frequently touch us in real profound ways, often much more than so-called "realistic" films. At the same time many also challenge conventional narrative forms of fairy tales. At least, the very best do. To be precise, within the field of filmic fairy-tale discourse there are major conflicts concerning how a fairy tale should be narrated and filmed and what the purpose of a fairy tale should be. In the third section there are three chapters: one that deals with such classical fairy-tale novels as *The Adventures of Alice in Wonderland*, *The Wonderful Wizard of Oz*, *The Adventures of Pinocchio*, and *Peter Pan and Wendy*; a second that introduces some unusual fairy-tale films from Russia, Czechoslovakia, and the former East Germany that have rarely been shown in the West; and a third that explores the role of the child as moral arbiter in some of the most innovative fairy-tale films of the past twenty years.

Originally, when I began this project about four years ago, I intended to include every significant fairy-tale film in the world. Little did I realize how prolific filmmakers have been in the cultural field of fairy-tale films, and I soon decided that I had to limit myself and focus mainly on the works produced by European and North American filmmakers. Otherwise, I might never have finished a project that was daunting in the first place. Wherever possible, however, I have included discussions of notable fairy-tale films from Japan, South Korea, Mexico, Australia, New Zealand, Hong Kong, and Singapore. I reluctantly abandoned my intention to write about the enormous amount of films based on tales from *The Thousand and One Nights*. They deserve a book-length study. Here and there I allude to some adaptations of stories from the *Nights* as when I discuss Lotte Reiniger's superb animated film, *The Adventures of Prince Achmed*. Unfortunately, I have not examined some works by several highly creative directors such as Ernst Lubitsch, Michael Powell, Emeric Pressburger, Terry Gilliam, Tim Burton, and some others. To make up for my "failure" to cover all the directors and films that deserve to be treated in my study, I have created a very large filmography that still has gaps but should be a helpful guide to those readers who want to explore the vast field of fairy-tale films.

Since any study of fairy-tale films necessitates references to the oral and literary traditions, I have stolen and included passages from some of my other books to provide historical background for the films. I have also fully revised and inserted a chapter on films derived from Hans Christian Andersen's tales that appeared in my book *Hans Christian Andersen: The Misunderstood Storyteller*. It is now much longer and contains discussions of many new films, one by the Danish filmmaker Jannik Hastrup, which I consider to be one of the greatest neglected animated films of the twentieth century. It was a surprise discovery for me.

Indeed, I hope there will be many surprises for readers of this book, and I wish I could spend a year or three as curator of a gigantic fairy-tale film festival that would include all the superb neglected films that I have discovered. They are truly inspiring and are informed by thousands of years of comforting and disturbing wisdom. If only I had three wishes . . .

Acknowledgements

The research for this book was made possible in part by a Professional Grant for Retirees from the Graduate School of the University of Minnesota for which I am most thankful. I am also grateful for the generous assistance of Kathleen Dickson and Steve Tollervey at the British Film Institute in London. Cristina Bacchilega, Marina Balina, Elliott Colla, Don Haase, Norman Klein and Rembert Heuser all took time from their own important work, read chapters of the book, or provided me with invaluable criticism and advice. Rob Craig, founder of Kindermatinee, an extraordinary website, was most helpful from the beginning until the end of my project. Erika Beckerman and David Kaplan, two wonderful experimental filmmakers, kindly shared their films and ideas with me. Charlotte Melin spurred me to apply for an important grant. The work on this book seemed at times almost like an eternal fairy-tale adventure and led to serendipitous encounters with numerous well-informed people who enabled me to discover important films and books. In particular, I want to thank Marina Warner, Pauline Greenhill, Jacqui Weeks, Christine Goelz, Brigitte Beumers, Deb Girdwood, and Isabelle Harder. Due to its size and complexity, the production of *The Enchanted Screen* demanded a great deal of care and attention to detail. I was very fortunate to have the great collaboration of Matt Byrnie, Stan Spring, and Carolann Madden at Routledge in New York, and Siân Findlay and Alice Stoakley in England. Matt helped me develop the project, encouraged me throughout the process, and was most understanding despite delays and changes in plans. Stan and Carolann prepared the manuscript, sorted the photographs, and contributed to the cover design for the book. Their assistance was indispensable. Siân dealt with all aspects of the final production of the book in a sovereign manner and magnanimously solved numerous problems. Alice is the most impeccable copy-editor with whom I have ever worked—perceptive, considerate, and scrupulous. Not only did she catch my errors, but she also grasped the full gist of the book.

As usual, my wife, Carol Dines, showed extraordinary patience when I went into other worlds during the last four years, and my amanuensis Vincenzo kept me grounded when I needed him most.

Prologue

At their best, fairy tales constitute the most profound articulation of the human struggle to form and maintain a civilizing process. They depict metaphorically the opportunities for human adaptation to our environment and reflect the conflicts that arise when we fail to establish civilizing codes commensurate with the self-interests of large groups within the human population. The more we give in to base instincts—base in the sense of basic and depraved—the more criminal and destructive we become. The more we learn to relate to other groups of people and realize that their survival and the fulfillment of their interests is related to ours, the more we might construct social codes that guarantee humane relationships. Fairy tales are uncanny because they tell us what we need, and they unsettle us by showing what we lack and how we might compensate for lack.

Fairy tales hint of happiness. This hint, what the German philosopher of hope, Ernst Bloch, has called the anticipatory illumination, has constituted their utopian appeal that has a strong moral component to it. We do not know happiness, but we instinctively know and feel that it can be created and perhaps even defined. Fairy tales map out possible ways to attain happiness, to expose and resolve moral conflicts that have deep roots in our species. The effectiveness of fairy tales and other forms of fantastic literature depends on the innovative manner in which we make the information of the tales relevant for the listeners and receivers of the tales. As our environment changes and evolves, so we change the media or modes of the tales to enable us to adapt to new conditions and shape instincts that were not necessarily generated for the world that we have created out of nature. This is perhaps one of the lessons that the best of fairy tales teach us: we are all misfit for the world, and yet somehow we must all fit together.

Fairy tales have an extraordinary, uncanny power over us, and the French critic Georges Jean locates this power on the conscious level in the way all good fairy tales aesthetically structure and use fantastic and miraculous elements to prepare us for our everyday life.[2] Magic is used paradoxically not to deceive us but to enlighten us. On an unconscious level, Jean believes that the most startling fairy tales bring together subjective and assimilatory impulses with objective intimations of a social setting that intrigue readers and allow for different interpretations according to one's ideology and belief.[3] Ultimately, Jean argues that the fantastic power of fairy tales consists in the uncanny way they provide a conduit into social reality. Yet, given the proscription of fairy-tale discourse within a historically prescribed civilizing process, a more careful distinction must be made between regressive and progressive aspects of the power of fairy tales in general to understand the liberating potential of contemporary tales for all human beings. Sigmund Freud's concept of the "uncanny" and Ernst Bloch's concept of "home" can enable us to grasp the constitutive elements of the liberating impulse behind the fantastic and uncanny projections in fairy tales, whether they be classical or experimental.

In his essay on the uncanny, Freud remarks that the word *heimlich* means that which is familiar and agreeable and also that which is concealed and kept out of sight, and he concludes that *heimlich* is a word the meaning of which develops in the direction of ambivalence, until it finally coincides with its opposite, *unheimlich* or uncanny, literally "unlike home," something unfamiliar.[4] Through a close study of E. T. A. Hoffmann's fairy tale "The Sandman," Freud argues that the uncanny or unfamiliar (*unheimlich*) brings us in closer touch with the familiar (*heimlich*) because it touches on emotional disturbances and returns us to repressed phases in our evolution:

> If psychoanalytic theory is correct in maintaining that every effect belonging to an emotional impulse, whatever its kind, is transformed, if it is repressed, into anxiety, then among instances of frightening things there must be one class in which the frightening element can be shown to be something repressed which *recurs*. This class of frightening things would then constitute the uncanny; and it must be a matter of indifference whether what is uncanny was itself originally frightening or whether it carried some *other* affect. In the second place, if this is indeed the secret nature of the uncanny, we can understand why linguistic usage has extended *das Heimliche* ("homely") into its opposite, *das Unheimliche;* for this uncanny is in reality nothing new or alien but something which is familiar and old-established in the mind and which has become alienated from it only through the process of repression. This reference to the factor of repression enables us, furthermore, to understand Schelling's definition of the uncanny as something which ought to have remained hidden but has come to light.[5]

Freud insists that one must be extremely careful in using the category of the uncanny since not everything that recalls repressed desires and surmounted modes of thinking belongs to the prehistory of the individual and humanity and can be considered uncanny. In particular, Freud mentions fairy tales as excluding the uncanny:

> In fairy tales, for instance, the world of reality is left behind from the very start, and the animistic system of beliefs is frankly accepted and adopted. Wish-fulfillments, secret powers, omnipotence of thoughts, animation of inanimate objects, all the elements so common in fairy stories, can exert no uncanny influence here; for, as we have learnt, that feeling cannot arise unless there is a conflict of judgment as to whether things which have been "surmounted" and are regarded as incredible may not, after all, be possible; and this problem is eliminated from the outset by the postulates of the world of fairy tales.[6]

Although it is true that the uncanny becomes the familiar and the norm in the fairy tale because the narrative perspective accepts it so totally, there is still room for another kind of uncanny experience within the postulates and constructs of the fairy tale. That is, Freud's argument must be qualified regarding the narrative machinations of the fairy tale. However, I do not want to concern myself with this point at the moment but would simply like to suggest that the uncanny plays a significant role in the act of reading, hearing, or viewing a fairy tale. Using and modifying Freud's category of the uncanny, I want to argue that the very act of reading, hearing, and viewing a fairy tale is an uncanny experience in that it separates the reader from the restrictions of reality from the onset and makes the repressed unfamiliar familiar once again. Bruno Bettelheim has noted that the fairy tale estranges the child from the real world and allows him or her to deal with deep-rooted psychological problems and anxiety-provoking incidents to achieve autonomy.[7] Whether this is true or not, that is, whether a fairy tale can actually provide the means for coping with ego disturbance, as Bettelheim argues,[8] remains to be seen. It is true, however, that once we begin reading, hearing, or viewing a fairy tale, there is estrangement or separation from a familiar world inducing an uncanny feeling which can be both frightening and comforting.

Actually the complete reversal of the real world has already taken place before we begin experiencing a fairy tale on the part of the storyteller, be it a writer or filmmaker. The storyteller invites the listener/reader/viewer to repeat this uncanny experience. The active process of reading, hearing, and viewing involves dislocating the reader/listener/viewer from his/her familiar setting and then identifying with the dislocated protagonist so that a quest for the *Heimische* or real home can begin. The fairy tale ignites a double quest for home: one occurs in the recipient's mind and is psychological and difficult to interpret, since the reception of an individual tale varies according to the background and experience of the recipient. The second occurs within the tale itself and indicates a socialization process and acquisition of values for participation in a society where the protagonist has more power of determination. This second quest for home can be *regressive* or *progressive* depending on the narrator's stance vis-à-vis society. In both quests the notion of home or *Heimat*, which is closely related etymologically to *heimlich* and *unheimlich*, retains a powerful progressive attraction for readers of fairy tales. While the uncanny setting and motifs of the fairy tale already open us up to the recurrence of primal experiences, we can move forward at the same time because it opens us up to what Freud calls "unfulfilled but possible futures to which we still like to cling in fantasy, all the strivings of the ego which adverse external circumstances have crushed, and all our suppressed acts of volition which nourish in us the illusion of Free Will."[9]

Obviously, Freud would not condone clinging to our fantasies in reality. Yet Bloch would argue that some are important to cultivate and defend since they represent our radical or revolutionary urge to restructure society so that we can finally achieve home. Dreaming which stands still bodes no good:

> But if it becomes a dreaming ahead, then its cause appears quite differently and excitingly alive. The dim and weakening features, which may be characteristic of mere yearning, disappear; and then yearning can show what it really is able to accomplish. It is the way of the world to counsel men to adjust to the world's pressures, and they have learned this lesson; only their wishes and dreams will not hearken to it. In this respect virtually all human beings are futuristic; they transcend their past life, and to the degree that they are satisfied, they think they deserve a better life (even though this may be pictured in a banal and egotistic way), and regard the inadequacy of their lot as a barrier, and not just as the way of the world.
>
> To this extent, the most private and ignorant wishful thinking is to be preferred to any mindless goose-stepping; for wishful thinking is capable of revolutionary awareness, and can enter the chariot of history without necessarily abandoning in the process the good content of dreams.[10]

What Bloch means by the good content of dreams is often the projected fantasy and action of fairy tales with a forward and liberating look: human beings in an upright posture who strive for an autonomous existence and non-alienating setting which allow for democratic cooperation and humane consideration. Real history which involves independent human self-determination cannot begin as long as there is exploitation and enslavement of humans by other humans. The active struggle against unjust and barbaric conditions in the world leads to home, or utopia, a place nobody has known but which represents humankind coming into its own:

> *The true genesis is not at the beginning, but at the end,* and it starts to begin only when society and existence become radical: that is, comprehend their own roots. But the root of history is the working, creating man, who rebuilds and transforms the given circumstances of the

world. Once man has comprehended himself and has established his own domain in real democracy, without depersonalization and alienation, something arises in the world which all men have glimpsed in childhood: a place and a state in which no one has yet been. And the name of this something is home or homeland.[11]

Philosophically speaking, then, the real return home or recurrence of the uncanny is a move forward to what has been repressed and never fulfilled. The narrative pattern in most fairy tales involves the reconstitution of home on a new plane, and this accounts for the power of its appeal to both children and adults.

In Bloch's two major essays on fairy tales, "Das Märchen geht selber in Zeit" ("The Fairy Tale Moves on its Own in Time") and "Bessere Luftschlösser in Jahrmarkt und Zirkus, in Märchen und Kolportage" ("Better Castles in the Air in Fair and Circus, in the Fairy Tale and Popular Books"),[12] Bloch is concerned with the manner in which the hero and the aesthetic constructs of the tale illuminate the way to overcome oppression. He focuses on the way the underdog, the small person, uses his or her wits not only to survive but to live a better life. Bloch insists that there is good reason for the timelessness of traditional fairy tales,

> Not only does the fairy tale remain as fresh as longing and love, but the demonically evil, which is abundant in the fairy tale, is still seen at work here in the present, and the happiness of "once upon a time," which is even more abundant, still affects our visions of the future.[13]

It is not only the timeless aspect of traditional fairy tales that interests Bloch, but also the way they are modernized, mediated by film, and appeal to all classes and age groups in society. Instead of demeaning popular culture and common appeal, Bloch endeavors to explore the adventure novels, modern romances, comics, circuses, country fairs, and the like. He refuses to make simplistic qualitative judgments of high and low art forms, rather he seeks to grasp the driving utopian impulse in the production and reception of artworks for mass audiences. Time and again he focuses on fairy tales as indications of paths to be taken in reality.

> What is significant about such kinds of "modern fairy tales" is that it is reason itself which leads to the wish projections of the old fairy tale and serves them. Again what proves itself is a harmony with courage and cunning, as that earliest kind of enlightenment which already characterizes "Hansel and Gretel": consider yourself as born free and entitled to be totally happy, dare to make use of your power of reasoning, look upon the outcome of things as friendly. These are the genuine maxims of fairy tales, and fortunately for us they not only appear in the past but in the now.[14]

Bloch and Freud set the general parameters for helping us understand how our longing for home, which is discomforting *and* comforting, draws us to folk and fairy tales, whether they be told, printed, or filmed. As we shall see, fairy-tale films continue to provide clues and reveal why we are attracted to the uncanny. As part of the culture industry, fairy-tale films can both obfuscate and illuminate the paths we must take to learn from one another and to learn what Bloch calls our ultimate goal—to walk with an upright posture.

I

1

Filmic Adaptation and Appropriation of the Fairy Tale

So we need to find a way of discussing adaptation and appropriation that will register influence but not assume it is a stranglehold, that will see possibility not prescription authored by what comes before, authored by our inheritance, both literary and genetic. The art of adaptation and appropriation has a potent influence and shaping effect in its own right. . . . No appropriation can be achieved without impacting upon and altering in some way the text which inspired the adaptation. So influential, indeed, have some appropriations become that in many instances they now define our first experiences or encounters with their precursor work of art.

Julie Sanders, *Adaptation and Appropriation*[15]

I don't like adaptations. I think it's very bad to make an adaptation. Perhaps, what I make is very bad, but I don't make adaptations. . . . On the other hand I have my own stories to tell. I am inspired by those roughly told anonymous tales, which are often poorly composed. I vamp the tales of folklore, and I make out of them what I want. I utilize them like ore from a mine, and I try to make jewels out of them. But I don't at all respect the ore of the miners. I think those people told tales in their time. Today, it's me who's the storyteller, and I do what I want with the heritage. I cite whatever has inspired me, but they are my tales. They are my guts, my heart, and all the rest.

Michel Ocelot, Interview with Christine Gudin[16]

Although numerous books have been written about the filmic adaptation of literary works, mainly novels and plays, the term adaptation in its strict sense does not fully capture how filmmakers have used and re-created fairy tales and folk tales for the cinema. As Robert Stam, one of the foremost scholars of film studies, remarks,

In the case of filmic adaptations of novels, to sum up what has been argued thus far, source-novel hypotexts are transformed by a complex series of operations: selection, amplification, concretization, actualization, critique, extrapolation, popularization, reaccentuation, trans-culturalization. The source novel, in this sense, can be seen as a situated utterance, produced in one medium and in one historical and social context, and later transformed into another, equally situated utterance produced in a different context and relayed through a different medium. The source text forms a dense informational network, a series of verbal cues which the adapting film text can then selectively take up, amplify, ignore, subvert or transform.[17]

Despite numerous adaptations of source fairy-tale texts, the majority of filmmakers have not relied upon a single text as hypotext to adapt a fairy tale. The hypotext is generally considered the pre-existing text upon which a film or hypertext is based. But it is difficult to find conclusive evidence that filmmakers studiously labor over a particular fairy-tale text, interpret it, and create a storyboard or a screenplay on which they base their films. On the other hand, it is clear that the filmmakers know some variant or variants of a fairy tale either after having re-read it, heard it, seen it in a book, viewed it as a film, or having recalled it from their childhood memories. Sometimes filmmakers do reflect upon a single text, but when a storyboard or screenplay for the film is conceived and created, other artists who work on the film will contribute their interpretations, perhaps based on their other readings, hearings, viewings, or memories, and thus, the story keeps changing because the hypotext is more a notion than anything else, somewhat like a meme carried about in our brains. Thus, as hypotext, the fairy tale is also a flexible or fluid text, or it consists of several variants of a tale type.

Whatever the case may be, there is no authoritative hypotext or *Urtext* upon which a filmmaker does or can rely, and this is because literary fairy tales stem from oral folk tales and have a long history of variation and dissemination in an oral tradition up through the present. Many literary fairy tales are already adaptations because they are translations that comprise some kind of adaptation in language and references to different cultural contexts. We need only think of Perrault's "French" tales, the Grimms' "German" tales, and Andersen's "Danish" tales from different centuries, not to mention the "Italian" tales of Straparola and Basile. They stem largely from tales told in dialect, are not purely French, German, Danish, or Italian, and have been adapted for small educated audiences. Numerous classic fairy tales and popular folk tales from the oral tradition have been translated, illustrated, and spread in diverse ways, but when published, they become so-called fixed texts—but only seemingly. This is also true of the American and British printed texts of fairy tales. The roots of most classical fairy tales in English begin with the European oral tradition of storytelling that led to the formation of the literary genre in the West.

The fairy tale as genre encompasses not only literary texts, but also operas, songs, poems, advertisements, cartoons, comic strips, graphic novels, comic books, ballets, dramas, radio plays, and hypertexts on television and the Internet and continues to be influenced by diverse forms of the oral tradition. In the case of classical fairy tales such as "Little Red Riding Hood," "Sleeping Beauty," or "Cinderella," the filmmaker may base his or her adaptation on a text by Charles Perrault, or the Brothers Grimm, or on a fusion of their texts. The screenplay may also simply derive from the memory of a tale. The filmic adaptation of a fairy tale follows no clear-cut rules except those long established by storytellers who appropriated what they heard and told stories to suit themselves and their listeners. And their styles and narrative representations were diverse *and* particular.

What then is a fairy-tale film if it isn't strictly speaking an adaptation of a particular literary text? To begin with, we must recognize that there are various types of fairy-tale films that can be categorized according to the cinematic techniques used: a silent black-and-white film shot with a fixed camera; the drawings, cells, puppets of animated films; the acting of live-action films; the mixed media of live-action/animated films; clay and wooden puppet films; paper-cut animated films; faux-historical films; documentary films of fairy-tale authors; and all kinds of digital films.

The technologies determine the extent to which a filmmaker can elaborate and expand upon a particular fairy tale or fairy-tale motifs and themes. The films are often based on an oral version, a literary text of a well-known tale, and another fairy-tale film and adapted to accentuate the ideas of the filmmaker and his or her collaborators. The fairy-tale source can also be an original screenplay or text conceived by writers in collaboration with the filmmaker and other artists. The fairy-tale film can be a remake of another fairy-tale film or contain intertextual references to other films. Some other distinctions can be made with regard to adaptation if there is a definite or explicit source of some kind: the fairy tale can be transformed into a musical as is the case with most Disney fairy-tale films beginning with *Snow White* in 1937, or it can be adapted from a Broadway musical such as James Lapine's and Stephen Sondheim's *Into the Woods* (1991), a collage of fairy tales, formed to produce a singular tragic–comic tale.There are also filmic adaptations of performances of ballets such as Tchaikovsky's *Sleeping Beauty* or *The Nutcracker* or of fairy-tale operas such as Rossini's *Cenerentola* or Dvořák's *Russalka*. Sometimes Humperdinck's music for his opera *Hansel and Gretel*, based on a religious libretto of the Grimms' text written by Humperdinck's sister, is used as background music for a modern adaptation of the text as in the case of the Canon production, *Hansel and Gretel*, and sometimes the opera is performed and filmed. One fairy tale may serve as the frame for others, as is the case with the Russian Boris Rytsarev's adaptation of Hans Christian Andersen's *The Princess on the Pea* (1976), which frames three other Andersen tales. There are also numerous adaptations of fairy-tale novels such as A. S. Byatt's *Possession* or Gregory Maguire's *The Confessions of an Ugly Stepsister*. TV cinematic productions have abounded such as the popular series *Beauty and the Beast*, which takes place in New York City during the 1980s, or Jim Henson's remarkable montage/collage films in the series titled *The Storyteller*; animated cartoons for television such as The Muppets fairy tales or the fractured fairy tales of Rocky and Bullwinkle maintain the early cinematic cartoon tradition of the 1930s, while other animated series such as *The Simpsons* and *Family Guy* often contain references to fairy tales or create pastiches and parodies. Some fairy-tale films such as Shelley Duvall's Faerie Tale Theatre productions or Tom Davenport's Appalachian adaptations of the Grimms' tales have been made as videocassettes and DVDs for schools and private showings in homes; short films, animation and live-action, have been produced for YouTube on the Internet or for Atom films.

A fairy-tale film is any kind of cinematic representation recorded on film, on videotape, or in digital form that employs motifs, characters, and plots generally found in the oral and literary genre of the fairy tale, to re-create a known tale or to create and realize cinematically an original screenplay with recognizable features of a fairy tale. Like any artistic genre that began in the oral tradition, the fairy tale has evolved from a print genre in constant commerce with oral tales and other art and commercial forms of fairy tales to be embraced by the technology of film. The fairy tale as genre is not "pure" and does not adhere to set rules and conventions. There is nothing essential about it. However, there are distinctive qualities, motifs, traits, aspects, topoi, plots, characters, and features that constitute its generic type either as oral narrative, literary text, or film. As Jessica Tiffin notes in her significant book, *Marvelous Geometry: Narrative and Metafiction in Modern Fairy Tale*,

> By identifying fairy tale by texture, I am thus invoking a range of characteristics which rely heavily on clean lines, deliberate patterning and a geometry of structure and motif, but also include style, voice, and some aspects of content and mimetic approach. This attribute of texture, rather than language or motif, renders a fairy tale intrinsically familiar and identifiable even through literary manipulation, and it is precisely this quality of identifiability which allows the form to provide such a rich ground for metafictional play.[18]

While maintaining these distinct characteristics, the fairy tale also borrows from other genres and incorporates motifs and techniques from other art forms to adapt to cultural expectations and changing conditions in the film industry. The fairy-tale film is only one example of how the genre of the fairy tale has adapted to technological changes of the twentieth and twenty-first centuries.

As human beings have sought to adapt to changing environments over the centuries, they have adapted their tales. To understand what adaptation means in a broader sense, we must think of other creative transformative processes that we employ such as appropriation, expropriation, translation, concretization, amplification, extrapolation, and reaccentuation.[19] Once again Stam is helpful in clarifying the many techniques of transformation and adaptation when he discusses the filmic adaptation of a novel:

> The filmic adaptation of a novel performs these transformations according to the protocols of a distinct medium, absorbing and altering the available genres and the intertexts through the grids of ambient discourses and ideologies, and as mediated by a series of filters: studio style, ideological fashion, political and economic constraints, *auteurist* predilections, charismatic stars, cultural values, and so forth. An adaptation consists in an interesting reading of a novel and the circumstantially shaped "writing" of a film. The filmic hypertext, in this sense, is transformational almost in the Chomskian sense of a "generative grammar" of adaptation, with the difference that these cross-media operations are infinitely more unpredictable and multifarious than they would be were it a matter of "natural language." Adaptations redistribute energies and intensities, provoke flows and displacements; the linguistic energy of literary writing turns into the audio-visual-kinetic-performative energy of the adaptation in an amorous exchange of textual fluids.[20]

A filmic adaptation in Stam's sense is the artistic and technical mode employed by the filmmaker to change and re-create a known or popular text. Whatever mode used, the adaptation always involves an expropriation and an appropriation, whether we are discussing novels or fairy tales. Both words, expropriation and appropriation, stem from the medieval Latin adjectives *propre* or *proper* indicating something that is peculiar, particular, belonging to, and appropriate. The nouns "property" and "propriety" are closely connected to notions of expropriation (to take something away) and appropriation (to make something foreign one's own). An oral folk tale, specifically a wonder tale, filled with magical and miraculous transformation, was at one time the "property" of a teller who told a proper tale to suit an appropriate occasion. It was also "proper" to his/her circumstances— cultural, social, pedagogical and belonged with the storyteller. This is still the case today, but it is more than likely that the oral tale, if it becomes popular, will be expropriated and appropriated by others to become a literary fairy tale. Writing and print culture have altered the effervescent "pristine" orality in a major way, and new media technologies have also transformed print culture in radical ways so that it is almost impossible today to hear or read a tale without already having viewed and heard it through the media of television, cinema, and the Internet. As Walter Ong has pointed out in his now "classical" study, *Orality and Literacy: The Technologizing of the Word,*

> Writing . . . is a particularly pre-emptive and imperialist activity that tends to assimilate other things to itself even without the aid of etymologies. Though words are grounded in oral speech, writing tyrannically locks them into a visual field forever. . . . This is to say that a literate person cannot fully recover a sense of what the word is to purely oral people. In view of this pre-emptiveness of literacy, it appears quite impossible to use the term "literature" to include oral tradition and performance without subtly but irremediably reducing these somehow to variants of writing.[21]

In view of the "pre-emptive and imperialist activity" of writing, it is necessary to emphasize the oral roots of fairy tales and their memetic power that continues to leave traces on our minds. The process of adapting a fairy tale for the screen has a long, profound, and complicated history that involves taking a tale out of its original socio-cultural context, literally to dispossess the owners of the tale and then to put one's own mark on it: expropriate to appropriate. For instance, an oral tale that originally had no title, as was the case with "Little Red Riding Hood," was probably a tale told in a French or Italian dialect in the seventeenth century by women about a girl who must demonstrate her prowess when confronted by a werewolf or wolf so that she can become initiated into a sewing society. In 1697, Charles Perrault, who may have heard some version of this oral tale from a wet nurse or governess, wrote this tale down in cultivated French, gave it a title, "Le Petit Chaperon Rouge," and placed an emphasis on the naiveté or stupidity of a girl who is violated by a wolf and blamed for her own violation. This tale circulated in print and was constantly reprinted and translated into numerous different languages. It also continued to be disseminated in some form in the oral tradition or re-entered the oral tradition in a variant of Perrault's text, but always in different forms. Once expropriated it was freed to become appropriated in innumerable unimaginable ways up through the present. In his ironic play, *The Romance of Little Red Riding Hood* (1862), Alphonse Daudet has poor Red Riding Hood sum up her treatment, that is, sum up the process of expropriation/appropriation of the tale, in a most amusing and appropriate manner when she addresses the pompous teacher Polonius:

> I want you to know, monsieur, that I've been devoured an infinite number of times, and each time it is my fault. There you have it! Four thousand years that I've had the same accident, four thousand years that I am revived, four thousand years, by an incredible fatality, I'm going to put myself inevitably in the paws of the wolf. What do you want? I always die very young, and when I return to the world, I only have a vague memory of my previous existences, very vague. . . . Oh, how interesting it would be to write and peruse that *Story of Red Riding Hood in all the centuries!* Monsieur Perrault has sketched but only one chapter. How fortunate is he who will write the others.[22]

Indeed, as I shall demonstrate in the chapter on "Little Red Riding Hood," many writers and artists have depicted Red Riding Hood's destiny since 1697 to form a fairy-tale discourse about this singular story up through the present and throughout the world. While violence may be done to the oral or literary source of a fairy tale when it is expropriated and written down or filmed in a different manner—folklorists have often talked about the contamination of a tale, film critics about fidelity to the text—the tale is preserved in some manner and in many cases enriched. If the hypotext or source text is oral, it has been preserved and can become part of a documented cultural heritage, but it is done, to be sure, according to the norms of the written language in different socio-cultural contexts. Even if it has been somewhat "violated," it has nevertheless been preserved as history. If the hypotext is a piece of writing by a particular author, it has often been transformed to address concerns of a different audience in a different socio-cultural context. Of course, it can be banalized and distorted, depending on the emphasis of the author/filmmaker who appropriates the hypotext.

Appropriation always involves translation of some kind. The appropriator or adapter of a source or hypotext must first interpret and translate the meaning of a story that is not of his or her own making. Adaptation always involves remaking. Once a fairy tale has been appropriated, the appropriated text necessitates translation, that is, the new hypotext will be transmitted to an audience with a new accentuation that addresses audience expectations. Fidelity to a so-called original text or hypotext is irrelevant because, first, it is impossible to be true to any source or text and, second, the entire purpose of adaptation is to renew, re-create, and re-present a commonly shared tale from one's own perspective. Every filmic adaptation of a fairy tale is a re-creation to be judged on its own merits and, of course, within the context of a critical standards and position-taking by artists, critics, and audiences in a given culture and period.

However, translation also brings with it a certain ethical responsibility to the source, hypotext, and audience. If a filmmaker claims or owns up to the fact that he or she is adapting a story that does *not* belong to him or her, he or she is obliged, in my opinion, to treat the tale as he or she would like to be treated, that is, interpreted and understood on some level. Even if a filmmaker is not adapting a fairy-tale source text or any hypotext, he is always translating something other to an implied audience, and he is translating himself at the same time.

In his insightful essay, "On Translating a Person," Adam Phillips, the innovative British psychoanalyst, makes the interesting comment that "the translator uses the text to reveal something about himself; but it depends upon there being something there to be faithful to. The comfort of the text is that it is there, and that it is as it is. The words themselves don't change around."[23] Obviously, there are many different questions one can ask about the translator to determine what his or her relationship is to the text, whether the text be fictitious, historical, religious, and so on. As I have already indicated in the case of the fairy tale, the text can actually be the spoken word, a folk tale, or it might be a literary tale written down a few hundred years ago or a few years ago. The first question to ask is why a filmmaker as translator chooses to translate a particular tale or collection of tales. Why does a teller of fairy tales replicate or re-create a tale? Why does a filmmaker feel impelled to create his or her fairy-tale film based on all sorts of tales that he or she has read or viewed? For the love of art? For money? To make the tale more available to audiences unfamiliar with the tale? Out of personal desire because the tale appeals to the translator and says something relevant about him or her that the translator wants to communicate to other people? Does the translator ever know his or her real motive? Can we? Is there an unconscious element of appeal that needs exploring and arises through translation? For instance, in the case of the Brothers Grimm, they began collecting the tales to help the poet Clemens Brentano, who wanted to produce a collection of folk tales after he had published a book of folk songs with his friend Achim von Arnim. Only after they began collecting and translating the tales into high German, for they were generally spoken in a regional dialect, and only after Brentano lost interest in the project did they realize the historical value of the tales that said something about themselves and their attachment to their family, friends, and German culture.

Translation is always concerned with our conscious and unconscious ties to the past and the present. However, the past is problematical because we both need it and need to transcend it. We must recognize its anachronistic features that may weigh upon us, and we must work through them and their ramifications to start anew. The present has no essential meaning without our conscious reflection and knowledge of the past. Without dealing with the past we cannot move forward. Adam Phillips cites both Karl Marx and Sigmund Freud, who believed that the past weighs like a nightmare on the minds of the living.

> Clearly the dead are never quite dead enough, but a nightmare, of course, wakes the sleeper up. Freud would say, it wakes the dreamer up with something from the past, the representation of which—the language of which—the dreamer cannot bear. He needs to return to so-called reality in order not to be overwhelmed himself; in order not to die. For Freud, in a sense, as for Marx, the past is both a nightmare from which we must awaken, but it is also our only resource. It is literally where we get our language from, where we learn it. To learn a language is to learn a history, and to acquire a medium from the past in which to reconstruct the past.[24]

Indeed, dreams need translation just as the past needs it. Translation can be an awakening and a means to make use of the past for a better life. The translator is compelled to step back into the past and step away from it. He or she appropriates a past text or tale of times past so it can be presented anew and readers can have a new look at what has occurred. In discussing what makes for a relevant translation, the French philosopher Jacques Derrida notes that a key to understanding the process of translation is the Hegelian notion of sublation or *Aufhebung*, which he translates in French as *relève*.

> Without plunging us deeply into the issues, I must at least recall that the movement of *Aufhebung*, the process of establishing relevance, is always in Hegel a dialectical movement of interiorization, interiorizing memory (*Erinnerung*) and sublimating spiritualization. It is also translation[25] . . . What the translation with the word "relevant" also demonstrates, in an exemplary fashion, is that every translation should be relevant by vocation. It would thus guarantee the survival of the body of the original survival in the double sense that Benjamin gives it in "The Task of the Translator," *fortleben* and *überleben*: prolonged life, continuous life, *living on*, but also life after death.[26]

Understanding a relevant translation as sublation or *Aufhebung* is crucial if we are to grasp how the process of translation works and what distinguishes a translation that brings about a relative understanding between source text and implied reader and a translation that prevents any understanding whatsoever and is self-serving. A relevant translation can provide a different perspective on history and on one's relationship to it in the present because it both negates certain anachronistic aspects of the source text and maintains usable aspects while forming a synthetic work which will endure as long as people in a particular culture need it. In some respects, translation is connected to evolution: translating is making something fit, and we re-translate something when older translations no longer fit.

Making a film fit a fairy tale and fit for audiences is a task that no filmmaker as translator can fulfill. This is the conclusion that Paul Ricoeur reaches in his short book, *On Translation*. Ricoeur claims that the translator can only find happiness when he "acknowledges and assumes the irreducibility of the pair, the peculiar and the foreign."[27]

Once the translator recognizes that there will always be a loss because he cannot capture the absolute meaning of a foreign text but can only provide an equivalence without adequacy, he can take pleasure in what Ricoeur calls "linguistic hospitality," "where the pleasure of dwelling in the other's language is balanced by the pleasure of receiving the foreign word at home, in one's own welcoming house."[28] By providing linguistic hospitality, the translator confirms the unique identity of the foreign text while showing signs of wanting to come to terms with the fact that every translation is unfinished, just as every adaptation is unfinished and must be left to others to continue to find mutual understanding. In his introduction to Ricoeur's work, Richard Kearney writes,

> it is only when we translate the wounds of strangers into our own language that healing and reconciliation can take place. This is ultimately what Ricoeur intends when he describes the ethics of translation as an interlinguistic hospitality. The world is made up of a plurality of human beings, cultures, tongues. Humanity exists in the plural mode. Which means that any legitimate form of universality must always—if the hermeneutic model of translation is observed—find its equivalent plurality. The creative tension between the universal and the plural ensures that the task of translation is an endless one, a work of tireless memory and mourning, of appropriation and disappropriation, of taking up and letting go, of expressing oneself and welcoming others.[29]

Earlier in the introduction Kearney maintains that "the work of translation might thus be said to carry a double duty: to expropriate oneself as one appropriates the other."[30] This is an interesting notion when one considers the labor of the filmmaker seeking to make something his own while taking away or perhaps giving away something of his own, expropriating what one has appropriated to share with others, to share in a struggle of understanding.

The struggle to understand human experiences through the filmic adaptation, translation, and appropriation of a fairy tale, whether it be oral or literary, stamps, in my opinion, the quality of the fairy-tale film. There can be no happy end in the best of fairy-tale films even if there is a happy end. The determination of its quality as a work of art is based on the artistic unraveling of our dilemma when we try to translate each other or translate a story. It must always be unfinished business or an unsuccessful struggle—a wisp of truth that can never be marked down for eternity. And yet, despite the "failure," there is a sweet relish, as if we can move closer not only to understanding something other than ourselves, but also ourselves.

Fairy-tale films transcend adaptation understood in a strict sense because they are all about our need to appropriate story to tell our own stories. In his essay, "Neo-Structuralist Narratology and the Functions of Filmic Storytelling," David Bordwell notes,

> a formal/functionalist approach [to film narrative] can usefully start from the premise that a film operates as a whole, in its individual parts playing determinate roles in a larger pattern. Recognizing that pattern and its possible functions also presupposes relations to broader historical norms. That is, a functionalist theory encourages us to explore functions and holistic patterns across a *body* of films. Within these contexts individual "figures" may fulfill conventional or unconventional purposes.[31]

While I shall not take a "formal/functionalist" approach to study the fairy-tale film, I am very much concerned in tracing holistic patterns in the films as they embody discourses about very particular fairy tales such as "Cinderella" or "Snow White" and reveal how deeply embedded these stories are in diverse cultures throughout the world. The body of fairy-tale films is vast, and even those films that may focus on, let us say, "Hansel and Gretel," can also be related to other fairy-tale films such as "Tom Thumb," because of the thematic issue of child abuse. Or, these films may function as horror films and enter into a discourse with other genres of fairy tales. Much will depend, as Bordwell points out, on the effect that the filmmaker seeks to induce.

When a filmmaker chooses to adapt and re-create a fairy tale or create an "original" film using recognizable fairy-tale characters, motifs, and topoi, he or she has several purposes, but I believe that the most important one in regard to fairy tales is to participate in discursive patterns "across a body of films" and to make a mark of some kind that will alter our view of the fairy tale, quite often to address social and political issues in the filmmaker's society and culture, or to speak to common socio-genetic and psychological phenomena in the civilizing process. It is over and through the body of the fairy tale that filmmakers and their crews engage with audiences, and active audiences engage with the cinematic fairy tale and the filmmakers. Fairy tales are perhaps the most vital staple in filmmaking, for we learn to communicate with them at a very early age. They are at the source of human cognition. If we were to study the sources of the narratives in thousands of films throughout the world, we would find that they are predicated on the narrative structure and patterns of different types of fairy tales. It is part of human nature that we appropriate and expropriate them, that we adapt and translate them, that we remake all that has been remade. We rely on cultural patterns of different kinds to know the world. I believe that, deep down, every filmmaker who decides to create fairy-tale films wants to be like Michel Ocelot and to make the tales his guts, heart, and everything else. And it is also true for those filmmakers, struck by the magic of a particular fairy tale, who feel the need to adapt and appropriate the tale that resonates within them.

But this is not the driving purpose behind all filmmakers. Many want to and have adapted and appropriated the fairy tale to use it as vehicle to celebrate his or her virtuosity, to make money, and to obtain power and fame. Some like Walt Disney sought to monopolize fairy-tale films so he would be recognized as a kind of master storyteller. Fortunately, there are numerous fairy-tale filmmakers who have contested the role of Disney and have revealed that the emperor is wearing no clothes, or put another way, that he is wearing flimsy clothes and has banalized the fairy tale with empty conventions. The body of films forming the frame of the fairy-tale film discourse is a body of conflicts. At the heart of all the conflicts are debates about the nature of storytelling and narrative, about the value and significance of human communication. As I shall indicate in the last chapter, the debate about fairy-tale films and storytelling is also a conflict that touches children as moral arbiters. Many fairy-tale filmmakers raise the question whether narrative has been taken away from children or how children can use the fairy tale to gain a sense of identity in dark times. It appears that these fairy-tale filmmakers are returning to the great oral tradition and encouraging spectators to adjust their vision and to learn to pierce the society of the spectacle and to tell their own tales. It is through what I call "de-Disneyfied" fairy-tale films that we learn to see reality for what it is.

In my opinion reality can best be understood paradoxically through artificiality, and in the case of the metaphorical fairy-tale film, we learn to view ourselves in artificially arranged images anew. The fairy tale is cinematically remade so that we can enter into particular and peculiar discourses that touch on audience concerns. Moreover, fairy-tale films are often remakes of other fairy-tale films built on discursive networks. There is an assumption in the fairy-tale remake that the "source" fairy-tale film is anachronistic or failed to interpret the source fairy tale sufficiently. There appears to be some lack or failure in the source fairy-tale film, which needs to be adapted and appropriated. The topic of fairy-tale remakes is very complex and raises a number of questions. In his highly significant work on film remakes, Constantine Verevis remarks,

> While there sometimes seems sufficient semantic and syntactic evidence to suggest that remakes are textual structures, film remaking depends, too (as does film genre), "on the existence of audience activity", not only prior knowledge of previous texts and intertextual relationships, but an understanding of broader generic structures and categories. In addition to this, film remaking is both enabled and limited by a series of historically specific institutional factors, such as copyright law, canon formation, and film reviewing which are essential to the existence and maintenance—to the "discursivation"—of the film remake. In these ways, film remaking is not simply quality of texts or viewers, but the secondary result of broader discursive activity.[32]

Verevis makes clear, in agreement with Rick Altman,[33] that film genres and remakes "depend on a network of historically variable relationships."[34] The genre of the fairy-tale film is itself part of the larger genre of the oral/literary fairy tale, and it is only by recognizing and tracing the extraordinary relations and discourses within the larger genre that we can begin to fathom the profound cultural meanings of fairy-tale films. We are always in the process of making and remaking ourselves, and in many respects, the making and remaking of fairy tales charts our struggles to be at home with ourselves and at home with the cultures that affect us. Filmmakers like the best of storytellers have sensed that "once upon a time" is a utopian concept, and the best of their fairy-tale films are remakes that open up alternative possibilities to form our own stories.

2

De-Disneyfying Disney: Notes on the Development of the Fairy-Tale Film

Indeed, there was something arrogant about the way the studio took over these works [*Alice in Wonderland* and *Peter Pan*]. Grist for a mighty mill, they were, in the ineffable Hollywood term, "properties" to do with as the proprietor of the machine would. You could throw jarring popular songs into the brew, you could gag them up, you could sentimentalize them. You had, in short, no obligation to the originals or to the cultural tradition they represented. In fact, when it came to billing, J. M. Barrie's *Peter Pan* somehow became Walt Disney's *Peter Pan*, and Lewis Carroll's *Alice* became Walt Disney's *Alice*. It could be argued that this was a true reflection of what happened to the works in the process of getting to the screen, but the egotism that insists on making another man's work your own through wanton tampering and by advertising claim is not an attractive form of egotism, however it is rationalized. And this kind of annexation was to be a constant in the later life of Disney. The only defense that one can enter for him is that of invincible ignorance: he really didn't see what he was doing, didn't know how some people could be offended by it, and certainly could not see that what was basically at fault was his insistence that there was only one true style for the animated film—his style.

Richard Schickel, *The Disney Version*[35]

As the studio most associated with manufacturing "family entertainment," Disney was a master at fostering and responding to this legitimating ideology of domestic amelioration. Certainly the theme pervades all of Disney's enterprises from *Snow White* on, but the insistence on the definition and containment of the adolescent woman is nowhere stronger and nowhere more specifically yet subtly articulated than in *Peter Pan*. Feminists like Chodorow attribute this attitude to the general condition of patriarchy: 'Men's location in the public sphere, then, defines society itself as masculine. It gives men power to create and enforce institutions of social and political control, important among these to control marriage as an institution that both expresses men's rights in women's sexual and reproductive capacities and reinforces these rights.' Few would question that Disney intended the studio to function as just such a controlling institution. But the more historically interesting question is, Why did this unusually strong insistence occur when it did?

Donald Crafton, "The Last Night in the Nursery: Walt Disney's *Peter Pan*"[36]

Although one could (and perhaps should) consider Georges Méliès, who produced highly innovative *féeries* at the end of the nineteenth century, as the founder and pioneer of the fairy-tale film, it is Walt Disney who became king of the fairy-tale films in the twentieth century, and though dead, his ghost still sits on the throne and rules the realm. Not only did Disney dominate the field of animated fairy-tale films, but many if not most of his live-action films followed the format that he developed for his animated films—a conventional reconciliation of conflicts and contradictions that engenders an illusion of happiness, security, and utopianism. Naturally, Disney did not do this by himself. He hired and organized gifted artists, technicians, and collaborators, not unlike the industrious virtuous seven dwarfs, who adapted fairy tales for the cinema by creating extraordinary cartoons and also developed the animated feature fairy-tale film in Disney's name so that his productions effaced the names of Charles Perrault, the Brothers Grimm, Hans Christian Andersen, and Collodi and became synonymous with the term fairy tale. There is scarcely an adult or child born in the twentieth century who, in the western world, has not been exposed to a Disney fairy-tale film or artifact. Our contemporary concept and image of a fairy tale have been shaped and standardized by Disney so efficiently through the mechanisms of the culture industry that our notions of happiness and utopia are and continue to be filtered through a Disney lens even if it is myopic. It seems that myopia has come to dominate both reality and utopia, thanks to Disneyfication, or that we are conditioned to view reality and fairy tales through a myopic pseudo-utopian lens.

Despite the domination of the fairy-tale film by the Disney Corporation, however, it would be misleading to consider the Disney productions as constituting a monopoly of fairy-tale films, or that they have totally twisted our views of reality and utopia, for there have always been competing films that offer a different vision of fairy tales and social conditions. As Pierre Bourdieu has made abundantly clear in *The Field of Cultural Production*, culture is constituted by different fields of production in which conflicting forces enter into a dialogue, often antagonistic, and seek to gain proper recognition and a stronghold for their views and beliefs in the field, and though the Disney fairy-tale films have been dominant throughout the twentieth century, they have never been without opposition. In fact, with the rise of filmmakers like Hayao Miyazaki, Michel Ocelot, Jan Svankmajer, Michael Sporn, David Kaplan, Matthew Bright, Guillermo del Toro, Tim Burton, Tarsem Singh, Anna Melikyan, Yim Pil-Sung, and many others in the late twentieth and early twenty-first centuries, it appears that the fairy-tale film may eventually become de-Disneyfied. But before I explain what I mean by de-Disneyfication, I want to comment on the evolution of the fairy tale from the oral to the cinematic, how this genre has expanded and morphed into the dominant form of fairy-tale film, and why the conflict in the cultural field of cinematic production is so significant.

Theses

1) The fairy tale began hundreds if not thousands of years ago as an oral form of storytelling created by adults, who told all kinds of tales in diverse settings in which adults determined the forms and contents. They told tales to communicate important information, and metaphor was highly significant in disseminating knowledge. The fairy tale was never a genre intended for children—and

it is still not a genre for children. With the advent of the printing press in the fifteenth century, writers gradually began to record and publish the oral forms of storytelling in print directed mainly at adult reading audiences. Adults have never stopped reading, producing, re-inventing, and experimenting with fairy tales.

2) It was not until the nineteenth century that the fairy tale was cultivated as genre and social institution for children in the western world and mainly for children of the upper classes. Notions of elitism and Christian meritocracy, along with the medieval notion of "might makes right," became staples of the stories, and a select canon of tales was established for the socialization of the young, geared to children who knew how to read. These notions are easily recognizable in most of the classical tales, especially those written by Hans Christian Andersen, who had become one of the most popular writers in Europe and America during the nineteenth and early twentieth centuries. The emphasis was on extraordinarily gifted individuals who owed their rise in fortunes to God's benevolence or miracles of destiny represented metaphorically through the intervention of a fairy or powerful magical people and objects. Another aspect that appealed to children and adults was the Richard Whittington/Horatio Alger attitude that encouraged taking advantage of opportunities and pulling oneself up by one's bootstraps. Although the fairy tale was altered to address the adult views of what a child should read, it was still read vastly by adults. Adults and children of the lower classes could not read these tales, but they circulated them in the oral tradition and in popular theaters.

3) Despite the rise of print materials, the fairy tale continued to be told widely throughout the western world for all types of audiences, and by the end of the nineteenth century in America and Great Britain, professional folklore societies were formed, and hundreds of collections of folk and fairy tales were produced in all the major European languages. One major purpose was to preserve the oral traditions (songs, tales, proverbs, legends, and so on) from folk cultures all over the world by printing them. At the same time the printed fairy tale with pictures gained more legitimacy and enduring value than the oral tale which "vanished" soon after it was told, unless recorded or written down. On the positive side, numerous educated Europeans and Americans made a dedicated effort to be true to the spirit or essence of the tales in their transcriptions, even though they were handicapped by the lack of adequate technology. On the negative side, many folklorists or transcribers regarded their informants and the people to whom the tales belonged more or less as primitives. What was considered essential to their world views and life styles by the different ethnic groups who used the tales to relate to one another was often viewed by the foreign transcriber as quaint, fantastic, and supernatural. Consequently, preserved oral tales were often revised, stylized, and censored to suit the Christian and middle-class ideology of the collectors and writers. Much of the collecting and preserving was completed at the beginning of the twentieth century in Great Britain and the United States during a period of western imperialism. It was only after World War II that a shift in the ideology of collectors and translators took place with more respect shown to the indigenous populations.

4) By the end of the nineteenth century and beginning of the twentieth century, the fairy tale was often read by a parent in a nursery, library, school, or bedroom to entertain and to soothe a child's anxieties because the fairy tales for children were optimistic and had plots with closure, that is, with a happy end. Fairy tales were among the first short narratives to be adapted as plays specifically for children and to be performed by adults and children and staged in the United States, Great Britain, and other European countries. In addition, they were read to children by librarians and teachers and made their way into school primers. Significantly, L. Frank Baum published his famous fairy-tale novel, *The Wonderful Wizard of Oz* in 1900, and J. M. Barrie produced *Peter Pan* in 1904 and had the character of Peter ask his adult audience whether they believed in fairies to save Wendy's life, and the audience responded with a loud vocal YES!

5) By the beginning of the twentieth century, the western classical fairy tales became established memetically as a canon and were disseminated through all forms of the mass media including books, postcards, newspapers, journals, radio, and film. The major tales were and still are: "Cinderella," "Little Red Riding Hood," "Snow White," "Sleeping Beauty," "Bluebeard," "Hansel and Gretel," "The Frog Prince," "Rapunzel," "Rumpelstiltskin," "Donkey Skin," "Tom Thumb," "The Ugly Duckling," "The Little Mermaid," "Beauty and the Beast," "Aladdin," "Ali Baba and the Forty Thieves," "Jack and the Beanstalk," and some other variants of these tales.

6) Although the plots varied and the themes and characters were altered, the classical fairy-tale narrative for children and adults reinforced the patriarchal symbolical order based on rigid notions of sexuality and gender. The types of characters, based on real professions, family figures, social class—often stereotypes, not archetypes—depicted in printed and staged versions of fairy tales tended to follow schematic notions of how young men and women behaved and should behave. Though somewhat of a simplification, most of the heroes are cunning, fortunate, adventurous, handsome, and daring; the heroines are beautiful, passive, obedient, industrious, and self-sacrificial. Though some are from the lower classes and though the theme of "rags to riches" plays an important role, the peasants and lower-class figures learn a certain *Habitus*, what Pierre Bourdieu describes as a set of manners, customs, normative behavior, and thinking, that enables them to fulfill a social role, rise in social status, and distinguish themselves according to conventional social class and gender expectations. The goal-oriented narrative of a classical fairy tale generally involves transformation of the major protagonist only to reinforce the social and political status quo. Implicit in the reconciliation of conflict is moral improvement. Evil is cleansed.

7) In printed form the fairy tale immediately became property (unlike the oral folk tale) and was regarded as a fixed text written by an author as proprietor. It was sold and marketed, and property rights were granted authors, collectors, and publishers. When bought, it could be taken by its "new" owner and read by its owner at his or her leisure for escape, consolation, or inspiration. An oral tale that once belonged to a community was gradually lifted from its context and deprived of its "original" social meaning and relevance. It is often difficult to establish the originality of a tale, but it is possible to study the process of expropriation and appropriation by tracing the histories of a particular tale as discourse with numerous variants. The oral tradition often takes revenge on the printed tradition by re-appropriating what has been stolen and expropriated from its culture.

8) There was always tension between the literary and oral traditions. The oral tales continued and continue to threaten the more conventional and classical tales because they can question, dislodge, and deconstruct the written tales and published texts. Moreover, within the literary tradition itself, there were numerous writers in the late nineteenth century such as Charles Dickens, George MacDonald, Lewis Carroll, Oscar Wilde, Laurence Housman, Edith Nesbit, and even L. Frank Baum, who questioned the standardized model of what a fairy tale should be.

9) It was through script by the end of the nineteenth century that there was a full-scale debate about what oral folk tales and literary fairy tales were and what their respective functions should be. By this time the fairy tale had expanded as a high art form (opera, ballet, drama) and low art form (folk play, vaudeville, and parody) and a form developed classically and experimentally for children and adults. The oral tales continued to be disseminated through communal gatherings of different kinds, but they were also broadcast by radio and gathered in books by folklorists. Most important in the late nineteenth century, as I have already mentioned, was the rise of folklore as an organized field of study and inquiry along with anthropology. It became a social institution and various schools of folklore began to flourish. There was hardly any literary criticism that dealt with fairy tales and folk tales at this time.

10) Though many fairy-tale books and collections were illustrated, and some lavishly illustrated in the nineteenth century, the images were very much in conformity with the text. The illustrators,

mainly male, were frequently anonymous and did not seem to count. Though the illustrations often enriched and deepened a tale, they were more subservient to the text and rarely presented alternative ways to read or look at a text. However, they clearly began influencing the way readers imagined the characters and the scenes of the tales. The heroines were largely blonde and beautiful with perfectly proportioned features; the heroes were gallant, handsome, and courageous, often with sword in hand and on a white horse. These illustrations, proliferated in the nineteenth century, marked the beginning of a major change for the fairy-tale genre.

11) The domination of the printed word in the development of the fairy tale as genre underwent a momentous change in the 1890s and early part of the twentieth century. The next great revolution in the institutionalization of the genre was brought about by the technological development of film, for the images now imposed themselves on the text and formed their own text in "violation" of print but also with the help of the print culture. This shift in adaptation of fairy tales can be viewed to a certain extent as the "incarnation" of fairy tales. As Kamilla Elliott points out,

> predicated on the Christian theology of the word made flesh, wherein the word is only a partial representation that requires incarnation for its fulfillment, it makes adaptation a process of incarnation from more abstract to less abstract signs. The words, which merely hint at sight, sound, touch, taste, and smell, tantalize readers into longing for their incarnation in signs offering more direct access to these phenomenological experiences.[37]

And here is where first Georges Méliès, the great magician, who used mixed media to create his films called *féeries*, Percy Stow, Ferdinand Zecca, Albert Capellani, Arthur Melbourne Cooper, Anson Dyer, J. Searle Dawley, Chester and Sidney Franklin, Herbert Brenon, Walt Disney, and other filmmakers enter the scene. They were among the first to realize how the fairy-tale genre might be enriched by film in unimaginable ways, and how film might be enriched by the fairy tale. In fact, their visions of the fairy tale became realized beyond their wildest dreams.

Fairy-Tale Film Narrative

In my opinion, the classical fairy-tale narrative stamped film narrative and the canonical Hollywood narrative long before Hollywood even existed. I would even argue that it laid the groundwork for classical European films, especially the melodramas. David Bordwell, one of the most astute film critics on film narrative, writes:

> Of all modes, the classical one conforms most closely to the 'canonic story' which story-comprehension researchers posit as normal for our culture. In fabula terms, the reliance upon character-centered causality and the definition of the action as the attempt to achieve a goal are both salient features of the canonic format. At the level of the syuzhet, the classical film respects the canonic pattern of establishing an initial set of affairs which gets violated and which must be then set right. Indeed, Hollywood screenplay writing manuals have long insisted on a formula which has been revived in recent structural analysis: the plot consists of an undisturbed stage, the disturbance, the struggle, and the elimination of the disturbance. Such a syuzhet pattern is the inheritance not of some monolithic construct called the "novelistic" but of specific historical forms; the well-made play, the popular romance, and crucially, the late-nineteenth-century short story. The characters' causal interactions are thus to a great extent functions of such overarching syuzhet/fabula patterns.[38]

It is a shame that Bordwell does not acknowledge the significance of the fairy tale for film narrative and the deep roots of the oral wonder tale and the literary fairy tale that generated the *féerie* plays of the seventeenth century up through the nineteenth century. Nor does he cite the importance of Georges Méliès, who was the prime "appropriator" of the *féerie* for the film industry in its infancy. Though there are many different schemata and patterns of fairy tales that involve normative ways of producing and viewing films, the conventional fairy-tale plot as outlined by Vladimir Propp in his famous book, *Morphology of the Folktale*, serves as a model for the commercial Hollywood films, Early European melodramas, and the Disneyfied fairy-tale films. Propp outlined thirty-one basic functions that constitute the formation of a paradigm, which was and still is common in Europe and North America. Though I have some reservations about the validity of Propp's categories because he does not discuss the social function of the oral wonder tale that engendered the literary fairy tale or their diverse aspects, his structuralist approach can be helpful in understanding plot formation and the reasons why certain tales have become so memorable. By functions, Propp meant the fundamental and constant components of a tale that are the acts of a character and necessary for driving the action forward. The plot generally involves a protagonist who is confronted with an interdiction or prohibition which he or she violates in some way. Therefore, there is generally a departure or banishment and the protagonist is either given a task or assumes a task related to the interdiction or prohibition. The protagonist is *assigned* a task, and the task is a *sign*. That is, his or her character will be stereotyped and marked by the task that is his or her sign. Names are rarely used in a folk or fairy tale. Characters function according to their social class or profession, and they often cross boundaries or transform themselves. Inevitably there will be a significant or signifying encounter. Depending on the situation, the protagonist will meet either enemies or friends. The antagonist often takes the form of a witch, monster, or evil fairy; the friend is a mysterious individual or creature, who gives the protagonist gifts. Sometimes there are three different animals or creatures who are helped by the protagonist and promise to repay him or her. Whatever the occasion, the protagonist somehow acquires gifts that are often magical agents, which are needed in conflict and can bring about a miraculous or marvelous change or transformation. Soon after the protagonist, endowed with gifts, is tested and overcomes inimical forces. However, this is not the end because there is generally a peripety or sudden fall in the protagonist's fortunes that is only a temporary setback. A miracle or marvelous intervention is needed to reverse the wheel of fortune. Frequently, the protagonist makes use of endowed gifts (and this includes magical agents and cunning) to achieve his or her goal. The success of the protagonist usually leads to marriage; the acquisition of money; survival and wisdom; or any combination of these three. Whatever the case may be, the protagonist is transformed in the end. The functions form a transformation.

The significance of the paradigmatic functions of the wonder tale is that they facilitate recall for tellers, listeners, and viewers. Over hundreds of years they have enabled people to store, remember, and reproduce the plot of a fairy tale and to change it to fit their experiences and desires due to the easily identifiable characters who are associated with particular social classes, professions, and assignments. The characters, settings, and motifs are combined and varied according to specific functions to induce *wonder* and *hope* for change in the audience of listeners/readers/viewers, who are to marvel or admire the magical changes that occur in the course of events. It is this earthy, sensual, and secular sense of wonder and hope that distinguished the wonder tales from other oral tales as the legend, the fable, the anecdote, the myth, and Biblical story; it is clearly the sense of wonder that distinguishes the *literary* fairy tale from the moral story, novella, sentimental tale, and other modern short literary genres. Wonder causes astonishment, and as marvelous object or phenomenon, it is often regarded as a supernatural occurrence and can be an omen or portent. It gives rise to admiration, fear, awe, and reverence. In the oral wonder tale, we are to marvel about the workings of the universe where anything can happen at any time, and these *fortunate* and *unfortunate* events are never to be explained. Nor do the characters demand an explanation— they are opportunistic and hopeful. They are encouraged to be so, and if they do not take advantage of the opportunity that will benefit them in their relations with others, they are either dumb or mean-spirited. The tales seek to awaken our regard for the miraculous condition of life and to evoke profound feelings of awe and respect for life as a miraculous process, which can be altered and changed to compensate for the lack of power, wealth, and pleasure that most people experience. Lack, deprivation, prohibition, and interdiction motivate people to look for signs of fulfillment and emancipation. In the wonder tales, those who are naive and simple are able to succeed because they are untainted and can recognize the wondrous signs. They have retained their belief in the miraculous condition of nature, revere nature in all its aspects. They have not been spoiled by conventionalism, power, or rationalism. In contrast to the humble characters, the villains are those who use words and power intentionally to exploit, control, transfix, incarcerate, and destroy for their benefit. They have no respect or consideration for nature and other human beings, and they actually seek to abuse magic by preventing change and causing everything to be transfixed according to their interests. The marvelous protagonist wants to keep the process of natural change flowing and indicates possibilities for overcoming the obstacles that prevent other characters or creatures from living in a peaceful and pleasurable way.

In some ways, filmmakers are similar to fairy-tale protagonists in that they want to keep the narrative tradition of wondrous storytelling flowing. They are the champion tellers and projectors of fairy tales. Some do this by relying on the canonic mode of telling and showing fairy tales as Disney came to do. Others, fully aware of the normative schemata of the canonical and/or classical fairy tales, have sought to contest the norms and introduce alternative ways of employing and visualizing fairy tales through film. Competing variants of fairy tales arose as soon as the tales began circulating, and as cultural fields of storytelling were formed thousands of years ago, there have been conflicts over the bodies of canonical tales, how to tell them, and how to achieve a certain effect. As we shall see in the course of conflicts, the Disney fairy-tale as commodified film and book rose to predominance in the twentieth century, but it was never the only narrative mode used by film-makers to try to "capture" the essence of fairy tales on film. The fairy tales and fairy-tale films have formed specific discourses about the meanings of particular tales and general discourses about the nature of storytelling. One thing is clear, however: film had a powerful impact on the oral and print tradition of fairy tales and has made the conflict within the genre of the fairy tale more intense and lively.

Spectacle, Film Production, Disneyfication, and the Fairy Tale

By focusing on how the advent of film technology changed the genre of the fairy tale, I am less concerned with the techniques of filmmaking and scholarly approaches that focus on film history and technology than I am with the issues of the adaptation and appropriation of the fairy-tale genre. That is, my concern is with the evolution of a specific cultural genre that has been most widely spread and promulgated through film, the mass media, and the Internet. The manner in which we appreciate, evaluate, and disseminate our understanding of all kinds of art, especially simple and short forms of fiction such as the myth, the legend, the anecdote, and the fairy tale, has undergone immense changes involving orality, literacy, and cinematography. Although all three means of communication—oral, print, and cinematography—are often combined with sound to convey a message and make an impression on our brains and imaginations, the image, moving and still, particularly the cinematic, TV, and Internet image, has superseded the other means of communication and conditions our perception of most art forms.

In the specific case of the fairy tale, I maintain that, throughout the world, in particular the world of globalized capitalism, children and adults are more apt to be familiar with cinematic versions of the fairy tale than they are with oral or printed ones. As Guy Debord has pointed out, we live in a world of the spectacle that causes our lives to be mediated and determined by illusory images.

Debord explains that "the spectacle is not a collection of images; rather it is a social relationship between people that is mediated by images."[39] In contrast to Walter Benjamin, who believed that art in the age of mechanical reproduction would lead to greater democratization and freedom of choice in society through the film and other forms of the mass media, Debord argued along the lines of Theodor Adorno's theses in his essay on the culture industry to show how the dominant mode of capitalist production employs technology to alienate and standardize human relations. In particular, he examined the totalitarian or totalizing tendencies of the spectacle or what he called the spectacular, because the spectacle is constituted by signs of the dominant organization of production and reinforces behaviors and attitudes of passivity that allow for the justification of hierarchical rule, the monopolization of the realm of appearances, and the acceptance of the status quo. Only by grasping how the spectacle occludes our vision of social relations will we be able to overcome the alienation and separation that pervades our lives. Debord insisted that

> by means of the spectacle the ruling order discourses endlessly upon itself in an uninterrupted monologue of self-praise. The spectacle is the self-portrait of power in the age of power's totalitarian rule over the conditions of existence. . . . If the spectacle—understood in the limited sense of those "mass media" that are its most stultifying superficial manifestation— seems at times to be invading society in the shape of a mere *apparatus*, it should be remembered that this apparatus has nothing neutral about it, and that it answers precisely to the needs of the spectacle's internal dynamics. If the social requirements of the age which develops such techniques can be met only through their mediation, if the administration of society and all contact between people now depends on the intervention of such "instant" communication, it is because this "communication" is essentially *one-way*; the concentration of the media thus amounts to the monopolization by the administrators of the existing system of the means to pursue their particular form of administration.[40]

Debord did not believe that the spectacle was impenetrable or that we all live in a glass bubble constructed by illusions. He wrote, as many critics have continued to write, to expose, contest, and negate the predominance of the spectacle and the social organization of appearances. His concept of the spectacle is particularly important for a critical understanding of how the fairy tale as film was "spectacularized," that is, how its signs and images were organized to create the illusion of a just and happy world in which conflicts and contradictions would always be reconciled in the name of a beautiful ruling class.

Almost all of Disney's films operate according to the "laws" of the spectacle. They impose a vision of life, the better life, on viewers that delude audiences into believing that power can and should be entrusted only to those members of elite groups fit to administer society. All the major, animated feature-length Disney fairy-tale films—*Snow White and the Seven Dwarfs* (1937), *Pinocchio* (1940), *Cinderella* (1950), *Alice in Wonderland* (1951), *Peter Pan* (1953), *Sleeping Beauty* (1959), *The Sword and the Stone* (1963), *The Little Mermaid* (1989), *Beauty and the Beast* (1991), *Aladdin* (1992), *Mulan* (1998), *The Emperor's New Groove* (2000), *Enchanted* (2007), *The Princess and the Frog* (2009)— follow conventional principles of technical and aesthetic organization to celebrate stereotypical gender and power relations and to foster a world view of harmony. The images, words, music, and movement lead to a totalizing spectacle that basically glorifies how technology can be used to aestheticize social and political relations according to the dominant mode of production and ruling groups that entertain a public spectatorship through diversion and are entertained themselves by a monologue of self-praise. There is virtually no difference in the "utopian" vision conveyed by these films that celebrates the actual standardized mode of production in the Disney Studios, its rationalization, hierarchy, and purpose. What is interesting is that the scheme of the Disney filmic narrative corresponds to its mode of production for the cinema.

Let us examine Disney's earliest animated feature fairy-tale film, *Snow White and the Seven Dwarfs*, and a later one, *Beauty and the Beast*, as examples. Each film is framed by a prince on a quest for the proper mate, essentially a young virginal woman, a trophy princess, who will serve his vested interests, and the quest ends with a marriage in a splendid castle, in which the prince and princess will be attended by admiring if not obsequious servants. The manner in which the prince attains his goal depends on the collaboration of the underlings, the dwarfs and enchanted objects, and the ingenuity and valor of this sympathetic prince. Songs are strewed along the plot as flowers to enliven and brighten the action, just as comic gags are used to divert us from the serious nature of the business at hand—ruthless competition for power. But everyone knows his or her role, and their roles are all geared to guaranteeing the happiness of their heroes, seemingly born to lead, take power, and to be admired, as fetishist objects. They will eventually reside in a palace, a utopian realm, that few people are privileged to inhabit, unless you are one of the chosen servants. The goal is not only a reconciliation of conflict and the defeat of evil, but also acclamation of those who deserve to rule by those who deserve to serve.

This crude, schematic description of how a Disney fairy-tale functions may appear to be overly formulaic, but the formula holds true: with slight variations, it can be applied to almost all the Disney fairy-tale films and the numerous live-action family films made by the Disney corporation up through its recent *faux* parody *Enchanted* (2007), a film that pretends to change the Disney model through burlesque and inane satire while pandering to consumerism. The model of most Disney films, even when they pay lip service to changing social and cultural values, reflects the actual structure of the operations in a Disney studio that have not been altered all that much over time. In the formative years of the Disney studio, those years that determined the work principles, ethics, and ideology, the guiding practices became set and were similar to other studios and corporations that participated in establishing what Debord has described as "spectacular" relations that stem from the mode of production and reification. Pictures and descriptions of the hierarchical arrangements in the Disney studios are widely known and widespread. By 1930 Disney had consolidated power in his studio so that he ruled without question, and he divided his workers into separate groups and departments who often worked side by side at desks, as though they operated mechanically serving a conveyor belt in a factory. They were organized according to their functions: cel painters, animators, musicians, gag men, storyboard producers, and directors. After 1935 Disney did not do any animating, composing, or screenplay writing and worked out of his own personal office. However, he supervised almost every film, large and small, and his decision was the final decision for almost all the early productions. To his credit, he sought out the very best collaborators and rarely stinted when it came to improving the technical quality of his productions. He also set the standard of hard work and showed great attention to detail. Most of all, he conceived many of the ideas behind the films and decided what project would move forward and which collaborators would work on a particular project. If there was a vision in a Disney fairy-tale film— and his spirit lived on well beyond his death—it was a shared spectacular vision of efficiency, exploitation, and expediency: how best to use a story to promote one's artistic talents, make money, market oneself, and promote a vision of how social relations should be ordered. The contents and history of the fairy tale were only a pre-text, that is, they provided the materials to be appropriated and adapted for production purposes that served market needs. Behind such purposes, of course, was an ideology commensurate with the capitalist mode of production and commodity fetishism that was intended to shape the vision of audiences so that they would want to see and consume more of the same.

Though it would seem that there is something utopian about the Disney vision of the world, one that was elaborated in collaboration with hundreds of mainly male artists, it is more apt, I think, to talk about the degeneration of utopia in Disney's schemes for fairy-tale films and how his corporation continued to cultivate it. Jan Svankmajer, the extraordinary Czech filmmaker of disturbing fairy-tale films, once remarked,

> Disney is among the greatest makers of "art of children." I have always held that no special art for children simply exists, and what passes for it embodies either the birch (discipline) or lucre (profit). "Art of children" is dangerous in that it shares either in the taming of the child's soul or the bringing up of consumers of mass culture. I am afraid that a child reared on current Disney produce will find it difficult to get used to more sophisticated kinds of art, and will assume his/her place in the ranks of viewers of idiotic television serials.[41]

But it is not only the taming of the child's soul and the commodification of children, and might I add, adults, that constitute the degeneration of utopia in the fairy-tale films of Disney, but also a carefully planned narrative that leads to the banalization of utopia. In one of the most significant studies of Disneyland, Louis Marin explained that

> the visitors to Disneyland are put in the place of the ceremonial storyteller. They recite the mythic narrative of the antagonistic origins of society. They go through the contradictions while they visit the complex; they are led from the pirates' cave to an atomic submarine, from Sleeping Beauty's castle to a rocketship. These sets reverse daily life's determinism only to reaffirm it, but legitimated and justified. Their path through the park is the narrative, recounted umpteen times, of the deceptive harmonization of contrary elements, of the fictional solution to conflicting tensions. By "acting out" Disney's utopia, the visitor "realizes" the ideology of America's dominant groups as the mythic founding narrative of their own society.[42]

Utopia, as most scholars from Thomas More to Karl Mannheim and Ernst Bloch have explained, does not exist; it is literally no place, and yet, numerous writers and artists have created and projected their image of utopia through their works to offer an alternative to the existing state of things. The fantastic images of utopia forge a space of play in which artists and writers experiment and invite their readers and spectators to play with the possibilities for changing social relations under real conditions of existence. Utopia demands an ideological critique of the status quo without limits, for the utopic knows no limits and offers no solutions or resolutions.

From the very beginning, however, Disney set limits on the possibilities of utopia that laid out a prescribed way of ordering the world and curbing the imagination. In fact, he sought to establish ownership of utopia. But his theme parks and plans for the perfect city were nothing but a continuation of degenerated notions of utopia in the fairy-tale films, for like the narrative of Disneyland outlined by Marin, they lead the viewer on a quest that legitimates a reality of violence and injustice by making it appear, through fixed stereotypes and values fostering violence and exploitation, that contradictions can be reconciled through a collective fantasy, namely the sets of images that constitute a Disney fairy-tale film. The telos of all Disney's fairy-tale films is to shape the vision of the spectators so that they are convinced and believe that they share in the values and accomplishments of the narrative, thus obviating any or all contradictions. The imagination of the spectators is thus curbed by the calculations of fantasy imposed by the film, and individual wishes are denied or caught in the snare of the fantasy. As Marin remarks,

> this brings about a rather violent effect on the imaginary by fantasy. The other side of reality is presented (Fantasyland is Disney's privileged place for this), but it emerges in the form of banal, routine images of Disney's films. They are the bankrupt signs of an imagination homogenized by the mass media. The snare I mentioned is the collective, totalitarian form taken by the "imaginary" of a society, blocked by its specular self-image. One of the essential

functions of the utopic image is to make apparent a wish in a *free* image of itself, in an image that can play in opposition to the fantasy, which is an inert, blocked and recurrent image. Disneyland is on the side of the fantasy and not on that of a free or utopic representation.[43]

If the Disney fairy-tale films constrain the utopic imaginary and fix our image of utopia through hallucinatory images, they have done this through the systematic dissemination of images in books, advertising, toys, clothing, houseware articles, posters, postcards, radio, and other artifacts that have mesmerized us into believing that the "genuine" fairy tale is the Disney fairy tale, and that the Disney fairy tale promises to fulfill what is lacking in our lives, to compensate for discomforting aspects of social reality, and to eliminate social and class conflicts forever. It plays pruriently upon the utopian longings of people by offering and selling set images intimating that special chosen celebrities and elite groups are destined to rule and administer just social codes that will make people happy and keep them in their proper places. Nothing is gray in the colored films of Disney, but the color camouflages the black-and-white view of good and evil in the world.

The Disney world view conveyed through the fairy tale is not, however, limited to Disney productions. In fact, most American fairy-tale films and many of the British and European as well as Japanese are variants of the Disneyfication process in the film industry. One need only view the majority of the films of the Faerie Tale Theatre produced by Shelley Duvall in the 1980s or the Cannon Movie series in the 1980s as well as the other numerous cheaply produced infantile films shaped by a myriad of minor film studios to dumb down children and their parents as well to understand how pervasive the Disneyfication of the fairy tale became in the twentieth century and how the Disney influence continues into the twenty-first. Yet, we must never forget that, just as drug addicts can save themselves through detoxification programs, the fairy-tale film—and the fairy tale in general—can save itself through de-Disneyfication programs, and perhaps we can also rescue ourselves and restore our vision so we can play with the fairy tale and social reality on our own terms.

The De-Disneyfication of Fairy-Tale Films

As I have already noted, the fairy tale began to be adapted in many different ways by filmmakers almost as soon as the movie camera was invented and put to use. Aside from the extraordinary work of Georges Méliès at the turn of the twentieth century, there were interesting experimental works produced by Émile Cohl, Chester and Sid Franklin, J. Searle Dawley, Max and Dave Fleischer, Anson Dyer, Paul Terry, Tex Avery, and many others up through the 1930s. Most of the films were short, five to ten minutes, and were produced to "warm-up" audiences, once feature films came into existence. They were shown before the main feature and were intended to induce laughs through the use of unusual twists to the plots and hilarious gags. In America, the cartoon became the most popular short in the cinema from 1930 through the 1960s, when television more or less brought about its demise in movie theaters.

Crucial for understanding the success and importance of the early fairy-tale cartoon is the gag. As Norman Klein points out in his superb book, *Seven Minutes: The Life and Death of the American Animated Cartoon* (1993),

> gags are more than random snatches of comic relief. They use the narrative code of late nineteenth-century popular culture. They are fables about surviving in an industrial world when the mind is still trapped inside a rural community (translated as the cartoon village caught inside the motion-picture machine). A plot of this sort, fractured by a variety of gags, has a unity based on dialectical confusion. The potential for hazards is never resolved, only examined, in chase after chase, disaster after disaster. Once again, the gag is similar to

Modernist theories from the twenties, on narrative, on epic theater, or defamiliarization. It is the Theater of the Absurd.[44]

Interestingly, Disney was a master of the gags and the chase plot in almost all his cartoons of the 1920s. In his Laugh-O-Gram fairy-tale films he displayed an unusul flare for the gag and anarchy. For instance, in *Puss in Boots* (1922), the young man who becomes a toreador to win the princess is assisted by the shrewd female cat to topple the king. The fairy tale of Charles Perrault is virtually transformed into a revolutionary gag with a young man from the folk overthrowing a popcorn-eating king who is exposed as a bumpkin and not capable of controlling the youth that knows how to use the latest technology to triumph over a feudal world view that is out of date. There were other anarchical live-action feature fairy-tale films in the 1920s, influenced by vaudeville, Chaplin, and other comedians, but they were not very successful. Even the animated fairy-tale films had difficulty finding and holding a niche in the market because they were expensive to produce, and because the cinema industry demanded quick and profitable releases. By the early 1930s the Disney Studio had become the dominant producer of fairy-tale cartoons using voiceovers, music, and Technicolor in stunning and adroit ways to set standards for the other studios and to prepare the way for production of the feature-length *Snow White and the Seven Dwarfs* in 1937. The reasons for the transformation of the fairy-tale cartoon are connected to the Great Depression of 1929, the development of rationalized workshops or studios influenced by Fordism, the invention of Technicolor and sound, and the political and cultural need, so it seemed, for strong leaders and harmonious living. In other words, the fairy-tale film was about to be domesticated in the mid- 1930s. As Klein states,

> a moral element is added to cartoons, which was relatively absent earlier. In order to add moral instruction, cartoon studios turned toward domestic melodrama, which also resembles stories in live-action cinema, and made primary use of fully animated faces and gestures. . . . The cartoon moved from vaudeville gags to movie melodrama, with cinematic references added. Now, audiences could see more cartoons about troubled consciences that needed mending. . . . Disney led the way in expanding personality animation to include melodrama. In fact, even after cartoon melodrama was exhausted and was replaced by the hyper-chase cartoon, by 1940, Disney hung on. For another twenty-five years, that high seriousness rarely left his work.[45]

In order to understand the significance of domestication and the high seriousness of Disney, most critics have focused on *Snow White* (1937), but I believe with Klein that the process started much earlier and that there are three fairy-tale films which document the process of domestication much better: *Three Little Pigs* (1933), *The Big Bad Wolf* (1934), and *Three Little Wolves* (1936). Not only did they perfect the gags by making them smoother and more didactic if not inane, but they incorporated them in much better synchronization with the storyline and music than ever before to bring about a fuller animation. As Michael Barrier has commented in his significant study, *Hollywood Cartoons,*

> None of the cartoons released on either side of *Three Little Pigs* in the spring and summer of 1933 come close to matching it in that regard. . . . Fairy tales and animal fables were sturdier raw material, and now that they were open to the Disney writers, there was no reason to hope that more cartoons would capture what most distinguished *Three Little Pigs* from any cartoon that had come before: its sense of balance and completeness.[46]

Although it would be an exaggeration to state that most fairy-tale cartoons up until 1933 had paid very little attention to the storyline and contents of the tale, it is clear that the emphasis had

Figure 1
Burt Gillett,
The Big Bad Wolf

always been on producing as many jokes and gags for their own sake, whether they fit the story or not, and on showing off the technical skills of the artists and cameramen. While the gags remained important in *Three Little Pigs*, more attention was paid to strengthening the story by making careful changes in the characterization of the wolf and the pigs, adding lyrics, and endowing the film with a message that quickly captured the sentiments of American audiences in 1933. The appeal of the film had a great deal to do with the Great Depression, poverty, and oppression, and how the story emphasized overcoming the voracious evil wolf at the door of the helpless pigs. It is thanks to the oldest brother pig that the younger ones can sing "Who's afraid of the Big Bad Wolf?" This ditty, which became a national song, was repeated in the two sequels in which the big brother pig always saves the day. It is through him that happiness is guaranteed and all conflicts are resolved. The house as home sweet home, as a sacred place that is to be defended at all costs, is celebrated, just as the big brother pig, whose industry, wisdom, orderliness, and strength are extolled as American values. It did not matter to Disney and his collaborators that the country was falling apart due to the values that counted more—exploitation, mismanagement, ruthless competition, violence, and corruption—they saw more of a need to submit to the protection of the individual owner, big brother pig. Though it may be stretching a point to compare this pig to the prince in *Snow White and the Seven Dwarfs*, they do play similar functional roles in that they as strong admirable characters provide the closure to the conflicts in the story and tidy up the mess that apparently is caused by greed and voracity. The spectacular image of the strong rational leader as rescuer concealed, of course, the real causes of antagonism and unhappiness in both the films and the social situation of the audiences of those times, for one must always ask why the wolf is impoverished and hungry and must resort to violence to survive, and why and how the pigs got their money and live comfortably in their own homes that the wolf cannot afford. One must also ask why little people are silly, stupid, and weak and cannot fend for themselves.

Once the Disney images and plots were set by 1937 and repeated throughout Walt's lifetime, they were not without their competition and opposition. For instance Max and Dave Fleischer produced a number of controversial and hilarious Betty Boop fairy-tale films already in the early 1930s, but the most fascinating fairy-tale animator was Tex Avery. Acknowledged as one of the most gifted if not provocative animators of the golden age of cartoons, Avery directed a good number of fairy-tale films for major film studios such as Warner and MGM and frequently undermined the studio approaches to animated fairy tales. In *Red Hot Riding Hood* he begins by having his characters (Red Riding Hood, the wolf, and grandma) protest against repeating the same old story and compel the director to change it. In *Swing Shift Cinderella*, the wolf chases Red Riding Hood across the credits until the girl points out that he is chasing the wrong woman and should be pursing Cinderella. If anyone can take credit for the term "fractured fairy tale," it should be Avery, for long before the Rocky and Bullwinkle fractured fairy tales, Avery was taking apart the traditional fairy tale and using motifs to delight audiences and unsettle the canonical tales. In *Red Hot Riding Hood* and *Swing Shift Cinderella*, aside from the brazen erotic depiction of the young women, the major twist in the plot involves sexy elderly women, the grandmother and the fairy godmother, who pursue the wolf, who never loses his lustful and predatory desire for young women. The frank portrayal of gender conflict and sexual proclivities with open endings were unique in Avery's times and remain somewhat unique today. Avery never made a feature-length fairy-tale film. The Fleischers made two, which were disasters. All three animators—and there were many more as I shall show in the following chapters—were important in the 1930s and 1940s, however, for demonstrating an alternative to the dominant conservative trend of producing fairy-tale films represented by Disney.

By Disney, I am not referring just to the man, who was a genial entrepreneur, but to a corporate manufacturing process that has continued well into the twenty-first century. A "good" example of the products that have been issued since 2000 by the Disney Corporation is *The Emperor's New Groove* (2000). It is truly a putrid and stale film filled with imitative gags and scenes reminiscent of Tex Avery's cartoons. (Even Avery can be co-opted and commodified.) The plot is offensive: it concerns a faux Inca emperor named Kuzco who is accidentally turned into a talking llama by his conniving evil advisor, the witchlike Yzma, because Kuzco fires her. Kuzco himself is a vain, despotic hipster, perhaps a model for the 1990s Silicon Valley types, who tramples upon his people for his own pleasure. However, he learns that he cannot survive without the help of a kind peasant, Pacha, whose village had been threatened by Kuzco, for the young emperor had ordered Pacha's village to be destroyed so that he could build a luxurious summer home called Kuzcotopia as a gift to himself for his eighteenth birthday. After numerous comic adventures, Pacha helps Kuzco regain his human form and turn Yzma into a kitten and her dumb lover into a Boy Scout leader. And Kuzco, who supposedly has learned how to become kind, builds his utopian summer house on a hill facing Pacha's village.

Figure 2
Tex Avery,
*Swing Shift
Cinderella*

The sentimental music and tendency of the drawings in each scene are intended to make the audiences feel sorry for the wise-cracking Kuzco and also to identify with the tender-hearted submissive Pacha. From an ideological perspective, the film is a disaster, for it displays South Americans in stereotypical forms and repeats the totalitarian message that almost all the Disney films have conveyed since their origin: the role of the peasants or little people is to help to reinstall kings, emperors, queens, princesses, and other celebrities so that they can rule more graciously. But rule they must and should. This is a stale message and a stale approach to fairy tales, and despite the moderate commercial success of *The Emperor's New Groove* and its television and DVD sequels, it may not be able to withstand the de-Disneyfying opposition of filmmakers, who seek to offer a fairy-tale vision of the world that will enable audiences to think for themselves and to grasp the forces that are degenerating their utopian longings. As the recent Disney production, *The Princess and the Frog* (2009), shows, the Disney filmmakers continue to produce for profit and the glory of the corporate brand, while more interesting and vital fairy-tale films are receiving a great deal of attention.

About the same time that *The Emperor's New Groove* was packaged for the market along with all sorts of books and articles to gain additional profit, the *Shrek* films and the Michel Ocelot and Hayao Miyazaki animated fairy-tale films appeared and began earnestly challenging the Disney reign. There were also several superb live-action films that made their mark in and beyond America. This was only the tip of the iceberg. Actually, there were and are hundreds of fairy-tale films, animated, live-action, mixed media, and digital that offer diverse perspectives on storytelling and fairy tales. In the following chapters, I shall endeavor to paint a clear picture of the debates and conflicts over the fairy-tale film and why we might see the world around us with more insight if we took off our Disneyfied lenses.

3
Georges Méliès: Pioneer of the Fairy-Tale Film and the Art of the Ridiculous

The divergence of the constructive and the mimetic, which no artwork can resolve and which is virtually the original sin of aesthetic spirit, has its correlative in that element of the ridiculous and clownish that even the most significant works bear and that, unconcealed, is inextricable from their significance. The inadequacy of classicism of any persuasion originates in its repression of this element; a repression that art must mistrust. . . . [The artwork's] ridiculousness is, however, also part of a condemnation of empirical rationality; it accuses the rationality of social praxis of having become an end in itself and as such the irrational and mad reversal of means into ends. The ridiculousness in art, which philistines recognize better than do those who are naively at home in art, and the folly of a rationality made absolute indict one another reciprocally.

Theodor Adorno, *Aesthetic Theory*[47]

Any discussion of the fairy-tale film must begin with Georges Méliès, and any discussion of Méliès must begin with understanding how he brazenly incorporated the ridiculous in his art not simply to parody the classical structure and contents of the fairy tale but to broaden our curiosity about the wonder and the enigma of the genre. In Adorno's brilliant assessment of the significance of the ridiculous in art, he claims that

the ridiculous, as a barbaric residuum of something alien to form, misfires in art if art fails to reflect and shape it. If it remains on the level of the childish and is taken for such, it merges with the calculated *fun* of the culture industry. By its very concept, art implies kitsch, just as the obligation it imposes of sublimating the ridiculous presupposes educational and class structure; *fun* is art's punishment for this. All the same, the ridiculous elements in artworks are most akin to their intentionless levels and therefore, in great works, also closest to their secret.[48]

Méliès' notion of fun was shaped by a keen intellect that had a political edge to it. As John Frazer has remarked in one of the best studies of Méliès' life and work:

> While the films created by Georges Méliès in his studio at Montreuil have a clear affinity with popular and folk traditions of the Belle Epoque, we must be cautious in identifying Méliès the artist with the tastes of the audiences he had chosen to please. Méliès was not, as used to be said, a naive folk artist. He was a showman who created broad farce for his own profit and for the pleasure of the masses, an urbane popular entertainer who was particularly sensitive to the unselfconscious tastes of popular culture. His films were made for the unsophisticated and their children. He loved that world and nothing pleased him more than the natural laughter and delight elicited by his magical turns. He was the ringmaster, the compère of a review, who always maintained his sensitivity which encompassed both the popular sensibility and the artistic traditions available to him at the end of the nineteenth century.[49]

Méliès was first and foremost a fanatic magician and man of the theater turned into an obsessed and inspired filmmaker, and once he discovered the potential of the camera to alter our perspective of reality, he became engaged in serious projects and experiments to test the constraints of artistic categories. At his best, he employed the mode of the ridiculous to expose the absurdity of rational actions in human striving and expectations. In doing this, Méliès put himself through a rigorous education, and it is important, I believe, to know something about his life,[50] before analyzing why he incorporated the ridiculous in his fairy-tale films and how the ridiculous enriched the fairy tale. In fact, Méliès's own life reads something like a fairy tale of a good sorcerer, who fell upon hard times when he could not compete with corporate magic. A version of his life was recently published as a kind of graphic novel, *The Invention of Hugo Cabret*, by Brian Selznick. Whereas Selznick makes Méliès into a mysterious, grumpy but loveable old man, Méliès in reality retained his dignity as an artist even as he was threatened by oblivion toward the end of his life.

The Merry and Sad Adventures of Georges Méliès

Born into a very wealthy bourgeois family on December 8, 1861, in Paris, Méliès was the youngest of three sons. His father Louis Méliès was a prosperous boot manufacturer; his mother, Johannah-Catherine Schuering, was the daughter of a well-to-do Dutch bootmaker at the Hague court. Her family moved to Paris after their factory had burned down. It was in Paris that Johannah-Catherine and Louis worked together, built their own workshop, and invented a new stitching process that enabled Louis to prosper in the boot business, buy properties, and become a multi-millionaire. By the time Georges Méliès was born, the family was rich enough to send him to two of the most prestigious schools in Paris, the Lycée Impérial at Vanves and the Lycée Louis-le-Grand. However, Méliès never enjoyed the privileges of a superior schooling; that is, he disliked the strict classical education because his time at both schools was heavily regimented. He was not an exceptional student and preferred to spend his time drawing, sketching caricatures, and creating puppet shows. By 1880 he managed to obtain the *baccalauréat*, the first in his family to do so, and was obliged to serve three years in the French army beginning in 1881. Fortunately, he only had to spend one year in service and began working for his father in the fall of 1882, even though he was not at all interested in manufacturing boots, if he ever was. He was always more interested in the fine and performing arts. After his official release from the army in 1884, he hoped to attend the École des Beaux Arts to become a painter. However, his father refused to support him and demanded that he continue to learn the trade of boot manufacturer. Consequently, Méliès was sent to London to improve his English, establish connections for his father, and become more experienced in commerce and the boot business. Though this assignment made him unhappy, his *séjour* in London turned out to be most beneficial for Méliès because he spent a good deal of his time frequenting the theater and magic shows. He was particularly taken by the spectacular performances at the Egyptian Hall in Piccadilly run by John Nevil Maskelyne and George Alfred Cooke, and he attended numerous pantomime and vaudeville shows based on fairy tales. In particular, he was strongly influenced by Maskelyne, who befriended him and mentored him in the art of magic.

Inspired by his experiences in London, Méliès hoped to become a magician when he returned to Paris in 1885. He soon began taking lessons from Émile Voisin and performing tricks in salons and before his family. That same year he married Eugénie Genin, illegitimate daughter of a wealthy friend of the family, and her dowry allowed him to spend more time studying art, theater, and magic. It was not until 1888, however, that Méliès could devote himself entirely to magic and vaudeville shows. This was the year that his father retired from the boot business and divided it among his three sons. Méliès immediately sold his share to his brothers and bought the famous Théâtre Robert-Houdin on Boulevard des Italiens in the center of Paris. This theater, which was especially constructed for magic tricks and contained trap doors, pulleys, ramps, and all sorts of mechanical devices, was named after the renowned magician Jean-Eugène Robert-Houdin (1805–1871), whose elegant performances and illusions had transformed the ways conjurers worked in the nineteenth century. Méliès was undoubtedly influenced by Robert-Houdin, but even more by his work in London with Maskelyne, who devised narratives and plays and elaborate sets to create a sense of enchantment and spectacle. From the time Méliès bought the Théâtre Robert-Houdin in 1888 until he sold it in 1915, he performed magic tricks, wrote skits and fairy-tale plays, designed all the sets, invented and built mechanical contraptions, including automats, directed and acted in plays, and handled all the business matters of his theater. Paul Hammond points out that

> from 1888 to 1907 Méliès invented thirty or so "theatrical compositions," many of them variations of older illusions (Maskelyne's), a number of which were put on the market by his friend, the theatrical supplier Voisin, who had helped him make a start in conjuring. In this way Méliès' illusions were seen in fairgrounds and music-halls long before his films were shown there. At the Théâtre Robert-Houdin many famous artistes performed in his (and their own) productions.[51]

In addition, Méliès occasionally dedicated himself to political causes to oppose ultra-conservative movements such as General Boulanger's endeavors to overthrow the Third Republic in 1888. Méliès drew cartoons for a journal that satirized the monarchical causes, and later he was a strong defender of the falsely accused General Dreyfus and made a series of provocative films about *L'Affaire Dreyfus* in 1899 that were banned by the French government.[52]

But what stirred Méliès's imagination most of all was the cinema. On December 28, 1895, he attended the first public showing of the Lumière *cinématographe* at the Grand Café, and he was so captivated by it that he wanted to buy a *cinematographe* from the Lumière brothers right away. When they declined his offer, however, Méliès traveled to London, where he bought a projector from Robert William Paul, a British inventor, and then modified it with the help of a French mechanic, Lucien Korsten. By April 4, 1896, he was able to present his first show at the Théâtre Robert-Houdin that consisted of short films by other filmmakers with seascapes, boxing kangaroos, and dancers. By 1896, Méliès made his first film about playing cards, and in 1897, he founded his own film company called Star Film Company and constructed the first film studio in Europe on family property in Montreuil, a suburb of Paris. His early films were very short and were largely documentaries or realistic films about daily life or important current events that were restaged. By 1899, however, he began to experiment with all kinds of narratives and also plays performed either at the Théâtre Robert-Houdin or at other locales. Soon, he began producing adaptations of fairy tales, science fiction, legends, and other fantasy stories that he created.

Among the early filmmakers and directors in the western world, it was Méliès who paved the way for fairy-tale films and experimentation with cinematic storytelling. Aside from his genial camera work and extraordinary set designs, Méliès brought a special element to independent filmmaking that has served as a model for numerous filmmakers who have followed him up through the twenty-first century. As the innovative Canadian filmmaker Norman McClaren has remarked,

> There is another aspect of Méliès that was remarkable and which must account for much of the freshness of his films when compared with those of his contemporaries. To quote Méliès himself, "I was at one and the same time an intellectual and a manual worker—that explains why I loved the cinema so passionately." An intellectual worker and a manual worker at the same time. He was not only his own producer, ideas man, script writer, but he was his own set-builder, scene painter, choreographer, deviser of mechanical contrivances, special effects man, costume designer, model maker, actor, multiple actor, editor, and distributor. While other producers tended to reply on assistants and studio personnel to carry out their ideas, Méliès wanted to do everything himself. He was not afraid of getting his hands dirty; in fact, to take a close and intimate concern with every facet of the job was an essential and vital part of the whole process of film making.[53]

Between 1896 and 1913, Méliès made over 520 films in his Montreuil studio, which was built to reproduce conditions in the Théâtre Robert-Houdin. Frazer gives a detailed summary of this gigantic glass structure that could adjust to natural lighting.

> Méliès had a pit three meters deep dug in the entire area where the stage was to be. The floor was modified and set up for stage fairy plays, with ramps, trap-doors, slots, set banks, elevator traps for apparitions, star traps, traps called "the tomb" and winches placed not above the stage as it is done in the theater but rather outside the studio which was then too narrow to put them inside.[54]

At the beginning, most of Méliès' films were shown at fairs. He also made advertisements, and many of the films were distributed overseas. Once nickelodeons and small cinemas became prevalent at the beginning of the twentieth century, there was a greater demand for his films. His most famous film, *Trip to the Moon* (1902), was so successful that it was often pirated. To protect himself from the illegal production of copies, his brother Gaston went to New York in 1902 and opened up an office to register the films for copyright in America. This meant that Méliès had to produce more films for both the American and European markets. Consequently, he had a second studio built in Montreuil, while his brother expanded operations in America. However, Méliès, who insisted in retaining quality control over all the films he made, began losing money in competition with larger studios like Gaumont, Pathé and Lumière in France and Edison in the United States, studios that could mass produce films. To help Méliès, his brother Gaston made some films himself in New Jersey and then moved to San Antonio, Texas, where he produced westerns in 1910 to keep pace with the larger corporations, but back in Paris, Méliès could not furnish enough films to keep Star Films profitable either in Europe or America. In debt, he signed a contract with Gaumont in 1910 to help with distribution, and in 1911, Méliès left Gaumont to sign a contract with Charles Pathé, who began distributing Star Films productions. At the same time, Méliès had to surrender artistic control over his films to Pathé, which began editing them under the supervision of the director Ferdinand Zecca. This change was very distressing for Méliès because Zecca butchered his films. Nevertheless, Méliès managed to produce one of his finest films, *The Conquest of the North Pole*, in 1912. Despite this success Pathé demanded new types of melodramatic and more realistic films, and audience tastes had also changed. When Méliès did not respond to new demands, he was obliged to abandon filmmaking in 1913, though he continued showing his films in the Théâtre Robert-Houdin until 1914. Then the outbreak of World War I forced all theaters to close for about a year, and by 1915, Méliès more or less abandoned the film industry, which was already in decline in France.[55]

When the theaters re-opened in Paris in 1915, he performed in magic shows and skits in the Théâtre Robert-Houdin with his daughter Georgette, his son André, and his mistress Jehanne d'Alcy. During the war, the studios in Montreuil were turned into a hospital and cinema. Many of his films were confiscated in Paris by the army and melted down for chemical use in boots. In 1920 Méliès delivered his final performance in the Théâtre Robert-Houdin, and three years later the theater was appropriated by the city of Paris and demolished to make way for the new Boulevard Hausmann. Méliès was meagerly compensated, and he also lost his studios and properties in Montreuil.

From 1923 until 1925, Méliès, who was heavily in debt and had rashly destroyed many of his negatives out of depression, performed in various variety shows and took on odd jobs to survive. But by 1925, his son and daughter, who had continued to act with him, had to leave him to earn a better living. At the age of 64, Méliès decided to marry his long-time mistress Jehanne D'Alcy, who had bought a small kiosk at the Montparnasse train station where she sold sweets, toys, and other trinkets. Méliès and his new wife worked in this shop from 1925 to 1932, and he sank into relative obscurity while living under poor conditions. However, there was one event that brought some light to his life in 1929, when a cache of Star Films was discovered among the property of a rich furniture owner, who had shown them in his store at the beginning of the century. Once the films were restored and new prints made, René Claire, Paul Gilson, and J. G. Auriol and two newspapers owned by the perfumier Coty organized a Méliès Gala at the Salle Pleyel in Paris on December 16 that brought attention to Méliès' great achievements as a filmmaker. Unfortunately, it did not bring about a great Méliès renaissance or help greatly in altering his living conditions. It was not until the mutual organization for people of the motion pictures (Mutuelle du Cinéma) gave Méliès a small apartment near Orly airport that he could stop working at the kiosk and live with his wife and granddaughter on a small pension. He spent the last years of his life writing scripts, drawing, meeting with film historians and admirers, and even acting with Jacques Prévert, Paul Grimault, and Jean Aurence in a publicity film. On January 21, 1938, Méliès succumbed to cancer, destitute but not forgotten.

Transforming and Adapting the Fairy Tale and *Féerie*

There is much to admire about Méliès' accomplishments, and he has certainly received due recognition in the past 30 years (finally) as one of the foremost pioneers of the silent film. Numerous books and essays have appeared and covered all aspects of his work. However, strange to say, very few film historians have written about his founding of the fairy-tale film as a genre. Of course, Méliès was not the only filmmaker at the end of the nineteenth and beginning of the twentieth century to adapt fairy tales for the cinema. There were others: G. A. Smith, *Cinderella and the Fairy Godmother* (1898); James Williamson, *The Little Match Seller* (1902); Edwin S. Porter, *Jack and the Beanstalk* (1902); Lucien Nonguet and Ferdinand Zecca, *La Belle au bois dormant* (1902); Ferdinand Zecca, *Ali Baba et les quarantes voleurs* (1902); Sigmund Lubin, *Le Petit Poucet* (1903); Lucien Nonguet, *Le Chat botté* (1903); Percy Stow, *Alice in Wonderland* (1903); V. Lorant-Heilbronn, *Le petit Poucet* (1905); Lewin Fitzhamon, *The Dollmaker's Daughter* (1906); Étienne Arnaud, *Barbe-bleue* (1907); Albert Capellani, *Cendrillon ou la pantoufle merveilleuse* (1907); and Percy Stow, *The Pied Piper* (1907), to name but a few of the directors and their films. But Méliès was by far the most innovative, the most intelligent, and the most prolific. Moreover, he more than likely influenced or spurred the other directors to adapt fairy tales, and his fairy-tale films have also continued to have an impact on contemporary filmmakers.

Of the 520 films that he made, there are about thirty or more that can be called fairy-tale films in a strict sense, that is, films based on the Perrault tales, melodrama *féeries*, vaudeville *féeries*, literary fairy tales, and original screenplays that he wrote. In some ways it is difficult to classify Méliès' films because almost all of them, except his documentaries about current events and short realistic films, involve magic tricks and miraculous transformation and could be considered fairy-tale-like. Nevertheless, it is helpful to try to distinguish the types of fairy tales and *féerie* plays he used to see the continuity of certain discourses and traditions and his contribution to the development of the fairy-tale film.

Many of his fairy-tale films are steeped in the tradition of the *féerie* in France. Katherine Singer Kovács notes:

> The *féerie* was born shortly after the French Revolution, when a new theater-going public composed primarily of uneducated spectators began to attend spectacle shows. This new public which sought thrills, excitement, and surprises in the theater enjoyed melodramas as much as *féeries*. In fact, in its earliest form the *féerie* was a type of melodrama in which acrobatics, music, and mime were the main elements. Like melodramas, the plots of most *féeries* pivoted upon a struggle between forces of good and evil. But while these forces remained invisible in melodramas, in *féeries* they were incarnated onstage by gnomes and witches. The plots of *féeries* were usually adapted from fairy tales in which supernatural creatures intervened in the lives of men. These creatures used magical talismans to effectuate the sudden metamorphosis of persons or things and the rapid replacement of one decor by another before the spectator's eyes.[56]

Actually, the origins of the *féerie* are older than the French Revolution. In his highly informative study, *La Féerie*, Paul Ginisty states:

> The origin of the *féerie* can be found in the court ballets of the sixteenth and seventeenth centuries, inspired in their action by stories and the marvelous. The Italian ingénues, summoned by Catherine de Médici, were the first to introduce the *féerie*. These graceful people were the great disseminators of the marvels. The court of the grand duke of Florence had been the school of intricate machine makers and decorators, Timante Buonacorsi, Baldassare Lancia, Nicolo Tribolo—they excelled in the offering of complicated and luxurious entertainments. Catherine de Medici placed Baltazarini in charge of the ballets, and this man of imagination responded to the confidence placed in him by calling the king's painter, Jacques Patin, the musicians Beaulieu and Salmon, and the royal poet La Chesnaie to collaborate in producing the ballet *Circé*. He hardly had enough money, for the ballet cost two hundred thousand ecus.[57]

Ginisty forgets to mention that this *ballet comique de la reine* was five hours long and danced by Queen Louise and the women of the court. Moreover, there were other developments in sixteenth-century Italy that may have influenced Catherine de Medici's penchant for the arts such as the reciting and enactment of fairy tales and myths at different courts.[58] In all the court entertainments in Italy and France during the baroque period, the spectacle was of utmost importance, and it consisted of magnificent displays based on myths and fairy tales that celebrated the glory and power of the court, which was likened to some kind of enchanted fairy realm. These ballets, masques, and operas were taken seriously at various courts in Europe; they often consisted of ten to fifteen tableaux or scenes; the stories were danced and sung by gifted actors and acrobats; machines and traps were invented and used to create illusions; characters such as fairies, witches, wizards, gnomes, gods, ghosts, devils, and noble protagonists were involved in plots that demanded the intervention of some good higher power, either a fairy, god, or goddess.

It should also be noted that, at the same time that these artful and serious spectacles were being cultivated, there were also comic representations that contained fairy-tale characters and themes and were influenced by the *commedia dell'arte*. By the time of Louis XIV's reign in the latter part of the seventeenth century it became common for the court to hold gala spectacles that certainly could be called *féeries* and for writers such as Corneille, Molière, and Lully to write plays based on myths and fairy stories. Moreover, the prose fairy-tale, influenced by the Italians Giovan Francesco Straparola and Giambattista Basile, became established as a genre in the 1690s thanks to the great vogue of fairy-tale presentations in salons and the publication of books of tales by Mme d'Aulnoy, Perrault, and other gifted writers, mainly women. This vogue continued well into the eighteenth century, but the fairy tale as play, ballet, opera, or narrative remained largely the entertainment of the upper classes. This is not to say that the lower classes did not cultivate the oral wonder tales and plays that involved fairy elements. But the *féerie* demanded lush scenery, acting, dancing, orchestras, and pomp that only the courts and upper classes could afford.

All this changed, that is, was transformed, after the French Revolution when a new audience consisting of different sectors of the middle and lower classes began attending the theater, vaudeville, and fairs throughout France and other countries in Europe during the nineteenth century. Among the types of plays preferred by this audience were melodramas and *féeries*. Most scholars have pointed to Alphonse Martainville's *Le Pied de Mouton* (*The Mutton Foot*, 1806), written with the actor César Ribié, as the classic example of the *féerie* in the nineteenth century. Ginisty remarks:

> *Le Pied de Mouton* is the model for the *féerie*, the *féerie* type. In truth, after its production, one could only repeat *Le Pied de Mouton* where one found the secrets of art, the battle among the fairies, each one endowing their protégés with talismans, the charming lover, and his grotesque rival, the explorations of marvelous worlds.[59]

This play opens with a monologue by Guzman, the charming hero, who has entered a forest to commit suicide because Leonora, the young woman he loves, is about to be married to a monstrous antagonist. Just as he is about to shoot himself, the pistols fly into the air, and a magnificent fairy appears from a flaming rock that opens right before his eyes. This fairy, who will protect him throughout the play, reprimands him and delivers a speech about the virtue, duty, and the preciousness of life. She gives him a magic mutton foot that will enable him to defeat his rival and save Leonora. Soon after Guzman embarks on his mission to save Leonora, he undergoes all sorts of trials in artificially arranged scenes with ballet and music and stage contraptions that make use of trap doors, smoke, and quick set changes. In the course of the action, there are many spectacular events that involve duels, moving portraits, the transformation of chaperones into guitarists, flying people, and disappearing food. All the magical effects are heightened to celebrate the power of true love and the triumph of good over evil that can only occur through the intervention of a fairy.

The success of *Le Pied du Mouton* was legendary, and during the first half of the nineteenth century there were many imitations, not only in France but also in Spain, where Juan de Grimaldi adapted *Le Pied du Mouton* and produced *La Pata de Cabra* (*Goat's Foot*) in 1829 with great success.[60] Spain had already established by this time its own tradition of *féerie* called *comedia de magia*. In England, James Robinson Planché, a dramatist and scholar of the history of costumes, continued the *féerie* tradition in England in various ways. In his memoirs he recalls a significant event while on a honeymoon in Paris in 1821:

> I saw, at the Porte St. Martin, the inimitable Potier in the "Comédie Féerie," by MM. Saurin and Brazier entitled, "Riquet à la Houppe," which was then in its first run, having been

produced about two months previously. I brought it with me to England, and fifteen years afterwards it formed the foundation of the first of those fairy extravaganzas which for so long a period enjoyed without one breakdown an almost unprecedented popularity.[61]

Planché made a name for himself with his fairy extravaganzas.[62] He also translated the French salon tales of the seventeenth century, and from 1836 to approximately 1854 he wrote and staged approximately twenty fairy extravaganzas in London such as *Puss in Boots* (1837), *Blue Beard* (1839), *Beauty and the Beast* (1841), and *Fortunio and his Seven Gifted Servants* (1845) that were comic melodramas, often parodies, bordering on the burlesque. They were known for their lush decoration, flashy music, fine acting, and tricks that were accomplished through machines and traps.

Both in England and in France, there was a movement away from the opera *féeries* and the pantomime *féerie* to the vaudeville *féerie*. Kovács remarks about the development in France:

> As the century progressed and vaudeville writers fixed the form and the conventions of the *féerie*, comedy became more important than poetry, and tableaux were more burlesque than beautiful. Authors began to devise more outlandish and elaborate settings for the *féerie*. The number of tableaux increased. By the end of the Second Empire in 1870, *féerie* contained as many as 20 different sets. In addition to the palaces, huts, underground caves and moving forests which the *féerie* inherited from melodrama, it acquired some new locales such as the sun, the moon, India, China, and Turkey.[63]

Méliès was familiar with the *féerie* in all its forms: melodrama, opera, ballet, and vaudeville. He grew up in the theater district of Paris, attended many different kinds of performance including those at fairs, and saw fairy-tale plays in London. As John Frazer notes:

> The ideas utilized by Georges Méliès for his major film productions did not, for the most part, spring sui generis out of the head of their imaginative creator, but were derived from a wide variety of specific theater pieces. The Méliès family home in Paris was for a long time on the Boulevard St. Martin, near the area that was the home for many of the theaters of Paris specializing in fantasies and spectacles. A few blocks away was the Gaîté-Lyrique, directed by Jacques Offenbach after 1862. Offenbach's musical productions were celebrated for the sumptuous decor and costumes that he, like Méliès at a later date, designed for his spectacles. Offenbach's fantasy operetta, *A Trip to the Moon*, was one of the inspirations for Méliès' best-known film, although that relationship was less important than the link between the film and the Jules Verne story. Méliès also adapted Offenbach's *Tales of Hoffman* as a magic illusion for the Robert-Houdin stage.[64]

Frazer could have also mentioned Offenbach's opera bouffa, *Bluebeard*, which premiered at the Théâtre des Varietés in 1866 and was performed frequently in Paris and in many other parts of the world. Fairy-tale operas and plays, as J. M. Barrie's *Peter Pan* (1901) and L. Frank Baum's musical version of *The Wizard of Oz* (1904) indicate, remained popular in Europe and America well into the early part of twentieth century. Though Méliès was not original in adapting the *féeries* and fairy tales, he was a consummate master of the forms, the designs, the costumes, tricks, and machines that made his films the most fascinating in this new filmic genre. Moreover, he had an astoundingly comprehensive knowledge of different types of fairy tales, wrote some of his own, and interpreted them in unique ways. Though he often used women as ornaments in his fairy-tale films and dressed them in spare costumes, he also endowed fairies with great powers, employed cross dressing, and clearly sympathized with mademoiselles in distress just as he generally favored small heroes and oppressed people. Whatever he did, he did with a twinkle in his eye and an eye for the ridiculous and preposterous in marvelous realms that he created in his Montreuil studios.

His fairy-tale films can be generally divided into three categories: 1) adaptations of Perrault's fairy tales; 2) adaptations of literary fairy tales; 3) re-creations of *féeries* and original *féeries*. I want to discuss a few films in each of these categories to demonstrate how Méliès used the techniques, machines, and tricks that he developed to embellish and exaggerate contradictions in fairy tales and to make social comments by ridiculing abuses of power. It is through his artful, comic, and careful staging of narrative contradictions and human frailties that Méliès demonstrated great originality and innovation. Clowning in Méliès' films was always a serious endeavor.

Re-Creating Perrault

Only three of Perrault's tales were used as hypotexts by Méliès: *Cinderella* (1899), *Little Red Riding Hood* (1901), *Bluebeard* (1901), and *Cinderella* (1912). Unfortunately, the 1901 version of *Little Red Riding Hood* has never been recovered. However, there is enough documentation (stills, synopses, sketches) to grasp Méliès' approach to all the tales by Perrault that he adapted. His earliest films are undoubtedly the most interesting and demonstrate his comic perspective.

The *Cinderella* of 1899 is a compact version of about six minutes with five tableaux in which clocks steal the show. In the first scene Cinderella is portrayed in a patched dress in a kitchen with a large fireplace and a big clock on the side. Her stepmother leaves. She sobs. All at once a fairy appears in the fireplace. She instructs Cinderella to let some mice out of a trap, and within seconds they become coachmen, and a coach manifests itself in the kitchen while Cinderella is transformed into a princess. The fairy points to the clock, and Cinderella is carried off in the coach that somehow is supposed to make its way out of the kitchen. The next scene is a ballroom that has a clock standing prominently in a corner. Cinderella arrives and enchants the prince. For the first time we see her two disgruntled stepsisters. As Cinderella is dancing with the prince a mischievous imp or gnome, played by Méliès himself, appears carrying a clock followed by the fairy, who changes her back into a young woman in rags. The entire upper-class society berates Cinderella. Immediately following this scene we are brought back to a neat living room with a distressed Cinderella returning home. There is a large clock in the room that begins to move. The imp reappears and taunts Cinderella with a huge clock. Then four gorgeous women pop out of the clock and dance with clocks that then

Figure 3
Georges Méliès, *Cinderella*

dance by themselves. Once they all disappear, the two stepsisters return home followed by the prince, who asks all the women to try on a leather slipper. Of course, it fits Cinderella, and the fairy appears to bless their union. The next scene takes place in a garden outside the prince's palace. The villagers with women cross-dressed as male peasants form couples with female shepherdesses to celebrate the wedding with a simple pastoral dance. The final scene is one of Méliès' favorite happy-ever-after scenes where Cinderella and the prince are seated on lavish thrones surrounded by courtiers in luxurious dress.

The film is more a spoof of "Cinderella" than a serious rendition about an abused step-daughter. Frazer notes Méliès may have been influenced by an 1896 pantomime that had been performed at the Théâtre de la Galerie-Vivienne and that Jules Massenet's opera *Cendrillion* was produced the same year as Méliès' film.[65] Whatever the case may be, Méliès makes light of the abuse that Cinderella may have received and focuses on her commitment to the fairy and the clock. Her fate, however, is never to be taken seriously, for Méliès was an optimist, who believed in the intervention of higher powers such as fairies, who would always take the side of the good. The clock as the overbearing and ridiculous symbol of order and duty plays no role in the end. Rather the kindness of the marvelous fairy and the love of the prince rescue her from poverty. Méliès constantly disrupts rational accounts and narratives to suggest that life is never run according to plan.

This is also the case in *Little Red Riding Hood* and *Bluebeard* of 1901. Both films are almost twice as long as *Cinderella*, and this extra time allowed Méliès to embellish his films with entertaining changes. Film was not simply an illusion for Méliès, it was also a theatrical laboratory in which artists could play with possibilities and display their imagination. In his hands, *Little Red Riding Hood* and *Bluebeard* become delightful family melodramas in which monsters are defeated and the slaughtered women rise from the dead. Red Riding Hood is the daughter of pastry makers, and when she wanders into the woods to grandma's house, there are scenes in which she goes dancing and other comic digressions. The wolf is a shaggy puppet and, unlike Perrault's fairy tale in which Little Red Riding Hood is gobbled up, workers from the pastry shop arrive to save her. The wolf escapes only to be shot by a gamekeeper. Then the beast is carried in triumph to the village square where he is comically roasted on a spit while the family celebrates a joyful reunion with their wayward daughter. In *Bluebeard*, Méliès makes some very important changes to the plot by showing how a greedy father forces his daughter to wed the monstrous Bluebeard, who is played as a bombastic buffoon by Méliès. In every scene, Méliès adds comic touches such as a parade through the kitchen where a worker becomes lost in a kettle, a gnome who jumps out of a book to entice Bluebeard's wife to open a secret door with a gigantic key, a nightmare filled with dangling keys and ghosts, and a finale in which Bluebeard is pinned to a post by a sword stuck in his chest and must watch his seven wives rise from the dead to be married to seven cavaliers. As usual, there is a final throne scene organized by a fairy, who has intervened throughout the action.

All the bizarre and preposterous events in both films are made even more bizarre and pre-posterous by hyperbolic acting and extravagant sets and costumes. Méliès sought to sweep his viewers away from reality so that they could indulge their imaginations. His films were intended to go beyond the actual telling or reading of a fairy tale. Spurred by the theater, which had the advantage of music and voice, Méliès sought to offset those technical advantages through stop-motion, dissolves, montage, and special machines that dazzled perspective and engendered laughter. But he was not always successful. His last adaptation of a Perrault tale, about twenty-eight minutes long, failed not only because Ferdinand Zecca of Pathé edited and ruined the final version, but also because Méliès desperately used trick after trick in boring scenes that had little comic relief. In fact, he followed Perrault's narrative too closely with the intent of making it into a melodramatic love story. Nevertheless, the film has its moments with the stepsisters actually beating and slapping Cinderella, a stunning fairy accompanied by other attractive fairies who turn into royal male servants in Cinderella's entourage, a foolish wild-goose search for Cinderella's slipper, and a slipper-trying contest in the middle of the village. It is interesting to note that there is only one scene in which a clock appears.

In all of his adaptations of Perrault's fairy tales, the influence of the *féerie* and vaudeville shows can be felt. But Méliès always added something to the magical drama to question stereotypes, audience expectations, assumptions of power, and notions of good and evil. Everything is relative in a Méliès film. Nothing can be defined with certainty even when there is a glorious happy end in most of his fairy-tale films. One must wonder whether these bombastic finales that ended in poses of grand majesty were nothing but the republican Méliès' last laugh at regal pomp.

Exploring Other Literary Fairy Tales

Other than adapting Perrault's fairy tales, Méliès used *The Arabian Nights* for *The Palace of the One Thousand and One Nights* (1905), a French fairy-tale witch for *The Fairy Carabosse, or The Fatal Dagger* (1906), and *The Surprising Adventures of Baron Munchausen* for *The Hallucinations of Baron Munchausen* (1911). Of course, there are various literary references and motifs in other films such as *Coppelia, the Animated Doll* (1900). In general, Méliès' adaptations of literary works reveal his disposition to recreate narratives freely with the comic perspective of the vaudeville and melodrama *féerie*. Time constraints also limited his ability to explore the themes of the narratives in depth.

The Palace of the One Thousand Nights is an eclectic borrowing of all sorts of Oriental motifs that Méliès shaped to form a simple frame story filled with numerous exotic scenes, which appear to be created only to foster a spectacle of *féerie*. The frame story involves the Prince Sourire (Smile), who seeks the hand of the Princesse Indigo from a mighty rajah. However, since Prince Sourire is not wealthy, the rajah rejects him and intends to give his daughter to a rich, old usurer named Sakaram. In despair, Sourire returns to his dwelling with his friends. He rejects their attempts to console him and compels them to leave him alone. (This beginning that features a despondent lover is typical of numerous *féeries* based on *Le Pied du mouton*.) In his despair, Sourire accidentally knocks a jar of incense from a table, and the sorcerer Khalafar appears from a cloud of smoke reminiscent of the Arabian Nights genii, who appears from the magic lamp. After hearing Sourire's tale of woe, Khalafar gives him a magic sword and tells him that if he is courageous enough, the sorcerer will lead him to a great treasure that will enable him to marry the Princess Indigo. Accompanied by his friends, Sourire manages to survive an abundance of tests and adventures and to gain a treasure from the fairy of gold in the palace of the one thousand and one nights. In the end, he returns to the rajah's palace just as Princess Indigo is to marry the old usurer, and he displays the great treasure that he has obtained. Of course, the greedy rajah breaks his pledge to the usurer, banishes him, and allows his daughter to marry the prince.

There are over twenty changes of scenes in this faux Oriental film, which is more interesting for its décor than anything else. Almost all the sets are elaborate surrealist "paintings" of sacred temples, rivers with strange creatures, the swan boats of a blue dwarf, a magical jungle, an ice palace with dancing skeletons, a grotto with fascinating animated puppet toads and reptiles, an underworld where women dressed in tutus perform a ballet, and a magnificent golden palace. As usual, the costumes are lavish, and the women are scantily dressed. There are comic incidents, but little dramatic conflict in this film that is too lush, predictable, and slow to be interesting.

In contrast, *The Fairy Carabosse, or The Fatal Dagger*, also known simply as *The Witch*, is a brilliantly designed and dazzling adaptation of French fairy-tale motifs and characters. Carabosse was the name given to a wicked fairy by Mme d'Aulnoy in her tale "La Princesse Printanière" ("Mayblossom," 1697). Until d'Aulnoy's time, fairies who acted like witches and malevolent fairy godmothers had generally been anonymous in the French oral and literary tradition. And they still are largely unnamed. But like the name of the great Russian sorceress, Baba Yaga, and names of other powerful fairy/witches, who could do both good and bad depending on their moods and whether they have been crossed, names added and add spice to a character, and Carabosse became well-known in France and even played a significant role in Tchaikovsky's ballet of *Sleeping Beauty* in 1890.

In Méliès' *The Fairy Carabosse*, the witch is indeed the central figure, and she is brilliantly played by Méliès himself as a crooked-nosed, diabolic hunchback, who is concocting a magic potion in the laboratory of a dilapidated castle in the first frame. A penniless troubadour appears out of the blue and asks the witch to read his fortune. She reads his palm and tells him that he will become very rich, but he does not want wealth, he wants to know the young woman who will love him. So, the witch has a magic mirror brought out by two clownish gnomes. All at once, a beautiful woman tied to a post appears within the frame of the mirror, and the troubadour is smitten. The witch has her disappear, and the mirror carried off by two bumbling gnomes. The troubadour declares that he is prepared to brave anything to rescue her. The witch offers him a magic four-leaf clover that will protect him, but she also demands a great sum of money from the troubadour, who cannot pay. When her back is turned, however, he fills a bag with sand and presents it to the witch as gold. After she gives him the clover, he runs off. Once she discovers she has been tricked, she creates a magic dagger from the blazing fire of a furnace that spurts smoke and will kill the person who tries to use it. She intends to give the "fatal dagger" to the troubadour so that he will kill himself, and she pursues him on her broom. Thus, the first of Méliès' chase scenes begins: the troubadour scurrying over desolate landscapes to a gloomy cemetery followed by the witch on a broom. In the cemetery of an abbey in ruins he is threatened by ghosts who arise from tombs through elevator traps. Though frightened, the troubadour wards them off with his four-leaf clover and manages to escape pursued by the witch on her broom. Finally, he arrives at the Tower of Despair, which is a castle in ruins where his beloved princess is held in captivity. The troubadour wants to cross a moat to rescue her, but he is confronted by huge animated puppets—a gigantic frog, a huge owl, and a dragon. Also, snakes start crawling toward him. When the troubadour tries to conquer the beasts and reptiles with his magic clover, he finds that it is useless. However, it does conjure up a powerful druid in a white gown, who looks a bit like Jesus on a pedestal. The druid gives him a sacred branch, which the troubadour uses to chase away the beasts and reptiles. At the same time, a tomb below the druid opens, and the Knight of Snow appears through an elevator trap. He is the savior of all the oppressed and the good people and offers the troubadour a magic sword that will protect him from the evil designs of Carabosse. Armed with the sword, the troubadour manages to climb into the castle, while the druid wards off Carabosse. After the troubadour escapes with the princess to a cliff overlooking Lake Azur, they are followed by the witch on her broom flying in the night against a marvelous backdrop of the moon and stars. As the couple embraces, Carabosse arrives to kill the troubadour, but the princess manages to use the clover to summon the druid, who pushes the witch over the cliff. Yet, before the witch falls, she magically calls one of her gnomes to help her. He arrives and is about to kill the druid with the fatal dagger that turns on him because it was enchanted by the witch to kill whoever wields it. In gratitude, the princess and the troubadour kneel before the druid to receive his blessings.

This action-packed eleven-minute film is a hodge-podge of fairy-tale motifs held together by the typical narrative structure of the *féerie*. Interestingly, there is no apparent reason why Carabosse should be punished in this fairy-tale film. After all, she reads him a good fortune, conjures up a beautiful woman, and gives the troubadour the magic clover, and then he cheats her. But in Méliès' films the world is always turned upside down, and so are fairy-tale narratives and characters. In *The Fairy Carabosse*, he mixes religious figures into the plot, and of course, the dark forces of evil represented by the witch must be defeated. The inconsistencies and the preposterous appearances of ghosts, a druid, a knight, and beasts, and reptiles are calculated to make spectators smile and ponder whether the absurdities on the screen can be so easily overcome as them seem to be.

The absurdities can also develop into ridiculous nightmares as in the case of *The Hallucinations of Baron Munchausen*. This film has little to do with the fairy-tale novel, which was originally published by an anonymous author in 1781, then translated into English and adapted by Rudolph Erich Raspe as *Baron Munchhausen's Narrative of his Marvellous Travels and Campaigns in Russia* in 1785, and made famous in another novel by the gifted German poet and writer Gottfried August Bürger in 1786 as *Wunderbare Reisen zu Wasser und zu Lande: Feldzüge und lustige Abenteuer des Freiherrn von Münchhausen* (*Marvelous Travels over Sea and Land: Campaigns and Funny Adventures of the Baron von Munchausen*). Each one of the versions contains tall tales and folk tales with fairy-tales told by the Baron to magnify his exploits. The book became so popular that there were well over 150 different versions in various European languages published in the nineteenth century not to mention several plays. (In the post-1945 period, the brilliant Czech filmmaker Karel Zeman, and the American-born British director Terry Gilliam, influenced by Zeman, produced fascinating film versions of *Baron von Munchausen*.)

Méliès decided to turn the book of preposterous tales into a series of nightmares experienced by the Baron and to break with the *féerie* tradition while creating a surreal fairy-tale dream sequence. The film begins with the Baron indulging himself at a small dinner party in an elegantly furnished parlor. When he becomes intoxicated, two of his guests lead him to his gilt baroque bed that has a huge gilt mirror right above it. After they tuck him in, he falls asleep and immediately begins dreaming and peering into the mirror that has its own stage. So, instead of dissolves, Méliès uses stop-motion action to change the scenes within the mirror. The viewer is viewing a stage and a stage within a stage. This technique allowed Méliès to sharpen the images that were not always clear in the dissolves or superimpositions.

Munchausen's dreams begin with a sweet vision of a minuet dance in a garden. Munchausen arises and wants to kiss the hand of a maiden, but the scene changes suddenly into a royal room where Cleopatra is reclining on a sofa. When Munchausen wants to approach Cleopatra, he is thrown back onto his bed by the attendants. Suddenly, there are three beautiful graces standing on a pedestal. Munchausen jumps back into the mirror to admire the women. (As usual, all the gorgeous women are scantily dressed or clothed in magnificent costumes to bring out their beauty.) As he is about to touch one of the women, they change into ugly reptiles and then devils and cast him back onto his bed. Munchausen wakes up and checks his mirror to determine whether he has been hallucinating or actually experiencing these episodes. Once he falls asleep again, he is transported by the bed to an oriental landscape where animated insects jump over his bed. He gets up and finds himself before a fountain where five half-naked women spout water. Soon it is winter, and before he knows it, Munchausen sinks to hell in a burst of smoke, and an extraordinary puppet dragon appears. Devils stick him back into his bed. Then there are several quick scenes featuring a woman spider with octopus tentacles, revolutionary troops that fire at him, an enormous moon that sticks its tongue at him that is transformed into an elephant's trunk, a horn-rimmed gigantic elephant, which sprays Munchausen with water. The water apparently wakes the baron, and he takes an armoire and throws it at the vision of the elephant resulting in Munchausen's falling out of the window. The next thing the baron knows is that he is impaled on a fence outside his home, one of the few scenes Méliès ever shot outside his studio. Servants run and fetch him inside, and he stands before a mirror examining his bumps and bruises with a sigh of relief.

This film is notable for its surreal images and display of scenes from fairy tales, myths, and history. The storyline is simple. Frazer thinks that the film is somewhat autobiographical. "No doubt Méliès sympathized with the poor baron who rages against demonic persecution. Méliès' demons of the moment were and the cause for his rages were Pathé's constraints on his artistic freedom and the expensive peregrinations of his brother Gaston."[66] This may be true to a certain extent. In 1911, when he made the Munchausen film, Méliès was in debt and was under obligation to Pathé. However, the film recalls the famous protagonist of Offenbach's *The Tales of Hoffmann*, who is constantly frustrated in his pursuit of true love. There is also something of the schlemiel in Munchausen's character. Of course, there is no pact with the devil, and Munchausen is more at the mercy of his hallucinations than of a demon. He survives his wild fantasies, and this is all that counts.

The Distinctive Film-*Féeries*

Munchausen is not one of Méliès's distinctive fairy-tale films. There are several much more characteristic of his style and ideology that laid the ground for the fairy-tale film, and those are based on folk and fairy tales that he wrote or on *féeries* that he created such as *The Devil's Castle* (1896/97), *The Philosopher's Stone* (1899), *The Rajah's Dream, or The Bewitched Wood* (1900), *The Sorcerer, the Prince, and the Good Fairy* (1900), *The Sorceress's Home* (1901), *The Enchanted Well* (1903), *The Sorcerer's Revenge* (1903), *The Kingdom of the Fairies* (1903), *The Enchanter Alcofribas* (1903), *The Grandmother's Tale and the Child's Dream* (1908), *The Marvelous Cobweb* (1908), *The Spirit of the Clocks, or The Son of the Bell-Ringer* (1908), *The Good Shepherdess and the Wicked Princess* (1908), and *The Knight of the Snows* (1912). I want to examine three examples of the typical Méliès *féerie*: *The Enchanted Well*, *The Kingdom of the Fairies*, and *The Knight of the Snows*.

Numerous folk and fairy tales feature wells. They were the gathering place in the center of villages. They were vital for peasants. Water was life giving. A trip to a well could be magical and catastrophic as we know in the well-known tale, "Mother Holle" in the Grimms' collection or Perrault's "The Fairies." It was a test to determine good girl/bad girl. In many versions of "The Frog Prince," the fountain is actually a well. And, in many folk tales involving wells, a tired old woman, who may look like a witch, is actually a fairy, and asks someone for water to see whether the person is kind enough to be rewarded. In Méliès' burlesque *The Enchanted Well*, the well is in a courtyard of a farm, and after several peasants pass by, a farmer wearing clogs arrives with a donkey played by an actor on all fours. The farmer is obviously the landlord. He kicks the donkey to his stall and begins to fetch water from the well when an old woman dressed as a crone appears and asks for alms.

Figure 4
Georges Méliès,
The Enchanted Well

The farmer rejects her and kicks her off the premises. Before she leaves, however, she casts a curse on him so that, when he takes a bucket of water from the well, the water turns into flames, and a demon pops out of the well to taunt him. The farmer hurls rocks at him, and he disappears down the well, which now shoots up several feet from an elevator trap and looks like a gigantic furnace with a tower. Animated reptiles and demons expose themselves and threaten him from all sides of the furnace while an enormous puppet snake endeavors to snare the farmer at the bottom. He escapes just as a demon appears on top of the well. The farmer takes a ladder and stick to get at the demon, but he falls down when the well itself collapses to its original size and four actors dressed in toad costumes jump out of the well and throw the farmer down into it. As the bedraggled farmer climbs out of the well, the well is dragged by rope and vanishes. All at once, the devil himself stands in the middle of the courtyard. He is attacked by the farmer and peasants with pitchforks. Once they surround him, however, he transforms himself into a bat and flies off.

Contrary to the typical ending of tales with wells and crones, nobody is rewarded in Mélès' film. In fact, one could call the film "The Witch's Revenge," and it is delightful. The actors are marvelous acrobats, and the puppets are goofy. The farmer is not a likeable character and certainly deserves to be punished for maltreating the crone, who does not seem to be wicked as in many of Méliès' other films. *The Enchanted Well* was made in 1903 just as Méliès had hit his stride as a maker of narrative fairy-tale films. This film, which has only one scene to it, one prop, and one backdrop, is a superb example of how Méliès was to frame his longer and more complicated fairy-tale films to incite laughter and to mock people who abuse their power. In and of itself, *The Enchanted Well* shows Méliès at his best as an original writer and designer of his own "ridiculous" fairy tales that have deep roots in folklore.

On the other hand, *The Kingdom of the Fairies* owes its form and contents to the theatrical tradition of the *féerie*, and many critics consider it one of his masterworks. Indeed, the film was enhanced by Méliès' acting. He performed the role of the major protagonist, Prince Bel-Azor, in this lush intricate *féerie* which has over eighteen different scenes and set designs and lasts close to twenty minutes. The plot itself is rather simple. The first scene takes place in the splendor of King Laurent XXIV's palace, where he announces the marriage of his daughter Princess Azurine to Prince Bel-Azor. Four fairy-godmothers arrive to endow the princess with gifts. All at once a nasty witch, who had not been invited to the celebration, arrives and curses the princess. The prince draws his sword

Figure 5
Georges Méliès,
*The Kingdom
of the Fairies*

to kill her, but she vanishes in a puff of smoke. In the very next scene that takes place in the sumptuous boudoir of the princess, the witch rises out of a trap door and tears apart a magic flower which was to protect the princess. With the help of spirited demons, whom she summons from the depths of the underworld, the witch abducts the princess. When Prince Bel-Azor learns about this, he is enraged and gathers together a company of armed knights in the cellar of the castle. As his men are departing the castle, he is left alone in the cellar for a moment. The witch appears and shows him a vision of the princess hoisted on to the tower of a distant castle by demons using pulleys, and she tells him that his rescue attempts will be useless. When he attacks her with his sword, he is easily thrust to the floor. The witch escapes on her broom. Then the fairy Aurore appears to grant him an invulnerable armor from the genie of invulnerability, a hump-backed dwarf, who does a somersault when he exits. Protected by this armor and also a magic sword, the prince and his men embark on a ship to the witch's castle. However, she casts a curse on the ship, which hits some rocks and is wrecked. All the men descend to the bottom of the ocean and appear to be dead. However, luscious sea nymphs alert King Neptune, who sends the water fairy in a chariot to rescue the prince and his men. She escorts them to the majestic palace of Neptune, who summons a gigantic puppet whale that will deliver the prince and his crew safely to the seaside of the witch's castle. Once they arrive, the prince valiantly storms the castle alone and rescues the princess from a castle set on fire by the witch's demons. The prince and princess rush to the edge of a cliff, where the witch attacks them. Once again, however, the fairy Aurore intervenes and pushes the witch over the cliff into the sea where she drowns. The last two scenes show the prince and princess receiving a joyous welcome in front of King Laurent's palace where the prince and princess are married. The final tableau is typical Méliès: it takes place in the kingdom of the fairies, arranged by the Fairy of the Airs and is composed of the prince and princess on gilt thrones, a ballet performed by fairies in tutus, and admiring people who are congratulating them in a glamorous pose.

Méliès' meticulous attention to detail in this film is what makes it so marvelous. All the costumes, the sets, backdrops, and machines combine to create an atmosphere of faerie splendor. There are set designs that rival surrealist collages and haunting painted backdrops. When the witch kidnaps the princess, Méliès depicts people from the court on a tower gazing at the witch. They are transfixed as they watch the witch and her demons in the moonlight rolling a chariot up a mountain; it is a scene that could even be likened to a weird composition in Chagall's paintings. There are other exotic images: the underwater scene of the shipwreck with a bizarre octopus stretching its tentacles while the fairy of the sea arrives in her chariot pulled by a gigantic fish and the scene of the enormous friendly whale that swallows the prince and his men while King Neptune gives his blessings. Méliès' imagination knew no bounds, denied formal and realistic rules of painting, and yet, was always thoughtfully suited to fit the canvas of fairy-tale narratives. Significantly, almost all his *féeries* were steeped in the French fairy-tale tradition of the 1690s when mainly female writers celebrated feminist longings and fantasies to change their worlds by focusing on the power of female fairies. Writers like Mme d'Aulnoy, Mme Murat, Mme Lhéritier and others cultivated the fairy tale subversively to question male prerogatives in the church and state. Méliès was by no means a feminist, and one might even label him some kind of sexist in the way he loved to focus on half-nude or beautifully dressed women and place them in all sorts of ridiculous poses as ornaments. On the other hand, Méliès remained true to the French salon writers by having fairies wield great power, even witches. They are the decisive force in almost all his *féeries*. Although he was always in charge of the artificially designed scenes in his films, he always gave a nod to the fairies in his finales as the "real" holders of power.

This is also true in one of the very last films he made, *The Knight of the Snows*. It is not entirely clear why the knight, Lord Gauthier, is called the Knight of the Snows, or the White Knight, except that he is identified with the good forces of light opposed to the brute Black Knight, who seeks revenge when King Majolic announces that his daughter, Princess Azurine, will marry the White Knight. Enraged, the Black Knight rushes to the dwelling of the sorcerer Alcofrisbas, who appears in other Méliès films. The sorcerer conjures up the demon Belphégor, who tricks the Black Knight into signing a pact with the devil. Soon after, the devil kidnaps Princess Azurine in a scene reminiscent of the kidnapping of Princess Azurine in *The Kingdom of the Fairies*. However, this time the princess is carted off in a cage drawn by an animated dragon up a mountain and lowered down into a dungeon in a gloomy castle. Once the White Knight learns about the abduction, he seeks help from the same sorcerer Alcofrisbas, who summons a fairy, who gives him a magic rose. In his pursuit he must cross an ocean and is accompanied by Neptune's daughters, Father Time, and a good fairy at the helm of a boat. After he arrives, he successfully rescues the princess and brings her back to the palace of King Majolic, where the White Knight accuses the Black Knight of treachery. Despite his pleas for mercy, the Black Knight is sentenced to be hanged. At the gallows he is surrounded by penitents in white sheets, and just as he is to be hanged, the devil appears and whisks him off to hell through a trap door.

Méliès appears to have run out of steam and joy in this last twenty-minute *féerie*. There are very few comic touches, and he borrows sets from other films. Nevertheless, *The Knight of the Snows* is a tightly-knit fairy-tale film that shows Méliès as a nimble master of the *féerie*, and it does have some unusual scenes and digressions from the traditional *féerie* plot. Amusing children play little demons who jump from a fireplace when the Black Knight enlists the help of the devil. The moveable cage drawn by a puppet dragon through the night is a wonderful surreal image as are the grottos through which the prince must swim to reach the dungeon of the princess. Once again, female fairies are the dominant driving forces who intervene to defeat evil and bring about harmony. Interestingly, there is no final pose of grandeur at the end of the film, which ends abruptly with the Black Knight dragged off to hell. If one were to read the film autobiographically, one might interpret it as Méliès' wish-fulfillment. By this time he was under contract to the Pathé Studio, which assigned people to edit Méliès' films. As defender of the realm of fairies, that is, imaginative films produced on stages in studios, Méliès fought to overcome the dark forces of corporate filmmaking to the bitter end. And, the end was indeed bitter for Méliès, for many new black knights were to rise up and declare his artworks anachronistic.

Méliès the Pioneer and his Contribution to the Fairy-Tale Film as Genre

Influence is difficult to trace and to register. Well-known during his productive years when he was the most prolific and original filmmaker of fairy-tale and fantasy films, Méliès set the bar for making fairy-tale films during the first decade of the twentieth century in Europe and America. It is difficult say whether he had an impact on filmmakers after this period, from World War I to 1930, or until the post-World War II period, when his films were rediscovered and re-circulated. But various filmmakers up through the present have mentioned that they were familiar with his works and that they were inspired by Méliès. What is more important in analyzing his contribution to the fairy-tale film is to comprehend his pivotal role in the evolution of the fairy tale from the oral to the literary to film.

Méliès used all the arts to explore how moving pictures could enhance the genre of the fairy tale. He was meticulous in every aspect of the film from writing the screenplay to acting in the plays that he directed and to drawing and painting the sets.

Not only did he adapt and appropriate literary and folk fairy tales, but he also transformed different types of *féerie* (vaudeville, melodrama, operetta) and recreated them for the cinema. He rarely stuck close to a particular text even when he adapted Perrault's tales. Indeed, he worked his magic on fairy-tale stuff with an unbridled imagination.

Due to his theater background, Méliès was among the first if not the first to emphasize narrative in his films, whether they were fairy tales, fantasy stories, or comic incidents that involved daily occurrences. A free thinker, Méliès shied away from ideology in his films, and he did not have a fixed concept of adapting fairy tales for the cinema. Rather, he worked from intuition and a particular disposition: to create films that would stun audiences and make them smile as they watched miraculous transformations and turn of events; and to reveal the ridiculous side of the abuse of power and fixed forms and perspectives. Méliès' fairy-tale films favor exploited and distressed young women, frustrated and dejected young men, beautiful, kind, and powerful fairies, cunning sorcerers who replace or foil kings, and optimistic dreamers, who want to cling to their visions. In short, he always took the side of the downtrodden or the little people and tended to grant them their wish-fulfillments, just as he provided hope for viewers of his films. He ridiculed the arrogance of the rich and punished mean and greedy kings, evil witches, demonic sorcerers, and pretentious aristocrats. It is true that his fairy-tale films generally did not call for radical social change, and they ended often with a grand finale in which there was a restoration of a monarchy. However, Méliès, who opposed a restoration of monarchical rule in France, saw morality in the fairy world as black and white, as an allegory of conflict between good and evil forces like the medieval *Romance of the Rose.* He saw good and evil in all classes of people and was not concerned whether a prince and princess married in his grand finales, which, as I have mentioned, were always somewhat ironic. Contradictions were part and parcel of Méliès' fairy-tale films. Good and kindness were most often invested in gorgeous fairies, whom he used to adorn his films in forms and shapes that would appeal to male fantasies. His sexist exploitation of women stemmed from an adoration of women, and male lovers basically served to obey fairies and rescue damsels in distress. What was important for Méliès was rectification of the abuse of power. As long as the fairies had power, evil could always be overcome.

Méliès' own magic power was the camera set in front of the stage that he designed. He rarely shot scenes outside his studio, and the comics of his scenes prefigured the early fairy-tale cartoons and animated films not to mention other live-action films of the 1920s, 1930s, and 1940s. Méliès interrogated the fairy-tale tradition and emphasized the ridiculous in the comic representations of the oral, narrative, and theatrical tradition of the fairy tale. The irrational happenings in his fairy-tale films that expose the limits of rational control and male domination lead to a playful if not utopian carnavalesque mirroring of the real world. Méliès mixed almost every known fairy-tale motif, character, and image to engender new visions and sometimes even nightmares. Whatever the case may be, he prepared the twentieth century for a great period of fairy-tale films that cover a range from pure kitsch to pure enlightenment. His form of enlightenment depended most of all on ridiculing social reality, and like all great filmmakers, he often stumbled as he sought to re-paint the world and to maintain his own integrity.

4
Animated Fairy-Tale Cartoons:
Celebrating the Carnival Art of the Ridiculous

The average cartoon runs approximately seven minutes, with subtleties that can easily be hidden from the viewer. Cartoons are a record of consumer rituals over the past seventy years: of transitions away from print media toward cinema, and then video; of the streets and stores where audiences shopped; and of the interior of consumers' homes. They are, above all, a narrative built around the expressive possibilities of the anarchic. They are another deterritorializing object, a tribute to the power of the naked line as transgressor.

Norman M. Klein, *Seven Minutes:*
The Life and Death of the American Animated Cartoon[67]

Cartoons—especially in their dominant Disney version—reformed, nestled up to the culture industry and changed their shapes correspondingly. The ideal reality that took on contours in Disney's fairy-tales showed nothing other than the momentary arrest of all possibilities for revolutionary social transformation. The idealized world moulded in Disney's fairy-tale reels made graphic the suppression of revolutionary hopes for social transformation in the 1930s and 1940s. Cartoon lines outlined political stances. Cartoon shapes and fantasies modeled social situations and the frustrations and joys that accompanied them. That there was a political edge to the cartoon line was expressed most dramatically in the now love affair, now skirmish, between Disney and the Nazis. The uses and abuses of the 'European' fairy-tale were at issue in the 1930s, as Nazi cabinet members, fascist filmmakers, communist critics, Europeans and Americans tussled over the bequest. These tussles, and others, reset the meanings of mass culture.

Esther Leslie, *Hollywood Flatlands: Animation,*
Critical Theory and the Avant-Garde[68]

Cartoons generated havoc for the genre of the print fairy tale as it made its way into the twentieth century. The seeds for what I shall call the carnival art of the ridiculous in fairy-tale films had already been planted in the French *féerie* tradition of the nineteenth century, the British extravaganzas, the vaudeville acts, the opera buffa, the shows at fairs, the magic performances, optical illusions, and comic strips. Georges Méliès, as we have already seen, relied on all these influences to create bedlam in his live-action fairy-tale films. But his work was only the tip of the iceberg.

The development of animation at the end of the nineteenth and beginning of the twentieth centuries opened up breathtaking creative possibilities for re-imagining and playing with the traditional fairy tales.[69] The great pioneers such as J. Stuart Blackton, Arthur Melbourne Cooper, Émile Cohl, and Winsor McCay, among others, demonstrated in diverse styles and techniques that live and inanimate objects could be drawn, molded, and sculpted and then arranged and rearranged to be photographed frame by frame. Once the frames were projected on film in some kind of narrative order or sequence, they appeared to assume a reality of their own. The created images or illusions were similar to the miraculous transformations within an oral and literary fairy tale except that, in this case, the fairies did not weave and control the magic, that is, the destiny of the characters and objects in a narrative. The animators were in charge, and they made sure that spectators knew who was acting godlike and creating the images that they were viewing and admiring. Consequently, it is important to consider the conditions of early animation in America and Europe and the role of the animator in general, for all this has a bearing on the animator's productive relationship with the fairy tale.

In his important study, *Before Mickey: The Animated Film 1898–1928*, Donald Crafton remarks that

> the early animated film was the location of a process found elsewhere in cinema but nowhere else in such intense concentration: self-figuration, the tendency of the filmmaker to inter-ject himself into his film. This can take several forms; it can be direct or indirect, and more or less camouflaged. . . . At first it was obvious and literal; at the end it was subtle and cloaked in metaphors and symbolic imagery designed to facilitate the process and yet to keep the idea gratifying for the artist and the audience. Part of the animation game consisted of developing mythologies that gave the animator some sort of special status. Usually these were very flattering, for he was pictured as (or implied to be) a demigod, a purveyor of life itself.[70]

As Crafton convincingly shows, the early animators literally drew themselves into the pictures and often appeared as characters in the films. One of the more interesting aspects of the early animated films is a psychically loaded tension between the artist and the characters he drew, one that is ripe for a Freudian or Lacanian reading, for the artist is always threatening to take away their "lives," while they, in turn, seek to deprive him of his pen (phallus) or creative inspiration so that they can take control of the narratives and their own lives. (Almost all the early animators were men, and their pens and camera work assume a distinctive phallic function in early animation.) The hand with pen or pencil is featured in many animated films in the process of creation, and it is then transformed in many films into the tails of a cat or dog. Sometimes the tails jump off animals to form exclamatory marks, weapons, or other signs. These tails then act as the productive force or artist's instrument throughout the film. For instance, Disney in his Alice films or Otto Messmer in his Felix the Cat films often employed a cat who would take off his tail and use it as stick, weapon, rope, hook, question mark, and so on. It was the phallic means to induce action and conceive a way out of a predicament. The Fleischer brothers, Walter Lantz, and other early animators were also fond of this technique that eventually led to Tex Avery's scenes of feisty fairy-tale characters in the 1930s and 1940s battling with the director of the film so that they could change their roles and forge their own plots and narratives. Ultimately, it was always the director or animator who had the last word, that is, image.

The celebration of the pen/phallus as ruler of the symbolic order of the film was in keeping with the way that animated films were actually produced in the studios during the 1920s. In America, where conditions were most propitious for cartoons and where the models for fairy-tale cartoons were set, most of the studios were at first located in New York and had become taylorized to save time and money. They were run by men who joined together under the supervision of the head of the studio to produce the cartoons. The American animators collaborated during the 1920s and 1930s to produce cartoons that dominated the world market, but they also competed and fought with one another because of their independent spirits, all seeking to make a mark so to speak through animation. Terrance Lindvall and J. Matthew Melton argue that the animator can be considered an *auteur*, especially if one considers the discursive nature of the cartoon.

> To have discourse, one must have communicating subjects, one of whom is the author (or *auteur*). This revived and reformed 'auteurist' approach must distinguish between the independent animator and the studio-driven, mass-produced cartoon. Yet, even in the latter, the voices of many authors whisper through the Studio Babel. The consciousness of the reader (his/her birth) occurs in encountering the author(s) in the words and images of the created text. The reader is neither a passive consumer of unyielding ideologies nor an independent constructor of brave new worlds, but one who seeks a meeting of the minds in the text. Cartoon authorship could involve a coterie of animators on Termite Terrace or just one *auteur* like the incomparable Norman McLaren, but the cartoon is a genre, like the avant-garde film, that highlights the name below the title. The authors leave their signatures or thumbprints on their work.[71]

It might be considered somewhat one-dimensional to examine all animated films as self-figurations, or embodiments of the animators' wishes and beliefs. However, to understand the importance of the producer and director of animated fairy-tale films that set a particular pattern and model as the film industry developed in the 1920s and 1930s, it is necessary to elaborate on Crafton's notions of self-figuration, for it provides an important clue for grasping the further development of the fairy tale as animated film driven by animators who made compromises with large studios to produce mass-marketed fairy-tale cartoons and who also resisted the conventions of the large studios, even though they might have worked within them.

Historical Transitions

One of the results stemming from the shift from the oral to the literary in the institutionalization of the fairy tale as genre was a loss of live contact with the storyteller and a sense of community or commonality. This loss was a result of the social-industrial transformations at the end of the nineteenth century with the *Gemeinschaft* (community) giving way to the *Gesellschaft* (society). However, it was not a total loss, for industrialization brought about greater comfort, sophistication, and literacy and new kinds of communication in public institutions. Therefore, as I have demonstrated in some of my other works,[72] the literary fairy tale's ascent corresponded to violent and progressive shifts in society and celebrated individualism, subjectivity, and reflection. It featured the narrative voice of the educated author and publisher over communal voices and set new guidelines for freedom of speech and expression. In addition, proprietary rights to a particular tale were established, and the literary tale became a commodity that paradoxically spoke out in the name of the unbridled imagination of the artist, who demanded that his/her uniqueness and individuality be recognized and respected. Depending on the mass market, artists and especially writers of fairy tales, who made claims for the integrity of their artworks, often spoke out against the market. Indeed, because it was born out of alienation to counter conditions that fostered alienation, the literary fairy tale engendered a search for new "magical" means to overcome the instrumentalization of the imagination. This quality, a utopian striving for a just and humane community, had always been and remains a strong component of the oral telling of fairy tales.

By 1900 literature began to be superseded by the mechanical means of reproduction that, Walter Benjamin declared, were revolutionary:

> the technique of reproduction detaches the reproduced object from the domain of tradition. By making many reproductions it substitutes a plurality of copies of a unique existence. And in permitting the reproduction to meet the beholder or listener in his own particular situation, it reactivates the object reproduced. These two processes lead to a tremendous shattering of tradition which is the obverse of the contemporary crisis and renewal of mankind. Both processes are intimately connected with the contemporary mass movements. Their most powerful agent is the film. Its social significance, particularly in its most positive form, is inconceivable without its destructive, cathartic aspect, that is, the liquidation of the traditional value of the cultural heritage.[73]

Benjamin analyzed how the revolutionary technological nature of the film could either bring about an aestheticization of politics leading to the violation of the masses through fascism, or a politicization of aesthetics that provides the necessary critical detachment for the masses to take charge of their own destiny.

In the case of the fairy-tale film at the beginning of the twentieth century, there are "revolutionary" aspects we can note, and they prepared the way for progressive innovation that expanded the horizons of viewers and led to greater understanding of social conditions and culture. But there were also regressive uses of mechanical reproduction that brought about the cult of the personality and the standardization and commodification of film narratives. For instance, the voice in fairy-tale films is at first effaced so that the image and printed words totally dominate the screen, and the words or narrative voice can speak only through the designs of the animator who has signed his name prominently on the screen. These images were intended both to smash the aura of heritage and to celebrate the ingenuity, inventiveness, and genius of the animator. In most of the early animated films, with some exceptions like Cohl, McCay, or Ladislas Starewitch, there were few original plots, and the storylines did not count. Most important were the gags, or the technical inventions of the animators ranging from the introduction of live actors to interact with cartoon characters, improving the movement of the characters so that they did not shimmer, devising ludicrous and preposterous scenes for the sake of spectacle, eccentric drawing, and so on. It did not matter what story was projected just as long as the images astounded the audience, captured its imagination for a short period of time, and left spectators laughing or staring in wonderment. The purpose of the early animated films was to make audiences awestruck and to celebrate the *magical* talents of the animator as demigod. As a result, the fairy tale as story was a vehicle for animators to express their artistic talents and develop the technology. The animators sought to impress audiences with their abilities to use pictures in such a way that they would forget the earlier fairy tales and remember the images that they, "the new artistic wizards," were creating for them. Through these moving pictures, the animators appropriated literary and oral fairy tales to subsume the word, to have the final word.

The early animators did not immediately turn to fairy tales as the stuff that they wanted to shape. The directors and producers of live-action films beginning with Méliès and a host of filmmakers such as Edwin Porter, Percy Stow, Albert Capellani, James Kirkwood, J. Searle Dawley, and many others were the first to explore the potential of the fairy tale for the cinema. Some stimulated the animators to take an interest in the fairy tale. By the beginning of the 1920s, the appropriation of the fairy tale by the cartoonists began in earnest, and three strong tendencies became apparent:

1) A carnivalesque approach to the classical fairy tales that sought to ridicule and play with the conventional forms and ideologies of the tales. This approach extolled the imaginative powers of the animators while endowing the tales with new meanings that often addressed contemporary manners and mores. While the carnivalesque animated fairy tale flowered in the 1930s and 1940s, it actually began with Bud Fisher and Raol Barré's *A Kick for Cinderella* and Walt Disney's *Laugh-o-Grams* in the 1920s and has persisted up through the fractured fairy tales of the 1960s and the recent raunchy cartoons of Seth McFarlane in the twenty-first century. The carnivalesque approach has also led to the creation of original fairy-tale films such as the live-action *The Princess Bride* (1987).

2) A non-reflective, standard, and conservative approach to the classical fairy tales that seeks to maintain the "original" meanings of the narratives. These animated fairy-tale cartoons were intended to show off the technological talents of the animators and cultivated an aesthetization of the contents to comply with the market expectations and dominant ideology of the times to set so-called high art values. The narrative sequences are predictable, the gags, infantile, and the characters, one-dimensional.

3) The creative experimental approach that employs silhouettes, puppets made out of cloth and wood, clay figures, marionettes, and other inanimate materials. This approach to the narratives of the classical fairy tales depended on the ideological and aesthetic perspective of the animator, who was often more intrigued by her/his exploration of technological inventions than making any explicit social or political statement through the experimentation. The fairy-tale narrative was a convenient vehicle for the art form. This is clearly the case in the films of Lotte Reiniger and Ray Harryhausen, who did not imbue their fascinating films with new meanings or even perspectives. But many experimental animators such as Starewitch and later Jan Svankmajer and Yuri Norstein challenged the manner in which spectators were to view and interpret fairy tales.

Before commenting in more detail about these tendencies, a word or two about the meaning of cartoon is necessary at this point. The English seventeenth-century word "cartoon" is derived from the Italian words *carta* (paper) and its augmentation *cartone* (which can also mean cartridge). It originally referred to a drawing on cardboard or heavy paper as a draft, design, or model for a painting, tapestry, or mosaic. By the end of the nineteenth century the word was also applied to a humorous illustration in a magazine, newspaper, or comic strip. At the beginning of the twentieth century, various kinds of machines and technological devices were invented that induced the movement of drawings in a certain arranged sequence, and these moving images were called cartoons. Two early examples of short animated films that were designated as cartoons were Émile Cohl's *Fantasmagorie* (1908) and Winsor McCay's *Gertie the Dinosaur* (1914). Essentially, they were graphic narratives without sound. Many early cartoons were derived from comic strips such as Bud Fisher's *Mutt and Jeff* or children's books such as Johnny Gruelle's *Raggedy Anne and Andy* books. Indeed, cartoons and live-action films "plundered" the print media for their ideas, narratives, and gags, and of course, they were greatly influenced by vaudeville. In his significant study of the cartoon, Norman Klein remarks that in animation, story is defined by the graphics and the vaudeville gag. "Character will adapt to whatever these two dictate. Disney redesigned these two in the thirties; and thereafter, the older use of story, what I defined as graphic narrative, was no longer appropriate. Disney was aiming for what he considered bigger game—a cartoon version of movie acting."[74] It was not until the 1930s that short animated comic films, generally seven minutes long, assumed their common meaning as cartoons and generally were fillers or shorts shown before a feature film in cinemas. It was also in the 1930s that lines were drawn, so to speak, to set up the conflicts in the cultural field of cartoons between the Disney standard approach to fairy tales and the carnivalesque approach to narratives exemplified in the works of Max and Dave Fleischer, Tex Avery, Friz Freleng, Chuck Jones, Bobe Cannon, John Hubley, and others. With the advent of television in the 1940s and 1950s, cartoons became a staple of television programs, generally for young audiences, and they were often lengthened to twenty-five or thirty minutes. Hand-drawn cartoons of different styles and techniques were dominant until the rise of computer-animated cartoons in the 1990s. Though the "world" of cartoons has been dominated by American filmmakers since the 1930s, this domination has basically been a market domination. Numerous animators from other countries produced cartoons throughout the twentieth century, and in recent years, Japanese and European filmmakers have created unique cartoons, particularly animated feature films, that have challenged the American hegemony.

The Carnivalesque Fairy-Tale Film

Carnivalesque fairy-tale films were prefigured in print by various authors who began writing and illustrating classical fairy tales from highly original perspectives. The emphasis in their works was on the humorous and ironic transformation of the characters and plots that revealed alternative possibilities for storytelling. The traditional meanings and forms of the fairy tales were contested by brazen writers and illustrators. For instance, F. W. N. Bayley published two illustrated volumes in verse, *Nursery Tales* (1846) and *Puss in Boots, Robinson Crusoe, and Cinderella* (1846), which were antic parodies of the classical tales. Incidentally, they were produced about the same time that James Robinson Planché was writing his vaudeville fairy-tale extravaganzas. At the beginning of the twentieth century Guy Wetmore Carryl published *Grimms Tales Made Gay* (1902), followed later by Edward and Joseph Anthony's *The Fairies Up-To-Date* (1923) with illustrations by Jean De Bosschère. Both books are filled with hilarious verse renditions of the Perrault and Grimms' tales. In 1925, Milt Gross, who drew comic strips and animated cartoons, brought out *Nize Baby*, a delightful Yiddish phonetic retelling of fairy tales. At the end of the decade, Johnny Gruelle, Thelma Gooch, and other famous artists collaborated in producing *The All About Story Book* (1929). One should also mention the great German illustrator and poet, Wilhelm Busch (1832–1908), whose comic strips of *Max und Moritz*, humorous broadsides, and illustrated fairy tales in the last half of the nineteenth century had a great influence on the development of comic strips in Europe and the United States in the twentieth century.

The graphic print narratives, especially the comic strips, sought to alter the reader's perspective on fairy tales, and the filmic cartoons have continued this tradition up through the present day. The mutual influence of comic strips/comic books and cartoons can be traced in the history of animated fairy-tale cartoons up through the present. However, given the multi-faceted technology of animation, the cartoonists have had greater technical liberty than the creators of comic strips and comic books to scandalize viewers' expectations of sweet tales with happy endings, especially when sound and color were introduced and enabled animators to add special effects. Moreover, they regarded themselves and projected themselves as dauntless "revolutionaries," ready to turn the world upside down through their drawings and mechanical puppets, dolls, clay figures, silhouettes, and so on. The two modes that added luster to the best of their cartoons—and they still do—are the carnivalesque and the ridiculous.

The notion of carnivalesque was developed by Mikhail Bakhtin in his important study, *Rabelais and His World*. Basing his literary concept on the carnival rituals and festivities celebrated in medieval and early modern Europe before Lent, Bakhtin argued that, as the rituals and festivities diminished and were modified, that is, as they were tamed in the civilizing process,

> the carnival spirit and grotesque imagery continued to live and was transmitted as a now purely literary tradition, especially as a tradition of the Renaissance. . . . In all these writings, in spite of their differences in character and tendency, the carnival-grotesque form exercises the same function: to consecrate inventive freedom, to permit the combination of a variety of different elements and their rapprochement from conventions and established truths, from clichés, from all that is humdrum and universally accepted. This carnival spirit offers the chance to have a new outlook on the world, to realize the relative nature of all that exists, and to enter a completely new order of things.[75]

Aside from using Rabelais as his main example of a carnivalesque writer, Bakhtin discusses Shakespeare, Lope de Vega, Grimmelshausen, Molière, and Diderot among others. He also maintains that the carnivalesque engenders a particular type of humor and laughter that characterizes certain animated fairy tales and cartoons and the responses to them.

> Laughter is essentially not an external but an interior form of truth; it cannot be transformed into seriousness without destroying and distorting the very contents of the truth which it unveils. Laughter liberates not only from external censorship but first of all from the great interior censor; it liberates from the fear that developed in man during thousands of years: fear of the sacred, of prohibitions, of the past, of power. It unveils the material bodily principle in its true meaning. Laughter opened men's eyes on that which is new, on the future.[76]

Ever since the Renaissance, the carnivalesque and the laughter that it generates have "invaded" all cultural forms of endeavor, high and low, and are a means both to open up readers/viewers to possibilities for overthrowing the holders of power and to throttle discontent because the carnivalesque can also provide a safety valve and channel the anger and outrage of people opposed to authorities. Certainly, carnivalesque fairy-films may do both: liberate and throttle while engendering laughter. A good deal depends on whether it tends to ridicule. That is, the ridiculous aspect of carnivalesque fairy tales must be taken into consideration, for it provides resistance against stale dominant forms of social and cultural relations.

As I have already shown in the chapter on Méliès, Theodor Adorno made some relevant comments about the ridiculous in his posthumously published book, *Aesthetic Theory*, that can help us grasp how profound many of the animated fairy-tale cartoons are because they embrace the ridiculous. To repeat part of the dense and complex passage of this book, Adorno writes:

> The rationality of artworks becomes spirit only when it is immersed in its polar opposite. . . . The progressive spiritualization of art in the name of maturity only accentuates the ridiculous all the more glaringly; the more the artwork's own organization assimilates itself to a logical order by virtue of its inner exactitude, the more obviously the difference between the artwork's logicity that governs empirically becomes the parody of the latter; the more reasonable the work becomes in terms of its formal constitution, the more ridiculous it becomes according to the standard of empirical reason. Its ridiculousness is, however, also part of a condemnation of empirical rationality; it accuses the rationality of social praxis of having become a means unto ends.[77]

For Adorno, every great work of art or any work of art that is to be considered truly artistic must somehow incorporate or sublimate the ridiculous (understood as silly, foolish, irrational, and clownish) in its form and content. The ridiculous aspect of a work of art prevents it from becoming stale, too rational, and too conventional. The ridiculous is a result of the unbridled imagination opposed to the instrumentalized imagination, curbed to serve a prescription or designed purpose. Adorno was always concerned by the manner in which the imagination was instrumentalized for explicit commercial purposes and rationally produced and disseminated works of art that were compromised by what he called the mediations and demands of the culture industry. Form and content of artworks are geared to serve market interests in the culture industry so that their systematic incorporation leads to a hollowing and standardization of art. Such rational creation, construction, and dissemination of art can only be opposed and subverted through the ridiculous that is expressed through the carnivalesque, irony, parody, the burlesque, and other comic modes. But, again as I have stressed before, Adorno was also aware that the ridiculous could itself be co-opted by the culture industry.

> The ridiculous, as a barbaric residuum of something alien to form, misfires in art if art fails to reflect and shape it. If it remains on the level of the childish and is taken for such, it merges with the calculated *fun* of the culture industry. By its very concept, art implies kitsch, just as by the obligation it imposes of sublimating the ridiculous it presupposes educational privilege and class structure; *fun* is art's punishment for this. All the same, the ridiculous elements in artworks are most akin to their intentionless levels and therefore, in great works, also closest to their secret.[78]

In short, the ridiculous in art can become trivial amusement and entertainment that has little depth to it and lacks an enigmatic quality as can be seen in most of the Disney cartoons and their hundreds of imitations in the culture industry. Fun is cotton candy, fluffy, sweet, and without nutrients. It is the staple of all the banal productions of the culture industry up through the present. Fun has nothing to do with carnivalesque laughter or the carnivalesque fairy-tale film, for the carnivalesque fairy tale ridicules fun and provokes reflection and self-reflection. The carnivalesque fairy-tale film tends to be crude and raw and sometimes participated in the fun business of the culture industry in its beginnings. The filmic adaptation of the print and illustrated fairy tale, however, tended to question the very nature and rational structure of the classical fairy tale and sought to impart new enigmatic meanings to the characters and plots. At the heart of all the intentional and unintentional questioning of the fairy-tale genre was and remains a questioning of the hierarchical arrangements of society, the seemingly rational stereotypes of gender and race, and the paradoxical process of the civilizing process that engenders just as much barbarism as it does humane behavior. At its best, the carnivalesque fairy-tale cartoon exposes the concealed mediations of the civilizing process that contribute to the society of the spectacle and ridicules and resists the instrumental formations conveyed in rational narratives.

It is one of the sad ironies in the history of the fairy-tale cartoon that Disney was first an anarchic animator who produced several fascinating carnivalesque fairy-tale films in the early 1920s before he began to mold and conventionalize the short fairy-tale films in the Silly Symphonies of the 1930s that were actually not silly or ridiculous enough. (They bowed to realism and naturalism.) During his brief stay in Kansas City, Disney produced six fairy-tale films between 1922 and 1923 called Laugh-O-Grams: *The Four Musicians of Bremen, Little Red Riding Hood, Puss in Boots, Jack and the Beanstalk, Cinderella,* and *Goldilocks and the Three Bears.* Russell Merritt and J. B. Kaufman remark,

> In many ways, Disney's first films in Kansas City seem as accomplished as his later Hollywood silents. We have to wait several years to find a film as well-paced, as thematically rich, or with backgrounds as provocative and well-drawn as his earliest surviving Laugh-O-Gram fairy tales such as *Little Red Riding Hood, Puss in Boots,* and *Cinderella.*[79]

The drawings were done by Disney, Rudolph Ising, Hugh Harman, Ub Iwerks, Max Maxwell, Lorrey Tague, and Otto Walliman, and they tend to be primitive if not childish, filled with ridiculous

Figure 6 Walt Disney, *Puss in Boots*

gags, topsy-turvy scenes, and unconventional plots that take place in a mix of contemporary worlds and ancient monarchies. By far the most fascinating and carnivalesque of the Laugh-O-Grams is *Puss in Boots*. Disney did not especially care whether one knew the original Perrault text or some other popular version. It is unclear which text he actually knew. However, what is clear is that Disney sought to undermine all versions with his animated rendition and that his cartoon is astonishingly autobiographical.

The setting is America of the 1920s. The hero is a young man, a commoner, who is in love with the king's daughter, and she fondly returns his affection while on a swing in the royal garden. At the same time, the hero's black cat, a female, is having a romance with the royal white cat, who is the king's chauffeur. When the large fat king discovers that the young man is wooing his daughter, he kicks him out of the palace garden and down the stairs, followed by Puss. At first, the hero does not want Puss's help, nor will he buy her the boots that she sees in a shop window. Then they go to the movies together and see a film with Rudolph Vasolino, a reference to the famous Rudolph Valentino, as a bullfighter, who spurs the imagination of Puss. Consequently, she tells the hero that she now has an idea, which will help him win the king's daughter, providing that he will buy her the boots. Of course, the hero will do anything to obtain the king's daughter, and he must disguise himself as a masked bullfighter. In the meantime Puss explains to him that she will use a hypnotic machine behind the scenes so he can defeat the bull and win the approval of the king. When the day of the bullfight arrives, the masked hero struggles in a ludicrous chase and fight scene but eventually manages to defeat the bull. The king is so impressed by his performance that he offers his daughter's hand in marriage, but first he wants to know who the masked champion is. When the hero reveals himself, the king is enraged, but the hero grabs the princess and leads her to the king's chauffeur. The white cat jumps in front with Puss, and they speed off with the king vainly chasing after them.

Although Puss as cunning cat is crucial in this film, Disney focuses most of his attention on the young man who wants to succeed in marrying the king's daughter at all costs. In contrast to the traditional fairy tale, the hero is not a peasant, nor is he dumb. He is certainly not a charming prince. Read as a "parable" of Disney's life at that moment, the hero can be seen as young Disney wanting to break into the industry of animated films (the king) with the help of Ub Iwerks (Puss), his friend and best collaborator at that time. The hero upsets the king and runs off with his prize possession, the virginal princess. Thus, the king is dispossessed, and the young man outraces him with the help of his friends.

But Disney's film is more than an autobiographical statement; it is a carnivalesque version of the literary fairy tale that upsets notions of royalty and employs technology to subvert the king's power. The cat and the young hero are "animated" by movie star Rudolph Vasolino, and they devise an electronic device to win the bullfight and then take away the willing king's daughter in the royal limousine. Many of the gags are word plays, or visual images such as the disrobed king in underpants or the king, princess, and cat eating popcorn at the bullfight. The tendency of the film is toward ridiculing the authority of the king and celebrating the inventiveness of the commoner and his female cat. The film delights in unconventional juxtapositions and the transformation of a predictable plot with a happy ending that includes a castle and a wedding into an unpredictable plot with scenes that displace the protagonists in various locations. The result is an open ending that makes spectators wonder whether this bizarre cartoon is the classical fairy tale they think they know or can even be considered a fairy-tale.

All of Disney's fairy-tale films in this period display upheaval and rupture that enable the young protagonists (who tend to be similarly drawn) to seek new horizons. Little Red Riding Hood flies off in a plane with her faithful dog and boyfriend pilot, who has rescued her from a predator, an evil magician. The four animals in the traditional Grimms' "Bremen Town Musicians" are kicked out of different towns because their music is terrible. They are pursued by a swordfish on land and ultimately find refuge by chasing bandits, who look like thugs, from their home. There are frenetic and chaotic chase scenes and nonsense that arbitrarily makes sense only when we are induced to laugh about tables being turned. Disney continued this type of carnivalesque work when he moved to Los Angeles and began producing his humorous Alice films that involved live action and animation. But when he turned to adapting fairy tales in the 1930s, he set the table for the conventionalization of the cartoon or the taming of the carnivalesque, and I shall discuss this shift later in this chapter. Right now, I want briefly to provide other examples of the carnivalesque fairy-tale film from the 1930s to the present to suggest that the conflict between the carnivalesque fairy-tale film and the conventional persists discursively up through the present. For my purposes I want to focus on the fairy-tale cartoons created and/or produced by the Fleischer brothers, Tex Avery, Friz Freleng, Chuck Jones, the UPA artists (Bobe Cannon, John Hubley, Ted Parmelee, Brad Case, Stephen Bosustow), Edward Norton (fractured fairy tales), Jim Henson (Muppet Babies), and Seth McFarlane. It should be noted that significant carnivalesque fairy-tale cartoons were also produced in Europe and elsewhere. Many are longer or shorter than seven minutes and continue to be created. I want to use the American development as my case study of the interaction between the carnivalesque and the conventional; some of the relevant European cartoons will be analyzed in the chapters on individual fairy-tale films.

Max and Dave Fleischer

The trait most characteristic of the Fleischer fairy-tale cartoons is irreverence. It is also this quality that characterizes the best of the carnivalesque fairy-tale cartoons up to the present. The Fleischers exploded the classical fairy tales, and out of the anachronistic dust, they created lively, absurd narratives that stretched the imagination beyond belief. They diminished the authority of Perrault's and the Grimms' fixed narratives and relativized their meanings. (This is also a trait in the oral tradition in which tales are always retold and deterritorialized.) All forms were to be re-formed and de-formed in split seconds and in improbable ways. In *The History of Animation*, Charles Solomon recounts the significance of the Fleischers' approach to animation in contrast to Disney's move toward realism:

> For many years, the studio least affected by Disney's innovations was the Fleischer studio, which also became its most serious rival. The Disney artists strove to break away from the loose rubber hose animation of the silent shorts. Their emphasis on fine drawing and the careful observation of anatomy and motion pushed the medium toward greater realism. The Fleischer animators took rubber hose animation to its logical conclusion: a loose-limbed, exuberant, metamorphic style, as fluid as a blob of mercury on a glass plate.[80]

In addition to their emphasis on constant gags, exaggeration, improbability, and transformation, the Fleischers used original fairy-tale narratives as the basis for cartoons that resembled raunchy and disjointed oral tales. They and their fellow animators paid no respect to the traditional fairy tales; they mocked, parodied, and twisted them out of shape. Their cartoons were outrageous and considered somewhat indecent for their time, especially the ones that featured Betty Boop.

Altogether the Fleischers made about eleven fairy-tale cartoons in a very short period from 1931 to 1936, if one disregards two minor films, *Mother Gooseland* (1925) and *The Wizard of Ants* (1941), which fall outside this date span. Betty Boop plays a major role in most of them, and she was the antithesis of your typical innocent maiden or persecuted princess. Created at the beginning of the 1930s first by Grim Natwick and modified by Dave Fleischer, Betty became a Hollywood celebrity up to her last cartoon in 1939 and beyond. John Grant has written a very apt description of this alluring cartoon figure:

> With her tiny mouth, big, big eyes, hugely oversized head, plunging décolletage, ever-shorter dress, and titillating garters, Betty was a conscious mixture of child and woman so that, however outrageous the goings-on, she preserved at the same time an aura of complete, childish innocence. It is very difficult to find offense in a Betty Boop short, although sure enough in due course, there would be those who would.[81]

And Norman Klein remarks,

> she was designed very well for movement to music. She could sway very delicately. Her arms and shoulders syncopated much the same way performers do when singing on stage. And she was a loveable victim, trapped somehow in her helpless body. She was often cheated, exploited, or cornered.[82]

Moreover, she was plucky, sassy, and courageous and spoke with a distinct New York accent. Depending on the fairy-tale film in which she appeared, Betty would adapt her "acting" and would change as her role changed. In *Dizzy Red Riding Hood* (1931) she is nonchalant and fearless and does not seem to mind when the wolf is about to seduce her. In *Snow White* (1933) she plays a defiant step-daughter, who outwits a vain, conniving witch. In *Poor Cinderella* (1934) she seems to be a helpless waif pleading in song for the sympathy of the audience. In some ways she is the pin-up girl of the Great Depression who maintains her good spirits no matter how dire the circumstances of her life are. These fairy-tale films are thus just as hopeful as the oral tales were, but the laughter they generate is gargantuan in comparison. The wonder they produce is gleeful. Since I shall be discussing the films that I just mentioned in other chapters, I want to focus here on an early black-and-white film, *Jack and the Beanstalk* (1931) to illustrate how the Fleishers transformed classical narratives into carnivalesque cartoons.

It is not known whether Dave Fleischer and his animators used any particular text of "Jack and the Beanstalk." It was not necessary since the story of the dumb peasant lad who sells his cows for three magic beans was well known. Scolded by his mother, Jack discards the beans outside the house. Overnight they sprout into a huge vine leading up into the sky. Jack climbs the vine, discovers a giant's castle and steals his prized possessions—the golden harp and the goose that lays golden eggs. The giant pursues Jack, who scrambles down the vine and chops it down causing the giant's death. Jack and mom become rich and live happily after. Ub Iwerks made a "Jack and the Beanstalk" cartoon a few years later, and Disney created an animated short, *Mickey and the Beanstalk*, in 1947. Both stick closely to the traditional plot, and while mildly humorous, they are both banal and conventional, an accusation that cannot be made of the Fleischers' cartoon.

Their film begins with the giant lying on a cloud with his castle popping up from behind his huge stomach. He is smoking a huge cigar, and as he is enjoying himself, he accidentally drops the cigar, named El Jumbo, which falls rapidly toward the earth. As it is in mid-air, it briefly becomes anthropomorphized and wonders what is happening. Then it crashes through the roof of a small cottage right into the mouth of a cow. It turns out that the cottage belongs to Bimbo, Betty Boop's adorable canine sidekick, and he is angry because of the damage caused by the cigar. He just so happens to have a can of magic beans that he opens, and once they begin to sprout, he climbs on top of a leaf of the beanstalk. By the time the sprout reaches the giant's castle, we see the huge giant devouring strings of spaghetti. Bimbo takes part of the vine and throws it into the strings of spaghetti so that he can reach the castle. Once he arrives he crawls into a spaghetti string and moves like a worm to the fireplace where he sees Betty working as a slave. Her foot is tied to a peg by a rope, and she must crack peas to make split pea soup for the giant. Bimbo helps her throw the split peas into a bowl and then falls into the soup. When the giant picks up the bowl and begins eating the soup, he cries out: "Fee fy fum, I smell the blood of a little bum!" The giant tries to capture Bimbo, but he untangles Betty and tangles the giant with the rope. Bimbo and Betty escape on the back of a gawky chicken that does not at all resemble a goose. A loyal mouse manages to free the giant, who begins chasing Betty and Bimbo, who are now driving off in a car. To catch them, the giant squeezes his feet into two cars that he uses as roller skates. However, he cannot control the skates and crashes into a mountain and sinks into the ground. Soon after this occurs, Betty and Bimbo's car flies off a cliff and suddenly is transformed into the huge chicken, who carries Betty and Bimbo as they joyfully kiss and fly away. Who knows what their destination is, but it is certainly to another cinematic adventure.

There is never a dull moment in the Fleischers' version of "Jack and the Beanstalk," and the viewer must pay close attention to every scene in the film because there are constant transformations and frenetic action. The re-presentation of the popular tale "Jack and the Beanstalk," which is generally told or pictured as a story about the luck of a country bumpkin, who accidentally and miraculously rises from poverty after a misfortune, is highly original and can be related to the social and economic conditions of 1931. Jack, played by Bimbo, is not a dumb bumpkin. Rather, he is a revengeful cunning protagonist, who seeks to topple the rich giant, who keeps his worker (Betty Boop) in chains. The giant lives above the earth in a magnificent castle. Jack is not interested in money—there are no golden harps or geese that lay golden eggs. He wants to pay back the giant for his wanton abuse and to free an attractive young woman. When Bimbo/Jack and Betty fly off, they are not richer than they were before, but they are free.

There is a strong utopian gesture in all of the Fleischer carnivalesque fairy-tale films. For instance, in another brilliant film, *Parade of the Wooden Soldiers* (1933), Betty is the spark that brings all the toys in a toy shop to rebel against a ferocious gorilla. This cartoon begins in live action with a shot of the famous violinist David Rubinoff playing Leon Jessel's "Parade of the Toy Soldiers" with his orchestra.[83] Soon after we see three factories that collapse after they produce a package, which is immediately carried by truck, train, and plane to its final destination. The package is dropped by parachute down the chimney of a toy shop and lands in the fireplace. Out pops a Betty Boop doll, who immediately comes to life and ignites all the wooden soldiers and other toys by singing a ditty, "I'm glad to be here." They all rejoice in a carnivalesque parade that leads to the crowning of Betty as queen. However, a gorilla, who may well have been the model for King Kong, wants to behead Betty and stick her head on a doll, whose head he had torn off. The soldiers come to Betty's rescue with canons and planes in another scene that foreshadows *King Kong*. Eventually, they capture and tie up the brutal monster and celebrate their victory in another parade.

All the exuberance and the antic transformations of the early Fleischer carnivalesque fairy-tale films were gradually brought to an end. Not only did the enforcement of the Hays censorship code of 1934 play a role in dampening their imaginations, but the more subdued and stream-lined model of the Disney cartoons began to have an effect. As a result, Betty Boop becomes sterilized or is made into a film goddess. Moreover, as Klein points out, the "cleansing" of the cartoons meant a rupture with vaudeville and imitation of live-action drama with its focus on celebrity.[84] In one of their most

Figure 7
Max and Dave
Fleischer,
Little Dutch Mill

sardonic non-carnivalesque fairy-tale films, *Little Dutch Mill* (1934), the Fleischers appeared to acknowledge their surrender to the film industry and censorship, but without throwing in the towel. This cartoon, filmed in Technicolor and with well-rounded figures that closely resembled stereotypical Dutch people, takes place in a friendly, clean Dutch village. Everything is ordered and regular. The children play in orderly fashion. Little do they know that an unkempt, dirty, large giant occupies one of the broken-down mills, where he stores stolen coins and grumbles. Two cute and tiny children, brother and sister, accidentally discover him as he counts his gold coins. He grabs hold of them and decides to cut out their tongues so that they will not reveal his secret. However, a duck, the children's companion, alerts the villagers, and they rush to save the children. Once they overwhelm him, they shave him, give him a bath, and dress him in clean clothes. In addition, they renovate and redesign his mill. Surprised by this kindness and harmonious regulation, the giant repays them villagers by giving them his golden coins.

This fairy-tale cartoon is a parody of sweetness, but it was also, for the Fleischers, a semiotic signal of their resignation; they were resigned to follow the path of least resistance and to join the Disney bandwagon. Impressed by *Snow White* in 1937, they tried to compete with Disney by offering three Popeye films—*Popeye the Sailor Meets Sinbad the Sailor* (1936), *Popeye the Sailor Meets Ali Baba's Forty Thieves* (1937), and *Popeye the Sailor Meets Aladdin and his Wonderful Lamp* (1939)—and also by producing a series of Raggedy Ann and Andy films in the 1940s. But these cartoons are lame and boring. They thrive on predictable plots, the same gags and tricks, and a patronizing view of children. The Fleischers' abandonment of the carnivalesque is a sad end to their experimentation of the early 1930s. Fortunately, there were other animators who continued their early "subversive" work.

Diverse Exploration of the Carnivalesque Fairy-Tale Cartoon

It should be noted that during the 1930s, 1940s, and 1950s, the so-called golden age of cartoons, most of the notable talented animators often changed studios, worked together, and knew about each other's techniques, concepts, and projects. Collaboration was essential in the field of animation, and so was experimentation with narrative, technique, drawing, color, and contents. No matter what studio they chose, the unconventional animators were primarily devoted to their art, and in the case of fairy tales, they wanted to use new techniques and technologies to represent them from innovative perspectives that would test accepted and approved versions. Many who followed in the Fleischers' footsteps opposed the Disney aesthetic and were soon to transcend the Fleischers, who became more conventional by the late 1930s. Not only were the drawings and characters of these other animators more artistic, but they were also more outlandish. Indeed, the most creative animators (Avery, Freleng, Clampett, Jones, Tashlin, Marcus, Gillett, and others) appeared to crave a certain amount of anarchy and sought to keep the carnivalesque spirit alive in their fairy-tale cartoons, even when they worked in the large corporate studios. In addition, these animators became enamored of the chase sequence as a function in the plot of the cartoon. It was not new to the cartoons of the 1930s, for we have seen that Disney had already used it in his fairy-tale cartoons, as did the Fleischers in the 1930s, but it became better designed and more effective in the plots by the end of the 1930s and 1940s. As Klein remarks,

> Chases were not necessarily faster because they ran faster. It soon became apparent that speed wasn't enough. Chases needed to look unpredictable and unreliable—even raw. Inside this rubberized room justice never prevailed, and revenge was always extremely sweet. A hapless war between incompatibles worked best: incompatible atmospheres, incompatible graphics, volumes, even ideologies. That's why a chase looks so very, very fast. Simply put: *The chase is the collision of improbables meeting on a field where only greed and invasion operate.* The more levels of collision in a single gag, the funnier it is. No wonder the form evolved more quickly after the war in Europe started and flourished during eras of military paranoia, during the Second World War and the early Cold War. Nor is the chase disorderly. It is a very orderly state of anarchy, because it is completely ruthless. It cleans house, wipes the slate clean.[85]

For instance, Tex Avery and Friz Freleng, who worked in different studios from the 1930s through the 1950s and with different artists, made brilliant use of the chase in their series of Little Red Riding Hood cartoons. Altogether they directed thirteen carnivalesque fairy-tale cartoons with Red Riding Hood and the wolf, which I analyze in Chapter 7 on the Little Red Riding Hood filmic discourse.[86] These fairy-tale cartoons cover the period from 1937 to 1955, and I want briefly to summarize some of their notable features that contributed to the preservation of the carnivalesque in the fairy-tale cartoons. From the outset it should be noted that all these Red Riding Hood cartoons are clearly parodies of the Perrault and Grimms tales as well as the Disney portrayal of the wolf and the dainty, stupid girl in the three Silly Symphony cartoons that depict the travails of the Big Bad Wolf. What is astonishing in the Avery and Freleng Red Riding Hood cartoons is that they rarely repeat the characterizations and the meanings of the narrative plots, even when the chase is somewhat repetitive. Havoc and irreverence are the essential qualities of their films.

Gary Morris has provided a succinct and precise description of Avery's work with fairy tales:

> He litters his work with sexual innuendo and distancing devices that replace the sense of reassuring archetypes with a modernist construct that merges the story with its audience, puts adult preoccupations (e.g., sex) in place of children's, and imagines characters not as clueless tabula rasas awaiting moral enlightenment but as sophisticated creatures with a bottomless bag of tricks. Avery's fairy tales jettison the whole idea of morality, along with other troublesome concepts like logic, sense, and sexual repression. He brings the "big bad wolves" and "red riding hoods" out of the sanctity of the linear narrative and into the service of the gag, creating in the process a unique world of self-conscious "cartoon characters" who know they're in a cartoon and freely comment on their status as fictional creations undercutting the story at every turn.[87]

Avery's carnivalesque Red Riding Hood cartoons are stunning and delirious. They are even "politically correct" in their exaggerated play with sexism by depicting strong feminine characters long before the feminist movement began to gather storm in the late 1960s. He portrayed three types of Red Riding Hoods: the sexy curvaceous singer who speaks with the voice of Katherine Hepburn in *Red Hot Riding Hood* (1943), *Swing Shift Cinderella* (1945), *The Shooting of Dan McGoo* (1945), and *Uncle Tom's Cabana* (1947); the diminutive, blonde doll-like girl in *Little Red Walking Hood* (1937) and *The Bear's Tale* (1940); and the scraggly farm girl in *Little Rural Riding Hood* (1945). All of them delight in showing off their bodies and cunning and in avoiding the clutches of the wolves. There are, of course, different kinds of wolves: the country bumpkin wolf; the suave wolf in a tuxedo; the pool-playing sleazy wolf; the pistol-slinging bandit wolf; the Simon Legree wolf. The grandmas dress in sleek nightgowns and chase the wolf, are depicted as fairy godmothers, persecute the wolf, or are old without teeth and are chased by the wolf. Often the chases lead to nerdy heroes protecting Red Riding Hood such as Egghead and Droopy, who hit the wolf over the head with mallets. Avery was fond of having his characters stop the action, argue with the director of the film, speak to the audience, and change the plot of the film. For instance, in *Red Hot Riding Hood*, the country wolf, the diminutive Red Riding Hood, and sick grandma are depicted in a style similar to the Disney characters, but they are disgusted with their roles and the story, stop the film, and demand that the director modernize the story. In *Swing Shift Cinderella*, the wolf and Little Red Riding Hood realize that they are in the wrong film when the title flashes on the screen. The wolf sends the little girl packing while he changes clothes and drives to Cinderella's house to seduce her. In *Little Red Walking Hood*, the grandma stops the chase scene when the phone rings and makes the wolf wait until she places an order with the grocer. All the sight gags and word plays with literal meanings undermine the conventional plot of the classical Little Red Riding Hood versions. Avery's cartoons reveal a tendency to make a mockery of male lust while celebrating a carnival spirit.

The same is true of Friz Freleng's four Little Red Riding Hood cartoons. In *The Trial of Mr. Wolf* (1941) the wolf, clearly a con man, is put on trial. Strangely, all the jurors are wolves, and the wolf is allowed to defend himself by telling a tale in which Little Red Riding Hood is a demonic predator who lures him to her grandmother's house to be killed. Grandma happens to be a furrier,

Figure 8
Friz Freleng,
The Trial of Mr. Wolf

and she and the sinister Red Riding Hood want his fur. As he finishes his obviously false testimony, he swears his story is the complete truth and declares, may he be run over by a trolley if it isn't. Of course, he is run over by a trolley that crashes through the courtroom. But it is not just the wolf who must pay for his "crimes" in Freleng's cartoons. Red Riding Hood is so obnoxious in *Little Red Riding Rabbit* (1944) that Bugs Bunny and the wolf ignore her and leave her suspended in the air so that they can continue chasing each other without disturbance. In *Red Rodent Hood* (1952) Freleng puts Sylvester the cat into the wolf's role, but he fails to capture tiny Timmy the mouse in a sequence of riotous chase scenes. Freleng returned to ridiculing the wolf in *Red Riding Hoodwinked* (1955). This time he revised the tale with the celebrity cartoon characters Tweety and Sylvester. In this delightful adventure, Little Red Riding Hood takes a bus and carries the smart little canary, Tweety, in a cage to her grandmother's house. She is pursued by the clumsy cat Sylvester, who must put up with an enormously dumb wolf, who keeps forgetting his lines and cues. Together Sylvester and the wolf kick Granny out of her house because they are not interested in her, only Little Red and Tweety. Totally incompetent, they cannot catch the girl and the bird in a raucous chase scene. The seemingly helpless girl and bird then depart for the city in a bus driven by granny and leave Sylvester and the wolf in their dust.

Almost all the fairy-tale cartoons from the 1930s through the 1960s introduced favorite celebrity characters such as Felix the Cat, Porky Pig, Bugs Bunny, Mighty Mouse, Popeye, Woody Woodpecker, Tweety, Daffy Duck, and Droopy into their cartoons to enact a carnivalesque fairy tale. Bob Clampett seemed to dare the censors to ban his cartoons, *Pied Piper Porky* (1939), *Ali Baba Bound* (1940), and *Coal Black and De Sebben Dwarfs* (1942), because they were often politically incorrect, but censorship was lax during World War II, and most cartoons were really not intended for the tender souls of children. Experimentation with the traditional narrative of fairy tales and techniques of drawing and representation thrived.

By the early 1950s, several animators, who had formed United Productions of America (UPA) after the bitter strike against Disney in 1941, began producing exceptional cartoons that were subtle and minimalist in design and content. The leading animators were Stephen Bosustow, Bobe Cannon, Chuck Jones, John Hubley, Ted Parmalee, Peter Burness, and William Hurtz, and their first fairy-tale cartoons were *The Magic Fluke* (1949), *Georgie and the Dragon* (1951), *The Wonder Gloves* (1951), and *The Emperor's New Clothes* (1951). In his informative and highly significant book *Cartoon Modern*, Amid Amidi remarks:

> UPA's far-reaching impact on the industry stems from the fact that it didn't propose a specific "UPA style" or a formula for others to follow. Rather, UPA championed the contemporary graphic language of the era and encouraged its adaptation to the animated medium. UPA promoted the idea of animation as a visual medium capable of being used for personal expression, and it revolutionized the field by proving that animation need not be restricted to the graphic clichés of mass-produced Hollywood animation. . . . There are enough consistencies in the UPA output to constitute a filmmaking idiom, if not a specific style of drawing. The artists preferred human characters over animals, satire over slapstick (the studio's disdainful term for violent humor was "hurt gags"), abstract and suggestive art over literal and representational, and a general commitment to being contemporary.[88]

Notably, the UPA artists did not seek to recreate the classical fairy tales. Rather, they either invented new narratives or used motifs from popular fairy tales or even operas, as in the case of the brilliant *The Magic Fluke*, to establish a more subtle and ironic style in recreating fairy tales for the cinema. (Incidentally, Paul Grimault, the genial French animator, had already begun doing this in France during the 1940s.) The two most innovative fairy-tale cartoons, in my opinion, were *The Unicorn in the Garden* (1953) and *The Fifty-First Dragon* (1954), both adaptations of literary works.

Figure 9
Peter Burness,
The Fifty-First Dragon

John Thurber's unusual fable/fairy tale, "The Unicorn in the Garden," first published in 1940, concerns a man who is eating scrambled eggs in a breakfast nook and observes a unicorn eating roses in the garden. Excited, he runs to wake his wife and tell her about this wonderful occurrence. She dismisses him by stating flatly that the unicorn is a mythical beast and returns to her sleep. However, the man goes out into the garden and feeds the unicorn a lily. Once again, he runs to his wife, who calls him a booby and threatens to have him put in a booby-hatch. So, he goes back into the garden. Since the unicorn has disappeared, he falls asleep in the garden. Meanwhile, the spiteful wife calls the police and a psychiatrist to report her husband. When they arrive, however, they find her story about a unicorn in the garden so preposterous that they subdue her and put her into a strait jacket. The husband denies ever telling her that he had seen a unicorn. The police cart the wife off to a mental institution, and the husband lives happily ever after.

The cartoon, directed by Bill Hurtz, follows Thurber's storyline carefully but also fleshes it out to reinforce the differences between husband and wife. The man is portrayed as a timid formal person, who is captivated by the unicorn and opens his imagination to allow a unicorn to enter into it. The wife is a closed and mean individual, who denies the possibility for unicorns to exist and obviously wants to get rid of her husband. While there is somewhat of a sexist tinge in the portrayal of the wife, the conflict is really about two individuals who have different perspectives on life, and the ironic ending demonstrates that people who have locked up their imaginations will be locked up for the rest of their lives if they dismiss the imagination. The childlike ink drawings against backgrounds that constantly change color are simple and charming. There are no chase scenes or violence, rather a gentle but an ironic depiction and defense of mild souls who are thrilled by the extraordinary in life.

The Fifty-First Dragon, directed by Peter Burness, continues the UPA's "anti-violent" and subtle carnivalesque fairy-tale program. (It is important to bear in mind that these films were produced during the McCarthy witch hunt, anti-communist hearings, and Cold War.) Written by the gifted journalist, Heywood Broun, in 1919, soon after World War I and published in *The New York Tribune*, "The Fifty-First Dragon" begins as follows:

Of all the pupils at knight school Gawaine le Coeur-Hardy was among the least promising. He was tall and sturdy, but his instructors soon discovered that he lacked spirit. He would hide in the woods when the jousting class was called, although his companions and members of the faculty sought to appeal to his better nature by shouting to him to come out and break his neck like a man. Even when they told him that the lances were padded, the horses no more than ponies and the field unusually soft for late autumn, Gawaine refused to grow enthusiastic. The Headmaster and the Assistant Professor of Pleasaunce were discussing the case one spring afternoon and the Assistant Professor could see no remedy but expulsion. "No," said the Headmaster, as he looked at the purple hills which ringed the school, "I think I'll train him to slay dragons."

Indeed, Gawaine, a mild-mannered and not very bright knight, learns a magic word "Rumplesnitz" to give him confidence, and he becomes an expert killer. He slaughters fifty dragons until he learns that the magic word is not magical at all, and he becomes fearful. Nevertheless, the Headmaster drags him to the forest to kill his fifty-first dragon, and from that day onward, he is never seen again. Though it is clear that he died from fright and that a dragon devoured him, the Headmaster conceals the truth and honors him as a hero.

Characteristically, the drawings in this UPA cartoon are sparse and depict mainly the major characters and dragons with very little background. The narrator, who recounts Gawaine's transformation, maintains an "objective" subtle tone, while Gawaine becomes a hideous if not craven killer. In unthinkingly serving the school to become a killer knight, he becomes a victim of its manipulative practices and is unaware that his glory is false. While Broun, a socialist, wrote his tale to comment on the treatment of American soldiers during World War I, the UPA animators certainly had the Korean War more on their minds.

The politics and ideology of the UPA animators had a great bearing on the designs and contents of their animated films, but they were not in keeping with the general trend of producing dim-witted fun that was the staple of the major film studios in America. Thus, their experimentation in adapting unusual tales was gradually abandoned. However, the studio did have success with the popular

Figure 10
Brad Case,
Prince Charming

Mr. Magoo cartoons. The loveable, near-sighted gentleman starred in four fairy-tale cartoons produced in 1961: *Red Riding Hood Magoo, Prince Charming Magoo, Goldilocks Magoo,* and *Magoo and the Beanstalk.* Word play and mistaken identities are typical in these intellectual cartoons. Magoo, wearing a red cap and gown, befriends and frustrates a stupid wolf by taking him to granny's house to celebrate a college reunion; he falls in love with a wooden mermaid and stirs the envy of an evil woman named Queenie, whose sailboat is destroyed when she tries to steal his boat; he causes a catastrophe for Mama and Papa Bears when he goes to their house dressed in a costume as a little girl; and he climbs a beanstalk in his garden and eludes the giant's son, Alfred E. Newman, the character from *Mad Magazine.* In addition to these delightful cartoons that have many unusual twists to them, Magoo starred in the feature film, *1001 Arabian Nights* (1959).

As the UPA carnivalesque fairy-tale cartoons were running out of steam, another group of animators, who developed the *Rockie and Bullwinkle* programs, began producing their inimitable four-minute fractured fairy-tale cartoons in 1959. From then until 1964, a total of ninety-one fairy-tale cartoons were filmed, all narrated by Edward Everett Horton. All were parodies of the classical and not-so-classical fairy tales, reconceived to provoke audiences with a blend of irony, minimalist techniques, and sophistication. Some of the tales such as "Jack and the Beanstalk," "Beauty and the Beast," "Snow White," and "Little Red Riding Hood" were fractured two or three times. For instance, in *Rumpelstiltskin* (1959) a young woman named Gladys will do anything to become famous. A tiny, weird character suddenly appears and informs her that he is a publicity relations man. All she must do is sign a contract that has a tiny clause in which she must promise to give him her first-born child. She signs, becomes famous thanks to the PR man's work, marries a prince, and has a child. However, Gladys finds a loophole in the contract and prevents the PR man from taking her son. He moves on looking for a girl who will make diamonds out of turnips. In *Rumpelstiltskin Returns,* the tiny PR man encounters a young woman who wants to win prize contests and become rich. She, too, signs a contract, and begins winning every contest imaginable, even one that allows her to marry a prince and have a son with him. She calls the boy Blunder. Since the PR man makes his money by recruiting boys for a rich summer camp, he returns to the princess when Blunder, an uncontrollable child, is about seven or eight. In fact, Blunder is so bad and mean that he causes catastrophes at the camp, and Rumpelstiltskin wants to bring him back to the princess, who refuses to have anything to do with her terrible son.

In both these cartoons, drawn as colorful comic strips, audience expectations are constantly reversed, and the conclusions are ironic morals that pertain to a modern sensibility and changed social relations. Thus, in *Sleeping Beauty* (1959), the princess only pretends to be asleep for twenty years while the prince and the evil fairy godmother make an amusement park out of the princess's castle and earn a good deal of money. Only when there is a great amount of money does the princess decide to awake and take her cut of the profits. In *Leaping Beauty* (1960), a princess jumps about and makes ordinary people happy, but she steps on the toe of an evil fairy godmother, who curses her by having her leap about and bore people to sleep. Eventually, she collides with a prince, kisses him accidentally, and breaks the curse.

The humor of these fractured fairy tales tends to be gentle; the cartoons are not as catalytic and raucous as the earlier carnivalesque fairy-tale cartoons. Very rarely are there chase scenes, sexual innuendos, or brazen politically incorrect references or scenes, though the traditional narratives and roles are questioned and mocked. The fracturing generally opens up the possibility for re-interpreting classical fairy tales, and the ideological twists in the plots tend to explore the contradictions in contemporary social relations. This approach has been greatly favored by Jim Henson and his collaborators.

From 1984 to 1990, Jim Henson's animated series *Muppet Babies* aired on CBS television. There were 107 thirty-minute episodes, and they were all framed in the same manner: the Muppets, drawn as infants about five or six years old, inhabit a large nursery supervised by an adult nanny, whose face and full body are never visible. Generally, the Muppets play at different games; Nanny checks on them and makes sure that they are not fighting or doing anything that they are not supposed to do. She leaves the room, and they engage in imaginary adventures. Frequently, they enact stories or make up stories. They confuse traditional plots, and scenes from other media such as popular films are woven into the action. The Muppets exchange roles and fall out of roles. They argue and settle their own disputes. At the end of the episode, the nanny enters to make sure that they are safe and sound.

Of course, during the episode, nothing is safe and sound from the imagination of the bizarre precocious Muppets. Among the episodes there are six carnivalesque fairy-tale cartoons: *Snow White and the Seven Muppets* (1985), *Beauty and the Schnoz* (1988), *The Pig Who Would be Queen* (1988), *Slipping Beauty* (1988), *Puss 'n Boots 'n Babies* (1989), and *Kermit Pan* (1989). One of the best, which can serve as an example of how the Henson creators worked, was *Beauty and the Schnoz*, a penetrating parody of "Beauty and the Beast."

The film opens with a frame of a woman painting. Her face is not seen, but it appears that she is giving lessons to the baby Muppets who are painting or drawing pictures on their scaffolds. Nanny enters, and the Muppets are eager to show off their paintings that are all diverse—abstract, naturalistic, penciled sketches. Miss Piggy, who always plays the antagonist in the cartoons and other Muppet films, objects to Gonzo's picture, but Nanny comments that sometimes one has to look closer to find beauty in something. This phrase will become the leitmotif of the cartoon. Once Nanny leaves the room, Skeeter brings out the fairy-tale book and announces that the cover is plain and the book is worn, but you can't tell a book by its cover. He opens it, and a beautiful realistic photo of a forest is shown. Then Skeeter reads "The Ugly Duckling," in which Gonzo is portrayed as a weird duck. The story is interrupted by a discussion about the real version of "The Ugly Duckling," and Gonzo argues that the ugly ducking, namely himself, grows up to be a rocket scientist. Then Gonzo is pictured in a montage shot of a real workshop. Once he returns to the nursery he squirts Piggy with an artificial flower filled with water to show her that you can never tell what is beneath a flower. Piggy chases Gonzo until they come across Kermit reading "Beauty and the Beast." As he reads aloud, the Muppets begin to enact the story which is totally changed. The merchant is a woodsman, played by Kermit, who has three daughters, and the most beautiful, Piggy, must go to the beast cave to save Kermit's life. The story collapses when Gonzo as the beast scares her and then tumbles off the shoulders of two other Muppets. Piggy calls Gonzo weird, but Gonzo wants to be loved by Piggy. The other Muppets encourage him to pursue her by singing a song: "Look a little closer, dig a little deeper, there's more to me, than just the outside of me." Given the large size of Gonzo's nose, the narrative now switches to *Cyrano de Bergerac*. Gonzo tries to court Piggy sitting on a balcony, and clips are taken from the TV series *Beauty and the Beast* and the films, *Frankenstein*, the 1938 black-and-white *Cyrano de Bergerac*, and *Roxanne* (1987), starring Steve Martin. The clips are interwoven with animated scenes that display Gonzo desperately endeavoring to charm Piggy. Meanwhile, the other Muppets are pictured in a movie theater commenting on Gonzo's approach to courting. Despite his flops, Gonzo decides just to be himself and tell Piggy that she's terrific. The Cyrano play within the nursery ends with Nanny returning to the room and Piggy stating that she cares for Gonzo and realizes that you can find something nice in the weirdest of things.

The cartoon is a highly sophisticated philosophical commentary on the meaning and appreciation of beauty. Two fairy tales and a classical drama serve as the subjects of creative play by the children who set the scenes, determine the narratives, and play different roles to explore the theme of beauty proposed by Nanny at the beginning of the film. The educational intent of the cartoon is clear, but the pedagogy takes second place to the use of complex aesthetic techniques and the creative exploration of the characters that takes place within a children's public sphere. Tender irony and spontaneity are hallmarks of the Henson style that mixes genres, plots, and roles to create an understanding of beauty that subverts the classical tale written ages ago by Madame Leprince de Beaumont.

Subversion is also what drives three recent cartoons, Seth MacFarlane's two-minute *The Frog Prince* (2008), made for his Internet site *The Cavalcade of Cartoon Comedy*, the episode of *Snow White* (May 10, 2009) in the TV series *The Simpsons*, and the delightful horror cartoon, *Granny O'Smith's Sleeping Beauty* (2008), shown on the Brown Bag Films website and nominated for an Academy Award. As usual, MacFarlane creates a lewd parody in which a princess walks by a talking frog sitting on a lily pad in a pond. She asks him whether he's one of those frogs who will turn into a prince if she kisses him. He suggests that she should kiss him to find out. She does, but he does not turn into a prince. Then the frog encourages her to feel the underside of his penis. She does this hesitatingly, but he still does not turn into a prince. She accuses him of being a liar and a pervert, while he claims he never told her that he was a prince. *The Simpsons'* version of "Snow White" is not as crude, but it is subversive. Marge takes her daughter Lisa to a beauty salon where they discuss whether a woman can be a kind of superwoman—beautiful, intelligent, and powerful. Lisa tells her mother the story of "Snow White," in which she stars as Snow White, but first she must argue with a Disney lawyer who claims that the tale is copyrighted by Disney and cannot be told. She protests by changing the characters and using her father Homer and his friends as the dwarfs. The comic antics of all the characters transform the classical fairy tale into a mock tale. In the end, Snow White, who had physically been forced to eat a poisoned apple, is saved by a female doctor and does not marry a prince. The wicked witch is lynched by the furious animals in the forest. In Phelan's *Granny O'Smith's Sleeping Beauty*, the grandma, voiced by Kathleen O'Rourke, comes trudging into a little girl's room. She seems to be asleep, but the stooped grandma with a heavy Irish accent stirs the girl with her cane so that she *must* hear a goodnight story. The poor timid girl with large bright eyes is afraid to say a word. Granny begins to read "Sleeping Beauty" in a soft voice, and images of the tale are flashed on the screen in bright soft colors. But Granny often interrupts her story with scowls and a gruff voice as she takes the side of the old ugly fairy who is not invited to the Christening of tiny Sleeping Beauty. The more she becomes invested in the tale, the more Granny raises her voice in anger. She puts down the book and peers at herself in the mirror. Enraged by the hip fairies and elegant crowd at the court celebrating the Sleeping Beauty's christening, Granny as the old fairy casts a curse on everyone and sentences them to die. Then she softens her voice and turns to the little dear in the bed and tells her the story is at an end. She wishes the terrified girl a good night and trots out of the room humming a weird lullaby. Not only is this cartoon a brilliant parody of conventional fairy tales, but it is a *tour-de-force* example of how storytelling itself can be modulated and explored for unusual purposes and effects.

There is no end in sight to the carnivalesque experiments with the fairy tale, whether it be conducted on the large movie screen, small TV screen, or the computer screen. At the same time, the conventional Disney approach continues to maintain a stronghold on many of the fairy-tale cartoons produced since the 1930s, and it is time we return to them to gain an understanding of why they are dominant and also serve as targets for the carnivalesque cartoons.

The Sweet Charm of Conventional Cartoons

From 1929 to 1939, Disney produced seventy-five short animated cartoons in a series called Silly Symphonies, originally intended to focus on musical shows, but the films quickly shifted their emphasis to serve as the basis for experimenting with different animation techniques, developing fuller, more realistic characters and plots, and inventing special effects. This new phase in Disney's work meant an abandonment of the carnivalesque cartoon for a more gentle and harmonious one that was connected to the way Disney viewed the world. On the positive side, Disney's desire to hire the very best artists and to improve his films had a great effect on the artistic quality of well-rounded films with lineal predictable narratives during the 1930s up until his death and beyond. As Solomon comments,

> All these diverse elements—the personalities of the animators, the improvements in drawing, the esprit de corps and even the practical jokes—are reflected in the films. With remarkably few exceptions, the Silly Symphonies from the mid to late 1930s remain as fresh and entertaining today as they were first released. The cartoons shimmer with the energy and enthusiasm of their youthful creators, who were testing their newly discovered powers and exploring a limitless medium.[89]

Yet, despite the improved artistic quality of the Disney cartoons, Solomon overlooks the move toward standardization and conventionality. In contrast, Klein analyzes the manner in which Disney fostered a mix of art nouveau with the gentle graphics of early twentieth-century picturebooks. He maintains that Disney's aesthetics were very different from the European art nouveau that contained neo-Gothic disturbing strains. As Klein explains,

> This "Disney Nouveau" had its own sources, a different track—not the European Art Nouveau or Arts and Crafts. Disney's animators followed more in the way Americans translated Art Nouveau. From the 1880s on, beginning with Howard Pyle, American illustrators and comic book artists came up with a much sunnier version of the Gothic Revival. In a way, theirs is a more harmonious reading of Japanese naturalism than the reception elsewhere. . . . European composition added an asymmetry that Americans designed to look smoother.[90]

Klein goes on to add that the Art Nouveau elements in Disney's films were combined with a Midwest spirit of urban planning, the simple grid village.

> In the mid-thirties cartoons, the backgrounds tended to be more paradisial. No matter how bad matters got, the world looked friendly, even hallowed, with an obvious message that could not be changed. The evenness of the background meant that goodness was inevitable. No threat could ultimately invade it, not even long enough to create much story conflict. Goodness was a constant fabric; only the story was changeable.[91]

Instead of reflecting upon the manner in which American society was formed and depressed at this time, the Disney fairy-tale cartoons of the 1930s projected images of ideal social orders in which life was ultimately rationalized according to patriarchal notions of meritocracy, and the conflict between good and evil was simplified by clear dichotomies. There is never a need to think about the complexities of good and evil in a Disney fairy-tale cartoon, even though many of the cartoons in the Silly Symphonies series were directed by different animators with different mindsets from Disney. Of the seventy-five cartoons in the series, there were approximately twelve that were based on fairy tales, and I want to discuss a few that exemplify the conventionalized approach to fairy tales. These fairy tales can be considered what Richard Leskosky calls the Reforming Fantasy:

> The defining elements of the Reforming Fantasy are threefold: (1) a series of specific sorts of actions performed by different character types in the cartoon; (2) a rigid ordering of these actions which admits only minimal variation; and (3) a set of global conditions which constrain the actions and characterization in the film.[92]

By far the most important fairy-tale cartoons Disney produced during the 1930s were the three films involving the Big Bad Wolf: *Three Little Pigs* (1933), *The Big Bad Wolf* (1934), and *Three Little*

Wolves (1936). Since I analyze them in detail in Chapter 7 on "Little Red Riding Hood," I want briefly to point out that all three well-rounded charming cartoons focus on the practical pig as master planner, who teaches his brothers and Little Red Riding Hood how to order their lives just as the cartoon itself is rationalized. They must reform their behavior. Disney's mission in the 1930s can be viewed as re-ordering the cartoon so that it becomes less chaotic, less provocative, and more harmonious. This mission can clearly be seen in the two versions of "The Ugly Duckling." The first version, directed in black and white by Wilfred Jackson, is roughly drawn, changes the plot of Andersen's tale completely, and is filled with conflict. A large plump hen hatches six chicks, but the seventh chick turns out to be a duck that quacks. The hen immediately disowns the poor duckling which is smacked around and spurned by the chicks and other animals. When a cyclone hits the farmyard, however, the duckling is the only one who can save the chicks in a henhouse swept down a river. Afterward, the little fellow is embraced by the hen. A simple cartoon without gags and cartoons, this fairy-tale cartoon is metaphorically a sentimental account of a good-hearted orphan child who wins the affection of "normal" people. It has none of the anarchic traits of the Fleischer cartoons, and by 1939, when the second version of "The Ugly Duckling" was issued and directed by Jack Cutting, there is no hint whatsoever of the asymmetry of the carnivalesque fairy-tale cartoon. Filmed in Technicolor, this film flattens the Andersen tale and transforms it into a cute re-presentation of Andersen's elitist tendency, that can also be found in most of Disney's films. The artwork and coloring are almost too perfect and smooth. The narrative concerns a female duck who hatches four dark ducklings, and when the fifth turns out to be a white "swanling," the father duck more or less accuses his wife of adultery. This joke is quickly dismissed, and the mother duck sets off into the water with her four children. The swanling is an outcast and cannot find anyone to care for him until a regal white swan swims by with four little swans and takes the outcast under her wing. In the end, the swanling snubs the ducklings.

Sweet and boring, this cartoon characterizes most of the fairy-tale films in the Silly Symphonies series. Even Disney himself could not provide an innovative and original approach to the fairy tale. He directed *The Golden Touch* (1935), which portrays a pompous fat King Midas, who sings "I never care for women, I never care for wine. Money is divine. Gold, gold, gold, I worship it. I wish I had more of it." Of course, he is punished suddenly by "Goldie the Elf," who gives him the magic touch, and after that, the king cannot eat any more because everything he touches turns to gold. In the end he gives up all his possessions for a hamburger. This trite, banal cartoon about a reformed king would have been much better if the king had cared for women and wine, but Disney had abandoned the carefree and inventive approach to fairy tales in the 1930s to set a moral and safe standard for the fairy-tale cartoons that followed his model in the postwar years.

Even though Ub Iwerks, who worked on some of the early Silly Symphonies cartoons, broke with Disney in the early 1930s to form his own animation company, he was enmeshed in the "Disney Nouveau." From 1933 to 1936 he produced ten fairy-tale cartoons that are artistically well-made but lack the verve and humor of the more carnivalesque cartoons of that period. Nevertheless, they are interesting because Iwerks clung to the transformative techniques and anarchical spirit of the Fleischers and other experimental animators while seeking to resolve conflicts in harmonious endings that made them less provocative. One of his more unusual creations was Willie Whopper, a stout boy, who constantly tells tall tales to boast about his prowess. For instance, in *Insultin' the Sultan* (1934), one of Iwerks' first independent black-and-white cartoons, Willie is in a classroom studying geography, and as he points out where Constantinople is on a map to a classmate, he tells a "whopper" of a tale of how he rescued his sexy girlfriend from a sultan's slave trade. Aside from an assortment of sight gags, there is a hectic chase scene that leads to Willy's escape from the sultan. Iwerks did not shy from using chase scenes whenever he could. In *Sinbad the Sailor* (1935), a ferocious pirate pursues and persecutes poor Sinbad, who is eventually rescued by a mammoth bird.

Iwerks' cartoons also delicately touched on the Great Depression. In *The Bremen Town Musicians*, a cartoon that deals lightly with unemployment, a farmer gets rid of a rooster, dog, cat, and donkey because they are bothersome and incompetent. They try their luck as wandering minstrels, but they are literally hounded out of the town because they sing so badly. When they return to the farm at night, they come upon a robbery and rescue the farmer from mean thieves. In gratitude, the farmer allows them to return and relax at the farm. In *Jack and the Beanstalk*, which raises the topic of poverty, Jack, his mother, the cow, and all the creatures on their farm are starving. In a close interpretation of the tale, Jack steals the magic harp, the hen that lays golden eggs, and the money bag from the giant. He is magically flown to earth by the beautiful maiden of the harp. The giant crashes to his grave. The final frame shows Jack and his mother voraciously eating a splendid meal in a royal setting.

There is a clear utopian tendency in Iwerks' fairy-tale cartoons. In *The Brave Tin Soldier* (1934), based on Andersen's tale, the poor tin soldier loses one leg and is discarded by the toymaker. When the toymaker goes to bed, all the toys in the shop come alive. They mock the tin soldier because he needs a crutch to walk, but the beautiful ballerina falls in love with him. A rude fat king interferes and kicks the soldier away. Then he tries to molest the ballerina, and the soldier manages to light a match that sends a rocket knocking over the king. In a mock trial conducted by Groucho Marx, the soldier is sentenced to death by firing squad. The ballerina attempts to save him, and both are executed. However, Iwerks follows Andersen in providing a sentimental ending with the two lovers rising to toy heaven where their hearts are united. The underdogs in Iwerks' fairy-tale cartoons always win or work together in solidarity. In his creative version of *Puss in Boots*, a peasant boy in patched pants saves three kittens from drowning. In gratitude, Puss in Boots, their father, promises to be his friend and help him whenever he can. Soon they learn that the king will give his daughter, the princess, to whomever can save her from a terrifying ogre, who has transformed the princess into a canary in a cage. The peasant boy tries to rescue her but is turned into a sparrow himself. Fortunately, Puss and his kittens are able to trick the ogre into changing himself into a rat. Then, they manage to catch him and put him into a cage and re-transform the princess and the peasant boy who are pictured kissing each other at the end of the film.

Iwerks was not able to maintain his independent animation studio, and by 1940 he returned to the Disney studios and was assigned, that is demoted, to work on special effects. His fairy-tale

Figure 11
Ub Iwerks,
The Brave Tin Soldier

cartoons were more or less buried, and he was not given any opportunity to work on other fairy-tale projects. Disney no longer trusted him, and Iwerks found himself working under the dominant aesthetic and ideological direction of Disney.

He was not the only one, for Disney Nouveau set the taste and tune of cartoons throughout the world and also conditioned audience reception and recognition of what constituted a fairy-tale cartoon. This domination can be seen in almost all the numerous mass-market fairy-tale cartoons manufactured for all types of screens that include the banal 1988 Grimm's Fairy Tale Classics, produced by Nippon Animation and aired on Nickleodeon, and the present-day drivel of the children's classic stories, *Hansel and Gretel* and *The Pied Piper* produced in 2008 by Abbey Home Media.

Unusual Short Animated Fairy-Tale Films

In the cultural field of cartoons, there has always been space for unusual short animated fairy-tale films that are not really cartoons in the American sense of cartoons, but they have been offered on television, the Internet, the video, and DVD markets as cartoons. Before I discuss them, however, I want to stress that the 1950s in America brought about a reinforcement of the opposition to the Disney fairy-tale cartoon. To cite Amidi once more,

> The new look of cartoons during the 1950s stemmed largely from the desire of animation artists to move beyond the slapstick routines and "hurt gags" that had been the stock-in-trade of American animated filmmakers up until that time, and instead use the language of animation to convey contemporary ideas and themes. Modern design was the ideal vehicle for delivering this new, mature brand of animated film, and it provided a way for filmmakers to instantly distinguish their cartoons from the conventional animated standard. Animation artists conceived a bold visual style that was derived from the modern arts, assimilating and adapting the principles of Cubism, Surrealism, and Expressionism into the realm of animation and in the process expanding and redefining the notion of the art form.[93]

Amidi cites a large number of new studios that produced cartoons, shorts, commercials, and advertisements, many based on fairy tales for television and the new media. Here I shall deal only with a few American and European animators whose work was not based on hand-drawn cells.

Among the more interesting fairy-tale shorts produced before the rise of computer animation were those by Lotte Reiniger, the Brothers Diehl, Jirí Trnka, Ray Harryhausen. and George Pal. They experimented with silhouettes, stop-motion and clay animation, and puppets and set models for numerous filmmakers who have come after them. They will be the main focus in this section, but it should be noted that there are numerous other animators who began experimenting with fairy tales at the same time. Their work will be considered in the chapter on animation. Reiniger, the Diehls, Trnka, Harryhausen, and Pal largely produced short films, and there are still many animators working with forms of stop-motion animation and puppetry that have invigorated the fairy-tale film tradition up through the present.

In his book, *Masters of Animation*, John Grant writes,

> Lotte Reiniger pioneered the art of silhouette animation; this art might not seem very important to the history of animation, but even today the earliest of Reiniger's animations possesses a beauty and fascination that far transcends anything on offer from most animators of that era, who were largely concerned with churning out productions of mind-numbing mediocrity that were just good enough to stop the audience from walking out. Reiniger's animations, by contrast, are touched by a love for the form and by a joy in the very act of creation, ensuring that they are today as magical as they ever were.[94]

This is certainly true of her artwork, but she was not particularly inventive when it came to questioning or changing the fairy-tale narratives that she adapted with her silhouette cutouts. The narratives are almost all lineal. She emphasized certain aspects of fairy tales that suited her ideological inclinations or changed the tales to make them more succinct. When asked by her friend and co-worker, Walter Ruttman, in 1923 why she had made the first feature-length fairy-tale animation film, *The Adventures of Prince Achmed*, in the midst of great inflation and political conflict in the Weimar Republic, she replied she didn't know. She was afforded the opportunity to do so and took advantage of it out of dedication to her art.[95] She did not favor agitprop art. Yet, Reiniger was very political and associated a great deal with communists and socialists including her husband Carl Koch, with whom she worked, and she took a strong stand against the Nazis. Denied a visa by England, she had to spend the war years in Italy and Germany and finally emigrated to England in the 1950s, where she continued her remarkable work as the foremost silhouette animator in the world. Altogether she produced approximately eighteen fairy-tale films from 1922 to 1961, all in the same elegant and subtle style that sought to enhance the features and struggles of oppressed characters. Her jointed cut-out figures were designed to move smoothly, and her protagonists were given special attention and were displayed in unique ways—at times through contrast with white backgrounds or through telescoping.

If one reviews her early films made in Germany from 1921 to 1947—*The Flying Trunk* (1921), *Cinderella* (1922), *The Count of Carabas* (better known as *Puss in Boots*, 1935), and *The Golden Goose* (1944/47)—it is clear that her protagonists struggle against authoritarianism, tyranny, and cruelty. In some cases she made significant changes in the narratives to bring out the abuse of power by kings and ogres. After World War II, she continued this tradition in *Tom Thumb* (1953/54), *Hansel and Gretel* (1953/54), *The Brave Little Tailor* (1953/54), and *Jack and the Beanstalk* (1955). Her stark shadow figures were like poetry in action. Among her best shorts are *The Golden Goose*, made at the close of World War II while Berlin was being bombed by Allied forces. In this short, she focused on the third and youngest son in a peasant family, called the Simpleton (Dümmling), notable for his kind heart, a traditional folk-tale character. In contrast to his brothers, Simpleton helps a poor old

Figure 12
Lotte Reiniger,
The Golden Goose

man in the forest who rewards him with a magic golden goose that causes people to become attached to one another when they try to pluck his golden feathers. Eventually, the young peasant drags a group of people and animals in front of a princess, who cannot laugh. Of course, she bursts into laughter, and though the king had announced that he would reward anyone who could make his daughter laugh with her hand in marriage, he rejects Simpleton until the golden goose obliges the king to give his consent. This short is narrated by an objective voiceover that does not speak down to a family audience, and the action is sparked by light folk music. All the backgrounds and the characters are depicted realistically so that the details of their dress, movements, and settings reflect the eighteenth-century towns and landscapes. Similar to the Reiniger's other films that focus on Tom Thumb, the brave tailor, and Jack, this short does not stress violence in overcoming authoritarianism but favors little people who use cunning to demonstrate hidden virtues that enable them to offset injustice.

Soon after Reiniger began transforming cutouts and collages into a cinematic art form that brilliantly captured the utopian spirit of fairy tales, the German filmmakers Ferdinand, Hermann, and Paul Diehl tried their hand at silhouette animation with an adaptation of Wilhelm Hauff's "Kalif Storch" (1930), but they were not very successful and soon switched to clay animation. During the 1930s and 1940s they made a series of successful stop-motion animation fairy-tale films and produced seven adaptations of the Grimms' tales: *The Bremen Town Musicians* (1935), *The Boy Who Went out to Learn about Fear* (1935), *Table be Covered* (1936), *The Seven Ravens* (*Die sieben Raben*, 1937), *The Wolf and the Seven Kids* (1939), *Puss in Boots* (1940), and *Sleeping Beauty* (*Dornröschen*, 1943). These films were produced in association with the Reich's ministry of education and tend to stress German customs, traits, and settings. Experts in the development of clay animation, the Diehls followed in Reiniger's footsteps by paying close attention to realistic details and sticking close to the original contents and plots of the Grimms' tales. The characters are dressed meticulously in clothes that befit their roles. The backgrounds and settings are naturalistic. Some of the villains such as the innkeeper in *Table be Covered*, or the sorcerer in *Puss in Boots* have Semitic features, but for the most part, the Diehls did not transform the tales into Aryan propaganda. Their shorts always had voiceovers, and their faithful interpretations basically demonstrated their great skills in the use of clay figures to enact the fairy tales as literally as possible.

The Diehls did not adapt any fairy tales after World War II, but Ray Harryhausen, who probably did not know about their work, began his experiments with stop-motion animation and clay figures in the immediate postwar years. He produced five shorts, *Little Red Riding Hood* (1949), *Hansel and Gretel* (1951), *Rapunzel* (1951), *King Midas* (1953), and *The Tortoise and the Hare* (1953). Like the work of the Diehls, his films are distinguished by their meticulous representation of realistic characters and sets, not for their narrative invention. Harryhausen filmed in radiant Technicolor, and his clay figures moved with greater fluidity than those of the Diehls. Moreover, he was able to provide greater facial expression by exchanging faces and parts of the clay figures. Harryhausen was most interested in displaying the possibilities of stop-motion animation to represent a straightforward narration of the tales rather than to enhance or transform them with an original perspective. There is absolutely no change in the plots. Red Riding Hood is rescued by a woodcutter. Hansel and Gretel return to their father. Rapunzel and the prince and are reunited in a happy end, and King Midas learns that greed can lead to misery. The shorts are more didactic than the original tales, and the narrator's voice speaks down to an implied family audience. Characteristic of all the shorts of Reiniger, the Diehls, and Harryhausen is their lack of humor, or, put more positively, they are gentle renditions intended to soothe the souls of family audiences.

This is not the case with the fairy-tale shorts made by Jirí Trnka and George Pal, two East European filmmakers, who are known for their eccentric irony, unpredictable narratives, and subversive approaches to fairy tales. Trnka, a Czech artist, was one of the foremost puppeteers and

Figure 13
Jirí Trnka,
*The Emperor's
Nightingale*

illustrators in Europe. An artist with great integrity and diverse talents, he began his film career right after World War II by producing three fairy-tale cel cartoons: *The Animals and the People of Petrov* (1946) about animals who defeat thieves to save the people of Petrov; *Granpa Planted a Beet* (1949) about a huge beet that needs an entire family to pull it from the ground; and *The Devil's Mill* (1949) about a veteran who chases the devil from an old mill and returns it to its rightful owner. Among the twenty short stop-motion animation films that he made with plaster and wood puppets, *The Emperor's Nightingale* (1948), based on Hans Christian Andersen's fairy tale, is perhaps his masterpiece. The design, setting, and puppets are highly imaginative as is the plot, based on a screenplay by Jirí Brdecka.

The story is set in contemporary Czechoslovakia, that is, the late 1940s, and begins in live action. A rich boy, dressed in a sailor suit, is to celebrate his birthday in a huge mansion. However, instead of being happy, he is sad because his parents are not present, and he is prohibited from leaving the grounds by a huge steel fence and wall that surrounds the property. A little girl about the same age, perhaps nine or ten, wants to play ball with him, but he cannot leave the grounds. The celebration of his birthday is a disaster, and in the evening he has a dream about the Chinese Emperor. At this point, the animation begins, and we are transported to China where the Emperor leads an extremely regimented life that suffocates him. It is not until a little girl brings him a nightingale that he begins to breathe and feel free. Thanks to her music and the friendship of the little bird, he begins to break with custom and routine to lead a more spontaneous and natural life. When the boy awakens the next morning, he immediately realizes the meaning of the dream, gets dressed, and runs outside. The film ends with a shot of him climbing over the fence to join the girl, who leads him into the nearby woods.

Trnka and Brdecka created this film immediately following World War II, when Czechoslovakia was undergoing massive social and political changes. Therefore, the emphasis in this film is not so much on the authenticity of art that saves an emperor, but how art can emancipate people from senseless tradition, strictures, and regimentation. Both the boy and the Emperor are incarcerated; they yearn for a different kind of life. It is through the dream sequences for the boy and through the music and companionship of the bird for the Emperor that they come to the realization that they have it within themselves to transform their lives. What makes this film especially effective and poetic is that no words are spoken. The action is narrated by a storyteller —it is interesting to note that in the English version of 1951, the narrator is the brilliant actor Boris Karloff—and there is unusual lyrical music throughout the film. Unlike many live-action/stop-motion films, there is no romance, no sentimentality. Rather, Andersen's tale is used to explore psychologically the suffering of an abandoned child, and how the imaginative power of art can work therapeutically to overcome depression brought about by containment and restrictions.

Pal, who was born in Hungary and worked in Prague before World War II, began using fairy tales in stop-motion animation action films to advertise the products of the Dutch company Philips. He called his shorts puppetoons and used wood-carved figures in stop-motion animation with light music, lavish sets, and dazzling colors to create unusual comic stories and parodies of fairy tales. Richard Neupert notes,

> the aesthetic differences between Pal's $25,000 Puppetoons and the cel animation of Disney, Fleischer or Warner Bros. are as instructive as they are striking. These stop-motion films featured hard-edged, brilliantly colored fantasy worlds that were realistically concrete and yet quite expressionistic; their overall visual layout today looks much closer to that of Pixar than to the classical cartoons of the 1940s.[96]

For example, in *Sleeping Beauty* (1935), he displayed how various heroes endeavored to save the enchanted princess without success over the course of several centuries. The would-be saviors are comic wood puppets, who are pictured in dazzling fashion dashing into a gigantic hedge of thorns and failing miserably. Then in the 1930s a dapper man arrives in a sports car with a Philips radio, plays some jazz music, and all the people in the castle awake, including the princess, who dances out to meet him. In *Aladdin and the Wonderful Lamp* (1936), the young Aladdin falls down into a subterranean cave that glitters with jewels and gold. Once he discovers the magic lamp, a grandiose genie appears and enables him to return to the desert and enjoy a sumptuous meal provided by the lamp. Then a sexy princess lures him to her father's palace, where he declares to the sultan that he wants to marry her but is rejected by the sultan because of his poor appearance. However, Aladdin changes his dress into a sparkling outfit and provides special lighting for the palace to make it modern thanks to Philips. Of course, he wins the princess, and Philips benefits from the advertisement.

In 1940 Pal emigrated to America, where he continued to make his puppetoons. One of his best fairy-tale parodies was *The Sky Princess* (1942), which mocks "Rapunzel," "Sleeping Beauty," and Disney's *Snow White*. The setting of the film also recalls science fiction tales. A sleeping princess is kept prisoner in a glass coffin in a castle in the sky. The witch is an exaggerated caricature of a hag. She instructs a tiny wooden puppet called Hokus that looks a bit like Disney's Dopey to guard the princess while she soars off into the sky on some mission. Then a sky boat elegantly glides to the castle; a charming prince alights and plays Tchaikovsky waltz music. The fearful and awkward Hokus is flabbergasted. The princess breaks out of the glass coffin to dance with the prince. At the same time the witch returns. Thunder and lightning shake the castle as the prince and princess kiss, reminiscent of the final scene in Disney's *Snow White*. The kiss causes the witch to be sent flying into space like a rocket. The prince and princess continue waltzing on a floor in the sky that resembles a glistening ballroom, and they set sail for his kingdom in the sky boat. The only character who speaks in this puppetoon is the witch and only briefly. Otherwise, the entire short is dominated by the music, and the characters move in rhythm seemingly tongue-in-cheek to comment on Disney's *Snow White* and the traditional fairy-tale endings. The film is a carnivalesque gem.

It is interesting to note that both Pal and Trnka employed carnivalesque techniques and perspectives to produce two remarkable anti-fascist cartoons that are among the best works they ever produced. Trnka uses cel animation in his fabulous short, *The Spring-Man and the SS (Pérák a SS*, 1946), about the Nazi occupation of Czechoslovakia. Though not exactly a fairy-tale cartoon, it is based on fairy-tale motifs and makes great use of miraculous transformations. The film begins with a large contingent of Nazis marching in columns down a city boulevard. A Nazi collaborator, who dresses and looks like Hitler, but acts more like a buffoon, peers from his window. He spies on all his neighbors including animals. With the help of the Nazis, he rounds up anybody or anything that is the least suspicious including a cat and a street sign and orders SS men dressed in black with skulls on their caps to cart them off to a prison. In the meantime, a chimney sweep views what has happened from a roof top, takes the springs from the cushions of a couch on which a couple is exchanging kisses, attaches the springs to his feet, and then causes havoc in the prison. He appears as a mysterious Tarzan, a masked man dressed in black, and bounces through the air to lead the Hitler collaborator and Nazis on a wild-goose chase through the city. The Nazis and the collaborator are mocked and ridiculed and either fall down manholes or are killed in accidents of their own making. Eventually they are driven away; the prisoners are liberated; and the chimney sweep returns happily to his work on the roof tops of Prague.

A few years before Trnka made his brilliant cartoon, Pal had produced a similar utopian cartoon in color called *When Tulips Shall Grow* (1942), which also had fairy-tale motifs. In this flamboyantly colored short, Pal portrays Jan and Janette, two stereotypical, blond Dutch youngsters, courting each other at a windmill. (Pal had spent several years in Holland.) They dance a lovely folk polka together and seem to live in a dreamland of tulips until suddenly they are attacked by the Screwballs, dreadful goose-stepping soldiers. Planes, tanks, canons, and trucks, all made out of metallic nuts and bolts, devastate the land, and Jan and Janette are separated. Jan manages to survive in a burned-out church. As Neupert comments, "Pal's story is not only excessively melodramatic in its frightening violence and gloom; the corresponding style with expressionist gestures, lightning, and camera angles, turns the tale into a modernist series of three-dimensional setups."[97] While Jan is in the church, he prays for help that comes in the form of a massive rain storm that causes the Screwballs to rust and retreat. Jan returns to Janette's devastated windmill, and to his surprise, he discovers Janette. Together they resume dancing a delightful polka, and as they dance down a road, the tulips begin to reappear, and a voiceover announces that tulips shall always grow.

Clearly the aesthetics and also the ideology of the silhouette and clay and wooden stop-motion animation shorts made from 1921 to 1955 were different from the "American" anarchic approach

Figure 14
George Pal,
*When Tulips
Shall Grow*

to adapting fairy tales and creating new fairy tales as cartoons. In the postwar period up to the present day, talented European, Canadian, and American animators such as Paul Grimault, Ernest Ansorge, Walerian Borowczyk, the Brothers Quay, Jiří Barta, Chris Maker, Karel Zeman, Herminia Tyrlova, and many others have used diverse methods of animation to retell and invent fairy tales. The distribution of their films remains a problem, and the cultivation of a sophisticated taste for fairy tales that are built on complex notions of humor and cognition has been difficult to forge in audiences accustomed to either the Disney aesthetics or the wild and wacky American cartoons that do not possess a carnivalesque spirit. Nevertheless, with the diffusion of fairy-tale cartoons and shorts through the Internet and through DVDs, the experiments with animated fairy tales will continue to offer unusual alternatives to those viewers seeking a deeper meaning and comic perspective on life and more than just fun and the dreary return of the same.

A Short Note on the Fairy-Tale Shorts of DEFA

The cinemas in twentieth-century Europe did not provide a conducive venue for the dissemination of short animated films. There had never been a widespread "ritual" of showing cartoons before a feature film as in the United States. But there were special programs and matinees, largely for children, that were well attended, and with the rise of television in post-1945 Europe, all types of animated shorts (cel, cutout, puppet, marionette) were produced for children and adults. And they continue to be produced. However, with few exceptions, there is very little information about these films, especially those that were made in East and Central Europe from 1946 to 1989.[98] Therefore, I want to add a note about the fairy-tale shorts created in East Germany by the Deutsche Film Aktiengesellschaft, otherwise known as DEFA, the state-owned film company.

Actually, DEFA is more famous for its live-action fairy-tale films, which I discuss in Chapter 14. But DEFA also built its own animation studio in Dresden in 1955 and went on to produce hundreds of animated films. Some of the more significant ones were fairy-tale shorts, and the DEFA production paralleled work that was done in all the Soviet bloc countries, especially Czechoslovakia, Poland, and Russia. It should be noted that there were just as many differences as there were similarities. But they all shared a common ideological starting point: the fairy-tale shorts were screened by state authorities and were obliged to follow the cultural policies of the communist regimes and emphasize pedagogical and moral aspects of the fairy-tale films. These policies kept changing, and the animators were always faced with arbitrary standards and censorship. Such a situation demanded that the filmmakers had to conform to cultural policy while trying to maintain artistic integrity and independent thinking.

The DEFA fairy-tale films represent an interesting case study because censorship was heavy-handed and because the East German animators managed to produce an unusual amount of fine fairy-tale shorts which sacrificed experimentation and innovation while avoiding pedantry and doctrinaire filmmaking. Joachim Giera has written a thorough historical analysis of the DEFA fairy-tale shorts, and he points out that, from the beginning, the animators consciously followed the conservative tradition of Lotte Reiniger and the Diehl Brothers.[99] In other words, the focus of the East German animators was artful exploration of texts or hypotexts, a respect for the narrative with an eye on the morals and ethics of the tale. They derived the material for their films from the classical works of the Grimms, Perrault, Andersen, and Hauff, but they also made a conscientious effort to be international, and the fairy-tale films stem from all parts of the globe. While not specifically "anti-American," the DEFA animators sought to distinguish their films from the fast-paced, violent American cartoons, through more gentle if not poetic styles. They worked with different techniques ranging from stop-motion animation and puppetry to hand-drawn cells. Their finest work is, I believe, in the field of puppet animation, influenced also by the great Czech masters

Jirí Trnka and Karel Zeman. Here I want to discuss four examples of films from different periods in East Germany: Johannes Hempel's *Jorinda and Joringel* (*Jorinde und Joringel,* 1958), Katja Georgi's *Sleeping Beauty* (*Dornröschen,* 1967) and *The Jungle Fairy Tale* (*Das Urwaldmärchen,* 1977), Werner Krauße's *The Fisherman and his Wife* (*Die Geschichte vom Fischer und seine Frau,* 1976), and Barbara Eckhold's *The Black Fortress* (*Die schwarze Burg,* 1987). These films were all geared to very young audiences, and yet they were made with great subtlety and sophistication.

Based on one of the lesser known Grimms' tales, "Jorinda and Joringel" concerns a shepherd named Joringel engaged to Jorinda. In the film, however, they are very young and are friends. Jorinda is lured by an evil witch into the forest and is transformed into a bird. Joringel is desolate, but he has a dream in which a magic flower appears to him. The next day he searches all over the forest until he finds it. Once he does, he seeks out the witch's castle, and by waving the magic red flower he dissolves the witch's power. Not only does he free Jorinda but many other children who had been turned into birds. There are no frills in the film. Hempel uses stop-motion animation with charming puppets. The imagery is exquisite, and the resolution of the conflict with a flower is typical of the unusual non-violent approach to dealing with tyranny. Hempel's style is also reminiscent of Trnka and Zeman. No words are spoken throughout the film. The graceful images speak for themselves.

This is also the case in Georgi's *Sleeping Beauty.* Similar to Hempel, she pays meticulous attention to the details of the castle and costumes of her puppets, and she stays close to the Grimms' version of "Sleeping Beauty," not Perrault's. There is no dialogue, only music. The thirteenth fairy turns into a witch, and when the valiant prince encounters her before the huge thorn bush, she turns herself into a dragon with three heads. This is the only major change made by Georgi, but again, the battle scene is short and simple, and flowers adorn the castle when the prince wakes the princess.

Georgi's other film—she made many more—*The Jungle Fairy Tale* is a magnificent film about a fearful odd-looking dragon, afraid of her own shadow. She speaks in a stuttering, timid voice, and when she meets the peasant boy Miguelito, he coaxes her to leave the jungle with him and to go on a quest. When he meets a princess in a castle in mourning, he learns that an evil witch has captured the bird of happiness. Everyone is sad. So Miguelito seeks out the witch in the jungle, and when he is hurt, the timid dragon must learn to use her wings to save him and the bird. At the end of the film they join the princess and restore happiness to the realm. Georgi's drawing of the dragon is reminiscent of some of Maurice Sendak's animals in *Where the Wild Things Are.* She is a combination of an armadillo and crocodile, but very gentle. The jungle is lush, not dangerous, and the other animals are seen playing freely while the dragon is afraid. The irony throughout the film is simple and subtle. The friendship between the outsider dragon and the peasant boy is the focus of the film, not the threat of the witch. Nor is marriage with the princess celebrated at the end. The three characters are just happy to be with one another.

The ending of "The Fisherman and his Wife", another Grimms' tale, is very different, but Krauße fills his film with gentle humor. His puppet fisherman is a humble man, happy to be with a cute dog, which accompanies him everywhere he goes. The fish he catches is a tiny striped one whose teeth grow sharper each time the fisherman returns to it to ask for yet another wish to be granted. Krauße's sea backdrop is a primitive paper-cut image, whereas the fisherman's hut, the mansion, and the palace are glamorous. The contrasts between the sea and the opulent buildings are drawn with clarity. The fisherman's wife is not particularly mean but he is insatiable. Whereas the wife wants to be Pope at the end of the Grimms' tale, she demands that the fish be brought to her so that she can continually have all her wishes filled. Of course, this does not happen. Her palace becomes a shack, and the poor fisherman is depicted fishing in a desolate spot.

As I have stated, the East German animators are more interested in exploring the tales and bringing out morals than they are in making political statements, but here and there a fairy-tale short addresses the contemporary political situation. In Eckhold's film, *The Black Fortress*, made in collaboration with the Czech animation studio in Bratislava, a tall lean soldier wearing a torn uniform returns to his hometown only to find that many of the townspeople have been turned to stone and that most of the buildings are in ruin. He has been away for many years, fighting in different wars, and returns without a penny. He soon finds out that living above the town in an old fortress is a monster who demands money, jewels, and treasures from the people. Those who cannot give are turned into stone. The soldier also learns that the monster has kidnapped his fiancée. With the help of the townspeople still alive, he uses a barrel as a kind of Trojan horse to trick the monster. Once he does battle with the monster, he makes his way into the gigantic belly of the monster and is joined by his fiancée. Together they plunge a sword into the heart of the beast. The enormous creature dissolves and his molten body paves the way for the rebirth of the town and liberation of the townspeople. While it might be an exaggeration to read the film as a German/Czech critique of the Soviet occupation, or as a critique of the communist state, it is clear that this fascinating fairy-tale film wants to impart a political message. The characters do not speak. It is as if actions speak louder than words. The accompanying music and the drawings of the town under siege create an atmosphere of doom. The soldier is not the hero of the film. It is only with the help of the other townspeople that he manages to defeat the monster. Learning how to get to the heart of the beast, if it has a heart, is key to his success. Made two years before the fall of the wall in 1989, this fairy-tale film seems somewhat prophetic. Like the best of the fairy-tale films that have come from East and Central Europe, it mixes humor, hope, and art to resist all kinds of tyranny.

5
Animated Feature Fairy-Tale Films

If the fairytale may be viewed as an explicit animated genre, it is not far to the idea of the "literary adaptation" as especially appropriate to the form. I have argued elsewhere that the "frame by frame" process in animated film-making has a particular minutiae and specificity of detail that directly echoes the construction of textual description and narrative imperatives, thus providing the most appropriate opportunity to represent the literary text in the most apposite of ways. Animation provides a particular model of adaptation in that in enunciating itself it foregrounds the concepts of *translation, transmutation* and *transition* not merely as the vocabulary of the animated form but as the process of taking a literary text and making it a moving picture. The centrality of the idea of "process" is crucial here, in the sense that if there is to be a view of literary adaptation in the animated form that differs significantly from adaptation in live action, then it is in the way that animation enables the fundamental movement within the text to find ready purchase, literally and metaphorically, in the chosen form.

Paul Wells, *Animation: Genre and Authorship*[100]

As we have seen in the previous chapters, the live-action silent fairy-tale films and the early cartoons and shorts paved the way for animated feature fairy-tale films that were slow to develop because of the painstaking and meticulous preparation they demand. For instance, in producing the first two great animated films of the twentieth century, *The Adventures of Prince Achmed* (1926) and *Snow White and the Seven Dwarfs* (1937), Lotte Reiniger and Walt Disney needed three to four years to conceive, design, and realize their projects. Once they did, however, they set models and indicated the potential of fairy tales not only to serve as fillers, advertisements, and special shorts to provoke and enchant audiences, but to serve as a unique artistic means to explore the deeper meanings of fairy tales through long narrative visuals.

The methods of animation applied to fairy tales have been diverse, and as Paul Wells has astutely remarked, they involve first and foremost *transformation.* In some European countries, animated films are referred to as "trick films" insofar as they perform magic before our eyes and can deceive our eyes and/or change our ways of viewing things. They are optical illusions, but illusions that can open our eyes through their artificiality to the truths and lies that govern our lives. The paradoxical purpose of the most serious and artistic fairy-tale animation is to puncture the false illusions of the society of spectacle with images and counter illusions so that viewers may focus on the real relations of production and consumption. That is, fairy-tale animation is artifice that seeks to expose the contradictions of reality in very specific and very universal ways. Unfortunately, some fairy-tale animation demeans this paradoxical purpose by reinforcing the spectacles of society and "tricking" viewers into believing that reality should be spectacle and that all our lives can turn into happy-ending fairy tales. This is what is known as the perverse transformation of the utopian tendencies of the fairy tale established by Walt Disney and his cohorts up through the present day. The Disney Corporation and other like-minded media companies have sought to establish a monopoly on happiness and on the distribution and consumption of joy and fun.

Fortunately, animators are not all like-minded, and they have used every means they can to interrogate the oral and literary tradition of fairy tales by wondrous thought-provoking animated feature films. Although the feature-length films may not be as experimental and carnivalesque as the fairy-tale cartoons and shorts, they have offered counter images of ourselves and narratives that have proposed alternatives to conventional modes of living and thinking. In the process the film-makers and animators have made use of hand-drawn (cel), stop-motion, silhouette, clay, puppet, model, abstract, and graphic animation along with pixilation and computer animation not to impress our eyes with their creativity but to open our eyes to diverse possibilities of viewing known and unknown fairy tales. It is important to bear in mind that animators may not work from or adapt a literary text when creating an animated feature. As I have argued in Chapter 1 on adaptation, filmmakers are so thoroughly conversant with so many different versions of oral and literary fairy tales that they may not feel the need to re-read and analyze texts. Re-reading may occur, but it is in the collaborative efforts of the animators to recall from memory and to re-visualize relevant tales, which still have a bearing on their lives, that the process of adaptation and necessary transformation takes place. And, in many instances, they have created their own fairy-tale films made from extraneous, but relevant, motifs and narratives.

The production of animated feature fairy-tale films has been prodigious throughout the twentieth and twenty-first centuries in all parts of the world, and it would be impossible to discuss the myriad of interesting films that have contributed to the formation of the cinematic fairy-tale genre.[101] Therefore, I shall limit my discussion to what I consider some of the key cultural productions and begin by discussing the pioneer work of Lotte Reiniger and Walt Disney. Then I shall examine some of the more unusual fairy-tale recreations that have infused the genre with their tenacious and vivacious spirit of experimentation up through the twenty-first century.

The Just Vision of Lotte Reiniger

Never before did any artist create an animated feature-length fairy tale with such refinement and invention as Lotte Reiniger did in producing *The Adventures of Prince Achmed* in 1926, and never after was she able to produce such an imaginative and original film with her silhouettes. As we have seen in studying her fairy-tale shorts, Reiniger did not greatly change the narrative plots of the classical fairy tales that she cut out in unique forms. She was more interested in embellishing stories that agreed with her ideological world view. For the most part, her films focused on the struggles of the underdog and closely followed the outlines of the original tales. However, in her very first major fairy-tale project she proved herself to be a most imaginative and impressive storyteller, who took great poetic license and wove strands of fairy tales from *The Thousand and One Nights* into a brilliant technical and ideological recreation. Her film, *The Adventures of Prince Achmed*, is a kaleidoscopic voyage into another world, an imagined Orient, filled with dreamlike, erotic and weird images and characters that constantly shape-shift into new constellations.

Very little has been written about Reiniger's sources for *Prince Achmed* and how she re-created some well-known and unknown tales from the *Nights* to form her own unique rendition of a cinematic fairy-tale film. The two Oriental tales that she used to form the frame of the film are "Prince Ahmed and the Fairy Pari-Banou" and "Aladdin and the Magic Lamp," which stem from the innovative French translation and adaptation by Antoine Galland (1646–1715). No other work of Oriental literature has had such a profound influence on the western world as *The Thousand and One Nights*. Translated first into French between 1704 and 1717 by Galland, a gifted Orientalist, the *Nights* spread quickly in French and other translations throughout Europe and then to North America. The amazing success of the *Nights* was at first due largely to the remarkable literary style of Galland's work, which was essentially an adaptation of an Arabic manuscript of Syrian origins and partially of oral tales that he recorded in Paris from a Maronite Christian Arab from Aleppo named Youhenna Diab or Hanna Diab. Galland's major contribution to European and Oriental literature was his translation or, one could say, "creation" of the *Nights*, which began during the 1690s when he obtained a manuscript of "The Voyages of Sinbad" and published the Sinbad stories in 1701. Due to the success of this work, he began translating and adapting a four-volume Arabic manuscript in French and added such stories as "Prince Ahmed and the Fairy Pari-Banou," "Aladdin," "Ali Baba," and "Prince Ahmed and His Two Sisters." By the time the last volume of his *Nights* was published posthumously in 1717, he had fostered a vogue for Oriental literature and had altered the nature of the literary fairy tale in Europe and North America.

At the beginning of the twentieth century, the *Nights* and other Oriental literary works were widely read and disseminated in Germany in different formats and translations. It is not known why Reiniger chose to adapt two of the best known tales from the *Nights* and why she employed motifs such as the flying horse, demons, and magic birds to create her own original fairy tale except to say that there was a great interest in the Orient among Germans at that time. What is significant is that Reiniger did not use one hypotext as the basis for her adaptation of the *Nights*. Instead, she threaded plots and characters from a variety of tales to form her own unusual "Oriental" version that bore her sentiments about justice and the autonomy of women.

Indeed, Reiniger wove her own tale that may be colored by the Orient but is stamped more by some of the struggles for democracy and the "new woman" in the Weimar Republic of her own time. Her film begins with a grand celebration of the Caliph of Baghdad's birthday attended by many dignitaries and his beautiful daughter Dinarsarde and his noble son Achmed. The joyous event is ruined, however, when a most powerful and sinister African sorcerer appears on a magic flying horse that dazzles the Caliph so much so that he wants to procure it. When the Caliph promises the magician anything he wants among his treasures for the horse, the sinister man shockingly chooses Dinarsarde. Since the Caliph cannot break his promise, the sorcerer starts to lead Dinarsarde away until Achmed, her brother, intervenes and declares he wants to test the horse. Once he mounts it, he pushes a lever on the horse's head and soars high into the sky and cannot return because he does not know how to make the horse descend. As he disappears into the heavens, the Caliph has the sorcerer thrown into prison as punishment for not having given Achmed instructions on how to guide the horse.

In the meantime, Achmed learns how to control the magic horse, and he lands on one of the magic islands of Wak-Wak. From here on, he has a series of exciting adventures. His first is in a harem with semi-naked women all desiring to make love with him. When they begin arguing with one another, he flees on his magic horse to another island, where he hides and observes three magic birds land, discard their feathers, and reveal themselves to be beautiful maidens. As they begin bathing in the nude, he falls in love with Pari-Banu, who is the ruler of the Wak-Wak islands. When he steals her feather dress, the other two maidens fly off, and Achmed asks Pari-Banu to go with him to his country, but she is unwilling and faints while trying to escape him. So, Achmed takes her and flies to China, where he proposes to Pari-Banu and promises to serve her until his death. Yet, Pari-Banu is fearful because of the power of the demons who will kill her for betraying them and leaving the realm of Wak-Wak. When Achmed claims that Allah will protect them if she becomes his wife, she decides to remain with him.

The next scene shifts to the evil sorcerer, who breaks out of the Caliph's prison to search for his magic horse. Once he determines where it is, he changes himself into a bat, flies off, and appears before Pari-Banu and Achmed. When the sorcerer tricks Pari-Banu and runs off with her feather dress, Achmed follows and becomes trapped in a gorge. The sorcerer returns to Pari-Banu disguised as a Chinese servant, abducts her, and sells her to the Emperor of China. When the Emperor tries to violate her, she rejects him. In his anger, he orders a hunchbacked dwarf to marry her. As preparations are being made for the wedding, the magician flies off to punish Achmed.

In the following scene the sorcerer captures Achmed with the help of winged monsters and carries him to the peak of the fiery mountain, where he places a rock on top of him. Afterward, he flies off to get hold of Dinarsarde. Fortunately for Achmed, the ruler of the fiery mountain is a hideous good witch, who turns out to be the sorcerer's arch enemy. Her bizarre slaves find Achmed and bring him to the witch. In sympathy with his plight, she decides to help him. On their way to the magic islands of Wak-Wak, they discover that Pari-Banu is about to be wed to the dwarf. They disrupt the marriage and carry off Pari-Banu. However, the demons from the islands of Wak-Wak manage to overcome Achmed and bring her back to Wak-Wak, where the gates of the islands are closed. The only way they can be opened is if Achmed possesses the magic lamp of Aladdin.

As chance would have it, Achmed saves the wandering Aladdin from a monster, and Aladdin tells his story, enacted by silhouette figures, of how he obtained the lamp, managed to marry Dinarsarde, and then lost the lamp and Dinarsarde to the evil magician. As Aladdin finishes the story, the witch arrives to inform them that the demons are going to kill Pari-Banu. The two young men are at a loss, for they have no way of saving Pari-Banu if they do not find the lamp. They plead with the witch to help them. Aladdin promises to give her the magic lamp if she finds and defeats the sorcerer. Consequently, she summons all her powers to bring the sorcerer before her. Immediately, they begin a fantastic battle, shapeshifting into different animals (reminiscent of "The Sorcerer's Apprentice"), until the witch manages to conquer the sorcerer and win the lamp.

Figure 15
Lotte Reiniger,
*The Adventures of Prince
Achmed*

Yet, this victory is short-lived because the demons are about to kill Pari-Banu. Another vicious battle ensues, and Aladdin and Achmed do their best to slay hundreds of demons and a ruthless dragon. In the end, it is the witch who guarantees victory by calling forth the forces of bright white spirits that conquer the black demons. Once Pari-Banu is rescued, the witch uses the magic lamp to bring back Aladdin's palace, and she transports the young lovers back to Baghdad, where they are reunited with the Caliph.

The film's narrative structure is even more complex than I have indicated in this synopsis, and remarkably, except for Aladdin's story, there is no tale in the *Nights* that resembles the phenomenal episodes in Reiniger's narrative. For instance, "The Tale of Prince Ahmed and the Fairy Pari-Banu" concerns a youngest son of a sultan of the Indies, who marries the omnipotent and ravishing fairy Pari-Banu, lives with her in a dazzling palace inside a mountain, and eventually has his father killed for betraying his secret alliance. The only similarity between Reiniger's film and the tale from the *Nights* is the emphasis on independent women and justice. In fact, the moral arbiter of the film is the atrocious-looking witch, who uses her magic for good. Though Reiniger focuses on the adventures of two stalwart young men from different social classes, a prince and a peasant, she makes it clear that they would not have survived and succeeded in regaining their true loves and status if it had not been for the strangely shaped, huge hag, who has compassion for their situation and is stirred to action. It is in the name of justice that the witch ironically uses her spells and magic power to rectify the malicious deeds of the slimy sorcerer.

The magnificent cutouts, their fluid and adroit movement, the backgrounds, the dissolves, and the montage were a work of collaboration with Carl Koch, Walter Ruttmann, Bertold Bartosch, Alexander Kardan, and Walter Turck. As Reiniger remarked,

> Koch was the producer and had control of the technical aspects, I cut out the figures and sets and animated them, assisted by Alexander Kardan and Walter Turck. Ruttmann invented and created wonderful movements for the magic events, fire, volcanoes, battles of good and evil spirits and Bartosch composed and cut out movement of waves for a sea storm, now a household word in animation but something quite new at this period.

In fact, the film was not only the first animated feature fairy-tale film, it was also the first avant-garde fairy-tale film and provided a model for filmmakers who sensed that animation provided a means to make oral and print tales come alive, that animated fairy tales could transform and perhaps transcend conventional narratives. Reiniger demonstrated that animation knew no boundaries when it came to exploring the depths of fairy tales. In contrast, Disney tried to set the boundaries in cement.

Disney's Recipe for Happiness

With the production of the cel or hand-drawn animated films, *Snow White and the Seven Dwarfs* (1937), *Cinderella* (1953), and *Sleeping Beauty* (1959), Disney sought to solidify the mode of adapting classical fairy tales and transform it into a special copyrighted formula that signaled a curse for fairy-tale experimentation with feature films. Fortunately, though other producers have fallen victim to this curse in trying to imitate the Disney aesthetic and ideology, the curse has largely only damaged the minds and imaginations of artists within the Disney corporation itself. Many other independent and international filmmakers have actually benefited from the curse by using the conventional Disney fairy-tale film as a model to be avoided, subverted, mocked, and disregarded.

Since I have already discussed Disney's first feature-length fairy-tale film *Snow White and the Seven Dwarfs* in some detail, I want to focus here on *Sleeping Beauty* because, as one of the last fairy-tale films he produced before his death in 1966, it is one of the best examples of how he and his huge staff of artists and musicians conventionalized the adaptation of fairy tales so that they became hollow and fluffy narratives and discredited original thinking, that is, the need to rethink the deeper meanings of the tales and their actual value for suggesting social if not artistic change.

The credits listed at the beginning of the film state that it is a "story adaptation from the Charles Perrault version of *Sleeping Beauty*." Nothing could be further from the truth, and Perrault would probably turn over in his eighteenth-century grave if he were to read this. Actually, he was not the originator of the literary tradition of "Sleeping Beauty." The first literary rendition of the tale was probably the fourteenth-century French prose romance *Perceforest*, which contains an episode entitled "The Story of Troilus and the Beautiful Zellandine" ("L'histoire de Troylus et de la belle Zellandine"). The romance was composed by an anonymous author, and it is in the grail tradition. In Chapter 46 of Book Three there is an episode that deals with the birth of Princess Zellandine. She is given various gifts by three goddesses but is sentenced to eternal sleep when one of them is offended. Zellandine is destined to prick her finger while spinning and then to fall into a deep sleep. As long as a chip of flax remains in her finger, she will continue to sleep. Troilus meets her before she pricks her finger and falls in love with her. The love is mutual, but Troilus must perform some adventures before seeing her again. In the meantime Zellandine pricks her finger, and her father, King Zelland, conserves and "protects" her by placing her completely nude in a tower inaccessible except for one window. When Troilus returns to King Zelland's court, he discovers what has happened to Zellandine, and with the help of a kind spirit named Zephir, who carries him up through the window, he manages to gain entrance to Zellandine's room. There, urged on by Venus, he gives way to his desire and has sexual intercourse with Zellandine. Then he exchanges rings with the sleeping beauty and departs. Nine months later she gives birth to a child, and when the child mistakes her finger for her nipple, he sucks the flax chip out of it, and she awakes. After grieving about her lost virginity, Zellandine is comforted by her aunt. Soon after, a bird-like creature comes and steals her child. Again Zellandine grieves, but since it is spring, she recovers quickly to think about Troilus. When she looks at the ring on her finger, she realizes that it was he who had slept with her. Some time later Troilus returns from his adventures to take her away with him to his kingdom. The episode between Zellandine and Troilus served as the basis for two Catalan versions, *Blandin de Cornoualha* and *Frayre de Joy e Sor de Plaser* during the fourteenth century. It is more than likely that Giambattista Basile was familiar with *Percerforest* or some oral tale, when he produced his fascinating sixteenth-century version, "Sun, Moon and Talia," in which a king "gathers the fruits of love" from the sleeping princess Talia. Then he returns to his wife and forgets about Talia, who bears him twins. Later, he recalls his amorous adventure with Talia and rides off to the forest to rekindle his desire. As time passes, his wife discovers his adultery and tries to kill the twins and Talia but winds up burned at a stake, punished by her husband. There is clear evidence that Perrault was acquainted with Basile's tale when he wrote "The Sleeping Beauty in the Wood" in 1697. However, instead of having his prince commit adultery, his hero wakes the comatose princess after a hundred years and then pays clandestine erotic visits to her in her pastoral palace. The result is the birth of two children, a girl named Aurora and a son named Day. Meanwhile, the prince's father dies, and his mother, a vicious ogress, reigns supreme and wants to control her son's life. When she discovers that he has been having an illicit affair and has two children and a lover, she orders the royal chef to cook them and serve them to the prince. However, the cook hides them, and the prince rescues his lover from his mother's claws and has his mother thrown into a copper vat filled with vipers, toads, adders, and serpents. Quite a saucy tale!

More prudish than Perrault, the Brothers Grimm wrote a very short, comic version of "Sleeping Beauty" that has no illicit affairs or violence. The princess and the castle are sent into hibernation for a hundred years, frozen until the right prince comes along. When he does, he gives the sleeping virgin a chaste kiss. She awakens, and with her, all the people in the castle. Prince and princess marry and live happily ever after. Basta. It is a boring fairy tale.

And so is the Disney film. It flattens the literary tradition and transforms a classical fairy-tale about an unusually complex love affair that in the course of a few centuries has involved rape, adultery, illicit love, jealousy and matricide into a banal adolescent love story in which a stereotypical nice-guy prince on a white horse rescues a pure blonde princess who awaits his blessed kiss while lying flat on her back. Certainly, one must give credit to the Disney team of artists for totally ignoring Perrault and developing their own interpretation of the tale in the "Sleeping Beauty" discourse. But their rendition is so stale, stiff, and stupid that one must wonder why the film was such a success when it premiered in 1959. Perhaps, by then, the Disney recipe worked to perfection in mass culture?

This recipe is easy to repeat, imitate, and digest.

1) Begin the film in the first frame with a beautiful gilded book that opens elegantly and a master voiceover as authoritative storyteller and make it seem as though the charming images represent a veritable fairy tale.

2) Add music of acclamation with brilliant lyrics such as "hail to the king, hail to the queen," and a glittering or stately castle.

3) Introduce three pudgy fairies to bless a new-born princess. Make sure that they are cuddly.

4) Threaten the bliss and the stability of the monarchy, and make sure that the threatening figure is an angry female called Malificent, is dressed in black, and has a raven as her as her crony.

5) Let the comic characters such as dwarfs, animals, or pudgy fairies provide a bit of frivolous relief.

6) Arrange a prince-meet-princess encounter and have the couple fall suddenly in love in the middle of the forest. Let the girl sing a catchy song, "Once Upon a Dream," that recalls Snow White's "One Day My Prince Will Come." Have her sing a duet with the prince and then dance to a musical score of Peter Ilyich Tchaikovsky's ballet, *The Sleeping Beauty*. Make sure that they don't know each other's identity.

7) Throw in some irrelevant comic scenes such as two kings and a jester drinking and arguing about their children. Paint them as harmless daddies, not kings, who dote on their children and act more like buffoons than kings.

8) Make it appear that the princess is doomed by the witch's curse when she is lured to a spinning wheel.

9) Add a little drama by having the witch capture the guileless prince and take him to a dungeon in the Forbidden Mountain.

10) Let the pudgy fairies come to the prince's rescue and encourage them to give him a sword and shield of virtue, truth, and courage.

11) Send the prince to battle the witch and make sure she turns herself into a fierce dragon before the prince kills her on a cliff.

12) Let everyone rejoice and celebrate that the prince and princess will unite two kingdoms and fulfill their parents' wishes. After all, it is important that elite groups preserve their legacies and are adored in acclamation. Make sure that the music is somewhat sacred.

13) Close the gilded book to signify a happy ending.

14) Remember the recipe: Make sure that the audience and characters in the film worship royalty and acclaim the beauty of a young girl, let her sing her wish for a man to save her, have her persecuted (generally by some one of her own sex), create a grand battle over her virginal body, let the best man win and elitism triumph.

Figure 16 Clyde Geronimi, *Sleeping Beauty*

Although the commentators in the two-DVD platinum edition of *Sleeping Beauty*, which celebrated its fiftieth anniversary in 2007, rave about the artistry and originality of the film, a few concede that it is very similar to *Snow White and the Seven Dwarfs*. Not only does Malificent look and speak like the vicious queen who wants to kill Snow White, but the animals and the forest are identical, and the arranged meeting and song of the young lovers imitate Snow White's encounter with her prince. Even the great battle between the prince and Malificent at the end of *Sleeping Beauty* is reminiscent of the dwarfs' battle with the queen. And, of course, the comatose virginal princesses are laid out identically on a decorative bier and sofa.

Great care was taken by many gifted artists and technicians in producing *Sleeping Beauty*, and in some respects it is technically *the* well-made animated fairy-tale feature film: intricate and decorative background designs, surreal color schemes, renaissance architecture, realistically drawn major characters, naturalistic movement, and classical music made modern. Yet, there is no substance or deep humor, just frivolity. The artwork crumbles because it cannot conceal an unimaginative narrative, and even the artwork is faux UPA graphic style mixed poorly with well-rounded, realistic characters. There is a Barbie-doll quality to the leading characters that is upsetting, and needless to say, the patriarchal perspective regarding Princess Aurora's role in life is disturbing.

Sleeping Beauty, a product of the silent, wonder years, the icy Cold-War climate of the 1950s, is very much in keeping with its time. The difficulty is that, even though the Disney Studios stopped producing animated fairy tales until the resurgence in 1989 with *The Little Mermaid*, the artistic and ideological recipe and approach to making animated fairy-tale films in the Disney Studio became cemented in 1959. No matter how the Disney artists and animators have tried—even when they have tried to mock themselves with the pitiful *Enchanted* in 2007—they keep producing the same kind of fairy tale. Basically, they have been reduced to selling a brand and maintaining a mass cultural taste for a particular brand of fairy-tale film. All the more reason that we consider some other examples of animated feature fairy-tale films.

Soviet Ambiguity and Utopian Conventionality

The rise of animated feature fairy-tale films in Russia is closely connected to the ideological organization of children's cinema and the control exercised by the Soviet government from 1919 to

1989. After the Russian Revolution, fairy tales were regarded at first as frivolous and antiquated forms of art that had little to do with the communist revolution. However, the perspective on folk and fairy tales soon changed. As Alexander Prokhorov points out,

> The fairy tale film provides an insight into the nature of the official Soviet utopianism. Stalinist culture had to rehabilitate the fairy tale film, which early Bolsheviks viewed with utter suspicion. . . . Stalinist cultural administrators changed the official line on folk culture, and the fairy tale became the legitimate film genre because it helped to visualize Stalinist culture's spirit of miraculous reality. Initially fairy tale films combined elements of animation with live action, but gradually the grotesque and caricature-like animation disappeared from the fairy tale film and was replaced by live-action cinema."[102]

While it is true that live-action fairy-tale films flourished in post-World War II Russian cinema—and I shall discuss them in Chapter 14— the animated films and cartoons never vanished and were not really replaced. Indeed, they also flourished with state funding up through the 1980s. In *Cartoons: One Hundred Years of Cinema Animation*, Giannalberto Bendazzi comments that the production of animated feature films began on a full scale after World War II, and that it was strongly influenced by the Disney aesthetic of round pleasing figures and remained conventional in its artistic approach to fairy tales and other literature. A special section for puppets and cutouts was founded at Sojuzmultfilm Studio in 1953, and while experimentation was limited, some very good films were produced. Bendazzi remarks:

> Unlike Russian live-action cinema, flourishing with Grigori Chujhrai's works, Soviet animation did not take part in the thriving period coinciding with Khrushchev's thaw. Notwithstanding the excellen˙ technical, narrative, and dramatic knowledge Soviet animators possessed, animation was considered (supported by Ivan Ivanov-Vano) as a public service, responsible for good entertainment and methodical teaching. Beside the traditional shorts, feature and featurette films were also produced. The main artists were Ivan Ivanov-Vano, the Brumberg sisters, Lev Atamanov, and Mikhail Tsekhanovsky.[103]

Despite the conservative artistic designs of the Soviet animated feature fairy-tale films, they were markedly different from the Disney standard films. The filmmakers tended to explore the ideological aspects of the narratives more deeply, use Russian customs and folk tales for their sources, and shied away from American slapstick humor and stereotypical musicals. The hand-drawn films were often water colored and resembled comic strips and were not as bombastic as the Disney films. The animated fairy-tale films were often simply and poetically told and did not focus on persecuted maidens. Ever since the late 1920s, the "assigned mission" of Russian animators was to address children in didactic but entertaining fashion, to impart a strong sense of Russian nationalism through the characters, designs, and background of their films, to focus on the collective rather than the individual hero, and to depict young characters who demonstrated proper ethical behavior that all good young Soviet citizens were to imitate. As Prokhorov makes clear,

> Soviet culture was to be inspired by folk art and to represent the wisdom of the common people. Soviet art embracing the popular spirit presumably was accessible to the Soviet people of all walks of life and allowed the entire Soviet community to keep in touch with the popular spirit as the metaphysical source of communal strength. The popular spirit obviously served as the source of wisdom for children.[104]

Given the ideological investment in the fairy-tale film and the goal of the Soviet state to build citizens dedicated to "communism," the fairy tale films, whether animated or live-action, were charged and filled with intense ambiguity and complexity. On the one hand, they wove moral instruction and socialist principles with Russian folklore and reinforced a Russian cultural heritage. Therefore, they tended to confirm the righteousness of communist policy and rule. On the other hand, many of the cinematic narratives that concern the overthrow of tyrannical czars, authoritarianism, and corrupt politicians had subversive implications. Whether they were intended to be contentious by the directors is not clear, but there is a great ambiguity in many of the films that have "utopian" endings. The utopian images can be read as representing real existing socialism as the fulfillment of the Russian people's wishes, or they can be read as a critique of Soviet society and as offering counter-images of possible ways to form democratic socialism. As Birgit Beumers writes,

> The fairy tale held a particular appeal for postwar Soviet culture in the 1940s and 1950s. First, the Russian fairy tale's hero answers for his fate: he is granted magic help as a reward for a good deed. The reward system of the magic realm offers, as it were, a recompense for the absence of such a system in socialist society. The fairy tale world functioned as a means of escape from the unpleasant reality of Stalin's tyranny, as well as a way of instructing children while turning both punishment and reward over into the realms of the magic world. . . . The animated fairy tale serves to instil moral, rather than ideological, values. In this lay the at-once orthodox and subversive function of the fairy-tale cartoon: it usurped a niche left by ideological instruction, namely that of teaching children a sense of right and wrong, and thus surpassed ideology.[105]

It is perhaps an exaggeration to maintain that the Russian fairy-tale films "surpassed" ideology. Nothing surpasses ideology. What is unusual about the Russian—and also many Eastern and Central European—fairy-tale films is that the ideological tendencies of the fairy-tale narratives, while approved and sponsored by the state and party, undermined the hypocritical announcements and pronouncements of the state and party. To a certain extent, the fairy-tale films proposed that children (and adults) should take socialist principles earnestly and try to realize them in real existing socialist societies. In this regard, they run counter to the Disneyfied "American" production of fairy-tale films that create charming elitist celebrities and illusions merely for the sake of promulgating spectacles glorifying the grandeur of "good" capitalist behavior. The Russian animated films, though artistically conventional and similar to the Disney-type films, can be considered somewhat of an alternative to them. Certainly, they address ideological and moral questions from a different perspective, and I shall try to deal with this difference in a brief discussion of several films directed by Ivanov-Vano, the Brumberg sisters, Mikhail Tsekhanovsky, and Lev Atamanov.

Among all the fine animators of the postwar period, Ivanov-Vano was considered the "patriarch" of Russian animation. Actually, he began his work in animation during the 1920s, but it was not until 1947, when he produced *The Humpbacked Horse*, remade in 1976, that he devoted himself largely to making animated feature fairy-tale films. Although he was responsible for directing such overly didactic films as *Twelve Months* (1956), based on a play by Samuil Marshak, in which a haughty princess is taught a lesson in humility, and *The Prince, the Swan, and the Czar Sultan* (1984), written by Alexander Pushkin, in which a stalwart prince demonstrates great moral rectitude, he was also the producer of two unusual films that are good examples of the ambiguous representation of utopia and allow for a contradictory view of state cultural policy.

The Humpbacked Horse was the first Russian animated feature film ever produced, and it was a popular success when it appeared first in 1947 and was later remade in 1976. The film's story has deep roots not only in the Russian folk and literary tradition but also in many other cultures throughout the world. Known by folklorists as tale type ATU 530 "The Clever Horse,"[106] there are hundreds if not thousands of oral and literary versions and variants worldwide. Typically, the plot is based on a combination of tales: "The Godchild of the King and the Unfaithful Companion,"

"The Golden-haired Maiden," and "The Clever Horse." A peasant boy, often the youngest of three brothers, goes on a search for a godfather or king. He manages to obtain a magic horse by performing a valorous deed. Along the way he picks up a glimmering feather or golden hair against the horse's wishes. When he eventually arrives at the king's court, he obtains a position as stable boy/groom thanks to the magic horse, or thanks to three magic horses. A jealous court official or another servant wants to get rid of the peasant boy who has become a favorite of the king, and he falsely reports that the boy had boasted he could find the bird that had lost the flaming feather, that he could bring the king a golden-haired maiden to become his bride, and other impossible tasks. Despite the immense difficulties of the tasks, the peasant accomplishes them with the help of the magic horse. When the princess is captured, she is unwilling to marry the king unless he or the peasant boy is tested by fire, boiling water/milk, or by the guillotine. The king demands that the boy submit to the test first, and the magic horse prevents the boy from being killed. Then the king must prove that he is as valorous as the peasant boy by completing the tests. However, he fails. The princess marries the peasant boy, or the magic horse turns into a princess and weds him.

The great flexibility of "The Clever Horse" tale type's structure, which allows the narrator to use a variety of recognizable motifs, has served to spark the imagination of many authors. In 1834, the Russian poet Pyotr Pavolich Yershov (1815–1869) adapted an oral tale and combined it with another Russian folk tale, "Prince Ivan, Firebird and the Grey Wolf" to form his fascinating poem, "The Humpbacked Horse," which became famous in his day and is still considered a classical fairy-tale poem in Russia up to today, even though it has been "relegated" to the realm of children's literature.[107] During the nineteenth century, the poem was considered somewhat seditious because the tsar is ridiculed, and for a time, the poem could only be published with the omission of certain sections. It was so famous in the nineteenth century that Arthur Saint-Léon used the poem as the basis of a ballet with music by Cesare Pugni for the Imperial Ballet in 1864, and it has been performed by different companies up through the twenty-first century.

Clearly, the tale of "The Humpbacked Horse" is deeply rooted in Russian culture, and thus it was not by chance that Ivanov-Vano decided to animate it and emphasize its Russian heritage. In the process, Ivanov-Vano made some important changes by effacing the Christian references in the poem, depicting the czar as a blundering buffoon, and exaggerating the role of chamberlain as vindictive villain. Of course, the poem, which Yershov wrote in charming but elevated Russian verse,

Figure 17
Ivan Ivanov-Vano/
Boris Butakov,
*The Humpbacked
Horse*

is transformed in comic-strip style to appeal to young people and is filled with traditional Russian medieval architecture, design, and ornaments to evoke an idyllic past. The hero of the fairy-tale film is the traditional Russian fool Ivan, more wise and lucky than foolish. (Some of the equivalent bumpkins in Europe are Pietro in Italy, Hans in Germany, Pierre in France, and Jack in England.) Ivanov-Vano's Ivan is interesting because he is a blond happy-go-lucky young man, who is daring, brave, and spontaneous. He wins the hump-backed pony, which speaks in a soft female voice, and two other magic horses by taming a magnificent white horse, which had been ravaging his father's fields. It is almost as if Ivan were representative of Russia. He takes great joy in life and has a hearty laugh but does not have a purpose in life. When his brothers cheat him by stealing his other two magic horses that he received along with the magic pony, he does not take revenge on them when they try to sell the horses in a market square. Instead, Ivan makes fools of them and gives them the money that he receives from the czar after he reclaims them and sells them. Once the czar, impressed by Ivan's ability to handle the magic horses, appoints him stable master, he must mature and demonstrate other qualities in various adventures before he can become the new czar. The driving force behind each adventure is the ex-stable master, now the evil chamberlain, who wants to get rid of Ivan because the boy took his position. So, the jealous chamberlain convinces the czar that Ivan can perform various deeds to enhance the czar's status. Ivan procures a fire bird, a beautiful fifteen-year-old princess, and a ring for the czar. But because the czar is old and ugly, the princess will not marry him unless he dips himself in three different cauldrons filled with cold water, boiling water, and milk to make himself young. The czar orders Ivan to test everything first to make sure he will not die. Ivan is desperate but the magic pony promises to help him. The evil chamberlain kidnaps the pony in a dramatic scene, but the pony escapes to help Ivan in the knick of time. Ivan is transformed into a very handsome tall princely man. On the other hand, the czar, who now thinks that he can survive the ordeal of the cauldrons and become young and handsome, is burned to death. The princess, who has always had an eye on Ivan, marries him, and the villagers rejoice.

The tale of Ivan and the magic pony has always had a certain carnivalesque if not revolutionary aspect to it, no matter when and where it has been told. A simpleton, a young man from the peasantry, rises with the help of good fortune in the form of a magic helper to become king and hopefully to bring about more justice and kindness in a sovereign realm. However, the replacement of one czar with another kinder czar does not add up to a revolution, nor does Ivanov-Vano's film suggest revolution or replacement of Stalin with a kinder ruler. Nevertheless, the film does harbor utopian notions of an anticipatory illumination—the wish image of eliminating a dictator. Unlike a Disney animation, this film does not center on true love and the rescue of a comatose princess, but on the struggles of a happy and honest young peasant to survive the machinations of a corrupt court. In addition, it is the beautiful princess and a feminine magic pony who enable him to mature and become a leader. This same theme is developed with clearer utopian tendencies in another of Ivanov-Vano's films, *The Adventures of Buratino* (1959).

Unlike Disney's *Pinocchio* (1940), based on Carlo Collodi's fairy-tale novel, Ivanov-Vano adapted Aleksey Tolstoy's *The Golden Key, or The Adventures of Buratino* (1936), which had already been brilliantly filmed by Alexandr Ptushko in 1939 and certainly influenced Ivanov-Vano's rendition. (I shall deal with Ptushko's live-action/animated film later.) Tolstoy's fairy-tale novel, which is regarded as a classic of Russian children's literature, is significantly different from Collodi's work. Though it, too, is basically a novel of education, Tolstoy's fairy tale is more about the education of a young boy who learns to act in a collective to bring about a new society, especially one in which actors can determine the roles that they want to play and how they act. In some respects, Tolstoy's work is also a *Künstlerroman*, a novel about art and the artist's role in society. Instead of elaborating Collodi's ideas about the necessity of education and literacy to enhance the development of a young "wooden" boy so that he becomes a good obedient human boy, Tolstoy emphasizes that the wooden puppet Buratino's education must be based on a learning experience with other people struggling to create conditions for an ideal society against tyranny. As Marina Balina points out,

> Buratino differs from both Pinocchio and the fairy-tale simpleton in the nature of the happiness he pursues. Both the folktale hero and Pinocchio selfishly seek rewarding solutions for themselves alone, whereas Buratino from the outset aims to achieve universal paradise, happiness for everyone. His goal is a world where not only his social status will improve, but the needs of the communal fantasy will be met. Pinocchio's transformation into a human realizes the central principle of the bourgeois work ethic: hard work finally brings rewards. . . . The moral transformation of Buratino, however, results from collective effort.[108]

Ivanov-Vano's animated film brings out the socialist utopian aspect of Tolstoy's work. Buratino is carved from magic wood by the kind and gentle Papa Carlo, who protects him from rats and makes a sacrifice of his winter coat to send Buratino to school. Interestingly, this wooden puppet has a long pointed nose and does not wish to be human. He is satisfied with his identity as puppet, and like Ivan in *The Humpbacked Horse*, he needs a mission that will make him more socially aware and responsible. When he passes by a puppet show on his way to school, he sells his school book and is eager to see the play. However, he interrupts the show because the malicious puppetmaster, Karabas Barabas, who looks like an ogre with a long black beard, maltreats the puppets. Karabas not only terrorizes the puppets, whom he exploits, but also the villagers. He corrupts the police and seeks a treasure that can only be unlocked by a lost golden key. Buratino, a free puppet, opposes Karabas's cruel treatment of the puppets, and even though Karabas captures him, he decides not to burn Buratino but use him to find the treasure which is hidden behind a painting in Papa Carlo's home. After Karabas gives him five gold coins that Buratino wants to use to buy a coat for Papa Carlo, he is pursued by Alice the fox and Basilio the cat, two comically incompetent swindlers, who want to steal his money. They also serve Karabas. Gradually, Buratino becomes aware of Karabas's quest to obtain the gold treasure. He joins forces with Malvina, a beautiful female puppet with blue hair, Pierrot, a sad singing puppet, and Artemon, Malvina's clever poodle. After he manages to get the golden key from Tortilla the turtle, he returns to Papa Carlo's home with his friends and opens a door that leads to a realm where all the puppets can live in freedom and perform the way they wish.

Figure 18
Ivan Ivanov-Vano,
The Adventures of Buratino

Ivanov-Vano's film was made after Stalin's death in 1953 and during the political thaw that briefly allowed more freedom of expression in the Soviet Union under Khrushchev until 1964. While there are no explicit references to this thaw, there is clearly a tendency in the film to emphasize greater freedom for "puppets," especially those with an artistic bent. The final images of the film, a happy audience enjoying the performance of free puppets without a tyrannical puppet master exploiting them, are clearly utopian projections that ran counter to conditions in Russia, even during the thaw. Ivanov-Vano drew upon the wish-fulfillment potential of fairy tales to make a loaded political metaphorical statement.

In one way or another most of the directors of animated fairy-tale films spoke out for freedom of expression and moral integrity while complying with or seeming to comply with the official Soviet policies. Valentina and Zanaida Brumberg made approximately fourteen long and short animated fairy-tale films from 1937 to 1972 that retained the didactic aspect of Soviet cultural policy while projecting subversive and utopian images. In *Fulfillment of a Wish*, also known as *When Wishes Come True*, made during the Khrushchev Thaw in 1957, they depict a good-natured woodcutter, a loner named Zebrino, who is blessed by a fairy with the power to make all his wishes come true after he has shown her great kindness. Unaware of his magical power and how he can help others, he makes a sad princess laugh when he rides into the city of Salerno on some wood that he has cut. Incensed that she has laughed at him, he wishes that she would fall in love with an honest hardworking lad like himself. Indeed, she falls in love with him, but the king, displeased because Zebrino is a peasant and appears to have magic powers, banishes him, his daughter, and a bungling minister to float on the sea in a small boat. Not fully aware of his magic power, Zebrino keeps making wishes to save everyone until he desires a palace without servants on a beautiful island. He refuses to be a king, and he wishes that the deceitful minister be sent back to Salerno to be a woodcutter. However, the princess feels sad because he is not in love with her despite treating her kindly. Apologetic, Zebrino genuinely cares for her and wishes that he could fall in love. The fairy, pleased by this wish, grants it and disappears from his life, and the woodcutter and princess embrace at the end.

A short film, graphically much different from Ivanov-Vano's work and closer to UPA style, *Fulfillment of a Wish* is an original interpretation of a unique fairy tale, "Zebrino the Savage" ("Zebrino le sauvage"), written by the neglected French writer Eduoard Laboulaye (1811–1883). Although the Brumbergs made some very small changes, they followed the plot of Laboulaye's narrative very closely and made it even stronger by not providing a reunion with the king's father at the end. The grand refusal of both Zebrino and the princess to return to Salerno and to remain in their magical realm can be interpreted to a degree as a rejection of Soviet conditions. Certainly, they remain true to their utopian vision.

Incidentally, the film has a venerable oral and literary tradition. Known as tale type ATU 675 "The Lazy Boy," the general plot involves a lazy simpleton, who releases a fish or supernatural being from captivity and is granted the power of making his wishes come true. After the simpleton takes a strange cart or oven that carries him through town, a princess laughs at him, and he wishes her pregnant. When she gives birth to a child and does not know who the father is, the king orders her, the child, and the simpleton, suspected to be the father, to be cast off in a barrel in the sea. They survive. The simpleton wishes for a castle. Later, the king accidentally discovers them while on a journey and is compelled to realize that he misjudged the simpleton. Such fine writers of fairy tales as Giovan Francesco Straparola, Giambattista Basile, Marie-Catherine d'Aulnoy, Christoph Martin Wieland, and the Brothers Grimm wrote interesting versions of this tale, all obviously interested in the manner that a ruler is forced to recognize the "nobility" of a simple man. Laboulaye's version, however, brings out the utopian and carnivalesque tendencies of the tale type.

Two cinematic adaptations of Hans Christian Andersen's fairy tales also seek to emphasize the utopian quest for a more just world: Mikhail Tsekhanovsky's *The Wild Swans* (1962) and Lev

Atamanov's *The Snow Queen* (1957). Both Tsekhanovsky and Atamanov directed numerous animated fairy-tale films, which tended to be highly didactic and emphasize the ethical education of young heroes. Tsekhanovsky's version of Andersen's "The Wild Swans" is interesting in the manner in which he combines minimalist UPA graphics with a Disney plot of true love and sentimental musical songs. The animation is at times stunning and unusual in its conception. A large crow, not unlike Grimault's wonderful crow in *The King and Mr. Bird*, narrates the story with wonderful irony and intervenes at various points. The depictions of the eleven princes and their sister are childish and cartoonlike at the beginning of the film, but once they are transformed into swans by their evil stepmother and forced to fly from their realm, they are drawn very naturalistically as is their sister and later the noble prince who wants to wed her. The melodrama is heightened by a stepmother queen/witch, who resembles Disney's witch in *Snow White and the Seven Dwarfs* and by the noble prince who must fight a duel against a black knight. Of course, the witch and the knight are overcome, and the princess, forbidden to speak, sews eleven nettle shirts for her brothers, succeeds in her task and declares her love for the prince. In the end, the princess and her brothers do not return to their father's corrupted realm. Instead, the young people remain in a new realm that has been cleansed and represents their hope for a more just world.

This is also true in Atamanov's *The Snow Queen*, which more or less follows the plot of Andersen's fairy tale closely. The major change is the elimination of all references to religion. Instead of the Lord assisting Gerda in finding Kai, it is Gerda's great valor and tenacity that enable her to liberate Kai from captivity. In addition it is the collective help of different people who enable her to reach the Snow Queen's realm. Atamanov's socialist–realist approach to the fairy tale stresses the innocence of youth, and therein lies its utopianism and also the utopianism in *The Wild Swans*. As Prokhorov notes,

> Thaw-era utopianism and the children's cinema differed radically from Stalinist views. Stalinist culture gravitated toward lifting the distinction between cinema for adults and for children, whereas Thaw culture cultivated both the distinction between the cinema for children and for adults and the distinction between the child's and adult's worldview. Children acquired the status of paragons of innocence and integrity as opposed to parents implicated in Stalin's crimes. The child hero became the protagonist not only in films for children but also in films for general audiences, because the child embodied the antimonumentalism as the key trope of de-Stalinization.[109]

Consequently, the thawing of the icy Snow Queen's realm and the thawing of Kai's heart, while not overtly stressed, are clear references to the need of a thaw in the Soviet Union if there is to be any hope for the young.

The Artful Hope of Resisting Fascism

In contrast to the American directors of animated feature fairy-tale films in the post-1945 period, European filmmakers, whether Eastern or Western, were greatly affected by World War II and its aftermath. Not only were they directly touched by fascism during the war, but they also had to struggle against totalitarianism in Eastern Europe and against the restitution of governments after the war that continued to aid and abet many of the same forces that had led to fascism. Two unusually gifted directors, Karel Zeman and Paul Grimault, provide examples in Czechoslovakia and France of how many animators sought to address political problems with great imagination and without succumbing to didacticism or sentimentality. The major contribution to animation lay in their ironic humor, artistic innovation, and projection of hope through compelling images that resonate even today.

Zeman (1910–1989), along with Trnka, was regarded as one of the great Czech pioneers of animation, and among his fascinating animation and live-action films, I want to discuss two, *King Làvra* (*Král Làvra*, 1948) and *Krabat* (also known as *The Sorcerer's Apprentice*, 1977), produced during two different time periods with different styles, but each commenting on political conditions of tyranny with defiant hope to change those conditions.

It is not by chance that Zeman chose to animate a satirical poem, "King Làvra," written by Karel Havlicek Borovsky (1821–1856), a teacher and journalist, who was exiled from Czechoslovakia at one point because of his political stance and dedication to the liberal national cause of the Czechs. Critical of the Russians and the Czech ruling classes, his poem basically mocked them as jackasses. Zeman's adaptation follows the broad outlines of Borovsky's work while making it even more satirical. The narrative concerns a king with donkey ears, and because he is ashamed of them, he grows his hair very long to conceal the ears. However, since he needs a haircut every now and then, he orders a barber to come to his palace to cut his hair. Since the barber must inevitably discover the donkey ears, the king always has him beheaded to make sure his subjects will not find out his secret. After his executioner has chopped off nine heads, King Làvra orders a young barber to give him a haircut. Fortunately, the barber is working on the executioner's hair when the king's order is sent. The barber quickly ties up the executioner, and after he goes to the king and gives him the haircut, the king cannot have him executed. So, he makes the barber swear that he will never tell a soul about the donkey ears. The barber agrees and is given a medal. However, the young man is haunted by the truth and tells the secret to some green twines growing in a field. Later, after some musicians come to the court and there is a celebration, one of the twines that has become a string on one of the musician's base makes a sound like a donkey, and the king's ears pop out of the crown. The king hides under the table in shame. To his surprise, his wealthy party guests clap and pander to him. The king realizes that he need not be ashamed of his donkey ears and returns to the feast at the table. However, he bans the folk musicians who set off into countryside. The king wants to include the young barber in the feast and as part of his retinue, but the barber discards his medal of honor and runs off to join the musicians.

Figure 19
Karel Zeman,
King Làvra

Zeman's stop-motion film uses wooden puppets that have tube-like arms and legs, perhaps made out of pipe filters. They move brilliantly to classical music throughout the film, and there is absolutely no dialogue. The music determines the rhythms of the puppets' gestures and movements. The facial expressions reveal their thoughts. The nineteenth-century town and dress of the people and courtiers at the castle have clear Czech designs. The miniature puppets live in a miniature Czechoslovakia ruled by a fat voracious king, concerned only about not appearing as a jackass. Interestingly, the king's ropey hair is red, and the cushion on which the scissors are carried by a servant to the barbers is red—an overt reference to the Communist Party. But Zeman's film is not an explicit critique of communism. The humor is wry and subtle, and the criticism of a jackass murdering ruler can be universally applied. Because of this, the film is all the more effective. In Czechoslovakia, however, it can be understood historically. Many loyal Czech and Russian communists who dedicated themselves to the state and party were often murdered because they knew too much. Zeman implies that the barbers are suffering the fate of those good people who do not resist tyranny. He makes a mockery of authoritarianism, and although the king remains in power at the end, he has been exposed as a jackass as are the sycophants who applaud him. All this is insufferable for the young barber. Unwilling to collaborate, he joins the folk musicians in the final image, a signal of resistance.

Resistance and hope are the key themes in *Krabat*, which Zeman made several years after the Russians put down the Cultural Revolution in the Prague Spring of 1968. Based in part on the German writer Otfried Preußler's 1971 novel, *Krabat*, the film has deep roots in European folk tradition. Categorized as ATU 325, "The Magician and his Pupil," this tale type recounts in diverse ways how a father apprentices his son to a duplicitous magician. The son learns all the magic tricks of the magician and manages to gain his release from his service before he has completed the apprenticeship. In a series of events, the magician tries to recapture the apprentice, and they have several transformation battles. Eventually, the apprentice wins by turning himself into a fox and biting off a rooster's head, which is actually the magician's head. In the end, the apprentice marries a princess. There are several films that endeavored to adapt this tale type with varying success. Among them are Disney's film *The Sorcerer's Apprentice* in *Fantasia* (1940), which is a comic adaptation of Goethe's mediocre poem *Der Zauberlehrling* (1797), made more vacuous in this musical animated short, and the South African *The Sorcerer's Apprentice* (2002), which is a weird live-action film that transforms the male sorceress into the evil sorceress Morgana and makes the conflict between Morgana and a young boy, Ben, into a trite battle of good and evil reminiscent of the medieval knights-of-the-round-table romances.

Zeman does not trivialize the folklore tradition the way these and other films do. He uses both folklore and Preußler's novel to form his own "contemporary" version of the tale type to comment on war, poverty, and tyranny. In his film, Krabat, the protagonist, is a fourteen-year-old orphan wandering about Saxony in late medieval Europe. War is everywhere, and Krabat, a vagabond, begs and looks for food and shelter. During the warm weather he is happy and manages to survive. However, the winter months are difficult. Starving, he is eventually lured to a mill by the sorcerer disguised as a raven. Once he arrives, he believes that he will work as a miller's apprentice. He soon discovers that he will be compelled to study black magic along with eleven other apprentices and to learn how to use it to help the evil sorcerer swindle people. At the end of each year, one of the apprentices is to challenge the sorcerer in magic, and whoever wins the battle of transformations kills the other. The sorcerer always wins by cheating. In the course of time, the sorcerer defeats a few apprentices, who are replaced by new recruits. Every now and then Krabat is allowed to test his magic in villages. On an Easter outing from the mill, Krabat falls in love with a maiden, whose name he never learns. As he visits her secretly over time, he grows more and more torn between his dedication to magic and his love for the maiden. The sorcerer learns about this love, whips him in front of the other apprentices, and warns him that he will be killed if he betrays the black magic. This whipping and another incident in which the sorcerer almost forces Krabat to kill his best friend make him realize that he must somehow read the sorcerer's forbidden magic book to become as adept at magic as the sorcerer. However, Krabat is puzzled by the last magic formula in the book that states "love is stronger than any kind of magic power." He tries to solve this formula, but before he does, the sorcerer changes all the apprentices into crows and intends to punish Krabat and kill him in a duel. Krabat resists the challenge, and just as the sorcerer is about to murder him, the anonymous maiden appears. The sorcerer declares that, if she can tell Krabat apart from the other eleven apprentices after he blindfolds her, he will let them go free. At first the maiden is troubled, but when she senses Krabat's anxiety and worry for her life, she succeeds in choosing him. As soon as she makes this choice, the sorcerer's head splits in two and a candle falls onto the magic book. The magic mill explodes into flames as if an atomic bomb had hit it. All the apprentices leave the mill as they were, young vagabonds without any knowledge of black magic. Krabat joins the unknown maiden in a starlit evening in the snow. Together they hold hands and walk off into the distant field.

In some respects, this film is similar to *King Làvra*; the narrative pits a young man against a tyrant. However, *Krabat* is first of all a longer film made with cel and cut-out animation, and it is a much more profound analysis of the deadly consequences of forced labor in the service of a dreadful, powerful tyrant, not a jackass king. The apprentices are all poor young men without hope and succumb to the lure or call of the magician. Just as the barbers are executed in *King Làvra*, these young men are also killed in a way that strengthens the sorcerer's rule of violence. Zeman's drawings are not realistic. The cutout figures have sharp angular contours; the perspectives of the frames are constantly altered with vividly colored backgrounds that constantly change and reveal different hues. Various motifs such as the wings of the bird, or Krabat's magic wings, are used in diverse ways. For Krabat, the wings are a possible means to escape prison, while the sorcerer uses the wings to attack and kill. Landscapes and architecture indicate mood and spatial freedom. The film is narrated in the first person by Krabat, and it commences with frames of a peaceful summer meadow suddenly threatened by soldiers and war. The music is solemn throughout most of the film. There is hardly any dialogue. The sorcerer utters harsh commands. Otherwise, the gazes of the characters indicate what they are thinking and feeling. Krabat never speaks to the anonymous maiden. They understand each other through intuition. The end is a silent snowy winter evening of peace. The beauty of Zeman's films of resistance and hope is that he weaves his tales with very little dialogue or commentary. The startling images speak for themselves and challenge viewers to think for themselves.

Figure 20
Karel Zeman, *Krabat*

Paul Grimault's adaptation of Hans Christian Andersen's "The Shepherdess and the Chimney Sweep" is also a thinking person's film. Although Andersen's tale is not well-known in the US and Europe, it is still extremely popular in France due to the brilliant cinematic work of Grimault, who actually made two versions, *La Bergère et le Ramoneur* (1950; English version, *The Curious Adventures of Mr. Wonderbird*, 1952)[110] and *Le Roi et l'Oiseau* (*The King and Mr. Bird*, 1979), which does not have an English version. In both films he collaborated with the talented poet and screenplay writer, Jacques Prévert.

Andersen's tale can be interpreted as a story about the fear of freedom. The shepherdess and the chimney sweep rebel against a tyrant and run away, but they are so overwhelmed by the outside world that they return to the safe and comfortable parlor, where they submit to its social code. Only by accident do they become happy, if they really do become happy. In contrast, Grimault's two films can be regarded as odes to freedom. In both renditions he celebrates the emancipation not only of the persecuted couple from a mean-spirited dictator but also the freedom of the oppressed populace living in darkness. First conceived in 1945, Grimault's two films hark back to World War II, the French occupation by the Nazis, and the atomic bomb. These events marked Grimault and Prévert to such an extent that they worked on the project for twenty-four years until they made the film as they desired and envisaged it. Since the 1979 version was Grimault's "final" statement about Andersen's "The Shepherdess and the Chimney Sweep," I want to summarize the plot of this film, written with Prévert, who died right before the final production, before examining how imaginatively he interpreted Andersen's work and contributed to the development of animation.

Figure 21
Paul Grimault,
The King and Mr. Bird

The film begins with the depiction of a cross-eyed vain king, who rules a mythical urban state modeled after a feudal kingdom and a quaint futuristic realm. The king's apparent hierarchical and authoritarian reign is reflected by the total submission of his subjects and by the pictures, statues, and designs that have his face on it. He is about to go hunting, his greatest avocation, and just when one of his servants sets free a tiny cute bird from a diminutive cage, a large crow-like bird with a top hat and vest swoops down all at once and saves the tiny one. It is the crow's son, and he taunts the king, who had recently shot and killed his wife.

The king is furious and retires to his royal apartments that are on top of a ninety-six-story building. One can only gain access to his rooms by a super-powered elevator. Once there he has another portrait in hunting attire made for himself and then executes the artist for making the painting too accurate by showing his crossed eyes. (Throughout the film, the king pushes buttons that open trap doors and sends people to their death.) Before going to bed that evening he uncrosses the eyes of the hunter/king in his portrait. Then he tours his collection of paintings, lusts after a sweet young shepherdess in one painting, and scowls at the dashing young chimney sweep in the neighboring painting. While he is asleep, the paintings come to life. The shepherdess and the chimney sweep declare their love for each other and decide to escape from their frames. As they are doing this, the hunter/king jumps from his painting to stop them. Neither he nor the statue of an old rider, who is supposed to guard over them, manage to prevent them. During the raucous chase, the sleeping king awakes and cannot believe his eyes when he sees what the hunter/king is doing. However, the hunterking uses the trap door in the floor to get rid of him forever and assumes his identity. The double replaces the original king, reminiscent of how the shadow replaces his master in Andersen's story "The Shadow."

With the entire palace on alert, the shepherdess and the chimney sweep, who marvel at the world outside and are enchanted to be free, are pursued by the royal police portrayed as flying bats and devious thugs. Only the intervention of Mr. Bird can help them for a time, but they are finally captured along with the bird and locked up in a dark underworld that resembles an impoverished Paris inhabited by common people who are all forlorn. The plight of the masses is represented by a blind man, who plays magical music on an organ grinder. At one point, the king arrives on top of a giant metal robot and threatens to have the chimney sweep and the bird killed unless the shepherdess promises to marry him. She is forced to accept, and while she is taken from them, they are sent to a dungeon, where the organ grinder has managed to tame ferocious lions and tigers with his marvelous music. Now the bird uses the music and his own oratory skills to rouse the lions and tigers to rebel against the tyranny of the king.

The animals virtually storm the palace to interrupt the king's marriage with the shepherdess. The pompous wedding guests scatter. The king flees with the shepherdess and takes her to a platform on his humongous iron giant, but he is pursued by the shepherd, who attacks him. Meanwhile, Mr. Bird takes control of the giant's levers and directs the machine's hand to pick up the king and toss him far into the wide universe. Immediately thereafter the machine begins to destroy the entire city. In the final scene, the machine sits alone in a pose that explicitly recalls Rodin's statue of *The Thinker*. The bird's little son is once again caught in a diminutive cage—the mischievous bird is always getting caught—and gently the hand of the iron giant reaches over, lifts the gate of the cage, and the little bird flies off into freedom.

Film critic Noel Megahey comments:

The animation is superb—beautifully designed sets and backgrounds full of technical marvels, wondrous caverns, towers, arches, Venetian canals and squares and vast palaces with Escher-like staircases. Each of the animators worked on their own characters, imbuing them with their own personality and characteristics—the king for example moves with the graceful fluidity of his creator, the chief animator Henri Lacam. Considering the amount of effort that went into acquiring a twenty year old film and the personal involvement that each of the creators put into the film, *Le Roi et L'Oiseau* is clearly a labor of love—and it shows. Rarely is animation so vital, so alive and so life-affirming—full of magic, wit, personality and imagination.[111]

Indeed, the 1979 *Le Roi et L'Oiseau* is an improvement over the 1952 version, which Grimault wanted to remake because he considered the first film artistically flawed. During the early 1950s Grimault had financial problems and arguments with the producers that prevented him from finishing the film the way he desired, and he disowned the 1952 production. This is why he obtained the rights in 1976, gathered some of the former animators around him along with additional animators, and ordered a new musical score written by the Polish composer Wojciech Kilar. The result is a masterpiece, perhaps one of the most insightful critiques of Andersen's tale and an extraordinary demonstration of how fairy-tale animation can be used to address contemporary social and political issues.

The reason why Grimault and Prévert re-titled the film "The King and Mr. Bird" is because the film is no longer about the love between the shepherdess and the chimney sweep but about the struggle between the small oppressed people represented by the bird and his offspring and the cruel dictatorial king. As Grimault himself said,

> the shepherdess and the chimneysweep, for example, are characters used as pretext: their very simple love will set off chain reactions. They are charming and nice, and everything that happens to them touches us. But it is the conflict between the king and the bird that gradually takes precedence. Moreover, it is the reason for changing the title of the film: *The Shepherdess and the Chimney Sweep* became *The King and Mr. Bird*—in regard to Andersen and the film *The Shepherdess and the Chimney Sweep*, the king and the bird assume much more importance. The bird, he represents liberty. He knows that the earth is round because he has taken a trip around it. What are borders for him? He doesn't care about them. He goes beyond them. He's at home everywhere. The only thing that he asks is that nobody harms his little ones. The king, he represents oppression: dictatorial, egotistical, megalomaniac, omnipotent.[112]

Clearly, Grimault and Prévert were influenced by the period of French and German fascism and were horrified by oppressive governments and the use of technology to intimidate people and cause mass destruction. Consequently, the tale in which Andersen re-confined his protagonists after they pursue freedom is changed into a struggle for freedom and a transformation of technology to support the cause of freedom and instill a sense of hope in its viewers.

American Postwar Experimentation

While European filmmakers of animated fairy-tale films embedded themes of war, fascism, totalitarianism, resistance, and hope in their works, most American animators followed Disney's model after World War II to create musical love stories filled with notions of elitism, meritocracy, violence, simplistic conflict between good and evil, and spectacle for the sake of spectacle. There were exceptions, of course, and unfortunately, though they endeavored to break the Disney model, almost all failed. For instance, UPA, the most innovative animation studio in the 1950s, tried to compete with Disney Studios, which produced *Sleeping Beauty* in 1959, with a feature-length film, *1001 Arabian Nights* (1959) starring Mr. Magoo. Though it was a clever parody of the traditional fairy-tale version of "Aladdin and the Magic Lamp" with Magoo playing a bumbling uncle, a lamp merchant, who unwittingly helps his naive nephew win and marry the beautiful princess Yasminda, the corny jokes and exaggerated caricatures of stereotypical fairy-tale characters become stale in the long predictable plot, and the unusual UPA graphics are wasted in a film that should have been a short cartoon. As Amid Amidi, author of *Cartoon Modern*, has remarked in his blog:

> I wouldn't go so far as to call UPA's feature *1001 Arabian Nights* a good film, but there is a lot of nice artwork in it. By the late-50s, UPA had squandered its reputation as a progressive modern animation studio, and the dumbed down storytelling and general immaturity of this film proved to be the final nail in its coffin.[113]

Despite the death of the UPA studio, it left a rich legacy and inspired many fine animators in the latter part of the twentieth century. Perhaps the most significant and fascinating American animated feature fairy-tale film of the twentieth century was *Twice Upon a Time* (1983), directed by John Korty and Charles Swenson. This film is so important that it is rarely referred to in the annals of animation as is the case with many rare animated films mainly from Europe and Canada. The reasons are complex, but it has to do with the limited distribution of the film in 1983, a dispute between the directors about which version should be shown on HBO in 1984, and the unwillingness of Warner Home Video to make a DVD after producing a limited number of video cassettes. It is also an animated film that goes totally against the Disney grain of fairy-tale films and demands close viewing and reviewing. The aesthetics and techniques of the film are stunning. Korty and Swenson used a new kind of stop-motion animation and cut-out animation that they called "Lumage." The American animator, Ward Jenkins, a great admirer of the film, has provided an ample description of the artistic work:

> The animation is quite impressive, especially when you take into account that it's all done with cut paper. It's stop-motion with effects done in camera. To make all of it look effortless is no easy task. The animators had to cut out each and every character in order for them to love. Mind numbing! Crazy technique, but I think it's worth it. There are some scenes that are really amazing to watch, with jaw-dropping and gorgeous scenery. I couldn't stop noticing all the beautiful layouts and colorful environments. The way the light filters through the translucent paper (pellon) gives the entire film a feel of a stained glass window coming to life, with rich textures and a warm glow. The characters are loveable oddballs, possessing some great voices from actors who were known for their improvisational skills and extreme dry wit and humor.[114]

Jenkins goes on to remark that the storyline is thin and does not devote any attention to it. But that is where he is wrong, because the conception of the story and characters is closely connected to the artistic perspective and animation. In fact, it is a complex carnivalesque film of over seventy-minutes. It begins with an introduction of the bizarre characters involved in a major conflict between the producers of sweet dreams in a realm called Frivoli and the producers of nightmares called Murkworks and ruled by the nasty Synonamess Botch. The people who are the target of Frivoli and Murkworks are introduced in photo collages: they are called "Rushers of Din," and appear to lead harried and happy lives, generally in the city of San Francisco. The man responsible for delivering sweet dreams is called Greensleeves or Greenie, and he resembles an Irish leprechaun. The dreams are pink adorable "figs," or figments of the imagination. Greenie and the figs are captured by black vultures, Botch's mercenary soldiers, and locked up. In the meantime two adorable *heroes manqués*, Ralph and Mum, are called upon to rescue Greenie and the figs. However, they are not ideally suited for the job. Ralph is a dog-like animal, who can change himself (somewhat incompetently) into any other kind of creature. He seems rational and blasé but constantly makes wrong choices. Mum is similar to the cartoon character Mutt, dressed in a frock, spontaneous,

Figure 22
John Korty/
Charles Swenson,
Twice Upon a Time

mischievous, and uncontrollable. They are easily duped by Botch who convinces them that they will help Frivoli by stealing the magic golden spring of the cosmic clock. Once they do this and give the spring to Botch all time stands still, and Botch will soon be able to drop bombs of nightmares on the human beings. In the meantime, a fluttering and petulant fairy godmother, known as FGM, appears out of nowhere to reprimand them and point out that they must recapture the spring and free Greenie and the figs to save the Rushers of Din from nightmares. They are joined in their quest by a vain flower, named Flora Fauna, who wants first and foremost to be an actress, and a muscle-bound Rod Rescueman, who had recently graduated from superhero school with a D average. He is the klutz version of Superman and Captain Marvel just as Flora resembles Olive from the Popeye cartoons. Though the fairy godmother, partly responsible for recruiting these untalented "heroes," does not believe they will succeed, they surprise her and manage to gain access to the Murkworks factory where they overcome Ibor, a King Kong gorilla television set and Ratattoie, half rat, half armadillo. Even Scuzzbopper, who is responsible for producing screams in nightmares, decides to help the misfits. The maniacal Botch becomes even more frantic and insane as he watches his defeat. He pushes the red button for one of his most trusted vultures to drop an atomic bomb to ignite all sorts of nightmares and to spread feelings of doom. But when Greenie and the figs are released and the spring is returned to the cosmic clock, the bomb detonates at the wrong place and wrong time. Botch is sent flying into space, and people wake up after experiencing sweet dreams and go on their happy ways.

The complex plot is filled with music and references to American popular culture, and the film is clearly a parody of all forms of the mass media and the illusions and spectacles that are fostered in daily life. Though the dead-pan humor and irony and the apparent caricature of the classical fairy tale make it seem that Korty and Swenson did not have anything serious to say, except to comment on people's needs to have sweet dreams to survive in a fast-paced world, nothing could be further from the truth. Whatever their intentions may have been, the directors and the artists with whom they worked were very familiar with the culture industry of Hollywood, and in many respects the film uses animation to subvert Hollywood animation and to offer a kind of self-critique, for they all played a role in producing artificial images to lure the American public into sweet dreams and daydreams. The great irony of *Twice Upon a Time* is that preposterous and fictive "heroes" save real human beings from so-called nightmares that might actually provide them with a more realistic understanding of their plight in a world that is running itself amuck at a fast pace. This is not to say that the crazy Botch and a gloomy vision should rule the world and the imaginations of people. But the film does raise the serious question about the role of the mass media and animation and how they disseminate sweet dreams and dumb down the American public. Many images in the film recall the dropping of atomic bombs, a Hitler-like or Mussolini-type maniac, ruins of buildings destroyed by war, and other ugly scenes that appear side by side with idyllic landscapes and pretty urban scenes. The sweet dreams of "Frivoli"—perhaps a code name for frivolous Hollywood—are intended to mask the consequences of the "cosmic" clock that appears to hold the conflict between nightmares and sweet dreams in balance. Yet, as the narrative is played out, only sweet dreams remain—images of the American mass media that conceal just as much as they reveal.

Japanese Utopianism

The very first endeavors in Japan to produce feature-length animated fairy-tale films are fascinating because they "Orientalized" Disney aesthetics in an endeavor to become independent from the Disney model and at the same time have the same public success. The result was mixed, but certainly the pioneer director, Taiji Yabushita, who made several fairy-tale films in the 1950s and 1960s, became a major force behind the great tradition of animated films in Japan and inspired the brilliant Hayao Miyazaki.

Yabushita's first film, *The White Serpent* (1958), also known in America as *Panda and the White Snake*, is based on the Chinese "Legend of the White Snake," which can be traced back to an oral tradition in the medieval period. It was a song that stemmed from the Southern Song Dynasty. Similar to the western narrative tradition of "Undine," in which a water sprite gives up immortality to marry a handsome young knight, this legend concerns a young scholar, who becomes enraptured by a beautiful woman without realizing that she is actually a white snake that can assume human shape. Though the maiden also falls in love with the scholar, it is a sin for a human to have a relationship with an otherworldly creature, considered a demon, and a monk tries to save the scholar's soul by throwing the white snake into a deep well. This simple plot was embellished over the years, and often the young scholar has known the white snake since childhood, and the white snake has a soul sister, a green snake, who often causes her problems. Indeed, many changes were made in the oral and literary tradition, and the legend has been transformed into a romance, short story, an opera, several films, and two TV series in China and Japan.[115]

Figure 23
Taiji Yabushita,
The White Serpent

Hiroshi Ôkawa, president of Toei Animation and producer of *The White Serpent*, encouraged Yabushita to make a film with a Chinese theme as a gesture of reconciliation with China and other Asian countries. To accomplish his goal at a time when feature-length animation had not been attempted in Japan, Ôkawa hired a few thousand artists, technicians, and animators to assist Yabushita. The film, made in only eight months, won honors at the Venice Children's Film Festival in 1959. But the edited American version, released in 1961, cut and ruined the film so that *Panda and the White Snake* received a poor reception. Only recently, in 2007, did the French bring out a beautiful DVD, based on the uncut original version, with a documentary and commentary about the making of the film.

Indeed, this animated fairy-tale film is a little gem. The hand-drawn backgrounds resemble picturesque Japanese watercolor paintings. The architectural designs of the temples, pagodas, and villages are realistically drawn in great detail. And yet, many of the scenes are surreal—the visit to the dragon king of the cosmos, the battle between the white snake and the monk in the skies, the underwater meeting of the young fish maiden with the Dragon King of the Sea. Tabushita's film alternates between tender scenes of gentle love and music and tense conflicts that include tempests, arrests, and battles. At the same time, there is a strong dose of humor, provided by comic animals, the pandas and their pals. This is the Disney comic relief effect.

The film is clearly directed at a family audience. The plot begins with a young boy named Xu-Xian going to market and buying a small white snake, which he keeps in a cage. However, his parents dislike his pet and force him to throw the snake away. Years later, when Xu-Xian is a handsome, mild scholar, who lives in a small village with two charming pandas, one black-and-white and the other a small red panda, he is reunited with the white snake, who is a storm spirit and has the ability to transform herself into a beautiful princess called Bai-Niang. This reunion is brought about through the efforts of a tiny friend of the princess, who is also a fish spirit. However, a monk named Fa-Hai, who has great magical powers, senses that there are strange demons lurking in the village and wants to protect Xu-Xian. What ensues is a series of events that involve the comic exploits of the pandas and the fish spirit, Xu-Xian's banishment to another village where he is punished and must perform hard labor, Bai-Niang's defeat in a major battle over Xu-Xian's heart, and Xu-Xian's accidental death when he falls off a cliff in resisting the monk. Due to her deep love for Xu-Xian, Bai-Niang flies to the Dragon King of the Cosmos, gives up her immortality, and carries the flower of life to Xu-Xian to resuscitate her lover. Of course, she is aided by the tiny brave fish maiden and the pandas and their gang. In the end, the monk realizes that the love between Xu-Xian and Bai-Niang is profound and genuine, and he blesses them before they set off into the sea on a bark. The last fame of the film is that of the two lovers in the distance on a blue ocean with a radiant rainbow above their heads.

Though it may seem a typical sentimental Disney ending, it is much different. In this film it is the beautiful maiden who saves a comatose hero. The so-called villain is not evil and is not killed. In fact, nobody is killed or violated in the film, and there is a serene quality to the conclusion, even in the comic and conflict scenes, suggesting that reconciliation can be brought about without violence. Peace and balance in the universe are restored, and the spirits of nature have been calmed. It is not clear at the end of the film where the bark will land. But it is clear that it is heading toward a place that the young couple has struggled to determine and attain with the help and guidance of friends, and this place is no-place called utopia.

This joyful utopian spirit infuses, I believe, almost all the animated films of Hayao Miyazaki. In particular, *Spirited Away* (2001) and *Ponyo* (2008), two of his best animated feature fairy-tale films, indicate the progressive and experimental manner in which he has gone way beyond Yabushita's utopian vision and made the perverse Disney images of utopia appear frivolous. Though *Spirited Away* is an original narrative based on experiences that Miyazaki had with his ten-year-old daughter and relies heavily on Japanese folklore, and *Ponyo* is a very loose if not radical adaptation of Hans Christian Andersen's "The Little Mermaid" and uses Japanese folklore and a contemporary eco- logical perspective to re-visit Andersen's tale, the two films have a great deal in common. As in most of Miyazaki's films, the major protagonist is a young girl, who struggles to name herself, that is, to establish her own identity in conflict with her family. Each girl must undertake an intense spiritual journey that leads her into chaos. She loses her name only to rename herself by confronting the "demons" that pose a threat to her welfare. Miyazaki focuses his films so that the camera's eyes and the animators' hands are linked to the emotions and perspective of young people throughout both films. Though intended to express the view of children, his fairy-tale animations are not children's films, but films about children that make an argument on their behalf—especially about their future and the utopian possibilities that must be maintained if they are to find the right path for self- determination. In discussing *Spirited Away* with Steven Horn, Miyazaki stated:

> The relationship between Chihiro and her parents is very typical of most family relationships in Japan. I was inspired to make this film when a daughter of mine turned 10. The most important thing for me in making this movie was to persuade the 10-year-olds that this movie was for them. I wanted them to be able to recognize themselves in the characters. I think I would like them to leave the movie theater with a sense of humility about the complexity and difficulties of the world we live in. I think an encounter with film is always an encounter with something new, so I think that the possibility for everyone in the world appreciating the film is there.[116]

Spirited Away is indeed complex and concerns a disturbed girl named Chihiro, angry at her parents because they are moving to a new home in unfamiliar surroundings. She is anxious and obviously would prefer to stay at her old home. As her parents drive with her to the new locale, they become lost and take an unpaved road to an abandoned old theme park. Once they go through a tunnel, they begin exploring the strange buildings, and everything becomes surreal. It is not clear whether Chihiro dreams or actually experiences what follows. Her parents are turned into pigs when they eat some food in a deserted restaurant; she meets a mysterious young boy named Haku, who

Figure 24
Hayao Miyazaki,
Spirited Away

helps her navigate her way through a town riddled by ghosts over a bridge to an enormous ancient Japanese bathhouse; Haku informs Chihiro that she must work for the large-headed witch Yubaba, dressed in a prim Victorian dress. She is the greedy and powerful owner of the bathhouse who dotes on a mammoth baby named Boh, who never leaves the bathhouse because of germs. Haku tries to help Chihiro free her parents and escape the world of the spirits, but first the young girl must work for Yubaba, who takes her name away from her, and she must now do drudge work with the name "Sen." Some very unusual-looking gods come to the bathhouse to cleanse themselves, and if Chihiro/Sen does not do her job properly, she will be turned into an animal, and her parents will remain pigs. Haku turns out to be a flying dragon and the river god of the Kohaku River that has dried up. He is under a spell by Yubaba. At one point he is wounded by the paper birds of Zeniba, Yubaba's twin sister, because he has stolen Zeniba's magical golden seal. To help Haki, Chihiro takes Boh and a faceless spirit with her on a trip to see Zeniba to save Haku. Once there Zeniba is friendly and forgives Haku, who appears at her house. They fly back to the bath house, and along the way, she recalls that she had almost drowned in the Kohaku River as a child and that Haku had saved her. This recollection enables Haku to recall his real name, and he breaks the spell that Yubaba held on him. But Yubaba will not free Chihiro until she identifies her parents among a herd of pigs. Instinctively, Chihiro senses that none of the pigs are her parents, and she is free to depart. Haku guides her to the bridge that leads to the human world and separates from her. As she crosses a verdant field, she meets her parents. It is as if Chihiro had gotten lost, and they had only been separated for some hours. Then, they go through the tunnel, get into the car and resume their journey. Chihiro is not certain that her experiences are real until she discovers a hand band that Zeniba had given to her as the car drives on in silence.

This brief summary does not do justice to the story, for it is filled with wry humor, extraordinary characters, unusual fairy-tale motifs, and references to Japanese folklore and rituals. The enormous and intricately drawn bathhouse serves as the dominant symbol of the film, which deals with cleansing—cleansing of the soul, cleaning the air, exploring the genuine essence of relationships and work. In some ways, Chihiro is a contemporary Alice in Wonderland, and once she enters the realm of the spirits, she learns to overcome her anxieties. Put to the test, to save her parents and Haku, she responds with great devotion and valor. In carnivalesque fashion, Miyazaki turns the normal world upside down into a bizarre counter-world, in which identical twin sisters appear to be dreadful and irrational and yet bring no harm to anyone. Everyone wants to take part in the cleansing. Nobody is purely clean. The world is chock-full of ambiguity. Deep down all the creatures want love and friendship. Humans, a spidery grandpa, ghosts, giant chicks, frogs, mice, and other creatures are drawn as unconventional characters that follow rituals without anything codified. The detailed depiction of the interior and exterior buildings is exquisite, and the images metamorphose before our eyes. The major transformation is Chihiro's character, but it is not the typical fairy-tale transformation: she does not become beautiful, marry a prince, or demonstrate outwardly that she has changed. She returns to reality and remains somewhat puzzled but with the confidence that she should be able to handle what comes. The world ahead of her might be difficult, but Miyazaki has shown what Chihiro—or any young person—can do when she has caring friends and is put to the test.

This same theme is repeated in *Ponyo*, not with the same depth and great artistry as in *Spirited Away*. Nevertheless, it is an interesting film because it departs greatly from Andersen's "The Little Mermaid" and reveals what a "feminist" director can do with Andersen's pathetic, misogynist narrative. The Disney corporation transformed the tale into a stupid pubescent musical that celebrated the spunk and illusions of a spoiled princess, who is awarded a handsome prince because she is so charming. Miyazaki shifts the focus to try to understand why differences can cause great familial disturbances that are also related to natural catastrophes. The film, clearly intended for very young audiences, is simple if not a bit too simplistic. Miyazaki sets the tale in contemporary Japan, and his two protagonists are five-year-olds, a boy named Sosuke, and a golden-fish-girl named Ponyo. Sosuke saves Ponyo when she becomes trapped in a bottle, and she licks the blood from a cut in his finger. As a consequence, she begins to develop a love for Sosuke and assume more of a human form. Her father, Fujimonoto, always dressed in a striped jacket and looking more like a bohemian sailor than king of the ocean, gains control of her and tries to prevent her from joining Sosuke. But with the help of her tiny sister fish, she breaks away from her father and causes an immense storm and flooding. Miscegenation does not seem to work and brings about an imbalance in the world. However, Granmamare, Ponyo's mother, a huge and beautiful queen, appears and calms her husband. They agree that, if Sosuke can prove he can love Ponyo as fish or girl, order will be restored in the world. The father makes one last attempt to prevent Sosuke from demonstrating his love. He fails, and there is a glorious ending in which the universe becomes calm and Ponyo turns into a little girl by jumping from the water to kiss Sosuke.

Despite the mediocre plot and the pretty paintings that resemble more the watercolored illustrations of a manga comic book or children's book without any depth or symbolic significance, the film deals with sensitive issues that touch very small children's lives. Both Ponyo, who refuses to be called by the name her father has chosen for her, and Sosuke are drawn to the "otherness" of each other. Miyazaki has totally transformed Andersen's tale of sacrificial love into a story of mutual trust and an acceptance of difference. Once again, Miyazaki minimizes violence and emphasizes patience and devotion as means to reconcile opposing views. The sea king is not a villain. Rather, he looks after the best interests of his daughters and wants to protect them. Humans, as he believes, will maltreat fish or creatures of the sea as some of the early scenes in the film indicate. But there is hope for change in the hearts of two five-year-olds, and the king needs to learn a lesson from the young. This is the utopian note sounded in *Ponyo*, and it is also a note clearly sounded in the French filmmaker Michel Ocelot's two films about Kirikou.

French *Joie de Vivre*

The real hope for children is clearly marked out in two of Ocelot's animated films, *Kirikou and the Sorceress* (1998) and *Kirikou and the Wild Beasts* (2005), which rely on two-dimensional hand drawings that recall the unusual paintings of Henri Rousseau. The protagonist of these two films is a tiny naked West African child who is born with wisdom beyond his years and also has the capacity to speak. He literally bursts from his mother's womb and scoots about the village to declare that he is there, ready to help the needy villagers. In the first film—and I shall focus only on this one— Kirikou quickly learns that his tiny village is threatened by the sorceress Karaba, who uses an army of robots and automats to take gold and kill any of the men who dare to oppose her. Kirikou decides to save the village, and everyone mocks him, but when he succeeds and outwits Karaba with his adroit speed and cunning, they begin celebrating him with songs that extol his deeds. However, the curious Kirikou does not only want to defeat Karaba, he also wants to know why she is so mean and evil. So he undertakes a perilous journey to seek advice from the Wise Man of the Forbidden Mountain. There he learns that Karaba had been violated by the men of the village and had sought revenge by using her magic powers to turn them into robots that served her. Her wickedness stemmed not so much from some innate evil quality but from the abusive behavior of the men who drove her to become an outcast. Once Kirikou learns all this from the Wise Man, he is able to free Karaba from her misery by pulling a thorn from her back. As he does this, he is magically transformed into a handsome young man, and the robots return to their human form and go back to the village. At first, the villagers cannot believe that Kirikou, too, has been transformed, but his mother recognizes him for the person he has become through the deeds that he has performed.

Figure 25 Michel Ocelot, *Kirikou and the Sorceress*

Aside from the artful depiction of lush colorful landscapes, bizarre mechanical devices, native animals and plants, and villagers who are bare-breasted and naked as they often are in West African villages, the film makes no attempt to westernize or Americanize the characters or plot. Based on various African folk tales, the fairy-tale film focuses on the extraordinary bravery, curiosity, and imagination of Kirikou. Ocelot, who studied animation in California and in France, was well aware of the Disneyfication of fairy-tale films, and he consciously endeavored to shape his film to respect the intelligence of his audiences of all ages. In an interview with Christine Gudin, he stated:

> At the beginning I did not have a precise audience in mind. I know that the film would also be for children because when one makes an animated film, there is only one audience on the market, the family audience, even if one does not willingly target this audience. For the moment, we are all condemned to this state of affairs. But it will change. I would not have found the money if I had proposed an animated film intended for adults. But the story [the West African tale] touched me. I truly had a great desire to tell it. I was very conscious of working for everyone, no matter what age, by evoking situations that only adults could decipher in a precise way, while children would comprehend half or would register it later. I am incapable of writing a scenario that doesn't touch me. I think that, to interest children, it's a very good method not to make a film for them, not to treat them as babies.[117]

Indeed, Ocelot's sophisticated film deals with rape, banishment, prejudice, revenge, and identity formation. Nothing is black and white, and there is no crude violence or saccharine melodrama. The village does not become a utopian realm at the end of the film; nothing is fixed or certain. But Ocelot touches on utopian longings and the potential in every tiny child to find his or her way through a morass of human relations degraded by a misunderstood magician/inventor and her command of technology. She takes men's bodies from them, takes away their identities, and embodies a monster that they have actually made. In contrast, Kirikou, the wonderful naked boy, embodies humane kindness and an exuberant *joie de vivre* that revives the village and the environment.

Richard Neupert has commented that Ocelot's films

> challenge our theorization of the cinematic body. Moreover, *Kirikou et la sorcière* is a particularly pertinent test case since its naked protagonist and topless women drew criticism

that their bodies' representations were inappropriate for children, and some cultural critics charged that they were racist representations. *Kirikou et la sorcière* never even received a full theatrical release in the United Kingdom or the United States due to these concerns. That these animated bodies can be feared and censored certainly proves that these painted forms are already regarded as bodies on legal, institutional, but also cultural levels.[118]

One of his more recent films, *Azur and Asmar* (2006), continued to provide substantial cultural difference in animation and to present bodies in unusual images and situations that challenge stereotypes and social prejudices. Set in the Middle Ages, the film takes place first in Andalusia, where a young boy named Azur is being nursed and educated by a North African woman Jénane because the infant's mother has died. Jénane has her own son, Asmar, the same age. The two boys play together and become close "brothers," despite class and ethnic differences. Ocelot depicts the relationship between the blue-eyed blond-haired Azur, and the dark-skinned, brown-eyed Asmar as natural and free of prejudice. The boys are both enraptured by a tale that Jénane tells them about the princess of the jinnis, who is encased in glass and needs to be saved by a valiant knight. As Azmur grows older, however, his father, a nobleman, abruptly and violently banishes Jénane and Asmar from Andalusia because he wants his son to receive a royal education appropriate for a young nobleman and believes that the dark son of a servant has had a bad influence on Azmur. Later, when Azmur has matured, he rebels against his racist father and sets out on a quest to free the princess of the jinnis, who resides, he believes, across the sea in Jénane's home country. Haunted by memories of his childhood, Azmur sets sail for Northern Africa. After he has an accident and is washed ashore, he finds himself in a country where people with blue eyes are regarded as dangerous because they bring evil. Everything appears strange and wondrous, and Azur pretends to be blind so that he will not be maltreated because of his blue eyes. Fortunately, he meets a cunning beggar named Crapaux, also a westerner, who speaks better Arabic than Azur. After some comic incidents, Capraux helps him find his way to Jénane's mansion. To Azur's surprise, he finds that Jénane has become a wealthy merchant and is highly respected. Reunited with his former nanny, who loves him, Azur is given a different reception by Asmar, who resents him because of the cruel way he and his mother were banished from Andalusia. Azur is also surprised that Asmar also wants to find the princess of the jinnis and win her for his bride. Now both are rivals, and as they prepare for their journey, Azur receives help and advice from a tiny princess, reminiscent of Kirikou, and a Jewish sage. He departs with Asmar, and along the way to the secret palace of the enchanted princess of the jinnis, they have various adventures and save each other's lives. Indeed, they become brothers again. The final sequence of events has Azur carrying Asmar to the princess of the jinnis and declaring that Asmar deserves her in a gesture of profound brotherhood. The princess of the jinnis has a dilemma and does not know what to do. She calls upon the mother/nanny, the tiny princess, the Jewish sage, and Crapaux to help her. They are all carried to her by a magnificent magic bird. Finally, her cousin, a princess of elves arrives. She is white and decides to marry the dark Asmar, while the dark princess of the jinnis chooses the blue-eyed Azur.

The plot is a pot-boiler of motifs from the western and Oriental fairy-tale tradition and recalls at times Lotte Reiniger's film *The Adventures of Prince Achmed*, especially when Ocelot makes great use of shadow puppets. Despite the predictability of the events and the obvious multicultural message of tolerance, the film evokes such an aura of marvelous enchantment with exotic landscapes, palaces, and caverns that the predictable and obvious are never heavy-handed. As in most of his films, Ocelot is interested in depicting the dignity of human beings and animals and generally enlivens his films with surprising characters such as the little princess who cuts in and out of her palace and speaks bluntly. Moreover, he has taken great care to research and represent customs, rituals, costumes, superstitions, and behavior of a different culture in a historical period when there was great conflict between East and West. Times have not changed much, as Ocelot has noted in interviews, and he originally intended to make a film that dealt with war. However, he shifted his emphasis to focus on tolerance. In an interview with Steve Fritz, Ocelot has commented:

> The inspiration [for *Azur and Asmar*] is what touches me or bothers me, here and now. There are rich and poor countries, and immigrants facing well-to-do citizens, and the West and the Islamic world, and people hating each other, when the contrary would be so much more pleasant. If I bring some dignity and a sense of lightness to people, I am satisfied. . . . I made up all the story, but I am aware that no story is totally original. My main source of inspiration for the graphic style was fifteenth-century and sixteenth-century Persian miniatures. I chose the medieval epoch because I wanted to talk about Moslem civilization at the time it was open and brilliant. I went to the late middle ages to use the beautiful costumes and architecture, even if it was a little late for the golden age of Moslem civilization.[119]

Fritz notes that *Azur and Asmar* resembles a brilliant Renaissance tapestry, but it is a tapestry of contestation and an example of how "other" fairy-tale animation is still being censored and banned throughout the world, but particularly in the United States. Ironically, this film about tolerance is not tolerated by media companies that dominate the network of film distribution. Ocelot had numerous problems having the two *Kirikou* films shown and distributed in America because of the nudity in the film, and in *Azur and Asmar*, he began the film with a sequence of frames showing Jénane breastfeeding the blond, blue-eyed Azur and singing a lullaby in Arabic and then breastfeeding her dark-skinned son Asmar. It is a beautiful, tender scene of solace and love. It is, however, a scene that has caused consternation among media conglomerates and censors that have limited the distribution of Ocelot's films. Fortunately, they do not have the last word, and though Ocelot's films and other animated feature fairy-tale films may never reach wide audiences in America, they continue to be disseminated and have offered models of contestation that continue to inspire animators to think and create their own tales and challenge audiences to see their social realities more clearly through fairy tales.

II

6

Cracking the Magic Mirror:
Representations of Snow White

Feminism has undone the mimetic mirror of masculinist culture. Whether by going through the looking glass or by smashing it to pieces, it has made the mirror crack. Feminist cinema has therefore profoundly transformed the traditional field of visual representation which "reflected the figure of man at twice its natural size" (Virginia Wolf), while the image of "Woman" remained diminished and distorted. Discarding and dismantling old forms of representation, feminist filmmakers have sought new ways of representing women's lives and experiences, of imagining female subjectivity, and of addressing the female spectator.

Anneke Smelik, *And the Mirror Cracked:
Feminist Cinema and Feminist Theory*[120]

Our fascination with the fairy tale "Snow White," originally written down in 1810, changed and edited by the Brothers Grimm over a period of forty-seven years, has very little to do with the trials and tribulations of the virginal protagonist Snow White, but much more to do with the passionate queen, her stepmother, and the queen's struggles with her omniscient and authoritative magic mirror. Despite its seemingly happy end, this tale is tragic: the beautiful queen has a major flaw in her character that leads to her downfall, namely her vanity. This is not to say that the character of Snow White is negligible in the story, but she is not the driving force. She is too pathetically good, too much the domestic, to be of major interest in the story. As is well known, the animators of the Disney film preferred to draw the evil queen because she was more real and complex as a woman, more erotic, and driven to desperate acts by her magic mirror. In fact, the tale should have been given the title "Cracking the Magic Mirror," for the mirror has a powerful hold on the queen and, to a certain extent, on Snow White. The queen's actions are determined by the mirror's representations of her as exemplifying beauty and evil, or associating evil and vanity with beauty, and these mirror representations are taken as the truth by the queen. Had she perhaps doubted and cracked the mirror, cracked the meaning of the mirror, she might still be alive today. As it is, she is still dancing herself to death in red-hot shoes in some printed version of the tale.

But what about the cinematic versions? She does not dance herself to death in the Disney animated feature film, and in many sanitized twentieth- and twenty-first-century printed versions for children, she is forbidden to dance herself to death for fear that she might damage the souls of putative innocent child readers/viewers. She either dies by accident, is banished, or disappears. Meanwhile, the magic mirror, the instigator of the queen's evil actions and the cause of her demise, continues to live in most cases without punishment and to reflect the standards of beauty throughout the world, much the same way that the Disney version of the tale of Snow White came to represent the ideal fairy tale and the ideal manner in which "Snow White" should be represented to children and adults.

One of the most interesting interpretations of the tale and its cultural legacy is a chapter in Sandra Gilbert and Susan Gubar's *The Madwoman in the Attic*, in which they argue that the tale dramatizes "the essential but equivocal relationship between the angel-woman and the monster-woman" of western patriarchy:

> The central action of the tale—indeed its only real action—arises from the relationship between these two women: the one fair, young, pale, the other just as fair, but older, fiercer; the one a daughter, the other a mother; the one sweet, ignorant, passive, the other artful and active; the one a sort of angel, the other an undeniable witch.[121]

Gilbert and Gubar strongly suggest, as do many other feminists, that the competition between the two women results from a patriarchal culture, represented by the male mirror, that pits woman against woman for the favor of a male. In other words, it would appear that women are victimized under social conditions beyond their control. Though Snow White might triumph in the tale, she will undoubtedly acquire a mirror after she marries, matures, and has children, and as the mirror reflects her aging and loss of beauty, she will be confronted by a young girl whose innocence and youth will spark her envy and hatred and perhaps drive her to eliminate her "competition." It appears as though there is a vicious cycle that entraps women up through today. Everything is played out under the male gaze.

Yet, the relations between the queen and Snow White have varied greatly in the hundreds of oral and printed versions from the sixteenth century to the present. For instance, in the handwritten Grimms' version of 1810, based on an oral retelling, the queen is Snow White's mother, and Snow White's father revives his daughter. In many instances, it appears that the young girl might also be fleeing her father. The conflict is between mother and daughter, and the father is the one who determines that his wife must die. But what remains dominant in almost all oral and written versions is the power of the mirror, and most important, in my opinion, is the relationship of the queen to the mirror that orchestrates her life. In many ways she becomes caught in a moving film of her life as she becomes absorbed in the mirror images that deceive her into believing that she is not the most beautiful woman in the realm and must act to regain and maintain her former status. Another way of describing her situation is that she becomes trapped in the spectacle of male illusions. Her identity and value as a woman are in large part determined by the refraction of the mirror. This is why the crucial relationship in all the tales and cinematic versions is that between the queen and the mirror, not between the queen and Snow White. If the queen had disregarded the mirror instead of gazing into it and becoming absorbed by it, her life might not have ended so tragically. What is fascinating about the tale that can, of course, be interpreted in many different ways, is that it reveals how we can all become enchanted by and obsessed by representations that reflect nothing more than the machinations of the apparatus. The mirror itself is never neutral and sets an arbitrary standard of beauty, for we know that there is no such thing as essential beauty. Nevertheless, the mirror appears to have some kind of divine authority, and it only derives its power because the queen acknowledges its authority. Snow White never gazes into a mirror, and thus she never becomes ensnared by a mirror reflection.

The cinematic discourse about "Snow White" is highly significant in this regard because it demonstrates how those filmmakers who have been attracted to some narrative or memory of "Snow White" have consciously and unconsciously endeavored to unravel the power of the mirror, that is, they have endeavored to question the hold that the mirror has on the queen and by consequence the hold that representation has on us, the spectators. At the same time, they question whether we are bound by one primeval text, or what German scholars have called the *Urtext*, about the queen and the magic mirror that ruins her life.

To demonstrate the significance of the mirror and representation of the queen's tragedy for filmic adaptations of the tale, I want to review some of the more salient "Snow White" films from 1915 to the present. The pre-1937 or pre-Disney films tend to be elaborations of the master narrative edited by the Brothers Grimm, while the films that follow the highly successful Disney film contend more with the master images and plot of the Disney film as well as with the Grimms' tale. It has been impossible, I believe, for any filmmaker not to be aware of the images and plot of the Disney film. Whatever the case may be, the driving force of the action and plot, even in Disney's *Snow White*, tends to be on the relationship of the queen to the mirror, although there are some notable exceptions.

Representing "Snow White"

But first, a brief excursion into the cinematic discourse of "Snow White" to illustrate the importance of representation in the genre of the fairy tale. All storytellers, writers, dramatists, illustrators, and filmmakers who re-tell, adapt, or re-present "Snow White" reflect in their minds that this story is in some way relevant to their lives and their audiences and that their representations are necessary because something meaningful may be missing in the tale to which they are referring, whatever the hypotext may be. The representation is thus an appropriation, a replacement, an elaboration, an enrichment, or a critique. In the case of film, the filmmakers do not want to efface the Grimms' or Disney version; they generally refer to them to stir our memetic minds and place emphasis on crucial motifs and elements of the well-known traditional plot to make us aware of aspects of the story that we may not have perceived. However, their point of reference is complicated because it is an intervention of some kind, a conscious intervention in the discourse about the meaning of fairy tales and one fairy tale in particular. Regardless of the source text, key elements of a tale that has stuck in millions of minds are touched upon in the representation to address social and cultural issues on a metaphorical level. "Snow White" is interesting because the tale has prompted film-makers to elaborate on the representation of beauty, who sets standards of beauty, why beauty is so important for women in men's eyes, and how the image and nature of beauty can be manipulated through the male gaze.

The cinematic discourse about "Snow White" and the essence of beauty began almost as soon as the film industry was established. According to some sources, there was an early 1902 silent *Snow White* and also a 1914 film, *The Legend of Snow White*; neither has been recovered or been restored. In 1916 two interesting full-length films directed by Charles Weston and J. Searle Dawley were produced; they depended heavily on the Grimms' printed version. However, Dave Fleischer's short animated *Snow White* of 1932 starring Betty Boop broke clearly with the traditional plot and turned the tragic tale into a hilarious comedy. Some of these early films may have influenced the Disney version of 1937, which was later parodied by Robert Clampett's provocative animated cartoon *Coal Black and de Sebben Dwarfs* (1943). The Disney film, however, had no impact on Howard Hawks' amusing live-action *Ball of Fire* (1941), in which Gary Cooper plays a timid scholar as prince and

Barbara Stanwyck, a gangster's moll named Sugarpuss, as Snow White. After World War II there were numerous live-action reproductions of "Snow White" in Europe that were clearly intended to cater to young and family audiences, for example Paolo William Tamburella's *The Seven Dwarfs to the Rescue* (*I Sette Nanni alla Riscossa*, 1951) in Italy; Erich Kobler's *Snow White* (*Schneewittchen*, 1955) and Kurt Hoffmann's *Snow White and the Seven Circus Performers* (*Schneewittchen und die sieben Gaukler*, 1962) in West Germany; and Gottfried Kolditz's *Snow White* (*Schneewittchen*, 1961) in East Germany. In addition, some European, Mexican, and South American directors produced adult, erotic, and horror live-action and animated films based on "Snow White" such as *Grimms Märchen von lüsternen Pärchen* (*The Grimms' Fairy Tales about Lascivious Couples*, 1969), *Snow White and the Seven Perverts* (1973), *Once Upon a Girl* (1976), *Stories Our Nannies Don't Tell* (*Histórias Que Nossas Babás Não Contavam*, 1979), *Snow White and her Seven Lovers* (*Blanca Nieves y sus 7 Amantes*, 1980), *Snow White & Co.* (*Biancaneve & Co.*, 1982), *Snow White . . . Ten Years Later* (*Biancaneve . . . dieci anni dopo*, 1999) and one animated feature film, *Snow White: The Sequel* (*Blanche Neige: La Suite* 2007). Among the more recent insipid American computer-animated films is *Happily N'Ever After 2: Snow White: Another Bite of the Apple* (2009), a sequel to the banal *Happily N'Ever After* (2007). In this made-to-make-money sequel that tries so obviously to imitate the success of the *Shrek* films, Snow White is portrayed as a spoiled rich kid who prefers discos, clothes, and partying to the philanthropic work of her dead mother Caroline. Her father, the merry King Cole, marries Lady Vain, who has a magic mirror that has the face of a magic genie with rings in his ears. She doesn't poison Snow White, but she uses magic to compel Snow White to spread vicious gossip about her friends and everyone in the kingdom. Snow White flees to the woods where she meets the dwarfs, who are boringly good Samaritans and teach her how to behave and improve her manners. In the end, she defeats Lady Vain and begins a romance with a handsome orphan, who is a stalwart knight. Aside from a stupid plot and poor animation, the recuperation of a sassy rich kid who retains her privileges by learning how to be as philanthropic as her dead mother is a dubious message to pass on to children, unless one believes that the rich always must be given a second chance to rule the world. This theme looms large in most filmic representations of "Snow White"—the virginal princess, abandoned by her mother in childbirth, who by virtue of her social status, innocence, and beauty, should always be destined to rise from the dead to rule a realm.

Almost all "Snow White" films are variations on this theme. In America there has been a tendency to transform "Snow White" into a musical comedy, following Disney. In 1961 Walter Lang produced *Snow White and the Three Stooges*, in which Carol Heiss, an Olympic figure skating champion, sings and stars as Snow White. The stooges, Larry, Moe, and Curly, are traveling entertainers who help a young man rediscover his identity as prince so he can eventually marry Snow White. Aside from a magic mirror that determines the fate of a stepmother queen, there is also a magic sword that enables the stooges to perform miracles. Other romantic comedies include the Faerie Tale Theatre version, *Snow White and the Seven Dwarfs* (1984), produced by Shelley Duvall, the Cannon Studio production *Snow White* (1987), and *Sydney White* (2007). Three more serious endeavors that grapple with the tragic aspects of the "Snow White" discourse are Michael Cohn's *Snow White: A Tale of Terror* and Tom Davenport's *Willa: An American Snow White*, which both appeared in 1996, and the Hallmark production *Snow White: The Fairest of Them All* (2002). Of course, there have been numerous short cartoons made for TV, videocassettes, and DVDs that either feature the "Snow White Tale," Snow White herself, or the dwarfs. For instance, the Muppet Babies have performed a "Snow White" play, in which Miss Piggy hogs the show, and there is a fractured "Snow White" in the Rocky and Bullwinkle series. In 1988 ABC produced a sitcom called *The Charmings*, in which the domestic life of Snow White and Prince Charming is depicted in a modern setting. HBO's multi-cultural series, *Happily Ever After: Fairy Tales for Every Child*

(1995–1998), narrated by Robert Guillaume, includes a *Snow White* in a Southwestern setting with White Snow as a Native American chieftain's daughter. In another TV mini-series, *The Tenth Kingdom* (2000), Virginia, the waitress-heroine, is given a magic mirror by the ghost of Snow White that she uses to discover her long-lost mother. But it is not only in America that "Snow White" has been disseminated through TV, video, DVD, and the Internet but in practically every country throughout the world. In Japan, for instance, Nippon Animation included Snow White in its 1987 TV series *Grimm Meisaku Gekijo*, produced in America as Grimm's Fairy Tale Classics, and Tatsunoko Animation Studio began a fifty-two-episode TV series, *Shirayuki-hime no Densetsu* (*The Legend of Princess Snow White*) in 1994. In addition to the television productions and showings of "Snow White," YouTube has well over a hundred different versions of "Snow White" from different countries, including banned and rare experiments with the classic tale and the Disney version. What becomes mirrored on YouTube is the profound widespread public interest in a tale that provokes retelling and reflection because it touches upon deeply rooted problems in every culture of the world ranging from what constitutes our notions of beauty to what causes conflicts between women, especially mothers and daughters and stepmothers and daughters. A close look at the role played by the mirror in some of the early "Snow White" films up through the 1937 Disney version will reveal, I believe, how filmmakers explored the representation of beauty through the mirror that is connected to the way we determine relationships through spectacle.

The Signifying Mirror

In J. Searle Dawley's 1916 *Snow White*, based on the stage version written by Winthrop Ames in 1912, numerous changes were made to the Grimms' plot that may have influenced Disney, who saw the film when it appeared.[122] Dawley enriched the tale by providing greater characterization, more intrigue, and clearer motivation. The film opens with Santa Claus leaving behind figurines on a dresser that come to life to enact the story of "Snow White." The initial scene depicts Brangomar, an evil and ugly lady of the court who wants to surpass Snow White's beauty. She makes a pact with a weird-looking witch who wants Snow White's heart in return for making Brangomar beautiful. Once they agree, Brangomar becomes beautiful and is also given a small magic mirror that will always tell the truth. If she breaks the mirror, she will become as ugly as she really is. Shortly after this, Snow White's mother Queen Imogene dies, and Brangomar becomes the new queen and sentences Snow White to work in the kitchen. During one of the girl's errands, she encounters Prince Florimond without revealing who she is. It is love at first sight. When Florimond appears at the court later, Brangomar thinks that he has come to propose to her, but, instead, he declares his love for Snow White. Furious, Brangomar demands that they wait a year and pretends that she is going to send Snow White to a boarding school for wayward princesses. Instead, she has Snow White imprisoned and demands that the huntsman kill her in the forest. Since Snow White is a dear friend of his children, he takes pity on her and sets her free in the forest where she is stalked by a lion. Fortunately she escapes in a wood that resembles a jungle and arrives at the cottage of the seven dwarfs who are absent. So, she tidies the place for them, and when they return from the mine shafts connected to their home, they agree to allow her to remain with them. In the meantime, the queen suspects the huntsman of betraying her and has him thrown into a prison next to his children. Then the mirror tells her what has happened, and the queen asks for a disguise so that she can kill Snow White. Her first try with a comb does not work, but the second with a poisoned apple supposedly kills her. She returns to her palace, but the huntsman has escaped with his children to alert Prince Florimond about the queen's evil deeds. The prince then escorts the seemingly dead Snow White in her coffin to the palace where she awakes because a little piece of the apple loosens in her throat. In anger, the queen breaks the mirror, and her evil face shows itself. However, she is not executed but banished from the court, while the dwarfs remain with Snow White.

Although the mirror is not anthropomorphized in this film, and although we cannot hear its stern male voice as in other movies with sound, it plays a crucial role in the film as truth-teller. Even after Brangomar has artificially become beautiful, the mirror responds to her question, "Mirror, mirror, in my hand, Who's the fairest in the land?" by answering: "You who hold me in your hand, you were the fairest in the land; but to-day, I tell you true, Snow White is more fair than you!" This occurs after Snow White adorns beautiful clothes, given to her by her seven maids of honor, and dances with Prince Florimund. Although it is clear that Snow White is indeed beautiful, the images of her seven maids and even the depiction of Brangomar make it difficult to determine who is the most beautiful female at the court, if one can ever determine a "beauty" queen with absolute objectivity. Beauty in oral and print fairy tales is never fully described. Generally, what constitutes beauty in traditional and classical fairy tales is character: a beautiful young woman must be innocent, kind, self-deprecating, hard-working, obedient, docile, sweet, guileless, and helpful. The mirror does not reflect physical beauty nor does it explain its judgment. Its words are to be regarded as the categorical truth, but we must remember that it is magic and a gift from a demonic witch who profits from the downfall of the queen. Truth is not told by the mirror, nor does the film expose the truth. Like the static camera that focuses only on what is presented on a deep proscenium stage, the images are framed to project a model of exemplary female behavior. The mirror rules as master narrator.

In contrast, Max and Dave Fleischer's 1933 version of *Snow White,* starring the inimitable sexy Betty Boop, reveals a talking mirror that is anything but objective and mocks the idea that one can know the truth through reflection and representation. The Fleischer film is a minor masterpiece, and like many of the cartoons of the 1930s and 1940s, their short seven-minute version dares audiences to think beyond boxes and stretches the limits of the imagination. Norman Klein aptly describes what accounts for the appeal of the typical Betty Boop film: Betty, whose motivation is generally primitive, breaks with propriety, causes trouble, and all hell breaks loose. The Fleischers rarely worked from a script, and even if they did, they would ad lib and change it beyond recognition. In their cartoons,

Figure 26
Max and Dave Fleischer,
Snow White

the Fleischers literally (graphically) broke down the screen into conflicting gags within the same frame, sometimes into fragments like a broken typology, at other times into a conflicting montage of foreground opposed to background (or a spoof of depth of field, I suppose). Instead of conflict, there was a rueful explosion of paranoiac disorder. Betty had endless bad luck, enough to drive Cinderella, Snow White, and Red Riding Hood to tranquilizers.[123]

In this *Snow White*, it is not so much Betty that causes trouble, it is the mirror. The film begins immediately with a series of frames that show the common-looking, conceited queen powdering her nose in front of a hand mirror. At one point the mirror actually polishes her nose as if polishing a shoe. When the queen asks who's the fairest in the land, the mirror turns into a male face singing that she's the fairest in the land. This is the first anthropomorphized depiction of the magic mirror in cinematic history, and the Fleischers add a great deal of personality to it: the mirror is saucy, frank, and rebellious, and the queen spends much of her time trying to tame and control the mirror. She wants absolute control over her representation and reflection of the world. Once Betty swoops and swaggers into the court, the queen commands the two clown figures Koko and Bimbo, dressed in armor, who appear in many Betty Boop films, to execute her. But they fall down into a strange underworld followed by Betty who slides into the seven dwarfs' house on a sled. The queen asks the mirror again whether she's the fairest in the place, and the mirror responds: "If I were you, I'd hide my face." Outside the palace, the witch turns the mirror into a shovel at the grave site of Snow White. Then she steps through the mirror as a witch and descends into the underworld, where she joins a funeral march to the music of Cab Calloway singing "The St. James Infirmary Blues." Once the march is concluded, the queen returns to her original shape and asks the mirror one more time who is the fairest in the land. This time the mirror sticks out its tongue with a duck attached to it and points to Snow White. The queen transforms herself into a snarling dragon and pursues Betty, Koko, and Bimbo in a hilarious chase scene. In the end, she is turned into a skeleton, and the three friends hold hands and dance.

The Fleischers' mirror makes no pretension to provide an impartial, objective reflection of reality. Nor does it set a standard of beauty. The mirror is cracked in the fullest sense of the word: it is whacky, and its perspective keeps changing. The queen wants to control it not because it is a truth speaker, but because it has the power to determine the meaning of signs: it is through the mirror, that is, through the image produced by the mirror, similar to images produced by a camera, that she can orchestrate her view of herself. It is through her own magic powers that she transforms the mirror to suit her purposes. The resistance that leads to chaos in the cartoon undermines her instrumental purposes. There is nothing smooth about the early images in the Fleischer cartoons, but the frenzy derives from a resistance to the norm. The Fleischers opposed traditional storytelling, especially sweet and saccharine retellings of fairy tales. Proper appropriated treatment of the classics—this they left to Walt Disney.

As numerous critics have pointed out, Disney's first feature-length animation of "Snow White" was the culmination of his early cartoon work that was geared to perfect the technology, sound, color, and artistry of animated fairy tales.[124] The rough illustrations of the Disney cartoons of the 1920s and early 1930s, ridiculous gags, disjointed primitive figures, lack of sound, flat scenes, and static camera were all more or less overcome by the time he came to make *Snow White*. At the same time, he simplified the plot for family audiences and re-cast the tragic–comic tale as a sentimental love story and musical promoting industriousness and innocence. We must remember that this film was created during the great Depression, and America's innocence and dedication to the Protestant work ethos were being put to the test. The test is reflected in the anthropomorphized mirror, who pits the stepmother queen against the rosy-cheeked princess, whose main role is to dream and sing about the prince who will come along and save her life.

Figure 27
Walt Disney,
Snow White

The very beginning of the film indicates, however, that the prince is nothing but an appendage to the story with two functions. He appears in the second scene to ignite Snow White's love and the queen's jealousy, and he appears at the end of the film to brush kiss the virginal girl's lips and carry her off to an exquisite castle painted as the princess's and every girl's utopian wish. But it is the first scene, which pictures the beautiful witch standing before the magic mirror, that sets everything in action. This mirror, much larger than the one in Dawley's silent film, is at first dark until a masked pale face appears, grim as death and projected among flames. The lips are partially purple as is the frame that holds the mirror. The colors, purple and black, will be associated with the queen, whereas white with a bit of royal purple is Snow White's color and that of the horse that carries her away. The mirror's voice is deep, male, and authoritative. It has previously told the queen that she is the fairest of the land, but in the opening scene, he declares that "Fame beside beauty, majesty, but hold a lovely maid I see, Rags cannot hide her gentle grace. Alas, she is more fair than thee." Now, it is somewhat strange that the queen believes the mirror, for the picture of Snow White reveals that she is a pretty pubescent red-cheeked ordinary girl while the queen is a stunning beautiful mature woman who might easily win a beauty contest. Leaving aside this question, it is apparent that the mirror as moral authority is prejudiced and appears to provoke the queen to take action as it will continue to do so throughout the film. It also remains intact.

Snow White is revered by the mirror because of innocence and good behavior. Like the protagonist in Dawley's film who is pictured initially as a scullery maid, Snow White is dressed in rags to gain our sympathy. The only time she sees herself in a reflection is when she peers into the well and is then joined by the prince. Their reflection is the announcement of true love at first sight. Ironically, the queen never sees herself in her magic mirror. She does not realize how beautiful she is. There is no reflection, only the representation of a male masked face that allegedly speaks the truth. The Disney film does not interrogate the Grimms' fairy tale or the Dawley film; rather it completes Dawley's innovations more artistically and efficiently relying on stereotypes: the evil witch, the virginal ingénue, seven amusing helpers, the prince on a white horse, and the truth-bearing mirror. These ingredients make for a delightful film with an antiquated and narrow notion of gender, love, and evil. People are not born vain, they are made vain through mirror images cultivated in the civilizing processes of diverse societies.

Post-1945 Snow Whites

Though some fairy-tale films and cartoons were made during World War II, most cinematic adaptations of "Snow White" commenced after 1945, and they can roughly be placed into two categories: conventional and experimental. The lines between these two categories are fluid, but there are some valid generalizations that can be made about each category. The conventional adaptations tend to follow the Grimms' narrative closely and add embellishments and motifs borrowed from the Disney film. Ideologically, they do not interrogate the questionable treatment of women, the role of the mirror, and the "happy" resolution that reinforces patriarchal rule. The conventional films are often made for younger audiences for commercial purposes. That is, the tale, "Snow White," is treated as a commodity that will sell well and contribute to the well-being of the young by focusing on the theme of jealousy and the generous help of the cute dwarfs as comic relief. Conventional films essentially mimic the Grimms and Disney. The experimental films, while often commercial as well, question the "essentialist" notion of representation and the arbitrary authority of the male mirror. The traditional Grimms' tale is often fractured to provide multiple and alternative perspectives about the story. While questioning proprietary rights to the tale, they often mock the Disney version and expose the dubious notions of innocence and pure heterosexual love. The experimental films challenge the dominant discourse about beauty and the authority of the mirror. To understand how the discourse about "Snow White" and the importance of the mirror has evolved, I want to consider several films made after the production of the Disney film under these categories.

Germany is a good starting point. Aside from some minor short cartoons, there have been four major films produced since the end of World War II: two in the former West Germany, *Snow White* (*Schneewittchen*, 1955) and *Snow White and the Seven Circus Performers* (*Schneewittchen und die sieben Gaukler*, 1962), one in the former East Germany, *Snow White* (*Schneewittchen*, 1961), and one in recently unified Germany, *Snow White and the Secret of the Dwarfs* (*Schneewittchen und das Geheimnis der Zwerge*, 1992). There are more common features in all four live-action films than differences. For instance, with the exception of *Snow White and the Seven Circus Performers*, the magic mirror, which sometimes speaks in the voice of a female, is always the omniscient truth-teller that sets the standards of beauty. At times, the queen can see herself in the reflection of the mirror and should be able to realize that she has a different type of beauty than Snow White. But she abides by the authoritative voice of the mirror. In each one of the films, the huntsman's role is expanded. He is always dressed in green like a typical Bavarian hunter, and he virtually becomes a substitute father and the moral voice of the film. The dwarfs are represented by children, real dwarfs, or small-sized men, who skip to and from work singing an idiotic song. They generously give up Snow White in her glass coffin to the prince, and the wicked queen is either killed by accident or humiliated and banished from the prince's court. Though one might expect major differences between the East and West representations of "Snow White," there are none. Instead, all three of the traditional German films are poorly acted, employ the same decor at the court and the same architecture of the palaces and dwarfs' cottages. Even the one exception, *Snow White and the Seven Circus Performers*, which takes place during Christmas in the early 1960s at an Austrian hotel in the mountains, imitates the basic scheme of the traditional Grimms' tale. In this case, however, we are treated to corny music and a sentimental story that features a striptease artist as the evil queen and a heating engineer as Snow White, who loves to talk to her poodle and associates with seven comic unemployed circus performers, whom she helps. Here the magic mirror is nothing but the plain mirror of a beauty parlor where Snow White gets her hair done, and the prince is reduced to an incompetent hotel owner. Kitsch rather than originality flavors all the German films, and the magic mirror's authority remains intact at the end of each one.

The conventional American films are not much different, but they were made with better acting, costumes, decor, cinematography, and clever inventions. Their concern tends, however, to focus on the sentimental love between the prince and the princess, and the mirror is used as a character to provide comic relief. For instance, in the Shelley Duvall's Faerie Tale Theatre production, *Snow White and the Seven Dwarfs* (1984) directed by Peter Medak, the mirror is delightfully played by Vincent Price, who also narrates the film. As commentator, he grins and grimaces and makes all sorts of faces throughout the film and seems to enjoy arguing with the evil queen played with relish by the gifted British actress, Vanessa Redgrave. The style and tone of the film make it clear that the director does not intend to explore the traditional tale in any critical or meaningful way. In fact, typical of Faerie Tale Theatre productions, all the major roles are played by celebrities, and the film tends to represent the celebrities for the sake of the celebrities and how they can put their talents to use to enliven a predictable and repetitive plot, well known to audiences. In this version of "Snow White," the mirror turns black in the end, and since the queen cannot see herself anymore, she tumbles to the ground in desperation. Apparently, she will drive herself crazy to the amusement of viewers, who will not discover anything about her dilemma in this film.

In the Cannon musical of *Snow White* (1987), there are once again some more talented celebrities such as Diana Rigg, Sarah Patterson, and Nicole Stapleton, but they must sing frivolous songs for their money. This film begins with the prince lost in the woods during the winter. He is returning with his entourage from some battle, and he decides to look for a path through the woods by himself and comes across Snow White in her glass coffin. Then one of the dwarfs begins to narrate the familiar Grimms' tale. In his account, Diana Rigg as the evil queen must glare into another male mirror, which has a ghostly white image and later frightens young Snow White when she sneaks into the queen's parlor to question it. However, in the course of the diegetic action, she really does not have to fear because the mirror will constantly reaffirm her beauty as the fairest in the land until she eats the poisoned apple. This event leads us back to the lost prince in the forest. He orders his men to place the glass coffin on a carriage and, of course, it falls. Part of the apple pops out of her throat. There is love at first sight. They return to his court and invite the queen to their wedding. Before she leaves, she shatters the mirror, and as the mirror falls apart, she grows older and appears as an old hag only to disintegrate when the mirror is completely shattered.

Not all American commercial adaptations of "Snow White" are as conventional and imitative as the Faerie Tale Theatre and Cannon productions. For instance, *Sydney White* takes place in the twenty-first century, and a cute girl named Sydney, raised by her widowed father, a plumber, on construction sites, goes off to college, where she competes with the ravishing rich blonde, Rachel Witchburn, to become the most popular girl on campus. Sydney, who is pretty, frank, funny and virginal, attracts Rachel's rich but decent former boyfriend. Consequently, Rachel vows to destroy her. So, using her power as sorority president, she humiliates Sydney and forces her to leave the sorority in which Sydney's dead mother had been a member. Poor weeping Sydney goes to live with seven dorky but eminently likeable students, all of them misfits and outcasts, in a dilapidated house. Sydney's juvenile fight with Rachel is mirrored on computer screens, not on mirrors. Eventually, the computer screens reflect the insidious plans of Rachel and her malicious character. This sweet predictable film drips with schmaltz, and the only thing that is represented is the American culture industry's tendency to produce dumbed-down happy fairy tales that reflect a serious cultural defect: the minimization of the problems at universities and the creation of a false sense of harmony. Mirrors do not always reflect that beauty in the form of goodness will always triumph.

On the other hand, there are three more serious American adaptations of "Snow White" which take the fairy tale itself and the problematic aspects of representation of beauty more seriously. In Michael Cohn's *Snow White: A Tale of Terror*, there are many mirrors in the castle of Count Friedrich Hoffman, who had lost his wife in a horrific wagon accident, forcing him to cut out the baby from his dying wife's stomach. He raises his daughter Lilly to become independent and strong-willed. Therefore, when he marries Lady Claudia, daughter of a witch, there is an immediate clash between the two women. Lady Claudia brings with her a magic mirror encased in a cabinet that has the potential to destroy anyone who looks at it, except Lady Claudia. Whenever she gazes at the mirror, there is a perfect image of her face, no matter what condition she herself is in. The mirror acts as a narcissistic reflection; yet it is not really Lady Claudia but an evil spirit that drives her to commit crime after crime. Eventually, the mirror's image takes possession of Lady Claudia, who brings about the death of her brother and some outcasts in the forest, where Lilly takes refuge from her. Maddened, Lady Claudia begins to torture her husband in an effort to bring her dead baby back to life, kills the servants in the castle, and murders a young doctor. Eventually, she accidentally burns herself to death as she endeavors to kill Lilly, who survives thanks to the help of a criminal outcast. The mirror is shattered and destroyed in the fire. The tension in this bleak adaptation is between Lady Claudia and the mirror, the legacy of her mother. There are hints throughout the film that Count Hoffman and the knights in his realm may have burned her mother at a stake, and they certainly maltreated the seven peasants hiding in the woods. Lady Claudia is bent on revenge of sorts and bent on living up to her mother's expectations. The mirror in this case does not represent a woman striving to meet standards of beauty, but to become at one with her mother and to carry out her mother's designs.

There is practically no reference to a mother in Tom Davenport's *Willa: An American Snow White* (1996), set in the South about 1915. Willa, a charming teenager, anxiously awaits the arrival of her stepmother Regina, a famous actress, who has retired from the theater. She is accompanied by her doting servant Otto, whom she treats like a dog. She also brings a large mirror with her that is covered by a velvet purple drape. Though aging, Regina is indeed beautiful, and each time she gazes into the mirror and sees her reflection, she hears the applause and cheers of an audience. Once Willa, however, shows her own thespian skills and beauty, Regina hears boos from the mirror and demands that Otto kill Willa. Good hearted, he lets Willa escape into a forest and cuts out a piece of his own flesh as proof for Regina that he has performed the nasty deed. In the meantime, Willa joins a traveling medicine side show composed of a dwarf, an Englishman, and an American dressed as an Indian chief named Tonka. They perform skits and sell a harmless alcoholic medicine that allegedly will cure any illness. But they are pursued by Regina who kills Otto after she discovers that he has betrayed her. Crazed, she almost kills Willa, who plays the role of Snow White in a skit, but Willa is ironically saved by the false medicine. Regina, on the other hand, burns herself to death. In the end, Willa heads West with a young man who wants to start his own motion picture company.

Davenport's use of the mirror is connected to the plight of Regina, who, as an aging actress, cannot bear to lose her beauty and appeal to audiences. The focus of his film is on her relationship to the mirror, that is, to the theater. She can no longer play the roles with the same grace and beauty that she had formerly done. She feeds upon the audience reception and keeps Otto, who adores her, virtually as her slave. The mirror reflects a loss of her powers and the anxiety of aging women, and Willa is a reminder that she will no longer be able to enchant audiences and play a dominant role on stage or in society. Her time has passed, just as the medicine side shows and theater will be replaced by the cinema. Davenport strikes a tragic note in depicting the fate of Regina, who becomes a figure of pity.

Her equivalent in the Hallmark film, *Snow White: The Fairest of Them All* (2002), directed by Caroline Thompson, cannot be pitied at all. This made-for-TV film has a most original plot. It begins with a peasant named John cutting a rose outside a cottage for his wife who has just given birth to a baby daughter. However, the wife dies right after childbirth, and he rushes through a blizzard with his daughter in search of milk. Along the way he falls, and it seems that he will be buried in the snow with his daughter. Tears stream down his face into the snow, and his tears melt

Figure 28
Caroline Thompson,
*Snow White: The
Fairest of Them All*

the snow and liberate a huge buried genie named The Green-Eyed One. In gratitude, the genie grants John three wishes: milk for his daughter, a castle in which to raise her, and a wife. It turns out that the genie has a wart-faced sister named Elspeth, whom he wants to marry off, and he gives her a magic mirror that will help her become beautiful and do many other things for her. Indeed, she is told to crack a mirror and send a shard into John's eye so that he will fall in love with her and not be able to see reality as it really is. At the same time that Elspeth does this, she transforms one of the dwarfs named Sunday into a figurine that is placed on the lawn outside her run-down shack. There is a subplot in this film. The dwarfs are simply kind people who live in the woods, and they are concerned about the missing gnomes who appear to have been lost. Actually, they, too, have been turned into figurines by the wicked Elspeth and resemble those ghastly cute Disney dwarfs that some people love to place on their lawns in America as if they were objects of beauty or hominess. The dwarfs themselves are named after the days in the week and are a motley crew that includes four tiny men, one small female, and a tall buffoon. They are obviously intended to make a mockery out of the Disney dwarfs and are comic appendages to the main plot. After sixteen years pass and Snow White has grown into a charming young woman, a prince named Alfred comes from overseas to propose to Snow White. However, Elspeth has apparently become tired of her husband John and wants to have Alfred for herself. Consequently, she orders a huntsman named Hector, who has the shard of mirror that pops out of King John's eye land in his, to kill Snow White. As usual, the huntsman cannot bring himself to do it. Snow White flees and takes refuge with the odd dwarfs. Elspeth uses her magic mirror to spy on Snow White and the dwarfs and eventually lures Snow White into biting the poisoned apple. The dwarfs can do nothing but freeze her in a chunk of ice. Now that Elspeth is once again the fairest in the land, her brother the genie comes to her and asks her to be a bit more merciful. She explodes in fury and throws her magic mirror at him. When it shatters, all her spells are broken. She becomes wart-faced. The gnomes regain their human shape and attack and kill her. The prince carries off Snow White on a white horse to his kingdom.

Though the plot of this adaptation of "Snow White" might seem to be ludicrous, the film is an unusual blend of horror and comedy. With the exception of a stilted Snow White, the acting is excellent, and there is depth to the characters, who are not stereotypical copycats of previous Snow-White films. Once again, it is the queen's relationship to mirrors that determines her fate and, to a certain extent, the fate of Snow White.

While these three American films are all flawed endeavors to crack open the mystery of the mirror in the Snow-White discourse, they all offer different artistic perspectives and approaches to the representation of a classical tale that they retell to explore how and why a woman of great beauty becomes consumed by her desire to be beautiful. They all try to break with the master narratives of the Grimms and Disney. In this regard, they follow more in the rebellious or resistant tradition of animated cartoons, and I want to consider some examples that followed Disney's 1937 adaption to demonstrate how stridently other filmmakers have questioned the sentimentality of Disney and the authoritative voice of the Grimms.

Resisting Authority

One of the first and most controversial challenges to the Disney version of "Snow White" was Bob Clampett's 1943 parody, *Coal Black and de Sebben Dwarfs*, produced by Warner Brothers. Condemned today for its racist stereotypes, the film is nevertheless a brilliant mock fairy tale that can be viewed as a carnivalesque rendition of "Snow White" that turns the Grimms' printed versions and Disney's cinematic adaptation inside out. Clampett intended his cartoon to honor black jazz and entertainment, and he was the first animator ever to use black characters and black idiomatic language and music to represent "white" fairy-tale characters. His female protagonist So White, a beautiful sexy young woman, is the antithesis of the red-cheeked stilted Disney Snow White, and her story is narrated not by a white male voice, but by a cheerful mammy, who begins by referring to the problem of hoarding during World War II by painting the witch as a hoarder. In fact, the entire cartoon has nothing to do with the condition or situation of blacks, nor does it cast aspersion on blacks. As Norman Klein remarks,

> most of all, *Coal Black* was intended as a declaration of personal independence. Black music was literally presented as an antidote to Disney sentimentality. The atmospheric Disney opening is dropped as soon as the story really begins. We leave the atmospheric plantation for a very contemporary castle, the queen with her stash of whitewall tires.[125]

The queen has huge muscles, big lips, a big rear end, and is the epitome of voracity. Her exaggerated stereotypical features are unfortunate as are others in the film, and yet, they can also be read as mocking racist stereotypes and are employed adroitly to ridicule the "whiteness" and predictability of the classical story and its characters. Moreover, the film addresses corruption, false patriotism, and gender stereotyping to transform the tale of "Snow White" into a unique social critique.

Mammy's tale is the opposite of sweet plantation narratives and depicts the queen as a food hoarder during a time when rationing had been instituted. The queen is fabulously rich and greedy, and when she looks into her magic mirror, she commands it to send her a prince six feet tall. As soon as he arrives in a limousine and with a smile that reveals dice-looking teeth, he cries out, "That mean ol' queen sho' is a fright/but her gal So White is dynamite!" He immediately begins to dance a minuet with So White that turns into a jitterbug. When the queen sees this, she hires Murder Incorporated to kill So White. Soon the hired killers arrive to kidnap her, and the prince exposes his yellow streak by not defending her. The killers take So White into the woods, where they set her free because she apparently allows them to fondle her. As she runs through the woods, she encounters seven little men in army uniforms at their military camp. When she declares that she's crazy about men in khaki, they hire her as a USO cook. She fries eggs and pork chops and sings a song to the tune of "Five o'Clock Whistle" and is happy as a lark. But the queen has discovered that she is alive and, when the little soldiers are absent in the woods, she poisons her with an apple. The dwarfs learn about this and pursue her in a jeep. When it appears that they won't be able to catch up with her, they stop and fire a dwarf that resembles Disney's Dopey in a war shell that stops in mid air. Dopey takes out a mallet and knocks the witch dead. However, So White is also dead, and the dwarfs sing:

> She's outta this world! She's stiff as wood!
> She's got it bad and that ain't good!
> There's only one thing that'll remedy this
> and dat's Prince Chawmin' and his Dynamite kiss!

Immediately the prince appears, but his kisses are to no avail. Dopey is the only one who can rouse So White with a dynamite kiss that is a military secret. With his second kiss, Snow White's pigtails turn into twin American flags to the tune of "Stars and Stripes Forever."

Produced at the outset of American involvement in World War II, *Coal Black and de Sebben Dwarfs* raises questions about social corruption, sexuality in films, the meaning of fairy tales, and patriotism. It minimizes the theme of beauty, its representation, and the power of the mirror. Intended for adult audiences, and specifically for American troops, Clampett's adaptation has a raunchy quality to it. There are sexual innuendos and gags throughout the seven-minute film; the movement of the characters is anarchical and erotic. The film is a challenge to propriety and authority, and like other cartoons of the 1940s it paved the way for carnivalesque adaptations for children, but only after the turbulent 1960s and 1970s, when propriety was exposed as hypocrisy in American society.

Two of the best carnivalesques are cinematic versions that explore if not explode Disney sentimentality and the "authoritative" meaning of "Snow White," made primarily for young viewers: *Snow White and the Seven Muppets* (1985) and *Rugrats: Tales from the Crib: Snow White* (2005). Given their artistry and sophisticated approach to storytelling, these TV films are more than just films for children, that is, they reveal the complex nature of films that have multiple levels of understanding and appreciation. Both are part of a series, and it helps somewhat if a viewer knows something about the Baby Muppets and the Rugrats, just as it helps to be familiar with the traditional Grimms' tale and Disney's adaptation. But this acquired knowledge is not absolutely necessary. Both films are hilarious parodies of authoritative representation of fairy tales and rely heavily on the Brechtian estrangement technique to liberate storytelling from the restraints of propriety and fidelity. In the case of the Rugrats film, it appears that some motifs were borrowed from the Muppets film.

The frame for *Snow White and the Seven Muppets* is important. The baby Muppets have just heard the fairy tale of "Snow White" told to them by their Nanny. Once she leaves them alone in the nursery, they decide to act out the story with Kermit the Frog as director. Immediately, there is an argument between Miss Piggy and Scooter about who will play the role of Snow White. Miss Piggy loses, and throughout the play, she vents her anger on all the Muppet babies, interrupts the action, and causes havoc. The Muppet babies construct sets made out of objects found in the room. If something is missing, they draw it on a piece of paper. One of the settings has a photographed beauty salon where the seven dwarfs live and where Snow White receives a beauty treatment. In one of the initial scenes Fozzie Bear plays the mirror with his head stuck inside a picture frame. Miss Piggy as the wicked queen declares: "I'm so cute I can't stand me." When she wants confirmation from the mirror that she is the cutest in the land, Fozzie replies: "I've got something you won't dig. Compared to Snow White, you're just a pig." In response, Miss Piggy smashes him, and she smashes him later when he tells her that she belongs in a zoo. In her rage, she hires insect terminators to get rid of Snow White, but they take pity on Snow White. The Muppets fall in and out of character and turn the sets upside down. In the end, the egocentric Miss Piggy is foiled in her constant attempts to steal the show and take over the direction from Kermit, who is constantly frustrated as director. Their play is only ended when Nanny hears their noise and asks whether everything is all right.

This same narrative frame is also used in the Rugrats film. In this case, the teenage babysitter Taffy tells the tiny Rugrats the story of "Snow White and the Adorable Minis," in which the bossy Rugrat, Angelica Pickles, plays the role of the wicked queen and her rival, Susie Carmichael, who is black, assumes the role of Snow White. During the telling, which is actually a ninety-four-minute made-for-DVD animated film with music, the baby Rugrats interrupt Taffy, who also leaves the room at one point to speak on a cell phone, and Angelica takes over as narrator to tell the tale from her perspective. One of the major characters in the film is the mirror who has the face of a black comedian. Snow White has a history of getting rid of mirrors who don't give her a high rating such as ratings for television stars and shows. This mirror, fearful of offending Angelica at first, calls her a babe and a fox, a cute chick, and the fairest in the room. He is reluctant to call her the fairest in the land because Snow White is. However, Snow White is suffering from loneliness and wants to find some friends. When the mirror finally confesses to the evil queen that Snow White is cuter than she is, the evil queen sends her off to become a babysitter for seven Minis who work in a diaper factory. Left alone in the castle, the queen tries different ways to get rid of Snow White for good against the mirror's protests. Finally, he quits, packs his bags, and walks out of the castle. In the meantime the queen succeeds in poisoning Snow White with an apple. The Minis put her in a plastic box that resembles the store toy boxes for dolls. When a prince, who resembles the pop singer Prince, comes along and wants to take the box with him, the box tumbles to the ground and a piece of the poisoned apple pops out of Snow White's mouth. She awakens, and she and the Minis agree to visit Prince's castle to play musical chairs. Once there, they find the mirror who formerly worked for the wicked queen, who also wants to join the fun. At first the Minis refuse but Prince and Snow White convince them to accept her. At this point Taffy ends the tale.

Both the Muppet and Rugrats adaptations break with the conventional focus on a sentimental love story. The mirrors become characters in their own right and reveal that they are helpless when the queen wants to take over the narrative for her own selfish reasons. The primary conflict is not between the queen and Snow White, but between the queen and the mirror. Even though the mirrors claim they know the truth, they are challenged and dismissed. They have little authority and power. The truth is difficult to uphold in the world of American babies, and both films depict the conflict over narrative authority that is threatened by the powerful will and desire of young females insistent on telling their own stories and gratifying their ambitions. Whatever the resolution may be, the animated "Snow White" films tend to take liberties with the truth and authority that directors of live-action films are often reluctant to trespass.

Perhaps the film that takes most liberties with the Snow White discourse is the Belgian animator Picha's *Snow White: The Sequel* (*Blanche-Neige, la suite*, 2007). It is the only animated feature film ever produced that deals with the happily-ever-after life that Snow White and the prince supposedly will lead, and it is so risqué, candid, and satirical that it has never been distributed in the USA. This may be due to the fact that there are scenes in which the dwarfs masturbate and later penetrate each other, the prince sleeps with the evil fairy godmother, an old hag with drooping breasts, and all the classical fairy-tale characters dance in the nude at a ball organized by Sleeping Beauty, who is trying to kill Cinderella and Snow White. There are many chase scenes and delightful sexual gags that hark back to the cartoons of the 1930s and 1940s. The prince feels it his duty to save and sleep with every princess in his realm and pursues them. A drunken huntsman is commanded to kill Snow White. A dumb ogre seeks to eat a naive Snow White. Sleeping Beauty wants to bed and wed the prince. The supposedly good fairy godmother is an evil old hag who also wants to bed the prince. Why all this action, one must ask, when Prince Charming is so abysmally dumb and Snow White so stupidly naive?

Figure 29
Picha, *Snow White:
The Sequel*

The animator Jean-Paul Walravens, otherwise known as Picha, explained in an interview quite clearly how he made the film to respond to the "lies" of Disney:

My ideas come to me just like that. I'm like a prolific hen. There aren't 36 questions. It just happens that from time to time the hen lays eggs. There are the winter months when the hen lays fewer eggs and lays more during the spring months. It also doesn't have to be during those seasons. I don't search for ideas, they come to me, and they become obvious and desirous because the idea is born, excites me and continues to develop itself. I don't have any other way of working. So, my subject had always been Snow White, for the film was Disney's first feature-length film and created the Disney myth. Well, since there's rarely been a success on earth that hasn't had its sequel, the idea occurred to me to do one. There hadn't been a sequel to *Snow White*, and nobody had written a sequel to it in reality, neither Charles Perrault nor the Brothers Grimm. I also liked the idea of turning something that Disney had brought to us and making it into a comedy, something that he brought me personally. Yesterday was the next to last day of the exhibit ["*Il était une fois Walt Disney. Aux sources de l'art des Studios Disney.*" *Exposition aux Galeries Nationales du Grand Palais à Paris de septembre 2006 à janvier 2007*] where there was a poster of Snow White, and I went to see it, and I realized to what extent Disney himself had borrowed everything, all the European iconography of the tales as well as the plots to adapt everything and grind it up in the American mill. It was in a very puritanical period that he did this, and these tales and designs did not have anything puritanical about them. Disney did not efface the violence and horror from the tales, but all his characters are totally asexual. This is indeed a perpetual lie where one embraces, one marries and little babies are born from a kiss, and other things like this! Prince Charming is some kind of a machine that is to give the first kiss to a dead or sleeping princess, and nobody can recall the slightest dialogue of Prince Charming because there is none except for the sentences of total transparency, and all this is very strange when one views the film again. And the other idea that came to me, one of the first that appeared with regard to Prince Charming, after I had become clear about that subject, was to use three tales, because Prince Charming is always the same in these three tales. He changes his looks a bit with curly or straight hair, but he has the same function. He always says very little. He does exactly the same thing. He's on his horse, and then, that's it. So this is what led me to mix three tales to create this sequel.[126]

Picha uses a male voiceover that seeks to maintain the propriety of fairy-tale plots, but he is opposed by a fluttering, plump, aged evil fairy godmother, who wants to sleep with the prince before his wedding night with Snow White. However, she is deterred, but so is the prince who must prove his sexual prowess to show Snow White that he is worthy of her. Once he leaves their charming cottage—not a magnificent castle—all hell breaks loose. Snow White, however, who always has cuddly animals around her and sings while she washes the prince's dirty underwear, is oblivious to all the sexual advances of the ogre, the dwarfs, and the huntsman, who invade her cottage while the prince is away. Meanwhile, the dumb prince blunders into affairs with Sleeping Beauty and Cinderella, and he finally blunders out of trouble after he sleeps with the fairy godmother and steals her magic wand. When he reconciles himself with Snow White, there is a mock depiction of the happy end promised by the Disney film that is impossible to contemplate after having viewed the sequel.

With some exceptions, the animated versions, whether cartoons or feature films, have a vitality and inventiveness that most live-action adaptations of "Snow White" lack. For instance, the UPA film *Prince Charming* (1961), directed by Brad Case, features a bizarre sailor witch, who is jealous of Mr. Magoo's sailboat. When she gazes in her hand mirror, which teases her, she learns that Magoo is out at sea, and she pursues him with a mermaid attached to the front of her boat. As she tries to destroy Magoo's boat, a tugboat of seven dwarfs who patrol the sea prevents her. Finally, she accidentally blows her boat up and is left holding on to planks in the middle of the sea while Magoo, oblivious to what has happened, sails off with the wooden mermaid. The total rewriting of "Snow White," which employs zany characters, mistaken identities, unusual settings, constant change, and unpredictable endings, compels viewers to rethink their notions of what is proper or normal in "Snow White." Cartoon fairy tales exude a vitality that stems from the curiosity of the filmmakers, who question the representations of the Grimms and Disney. They exude independent thinking.

Such is also the case with the Portuguese director João César Monteiro, who created an unusual film in 2000, *Snow White* (*Branca de Neve*) based on an anti fairy-tale play, written in 1904 by the Swiss German writer, Robert Walser. This film is basically a recital without images. The screen is black for the most part as actors read the play in Portuguese, or one can "see" and read the film with English subtitles. Walser's brilliant play takes place after Snow White has been resuscitated. Her mother, the queen, is still alive, and there are a series of dialogues between the queen, Snow White, the huntsman, and the prince, who all have different perspectives about whether the queen really intended to kill Snow White, why, and what they should do after the thwarted attempt at murder. Very early on, the queen declares:

Oh, do not trust the craven voice
That whispers sin which is not there.
Oh, trust the right and not the left—
I mean the false—ear which presumes
To make the wicked mother of me,
Envious of beauty. Come, do not
Pay heed to the preposterous yarn
Which pours into the world's all too
Receptive ear the news that I
Am crazed with jealousy, by nature bad—
While all of it is empty talk.

I love you. No confessing has
Confessed more genuinely yet.
Your beauty only makes me glad,
Beauty in one's own daughter is
Like balm to a mother's flagging joy,
Not goad to such repulsive deed
As fantasy has underlaid
This fable here, this spectacle.
Don't turn away, be a dear child,
Trust parent word like your own self.[127]

In the course of the action, Snow White comes to consider herself a sinner and pardons her mother, who evidently is in love with the huntsman. The prince who is an adolescent weakling falls in love with the queen. Snow White is clearly not in love with him and does not believe that he kissed her awake. The incidents of the traditional Grimms' fairy tale are examined, interrogated, and questioned until the tale is declared a lie. In one of the last dialogues between Snow White and the huntsman, whom she trusts because he was so compassionate and did not kill her, we hear:

Huntsman

> That she enflamed me to the crime
> With fiery kisses is untrue.
> The fairy tale that says so, lies.

Snow White

> How could it *be* truth when you call
> It lie. Go on, I am convinced.

Huntsman

> That she detest you like an adder
> For your fresh beauty's sake, that is
> A lie. Why, is she not herself
> As splendored as a summer tree?
> Look at her now, and call her fair.

Snow White

> Fair—oh, how fair. The lavish splendor
> Of spring is not so exquisite.
> Why, her magnificence excels
> The polished marble given shape
> By an accomplished sculptor's hand.
> Sweet as a mellow dream is she,
> The fervid sleeper's fancy can't
> Imagine such a fairy shape.
> And she, they think, is envious
> Of me, who like the winter maid
> So still and cold stands by her side?
> That's past belief. How could it be?
> Continue then, you see I am
> Quite of your mind in this affair.

Huntsman

> Beauty does not hate beauty so
> As fairy tales have given out.[128]

Snow White is in agreement with the huntsman, and when her father finally appears on the scene for just a few minutes, she tells him not to worry because the quarrel has been settled, despite the fact that the prince still regards the huntsman as a villain and believes that a crime was committed. He leaves in bitterness while the king wants to celebrate in universal bliss.

It is questionable whether the "happy end" of this play provides "blissful" resolution to the conflict and whether the truth about the attempted murder can be known. The king wants to sweep everything under the table, and the queen and Snow White appear happy to do this. However, neither Walser nor Monteiro want to sweep anything under the rug. Rather they seek to crack the mirror of representation in the classical tale by exposing what cannot be represented. Monteiro's startling choice to use a black screen and monotone, soft voices with interludes of blue skies and electronic music does not make for pleasant movie viewing. His film, which begins with still photos of Walser dead in the snow of Switzerland, is frustrating. But that is exactly the point: beauty cannot be represented, nor can the classical tale be represented as a truthful fairy tale because the mirror does not represent the truth and mother and daughter must learn to live with the repression of the truth. That is, they must live with the tension between truth and falsehood.

The "Snow White" cinematic discourse about mirrors, reflections, and the representation of beauty, what beauty might mean, will always be an open-ended discourse, even when many "Snow White" films end on a happy note. The cultural standards of beauty cannot be standardized. They are continually in flux even when the mass media seeks to set hegemonic definitions on all types of screens. Women cannot determine their beauty when they look into male-determined and mass-mediated mirrors. Mirrors are not the bearers of truth. They have no authority, but perhaps they can inform us about what we lack or what we need. Filmic representations of mirrors reflecting beauty as in the case of the fairy tale about Snow White are clearly most delightful and helpful when they endeavor to crack those mirrors and compel us to look a bit askance at all mirrors that claim to possess the truth.

7

The Trials and Tribulations of
Little Red Riding Hood Revisited and Reviewed

> I want you to know, monsieur, that I've been devoured an infinite number of times, and each time it is my fault. There you have it! Four thousand years that I've had the same accident, four thousand years that I am revived, four thousand years, by an incredible fatality, I'm going to put myself inevitably in the paws of the wolf. What do you want? I always die very young, and when I return to the world, I only have a vague memory of my previous existences, very vague. . . . Oh, how interesting it would be to write and peruse that *Story of Red Riding Hood in all the centuries!* Monsieur Perrault has sketched but only one chapter. How fortunate is he who will write the others.
>
> **Alphonse Daudet,** *The Romance of Little Red Riding Hood*

When Alphonse Daudet wrote his ironic play about Little Red Riding Hood's "accident," which many writers and critics have been explicitly referring to as rape for many years now, he had no idea how many "fortunate" writers would continue the tradition of writing other versions about her fate. Certainly, he could not have anticipated Angela Carter, who not only wrote one unusual rendition, "The Company of Wolves," but also two others, "The Werewolf" and "Wolf-Alice," all three published in *The Bloody Chamber and Other Stories* (1979), a tantalizing book that was intended not only to subvert the classical patriarchal fairy tale but also to subvert standard notions of sexuality, archetypes, and stereotypes. As was her wont, Carter often wrote two or three experimental versions of one classical fairy tale to explore its peculiarities from different perspectives and to demonstrate how the plots and characters might be fleshed out and deployed to make discoveries about social relations in the present. Thus, her "Beauty and Beast" tales probe father/daughter relations and the bartering that constitutes marital relationships. Her "Cinderella" triad of short pithy tales delves into the mother/daughter relations of dependency and projection. At the bottom of her profound interest in fairy tales was a fierce ideological commitment to overcome false dichotomies that separated the sexes and led to male dominance in all spheres of life, public and private.

In her controversial book, *The Sadeian Woman: An Exercise in Cultural History*, published the same year as *The Bloody Chamber*, Carter drew an interesting connection between graffiti and pornography that is very much related to her feminist revisions of "Little Red Riding Hood." In the schema of graffiti, she asserted,

> as in the mythic schema of all relations between men and women, man proposes and woman is disposed of, just as she is disposed of in a rape, which is a kind of physical graffiti, the most extreme reduction of love, in which all humanity departs from the sexed beings. So that, somewhere in the fear of rape, is a more than merely physical terror of hurt and humiliation—a fear of psychic disintegration, of an essential dismemberment, a fear of a loss or disruption of the self which is not confined to the victim alone. Since all pornography derives directly from myth, it follows that its heroes and heroines, from the most gross to the most sophisticated, are mythic abstractions, heroes and heroines of dimension and capacity. Any glimpses of a real man or a real woman is absent from these representations of the archetypal male and female.[129]

In many respects Carter's fairy tales in *The Bloody Chamber* were written to endow the characters with flesh and blood and the plots with more intricacy, particularly if they dealt with the persecution and violation of women. "The Company of Wolves," which she adapted for the cinema with Neil Jordan in 1984, is particularly significant because it shifted the literary and filmic discourse about the character and dilemma of Little Red Riding Hood from that of passive victim to a young woman, curious and confident, unafraid to fulfill her own desire. In the world of cinema, most "Little Red Riding Hood" films had generally been based either on the Perrault and Grimm versions or a mélange of the two up to 1984. After this date, thanks to Carter and other feminist writers, there is a marked difference in the way that this girl is more fully and sensuously portrayed in literature, the fine arts, performing arts, and cinema. In particular, the filmic discourse about Little Red Riding Hood's "accident" is most significant because it has employed every possible means—script, voiceover narration, puppets, drawings, music, and digital composition—to question whether Red Riding Hood herself is at fault for her repeated rape. In fact, the films based on her story have almost come full circle and returned to its oral antecedents of the seventeenth century in which there was no such thing as a red hood, cap, or spoiled girl but simply a young peasant girl who outwits a werewolf and knows how to take care of herself.

There appear to be two major phases of the filmic adaptation of the classic Perrault and Grimm narratives. The first begins 1901 with Georges Méliès and encompasses the silent film period, the cartoons of the 1940s and 1950s, and the live-action films up to the publication of Carter's 1979 "The Company of Wolves" and focuses on the gullibility of Little Red or the rapacity of a stupid wolf, both who need governing and policing by an armed huntsman. In the second phase, after 1979, with some exceptions, the films are more concerned with depicting a more forceful young woman intent on following her desires and breaking with the male gaze of domination. Of course, it is not solely to Carter's credit that there is a subversive if not radical way of looking at Little Red and her accident. Her own work coincides with a resurgence of feminism in the 1970s that has continued to bear fruit up through the twenty-first century. But, before I examine the Red-Riding-Hood films of this period, I want to discuss how the foundations of a cinematic Red-Riding-Hood discourse were laid by the silent films, cartoons, and traditional live-action films from 1901 to 1979.

Silent Films, 1901–1929

One of the difficulties recording the history of the silent films about "Little Red Riding Hood" is that many of the films have been lost or damaged. Consequently, we do not have complete accounts of the plots, interpretations, and production qualities. According to my records, there were approximately nine live-action silent films that dealt with "Little Red Riding Hood," most of them very short and based on the traditional versions of Perrault and the Grimms. There appears to be a tendency to transform the classic tales into sentimental family comedies, even though Perrault's text ends on a tragic note, and even though the Grimms' tale does not reunite Little Red with her mother and father.

For instance, in the very first silent film about the naive girl, *Little Red Riding Hood* (1901), Georges Méliès's went to great lengths to transform Perrault's text into a comic adventure with a happy ending. As he wrote in a special note to the film:

> I took great care in producing this new creation: the details of the drama have been ordered with great attention, and the sets and scenery have been constructed and completed in the most original and artistic fashion possible. I made a very complicated play out of a tale that is simplicity itself. Therefore, I owe some words of explanation to the professionals. Committed to following Perrault's tale very closely, a tale known throughout the world, I had to enhance and adorn the comic scenes or the picturesque episodes due to theatrical exigencies. Without doing this it would have been impossible to create an interesting scenario, for the filmmaker only addresses himself exclusively to the eyes of the spectator.
>
> The tale, scrupulously respected in all its essential parts, finds itself framed in a very humorous and amusing fashion. However, I allowed myself to vary the ending, and here's why.
>
> The public will very much accept viewing how the poor grandmother is eaten, because this episode is treated in a comic fashion. But to view the wolf eating Little Red Riding Hood (a sympathetic character, spoiled but charming child) would certainly be a disagreeable spectacle, even odious that would badly terminate a play destined to entertain more than anything else. Moreover, this ending would not have any dash to it and would leave a troublesome impression on the spectators.
>
> The terror experienced by Little Red Riding Hood is, in addition, sufficient punishment for disobeying the advice of her father, and I believe, I am even certain that the public will be delighted to see the bad wolf punished as he deserves to be, and the final chase scene, the parade and the triumph of Little Red Riding Hood, would find the public's approval and . . . its applause. Moreover, my only goal was to create an amusing and presentable spectacle for all audiences.[130]

Méliès divided his short film into twelve tableaux that were shot on the stage of his Robert-Houdin Theatre, and despite his minimizing the changes that he made, he greatly altered Perrault's "tragic" tale in which Little Red Riding Hood is devoured by the wolf and blamed in the moralité for causing her own rape. In contrast, Méliès portrays a different story. Little Red Riding Hood's mother and father own a pastry shop, and when her parents depart briefly, she causes a ruckus. Upon their return, her parents scold her, and she is ordered to take some butter and galettes to her grandmother. She skips off into the woods and begins to gather flowers. When the wolf approaches, she is afraid, but he reassures her that he means no harm and makes a wager with her about who can arrive at grandmother's house first. As usual, the wolf takes a short cut, while Little Red Riding Hood gathers more flowers and dances with schoolmates in the field. Then there is some comic relief: a digression that has nothing to do with the plot and involves a miller, who is upset by a stubborn mule that dumps sacks of wheat on a hill and scrambles the wheat. In the next scene we are transported to grandmother's house, where the wolf devours the poor old lady and gets into her bed. Shortly after Little Red Riding Hood arrives and begins asking the formulaic questions, and just as the wolf is about to eat her, the workers from the pastry shop arrive to prevent the disaster. They had been sent by the worried parents. The house is turned upside down in a comic chase scene that leads into the woods. Meanwhile, the game-keeper, who had been alerted by the country folk, hides behind a rock and shoots the wolf who falls from a bridge into a river. The workers arrive and carry the dead wolf on a stretcher to the town where there is a huge comic celebration attended by all the dignitaries and capped by the roasting of the wolf on a spit.

Typical of Méliès style, this film mixes horror with absurd humor. His grand finale with a parade and pose is an expression of joy—the family is reunited, and Little Red Riding Hood is forgiven. The emphasis on the happy end, a romantic picture of the family, and the minimization of the violent rape or eating scene can also be seen in James Kirkwood's *Little Red Riding Hood* (1911), which starred Mary Pickford. In this film the serene family is depicted as a harmonious unit at the beginning. Little Red Riding Hood goes off to bring goodies and supplies to her granny, who has just moved into a new home. Along the way, Little Red Riding Hood becomes tired, lies down, and falls asleep. Her encounter with the wolf, a trained dog, takes place in her dream. Due to a faulty restoration of the film, it is not clear whether the father kills the wolf in the dream or after the dream. What is clear, however, is that Little Red Riding Hood wakes up from her dream with her family surrounding her. Again, the implication is that Little Red Riding Hood's flawed behavior causes a near catastrophe.

Aside from the silent films that focus on a girl who must be rescued and returned to the family fold, there were also some slapstick comedies such as Leo McCarey's *Big Red Riding Hood*, featuring the famous comedian Charley Chase, playing his bumbling hero, Jimmy Jump. In this short film, Jimmy Jump flirts with the daughter of the owner of a bookstore while reading the book, *Little Red Riding Hood*. When he is given an assignment by the Swedish Consulate to translate "Little Red Riding Hood" into Swedish for educational purposes, he returns to the bookstore only to find that the only copy of the book has been sold. Coincidentally, the man who bought the book pursues some car thieves, and Jimmy joins the pursuit on his bike only to read the book in the man's car so that he can translate it. Wacky with no rhyme or reason, this live-action film was more an exception than the norm. The focus is on the unusual character Jimmy Jump created by Charley Chase rather than on "Little Red Riding Hood," which was just a vehicle for Chase's slapstick performance rather than anything else. Actually, the most outlandish and serious interpretations of the tale were created by the great animators in Hollywood during the first half of the twentieth century and not by the directors of live-action films.

Cartoons 1922–1979

Walt Disney was the first animator to adapt the tale of "Little Red Riding Hood" in 1922, and he returned to it in *The Big Bad Wolf* (1934), which was the second in a trilogy based on the animal fable/fairy tale, "The Three Little Pigs." The contrast between Disney's own two cartoons is great and reflected the monumental shift in animation that took place in the 1930s. The 1922 *Little Red Riding Hood* opens with the mother baking a pie in the kitchen with a cat patrolling the room, a rifle on his shoulder. As the mother kneads the dough, she throws pieces into the air that the cat shoots so that they fall into a pot. A picture of the grandfather on the wall becomes animated so that the grandfather makes faces. The cat eats some bad dough, has a stomach ache, falls to the ground, and must be carted away by an ambulance. In the meantime the mother has finished making the pie, goes outside, and whistles for Little Red Riding Hood. The tunes of the whistle dance off into a field. Little Red Riding Hood arrives and takes the basket with the pie from her mother. After she goes to her garage, she drives out in a tiny cart-like vehicle pushed by a dog. On her way to granny's, she meets a dapper man driving a much larger car. He asks where she is going, and she tells him. Then she drives off. The man's car literally flies through the air to granny's house. In the meantime Little Red Riding Hood stops her car near some fields and picks flowers that run away from her. When the dapper man arrives at granny's house, he shrinks his car through some kind of magic spell and then tucks it into his pocket as if it were a toy car. He finds a note on the door written to Red Riding Hood by her grandmother, saying that she has gone to town. He enters. Soon after, Little Red Riding Hood arrives and enters the house with her basket. All at once there is a commotion. The house shakes. Cries of help come from the house. The dog takes off with the cart and unhooks himself from the harness to run for help. We then see a young pilot standing next to his plane and looking through binoculars. He spies the dog running toward him. The dog arrives and tells him what has happened. They jump into his plane. The dog sits behind the pilot. When they arrive above the house, the pilot drops a line and lifts the house so that only the two figures of Little Red Riding Hood and the dapper man are left standing below. The dapper man pulls out his car from his pocket. It becomes large again, and he drives off. The pilot swoops down and pulls up Little Red Riding Hood into the plane. They pursue the dapper man in his car. Eventually, the pilot drops his line again and hooks the car and then drops it into a lake. Then he flies off with Little Red Riding Hood kissing him.

Though the gags are not particularly clever, the film has a delightful manic tempo. The storyline is that of a typical chase film, featuring a girl who needs to be saved by a dashing hero. The cat and dog are used for comic relief. The villain is not particularly lecherous. He has magic powers, but does not use them to dominate the girl. There is no obvious reason why he wants to seduce Little Red Riding Hood. He has plenty of time to violate her, but his attacks do not seem to have much success in the shaking house. The raw quality of the animation, the disjointed plot, the focus on the lecherous male, and the constant disregard for the rules of the well-made narrative were typical of most cartoons in the 1920s and 1930s. However, Disney changed his perspective on animation when he began developing his Silly Symphonies, the 1930 cartoons that favored smooth transitions, carefully composed characters and sets, a rational plot, and appropriate gags for family audiences that barely had a trace of sexual innuendo.

For instance, Disney's *The Big Bad Wolf* followed the pattern set by *Three Little Pigs* produced in 1933. As usual, the oldest pig is constructing something and pictured high above his two brother piglets when Little Red Riding Hood comes along. She is characterized as a sweet simpleton, and when the two piglets want to accompany her to grandma's house, they are warned by the master

Figure 30
Walt Disney,
Little Red Riding Hood

Figure 31
Burt Gillett,
The Big Bad Wolf

inventor and builder to beware of the big bad wolf. Their response is typical; they sing the famous song, "Who's Afraid of the Big Bad Wolf?" And, of course, they are scared to death when they meet him in the forest. In truth, however, the wolf, who disguises himself as a transvestite, is ludicrous, and not even your grandmother would be afraid of her. While he chases the little girl to grandma's house, the piglets run to their fatherly brother, and he takes his tools to teach him a lesson, not to kill him. When he disappears, the final scene is set in home sweet home with the piglets and Little Red Riding Hood singing "Who's Afraid of the Big Bad Wolf?" Everything is regulated—form and content.

By complying with notions of a well-made suitable film for young audiences, Disney outraged many animators, who still believed that the animated cartoon was the art form that defied harmony and synchronicity and raised provocative questions about social decorum and propriety. Moreover, they preferred off-color jokes and ambivalent acts. In the case of "Little Red Riding Hood," many of the animators objected to making the wolf harmless and to creating a sense that all was well with the world, especially during the years of the Great Depression. Their cinematic versions of "Little Red Riding Hood" differed greatly from Disney's, and though not all of them departed clearly from Disney's fixed characterization of the wolf and the dainty little girl, there was certainly a debate if not a battle over these two characters and how they should be represented with more focus on male desire, guilt, and stupidity.

The "battle" over property rights to the correct version of the text and its two famous characters took place mainly in America, and there were approximately seventeen important different animated versions about Little Red Riding Hood's accident from 1930 to 1968 that focused more on the wolf's rapacity than on the gullibility of the spoiled child. In 1931, even before Disney produced his characters as the official brands to be copied, Dave Fleischer created an unusual black-and-white cartoon, *Dizzy Red Riding Hood*, with Betty Boop as Little Red. This film begins with a narrator mocking the voice of a loving father:

Listen my children and you shall hear an exciting story of a little dear. There've been red rumors of Riding Hood. Some are bad, and some are good. Why do they pick on the poor little kid? Some say she didn't, and some say she did. You surely heard the story before. She tried to keep the wolf from the door. How really true can the story be? Well, watch my dears, and you'll hear and see.

The opening scene shows Betty taking a fish and hot dogs from a refrigerator to put into her basket that she's going to carry to granny. Her famous pet companion, the talking dog Bimbo, eats the food before Betty can put it into the basket. When she locks the door to her house, Bimbo asks whether he can go along, and Betty replies that her mother wouldn't want him to accompany her. So, she struts off to the woods in her inimitable gait wearing a short dress with her garters showing. The trees warn her to beware of the wolf as does Bimbo, who follows her. Betty is totally nonchalant, even when a wolf appears and skips right behind her. Finally, the wolf offers her flower seeds that she begins to plant in the ground. Then he takes out a knife and fork and sharpens them while singing that they should break the news to granny that Betty won't be arriving because he will eat her. However, Bimbo prevents the wolf from eating her by dragging him to a hollow tree trunk where he skins him. The wolf's skeleton runs off, and Bimbo takes the wolf skin and disguises himself as the wolf remarking that Betty loves wolves. He runs off to granny's house which is empty because the old lady has gone off to the fireman's ball. When Betty enters, she jumps on the bed and sings a jazz version of the questions and admires the wolf's muscles. Finally, Bimbo reveals himself, and they embrace and kiss. The film ends with them kissing on a moon that turns into a hammock.

Though not one of the Fleischers' most audacious films, it is nevertheless a good example of how numerous animators were going to stress the sexuality of the story with emphasis on the wolf's uncontrollable desire to possess and violate a young woman. Moreover, the young woman will be sensual, smart, flirtatious, and aware of who is causing the accident. In the case of Betty Boop, who was already regarded somewhat of a sex queen by audiences, she shows no fear of the wolf, and at one point, outside granny's house she loses the garters on both legs, and Bimbo lustfully watches her as she bends over to find them. Immediately, he is whisked away by a clothesline that apparently does not approve of his lewd behavior. Yet in the end Bimbo and Betty romp in grandma's bed, and their enjoyment in kissing each other was certainly not commended by the censorship board, which enforced the Hays Code that took effect on July 1, 1934. This production code was aimed to prevent the lowering of moral standards and did cause animators to tame some of the antics of their films such as making Betty Boop more presentable in a housewife skirt. Nevertheless, the best of the animators found ways to subvert the code, and in the case of Little Red Riding Hood films, sex was always on their minds and in their images.

The plots of some of the more unusual Red Riding Hood cartoons are indicative of the discourse that ensued from 1930 to 1979. For instance, in the Van Beuren Studio's *Little Red Riding Hood* (1931) directed by Harry Bailey and John Foster, the sick grandmother is pictured at home in bed. The doctor gives her some medicine that is "jazz juice" and departs. Then granny douses herself in the juice and is transformed into a sexy young woman. Soon after the wolf arrives, he is astonished when she tells him that she is granny. "Wow, some granny!" he says and sits down at the piano and plays a swinging song to which granny sways her hips. Red Riding Hood arrives and peeks through the window. She cannot believe her eyes and runs and tells the wolf's wife, who comes thundering after him and chases him down a road with all their wolf cubs in pursuit. In Sid Marcus's *Red Riding Hood Rides Again* (1941), the wolf's plans are also thwarted. After he persuades Little Red Riding Hood that he is a good police dog, she indicates where her granny lives. But she is not at home when he arrives because her boyfriend has taken her dancing. Now the wolf's attention shifts to Little Red Riding Hood; however, he is foiled by a postman who delivers a draft induction notice. So the wolf must depart to join the army.

Foiling the wolf became the key motif in most of the cartoons up through the 1970s. Friz Freleng directed four cartoons, *The Trial of Mr. Wolf* (1941), *Little Red Riding Rabbit* (1944), *Little Red Rodent Riding Hood* (1952), and *Red Riding Hoodwinked* (1955), all of which focus on male deviousness, desire, persistence, and competition. In some ways the story about Little Red Riding Hood becomes more a story about the plight of the wolf who wants to become bad but fails, or a

Figure 32
Friz Freleng,
The Trial of Mr. Wolf

comic depiction of the male biological urge that borders on rapaciousness and is made to look silly. The focus is almost entirely on the wolf. In *The Trial of Mr. Wolf,* the wolf takes the stand in self-defense and tells how Red Riding Hood, who speaks in Katherine Hepburn's voice, stalked him in the woods, drove him to her granny, who is a furrier and wants his skin for a fur coat. As the wolf ends his self-defense by depicting granny attacking him with a mallet, he swears that if his story is not the truth, he hopes to get run over by a streetcar. Of course, the streetcar comes crashing through the courtroom and runs him over. In *Little Red Riding Rabbit,* the usual demure girl is transformed into an obnoxious spindly-legged girl carrying Bugs Bunny to her grandmother "to have." However, granny is at a swing shift at the factory, and the wolf is more interested in eating a rabbit than eating Red Riding Hood. Once he dons granny's nightgown and bonnet, he kicks Little Red out of the house and begins chasing Bugs Bunny, who enjoys toying with him. Their male games, however, are constantly interrupted by Little Red Riding Hood, who keeps knocking on the door to ask the wolf the appropriate questions according to the standard storyline. Finally, the wolf and Bugs are so irritated by her interruptions that they pile furniture and weights on top of her as she is spread-eagled over burning hot coals. In *Little Red Rodent Riding Hood,* a grandma mouse tells her little grandson a bedtime story which features Sylvester the cat as a preying wolf, and she ends it by throwing a fire cracker through the mouse hole that devastates Sylvester. In a variation of this cinematic tale, *Red Riding Hood Hoodwinked,* Freleng portrays a nonchalant Little Red Riding Hood with blonde hair leaving her house in the city to carry Tweety, the tiny bird, in a cage to her granny's house in the country. Sylvester the cat spies her and wants to devour Tweety. But Little Red takes a bus, and in the forest she meets a dumb wolf, who continually forgets her name and how to follow the script of the traditional tale. Both cat and wolf join forces and kick a feisty grandmother out of her house so that they can deceive Little Red and devour her and the bird. Once she pops the question, there is a wacky chase scene in which cat and wolf hamper each other. Finally, Little Red escapes with Tweety, and as they board the bus back to the city, the cat and wolf are prevented from getting on the bus by the strong-willed granny, who kicks them out.

Freleng belonged to a large coterie of animators and directors who made cartoons mainly for adults and took the revision of fairy tales very seriously. They assumed that their audiences were

Figure 33
Tex Avery,
Little Red Walking Hood

familiar with the classical tales and with the Disney imitations of these stories. They challenged themselves to be as inventive and as innovative as possible and to distort and explore aspects of the tales that would stun their viewers and "animate" them to re-view them afresh in the spirit of modernity. Therefore, the music and songs of the films were generally taken from hit sings, popular music, or unusual excerpts of classical music. The visual gags were startling even though they always included predictable chase scenes. The personalities of the characters changed with each film as did the plots. The hilarity of the cartoons depended on a profound insight about the incorrigible nature of the wolf.

The animator who understood the wolf's character more than any other artist was the controversial and talented Tex Avery who produced five tantalizing cartoons, *Little Red Walking Hood* (1937), *Red Hot Riding Hood* (1943), *Little Rural Riding Hood* (1949), *The Shooting of Dan McGoo* (1945), and *Wild and Woolfy* (1945), which depicted the antics of a panting delirious wolf who never captures his prey. He also made additional use of feisty Red Riding Hoods in *A Bear's Tale* (1941), *Swing Shift Cinderella* (1945), and *Uncle Tom's Cabana* (1947). For the most part, however, Avery and his animators delighted primarily in exploring the male libidinal drive.

His first cartoon, *Little Red Walking Hood*, begins with a wolf playing a pinball machine in a pool hall and losing. As he complains, a miniature, blonde-haired, blue-eyed Red Riding Hood walks by outside the pool hall. She looks like a delectable doll, and the wolf immediately runs out, jumps into a long limousine convertible, and drives slowly next to her. As he utters sweet words, often to a popular hit tune "Gee, but you're swell," she dismisses him in a Katherine Hepburn voice, which Friz Freleng later copied, and tells him to scram. She often breaks the fourth wall and speaks directly to the audience to comment on the wolf's behavior. Every now and then, a strange man named Egghead, a famous cartoon character, who has a red nose, whistles, saunters, and carries a violin case, breaks the action and keeps following the wolf, who speeds off to granny's house. Once he storms into the house, he begins chasing an old lady without teeth, and at one point, she calls time out to answer the phone and order something from the grocer's. Then she merrily signals to the wolf to continue the chase until she finds herself trapped in a closet with the wolf. Suddenly, there is a loud knock at the door, and the wolf hurriedly asks her for her bonnet and nightgown. Granny obliges, and the wolf jumps into her bed. When Little Red asks the famous three questions, another

Figure 34
Tex Avery,
Red Hot Riding Hood

chase scene begins, interrupted by the shadow of a spectator who has arrived late and moves to a seat in the audience. Once the action resumes, Egghead appears again, and the angry and frustrated wolf asks him who he is. In response, Egghead takes out a mallet from the violin case, hits him over the head, and announces that he is the hero of the film.

All of Avery's unusual techniques that he would hone in later films can be seen in this early cartoon: the parody of Disney's infantile depiction of the innocent girl and bumbling wolf, the effective use of popular songs and music which he transforms into spoken dialogues, exaggerated machines and colorful landscapes that are constantly changing, and the interruption of the action at key moments. Avery was a genius of timing, and without knowing the Brechtian alienation effect, he often had his characters stop, step out of their roles, and confide in the audience. He insisted on a thinking audience in tune with his ironic humor. Perhaps the best example of his use of the alienation effect was his masterpiece, *Red Hot Riding Hood*. This film begins with Little Red Riding Hood visiting her grandmother and the wolf lurking in the woods. The narrator's voice is a mock version of the sweet uncle speaking down to children. All the drawings of the characters resemble Disney's typical figures. At one point, however, the characters stop the action and complain that they are fed up with the usual plot and go on strike. They argue with the director, who relents and allows them to transform their roles and the setting. All at once, we are transplanted to a glittering Hollywood scene. Grandma, a rich sultry lady, who lounges on a sleek sofa, lives in a penthouse apartment. The wolf is a dapper gentleman in a tuxedo, who enters a strip joint, and Little Red Riding Hood is a svelte sexy singer who struts on stage and sings an adaptation of the popular song "Daddy." Instead of "Daddy," however, she sings "Oh, wolfie," and the wolf can barely contain himself from racing to the stage and ravaging her. When she finishes her song, he grabs hold of her and makes her sit at his table. In a voice with a French accent that recalls the actor Charles Boyer, he tries to seduce her. She responds superciliously in Katherine Hepburn's voice. Since the wolf is relentless, she must finally hit him over the head with a mallet and rushes off, supposedly to granny's. The wolf pursues in his limousine, and once he arrives at granny's, he is stunned to find a granny who is highly excited and wants to seduce him. She chases him in and out of the doors until they both crash through a window. We never learn what happens to granny, but the wolf appears at the nightclub again, swearing that if he ever falls for another woman again, he will shoot himself. However, as soon as Red Hot Riding Hood appears onstage, he gapes at her and goes

Figure 35
Tex Avery, *Little Rural Riding Hood*

bonkers. Then he takes a gun and blows his brains out. Despite his death, his ghost appears and continues to ogle and vociferously express his desires.

For Avery, as for most of the male animators of his time, the wolf was the force that drove the story. Implicit in *Red Hot Riding Hood* is the idea that the male biological urge could not be curbed. Like bulls, men charged wildly when they saw red. Even as ghosts, men would bounce back and try to possess women. In *Little Rural Riding Hood* (1949), based on the animal fable, "The City Mouse and the Country Mouse," a country wolf discards a country bumpkin Red Riding Hood, travels to the city to visit his cousin, falls in love with Red Hot Riding Hood at a club, and must be dragged back to the country by his cousin because he cannot contain himself. Yet, when they arrive, the city wolf goes gaga over the Rural Riding Hood and must be dragged back to the city. In the two cartoons, *The Shooting of Dan McGoo* and *Wild and Woolfy*, the tiny dog Droopy must put the wraps on a wolf out of control. Clearly, the interest of animators in *Little Red Riding Hood* is a kind of quest to grasp their own animal desires. From the male perspective, it was important to make the wolf seem harmless and to minimize rape, and this theme continued to play a major role in the fractured fairy tales, *Little Red Riding Hood* (1959) and *Riding Hoods Anonymous* (1961), which came later in the Rocky and Bullwinkle show; the focus is always on the wolf. Even though he resolves to abstain from eating Red Riding Hoods in *Riding Hoods Anonymous*, he cannot resist pursuing grandmothers, and eventually blows himself up through his own stupidity.

Live-Action Films 1950–2009

Whereas the cartoons and animated feature films from the postwar period through the twenty-first century tend to mock if not rationalize outrageous male behavior by minimizing the danger of the wolf in men and portraying the wolf as stupid and bumbling, the live-action films since the 1950s have tended to recount and review the traditional story generally through two different lenses with a focus on the shame of the young girl/woman: either they present Little Riding Hood conventionally as naive and irresponsible and thus culpable for enabling the wolf's actions; or they portray a clever and alert young woman, who is fully aware of her circumstances and can fend for herself. Sometimes she is even bent on revenge for the violation that she has experienced. In fact, there have been several "raging" Red Riding Hoods since the 1980s, but first I want to focus on some of the more conventional representations of the ignorant but fortunate girl.

In the early 1950s and 1960s several seemingly different films appeared in France, Germany, and Mexico that all had the same message and were all somewhat bizarre and kitschy. In France, Raoul André directed *Good Enough to Eat* (*Une fille à croquer*, 1951), in which a young heiress named Rose Chaperon is given the task of delivering jewels to her sick grandmother, Mme de Megrand, and she allows herself to be lured by the charms of a fortune-seeker named Jean-Louis dit Loup. In Germany, three high kitsch films for family audiences all called *Little Red Riding Hood* or *Rotkäppchen* were produced in 1953, 1954, and 1962, the first two in West Germany directed by Walter Janssen and Fritz Genschow and the third in East Germany by Götz Friedrich. All of them reek with sweetness and follow the Grimms' version slavishly even if they embellish the plot with tidy ornamental homes, puppets and actors dressed as cute or ferocious animals, stalwart father figures, and mothers who are exemplary housewives. No matter whether she is blonde or dark-haired, Little Red Riding Hood is eaten because she strays from the straight path, but she rises from the wolf's tummy to be embraced by a tight-knit family. The emphasis on community and home were part of the ideological tendencies in both East and West Germany during the postwar period and the beginning of the Cold War. This "homey" and conservative tendency can also be found in three incredible versions of the classical tale: *Little Red Riding Hood* (*La Caperucita Roja*, 1960), *Little Red Riding Hood and her Friends* (*Caperucita y sus Tres Amigos*, 1961), *Little Red Riding Hood and Tom Thumb against the Monsters* (*Caperucita y Pulgarcito contra los Monstruos*, 1962), which were all produced and distributed in America by K. Gordon Murray to be played at kiddie matinees. In each one of the films, Little Red Riding Hood, played by the talented Marcia Gracia, saves the wolf's life because of her Christian charity, and if it were not for the zany behavior of the ridiculous wolf and his friend, Stinky the Skunk, and for the exaggerated magical characters that include fairies, bad queens, ogres, murderers, and gypsies, who are taken from pagan beliefs and superstitions, the films could easily be dismissed as didactic religious cinema. But Rodriguez's films, often changed somewhat by Murray, represent unique experiments in recreating a classical European tale for Mexican children with a focus on community. In the first film the village wood-cutters save Red Riding Hood from the paws of the wolf whom they want to kill, but she intercedes and asks that he be given a second chance and made keeper of the forest so that he can become a useful citizen. In the second film, the wolf and the skunk soon become bored by protecting the villagers and the forest and leave their jobs. Meanwhile, Little Red Riding Hood is kidnapped by gypsies whom she had befriended in the woods. At one point the wolf accidently shoots and wounds some men who are illegally chopping wood. Once again he is hunted, but Little Red comes to his rescue and also begs the villagers to forgive the gypsies. In the third film, the Queen of Badness, who lives in a gloomy castle deep in a haunted forest, seeks to capture the only two truly good people left on earth, Little Red Riding Hood and Tom Thumb. However, because of their faith in God endorsed by the Fairy of Dawn, Little Red and Tom Thumb not only save the wolf but also the entire community, which sings a song about how faith, hope and charity can always conquer evil when it arises in the world. In his Kiddie Matinee website, Rob Craig maintains that *Red Riding Hood and the Little Monsters*

is more bizarre, imaginative, harrowing and grotesque than any other film ever made expressly for children. The hybrid of wacky fairy tale and gothic horror movie has never been done as successfully as in this stunning film. Played almost entirely like a horror film, with scenes that still shock and unnerve today, this amazingly grim fairy tale must have scared the pants off of little Mexican kids during its original release. . . . The assortment of monsters here is a veritable catalog of monster movie icons: witch carrot monster, Frankenstein, ogre, vampire, robot, skeletons, man-eating plant, dragon, animal people. These monsters range from cartoony to highly effective, and some are straight out of Mexican horror film productions.[131]

Ironically, what remains stable in this film—and in the first two of the series—is the saintly child, whose "original sin" enables her to transform the criminal wolf into a do-gooder, who learns the virtues of good citizenry.

Unfortunately, most of the conventional films, produced in America from the 1960s to the present, slavishly show how Red Riding Hood must learn from her mistakes and are not as unusual and fascinating as Rodriguez's works. For instance, there are two musicals, *The Dangerous Christmas of Red Riding Hood* (1965), directed by Sid Smith, and *Little Red Riding Hood* (1989), directed by Adam Brooks, which are unusual adaptations but continue to stress the same message about the girl's guilt. *The Dangerous Christmas of Red Riding Hood* was a TV special that featured such stars as Liza Minnelli, Cyril Ritchard, Vic Damone, and the rock group, The Animals. The debonair wolf sits in a prison cell and narrates his version of the story; how he attempted to befriend Little Red, and how he was betrayed. His version is acted out in song and dance as a conventional light parody of the classical Grimms' tale. Though delectable commercial fare, the TV film displays Little Red Riding Hood as simplistic and foolish. The result is that she must be saved from her fate by the handsome swooning Vic Damone. Little girls always need a male savior. In *Little Red Riding Hood*, one of the Cannon Studios set of fairy-tale adaptations, there is a more complicated plot. The story takes place during the Crusades, and the girl known as Lynette is a kind of tomboy, raised by her mother among peasants because she wants nothing to do with rich society and the evil prince, her brother-in-law, who has sold his soul to a demonic werewolf to gain power and the throne. Her husband, the rightful heir to the throne, went off to the Middle East and has been absent seven years during the Crusades and is considered dead by most people. Despite the fact that her mother has raised Lynette to be "fearless," the girl falls into a trap created by the werewolf. And, of course, she can only be saved by her long-lost father, who returns just in time from the Crusades to rescue her and to kill the werewolf. All's well that ends well in this strange melodramatic and predictable musical fairy-tale film that once again delivers a message about the gullibility of a young girl.

Even stranger is the Hungarian/Canadian film, *Bye Bye Red Riding Hood* (1989) directed by the Hungarian filmmaker Márta Mészáros and based on the novel *Bye Bye Chaperon Rouge* by Viviane Julien. Although some critics see this film positively as a feminist initiatory film,[132] it is so pretentious, long, and boring and portrays Red Riding Hood as such an unlikeable character that one is tempted to hope the wolf will keep the girl in his tummy after he devours her. The acting is stilted; the plot is overly contrived; the shots contrasting city and country are artificial. The story concerns Fanny, who at four was traumatized by the separation and divorce of her parents, while living in the city. Then the film jump cuts about eight or nine years to Fanny's adolescence. She has been schlepped to live in the woods where her mother works as a meteorologist and her grandmother and great grandmother on her father's side also reside in a cabin on a hill. Why they are there and how they earn a living is never explained. Always dressed in red and shown in red hues with stuffed animals, Fanny continually visits her grandma and great grandma, strikes up a friendship with a real four-legged talking wolf, who is more comical than dangerous, encounters a man who might be her father but is really her mother's new lover, and begins an adolescent romance with a boy named Nicholas from the city. Throughout most of the film the grandma sits on a wooden throne as some kind of wise woman who has magic powers, but she cannot prevent her own daughter and Fanny from being swallowed by the wolf whose stomach resembles that of a giant whale made on a Hollywood set. The depiction of Fanny and grandma in the wolf's tummy is ludicrous as is most of the film. And yes, both her mother's unnamed lover and Nicholas must save the females.

Mészáros's film is almost as stupid as the Shelley Duvall Faerie Tale Theatre production *Little Red Riding Hood*, directed by Graeme Clifford in 1983. In this outrageously sexist film, Little Red Riding Hood hangs oedipally on every word her father utters and is portrayed as a moron as is her mother. This filmic interpretation which includes a comic wolf with a British accent has no redeeming value to it. It blithely recounts the traditional Grimms' tale placing total blame on the insipid Rid Riding Hood, who whines happily when she is rescued by her father. While the Faerie Tale Theatre production might win the competition for the worst recreation of the Red Riding Hood tale, there are others that might give it a run for the money. For instance, Giacomo Cimini's *Red Riding Hood* (2003) is an Italian horror film made with revolting bad taste. The "heroine" of the film, a twelve-year-old girl named Jenny McKenzie, is abandoned in Rome and goes on a killing spree to clean the city of criminals and derelicts. Reminiscent of Fanny in *Bye Bye Chaperon Rouge*, Jenny is a spoiled brat who rationalizes her lust for blood and gore by believing she is on some kind of ethical mission. This poorly acted, imitative horror film made simply for horror's sake adds nothing new to the genre and certainly nothing new to the Red Riding Hood cinematic discourse. The transformation of "Little Red Riding Hood" into a kind of horror film was more or less initiated by the Jordan/Carter adaptation, *The Company of Wolves*, in 1979 and has resulted in several lame and simplistic recreations that drown in the sweat and blood of the producers and actors. For instance, even before Cimini's plodding film, Charles Cornell produced *In the Deep Woods* (1992), a stalker film, which thrives and preys upon the anxieties of women as victims of a psychopath; the British director, Will Gould, tells a pathetic love story about young gay men, outcasts of society, suspected of eating girls in *The Wolves of Kromer* (1998), while all they want to do is to make love with each other; and the French director, Lionel Delplanque, designs a haunted mansion in *Deep in the Woods* (2000), in which young actors are hired to perform a play about Little Red Riding Hood, but are subjected to gruesome idiotic murders that merely serve to thrill audiences with blood and gore. More recently, Harry Sparks has unfortunately produced *Rotkäppchen: The Blood of Red Riding Hood* (2009), a soft-porno horror film, in which a poor German girl named Rose comes to America to visit her grandmother, but instead of having a pleasant time with granny, the unlikely eighteen-year-old virgin must endure the brutality of her LA sex-obsessed classmates and some gruesome murders by an anonymous beast. This film, filled with gratuitous sex scenes, wins the award for outrageous stupidity and pretentiousness. Rose, who is pregnant after her survival, seems to deserve what she gets.

On the lighter side of commercial filmmaking that does not thrive on horror, there is Randall Kleiser's musical comedy, *Little Red Riding Hood* (2004), hastily made, which can also be rapidly devoured as another stale production that pretends to be unique through the use of sets of live 3D virtual reality, hip allusions to contemporary life style and technology, Hollywood song and dance, and a feminist grandmother. However, in the end, the plot repeats the conventional story of a handsome hunter with a musket riding a white steed who must save Red Riding Hood from herself.

Experimental Films 1984–2009

In contrast to the predictable Little Red Riding Hood films of the past sixty years, the experimental filmmakers, who have been strongly influenced by the feminist movement, have given greater thought to the problem of rape and responsibility for rape than the more conventional directors and producers, who have often just used the tale as a vehicle to make money, show off their cinematic skills of imitation, or to repeat irresponsibly a so-called good message of warning to little girls who stray from the right path of propriety. As I have previously maintained, Angela Carter's story, "The Company of Wolves," published in 1979 and Neil Jordan's filmic adaptation of Carter's tale in 1984 are important markers in the shift of the cinematic discourse that becomes more graphic, profound, and original since the 1980s and tends to include Red Riding Hood's desire, rage, and revenge in the discourse. Beginning with Jordan's *The Company of Wolves*, I want to discuss the nature of a destabilizing process that focuses more on the complexity of desire and anger, female and male, than the fears, gullibility, and guilt of a young woman. The films I shall examine are Garri Bardin's *Grey Wolf and Little Red Riding Hood* (*Seryy Volk end Krasnaya Shapochka*, 1990), Matthew Bright's *Freeway* (1996), Jan Kouren's *The Last Red Riding Hood* (1996), David Kaplan's *Little Red Riding Hood* (1997), Pieter Van Hees's *Black XXX-mas* (2000), David Morwick's *Little Erin Merryweather* (2003), David Slade's *Hard Candy* (2005), Rajneel Singh's *Big Bad Wolves* (2006), and S. J. Chiro's *Little Red Riding Hood* (2006). First, I want to turn to *The Company of the Wolves*, and I want to begin by registering a complaint.

Though the screenplay was written by Carter and Jordan, the final edited film is solely Jordan's work, and he made numerous infuriating changes that contradict the printed story, screenplay, and tendency of the dream that celebrates a young girl's taming of a wolf and her own desire to become wolflike. In Jordan's hands, the frame of the film is wooden, symbolically blunt, offensive, and, in the end, a pathetically flawed strategy to encase a series of related tales. There is also something faintly comic about depicting a young girl who is having her first period, tossing and turning and dreaming about herself as a fearless young girl and then showing her frightened out of her mind by hairy Belgian shepherds, who no more resemble wolves than my curly standard poodle does, and who stampede like wild cattle and crash through a window into the poor girl's room causing the poor ruby-red-lipped girl to scream in terror, as if to say menstruation is a bloody horrifying affair.

The Carter/Jordan screenplay, which employs a different frame, is much more in keeping with her original story. The screenplay portrays a young girl named Alice, and her sister is younger, not older as in the film, and plays a negligible role. Alice is disturbed, and there is a "sense of oppressive and unfocused sensuality, adolescent turbulence"[133] in the bedroom. She lies on her bed surrounded by toys, dolls, and fairy-tale books, one which exhibits Gustav Doré's illustration of "Little Red Riding Hood," and there is also a film poster picturing a werewolf. Her first dream is a nightmare in which she envisions herself moving from an artificial forest of dolls and toys to a real forest where she is attacked and killed by a wolf. The death of the dream-Alice brings about a transformation: the birth of Rosaleen, Alice's dream persona, who will face down wolves and determine her own destiny. At the end of the screenplay, Rosaleen tells a tale to soothe the werewolf while cradling him in her arms. "I'll tell you a story, you pitiful creature, though you showed my grandmother no pity, did you? Yet now you're worse off than she . . . I'll tell you a story about love between two wolves."[134]

Her story is once again different from that told by the Rosaleen of Jordan's film. It concerns an old wolf who brings a priest to his dying mate for a blessing. When the priest touches her forehead, the dying she-wolf is transformed into an old woman. As this occurs, the male wolf becomes an old man dressed in rags. Both are outcasts. Then he kisses the old woman's forehead. Rosaleen concludes her tale by saying: "So then the priest knew what any wise child could have told him, that

Figure 36
Neil Jordan,
*The Company
of Wolves*

there are no devils, except the ones we have invented."[135] Following this event Rosaleen herself is transformed into a wolf and bounds through the forest, joined by another wolf (ostensibly the werewolf, whom she loves). They run through the magic forest past the doll's house toward Alice's room. The concluding passage of the screenplay reads:

> Alice stands up on the bed. She looks down at the floor below the bed. She bounces a little on the bed, as if testing its springs. A long howl can be heard—this time somewhere beyond the open door. Alice suddenly springs off the bed, up into the air, as if off a diving-board. She curls, in a graceful jack-knife and plummets toward the floor. The floor parts. It is in fact water. She vanishes beneath it. The floor ripples, with the aftermath of her dive. Gradually it settles back into the plain floor again.
>
> We see the room, for a beat, half-forest, half-girl's bedroom. There is a whining at the door. It opens, under the pressure of one wolf's snout. First the he-wolf enters, then the she-wolf. They nose their way around Alice's things.[136]

The ending of the screenplay is significant for it emphasizes, in the spirit of magical realism, the disappearance of the disturbed, fearful Alice, who is replaced by Rosaleen in the form of a wolf accompanied by her lover, who sniff the remains of Alice's childhood. Alice's transformation to a woman is complete, and her immersion with the fluid floor symbolizes the fluidity of her future identity. On the other hand, the film ends on a blissfully ignorant note paraphrasing Perrault's sexist *moralité* in a voiceover spoken in a sweet and soft female voice:

> Little girls, this seems to say,
> never stop along your way.
> Never trust a stranger friend.
> No one knows how it will end.
> As you're pretty, so be wise.
> Wolves may lurk in any guise.
> Now as then 'tis simple truth.
> Sweetest tongue has sharpest tooth.

This scene and verse are a revolting contradiction that belies the screenplay and Angela Carter's original story and screenplay. That being said, the film has its merits, for it probes the consciousness-raising of a young girl named Rosaleen with subtle irony and sensual erotic symbols through storytelling that blends horror with humor. Dropping the frame which is useless, we begin with the grim depiction of Rosaleen's older sister who enters a dark forest and then is attacked and devoured by wolves. This gruesome event sets off a series of storytelling and questioning about wolves and violence that prepares Rosaleen for her encounter with the werewolf and her decision to pursue her attraction and to become a wolf. As Charlotte Crofts points out in her astute essay,

> the film's foregrounding of storytelling serves a double function, first by contextualizing the violent tales of male agressivity in the mouth of Granny, the "prohibitive mentor", and second by allowing Rosaleen to speak for herself. In fact, by giving the main female protagonist a more vocal role, the film could be seen to offer a greater space for the articulation of female subjectivity and desire than is available in the short story.[137]

In fact, the film, which employs gadgets and gags from popular horror movies, could be viewed as a storytelling duel between a grandmother, who spreads idle superstitious lies to scare her granddaughter so that she will distrust men and sex, and her granddaughter who creates tales about outcasts who need more love and trust in the world, otherwise they will continue to be marginalized. Intervening in the storytelling from time to time is Rosaleen's mother, who reinforces Rosaleen's quest to find her own way through the woods and saves her life at the end of the film. To a certain extent, the film "justifies" the werewolf's devouring of the bigoted grandmother, whose aggressive storytelling is antiquated and needs to be replaced by her granddaughter's.

The imagery in the film is startling. The forest pulsates with phallic snakes and plants and womb-like wells and fertile eggs. The village resembles Robin Hood's hideout in a dense, almost jungle-like forest, and the scenes are reminiscent of peasant images in Breughel's paintings. The vigorous life of the peasants who live with the threat of wolves in the forest corresponds to the surging sense of sexuality in Rosaleen. This is a film, if we discard the frame, that explores how male violence might be overcome by female desire and employs unusual storytelling and dreams to posit the possibility of taming the wolf that lies within all of us.

Taming the wolf is also the central theme of the Russian filmmaker Bardin's dynamically animated film, *Grey Wolf and Little Red Riding Hood*, a scintillating parody of the ravaged Russian way of life and the hopes of Russians after 1989. Though it does not deal so much with female desire and sexuality, it does raise the issue of rape and identity—the rape of Russia and the potentially new identity of Russians. Following the carnivalesque tradition of cartoons, Bardin ridicules the former oppressors of the Soviet people by transforming them into a single character, a grey spindly wolf, whose teeth have been extracted to eliminate his danger. He is characterized as a dangerous con man as he sings a song about his "unjust" fate to the tune of "Mack the Knife" from *The Threepenny Opera*: "I'm Grey Wolf, once tough and ruthless./But now I'm just rough and toothless./I'm supposed to have adventures./But life's empty without dentures." It is clear that communism is not dead in the "new" Russia, and the cunning ferociously comical beast manages to terrorize a dentist and force him to implant a new metal mouthpiece so he can devour whomever he wishes. Indeed, he swallows the dentist whole as soon as he has his mouthpiece, and then he begins to gobble up whomever he encounters. All the characters are pictured in the wolf's growing belly. At the same time that he is recovering from changes in the Soviet Union, a cute and delightful petite Red Riding Hood is depicted with her large bosomy mother making a pie in a kitchen. As they work and bake, they sing a song about liberty, overcoming fears of the wolf, and longing for grandma in gay Paris. The mother proclaims: "There are no longer borders to friendship, my beauty./ To visit Paris, we now have a duty./ But danger is lurking./ The wolf's been freed upon the heath./ Though they sentenced him to lose his teeth/without good people's help, he can't survive." As soon as the pie is finished, the mignon Red Riding Hood starts toward Paris to deliver the pie on foot. In the middle of the woods, she encounters the wolf dressed in a tuxedo, but she escapes him, thanks to three marching huntsmen. Both cross the border, the wolf by bribing the guards, Red Riding Hood by legal means. Along the way the wolf eats a minstrel, the three pigs, and the seven dwarfs. He beats Red Riding Hood to the granny's cottage near the Eiffel Tower and devours her. When Little Red Riding Hood appears, she is helpless, and the wolf knocks her down and tries the pie before eating poor Little Red Riding Hood. However, when he bites into the pie, it is like stone, and he loses his denture. Now toothless, there is a revolution in his belly that expands into a gigantic balloon that bursts. All the occupants march out singing "Let the world be sunny all over!" They carry peace signs and trample over the wolf, who is left in chains, as they head toward the future.

Bardin's transformation of "Little Red Riding Hood" into a political film about freedom and the assumption of a new identity bursts with good humor and artful design. All the characters are made out of clay, and Bardin has developed an unusual technique so that their movements are fluent and flexible. He uses old popular songs in original ways with new lyrics. Aside from the wolf singing "Mack the Knife" as his leitmotif, he also has a seductive ditty based on "Tea for Two"; Little Red Riding Hood and her mother are associated with Russian folk music; granny sings a song from her bed to the tune of "La Vie en Rose"; and the final marching song is a composition based on "Auld Lang Syne." Though Bardin is skeptical about the new Russian identity, his film is filled with carnivalesque hope. With the wolf leveled, Little Red Riding Hood strides forward in solidarity with an eccentric group of people who believe in peace and must still be on the alert against wolves.

The situation in the 1990s in America was, of course, very different. But there were also struggles, and one was the feminist confrontation concerning the backlash against feminism. Whether this was what impelled David Kaplan to make a brilliant short, black-and-white film, *Little Red Riding Hood*, which recounts an oral version of the "Little Red Riding Hood" classical tale, is unclear. But there is nothing ambiguous about the emphasis of the film: it focuses on female desire and a female gaze that rejoice in a young woman's artful and playful way in which she seduces an androgynous wolf. Kaplan's film, which is narrated by a male voice with background music of Ravel and uses an 1883 text of a hybrid oral tale composed by the French folklorist Paul Delarue, begins with a young woman looking into a pond and admiring herself. Gazing narcissistically at herself she is sure of herself and will pursue what that self desires. As she moves into the forest, she spies a strange-looking wolf dancing in a meadow and observes him from behind a tree. Once she makes herself noticed, the wolf asks her where she is going, and she indicates the way to her granny's house. Interestingly, Kaplan's images and the actions of the characters often contradict the words spoken by the narrator. Nobody speaks in this film except the narrator, and his words are countered by the movements of the characters beyond his control. For instance, the wolf is a hairy, intense ballet dancer, whose gestures are graceful. Little Red Riding Hood is confident, clever, and sensual and contemplates each step she takes. When the wolf invites her into bed, she performs a striptease, and once in bed she appears to intimidate the wolf. As soon as he announces that he wants to eat her, she tells him that she must go outside and make kacka. Disappointed, the wolf ties a rope around her ankle and lets her go into the courtyard. Then she escapes, watches the lamenting wolf from a distance, and runs toward her home. The narrator states: "He followed her but arrived at her house at the moment she entered." The narrator implies that she has entered the house and closed the door, while the film's last frame has the wolf's claw tenderly stroking the girl's face.

Kaplan's film is filled with references not only to the printed oral text but also to the illustrations of Gustav Doré. Whereas it is clear that the androgynous wolf lusts after Little Red Riding Hood, it is her desire and bemused attitude that determine the course of the narrative in this film. Little Red Riding Hood is firmly in control of her destiny, and she enjoys every moment of her interaction with the wolf. There is no hint of violence even if the wolf does destroy the feeble grandmother in a comic

Figure 37
David Kaplan,
Little Red Riding Hood

Figure 38
Matthew Bright,
Freeway

scene. In French folklore studies the death of the grandmother has been explained by the fact that she has become too old to defend herself and serve the community, and thus, she must die and be replaced by her granddaughter. In the film, this is a tragic–comic incident. What counts most is the manner in which a young girl proceeds to plot and fulfill her own sexual drives.

This is also true in Matthew Bright's film *Freeway*, but she has no choice but to react violently to the violation of her life. In this film Little Red Riding Hood is poor white trash, a juvenile delinquent teenager named Vanessa Lutz, who lives transiently in southern California, land of the freeways. Her mother is a prostitute; her stepfather, a crackhead. Her boyfriend is black and packs a gun because of a running feud with Latino hoods. The film begins with the non-literate Vanessa trying to read a sentence on a blackboard and being rewarded with a luscious kiss by her boyfriend Chopper when she does. Soon after she watches her mother and father being dragged off by the police because of illegal solicitation and drugs. Vanessa promptly escapes a social worker because she does not want to go to yet another foster home. Instead, she decides to travel up north to her grandmother whom she has never seen, in the car that she has stolen from the social worker. Before she departs, Chopper gives her a pistol to protect herself. Immediately after he is gunned down by some hoodlums. On the freeway, Vanessa's car breaks down, and she is rescued on the I-5 by a kindly psychologist named Bob Wolverton, who gives her a ride. However, he is not as kind as he seems. He is a notorious serial killer, who has murdered several young women on the freeway. This time he is unfortunate because Vanessa, clever beyond her years, outwits him. She forces him to an isolated side road, with Chopper's pistol, shoots him many times, and leaves him for dead. Soon after she is arrested and brought to a juvenile center. Somehow Wolverton manages to survive but is grotesquely deformed and sexually handicapped. He and his wife, who appear to be decent middle-class citizens, want Vanessa sentenced to death. At first two detectives believe their lies, but as they gather evidence against Vanessa, they gradually realize that the evidence points to Wolverton as the depraved serial killer. In the meantime Vanessa manages to flee the detention center in a bloody escape. When she finally arrives in northern California, she discovers that the maniacal Wolverton has beaten her to grandma's house and killed her. Infuriated, she attacks Wolverton and beats him to death in a fierce comical fight scene. The two detectives show up at the scene fearing for Vanessa's life, but she emerges from her grandma's trailer, and the film ends with her taking a cigarette from the detectives and smiling.

As James Berardinelli wrote when *Freeway* was released in 1996,

> The film works—and does so manifestly—because its intentions are clearly delineated. Using black humor, blood, and a pair of tremendous performances, *Freeway* hones in on its targets and calculatedly skewers them one-by-one. First up is America's welfare system. Then the

judicial system. Then the penal system. And when you put all the pieces together, you realize that *Freeway* is making a penetrating statement about the general populace's endless fascination with the lurid and violent. And, unlike Oliver Stone's *Natural Born Killers*, which was torpedoed by interference from the director's ego, *Freeway* drives home the point effectively. This movie is both grimly funny and thought-provoking.[138]

Moreover, I would add, it is one of the more innovative and politically meaningful recreations of the Red Riding Hood fairy tale. Beginning with the cartoons that sketch the story as the credits flash on the screen, the film focuses on changing the viewers' perspectives not only on the tale of "Little Red Riding Hood," but also on rape and rage. Bright is a provocateur, and many of the scenes in the film are aimed at causing a sense of unease, revulsion, and horror. For instance, Vanessa viciously attacks a black detective who insults her and implies that she is a racist. Later, she breaks the nose of a prisoner who tries to intimidate her and almost murders her. Then the very same prisoner slits the throat of the female warden helping Vanessa escape from the juvenile center. Each scene is framed as negatives to expose the tendencies of social institutions to brand Vanessa guilty before she can defend herself. Though Vanessa has been victimized from birth, she is not a victim. What makes this "Little Red Riding Hood" different is her outrage and ability to adapt to and survive the most excruciatingly unjust conditions. Vanessa does not need a hunter or the police to rescue her. However, the sad fact is that her rage does not bring a deep sense of fulfillment or a new meaning in her life, just temporary relief.

Rage, though warranted, is self-defeating when raped girls seek revenge in Red Riding Hood films. A good example is Tzang Merwyn Tong's *A Wicked Tale* (2005). This psychodrama and surrealistic revision of "Little Red Riding Hood" begins in a hospital with a Caucasian young man as a patient who unwillingly takes some pills from a Chinese nurse. (All the actors except the patient are Chinese.) He apparently needs to be sedated. Gradually he begins babbling to recount his story about bestial behavior, and there is a flashback to the house of a young girl named Beth dressed in a white gown who is sent to her granny's house in the forest. She is the epitome of innocence and naiveté. Along the way on some railroad tracks she meets the Caucasian dressed as a friendly monk. She is attracted to him, but her Uncle Charlie appears and warns her to stay away from him. He works with a grass cutter to clean the tracks and appears to be somewhat ornery himself. Beth dismisses him. The Caucasian leaves, rushes to granny's house, where he beats her to death in a gory fight and drags her bloody body beneath a bed. When Beth arrives, she is about to succumb to the seduction of the Caucasian. However, Uncle Charlie arrives and engages the Caucasian in yet another bloody battle. Charlie is killed. The Caucasian lies exhausted on the floor. Beth, who has seen her dead grandmother beneath the bed, has now realized what a demon her would-be rapist is. She takes the grass cutter and cuts off the Caucasian's legs. Then, in her rage, she sadistically sits on him and has intercourse. Once again at the hospital the Caucasian patient is now the traumatized victim, and his nurse Beth sadistically enjoys her revenge.

Or does she? Can she? This short experimental film, though gruesome, is a terse and significant comment on what happens when the persecuted heroine becomes a rapist herself. Though Vanessa Lutz killed in *Freeway*, she did this in self-defense and never intended to exploit or violate anyone. Beth could have simply killed the Caucasian, but she chose to mutilate and rape him. Later she will haunt him every day as his nurse. The disastrous reversal of roles may also be interpreted as some kind of political allegory. Tzang Merwyn Tong is a Singaporean filmmaker, and perhaps one could view the film as a critique of western colonization. The difficulty with any conclusion that one draws from this film is that one must raise the question: who benefits when victims become just like their victimizers?

This question is also central to David Morwick's morbid horror film *Little Erin Merryweather* (2003). The opening scenes that introduce the credits reveal the background history of Erin

Merryweather, who was raped many times by her father. Later, in the small college town in which she has grown up, Erin takes out her revenge by dressing in a red cape and slashing male college students, including the police chief, who is close on her heels. In a bizarre ending, a female psychologist and one of Erin's male friends pursue her into the forest, but she appears to disappear in smoke and dust. Never caught, I fear that Erin might return to us in a sequel. This corny, predictable slasher film is, nevertheless, significant despite its predictability and some wooden acting. Morwick's depiction of the incest scenes is chilling, and his portrayal of the crazed and desperate mental condition of Erin is convincing. Clearly, Erin is not satisfied by her killing. In fact, she is insatiable, seeking revenge in wild acts to draw attention to her own violation that can never be redeemed.

Related to Erin, the fourteen-year-old Hailey in David Slade's *Hard Candy* is more cruel, clever, and complex. It also seems that she is satisfied with her ghastly deed at the end of the film. But nothing is really clear in this exploitation film except that Hailey, dressed in a red sweatshirt with a red hood, drives a confessed pedophile to suicide. The film begins with Hailey exchanging messages in a chat room on the Internet with a thirty-two-year-old photographer named Jeff. They meet in a cafe. They go to Jeff's ultra modern condo in the hills of Los Angeles. She manages to dope his drink so that he falls unconscious. When he awakes, his is bound to a chair, and Hailey accuses him of murdering her missing friend Donna Mauer, another teenager, and begins to torture him and make him confess. In one graphic scene after another, including one in which she pretends to castrate him, he confesses to having taken a photo of Donna and watching her murder. Right before she compels him to commit suicide by hanging himself from a rooftop, she reveals that her name might not be Hailey, her father might not be a doctor, and Donna might not be her friend. He will never know who she is, but she declares that she represents every girl he has photographed, seduced, and fucked. After he hangs himself, she is seen escaping through some nearby woods, cheerful and content. She seems to be like any other teenager in her red sweatshirt and hood walking down the mountain.

This film could be titled "The Ultimate Revenge of Little Red Riding Hood," but we can never be certain whether Hailey herself was ever violated, whether she was Donna Mauer's friend, and whether she is justified in taking the law into her own hands. In a couple of instances she tells Jeff that she is insane and sees a therapist. At times she appears to be completely rational. Other times, she has a stony maniacal look. She had definitely stalked Jeff for some time before making personal contact with him. She is frighteningly lucid, and his murder is premeditated murder, intended to set an example for future pedophiles and rapists. The film is disturbingly non-committal on this point. Viewed within the context of the development of the Red Riding Hood cinematic discourse, the film could be interpreted as the only response to the brutal molestation and rape that threaten women throughout the world every day.

Three other late twentieth- and early twenty-first-century films appear to provide evidence for how women are ceaselessly plagued by rape and may have no other choice but to strike back with violence. In the surrealist musical, *The Last Red Riding Hood*, directed by the Dutch-born French filmmaker Jan Kounen, there are strong echoes of Jacques Demy's *Donkey Skin*, a light-hearted bizarre parody of Perrault's tale of incest that makes use of sentimental music and dream scenes. Kounen, who is also known for his strong interest in Shamanism, goes one step further in his thirty-minute film that resembles more a horrific hallucinatory trip in which a machine monster maims and murders girls before the credits are shown. The last young woman he maims is a Red Riding Hood, who manages to destroy the monster and then continues to live in a laboratory where she seemingly takes the blood of animals. Once the film begins years later, we are transplanted to an enchanted forest filled with dancing mushrooms, a cute rabbit, and a wolf dressed in black tie wearing a muzzle. The wolf is encouraged to push a button on a time capsule, and a young ravishing

Red Riding Hood appears. She sings a song about her desire for a tender love and dances in a glade. The wolf falls in love with her. A threatening machine monster appears and kidnaps the rabbit. It appears to be a contraption invented by the old grandmother. The wolf rushes to her laboratory that is located deeper in the forest. He strangles the grandmother, who is operating on the rabbit, just as Red Riding Hood knocks at the door. Once she enters, the wolf discards his muzzle, and they dance an amorous *pas de deux* that abruptly changes into a violent rape scene. As the terrified Red Riding Hood breaks away from the wolf, his face resembles that of a werewolf. She asks three questions, and he viciously devours her.

Kounen's stark and enigmatic reverie about the tale that keeps repeating itself even when it appears to be buried is terrifying. The sudden transformation of the wolf's apparent tender love for Red Riding Hood, who appears to be a beautiful innocent flower in an enchanted world, reflects upon the brutality that is closely connected to feelings of love that men may have for women. In Kounen's film male love is connected to a ravenous appetite that needs a muzzle. When unmuzzled, there is no telling how the wolf-like man may react. In this film sweet hallucination yields to a grim reality, and it seems that men cannot stop themselves from raping.

Though Kounen's surrealistic film may seem cynical, Pieter Van Hees, a Belgian filmmaker, has made an extraordinary eleven-minute film *Black XXX-mas* (2000), which makes *The Last Red Riding Hood* look like a sweet melodrama. The film is framed by two scenes showing God in heaven surrounded by sexy women, playing with a computer game in which he will manipulate events on earth. After the first shot, the camera swings to an apartment in a ghetto, to the reality described by the voiceover of a young black girl, as a world in which there are no good guys or bad guys. There are just bad guys and guys that are worse. This is the world according to her father, who is a burglar and is preparing to set out on Christmas Eve to rob a few homes. Before he leaves, he warns his daughter, an obvious Red Riding Hood character, not to leave their apartment because there is a "fucken jungle" out there. However, in the very next scene we see her entering a dangerous street to buy some weed, while her mother, who is white, remains at home watching television. Red Riding Hood walks down the street smoking a joint and is stopped by a white police officer, played by God, who is now called Wolfgang Schutzwald and speaks with a German accent. Van Hees plays with the name Schutzwald, which can be translated as protector of the woods. The police officer, who prefers to call himself Wolfie, is more interested in fondling Little Red Riding Hood than arresting her. When some tourists snap some photos of Wolfie molesting the girl, he shoots them dead. And because he does not want any witnesses, he knocks the girl unconscious and begins to eat her to do away with the evidence. Meanwhile her father, dressed as Santa Claus, invades a rich apartment, painted in glaring white colors, slaps a young boy and begins stuffing his bag with valuable objects. When the woman of the house appears, she disrobes, and she begins having sex with the black Santa. In another scene about the same time, Santa's wife, that is Red Riding Hood's mother, makes love to an Italian Stallion. As Santa is enjoying sex, the door to the apartment opens, and Wolfie, who is the husband of the woman, enters and accidentally shoots his wife. Santa grabs a gun from above the fireplace and blasts the head off Wolfie. Then he hears a voice coming from inside Wolfie's body and cuts it open to find his daughter. In the next to last scene, we see Santa, his wife, and his daughter standing in their apartment before a Christmas tree and singing a Christmas carol. They are the picture-perfect image of the happy bourgeois family. Finally, the camera takes us back to heaven where God is draped by two beautiful women and plays with his computer game. Addressing the spectators, he smiles and declares that "Life is a bitch."

As gruesome as this film is, it is also very funny. It is a film literally motivated by black humor that pictures an immoral God taking sadistic pleasure in playing with people's lives. Everyone is corrupt and cheating on one another. The rape scene turns into cannibalism. Blood is splattered in the ghetto and in the lily-white apartment. Survival is all that counts. The next-to-last final scene of father, mother, and daughter singing "Silent Night" is the ultimate parody of the normal pious, bourgeois nuclear family. There is no lesson to be learned from this film.

However, in Rajneel Singh's *Big Bad Wolves*, produced in New Zealand, there is an educational lesson in the story about Little Red Riding Hood. This amusing eleven-minute film depicts five Mafiosa-type American gangsters sitting around a table in a restaurant, smoking cigarettes and cigars, and discussing the true story or virtue of telling the tale about Little Red Riding Hood. The leading gangster who also narrates the story wants to convince his friends to take the tale seriously because of its sex educational value. As he begins telling the story, the scenes are enacted and interrupted by curious and ignorant comments by the gangsters. The narrator insists that the mother is a neglectful parent because she does not educate her daughter about sex and sends her to the grandmother to learn about the secrets of sex. The father is supposedly dead and not important for the story. What is important, according to the narrator, is that the mother shirks her responsibility and thus causes her daughter's death. The gangsters discuss phallic symbols, menstruation, and types of kinky sex as the narrator brings Little Red, a gorgeous blonde, to grandma's cabin where the young man in bed tells her to take her clothes off and throw them into the fire because she won't be needing them anymore. She gets into bed, and the man begins to have sexual intercourse with her. When she asks the three questions, the intercourse turns into rape and murder, and the story ends. The last image of Little Red is that of her spread naked on the bed with blood on her mouth. The gangsters ask about the woodcutter, and the narrator responds that he doesn't think that the woodcutter shows up. It ends with Little Red's death because her mother did not teach her about sex. Then the men stand up, pay the bill, and as they leave the restaurant, the narrator asks them whether they know the story about Goldilocks and the Three Bears.

Singh's film tends to portray the men discussing the lesson of Little Red Riding Hood as harmless stupid caricatures. Their talk recalls the talk of locker rooms or card playing parties in which men discuss sex and often boast about their experiences. Ironically, in this film the lesson that Little Red Riding Hood needs to learn is a lesson that the men should learn, but it is twisted to put the onus on the mother and daughter. It is assumed that men will always be wolves and that women must always be on their guard. The narrator does say at one point that the wolf is a "perverted mother fucker who likes little girls," and there is a condemnation of the predator. However, there is ironically no sense of culpability on the part of the narrator and his listeners. Some men are perverts, it seems, while the men at the table believe that they are normal. They never realize the danger that they represent to women or the society in which they commit their crimes. The film as spoof of men's ignorance or inability to see how the story of Red Riding Hood might relate to their own lives is almost as horrific as the horror films that have openly dealt with the story as a tale of rape.

Since it appears that most men will never learn to control their urges, women must be prepared at a very early age to defend themselves, and this is the message of a short unusual film made by the Seattle-based independent filmmaker S. J. Chiro. Her 2006 beguiling black-and-white version, *Little Red Riding Hood*, begins and ends with a pregnant woman, filmed in color, who sits in a rocking chair under a magnolia tree and dreams. It seems that she dreams about what might happen to her daughter after she is born, for the black-and-white dream depicts a caring mother who sends her six- or seven-year-old daughter into the woods to visit her grandmother. There are no spoken words in the film that recalls the early silent films with interspersed dialogues. The tiny girl is told not to dilly daddle and makes her way into the forest where she gets lost because she is curious and explores the woods. At one point she encounters a wolf, who looks more like a burlesque creepy pedophile than a dangerous wolf. He points her to grandmother's house and takes a path designated "short cut," an additional comic touch by Chiro. When the girl arrives, it is clear that the wolf is in the bed. It is no surprise, but it is a surprise when the little girl adroitly uses her karate skills to flatten the wolf. Then grandma arrives to twist the arm of the pedophile and throw him out. Afterward, she and her granddaughter enjoy the goodies that Little Red has brought her. Though the use of karate appears to be an abrupt "feminist" tactic and message, the film succeeds because of the ironic dream that has an estrangement effect. As a result, the "Red Riding Hood" tale becomes a wish fulfillment in stark and simple black and white. The girl and grandmother need no help from anyone to determine their lives. The dreamer can smile at the end. If there is danger from a predatory male in the future, she knows her daughter will be able to fend for herself.

Almost all the more serious and innovative films in the cinematic discourse about "Little Red Riding Hood" since Jordan's filmic adaptation of *The Company of Wolves* appeared in 1984 have explicitly interrogated the classical tale as one about rape. Most of them are concerned with finding and demonstrating responses to rape that might change attitudes of spectators or draw responses from spectators so that they will reflect upon conditions that foster rape. Interestingly, all the films—with the exception of Chiro's work—have been directed by male filmmakers, and they have either explored female desire and subjectivity or the rage and anger with which women have to live in societies that have failed to cope with rape despite the gains made by feminism in the last forty years. The flaws of the films reveal the misunderstandings about women's subjectivity and the need to continue to address the violation of women's equal rights to live as they desire. It is through the imagining and images of the Little Red Riding Hood tale that possibilities for recreating the story and real social conditions are manifested in a way that Alphonse Daudet never suspected they would be. The "accident," which Daudet's Little Red Riding Hood experiences time and again, is, for the most part, no longer regarded as the girl's fault, nor is it just always the same "accident." The cinematic Red-Riding-Hood discourse has undergone a major change that has led to sober re-evaluations of why rape comes about and who is responsible. The answers that the future films about the girl and wolf try to provide will reflect, in my opinion, the moral value of the efforts we make to reduce the barbaric nature of our present civilizing process.

8

Bluebeard's Original Sin and the Rise of Serial Killing, Mass Murder, and Fascism

> Bluebeard's problem, then, is analogous to Yaweh's, in the sense that he is threatened by his wife's ascent into likeness and equality. His solution has to be different, however, precisely because, as a mortal ensconced in human society, he lacks the resource of a god; he can neither retreat into a unique attribute that his wife lacks nor resort to banishing her from his domain. To restore the regimen of inequality, he has but one secure option, the retributive position enunciated by Yaweh with respect to the fruits of knowledge: "the day when you partake of them, you will surely die" (Gen. 2:17). So Bluebeard's instant move from verdict to death sentence is entirely consequential: to hold power based on privileged knowledge, he must deny that knowledge once and for all to his rival; to reestablish his authority when she overturns the denial, he has no recourse other than to reimpose not-knowing on her. That he can only do by killing her.
>
> **Philip Lewis,** *Seeing Through the Mother Goose Tales*[139]

We like to point to Bluebeard as abnormal, repulsive, and criminal. We like to track the source of Charles Perrault's invented text, "Bluebeard" (1697), to real history, mainly to the history of Gilles de Rais, a sadistic mass murderer of children in the fifteenth century. We want to know fully the causes of atrocious and scandalous behavior. Are monsters born monsters, or are they created by circumstances? Are men brutes by nature? Perhaps they become brutal because they are treated brutally when they are young, or they are too easily provoked by women? Perhaps some have insulted a fairy and been turned into a beast? Some scholars have traced motifs in Perrault's tale to the Bible and Greek and Roman myths that deal with the curiosity of women such as the story of Adam and Eve or Pandora's Box. Ute Heidemann, an astute German scholar, has maintained in her intertextual analysis, "La Barbe bleue palimpseste," that Perrault was in dialogue with Vergil's *Aeneid* (first century BC), Apuleius's "Cupid and Psyche" in *The Golden Ass* (second century), and Paul Scarron's burlesque *Le Virgile travesty en vers burlesques* (1648–1659).[140] Folklorists have linked Perrault's narrative to the oral tradition such as two tales in the Grimms' *Children's and Household Tales* (1812–1815), "The Robber Bridegroom" and "Fitcher's Bird," in which a clever maiden outwits a mass murderer. Versions and fragments of these tales pre-date Perrault's carefully sculpted printed text. Whether named or anonymous, fiends like Bluebeard thrive in oral and literary traditions, and most critics and folklorists are very astute in detecting how Perrault may have relied on them or generated great stuff for generations of storytellers, writers, and artists to come, not to mention filmmakers. But very few, with the exception of Philip Lewis's highly sophisticated study, *Seeing Through the Mother Goose Tales: Visual Turns in the Writings of Charles Perrault*[141] have struck upon the heart of the matter—Bluebeard's original sin.

In my essay, "The Male Key to Bluebeard's Secret,"[142] I endeavored to develop some of Lewis's ideas by exploring the notion that Perrault's text conceals Bluebeard's secret by rationalizing his motive and leading us to believe that he simply wants to punish his wife for disobeying him and exerts male privilege. Lewis demonstrates that there is more at work here that we can see if we ask the question about Bluebeard's original motive or original sin: What prompted him in the first place with his first wife to test and to kill her and leave her corpse in the first room? Lewis argues that there was nothing in the room when Bluebeard's wife entered it during his absence and that her *discovery* was that nothing legitimated his male power or right to have power over her. Bluebeard kills her because she realizes that there is nothing to justify male domination. Her death and the continual murder of women is meant to drive fear into would-be wives. His murdering her is an exemplary act, a model that serves to warn women what will happen to them if they cross certain lines. In this regard, Bluebeard is a hero for all men, even if he always dies. The more women live in fear, the more men can exercise control either as murderers or saviors. Though Bluebeard is almost always caught and killed in the thousands of oral and literary versions that followed Perrault's tale, his original sin is rarely discussed or explored.

Of course, Perrault's "Bluebeard" is very much a product of his times and is also a not-too-subtle critique of marriages of convenience. In his text, the young woman, who marries the mysterious man for his money, should have realized the danger. His blue beard already marked him as suspicious, perhaps a *noveau riche*. However, her aristocratic family has fallen on hard times, and she is enchanted by this wealth. As for Bluebeard, he obviously seeks a wife who will be completely submissive to him, and the only way he can learn whether she will surrender herself to him is by testing the young woman with his keys, wonderful phallic symbols. She fails, and he will exercise his right. In 1697, when absolutism was celebrated by King Louis XIV, women had very few rights, unless they belonged to the aristocratic class or high bourgeoisie. Even then, they were at the disposition of their fathers and husbands. Women were "civilized" to live in fear of male tyranny and had to learn to use cunning to cut into the laws and manners arranged to privilege white male power. They did not dare to question Bluebeard's original sin. It was part of the French civilization process and was cultivated by every country in Europe and North America.

No wonder this tale has taken root in almost every culture of the western world, and no wonder that films have continued the oral and literary fairy-tale discourse about Bluebeard.[143] We are still perplexed and disturbed by the motives of serial killers and mass murderers. It seems that we cannot put a stop to the raping and murdering of women even with all the laws and social codes established to prevent such actions. Not a day goes by without some husband striking out at his wife and killiing her. Not a day goes by when mass murders and serial killing do not occur. Women continue to live in a state of induced fear and are protected by the very men who may strike them down.

In the cinematic discourse, filmmakers, mainly male, have continued the discourse about Bluebeard in a variety of ways. Some have transformed the tale into a burlesque play in which Bluebeard is mocked. Others have adapted Perrault's version and stuck close to his text. A few filmmakers have modernized the tale to portray contemporary kinds of bluebeards. Finally, there are some films that touch upon the connection of serial killing to fascist behavior. I want briefly to discuss some of the comedies and contemporary adaptations before turning to filmic experiments that endeavor to draw a connection to mass murder and fascism, for it is there that Bluebeard's original sin is clearly exposed.

Bluebeard the Bumbler

It is not by chance that, among the very first fairy-tale films ever made, Georges Méliès's *Bluebeard* (*Barbe-bleu*, 1901) set an extraordinary comic model for treating the distasteful topic of the serial killer. Not only was Méliès familiar with all of Perrault's fairy tales, but he more than likely knew Jacques Offenbach's *Bluebeard* (1866), an opéra bouffe, which was very popular at the end of the nineteenth century. More important, perhaps, he was well aware of the Jack the Ripper murders of 1888 and lived during a time when the newspapers and mass media were reporting similar sensational crimes. While Méliès' film does not depart much from the traditional plot of the Perrault tale, it is a brilliant work cinematically because of its technical invention, imaginative sets, elaborate costumes, jump cuts, and humorous critique of a tyrannical count, who is just as much a buffoon as he is a dangerous killer. Méliès' most favorite trick in dealing with villains in all his films was to disrobe them so that they would appear ridiculous and preposterous and trip over their own feet.

In Méliès' adaptation of Perrault's "Bluebeard," the tyrant lives like a king. He has already married and killed seven women. In his old age he seeks to wed yet another young woman, but this time he miscalculates his own power and is eventually killed by his young wife's two brothers. From the very first shots in Bluebeard's lavish castle, we see that Bluebeard is repugnant and is rejected by lines of women whom he has selected as candidates to marry. Instead of having a young woman marry him for his money, Méliès creates a greedy father, who forces his daughter to marry. He literally drags his daughter to accept Bluebeard, who offers him a huge sum of money. Later, after their marriage, when Bluebeard pretends that he must leave for a voyage of six weeks, Méliès invents a male demon, who jumps out of a book to prompt her to yield to her curiosity. In other words, her fate is framed by men who manipulate her or save her. Her only hope is a fairy, another Méliès

Figure 39
Georges Méliès,
Bluebeard

creation, but the fairy's role is minimal within the male struggle over her body. There are comic touches in each one of Méliès's scenes such as the very first one in which Bluebeard refuses to pay the notary for the marriage contract and kicks him out of his hall. In the very next scene Bluebeard's young wife is led through the kitchen, and the cooks begin fighting with one another as they prepare the marriage banquet, and one of the cooks becomes lost in the kettle of stew. When the young wife dreams, she envisions the dead bodies of Bluebeard's former wives and oversized keys dancing above her. Méliès also used montage and surreal effects to create tension, and the final scene in which Bluebeard is pinned to a stake by a sword while he watches his former wives come to life is worthy of the best vaudeville burlesques.

Clearly, Méliès did not alter the major stereotypical gender roles of Perrault's tale very much. Bluebeard's young wife, however, does not marry for money and is not calculating. Rather, she is a victim—also a victim of her own curiosity when she gives in to it and is reprimanded by the fairy. Bluebeard's power is represented by enlarged keys and the phallic symbols such as the swords throughout the film. Knowing how to use the keys and swords will determine the fate of women. Yet, Méliès's critique of arbitrary power and oppression is clear. Bluebeard is a preposterous figure whose actions are so outrageous that one is compelled to laugh. Méliès' use of comic antics subverts the pomposity and pretension of the wealthy classes in almost all his films, and the possibility for transformation is mediated by the magic tricks. In many respects, Méliès followed in the burlesque tradition of Bluebeard interpretations and kept the door open through his comedy for other artists to grapple with the serious implications of how men defiantly sought to maintain the secret of their original sin through violence.

In some of the other silent live-action films produced in the early part of the twentieth century, such as J. Searle Dawley's *Bluebeard* (1909), Charles Giblyn's *Monsieur Bluebeard* (1914), and Hans Otto's *Landru, the Bluebeard of Paris* (*Landru, der Blaubart von Paris*, 1922), there is very little comic depiction of the mass murderer that exposes his monstrous behavior as moronic bumbling. Méliès's comic style and approach to "Bluebeard" was pursued largely by animators and a few directors of live-action films. Cartoons such as *Bye, Bye Bluebeard* (1949) featuring Porky Pig and directed by Arthur Marcus generally follow the typical plots with chase sequences and make light of murder of any kind. Some live-action films transform the Bluebeard character into a harmless or falsely accused hero. For instance, Scott Dunlap's *Bluebeard, Jr.* (1922) is a delightful farce in which a young businessman is suspected of killing young women, while he is merely using a substitute wife to gain 50,000 dollars. His real wife returns to him and rescues him in the end. Ernst Lubitsch's *Bluebeard's Eighth Wife* (1938) is a charming comedy, in which Gary Cooper plays a likeable, happy-go-lucky multi-millionaire, who has divorced seven times and is pursuing his eighth wife, Claudette Colbert, a marquis's daughter, who teaches him numerous lessons. He is the foil to her sharp wit, but the comedy is so predictable that it falls on its face.

In contrast, three remarkable animated films, Jean Painlevé's *Blue Beard* (*Barbe-bleue*, 1936–1938), Vladimir Samsonov's *Very Blue Beard* (1979), and Alexander Bubnov's *The Last Wife of Bluebeard* (*La dernière femme de barbe bleue*, 1996), continue Méliès' tradition in most unusual ways. As Patricia Hutchins points out in an article on Painlevé's film published in *Sight and Sound* (1938),

> This color version of Perrault's *Blue Beard*, produced by the scientist Painlevé and realized by the sculptor René Bertrand and his children, is not a puppet film in the Pal, Starevitch, or "New Gulliver" tradition. In the use of a new plastic material to give a striking effect of three-dimensional reality, its deviation from accepted methods, and close study of natural movement, the film carries forward the work of many half-forgotten enthusiasts who foresaw the future of satire and fantasy in the cinema.[144]

Painlevé, who was responsible for the concept and entire production of *Blue Beard* and was very familiar with Méliès' films, brought together Bertrand with the musician Maurice Jaubert and the lyricist Jean Vincent Bréchignac to create a hilarious opera buffa. The bright colors of the puppets are extraordinary, and the music reinforces the terse hyperbole of the lyrics. When Bluebeard is presented as a grimacing clay puppet, we hear the chorus sing: "Here comes Lord Blue Beard. What a moustache! He is hideous. And what a beard! He is frightful." Indeed, he is ugly and nasty and announces: "My six wives are dead. And my castle is bleak. Your two daughters are beautiful, and their innocence is futile." He offers another older aristocrat thirty pearl necklaces and a thousand silk dresses to marry one of daughters. Soon after Bluebeard marries, he goes off to fight the Saracens, and in the battle scenes, he lops off heads and demonstrates how brutal he can be. In the end, however, the film shows that he who lives by the sword will die by the sword, for the brothers of Bluebeard's wife arrive just in time to save their sister.

Painlevé's interpretation of Perrault's tale and Méliès' film is not very original, but he is highly innovative in his creation of an opera buffa. The movement of the clay figures is intricate; the chanting of the chorus and the singing of the individual figures are deadpan and are in contrast to the lavish scenes and pomposity of Bluebeard's castle and battle scenes. His death is farcical as it is in Méliès' film, and we are left with a strange moral: "Curiosity, however enticing, often brings regrets, often brings, often brings regrets!" This moral is not at all in keeping with the story that ends with the rescue of Bluebeard's wife, who will certainly benefit from his death. Indeed, her curiosity is rewarded, while Bluebeard is punished for his crimes. The film suggests that it is better to be curious than to live in fear of the constraints of one's husband.

In contrast to Painlevé's ironic moral, there are no didactic morals in Samsonov's *Very Blue Bluebeard* and Bubnov's *The Last Wife of Bluebeard*, two intriguing animated films. There are, of course, lessons to be learned. Samsonov's film spoofs American musicals, detective cartoons, comic strips, and Perrault's tale all at the same time. A cartoon character who resembles Dick Tracy with a tiny head and large body decides to go hunting for Bluebeard when he finds a strand of his hair. While on his search he calls his wife from a telephone car, and she complains that he will be late for dinner. But the detective dismisses her complaints and follows some clues that lead through a subway. Accompanied by a dog, he lands in a surrealistic landscape and encounters a royal Bluebeard, who appears to step out of a Modigliani painting in a Modigliani palace. Bluebeard admits his guilt but pleads innocent because of extenuating circumstances that drove him to murder three wives. All of a sudden, the dog is transformed into a court singer, and Bluebeard tells how his first wife Marianna, a high-fashion lady, drove him mad by changing the style and decor of his castle. He killed her by stepping on the tail of her pet dragon, which burned her to death with a flash of fire from his tongue. His second wife, Lilianna, changed his diet to curb his lust, and she was eventually killed by a poison apple. His third wife, Didianna, was a fairy, who believed in free love, and slept with another man while Bluebeard went hunting. He returned to kill her and the man. While telling the stories of all three marriages, there are song and dance routines. Bluebeard is compelled to shave his beard by his wives, and it only grows back when he is enraged. The detective finds the stories convincing and does not arrest Bluebeard. On his way home in his car he telephones his wife who accuses him of having an affair because he is so late. As he argues with her over the phone, a blue beard grows so rapidly on his face that it spreads out of the car as the detective rushes home.

Samsonov's moral, if there is one, is somewhat misogynistic, and ironically it touches on Bluebeard's original sin. If, indeed, there is a bluebeard in every man, it will show itself at various points in a relationship with women. Yet, this does not mean that women cannot defend themselves as Bubnov shows in his very clever short cartoon. His Bluebeard character is a contemporary serial killer pictured shaving and preparing himself to embark on a new adventure. He has an elongated neck with teeth on it and a short cropped blue beard beneath it. As he prepares to leave his castle, we are shown a room filled with bones and all kinds of instruments that he has used to murder his former wives. Once he is outside, he strolls through a park in a metropolitan setting and tries to pick up a new victim. However, he is rejected by two lesbians, beaten by one woman, and maced by another. Finally, he meets a woman on a bench, who is open to his flirting. They quickly wed, and when Bluebeard brings his new wife to his castle, she reveals herself to be Medusa with green snakes curling on her head. The tables are turned, for she can easily turn him into stone with flashes of lightning from the snakes if he does not obey her every wish. He becomes her servant, and when he is fed up and tries to kill her one night, he is thwarted and thrown out of the castle. In a bar, he meets a chunky man and pours out his sorrows over beer. The man turns out to be a modern-day Cupid and promises to help him. They return to the castle and the plump man undresses; wings sprout from his back; he manages to fly to a branch though overweight; after a few tries he sends an arrow into Medusa's heart. The snakes turn into flowers, and immediately she falls in love with Bluebeard, who wants to kill her with a razor. However, Cupid remembers to shoot him with an arrow, too. Husband and wife are now enchanted with one another and begin to make love in a large bed. All of a sudden, there is a huge cry of pain from Bluebeard, who is pictured in the nude running down a road away from the castle. The last frames show Medusa in the nude looking down at the small green snakes covering her vagina like pubic hairs.

In contrast to Samsonov's "sexist" version of "Bluebeard," Bubnov's film, made about twenty years later, is partial to a feminist interpretation of the world. Perhaps women will not be able to change men or even discover their secret, but they can protect themselves without the help of men. Almost all the comic films in the Bluebeard filmic discourse picture men with contradictions and foibles that puncture their "infallibility" or their representation of intractable power. The comic approach to "Bluebeard" always tends toward representing tyranny as resistible, but the deep roots of serial killing and mass murder are never fully exposed.

Psychopathic Husbands and Terrified Wives

Most filmmakers shy away from depicting the character of Bluebeard as a buffoon and have tried all sorts of ways to alter his story and present him as some kind of psychopath. In particular there were a series of films produced during the 1940s and well into the 1960s that recalled Perrault's "Bluebeard" or referred to the tale directly; they are significant because they seem to have arisen from the social and marital crises caused by World War II. In her significant study, *Secrets Beyond the Door: The Story of Bluebeard and his Wives*, Maria Tatar explains that the marriages of many men and women were upset by the war leading to divorce, separation, and estrangement, if not murder. Consequently, filmmakers used these experiences as the basis of numerous films. The plots generally involved a husband, homecoming hero, or stranger, who seems to be the perfect mate but turns out to be a killer with a mysterious past that haunts him and makes him demented. Trauma is the basis of the drama, and most of the so-called "Bluebeard" films that Tatar discusses are horror films of some kind: Alfred Hitchcock's *Rebecca* (1940), Alfred Hitchcock's *Suspicion* (1941), Alfred Hitchcock's *Shadow of a Doubt* (1943), André de Toth's *Dark Waters* (1944), George Cukor's *Gaslight* (1944), Robert Stevenson's *Jane Eyre* (1944), Alfred Hitchcock's *Spellbound* (1945), Jacques Tourneur's *Experiment Perilous* (1945), Vincente Minnelli's *Undercurrent* (1946), Fritz Lang's *Secret beyond the Door* (1948), and Max Ophüls' *Caught* (1949).

In light of these films Tatar maintains that

Bluebeard films of the 1940s form an extraordinarily intricate cinematic network, taking cues from each other in such obvious ways that they sometimes appear more closely related to each other than to any primal originating narrative. Like the tales in the folkloric sea of stories, they do not really refer to a foundational narrative but participate in what Roland Barthes has called "a serial movement of disconnections, overlappings, variation," revising, adapting, and reimagining the story embedded in previous films. To be sure some of the films nod in the direction of Charles Perrault's "Bluebeard," but most of them seem to be paying homage to a narrative tradition that is in the air, that has circulated in Anglo-American and European cultures as folktale, folk wisdom, children's story, adult melodrama, and song, and that settled into film as a natural resting place."[145]

The difficulty with Tatar's thesis is that any "horror" film that evokes fear and involves a murderous husband from the films of the 1940s to Charles Laughton's *The Night of the Hunter* (1955), Joseph Ruben's *The Stepfather* (1987), William Malone's *House on Haunted Hill* (1999), to a series of domestic violence films in the 1990s such as Robert Iscove's *Shattered Dreams* (1990), Joseph Ruben's *Sleeping with the Enemy* (1991), John Powers' *Fatal Vows* (1994), Karen Arthur's *Dead by Sunset* (1995), William Graham's *Sleeping with the Devil* (1997), and Bethany Rooney's *The Promise* (1999) can be considered a "Bluebeard" type of film. By broadening the category of the Bluebeard cinematic discourse, there is a danger that the problem concerning the mystery of Bluebeard's original sin will become dissipated. Certainly, Perrault's "Bluebeard" touches on crimes such as serial killing and domestic violence that have been haunting us for centuries. But it is also very particular in that the tale demands the investigation of Bluebeard's original sin. It asks and continues to ask in the Bluebeard discourse, what makes a bluebeard tick? It raises the question, as the animated *Very Blue Beard* does, whether there is a bluebeard in every man.

The 1940s did more than produce films about unsettling marriages that alluded to Perrault's "Bluebeard," but they also gave rise to two significant films with a more direct connection to the tale: Edgar Ulmer's *Bluebeard* (1944) and Charlie Chaplin's *Monsieur Verdoux* (1947). Since Chaplin's film also refers to the history of a famous serial killer, Henri Landru, called Bluebeard by the mass media, and generated other films about this serial killer of women, I want to focus first on Ulmer's *Bluebeard* and discuss three other notable films that were intentionally made to comment on Perrault's "Bluebeard": Christian-Jaque's *Bluebeard* (*Blaubart*, 1951), Edward Dmytryk's *Bluebeard* (1972), and Catherine Breillat's *Bluebeard* (*Barbe-bleue*, 2009). Then, I should like to turn to films that link Landru with Bluebeard.

Figure 40
Edgar Ulmer,
Bluebeard

Ulmer's *Bluebeard* was produced just as World War II was coming to an end, and it recalls an ethical problem that began haunting men and would continue to haunt them ever since Perrault wrote his tale: how to maintain godlike power when women seek to be real, equal, and intimate without killing to defend one's illusions. Set in Paris during the nineteenth century, Ulmer's film is a study of a pathological artist named Gaston Morrell. The reason for his demented mind and behavior is, according to him, a woman. Morrell, whose ambition was to become a great painter, had found a sick woman named Jeannette on the streets of Paris, and as he was nursing her back to health, he painted her, and his work became a masterpiece, but when Jeannette recovered and left him, he searched for her, only to discover that she was a prostitute. Morrell thought she had defiled his work, and therefore killed her and sold the painting through a well-known art dealer named Lamarté. Now it is only through killing women that Morrell discovers that he can continue painting extraordinary works and making money through Lamarté. All of Paris is now terrified of Morrell, now known as Bluebeard. However, he falls in love with a young costume maker named Lucille and desperately seeks to mend his ways by not painting her and working primarily as a puppeteer. But Lamarté continues to put pressure on him to paint portraits for profit, and Morrell accidentally murders Lucille's sister while she is working for the police in order to capture the notorious Bluebeard. Lucille bravely seeks him out when she suspects that he has killed her sister, and when he confesses his crimes, he expects her to continue to love him. She is repulsed and is almost murdered. However, the police rescue her, and Morrell drowns in the dark waters of the Seine as he attempts to escape the police.

Ulmer, a Czech director, who had studied under Max Reinhardt in Vienna and also worked under Fritz Murnau and other talented European directors, came to America in the 1930s and quickly made a name for himself as a young director of morality films. Steeped in European culture and influenced by socialist ideas and the New Deal, Ulmer began making all kinds of films about different ethnic groups as well as documentaries, film noir, and morality films. *Bluebeard* was a combination of the morality play with film noir, and it is particularly interesting because Ulmer intended to expose the misogynous nature in men who seem to idealize pure women. Morell appears to be contradictory: a murderer but a haunted romantic artist who, like the hero of E. T. A. Hoffmann's brilliant tale "Madame de Scudèry," which also takes place in Paris, kills to preserve the genuine nature of art and his own soul. But as Erik Ulman points out, Morell's contradictory character is not really contradictory at all because that idealization is only the other side of misogyny, and "Ulmer demonstrates Morell's propensity for murder not only with his normal desires, but with something self-willed in his economic condition as well."[146]

Morell is not a victim of uncontrollable and irrational forces. Rather, he makes choices based on economic profit and kills for profit. While it might be an exaggeration to argue that Ulmer saw in this Bluebeard figure a prototype of the fascist killer, there is no doubt that he abhorred war and the rise of fascism in Europe and spoke out against murder in the name of idealism or any kind of ism. His representation of manhood in the figure of Bluebeard at the close of World War II reflects a condemnation of men who violate women, live for their illusions, and thus represent a danger to civil society. Morell is caught in his fantasies of women—what they should be like, how they should behave.

Morell is not only a painter, but a puppeteer who forgets that pulling the strings of puppets is different from negotiating relations with women. It is because he cannot accept the difference between art and reality that he turns into a pathologic bluebeard, unable to cope with women as real human beings.

In contrast, Christian-Jaque's portrayal of "Bluebeard" recalls the earlier comic work of Méliès, but his film is more a dark comedy. Jaque, whose real name was Christian Maudet, directed some seventy films during his lifetime, among them *Fanfan the Tulip* (1952) with Gerard Philippe and

Babette Goes to War (1959) with Brigitte Bardot, sets his film in the Middle Ages. The Count Amédée de Salfère, otherwise known as Bluebeard, has just become a widow for the sixth time and embarks on a search for his seventh wife. The people in the count's village are terrified because the count is known to be a murderer and a tyrant. Every marriageable girl is hidden from his sight with the exception of Aline, a perky young woman, daughter of the tavern keeper, who has no fear whatsoever and is curious to find out what the count is really like. She breaks away from her boyfriend Giglio, a young blacksmith, attends a ball, charms the count, and weds him. However, she does not consummate the marriage on the wedding night. Instead, she persuades the count to tell her about how he killed his six previous wives and then rocks him to sleep. The next morning the count must follow tradition and ride off on a hunt. While he is gone from the castle, Aline discovers that his six wives are happily living together in a hidden room. When the count returns and realizes that Aline knows that he is not a tyrant and killer, he decides to murder all his wives and begins with Aline. However, before she can be executed, she is rescued by her sister Anne and Giglio. Moreover, some cavaliers are sent by the emperor to arrest the count for the murder of his other six wives. Fortunately, he can prove his innocence and is banished from the realm. Meanwhile Aline is now free to marry Giglio.

Christian-Jaque's film has unfortunately not received the attention from film critics that it deserves, and it may be due to the fact that it is somewhat flippant and does not take Bluebeard seriously as a serial killer. Christian-Jaque made two versions of this film, French and German, and employed two gifted actors in the major role, Pierre Brasseur and Hans Albers. Each plays the count alternatively as buffoon and tyrant. Giglio is depicted as a pouting teenager. Aline performs a striptease to entice the count, and when the count tells six tales about the murders of his six wives, they are enacted with black humor. All the sets are meticulously decorated and filmed with pastel colors that evoke an unreal atmosphere. Nevertheless, Christian-Jaque touches on an important element of Bluebeard's original sin—his power is nothing and based on an idle threat. That is, only after Aline discovers his deception and false claims as murderer does he turn into a bluebeard, ready to murder to conceal his secret. Banishment is Bluebeard's fate, not murder or execution. In true comic tradition, Christian-Jaque proposes that men's brutal tendencies can be resisted.

The possibility of resistance and forgiveness does not exist in Edward Dmytryk's *Bluebeard* (1972), a film so stupid, ridiculous, and insulting that it cannot even be designated as "camp." In a pithy review of the film, Chris Kirkham writes,

> An odd duck of a movie, *Bluebeard* doesn't fit neatly into any one cinematic category. It isn't a horror film, although there are certain horror elements in it. It's not a comedy, black, bedroom or otherwise. It doesn't even quite qualify as exploitation, although there's plenty of skin to be sure. If forced to do so, the best three word description I could come with would be "fantasy suspense misfire."[147]

The grim, stoic Bluebeard, played by the illustrious British actor Richard Burton, is Baron von Sepper, an Austrian aristocrat and ex-World War I flying ace, whose face was burned in a crash, and thus he sports a strange blue beard. Moreover, he may have lost more than skin in the crash because he is clearly impotent, something we learn later during the course of action in the film. Most of the events take place near his castle during the 1930s, when he has become a ruthless fascist leader of some kind. (Curiously Dmytryk has the Baron and his friends don black uniforms and wear armbands with symbols that seem to be the swastika but are some other insignia.) Flashbacks enable us to see how he destroyed Jewish homes and businesses and how afterward he is pursued by a Jewish violinist whose family he had destroyed. But the film centers on his relationship with his seventh wife, a spritely American dancer and singer, who discovers the Baron's former wives frozen in a secret chamber, while he is absent from the castle. Of course, he returns and catches her. But she is clever and pretends to be concerned and caring and convinces him to tell her what happened to the other six wives. (This ploy may have been borrowed from Christian-Jaque's film with which Dmytryk was probably familiar.) What follows are six ludicrous flashbacks in which six international actresses, Raquel Welch, Virna Lisi, Nathalie Delon, Marilù Tolo, Karin Schubert, and Agostina Belli, known for their sex appeal, are murdered by the Baron in comically horrific ways: they are shot, guillotined, stabbed by the tusk of a rhinoceros, clawed to death by a falcon either because they ridiculed him or betrayed him. For instance one of his wives is kinky and has sex with another woman. All the sex scenes are gratuitous exploitation of the star actresses, obviously to guarantee the film some commercial success. Predictably, after the Baron tells these ghastly revolting tales, he is killed by the Jewish violinist, who also rescues Anne from the refrigerated chamber in which she would have died.

Dmytryk had been blacklisted in the 1940s as one of the famous Hollywood Ten and had emigrated for a short time to England. Then he returned to America in 1951, only to reveal the names of members of left-wing groups in Hollywood so he could work there again, and he obviously intended this film to be taken seriously. Also, at the beginning of the 1970s, he probably wanted to make some kind of statement about women's liberation and the threat it posed to seemingly potent men. It is insulting, however, that he transformed Bluebeard into an impotent "Nazi" and implied that fascism can somehow be connected to male impotency and impotent men can be held responsible for the Holocaust. As Klaus Theweleit has demonstrated in his significant study, *Male Fantasies*, the psychological problems of men who fought for Nazi Germany are much more complex and are connected to an idealization of a particular female type that had to be protected, saved, and kept pure at all costs. Nevertheless, Dmytryk's film does reveal how male fantasies about women have been troubled by women who question how men imagine them and want to control them. Relations between men and women have been undergoing major shifts in the last sixty years, and while masculine domination remains a key factor in most western societies, the rumbling of feminist resistance can be detected in all force fields of cultural production.

In the fairy-tale discourse about "Bluebeard," Angela Carter marked a major shift in the title tale of her collection of provocative tales, "Bloody Chamber" (1978), in which a stalwart mother arrives in the nick of time to shoot a lascivious count dead before he can murder her daughter. It has taken thirty years for a filmmaker to follow in her footsteps, but it has been inevitable, given the changes that the feminist movement has brought about during this time. In this case, the *provocatrice* is the French filmmaker, Catherine Breillat, who produced her film *Bluebeard* (*Barbe-bleue*) for French television in 2008.

Breillat sets her unusual adaptation of Perrault's narrative some time during the 1950s in France and uses a complex narrative frame to offer two re-tellings of "Bluebeard" at the same time. Two girls of about six and ten, Catherine and Marie-Anne, are depicted playing in an attic, and the younger of the two, Catherine, rebellious and plucky, seeks to frighten her sister as she reads the tale of Bluebeard to her. While they are engaged in the reading and often debate the meaning of Catherine's reading, which is *not* based on Perrault's text, the scene shifts back and forth to seventeenth-century France, exactly when Perrault wrote his story, and Catherine weaves a tale about two adolescent sisters who are thrown upon hard times when their father dies. They are compelled to leave a private convent school, and since they have no dowry, Marie-Catherine, who resembles the contemporary Catherine in character, decides to marry a nobleman named Bluebeard, despite the fact that several of his previous wives have mysteriously disappeared. For his part, Bluebeard, who acts like a gentle ogre, is impressed by the pert Marie-Catherine and is enticed by her honesty and innocence. Once they marry, he apparently wants to trust her and teach her about plants and the stars. At one point he leaves and gives her the keys to all the rooms without restricting her. She senses that she has control of him and always gets her way. After he returns, he leaves again, but this time he gives her a small golden key and tells her not to enter a small chamber. This will be a major test. In the meantime, the two "contemporary" sisters have been fighting about the telling of "Bluebeard," and the older sister, Marie-Anne, does not want to listen and calls her young sister weird. Their interaction is projected into the seventeenth-century revision and projection by Catherine. There, the young wife cannot control her curiosity, and when she enters the chamber, she finds the dead bodies of Bluebeard's former wives and walks on the blood-stained floor. What is significant about this scene is that the image of Marie-Catherine is transformed into the image of the girl reading the fairy tale until Bluebeard returns home and discovers her "betrayal." He blithely expects her to accept her death sentence even when she asks for pity. Instead of killing her right away, he hesitates and allows her to play psychological games with him to stall and wait for the musketeers to arrive. Indeed, Marie-Catherine proves to be more than his match, and it is Bluebeard who loses his head. There is horror in the suspense. At the same time, as little Catherine is reading the final terrifying scene, her older sister Marie-Anne is petrified and does not want to listen. She backs away from Catherine, who moves toward her until Marie-Anne falls to her death through an open hatch in the attic and lies on the floor beneath. Their mother arrives and seems strangely unaware of her older daughter's death, even though she stands directly above the girl's body. The final shot of the film returns to the seventeenth century with the elegantly dressed and somber Marie-Catherine portrayed stroking the head of Bluebeard on a platter as if he were a piece of fruit in a bowl in a classical oil painting.

The interplay between the 1950s and the 1690s involves a critique of both periods in which women were deprived of their rights. And perhaps Breillat is inferring that young women are still threatened by bluebeards. But Breillat's focus is more on the two sisters, especially Marie-Catherine/Catherine, and the double narrative than it is on Bluebeard and his original sin. For Breillat, the "original sin," if there is one, concerns the fragile and strong female psyches and competitive sisters. Her ambivalent heroine in both stories is a defiant young female, who takes charge of her own destiny. She is not necessarily vicious but cunning and assertive. Though she loves her older sister, she is also so competitive that she will stop at nothing to gain her way. Accidents may happen, but a young girl must learn to seize the opportunity. If men are ogres and brutal, there appears to be no way but to use their violence psychologically and physically against them. This is a disturbing choice, but Breillat implies that men have been disturbing women's lives for hundreds of years, and violent resistance may be the only answer to male domination, especially when men show no remorse.

From Bluebeard to Landru

The history of Henri Landru, a notorious French bluebeard, may serve as a case in point for Breillat, for he remained an unrepentant killer of women until his execution in 1922. Born in Paris in 1869, Landru joined the French army in 1887 after graduating from high school. Upon leaving the army in 1891, he had an affair with a cousin, who gave birth to a daughter, but he did not marry her. Instead he wed another woman named Remy with whom he had four children. By this time he was working in a small business and was cheated by his employer. Landru was supposedly so angered by being cheated that he decided to become a swindler himself. However, he was caught by the police in 1900 and served two years in prison. Once released, he continued to swindle in many different ways and eventually became rich by placing personal ads in the lonely hearts section of newspapers enticing rich widows with a promise of eventual marriage. His ads during World War I were particularly effective because many women had lost their husbands in battle and sought new husbands. He would put on a show for these widows by inviting them to his luxurious villa and seducing them. After he married them, he would either strangle or stab them to death and then burn their bodies in an oven. Landru, who also had well over 200 mistresses, killed at least twelve women between 1914 and 1919 and escaped the police by using many different aliases. However, the sister of one of his victims eventually discovered him and brought charges of embezzlement. Though there were no bodies to be found, the police investigating the frauds found evidence enough to convict him of murdering eleven women. He denied the charges but was convicted of murder in November of 1921 and guillotined in February of 1922.

As soon as he was executed Hans Otto (Löwenstein), the talented Austrian director, made a feature film about him in 1922 with the title *Landru, der Blaubart von Paris* (*Landru the Bluebeard of Paris*). Unfortunately, the film tends to be overly didactic and was produced to educate audiences about the vices of con men. Otto did not shy away from blood and gore in depicting Landru's murders—women were chopped up and stuck in stoves. At least Otto had his Bluebeard repent his crimes. What is significant about the film is the immediate identification of Landru with Bluebeard and the audience interest in a bloodthirsty killer, mainly interested in murdering wives for their money.

The association of Landru with Bluebeard in the cinematic film discourse has not abated. Several films about Landru as special type of Bluebeard have been produced since 1922: Charlie Chaplin's *Monsieur Verdoux* (1947), W. Lee Wilder's *Bluebeard's Ten Honeymoons* (1960), Claude Chabrol's *Landrou* (1963), also known as *Bluebeard*, Juan José Gurrola's *Landru* (1973), and Pierre Boutron's *Désiré Landru* (2005). By far the two most significant films are those by Chaplin and Chabrol, and each director takes a different view of Landru's lack of remorse.

Chaplin's brilliant dark comedy *Monsieur Verdoux* cynically suggests that society is more a danger to humankind than men are to society, and there is no reason for Verdoux, the Landru character, to repent his crimes. In fact, this film is highly relevant today because it concerns a man, who is "stiffed" and resigns himself to the overwhelming economic and military forces that are about to bring about the mass murders of World War II. On trial for having murdered over twelve women, Monsieur Verdoux bitterly defends himself by explaining that he was only carrying on the same ruthless business that individual corporations constantly conduct en masse and that in comparison with the contemporary world which is "building weapons of mass destruction for the sole purpose of mass killing," he is only an amateur.

Chaplin made this film in 1946 after the atomic bombs had been dropped in Nagasaki and Hiroshima and during the hearings of the House Committee on Un-American Activities. In fact, he

Figure 41
Charlie Chaplin,
Monsieur Verdoux

purposely had one of the first showings of the film in 1947 take place in Washington DC to stir controversy and to support one of his friends, the communist musician, Hanns Eisler, who was about to be deported from the United States. The film makes a blunt didactic statement to support freedom of speech and small people exploited by the government and big business, and thus it was banned in many states and received an unjust if not hypocritical treatment by the press.

Chaplin set the film in Paris right after the Great Depression, and it begins in a cemetery. In the first frame the camera glides by the gravestone of Henri Verdoux, born 1880, died 1937, and it is his voice that we hear, explaining that he had once been an honest bank clerk, who had worked hard for thirty years, until he was suddenly fired by the bank in 1930 soon after the Depression started. To support his invalid wife and young son, he tells us, he had to go into business by killing wealthy women, but he ironically adds that the career of a bluebeard is not profitable, and he proceeds to narrate his history to demonstrate why he failed in his business. The very next clip shifts to the crude, somewhat revolting members of the Corvais family in the North of France who argue about what they should do about their missing sister Thelma. Though they are concerned that her new husband is a gold-digger and might have harmed her, they are obviously vulgar people and represent the greedy merchants who are part of what is wrong in society. Right after we are introduced to them, we are brought to the South of France, where Monsieur Verdoux is in a luscious flower garden clipping roses. Just as he has finished, he almost steps on a caterpillar, but he daintily avoids it and places it in a safe place. As he enters his villa, there is black smoke coming from an outside incinerator, and we can easily surmise what has happened to poor Thelma. Though Monsieur Verdoux appears to be a refined, gracious, and amiable man, he is only playing a role to conceal the ferocious anger that has driven him to become a serial killer.

Chaplin makes no excuse for Verdoux. This is not a film that justifies male brutality toward women. Rather, it is a film about a man who has lost his identity as an honest worker and falls in and out of his role as a misfit murderer, who eventually—after his wife and son die—abandons the business of murdering because he doesn't see how anyone can set a moral "example in these immoral times," as he himself puts it. What makes this film so exceptionally poignant is that Verdoux is depicted clearly as a cog in the wheel of an economy and society that drive people to death, while the comic touches and interludes reveal the touching human side of Verdoux that he cannot help but express. Not only does he stumble about as he woos and kills his wives, plays the stock market, races by train from place to place to expedite his calculating plans, but he also visits his invalid wife and son, helps poor animals, and takes in a young woman in distress, who ironically marries a munitions manufacturer by the end of the film. If Verdoux has a secret he does not keep it from himself, nor can he keep it from others. He is the shafted man, the man who has no power, and he does not attribute his loss to women. They are unfortunately easy victims, objectified and convertible. Even here, the women are not simply passive and obedient but represent different types like the outrageous Annabella Bonheur and dignified Mme Grogney, whom Verdoux fails to trap.

In the end it is Verdoux who is trapped. But stripped of his disguises, he becomes more noble than ever before, and in the last frame we watch as Verdoux walks toward the guillotine and recalls the figure of Chaplin's tramp, defeated but aware of what the forces are that have taken away his integrity.

Claude Chabrol was very familiar with Chaplin's Verdoux and his fate, and thus his decision to make an entirely different film in 1963 about the historical Landru was somewhat of a corrective to Chaplin's portrait—and it was perhaps a bitter reflection of what was occurring to the image of men in France in the 1960s. Instead of portraying Landru as a philosophical murderer, Chabrol depicted him as merciless trickster, who supports a nasty family that he detests as much as they despise him. Instead of using the Great Depression as his backdrop, Chabrol has the action take place during World War I, when the real Landru committed most of his crimes.

Figure 42
Claude Chabrol,
Landrou

Chabrol has stated that he doesn't

like stories which attempt to demythify a myth. But Landru . . . is he a myth or is he a man? A man transformed into a myth. So when one makes a film about Landru does one transform the myth into a man, or must one transform the man into myth? That's the question! So there are both in this film. For the first time in world cinema, we see before our very eyes the metamorphosis from man into myth![148]

The difficulty is that Chabrol is unable to capture the personality of Landru or the compelling motives for his gruesome acts. As we know, Landru was a common crook, who evaded the police in 1914 and went on to murder over twelve women. Chabrol shows how he would place ads in the personal sections of newspapers, lure wealthy middle-aged women to a villa, kill them, chop their bodies into pieces, and then burn them. As his crimes became known between 1914 and 1919, Chabrol interweaves shots of the battlefields and unpleasant visits that Landru made to his family. In the meantime the mass media made him into a mass murderer and bestowed the name of Bluebeard upon him. However, after he is arrested and put on trial, Landru insists that he is innocent and not a pathological killer. He shows no remorse for his crimes and goes to the guillotine in February of 1922.

If there is a value to Chabrol's film, it resides in his resistance to portray Landru as a "mythic" and compelling figure, something that Chaplin's film tends to do. Chabrol's Landru is banal. He kills solely for money and for survival. He is petty and unlikable, never concerned about other people, the war, or the immorality of his acts. He is a non-reflective man, who does not bother himself to probe the meaning his vicious acts and clings to his secret even when it is exposed. It is this intransigent position, the murderer who believes that he has not murdered and maintains an illusion of innocence, that is most frightening in this film and most frightening in general when one thinks of leading politicians throughout the world, who foster war crimes while pleading innocence. Chaplin put his finger on Bluebeard's original sin when he linked the personal to the political.

9

The Triumph of the Underdog: Cinderella's Legacy

Cinderella has come a long way—from riches to ashes to riches and a marriage to a charming prince in his magnificent palace. Who would have thought that this abused young woman, orphaned by her mother and abandoned by her father, would have had a chance against a vicious and conniving stepmother and two spiteful stepsisters? But fortune has always been on her side throughout history, and it has taken various forms: a fairy godmother, her reincarnated mother in the form of helpful animals and birds, magic plants, and helpful men. And she has also been driven by her own indomitable spirit and desire to claim her rightful place in the world. Though she has often been portrayed as meek mouse, she is not a wimp. Cinderella is a survivor par excellence, and she has assumed various guises from persecuted stepdaughter to feisty orphan and underdog. Indeed, there is a multitude of "Cinderella" types, and this makes it extremely difficult to explore the filmic discourse about her tale of woe and happiness, for it is not based on one or even two hypotexts.

"Cinderella" is probably the most popular fairy tale in the world. There are thousands of oral and literary versions. Indications are that the tale may have originated in ancient China or Egypt. The shoe or slipper test may have been connected to a marriage custom in which the bridegroom takes off the bride's old shoes and replaces them with new ones. But this thesis has never been completely verified, and depending on the society and customs, shoes are used in many different ways in marriage celebrations and tests to determine authenticity. In the various literary and oral versions the shoes are leather, gold, silver, and glass. Charles Perrault invented the glass slippers in 1696 most likely as an ironic joke since a glass slipper was likely to break if it were to fall off a foot. What most of the tales, oral and literary, have in common is the conflict between a young girl and her step-mother and siblings about her legacy. Cinderella must prove that she is the rightful successor in a house in which she has been deprived of her rights. She is to be tested in a kind of initiation ritual common to many cultures as Vladimir Propp has explained in his posthumously published book, *The Russian Folktale*.[149] She receives help from her dead mother in the guise of doves, fairies, and godmothers. Belief in the regeneration of the dead who can help the living in the form of plants or animals underlies one of the key motifs of the fairy tale. In the European literary tradition, which first began with Bonaventure des Périers' *Les Nouvelles Recréations et Joyeux Devis* (*New Recreations and Joyous Games*, 1558), it is clear that Giambattista Basile's "Cat Cinderella" (1634) played a role in influencing Charles Perrault's "Cinderella, or The Glass Slipper" (1697) and Marie-Catherine d'Aulnoy's "Finette Cendron" (1697). They, in turn, had some effect on the Grimms' "Cinderella" of 1812 as did Basile. Significant in Basile's tale is the active role that Cinderella plays in determining her future: she kills her first stepmother (only to be exploited by her second one) and stops her father's ship from returning from Sardinia. Some of this activism, in contrast to Perrault's narrative, can be seen in the Grimm brothers' version of 1812.

Since there were so many different versions by the time the Grimms composed their "Cinderella" —for instance, they may have also been influenced by the Bohemian version "Laskopal und Miliwaka" in *Sagen der Böhmischen Vorzeit aus einigen Gegenden alter Schlösser und Dörfer* (*Legends of the Bohemian Early Period from some Regions of old Castles and Villages,* 1808)—it is difficult to establish one source for their work in particular. Clearly, many different literary and oral tales fostered a huge Cinderella cycle in the East and the West. Alan Dundes' *Cinderella: A Folklore Casebook* (1982)[150] provides valuable background information and discussions about the cycle and different interpretations. The early literary work of Basile, d'Aulnoy, Perrault, and the Grimms certainly played a role in the creation of nineteenth-century plays and musical adaptations such as Nicolas Isouard's popular fairy opera *Cendrillon* (1810), as well as in the equally successful operas *La cenerentola* (1817) by Gioacchino Rossini and Jules Massent's *Cendrillon* (1894), not to mention the various vaudeville and melodramatic *féerie* adaptations and children's plays produced during the nineteenth century.

The cinematic discourse of "Cinderella" was closely connected to the theater and to the texts of Perrault and Grimm, sometimes an amalgamation of Perrault and Grimm. Perrault's tale begins:

> Once upon a time there was a gentleman who took the haughtiest and proudest woman in the world for his second wife. She had two daughters with the same temperament and the exact same appearance. On the other hand, the husband had a daughter whose gentleness and goodness were without parallel. She got this from her mother, who had been the best person in the world.[151]

The Grimms' tale begins:

> The wife of a rich man fell ill, and as she felt her end approaching, she called her only daughter to her bedside and said, "Dear child, be good and pious. Then the dear Lord shall always assist you, and I shall look down from heaven, and take care of you." She then closed her eyes and departed.[152]

Perrault endows his heroine with innate qualities while the Grimms' young girl must earn these qualities. They are both well-born, that is, they come from well-to-do homes. Perrault makes no reference to a god, while the Grimms have "Christianized" a secular tale that had no reference to a "dear Lord" in their own original manuscript. Whatever the case may be, both tales enter the civilizing process of Europe to set a model of comportment: girls are to be gentle, pious, and good, and their beauty and happiness depend on their spiritual qualities. Though they are not total orphans, they become complete orphans due to the ineptitude of their fathers or their unwillingness to protect their biological daughters. As a result the Cinderellas of Perrault and the Grimms are viciously treated and brutally attacked by their stepmothers and stepsisters. The only defense of these poor rich girls is their virtuous behavior, patience, and tenacity. Ultimately, they are rewarded by a higher power, and they *regain* their status in life through marriage to a prince. Neither the Perrault tale nor the Grimms' tale is a rags to riches story. Both belong to the category of didactic and moralistic fairy-tale exemplars that set models for girls of the upper class who need to show off their beauty and docility to win the appropriate mate.

The fairy-tale films of the twentieth century seek to alter the narrative while following the traditional patriarchal narrative. That is, most of them discard fathers who enable their second wives to maltreat a stepdaughter; most of them omit the fact that Cinderella was born into a well-to-do family; most of them dispense with religious connotations. They patch up the narrative in response to the changing role of women, but they still insist that Cinderella use her talents and beauty in a public spectacle so that she can impress a young man and wed him. The major shift in the majority of the films beginning with Georges Méliès' two versions in 1899 and 1912 is to create an underdog survivor, whose kind demeanor attracts a fairy, who intervenes in her behalf so that she can move away from her persecutors to marry a rich man. The other tendency is to create a savvy heroine who outwits her stepmother and stepsisters and determines her own fate without the help of some higher power. At the bottom of the conflict in most of the films is the unspoken biological disposition of parents to devote more time, emotion, and attention to promote their own offspring rather than care for their non-biological children, and this disposition, common throughout the world, explains the popularity of the tale, and it helps explain the competition among siblings who are not born of the same parents. In this regard, the morality of the Cinderella films, that is, the triumph of the *good* Cinderella, is designed to demonstrate in its narrative how a child, who has the odds stacked against her, must develop strategies for dealing with the brutal treatment by stepmothers and stepsisters, who test her. Her magnanimous triumph at the end of her predictable rise to fortune does not put an end to the real social problem of unjust discrimination, but films, just like their literary and theatrical forbears, can pose alternatives to object relations in families that no longer resemble the so-called norm of the bourgeois nuclear family. Put another way, many films propose that discrimination that stems from social and biological forces can be cured by culture or cultivated differently in the civilizing process.

Since there were well over 130 different kinds of Cinderella films made during the twentieth and early part of the twenty-first centuries, it would take a book to examine how the cinematic Cinderella discourse has developed. Consequently, I want to examine mainly those films that have "punctuated" the discourse in original and innovative ways and shed light on how and why the narratives that stem largely from Perrault and the Grimms have been transformed in response to cultural changes, especially in light of gender formation and family conflict. For the most part, the transformations tend to be modern remakes with a faux feminist touch. I shall begin first by discussing a few silent films, followed by an analysis of cartoons, musicals, and live-action films.

Melodramatic and Modern Cinderellas

As I have already discussed in the chapter on Georges Méliès, he was the first to adapt "Cinderella" in two different cinematic versions in 1899 and 1912. Neither film is exceptional with regard to transforming the Perrault narrative, but each demonstrates particular tendencies that become clearer in most of the silent film versions of "Cinderella." In both of Méliès' films, the father is totally eliminated from the plot, and the girl's true test is whether she will live up to the fairy's expectations, overcome the oppression that she suffers, and find some kind of happiness. She is not taunted by her stepsisters in Méliès' 1899 film; only in the second film is she slapped and maltreated. The setting is more nineteenth century than it is seventeenth in both films, and they also feature love at first sight and a lost slipper followed by a slipper test. The character of the prince plays a negligible role. Though there are delightful comic antics in the first film, Méliès was more interested in creating a melodrama in both films that was to move viewers to shed a few tears for the persecuted heroine and to smile when she triumphed in a grand finale. Méliès was too fixated on recapturing the traditional Cinderella story in hyperbolic form with his usual antics of sexy women and mischievous imps to explore deeper meanings in the story.

It is this emphasis on melodrama that marks almost all of the Cinderella silent films that followed Méliès' productions. For instance, one of the notable early films, James Kirkwood's *Cinderella*

(1914), starring the great actress Mary Pickford, strengthens the plot by emphasizing the moral goodness of Cinderella in an overly didactic way. In the initial scene, the stepmother and step-daughter refuse to give alms to a poor old woman (who incidentally is dressed in black and resembles a witch) outside their mansion. Soon after, the sweet Cinderella appears and provides the old woman with something to eat. All at once, the woman turns into a tall, beautiful fairy who will protect Cinderella throughout the film. Soon after, Cinderella, dressed in elegant rags and high heels, meets the prince by chance while she is gathering wood in a forest. They fall in love, but they must separate. He returns to his castle, she, to her large mansion where she is mercilessly mal-treated by her stepmother and stepsisters. Little does she know, however, that she has won the favor of the fairy godmother, who continues to help her at crucial times without making herself visible. Cinderella also continues to show her pious nature by praying and turning the other cheek. When a ball is organized by the prince to find a wife, Cinderella is, of course, cruelly prevented from attending. In a comic scene, the stepsisters see a fortune teller, who announces that one member of the family will marry the prince, and they mistakenly believe it will be one of them. After they depart for the ball, Cinderella is surprised by the visit of the fairy godmother, and the plot basically follows the Perrault script. At the end, when Cinderella, despite being a poor maid, wins the prince, he tells her that he would like to behead her stepsisters, but Cinderella rejects the idea. Then, the fairy appears to bless her and her prince.

Kirkwood tries to remain true to the spirit of the Perrault text, and thanks to the length of the film (fifty-two minutes), he can expand the love story and exaggerate the trials and tribulations of his heroine. Typically, she is the kind and dutiful orphan, whose pure soul glimmers through her rags. Both the fairy and the prince recognize this purity, and Cinderella, as the good, untarnished virgin, is blessed for more or less *not* speaking out against her victimizers. But, in 1914, times were about to change, and a new woman was on the horizon.

Aside from the usual melodramatic representations of the Perrault text in the silent-film era, there were also several films with the same title that indicated the representation of a different Cinderella: Percy Stowe, *A Modern Cinderella* (1908), J. Stuart Blackton, *A Modern Cinderella* (1910), J. Searle Dawley, *A Modern Cinderella* (1911), Eleuterio Rodolfi, *A Modern Cinderella* (1913), and John Adolfi, *A Modern Cinderella* (1917). There were also others such as C. J. Williams's *A Reluctant Cinderella* (1913), Sidney Morgan's *A Lowland Cinderella* (1922), and John Daumery's *Naughty Cinderella* (1933). They all served notice that women were coming into their own and becoming more independent thanks to the suffragette movement, World War I, and the modern industrial transformation that opened up new opportunities for women in the work force, including Hollywood itself. Cinderella began to take destiny in her own hands, and only here and there did she need a little help from friends.

One of the most interesting films during this period was *Ella Cinders* (1926) directed by Alfred Green and starring Colleen Moore and Lloyd Hughes. The film was based on a syndicated comic strip written by Bill Conselman and drawn by Charles Plumb that originated in 1925 and ended in 1961. It featured a wide-eyed pert girl with black hair in a dutch-bob haircut named Ella, who must carry out all the housework in a dysfunctional family run by the tyrannical Myrtle "Ma" Cinders and her two nasty daughters, Lotta and Prissy Pill. Though not beautiful, Ella wins a beauty contest, and the prize enables her to leave the small town of Roseville with her kid brother Blackie and head for Hollywood, where she discovers that the film company which had sponsored the contest no longer existed. However, she stays in Hollywood and endeavors to make a name for herself during the next thirty-five years in all sorts of comic-strip adventures in the West and a marriage to a young man named Patches, who has his own sort of amusing experiences. In the process of producing a comic strip over years, the core Cinderella story was dropped in favor of a series of brief tales depicting a smart young woman who would fall into and out of trouble.

In contrast, Green's *Ella Cinders* retains the core Cinderella plot transformed into an exceptional farce that focuses on class differences and reinforces the personality of Ella as a young woman with determination, a great sense of humor, and pride. Green discards the brother as best friend in favor of Waite Lifter, who is a handsome iceman/fairy godfather. Although Ella knows how to fend for herself, she does need some protection and encouragement from Waite to enter the beauty contest. When she must submit a picture to the judges, her photographer submits one in which she makes a funny face. The reason she wins the contest is because the down-to-earth judges value personality and humor above beauty. They are also apparently critical of the pretentious class climbers represented by Ma Cinders and her daughters. There is no love lost between Ella and her stepmother and stepsisters. They do not part on good terms. But it is clear that she and Waite are in love with each other as he drives her to the train station and she departs for Hollywood. Shortly thereafter, we learn that Waite is actually from a very rich family and the star of the Illinois football team. He rebels against his father and follows Ella to Hollywood, where we see her sneaking into a Hollywood film studio, determined to become a star even though she has no connections. In an amusing scene in which she busts through the gates of a studio and interrupts the shooting of a film, Ella shows her acting talent and becomes a "discovered" young star. In another amusing scene, Waite arrives to rescue her from what he thinks is her impoverished existence, and he, too, interrupts the shooting of a scene to propose to her.

There are no miraculous transformations in this fairy-tale film. Instead, we have fortunate accidents that enable a young woman from the lower classes to discover her profession and to find a young man who accepts her for what she is: frank, funny, forceful, and talented. It is true that she abandons acting for marriage and a family, but she makes the decision to follow her heart. The "modernization" of Perrault's tale and the adaptation of the comic strip are effective. Green does not dabble in melodrama. The action combines elements of Méliès' burlesque humor with a touch of Chaplinesque comedy, especially when the gifted actress Colleen Moore makes faces at the camera. Indeed, she brought a new face to Cinderella.

As I have already mentioned, there were other silent films that "modernized" Cinderella. Two others of note are Herbert Brenon's *A Kiss for Cinderella* (1925) and King Vidor's *The Patsy* (1928). Though Brenon's film does not depict a "new woman," his film, based on J. M. Barrie's play, does feature a servant maid who realizes her dreams of becoming Cinderella in war-time London. In King Vidor's comedy, based on a play written by Barry Conners, Patsy, played by the famous actress Marion Davies, is the younger mistreated daughter, who must do all the chores in the house, even though her father favors her. She is in love with her older spoiled sister's boyfriend, and eventually, after the boyfriend gives her advice on how to catch a man, she catches him. Vidor does not bother following the plot of any traditional Cinderella story. For him, as for many other filmmakers from the 1930s onward, the association of a disowned, downtrodden, maltreated lower-class female (and sometimes male) was enough to recall the Cinderella fairy tale. The traditional plot would be stretched out of shape, but not entirely. It was up to the cartoons to challenge and distort the conventional narrative, and they began doing this in the 1920s.

Unfettered Cinderellas

While it is true that live-action silent films were the first to introduce Cinderellas with new faces and personalities, the cartoons kept pace and were quick to let her take away her bonds and reveal herself/himself in preposterous and provocative ways. Three early animated films indicate that the traditional manner of telling the "Cinderella" story had to be challenged: Bud Fisher's *A Kick for Cinderella* (1924), Lotte Reiniger's *Aschenputtel* (*Cinderella*, 1922), and Walt Disney's *Cinderella* (1922). All three films are exceptional experiments and twist and turn the plot of the traditional fairy

Figure 43
Bud Fisher,
A Kick For Cinderella

tale in original ways. Fisher's film is based on the comic strip characters of Mutt and Jeff. The tall Mutt decides to give a Charleston exhibition and leaves the desolate Jeff at home before a fireplace. As he weeps, a fairy appears and gives him magic slippers and a limousine that drives through the wall of the house to take him to the dance hall. He is warned that he must return by midnight. Once he appears, he dances solo and outdoes Mutt, who had made a grand impression on the audience. As he is showing off, however, Mutt ties his coat tails to a large plant, and Jeff sees the clock about to strike twelve. He springs onto the clock and struggles to prevent it from moving. He loses, and he also loses his clothes to his embarrassment. Then, all at once, he is struggling with a pillow in front of the fireplace. He had been dreaming, and Jeff appears to call him a sap!

Not only is the cartoon unusual because the main character is a male, but also because it ends abruptly with a disappointed "Cinderella man," who does not realize his dreams. And there is certainly no marriage on the horizon. Unlike many early cartoons, there are no chase scenes. The adroitly drawn characters dance in a delightful way, and their facial expressions reveal their jealousy and competitive spirits. However, Fisher's film pales when compared with Lotte Reiniger's silhouette animation. She based her film on an adaptation of the Grimms' fairy tale, and the black-and-white figures are all uniquely cut to express the personalities of the figures. The film plays upon the motif of cutting, "snip snap," and Reiniger introduces an estrangement effect by having the scissors first cut the figures before they are animated. The screen is predominantly black with white boxes opening as if they were stages to reveal the story of Cinderella with a touch of humor. The fat stepmother and the spindly stepsisters are comic figures while Cinderella is shaped as a noble, graceful character. Reiniger eliminates the father figure and gives the doves a major role in helping Cinderella. At the ball the prince is so much in love with Cinderella that he kisses her, falls on his knees, and proposes to her. However, she must flee in her coach that shrinks when she arrives at the tree where her mother is buried. The prince follows but does not recognize her. When he returns to the palace, he sends out some droll messengers who fail to do anything. So, the prince returns to Cinderella's house, where the sisters cut off parts of their feet to fit the slipper. In the end, Cinderella triumphs, and the stepmother is so distraught and angry that she splits herself in half.

Reiniger's humor was always subtle, just as her Cinderella is silently and gracefully strong. In contrast, Disney's reworking of "Cinderella" is raucous and delirious. He sets his story in America of the 1920s and quickly introduces the characters in different contexts. For example, Cinderella works in the kitchen with her only friend, her cat. Incidentally, Disney's major characters, Cinderella, the cat, the dog, the prince, and the king, had already been drawn with more or less the same traits in his remarkable *Puss in Boots* of 1922. The difference here is that the prince is much more active and has a dog as a friend, not a cat. He is first pictured on his horse hunting a bear. To show his mock heroism, Disney has him gallop to a cave where the bears had merrily been playing music, and the prince manages to capture them all and drag them back to his palace. Next we are informed that there will be a ball on Friday the 13th. In another comic scene in the kitchen, a fairy godmother who looks more like a witch than a fairy appears and provides Cinderella with a dress and a limousine driven by her cat. She appears at the ball dressed as a flapper, and the prince immediately falls in love with her. The bearded king dressed in shorts and a gown approves. (He had been the tyrannical villain in *Puss in Boots*.) In addition, the dog falls in love with Cinderella's cat and dances with her. As usual, Cinderella must flee at midnight, and as usual the prince discovers who she is and embraces her in the end. Of course, the dog also embraces the cat. Disney's upbeat film that favors the underdog was characteristic of all his early cartoons and later feature animation films. Here the modern Cinderella is confident that she will win the prince, and the storyline does not disappoint her expectations or those of the viewers.

In Dave Fleischer's *Poor Cinderella* of 1934, the expectations are also fulfilled but gently mocked at the same time. Betty Boop stars in this film and begins by singing a sweet melodramatic song that will be repeated throughout the cartoon:

> I'm just a poor Cinderella.
> Nobody loves me it seems.
> And as I am the poor Cinderella,
> I find my romance in dreams,
> for that's where I meet my prince charming.
> I'm just a poor Cinderella,
> but I'll be a princess some day.

Since Betty, who is not very sexy or provocative in this film due to a more vigorous enforcement of censorship, is the star of the film, there is no mean stepmother, nor do the nasty stepsisters play a role. A charming blue fairy sets her on her way. Her horses sing her theme song. Cupid must hit the prince over the head with a hammer. Betty's foot glides into the lost slipper and she is driven off in a coach with a "just married" sign.

This whimsical cartoon is untypical of the more provocative cartoons that deliberate the fate of Cinderella. In the Terrytoon production of *The Glass Slipper* (1938), the film begins with Cinderella speaking on a phone with a New York accent to her friend Sadie. Dressed in rags, Cinderella recounts how a fairy dressed like the sexy Mae West appeared and sent her to the prince's ball in royal clothes. The people at the ball are dancing to jazz music. The prince resembles a clown and gallops to Cinderella. In the end, when he goes searching for the young woman whose foot will fit the slipper, he visits Sadie, who hangs up the phone expecting to become a princess. However, the fairy Mae West appears and steals the prince concluding the film with her famous line: "I always get my man."

The explosion of audience expectations—always a critique of sentimental love—is characteristic of two cartoons directed by Tex Avery: *Cinderella Meets Fella* (1938) and *Swing Shift Cinderella* (1945). Both films show Avery at his controversial best. In *Cinderella Meets Fella*, he depicts the heroine alone as a tiny doll-like creature dressed in rags. When the clock strikes nine, she becomes irate, picks up the phone, and yells at the police in a harsh voice to go and search for her fairy godmother, who is late for their appointment. The police pick her up. She is drunk and makes

Figure 44
Dave Fleischer,
Poor Cinderella

mistakes when she uses her magic wand. Cinderella, now in an elegant gown, must drive to the ball in a western coach driven by a cowboy. The prince turns out to be the tipsy Egghead, who appears in other Avery cartoons. They dance to an overly sentimental tune of "Boy Meets Girl," and as the hands of the clock approach midnight, a bird tries to stop them from striking twelve. Before Cinderella dashes off, she purposely drops a slipper right before Egghead's eyes. When he arrives at her house illuminated by fluorescent lights, he finds a note saying that Cinderella got tired of waiting and went to the movies to see a Warner film. Egghead rushes to the movie house and is pictured on a screen with Cinderella in the audience. She then jumps into the screen and drags Egghead back into the audience so that they can watch a newsreel together.

Avery typically uses every technique possible to estrange the audience from the story, especially to prevent viewers from identifying with any of the characters. The viewers must be conscious that they are watching something artificial and are sharing the jokes that nevertheless will surprise the viewers because anything is possible in an Avery cartoon. In *Swing Shift Cinderella*, loosely based on his *Red Hot Riding Hood*, the film begins with the wolf chasing a tiny bratty Red Riding Hood until the wolf realizes it is the wrong character. So, he ditches Little Red Riding Hood, transforms himself into a debonair gentleman, and drives to Cinderella's house. Cinderella is a voluptuous blonde, and he attempts to invade her house. She calls upon an older grandma fairy godmother to protect her. Eventually, Cinderella goes off to perform in a nightclub, and the fairy godmother tames the wolf and brings him to the nightclub where Cinderella, reminiscent of Red Riding Hood in *Red Hot Riding Hood*, struts and sings, "All the little chicks are in love with a groovy wolf. Oh, Wolfie, Oh Wolfie!" In the end, she escapes, returns home, and changes into factory clothes for her swing shift. When she boards a bus, she thinks she is free of the wolf, but the passengers all turn out to be wolves who ogle her.

Avery's Cinderellas are cunning, strong, and feisty young women. Marriage is far from their minds. Even in cartoons in which Cinderella marries, it is clear that she refuses to be a wimp. In *Señorella and the Glass Huarache* (1964), directed by Hawley Pratt, Cinderella becomes a sexy Spanish dancer and marries the handsome son of Don Miguel. In this cartoon that features an unidentified cowboy in a saloon, who tells the "sad" story of Cinderella, we learn that the story is sad because the storyteller had married the mean stepmother. Of course, irony is key to two versions of "Cinderella" that appeared as fractured fairy tales in the Rocky and Bullwinkle TV series: *Cinderella* (1960) and *Cinderella Returns* (1960). In both films Cinderella must sign a contract with a short plump fairy godmother before the woman agrees to help her. In the first cartoon Cinderella, who must sell pots and pans if she is to marry a rich prince, is unaware that the prince is broke and wants to marry a rich heiress. In the end, he turns into a Fuller brush man, selling brushes from door to door. In the second film, the prince wants to marry a commoner and leave the castle, and Cinderella pretends to be rich and beautiful and ignores the fairy's warnings that she should be her common self. Here, too, Cinderella loses the prince. This time to the fairy godmother.

It is due, in great part, to the cartoon tradition that the wishes and dreams of Cinderella are made to seem ridiculous or are never fulfilled in the way that Cinderella hopes. Even though she fails in winning a prince, Cinderella is more often depicted as an assertive and opportunistic young woman than a passive servant. She senses deep down that she has the wits, charm, and determination to change herself and her status. Yet, some filmmakers question whether it is better for her to be so independent or whether she should assume the role of a demure, humble, and helpless victim. Kindness, piety, and purity, so many a young woman has learned, is the good girl's way to success and marriage.

Glorification of the Good Cinderella Through Music

In the postwar years, the pious, victimized Cinderella has been celebrated in musicals by the Disney Corporation, Rogers and Hammerstein, the Sesame Street Studio, and repeat performances of Rossini's *Cenerentola* and Prokofiev's ballet *Cinderella*. As I demonstrated in the chapter on Méliès, it is important *not to underestimate* the role of theater, vaudeville, and opera in the development of the cinematic discourses of particular fairy tales. In addition, the adaptations made for television and the market for DVDs are also significant. However, it would be misleading to lump all the different kinds of musical "Cinderellas" together because many of the repetitive productions of the same opera, play, or book adaptation interpret the libretti and scripts in diverse ways. Nevertheless, there is a dominant sentiment in the filmic representations of Cinderella that echoes throughout the history of the adaptations—poor Cinderella as stereotype of the persecuted heroine who *cannot* take charge of her life and who needs the help of magic powers and men to bring her happiness in the form of marriage. Almost all the musical versions follow in Perrault's tradition, which extolled the model of the pious, good-hearted young woman.

Though Rossini's libretto of *Cinderella* (1817), written by Jacopo Ferretti, brought about great changes in Perrault's plot and characters, it basically upheld the conservative role that women were to play in society. As is well known, Ferretti introduced a stepfather as villain and replaced the fairy godmother with the philosopher Alidoro, the prince's tutor. In addition, the prince is disguised as his own valet, and the valet, as the prince. The opera is enlivened by a series of mistaken identities and the prince falls in love with Cinderella from the time he catches a glimpse of her. It is her pure heart that wins the day, and the prince rescues her from a life of drudgery. Prokofiev's ballet of *Cinderella* (1945) was much more traditional than Rossini's opera and basically reproduced Perrault's tale through a remarkable musical score. The major change that he made was to introduce the fairy as a beggar at the beginning of the play, something that Kirkwood had also done in 1914. Otherwise, Cinderella was to dream and dance her way into the prince's heart.

However, the musical adaptation of Perrault's tale that truly ignited filmgoers' hearts was Disney's animated *Cinderella* (1950) followed much later by two direct-to-video film sequels *Cinderella II: Dreams Come True* (2002) and *Cinderella III: A Twist in Time* (2007). It is difficult to understand why this film, which resuscitated the Disney production of fairy-tale films, had so much success.[153] The music is mediocre; the plot is boring; and the themes are trite. The character of Cinderella, who loses both her parents within minutes of the beginning of the film is that of embodied sweetness and helplessness. If it were not for the animals, the two cute mice Jaq and Gus, the wonderfully mean cat Lucifer, and the loyal dog Bruno the bloodhound, not to mention the bumbling king, who dreams of his son marrying a beautiful princess and looking after his grand-children, the film would not be worth mentioning in the Cinderella discourse. However, it is important to note because it contributed to the development of the musical melodramatic tradition that stems from the *féerie* of the nineteenth century. The Disney Corporation tried to rectify the mistakes made in the original *Cinderella* with its two sequels by making Cinderella more active. For instance, in *Dreams Come True*, Cinderella plays a sort of matchmaker and tries to help her stepsister, Anastasia, who has fallen in love with a common baker. Once again, the mice steal the show in their conflict with Lucifer. The stepmother and stepsisters are incorrigibly nasty. In *A Twist in Time*, Cinderella and the prince celebrate their first wedding anniversary when Lady Tremaine, the evil stepmother, steals the fairy godmother's wand and uses it to send everyone on a trip back in time before Cinderella married the prince. Lady Tremaine wants to re-do everything so that her daughter Anastasia will be chosen to marry the prince. However, the mice save the day again; the prince blocks the wand's power; Anastasia has a change of conscience, takes the wand from her mother, and gives it to Cinderella, who then returns it to the fairy godmother, who restores order and enables Cinderella and her prince to remarry. Though Cinderella is more active in this film, about the only thing the film really wants to do is to recreate interest in other Disney films about Cinderella and to pull on the purse-strings of children and adults.

The goals of other musicals are about the same: to create hollow entertainment. A classic example of live-action trash is the Richard Rodgers and Oscar Hammerstein made-for-TV production of 1957. This film features a mousy Cinderella, who constantly looks at the prince with goggle eyes, and a prince, who stiffly rides a horse and wards off his parents who want him to marry some wealthy princess. The major shift in emphasis regards the prince. Almost all the post-1950 films to the present seek to develop a prince who is much more democratic and aware of his sentiments for Cinderella, whom he meets accidentally at the beginning of the film. In the Rodgers and Hammerstein musical, the plot is so artificial and contrived, and the songs so mushy and saccharine, that one wonders why such an adaptation has been reproduced two other times on television in 1965 and 1997.

In contrast, *The Slipper and the Rose*, a British musical of 1976, directed by Bryan Forbes, is a delightful farce that raises some serious questions while mocking social prejudices in England and spicing the Cinderella story with whacky humor. The film takes place in the tiny kingdom of Euphrania during the seventeenth or eighteenth century, and the bumbling king and his lord high chamberlain are intent on arranging a marriage for the prince to a princess of a powerful nation to

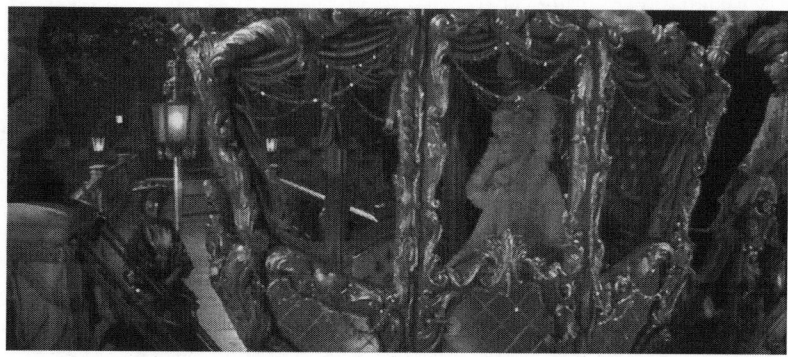

Figure 45
Bryan Forbes,
The Slipper and the Rose

protect Euphrania. However, Prince Edward will have nothing of this. Indeed, the film is more about him than about Cinderella, who is cruelly sent to the kitchen cellar after her father dies. Once again, we have a poor waif, who is helped by a witty godmother. If it were not for her humor and the many comical scenes that reveal how the prince is revolted by his father's plans, and how his father and his stupid courtiers foul up their plans, the film would be totally boring, for the music and songs are monotonous. In contrast to the bland American melodramatic musicals that take the sentiments of a meek Cinderella seriously, this British musical, despite the grand finale of a happy ending, rescues itself by not taking itself seriously and transforming the Cinderella story into a vaudeville play.

The most hilarious vaudeville musical, however, is the Sesame Street version, *Cinderelmo* (1999), directed by Bruce Leddy. Perhaps it should be called a "mock Cinderella," for the hero is the downtrodden, easygoing, red-headed Elmo, who dreams of dancing with the princess. In typical Sesame tradition, the film mixes humans with Muppets as though a multicultural, multiethnic, and animistic world were normal. Most of the familiar Muppets from the Sesame Street TV show are in this film, and role reversals are the rule. Elmo's stepbrothers are Muppets and his stepmother a human played in burlesque style by Kathy Najimy. Princess Charming, who is turning eighteen, must marry by the end of a ball otherwise her parents will lose the kingdom. She, too, is human and takes everything in her stride with good humor. Since she has never found anyone she would like to marry, her parents agree to invite everyone, including monsters, to the ball. Elmo receives the help of a gentle but clumsy godfather, who turns the dog into a prince and the dog's bowl into a coach. After much commotion at the ball, Elmo dances with the princess and impresses her. When he loses his silver slipper, she pursues him and discovers that he is much too young to marry—he is only three-and-a-half—but the fluffy dog is re-transformed into a prince at the end, and it appears that he might fit into this bizarre kingdom. The song-and-dance routines are lively and are part of the jests. For instance, when the stepmother uses binoculars to spy on the princess, she sees her jumping about and trying to shake water out of her ears, and she thinks this is a new dance. So, she teaches it to her Muppet sons, and the dance and song become the hit at the ball. Throughout the film, transformations and mutations and mistakes provide opportunities to see the "Cinderella" story anew without melodrama and a sentimental ending. The humor that borders on the ridiculous is in tune with the cartoon depictions of the "Cinderella" tale, but here, in contrast to the cartoons, the humor is always gentle.

One other semi-musical worth noting is the black-and-white Russian film *Zolushka* (*Cinderella*, 1947), which has become a classic. The film features a cute diminutive Cinderella, whose father adores her but is too weak to help her confront the tyrannical stepmother. The most interesting character is a bumbling king who keeps losing his wig as he does his best to find a perfect young woman for his son, the prince. The songs, mainly sung by Cinderella, are melodic and the dancing is entertaining. But the film is nothing but a traditional melodrama that must have lightened Russian hearts after the devastation of World War II.

Diverse Postwar Cinderellas in Europe and America

Numerous melodramatic live-action Cinderella films continued to be produced after World War II, and they reflect shifting cultural differences with regard to the character of Cinderella, that is, the role young women were expected to play, and cultural attitudes toward the traditional tales. In Europe, there was a strong tendency to stick closely to the narrative of the Grimms' version. Strange to say, Perrault's version was rarely adapted, even in France.

During the 1950s Fritz Genschow directed a series of fairy-tale films in West Germany that were directed at young audiences. In 1955 he filmed a live-action cute if not kitschy *Cinderella*, in which a very meek and persecuted young girl is helped by a fairy godmother, who springs from a tree planted at her mother's grave, and by a collective of real animals. The film is narrated by a male voiceover storyteller, and there is a comic forest spirit, who assumes different guises to enliven the film. The father is kept alive in this version only to absent himself when his daughter is maltreated by his new wife and stepdaughters. Cinderella is a pious child, who never speaks back to her victimizers and spends more time at her mother's grave than in the house. Ultimately, her piety wins the day, and after her stepsisters cut off a toe and a heel in a vain attempt to win the prince, Cinderella is asked how they should be punished. Instead of having their eyes pecked out by pigeons, she sentences them to one year of hard labor so they can realize what it is like to be a serf. While the acting is at times condescending to children, the film is well made and is an endeavor to keep the legacy of the Grimms' version alive and well in West Germany. The difficulty with this depiction of a staid young Cinderella is that it continued to foster myths about fixed gender roles in West Germany that oblige marriageable girls to silent observance.

Short mention should be made about the animated Russian film *Cinderella* (1979) directed by Ivan Aksenchuk and produced by the Soyuzmultfilm Studio. Short because the film, though in color, is a drab imitation of the Disney plot and structure, despite the Cold War. In this film a totally passive young girl watched over by the dark portrait of her dead mother lets everyone boss her around or push her to her destiny. She is dressed according to standard—a patched dress and clogs—and has blonde hair and blue eyes. The drawings are black-line cartoons with sweet music. If there was a feminist movement in the Soviet Union during the 1970s, this film certainly contributed to its setback.

The same could be said about the German/Czech *Cinderella* (1989), directed by Karin Brandauer, which more or less repeated the Genschow literal interpretation of the Grimms' tale, though Cinderella appears to be a bit more active. This may be due to the fact that her father is a total fool and refuses to recognize how badly his daughter is treated by his new wife and stepdaughters (similar to the animated Russian film). Yet, out of reasons of respect—one does not talk back to one's brutal stepmother—Cinderella cannot contradict her stepmother in front of her father. Once again we have a pious daughter looked after by a tree and pigeons. Her visits to her mother's grave and a few prayers enable her to win a prince. In both the German films, the prince is basically a handsome appendage as he is in the Grimms' tale. He functions as the "pretty" reward that is due to Cinderella once she passes the test of obedience and fidelity.

The only European film that resists conforming to the Grimm hypotext of "Cinderella" is Václav Vorlícek's *Three Wishes for Cinderella* (1973). The title in Czech is *Tri orísky pro Popelku* or *Three Hazelnuts for Cinderella*, and the reason it resists the Grimms' version is that the film is based on a fairy tale written by Božena Nemcová, one of Czechoslovakia's great writers of folk and fairy tales in the nineteenth century. Vorlícek, the most prolific Czech director of fairy tales, spiced this dynamic tale with clear feminist ingredients in his film that corresponded to the changing role of women in postwar Czechoslovakia. Moreover, he was fortunate to find the talented actress Libuse Safránková to play Cinderella. She brought a charming rebellious spirit to her role and was so captivating that the film became a cult classic in Europe.

True, the film, which takes place in eighteenth-century Czechoslovakia, does not break greatly with the melodramatic tendency in the Cinderella filmic discourse, but it does display a modern Cinderella, who takes her destiny in her hands with alacrity. (In part, this may be due to Nûmcová's text which was imbued with an unusual ideological impulse. She herself was a socialist, who struggled against oppression in her country.) In the film, Cinderella is an orphan who has undeservedly been cast out of her family mansion on a large estate by a greedy stepmother and her nasty plump daughter and forced to work like a serf. Nevertheless, the spritely Cinderella shrugs off the maltreatment and is supported by all the workers on the estate, along with her dog Casper, her

Figure 46
Václav Vorlícek,
*Three Wishes for
Cinderella*

horse Nicolas, and an owl named Rosalie. Indeed, she has a great love for nature and loves to spend a great deal of time in the forest. Moreover, she is an expert rider and hunter, thanks to her dead father, and when she first meets the prince in the forest, she embarrasses him by preventing him from shooting a deer. In another instance, disguised as a forester, she defeats the prince in a shooting contest. Baffled, the egotistical prince, who is somewhat a rebel himself, wants to become better acquainted with her, but she outwits him and always manages to escape his grasp. Still, it is apparent that the prince, who does not want to wed, is similar in spirit to Cinderella. When he is finally forced by his well-meaning parents to find a wife, a ball with beautiful women is held, and of course, Cinderella, aided by three magic hazelnuts given to her by a coachman, charms him. The rest is history.

Vorlícek's film, though sentimental, succeeds because he does not force the humor of mistaken identities, nor does he use magic tricks to create a false sense of enchantment. For instance, there are no rats, mice, lizards, or pumpkins. Cinderella rides to the ball on her own horse. The scenes at the country estate, the palace, and the forest are stark and realistic. Vorlícek reveals that work was rough. General living conditions were hard. The images of nature are contrasted with the cluttered courtyard and artificiality of the palace. Cinderella and the prince are free spirits. Though Cinderella receives help from friends and animals, it is because they naturally respond to her courage and good will, not because she is helpless. Their help also signifies that one talented individual cannot succeed alone. At times the music is schmaltzy, and the shots of Cinderella galloping through the snow with her prince are overly romantic. But overall *Three Wishes for Cinderella* is a contentious film that challenges traditional assumptions about Cinderella as a poor helpless waif. She will wed out of love not out of necessity, and it is clear that she has come into her own.

Whereas most European directors—perhaps because they are more historically inclined—have chosen to set the Cinderella story in the baroque period, American and British filmmakers have tended to adapt Cinderella stories and novels for the screen in innovative ways to use the story as a vehicle for some well-known actor or actress, and to relocate the action to a more modern setting and attract teenage audiences by showcasing a teenage star as representative of girl power. In almost all the films, the emphasis is not so much on Cinderella's claim to her legacy but on the maltreatment by non-biological stepmothers and stepsiblings. In every case the underdog triumphs against odds with or without the help of friends. In the worst cases—and there are many—the fairy tale is transformed into melodramatic spectacle for the spectacle's sake.

The cinematic adaptations of prose works are among the most interesting if not the most creative interrogations of underdogs in the modern Cinderella cinematic discourse. For instance, Babette Cole's idiosyncratic picture book, *Prince Cinders* (1987) was adapted and made into a highly amusing animated film by Derek Hayes in 1993. The film is a close rendition of the book which concerns a skinny, hardworking boy exploited by his three muscle-bound brothers. Turned into a goony ape by an incompetent fairy, Prince Cinders accidentally wins the heart of a down-to-earth princess while his brothers are turned into fluttering winged fairies who must do household chores. In another made-for-TV British mini series, *I Was a Rat* (2001), Philip Pullman's delightful 1999 novel provides another original twist to the Cinderella tale. This time a pageboy who appears at the door of an aging couple explains that he had once been a rat and that the fairy had not re-transformed him after Cinderella had married and become Lady Ashlington and then Princess Aurelia. The couple take him in, name him Roger, and send him to school, but he continues to behave like a rat. The head of the school wants to beat him because of his disobedience, but Roger escapes and is portrayed as dangerous vermin by the mass media. The film, set at the beginning of the twentieth century, expands upon the novel set in the second half of the nineteenth century, and the director, Laurie Lynd, adds a touch of Charles Dickens' social realism mixed with fairy-tale motifs and some slapstick humor. For instance, Roger is captured by the police and taken to a royal medical laboratory where experiments are done to determine whether he is a monster and should be exterminated for the good of the people. Only Princess Aurelia, who knows the truth about his background, can save him and reveal the stupidity of the people and the press that want to persecute a simple boy. The film explores the entire question of identity and whether it is better to remain a simple kitchen maid or a rat rather than to rise in society. The figure of Cinderella is an auxiliary in this instance, but the film does raise questions about the manipulation of identity at a time when the media spreads more "myths" about people than truth.

In another more serious film made for American TV, *The Confessions of an Ugly Stepsister* (2002), Gregory Maguire's complex and riveting 1999 novel is transformed into an equally compelling film about a Dutch Cinderella viewed from the perspective of a mute ugly stepsister. Actually, the story is less about a Cinderella type and more about a complicated stepmother. Maguire set his story in the small city of Haarlem in seventeenth-century Holland, and he has a great eye for capturing the customs and living conditions of the time. The film follows suit and produces a nuanced historical portrait of the times; the images do not form a magical enchanting tale. The narrative concerns the return of the widow Margarethe Fisher from England with her two daughters, Ruth, an awkward but gentle mute, and Irene, a plain but gifted and compassionate girl. Fierce in her determination to protect her daughters and to provide a livelihood for them, Margarethe finds a job as a servant for a master painter and then as head of the wealthy van den Meer household, where Irene is giving English lessons to a beautiful and anxious girl named Clara, who had been abducted and saved from her kidnappers when she was a child. Eventually, her mother Margarethe takes over the household and marries Cornelius van den Meer after the death of his wife. From this point on she rules the domestic affairs of the house with an iron fist. Ruth's "confession" is a true story mainly about her mother and her ambitious striving to make sure that her own genetic daughters would have a better life. She acts out of desperation and tries to overcome poverty by any means she can justify as the Dutch merchants ruthlessly deal with one another in the town of Haarlem. It is a dog-eat-dog world that the film depicts, and it is no surprise that the crude and domineering Margarethe is not punished in the end but lives on to represent the indomitable will not just of stepmothers, but mothers obsessed with protecting their daughters.

While the cinematic adaptation of Maguire's work remained close to the original novel, this is not the case with *Ella Enchanted* (1997), written by Gail Carson Levine. The book, which won the esteemed Newberry Award, is a straightforward fairy-tale novel about a young girl named Ella, who lives in the kingdom of Frell and is granted the gift of obedience by a fairy named Lucinda. This gift creates grave problems for her when she turns fifteen and her mother dies. At the funeral she makes the acquaintance of Prince Charmont (Char), and they become friends. But Ella is now sent to a boarding school, and two nasty sisters, spoiled daughters of Dame Olga, take advantage of her after learning about her spell of obedience, which is more a curse than a gift. To break the spell Ella goes in pursuit of Lucinda, who refuses to rescind the gift of obedience. Ella is almost killed by ogres but is saved by Char. In the meantime, Ella's father, who is in debt and needs a rich wife, marries Dame Olga, and when her father leaves to conduct some trading business, her life becomes hell. Her only hope is to marry Char, who proposes to her. She refuses because her curse of obedience would endanger his kingdom. Now the fairies Lucinda and Mandy come to her rescue and enable her to attend a ball, break the curse, and agree to marry Char.

This convoluted plot is made even more convoluted in the film by the addition of an evil uncle named Sir Edgar, who rules Frell as regent and has a vicious snake. Edgar wants to kill Char, whom Ella more or less saves. There are all sorts of struggles involving ogres, giants, and elves. In the end, however, Ella gets her man, and the film, which stars Anne Hathaway, is fluff entertainment that adds a touch of feminism to make it more fashionable.

Cinderella films have often been used as vehicles for celebrities or potential celebrities to charm and delight audiences while seemingly probing the meaning of assumed Perrault and Grimm hypotexts. A good example is Frank Tashlin's *Cinderfella* (1960), which stars Jerry Lewis as a goofy innocent heir to millions and Ed Wynn as a fairy godfather, who explains to him how women have taken advantage of simpletons like himself for centuries. Tashlin, who worked as an animator in cartoons before turning to live-action films, directs Lewis in song-and-dance numbers that enable Lewis to show off his slapstick routines. While amusing, the film is more notable for its stupid misogyny than anything else.

The "celebrity" film that may have caused a rash of other sentimental films, such as *Cinderella* (2000), featuring Kathleen Turner as a vicious femme fatale, *A Cinderella Story* (2004) featuring Hilary Duff as a victimized waitress in a diner, and *Another Cinderella Story* (2008) featuring newcomers Selena Gomez and Andrew Seeley as dancing Cinderella and prince, is undoubtedly *Ever After* (1998) with its star-studded cast of Jeanne Moreau, Drew Barrymore, Angelica Huston, and Dougray Scott to name but a few of the stellar actors. This film directed with great craft by Andy Tenant wakened a new interest in the "Cinderella" story, I believe, not only because of its box-office success, but, like *Three Wishes for Cinderella*, because it was also intent on displaying a tom-boy young woman with power who could control her own destiny, and in this case, pursue her utopian dreams. Both films—and there is an apparent influence of the Czech film on *Ever After*—were designed to speak to the problematic condition of late-twentieth-century young women, who no longer need men to save them while they must still abide by conventions and conditions set by men.

Ever After has a particularly clever frame. The initial shots show the Brothers Grimm arriving at the home of the elderly Grande Dame of France played appropriately by the great actress Jeanne Moreau, the grande dame of late-twentieth-century French cinema. She has invited them to her elegant mansion to tell them a "true" story about her great-great grandmother, Danielle, and to correct their version of "Cinderella." There is also an implicit critique of Perrault's version. She begins her tale as the brothers admire a beautiful oil painting of a young woman. The Grande Dame indicates that there is a story behind the painting. The brothers' curiosity has been piqued, and of course, the audience is curious, too, but is aware that a few games are being played when the Grande Dame begins her "true" story because we all know that there is no authentic "Cinderella" tale.

According to the Grande Dame, however, Cinderella's real name was Danielle de Barbarac, and she narrates in a flashback what actually happened in the seventeenth century. The plot, which incorporates motifs and characters from previous Cinderella films, albeit from a much more pronounced "feminist" perspective, can easily be summarized: Danielle is raised solely by her father after her mother's death (which accounts for her tom-boy attributes); when she becomes a young woman, her father surprises her by marrying a baroness with two comely daughters, one nasty, the other kind; the father unexpectedly dies from a heart attack; the Baroness Rodmilla de Ghent takes over the household and reduces Danielle to the status of a maid; Danielle accidentally meets and embarrasses Prince Henry of France in a field; Danielle pretends to be a comtesse; Danielle rescues Henry from gypsies; the Baroness keeps treating Danielle in a mean-spirited way and plans to have her nasty daughter marry Prince Henry; the king and queen, desperate to create a line of heirs, want Prince Henry to marry a Spanish princess; Prince Henry refuses but agrees to choose a bride at a masquerade ball; Danielle is almost prevented by her stepmother from attending the ball, but servants help her to appear at the ball; however, Danielle is humiliated when her stepmother reveals that she is not of noble blood; Prince Henry deserts her; Leonardo da Vinci, the great painter, reprimands him; Danielle is sold to a sinister nobleman; Prince Henry decides to break off his engagement to the Spanish princess and save Danielle from the sinister nobleman only to find that Danielle has freed herself; Prince Henry apologizes and proposes to Danielle; the stepmother and one of her daughters are sentenced to work in the royal laundry; the kind stepsister is given a position at the court; Danielle and Henry wed and supposedly live ever after; Leonardo da Vinci reveals a painting that he has made of Danielle.

There are other events in this finely acted film shot as a period piece. In the end, the Grande Dame has the final word and displays the glass slipper that Danielle had worn to the masquerade ball. The brothers are bedazzled and convinced. They ride off and appear to have been taught a true historical lesson on the screen, while people in the audience can delight in being part of a joke that has been played on the poor brothers. Of course, spectators can also be delighted in having watched images of a headstrong young woman, who reads Thomas More's *Utopia* as a bible and fights for the liberation of slaves and indentured servants.

But can they? In one of the more insightful critiques of the film, Christy Williams declares:

> *Ever After* assumes a feminist stance, but offers a mass-mediated idea of feminism in which individual women can be strong and achieve equality through personal actions that do not, however, work to challenge or change the underlying patriarchal structure of society. And these heroines can still be (sexually) desirable and marriageable in doing so. The problems identified in second-wave feminism are simplified, emptied of radical critiques of gender inequality, and marketed to young women. This limited version of feminism, which draws on girl power and liberal feminism, reinforces patriarchal authority by its focus on individual achievements and by isolating one woman, the heroine, as an exception to standard feminine behavior. To denaturalize the idea of feminism *Ever After* projects, I will focus on the limited power of Danielle's action within the film's dynamics of narrative authority, the highly gendered representations of Danielle, the reversal of the damsel-in-distress plot, and the re-gendering of the fairy godmother as male. The fragments of the "Cinderella" tale that are maneuvered most consistently in *Ever After*—the phrase "once upon a time," the dress, the rescue, and the godmother—placate a late twentieth- and early twenty-first century audience's expectations of popular feminism, but fail to move the "Cinderella" story beyond the structural misogyny bound up in the tale's plot.[154]

Though I agree with many of Williams' arguments, I believe that she exaggerates the extent to which *Ever After* is complicit in furthering misogynistic tendencies in contemporary society. If anything, the film, I believe, tends to problematize feminist aspirations and reveal how undependable male love and dedication are when confronted with a young woman with unabashedly democratic ideals and a zest to make social reforms. Moreover, the very frame of the film raises important questions of authenticity and narrative appropriation that Williams appears to misinterpret. The Grande Dame summons the Brothers Grimm to *her* space, where she re-appropriates the "Cinderella" story, told from a female perspective. Or, in other words, she wants to recapture her legacy and confronts the Grimms and history by telling about the accomplishments of her greatgreat grandmother. In the face of the evidence, the Grimms do not protest. Rather, they ride off and are apparently jostled by the "truth." In this respect, *Ever After*, while showing the limits of the second wave of feminism, destabilizes the traditional patriarchal narrative while also showing the compromises that young women still make (or must make) to take part in a socio-economic system that will not allow them to act radically in a political or personal way if they want to be part of the ruling hierarchy. The best that they can hope for is minimal reform, and *Ever After* shows this by making the stepmother and her daughter complicit with the sinister nobleman. They are not the real villains in history though they may be portrayed as the villains in the film. As we know, the real cads in history were men like Prince Henry and his successors, and the real heroines were never Cinderella-type young women, anxious to marry well.

What is relevant always depends on who gets to tell his or her story, who is authorized to make his or her film, and who controls the distribution of stories and films. For instance, another film that rivals *Ever After* in its "feminist" significance, one that raises issues rather than proposes a complete answer, is *Ashpet: An American Cinderella* (1990) directed and produced by Tom Davenport. During the 1980s and 1990s Davenport made original use of the fairy tale and film to enhance viewers' understanding of storytelling, politics, and creativity and *Ashpet* is one of his best endeavors. This cinematic version is about a young white woman named Lily, who learns to reclaim her rights and heritage through the help of a wise black woman whose sense of history and knowledge of oppression empowers the "enslaved" Lily to pursue her dreams. The action takes place in the rural South during the early years of World War II, when people were making sacrifices and forced to separate because of the military draft. But Lily manages to find the strength to overcome isolation and exploitation by piecing together a sense of her own story that her stepmother and stepsisters had taken from her. Consequently, Davenport's Cinderella story is no longer history in a traditional male sense, that is, no longer the Grimms' story, or a simple rags-to-riches story. Nor is it a didactic feminist interpretation of *Cinderella*. Instead, Davenport turns it into an American tale about conflicts within a matrilineal heritage in the South, narrated from beginning to end by a well-known Afro-American storyteller, Louise Anderson, who plays the role of Dark Sally, the magical conjurewoman and fairy godmother. The focus of the film becomes Dark Sally, and it shows how her storytelling can lead a young woman to recover a sense of her history and give her the strength to assert herself, as many women are doing today.

Mounting and Dismantling Cinderella

The question of voice, control of the narrative and the camera, and representations of ideological conceptions of success and happiness are crucial in the creation of all fairy-tale films, especially those with heroines similar to Cinderella. *Ashpet* was made during the late 1980s, when the first phase of the feminist movement had made its mark, and the second phase (of many more to come) was in the process of solidifying gains and also receiving a backlash. Some of the gains and losses are reflected to a certain extent in three mainstream Hollywood films with "Cinderellalike" protagonists: Howard Deutsch's *Pretty in Pink* (1986), Mike Nichols' *Working Girl* (1988), and Gary Marshall's *Pretty Woman* (1990).[155] Each of these films depict the travails of lower-class women, all white, who use their elbows, cunning, and sensitivity, to scramble to the top. In *Pretty in Pink*, Andie, a working-class teenager in Chicago, falls in love with a rich preppie named Blane McDonough. Their class differences lead to class conflicts, but Andie eventually gets her man at the school prom when she exhibits a love that helps him rise above class arrogance. In *Working Girl*, Tess McGill, a working-class secretary from Staten Island, seeks to become an executive in a Wall Street firm, but she is victimized by her female boss, Katharine Parker, who steals one of her wonderful business ideas to raise her prestige. However, while Katharine is cooped up in her apartment due to a skiing accident, Tess accidentally meets her boss's fiancé, Jack Trainer, an executive at another corporation, pursues her business idea with success, and falls in love with Jack at a wedding party. When she is seemingly exposed as a fraud, Jack sticks up for her, and Tess gets her man and a promotion to an executive position. In *Pretty Woman*, which takes place in Los Angeles, Edward Lewis, a ruthless New York corporate executive, arrives to take over and exploit a small family business. He accidentally meets a good-natured prostitute, lower-class Vivian Ward, who helps him find his way to his hotel. At first Edward does not realize that Vivian is a prostitute, and when he does, he decides to employ her (because of her beauty) so that she can help him in a business deal. She learns manners and culture in the process, and he learns how to soften. After some misunderstandings and an attempted rape by a business associate, Edward makes a decision to give Vivian what she wants, which is "the fairy tale."

All three films are loaded with super Hollywood stars: Molly Ringwald, Melanie Griffith, Harrison Ford, Sigourney Weaver, Alec Baldwin, Joan Cusack, Richard Gere, and Julia Roberts. Typically Hollywood, these films are not works of art but vehicles for the actors to attain more celebrity and commodities for the producers to increase their profits in the film industry. All three were directed by male filmmakers who used male cinematographers to realize their male fantasies. The sites of the films cover America's dream cities: Chicago, New York, Los Angeles. The plots that drip with sentimentality and conventionality are predictable: lower-class struggling girl (Cinderella) meets wealthy cultivated male (prince); lower-class girl wants to find a place in the opulent world of the rich and famous; she needs helpers (fairy godmothers) to show her the way to her goal; she passes various tests and overcomes obstacles to show that she is worthy of moving up in the world; she claims her prince as trophy.

It is ridiculous to try to salvage these films for contemporary feminism by analyzing how all the Cinderellas in these films demonstrate their talents and are active, humane, thoughtful, and assertive, as some critics have done. Such "salvation" merely rationalizes the sequence of demeaning behavior that the female protagonists must exhibit: they must obsequiously learn the male rules of the game to attain status and wealth, while believing they are making a stand for women's souls. A true rebellion is out of the question. They mount their male trophies while being mounted themselves as complicit in ways males fantasize about new kinds of Cinderellas.

However, can a Cinderella girl act any differently in a socio-economic system that lays traps for her in every game situation? Can a filmmaker depict other valid possibilities other than complicity? These are the questions asked by Ericka Beckman, an independent filmmaker, in her highly experimental and provocative short film, *Cinderella* (1986). In the process she dismantles the traditional nineteenth-century and Hollywood narratives of "Cinderella" and positions a young working woman on the verge of self discovery. There will be no closed happy end in this film.

Beckman's story gives the girl Cinderella and the tale itself a total remake. Before the title is flashed on the screen we see a farmer heading toward a small wooden building with FORGE written in large letters. Then the title appears indicating that we are to view a Cinderella story. Indeed, we shall see a forgery of the traditional "Cinderella" that will be forged before our eyes, but the forgery will ironically lead to the forging of a new "Cinderella," truer to the position of women in the contemporary western world, for this forgery is a woman's appropriation of male fantasizing and

Figure 47
Ericka Beckman,
Cinderella

an assertion of a female, if not feminist, voice. Inside the forgery there is an accordion player chanting and squeezing a papier-mâché accordion while a couple of blacksmiths are working in tune to the music and chants. Cinderella, dressed in working clothes, pumps papier-mâché bellows fanning the fire in the glowing furnace. Suddenly a voice is heard that announces: "Cinderella. Now's the hour. From the fire comes your power!" Soon a gift-wrapped box comes tumbling out of the furnace. Once Cinderella opens the box she discovers a green satin dress with a crinoline. Female voices sing that the game is about to begin and that she must use the dress to win the prince. However, no sooner does she wear the dress than the chorus accuses her of being a robber and announces that she must be put in her place. Then Cinderella is pictured in her work clothes back at the bellows. A few moments later, another gift box appears, and it now becomes clear that Cinderella is being tossed into a computer-generated game on a grid that, at times, resembles a spider's web as does the crinoline frame of her dress. She is fired up, so to speak, and enticed. If she wants to win the game and the prince, she must learn the right moves, and as she tries three times, she is taunted and also instructed by the chorus what she must do to become perfect. As a "Greek" chorus, the voices can be likened to the messages of corporate America that set the standards for marketing and consumption. To rise from her working class and to succeed, Cinderella is expected to conform to these standards. As Vera Dika observes in an astute review of the film,

> eventually. . . Cinderella learns how to model herself after the prescribed image of woman— which the film presents as a sort of consumerist princess-cum-Barbie doll—and at last she wins. Playing by the rules, she gains the prize and literally acquires her own voice. In the final segment of the film, Cinderella's singing voice is dominant, virtually replacing the chorus and the titles. But her victory is bittersweet. Growing in awareness, Cinderella sees that the prince is more interested in her image than in her self, and so she finally rejects the game, the prince and the dress, which serves as a metaphor both for her sought-after conventionalized image and for her entrapment.[156]

In many respects, Beckman's film can be likened to a Brechtian learning play without the didacticism of Brecht. The startling images of Cinderella's repeated endeavors to win the game, which is really a game of entrapment, are closer to surrealism than to the social realism of Brecht.

An animated clock jostles and intimidates her and sounds warnings. She is frightened into minting money. Robots and machines appear to test her as if she were a laboratory guinea pig. Yet, the images that dissolve into one another meld structures and space. Indeed, Cinderella is like a lovely Victorian Alice in Wonderland that makes no sense, but this time it is a contemporary working-class Cinderella caught in a computer game, and as she unravels the grid and the straight-jacket of the crinoline, she begins to sing for herself and the film ends on a strident note:

> Let me set the record straight,
> How I played it differently.
> If I can't change what I see,
> Change it in my memory.
>
> I see there's no end to this game.
> When it's over, it starts up again.
> Lift up your skirts. He's attracted to you.
> He'll give you money for a copy or two.
> The company will tell you what to do.
> Residuals are too good to be true!
>
> Listen to the record, spinning like a top,
> I can put my finger down. I can make it stop.
>
> I feel something rising up,
> rising, rising through the cracks.
> Pushing it's way to the top.
> Nothing's going to hold me back!
>
> A song is rising, rising from the cracks.
> It's been tied down so long,
> it's striking back!
> NO NO NO . . .
> All these circles, these tattoos,
> my skirt records what I live through.
> I'm rising up, I'm turning round.
> My skirts will never be let down!

NO, NO, NO . . .

Though produced in 1986, Beckman's brilliant film is still very topical and definitely more significant for the Cinderella filmic discourse than the other faux "feminist" Cinderella films of the 1980s and 1990s. The dreams of underdogs, whether they be female or male, who seek to liberate themselves from the oppression of wicked stepmothers, stepsisters, and dysfunctional fathers and from an "evil" social system, are both real and valid. The interference and intercession of helpers are also necessary if an underdog is to understand how games work. Yet, if the oppressed do not want to join the wealthy upper class to become oppressors, they must learn how to resist conformity while maintaining their integrity. As Beckman's film demonstrates, there's no end to the game as it is played now, and resistance is the first step toward recreating a Cinderella tale with the possibility of self-definition.

Resistance and self-definition are the keys to understanding the unusual film, *Year of the Fish* (2007), directed by David Kaplan, another independent filmmaker, who uses rotoscopic animation to depict the desperate situation of a young Chinese woman, Ye Xian, in a massage parlor in New

York's Chinatown. The rotoscopic process involves tracing over live-action film that gives the pictures the effect of a watercolor painting and a graphic novel. It also creates an estrangement effect that is perfect for the narrative perspective: an estranged young woman viewing a strange "new world." After her mother's death, Ye Xian, who can barely speak English, has been sent to New York by her impoverished father to help support him and his family. Misled by relatives, Ye Xian believes that she will be working in a professional studio of some kind. However, once she signs a contract with Mrs. Su, the owner of the parlor and the "wicked stepmother," she soon realizes that she is supposed to be a sex worker. But Ye Xian refuses to pleasure men and is thus forced to work as a maid in the parlor to pay back the money. Mrs. Su, who is called Mama by everyone in the parlor, mistreats her and tries to force her to marry her degenerate brother. As Ye Xian tries to make sense out of the strange "culture" in Chinatown, she meets a bizarre "fairy godmother," Auntie Yaga, who has traits of a bag lady and the Russian witch Baba Yaga. This eccentric woman appears and disappears throughout the film. In her initial meeting with Ye Xian, she offers the young woman a gold fish as a good luck charm and later helps her after Mrs. Su kills the gold fish and serves it as a meal to her family of sex workers. Ye Xian also encounters a seemingly demented old man, who mysteriously instructs her and helps her find her way through the morass in Chinatown. At the same time that all this is happening, she falls in love with a young musician named Johnny, her "prince." Attracted by his accordion music, she keeps bumping into him on her errands in Chinatown. Eventually, after they meet at a celebration of the Chinese New Year, he helps her leave the massage parlor.

While Kaplan follows the linear narrative of the traditional "Cinderella" story, he probes the tale and deepens its significance by relating it to the experiences of a young woman trying to make sense of strange signs and customs in an unfamiliar culture. The Chinese world in which she lands in New York is not what she expected. Prostitution, sweat factories, and a vicious employer are what she encounters. Yet, she has a remarkable spiritual resolve so that she remains true to herself and protects her integrity at every step toward her freedom. Kaplan focuses entirely on the honest and strong moral character of Ye Xian. The camera reflects the world as she sees it and feels it. She is saved by herself and helped by a few kind people who understand her plight. But the happy ending is, as Kaplan hints, just the beginning of a new life in a Chinatown, which will not change. Like Beckman's Cinderella, however, Ye Xian has learned what kinds of exploitative games people want to play with her, and her resistance to such manipulation can only become stronger.

10

Abusing and Abandoning Children: "Hansel and Gretel," "Tom Thumb," "The Pied Piper," "Donkey-Skin," and "The Juniper Tree"

Issues of child abuse and abandonment have formed the crux of many different kinds of stories ever since humans began to speak. The Greek, Roman, and Egyptian myths and the Bible are full of them, not to mention the thousands of legends and initiation stories that have been gathered from indigenous tribes throughout the world. How old they are is anyone's guess, but given the continual abuse and abandonment of children up through the twenty-first century, it is clear that the perpetual "problem" of raising, nourishing, and caring for children will occupy our hearts, minds, and stories for years to come. Thus, it is not by chance that filmmakers have adapted various fairy tales such as "Hansel and Gretel," "Tom Thumb," "The Pied Piper," "Donkey-Skin" and "The Juniper Tree" to comment metaphorically on modern attitudes toward the maltreatment of children, the causes of physical abuse and violence suffered by young people, and the trauma of incest. Though many other types of stories touch on these themes, I have selected some of the more prominent fairy tales and their cinematic adaptations to understand how filmmakers have endeavored to create new discursive and cinematic strategies to shed light on abuse and abandonment.

In the particular case of "The Pied Piper," it may seem inaccurate to regard this legend as a fairy tale, but I want to argue that, in the course of the nineteenth and twentieth centuries, "The Pied Piper" has gradually assumed more characteristics and motifs that make it similar to a fairy tale; they include the mysterious stranger with extraordinary powers, a magic flute, an impossible task, a miraculous transformation, and betrayal that ironically causes the fall of fortunes of the town of Hamelin. The fluidity of short narrative genres has always been invigorating for storytellers who borrow, change, and retell tales without a bow to "absolute" laws of a putative fixed genre. Filmmakers have bent every narrative rule in the book to adapt distinct fairy-tale plots that have become memetic to convey their impressions of child abuse and abandonment, and the fairy tale has served them well.

Hansel and Gretel: There's No Place Like Home

No other fairy tale in the Grimms' collection has been as celebrated in the popular imagination so much as "Hansel and Gretel" for its sanctimonious representation of brotherly and sisterly love, its idolization of a compassionate father, who opposes a witch/wife, and its picture of home sweet home made sweeter by treasures stolen from a cannibalistic witch. Yet, there are many fissures in this well-made narrative about the struggles of two abandoned children to return home and honor a father, who has betrayed them, and numerous writers and illustrators have questioned the reconciliation and the idyllic ending of the Grimms' tale about childhood abandonment. In one of my recent essays, I pointed out that the Grimms recorded this tale after hearing it between 1808 and 1810, and the narrative was very different from the one which they published in 1812.[157] In the hand-written text of their Ölenberg manuscript of 1810, the children are not given lovely names; their mother is their biological mother; the children do not need the help of God to save themselves; they automatically return home with money that will guarantee a warm welcome. Indeed, the Grimms changed this oral tale that they had recorded, and in the process they demonized a stepmother, transformed the children into two pious innocents with cute names who trust in God, and added a silly duck that helps them across a pond to sooth a sobbing father, who does not show any grief about his dead wife, nor does he apologize for abandoning them.

The Grimms, mainly Wilhelm, kept changing the text of "Hansel and Gretel" through seven editions of their classic work, *Children's and Household Tales*, and the final text of 1857 is a highly significant, ambivalent, and memetic fairy tale because it raises more questions than it answers. It is significant because the tale reveals the ambivalence that parents feel when they are confronted with decisions that involve their own survival in hard times and their ties to their offspring. To put it bluntly, the tale asks whether children are a burden or a blessing when the going gets rough. It asks what the real nature of home is, and whether children can trust their parents. In addition, it tends to associate cruel and harsh treatment of children with stepmothers and witch/women and to sanctify the benevolent father. It is a narrative that creates a longing for a home and a protective father who promises eternal security. It is a text that promises something durable that it cannot fulfill, nor can we fulfill this longing in our social reality. Its significance is in its anticipatory illusion of a home that we must somehow build by ourselves. The text contradicts its own illusion by concretizing happiness and equating home solely with a father, and the best of the fairy-tale films explore the contradictions of such a conception. All the filmic revisions of "Hansel and Gretel" have a memetic quality connected to our need to develop and remember strategies for escaping cruel treatment, adapting to unfamiliar surroundings, and our profound drive to transform the unfamiliar into the familiar, that is, to be at home with ourselves.

For the most part the Grimms' final 1857 text of "Hansel and Gretel" is the hypotext or the reference for most of the Hansel and Gretel films produced in the twentieth and twenty-first centuries, but numerous films also show a strong influence of Engelbert Humperdinck's opera, *Hansel and Gretel* (1893), based on a pious Christian libretto written by Adelheid Wette, Humperdinck's sister. This very popular opera has been performed hundreds of times and continues to be produced throughout the world and has been reproduced as a film in different versions in the cinema, on television, and on the Internet. Wette, a deeply religious woman, made profound changes that greatly altered the Grimms' text. Instead of pointing the finger at the parents for abandoning their children, she wags her finger at the children who are referred to as "little sinners." They are not abandoned by their parents but chastised for breaking something in the house and then sent into the woods to look for strawberries. They become lost; their parents search for them; and they are discovered deep in the forest after Gretel cleverly pushes the witch into the oven with God's help. The final scene, the rescue of the children, sums up the didactic message of the opera:

Mother: Children!
Father: There they are, the little sinners! (*Joyful reunion. Meanwhile two boys drag the witch in the form of a large gingerbread figure out of the ruins of the magic oven. Upon sight of her everyone begins to rejoice. The boys place the witch in the middle of the stage.*)

Father: Children, look at this miraculous sight,
           How the witch has lost her might.
           how hard,
           crispy hard
           she herself is now a cake.
           See how Heaven's judgment works:
           Evil deeds do not last!
           When our need is at its most,
           The Lord our God gives us a helping hand!
Everyone: When our need is at its most,
           The Lord our God gives us a helping hand![158]

Wette's libretto reinforces a dimension of the tale that exculpates the parents. It is a narrative perspective that I have called the rationalization of abuse in fairy tales.[159] There is an overwhelming tendency in all folk tales and fairy tales and fairy-tale films to tell the story of child abuse and abandonment from an adult perspective that diminishes or excuses the consequences of adult actions harmful to children. Even if the tale may point to the parents as culpable, there is always a certain amount of rationalization of guilt and responsibility that shapes the telling of the tale. The aesthetics are formed by the ideological perspective of the storyteller. Whereas the Grimms held at least one of the parents, a stepmother, accountable, and also cast blame on a female witch, Wette implies that the children bring abuse upon themselves. They are little sinners who must be saved from themselves. At the very least, they need God's helping hand.

At the same time that Wette and Humperdinck were spreading their revised version of the Grimms' tale through numerous performances and adaptations, another story about abandoned children, "Babes in the Wood," undermined the rationalization of childhood abandonment. Well known in England, it is not as famous as "Hansel and Gretel," and this may be due to its blunt depiction of how adults exploit and maltreat children. The story may have been based on a real incident and was first published in Norwich as a ballad by Thomas Millington in 1595. Later it was frequently adapted in prose chapbooks and reprinted as a poem in Mother Goose books. By the end of the nineteenth century, Joseph Jacobs included it in *More English Fairy Tales* (1894) with the title "The Children in the Wood."[160] The tale concerns a wealthy couple in Norfolk with two tiny children. When the parents die, the father bequeaths a good deal of money to his children, and his brother is placed in charge of them. However, after a year, the uncle, who wants their money, devises a plan to have the children killed. He hires two ruffians to take them into the woods. One of the assassins refuses to do the nasty deed. The two men quarrel, and one kills the other. The "kind" ruffian tells the children that he will go into the town to seek provisions, but he never returns. The children die, and robins cover them with leaves. In some versions, it is simply the uncle who abandons the children in the woods, where they die and are buried with leaves by birds. Sometimes the uncle is punished for his crime, but in the original ballad, there is no retribution.

Interestingly, there are two early filmic versions of "Babes in the Wood," one silent in black and white directed by Chester and Sidney Franklin in 1917, and the other, directed by Burt Gillett in color and animated in 1932 as part of Disney's Silly Symphonies. The Franklin film is particularly important because it combines the plots of "Babes in the Wood" with "Hansel and Gretel" in an unusual if not bizarre manner. In this film two tiny children about six or seven years old, clearly blond and dressed like old-fashioned dolls in aristocratic clothes, watch their father dying, and then they overhear their wicked uncle talking to their evil stepmother and plotting to kill them. Taken into the woods by two "bad men," they are protected by a fairy who causes the bad men to fight. After the more evil of the two dies, the other bad man leaves the children in the forest where they enjoy a deep sleep and pleasant dreams thanks to the fairy. However, their troubles are not at an end. A robber prince with a moustache, who is about their age, wants to marry the petite girl. Again the fairy protects the children by paralyzing the robber and his band and sending brother and sister across a river on the back of a swan. It is at this point that we are informed that the children's names are Hansel and Gretel, and it is at this point that "Babes in the Wood" merges with "Hansel and Gretel," for the robber prince enlists the help of a witch, who captures the brother and sister by luring them to her gingerbread house with a dove. As usual, Gretel pushes the witch into the oven before she can eat Hansel. Then brother and sister use a magic wand to break an evil spell and to free the gingerbread men, who are the king's soldiers. The fairy provides a coach to take them to their village, but the robber prince and his band attack and capture them. Gretel refuses to marry the robber prince, who decides to poison Hansel. Fortunately, the king's soldiers arrive to save brother and sister. Hansel kills the robber prince by shoving him off a cliff. Then he and Gretel return to their village where they tell an old man, probably the mayor, what happened. The villagers storm the wicked uncle's house and drag him and the stepmother to the village square where they are placed in stocks on a platform. This punishment is the final scene of the film.

Viewed today, this remarkable melodramatic film is hilarious. The Franklins employed child actors in the Black Forest to perform the roles of the fairy, robbers, and soldiers. Despite exaggerated gestures and grimaces, the acting is unusually good; the chase scenes are lively and reminiscent of those in other early silent live-action and animated films. However, many of the shots are unintentionally comic. For instance, the fairy queen, a young pre-teen girl, is dressed in a white gown with wings and pops in and out of the film with a flash of smoke; the six-year-old robber prince is fond of twitching his moustache; the swords are almost larger than the robbers and soldiers. The overly dramatic emotions of Hansel and Gretel are difficult to take seriously. Nevertheless, the plots of "Babes in the Wood" and "Hansel and Gretel" are woven together effectively in the film and raise interesting questions about the safe home that the two orphans seek and need. In the end, they are left with money and a mansion without parents or guardians. Justice is served, and perhaps this is all that we need to know. The final scene depicting the evil uncle and stepmother in stocks on a platform in the town square is in some ways more satisfying than having Hansel and Gretel return to their father with treasures.

The Disney cartoon *Babes in the Woods* (1932) dispenses with mean parents and a search for home altogether. In this short animated film, the camera focuses first on a strange rock formation that resembles a witch on a broom, and a voiceover begins to tell us and sing about the story of the "witch rock." The next frame introduces us to two blond children, who are wearing wooden shoes and resemble stereotypical pictures of cute Dutch children. They are lost in the forest, and as they move deeper into the woods, they discover a glade filled with bearded elves who invite them to join their merry dance and festivities. After a few minutes of amusement, the celebration is broken by an ugly witch flying on a broom who lures the children to ride with her back to her gingerbread house. Once there, the witch throws the children into the house where they are frightened by spiders, rats, lizards, and cats who are in cages or in chains. The witch declares she is going to change them into reptiles and insects and manages to transform the boy into a spider with a magic potion. The girl resists and is helped by her brother. Suddenly, the elves arrive in full force and attack the witch. The girl and boy find an antidote in a bottle and pour it on the caged beasts and insects who become lively children. In the meantime, the elves shoot the witch in the air, and she falls into a boiling cauldron that turns her into a rock. The children and elves celebrate, and the final frame depicts the witch rock.

Though the Disney film probes neither the ballad "Babes in the Wood" nor the Grimms' "Hansel and Gretel," the references to both works are abundantly clear. It appears as if Gillett solved the problem of childhood abandonment and abuse by focusing merely on the witch. The children are drawn simply as innocent babes in the woods. They do not seem to have parents, and they join with other children whom they have saved and the bearded elves who saved them to celebrate the defeat of evil. This film was produced during the Great Depression, and one could possibly draw parallels to numerous lost and abandoned children during the 1930s. Whatever the case may be, it avoids addressing the causes of evil by arbitrarily introducing the stereotypical witch who is symbolically frozen into a legendary figure as the eternal threat to children.

Filmic Narrative Strategies

Aside from incorporating motifs from "Babes in the Wood," the filmmakers, who have been engaged in the discourse about "Hansel and Gretel" and abandoned children, have devised many different narrative strategies to address the problematic actions of the parents, the cruelty of the witch, and the search for a safe and happy home. Whether live-action or animated, the films involve: 1) close adherence to either the Grimms' text or the Engelbert opera as hypotexts that focus on the reconciliation of the children with their father or parents in a safe home; 2) mock versions that parody "Hansel and Gretel" as innocent children and question the canonical tale in diverse ways; and 3) contemporary adaptations that often diverge greatly from "Hansel and Gretel" to focus on the trauma of the children and recreate the incidents as horror or uncanny experiences. They clearly raise controversial questions through horror about how children are treated today.

Despite their conservative tendencies, some of the films that adhere closely to the Grimms and Humperdinck plots are highly artistic and technically innovative. Ray Harryhausen's *Hansel and Gretel* (1951) and Lotte Reiniger's *Hansel and Gretel* (1955) are good examples. Harryhausen used stop-motion and model animation with realistic figures to portray two industrious and tidy children who clean house furiously to help their widowed father, a poor woodcutter. When Gretel accidentally breaks a pitcher of milk, the family has little left to nourish itself. So, she and Hansel set out into the forest to gather berries. They become lost; the witch sees them and magically creates a delightful gingerbread house to trap them. After Hansel is locked in a golden cage, Gretel pushes the witch into a fiery oven. All at once, the house disappears. A charming rabbit shows the children the witch's treasure of jewels and gold. The father, who had been searching for them, arrives to share in their good fortune.

The backdrops of home, forest, and gingerbread house are painted with meticulous care. The movements of the model figures are flawless just as the voice of the narrator is soothing. The narrative is one of sweet reconciliation, but it is clear that the father has played no role in the dilemma of the children. Nor is there an idyllic image of home in the end. The reunion of the father takes place in a "liberated" forest.

The final image in Lotte Reiniger's version of "Hansel and Gretel" is slightly different. There is no treasure at the end of her story. Rather, Hansel and Gretel return home to their loving parents and bring with them the squirrel and goose that helped them overcome a wicked witch. In contrast to Harryhausen's clay figures, Reiniger's silhouette puppetry does not allow viewers to see the expressions of the characters.

Everything depends on the movements and actions of the shadow puppets narrated by a voice-over that assumes different vocal roles. Interestingly, there is no major conflict with the parents in this film. Hansel and Gretel want to play outside the house in a meadow, and their anxious mother asks them to stay close to home. However, they stray into the forest when a squirrel drops a nut near them, and they chase it until they are lost. Later, the squirrel and a goose help the children break the witch's magic wand causing her to explode into a thousand pieces. Reiniger's film is more comic than Harryhausen's pristine portrayal of a brother and sister, who are overly nice and obedient children. And, of course, the films are technically very different. Yet, their similarities in ideological perspective are greater than their artistic differences. Each one focuses on sweet reconciliation and the warmth of caring parents. This image of care is clearly connected to postwar sentiments about family and national togetherness in postwar Europe and America and the "silent" 1950s.

There were many other films produced during this epoch that did the same. For instance, two West German productions made specifically for German families in 1954 reflect a tendency in the German film industry to produce films calling for a creation of a sense of *Heimat* or home after World War II. Walter Janssen's *Hansel and Gretel* depicts an impoverished but happy family of basket makers hounded by a nasty landlord. They dream of a better life, and Hansel and Gretel leave home to find a witch's treasure. Later, after they defeat the witch, they return to their parents in a show of solidarity. In Fritz Genschow's *Hansel and Gretel* there is another hard-working family threatened by a famine. The parents are compelled to abandon their children in the woods, but after Hansel and Gretel defeat the witch, they free a large group of children who had been turned into gingerbread figures, and they all sing as they march back into the village where the children are greeted by their parents. Implicit is that Hansel and Gretel will also return to their parents. Both these films are filled with decorative nature scenes, idyllic villages, and sturdy people in country costumes. Made during the period of the economic miracle in West Germany, the "new" versions of "Hansel and Gretel" are tied to the old themes of national bonds and family harmony.

Aimed at family audiences, most of the films produced in Europe and America in the 1950s and 1960s do not raise serious questions about abandonment but rather use the "Hansel and Gretel" story to create images of loving parents and a feeling of security in stable homes. This tradition has continued well into the twenty-first century. For example, Tom Davenport's first educational film produced in 1975 was a short Appalachian version of "Hansel and Gretel" set in the 1930s during the Great Depression. Though well-intended, he sticks too closely to the Grimms' text and associates the stepmother with the evil witch—the same actress almost always plays the stepmother and the witch—and thereby he obfuscates the real causes of poverty. To his credit, Davenport does capture the misery, despair, and poverty of the people in Appalachia during the Depression, but there is no hint of rethinking and recreating the tale so that viewers might reflect about the possibilities for transformation. This film, like many children's books and other more commercial films, ends with the father's embrace of his children, a loving but deadly embrace of home as closure.

It is striking that most of the cartoons and longer animated films produced in the latter half of the twentieth century tend to repeat the Grimms' message that home needs to be recreated by guiltless parents or by father alone. In a delightful cartoon, *Hansel and Gretel* (1952), Mighty Mouse rescues two tiny mice, shrinks the witch, and delivers the cute mice to their father. Not only does he save them but he also gives their father a magic axe that will enable him to cut down all the trees in the forest and lift the family out of poverty. In *Mr. Piper and the Story of Hansel and Gretel* (1963), part of a Canadian TV series, narrated by the opera singer Alan Crofoot, we are presented with a hybrid sentimental version of the Grimms and Humperdinck stories with mediocre images. The children are at fault in this flimsy story, and Crofoot reminds his audience at the end that all children should always listen to what their parents have to say. In the German Simsala series, the 1999 *Hänsel und Gretel* is framed by the adventures of two amusing animal characters, Doc Croc and Yoyo, who clumsily and merrily intervene in all the Grimms' tales. In this film, the father is henpecked and sent off by the stepmother to find a better job, and then she abandons Hansel and Gretel in the forest. Despite their clumsiness, Croc and Yoyo save the children and return them to their father whose wife has left him because of his inability to find work, but the children have brought him a treasure. The British Britannica version, *Hansel and Gretel* (2005) is only slightly different in that the father takes a trip to procure more food for the family. While he is gone, the stepmother abandons Hansel and Gretel in the forest. When they return home, the stepmother is sent packing by the strong father who has returned from his trip to support his children.

The non-critical approach to the Grimms and Humperdinck versions of "Hansel and Gretel" also marks most of the commercial, live-action family films. For instance, James Frawley's *Hansel and Gretel* (1982), part of Shelley Duvall's Faerie Tale Theatre series, basically uses the traditional tale to exhibit Hollywood celebrities to show off their talents. Joan Collins takes delight in starring as both the evil stepmother and the even more evil witch, who is, of course, sent to her death by the brother and sister in a typical imitative interpretation of the Grimms' "Hansel and Gretel," backed by melodic music reminiscent of Humperdinck's opera. The opera was used as the basis of the Cannon Movies production, *Hansel and Gretel* (1988), directed by Len Talan, a hastily made film that drips with sentimentality even if it represents a more realistic picture of the children's mother. Just as the Faerie Tale Theatre films always wink at adults to make preposterous if not infantile jokes and gain approval for "harmless" retellings of fairy tales, this film, too, is filled with sentimental scenes and pathetic humor. The most stupid of all the comic versions, however, is Gary Tunnicliffe's *Hansel & Gretel* (2002), which poorly resembles a fractured fairy tale that turns all the traditional motifs inside out. This film is framed by a concerned father reading a musty magic book to his two children who have recently lost their mother, and he changes the tale therapeutically à la Bruno Bettelheim to help his children overcome their trauma. In this version of "Hansel and Gretel," a bossy and bumbling stepmother takes two children, clearly contemporary American kids, who are spunky, witty, and powerful, into a magic forest. Abandoned, the children meet a gay sandman, a sexy wood fairy, and a dumb troll, and then à la *The Wizard of Oz*, the children manage to defeat the British actress Lynn Redgrave, whose parody of a witch only makes a mockery of her own choice to be in the film, one of the most insipid adaptations of "Hansel and Gretel" to date.

In many respects, Tunnicliffe's *Hansel and Gretel* can be considered a caricature of good parody that falls flat on its face. Perhaps, because of the seriousness of the classic tale and the theme of child abandonment, "Hansel and Gretel" has been difficult to parody. The fractured fairy tale of "Hansel and Gretel," which appeared in the Rocky and Bullwinkle television series in 1960, is one of the better parodies. In this short skit, Hansel and Gretel's mother wants carbohydrates, amino acids, and riboflavin, and she is driving her woodchopper husband and children crazy to find food for her. The woodchopper only brings back logs instead of food. So, the children go into the forest to placate their mother. Instead of finding a wicked witch, they find a clumsy one who turns Hansel into an aardvark to uphold the witch's tradition. However, she cannot fly a broom, and Gretel promises to teach her if she will change Hansel back into his former self. The witch agrees, but once she starts flying, she cannot stop and zooms around the earth in orbit where she still is to this day. Hansel and Gretel return home with the help of a French talking duck. Their father has turned into a hunter and now can supply the family with food, but the mother is somewhat anxious because of the stray bullets that fly about the house.

This light parody mocks all the stereotypical characters in the Grimms' tale and concludes with an ending that is the beginning of another problem in the family—hunting. The jokes and gags are dependent on word play and ironical twists in the action. The woods are not dangerous, nor is the witch. In another parody, *The Wacky Adventures of Hansel and Gretel* (1999), the story is narrated by a demure looking puppet bird on a branch. The major characters are all marionettes filmed in natural or real settings. Hansel and Gretel live with their lumberman father; they are nerdy children who go into the forest to save a moose. Instead of saving a moose, they rescue a small dog with a deep voice that was caught in a net. He takes them to the underground laboratory of the weird Professor Cranium, who shows them his experiments with robots. When the children leave to return to their father, they encounter the witch living in a candy trailer home in the middle of the forest. She traps them in a pit with Ratso the reptile. They escape on the witch's broom and eventually return to their father.

Invariably, the parodies expose the witch as harmless and make light of the idea of child abuse. But there are also some other films that seek to deal with the trauma of abandonment and also border on being parodies. For example, *Whoever Slew Auntie Roo?* (1971), starring Shelly Winter as a psychotic American mother and ex-vaudeville star, who lives in England during the 1920s, intends to be a thriller but is more humorous than terrifying. The insane mother turns into a kind of witch and plunders an orphanage to capture children. Later she is burned to death in her mansion. Winters is so ridiculous and comical as a would-be witch that the film becomes more camp than horrific. In another film, *Criminal Lovers* (1999), which is truly a horror story, the French filmmaker François Ozon does not refer directly to "Hansel and Gretel," but there are clear allusions to the classic tale. Here two teenagers kill an Arab schoolmate and flee to a forest, where they are captured by a lonely huntsman, who is more dreadful than any witch could be. He treats the unassuming teenagers in brutal and sadistic ways. Eventually, the girl is killed by the police who have pursued the pair, while her friend and the hunter are arrested. Unlike "Hansel and Gretel," which provides motivation for the cannibalistic witch, the arbitrary violent acts in this film are enigmatic and are horrific representations of how the random acts of violence by teenagers can generate a retribution that is more violent and perverse than the murder they have committed.

Criminal Lovers endeavors to be a more serious depiction of the trauma experienced by two young people lost in a dangerous forest, but it does not deal with abandonment and the search for home. As I have mentioned above, the film touches only tangentially on the major themes of the Hansel and Gretel filmic discourse. Three other contemporary films, Alex van Warmerdam's *Grimm* (2003), Christoph Hochhäusler's *This Very Moment* (*Milchwald: Ein Märchen in Angst und Farbe*, 2003), and Yim Pil-Sung's *Hansel and Gretel* (2007), are more significant contributions to the Hansel and Gretel filmic discourse because of the innovative and critical manner with which they explore the consequences of abandonment for young people.

Van Warmerdam's macabre film begins with a shot of a dog in an alley sniffing for food during a bitter cold winter evening somewhere in Holland. In many ways the film is about starving "dogs" living off the refuse of society. The camera then leads viewers through desolate streets to a brick farmhouse. Inside, we witness a bitter dispute between the parents and their two hungry children, who are in their early twenties. There is no food, and the children are sent to bed by an angry and glum father. The next day the sullen father takes them into the bare forest to fetch firewood as their mother watches sadly from a window. The parents have apparently made an ominous decision. From this point on the camera's view will be similar to the detached gaze of the mother in the window frame looking out at her children and wondering what will become of them.

Figure 48
Alex van Warmerdam,
Grimm

Deep in the bare forest, the father abandons his children. Jacob, the older sibling, finds a note in his pocket written by their mother that tells them to go and visit their Uncle Ramon in Spain where it is warmer. Marie, the sister, asks, "How do we get home?" And Jacob replies, "Home? Marie, he abandoned us. Bastard. He couldn't handle us."

It appears that Jacob and Marie will have a grim destiny, and van Warmerdam plays upon the name grim throughout the film: Jacob is the name of the older brother Grimm; Marie is the first name of one of the best storytellers who contributed tales to the Grimms' collection; motifs from the Grimms' "Hansel and Gretel" and also "Brother and Sister" that are to lead to happiness are woven grimly into a dark comedy. Indeed, the adventures of Jacob and Marie turn grotesquely humorous soon after their abandonment. As they trudge through the woods into the night, they are starving. They manage to trap a farmer's dog and roast it over a fire. Meanwhile, the farmer, alarmed by Marie's cries, comes upon them and takes them to his house, where Jacob is forced to have intercourse with the huge homely wife of the farmer because the farmer cannot perform according to his wife's expectations. It appears that Jacob will be kept as a stud, but he and Marie invent a bludgeon that swings and knocks out farmer and wife, and they make a comic escape.

From this point on, there are a series of episodes in which van Warmerdam portrays Jacob and Marie as scavengers, who act on impulse and destroy any possibility to endow their lives with meaning. For instance the very next scene is in a desolate part of a Dutch city where they are living in a tent. They have no money or food, and when a seemingly well-to-do stranger comes upon them, Marie is willing to prostitute herself for twenty euros. Once again, things go awry when Jacob takes a pistol and tries to rob the stranger. In a comic fight scene with the bare-assed stranger, brother and sister accidentally kill him and find that he only has ten euros in his pocket. Their only choice now is to flee to Spain where they have one absurd adventure after the next.

Upon discovering that their Uncle Ramon is dead, Marie separates from Jacob and goes to the home of a wealthy handsome surgeon named Diego, who lives with his sick sister Teresa outside the city in a huge mansion on a hillside. Most of the settings and landscapes in the film are desolate. Jacob follows and is obviously jealous of his sister's affair with Diego, and he also resents the supercilious behavior of Diego and his sister's desire to be part of rich society. When Jacob discovers a locked door, he becomes suspicious that Diego may have some sinister plans. In fact, he does, for he overcomes Jacob, injects him with a serum that makes him unconscious, and imprisons Marie in a cell-like room. Then he operates on Jacob and takes out one of his kidneys for his sick sister. After he abandons Jacob for dead in the hills, it seems that he may kill Marie. However, she escapes and finds Jacob in a dilapidated car that he has stolen. Diego pursues them in his slick black car, but he accidentally drives over a cliff during the chase and is left for dead. Wandering in the desert, Jacob and Marie stumble on a ghost town that resembles a Hollywood Western set, where Marie nurses Jacob back to health. After several days, Diego, who has risen from the dead, suddenly appears with a shotgun, and Jacob takes a bow and arrow to defend himself and his sister. In a mock duel on lonely Main Street, Jacob shoots Diego in the heart with an arrow. As Marie and Jacob are burying him outside a saloon, they are about to cover his head with dirt as dogs might do, but they cannot finish because two Spanish police show up. In a scene filled with droll black humor, brother and sister must place a bucket over Diego's head so that the police will not discover the body. Once the police leave, Jacob and Marie are pictured throwing rocks into a small lake at the bottom of a rocky hill. They are silent until Marie says, "I want to go home." In the very next shot they are pictured moving up and over the rocky hill with a donkey supposedly on their way home.

Jacob and Marie are not the brightest people in the world, even if they somehow speak perfect fluent Spanish—one of the many unbelievable inconsistencies in the film—they are survivors despite themselves. They bungle all the opportunities they have to lead stable lives. They have absolutely no morals, and they do not seem to have feelings for other people except for each other.

Even their love for one another borders on comical incest. They always sleep in the same bed, and they bathe together. Yet, they never seem to consummate their apparent desire for each other. They always blunder. Indeed, they pout and argue their way through the absurd episodes like two infants. Though in their early twenties, neither has a job, nor do they seek jobs when they are abandoned. It appears as though they are stunted in their growth and maturity, and perhaps they have been overly protected by their parents, who can no longer protect them.

Van Warmerdam is disposed to play with clichés in this film, as in his other films. As we know, the fairy tales "Hansel and Gretel" and "Brother and Sister" end happily and depict a pristine relationship between brother and sister. Van Warmerdam's fairy-tale film is more an absurd nightmare than anything else, and though comical and critical of typical feel-good narratives, the film is filled with too many improbabilities that prevent the bizarre scenes from becoming somewhat credible or even humorous. The final scenes in the ghost town seem tacked on to the film and are feeble attempts to mock American Westerns. Van Warmerdam relies too heavily on playing with stock characters such as the macho Spaniard, the silent black maid, the devoted polite servant, the plotting sister, and the dumb Dutch peasants without offering any substantial insight into the plight of young abandoned teenagers. Is van Warmerdam concerned about the amorality of young people today? Does he explore what home might be and what Jacob and Marie envision as home? Is life merely an existence to be survived? It is difficult to say what van Warmerdam wants to convey by depicting the chaotic adventures of Jacob and Marie except to say that he has lost himself in the maze of spoofs that he has created.

This is not the case with Christoph Hochhäusler's *This Very Moment*, which is a much more serious social and political treatment of abandonment. This stark film begins with a long-distance shot of two children walking slowly along a flat country road lined by telephone poles. Their features are indistinguishable, but as they move toward the camera, the viewer can see a girl and boy about nine and seven carrying school backpacks. They are stragglers in a bad mood because their stepmother apparently did not pick them up at an appointed place at the right time. They are German children somewhere in the former East Germany on a road near the Polish border. At the end of the film, these same two children are filmed walking away from the camera on a road in Poland toward Germany. They have been chased out of a Volkswagen van by a good-natured Polish worker, who has been frustrated by them. They walk down the middle of a lonely road toward an unknown destination and destiny until they disappear over a hill.

Hochhäusler's bleak but brilliant film about the accidental abandonment of two children, Lea and Constantin, picks up on a theme from van Warnerdam's *Grimm* that was not fully developed— the incapacity of parents in our post-industrialist world to provide the young with the nurture and care that they need. Hochhäusler's film is a poignant comment and vivid depiction of anxiety

Figure 49
Christoph
Hochhäusler,
This Very Moment

and alienation. The plot is simple and straightforward: a young woman named Sylvia has become a stepmother by marrying an older man named Joseph, a widower, who has two children. They are clearly well-to-do in the former East Germany and have recently moved into a suburban house still in the midst of a renovation. Everything is white, sterile, and unfinished inside the house, and Sylvia has obviously not adjusted to the house and the two stepchildren who resent her. The unprepared young wife married to a rich professional can easily be interpreted as a representation of contemporary East Germany after the fall of the wall in 1989. The young stepmother is not up to the task of raising children who do not belong to her. When she does pick them up after the initial scene on the road and drives them to do her shopping in Poland, where it is cheaper than in Germany, she has an argument with Lea, the daughter, and abandons both of them temporarily on the road to the shopping center. The abandonment turns out to be permanent when the children wander into a forest and become lost. Sylvia returns home to the sterile house and lies to her husband by telling him that she had not seen the children in the afternoon and that they must have gone to a caretaker's home. The caretaker knows nothing, and soon there is a police hunt for the children. In the meantime, Lea and Constantin stumble upon the van of the Polish worker named Cuba, who delivers cleaning fluid to different hotels in this western region of Poland. He intends to take them to the police the next morning and provides for them during the evening. Meanwhile, the stepmother Sylvia becomes more and more morose, depressed, and anxious. She clings to Joseph, who leads a search and posts a reward. When Cuba hears about the reward, he wants to collect it, but he himself had abandoned them to the care of some religious pilgrims in the middle of a small Polish town. Lea and Constantin try to return home by bus but fail. They become separated and are finally "re-captured" by Cuba, who has set up an appointment to meet their father in a parking lot outside a highway restaurant in Poland. Joseph drives with Sylvia to the restaurant, and Sylvia collapses out of fear that Joseph will learn the truth about her treatment of his children. Cuba cannot control Lea and Constantin, who are scared that he will not take them home. So, Lea tries to poison him. Finally, Cuba realizes that the children are not worth all the trouble that they have caused him, and he chases them out of his van and sends them packing back to Germany.

In an interview included on the DVD of the film, Hochhäusler remarks that he has always been attracted to the enigmatic quality of fairy tales. For him, "Hansel and Gretel" has too much of an abrupt happy ending that appears to be forced. Therefore, in his contemporary adaptation of the tale, he wanted more to capture the enigma of the tale and to stress that the difficult conditions in the German family will persist in the post-1989 period. There is no happy end in his film. Hochhäusler also stated that the family is a community of anxiety within a cruel world. The children in his film are left to their own resources because anxiety and alienation cannot create bonds of support for the young. Misunderstanding is the way people communicate whether it be in the former East Germany or Poland, and certainly the language and cultural misunderstandings contribute to the conflicts between Cuba and the children. Silence and repression are also contributing factors to the dilemma of the family. Sylvia cannot express her rage or articulate how alienated she feels, while Joseph assumes that the way he has re-ordered his family after his wife's death will work, that is, until the fissures are exposed. Certainly, the children are not willfully abandoned in this film, but they have been psychologically abandoned, and though they head for home at the end, it is questionable whether they can find home in a world of lies and miscommunication.

Though it may be wrong to generalize and discuss the problems of the young in "Hansel and Gretel" films as representative of world-wide problems in a globalized world, these films do give pause for thought about how children are being similarly maltreated in different societies, even though the cultures may be very different. Interestingly, the most chilling and relentless critique of adult abandonment and abuse of children engaged in the "Hansel and Gretel" filmic discourse comes from South Korea. Yim Pil-Sung's *Hansel and Gretel* is a fascinating and disturbing if not surreal guilt trip about the criminal and brutal treatment of children in a world that pays no heed to their cries of despair. Pil-Sung purposely chose a German fairy tale and European magic realist style that would be unusual for Korean audiences and more familiar to western audiences. Indeed, it is striking to view a Korean director's use and adaptation of European folklore and western fantasy films to challenge Korean spectators. The result is a remarkable haunting and unforgettable film: Yim Pil-Sung adds a dimension to the "Hansel and Gretel" filmic discourse that continues to ask many of the questions raised by Hochhäusler, but in a more harrowing way.

Pil-Sung's *Hansel and Gretel* begins with the voiceover of the major protagonist of the film, a young man named Eun-Soo, who, as he is running frantically through a forest, tells us: "In this world a strange place that couldn't possibly exist, a deep forest where anyone can get quickly sucked into, might exist somewhere. Everything started in that deep forest." Actually, everything begins in the first scene, once again, on a road through a forest. It is in the middle of winter near Christmas. This time Eun-Soo is pictured driving and speaking to his pregnant girlfriend on his cell phone. She is angry because she is about to give birth, and he has left her to go to his mother whom he dislikes but who is ill and perhaps is dying. Distracted, Eun-Soo tries to avoid hitting an animal, drives off the road, and the car turns over. When Eun-Soo awakes after the accident, it is dark, and as he tries to make his way out of the forest, he suddenly sees a strange young girl about twelve wearing a white dress and red cape. Perhaps she is Red Riding Hood lost in the forest? She is holding a lantern and leads him to a large Victorian house deep in the forest. Outside there is a barely visible shabby sign that reads "House of Happy Children," a warning to the viewers that we should expect a good deal of unhappiness.

Pil-Sung, a meticulous, artful director, had a special house built in the middle of the forest that resembles many haunted houses on the outside, but inside the decor and rooms resemble more a typical Victorian nursery or dolls house with flowery wallpaper and pictures of cute and weird rabbits and toys, trinkets, and dolls scattered on the floor and throughout the house. There is also a brightly lit Christmas tree with ornaments. Instead of finding a witch, ghosts, or vampires, Eun-Soo is introduced to what appears to be the model contemporary bourgeois family sitting on a couch and smiling as if posing for a photographer. They are all primly and properly dressed, almost as if they were dolls: a well-dressed mother and father, Young-Hee, the demure girl who found him, her sister aged about seven named Jung-Soon, and her brother Manbok aged about fifteen. Their smiles, however, are creepy and chilling. The parents speak as if they are afraid of making a mistake and displeasing the children. When they eat, they stuff themselves with cake and candy. Eun-Soo is perplexed, but everyone appears to be kind and helpful. He plans to leave the next morning, but

Figure 50
Yim Pil-Sung,
Hansel and Gretel

there is no phone in the house and no way to make contact with the outside world. He has no idea where he is, and when he sets out to leave the forest the following morning, he wanders the entire day until he sees a light in the evening and realizes that he has returned to the Victorian house.

By now Eun-Soo feels very uneasy and suspicious that something strange if not an evil force is lurking in the forest and in the house. Viewers, already clued by the title of the film and the first shot of Eun-Soo running for his life, must feel that the house may indeed be the witch's gingerbread house. However, it is never clear what the house is and whether what happens actually takes place in reality. For six days Eun-Soo tries to find his way out of the forest so that he can get to his mother and return to his girlfriend. Each day something happens that frustrates and prevents him from finding the correct path. The parents disappear after they make some disparaging remarks about the children, who continue to remain overly sweet and are often referred to as angels. When questioned about the disappearance, the children state, "We're not bad kids," a refrain that they will repeat throughout the film. They begin to call Eun-Soo uncle and question why he wants to leave them. On one of his excursions during the third day he encounters a Christian deacon and his wife who are taken to the Victorian house because their car broke down on the highway. The deacon behaves as though he were possibly in league with a sinister God or the devil himself. He seeks to take over the house. His greedy wife disappears. Eun-Soo discovers the mother from the first day in the labyrinth of the attic. Later she is transformed into a doll. Meanwhile, Eun-Soo also finds a copy of *Hansel and Gretel* with eerie figures and scenes. He senses that there is a mystery that needs to be solved and that maybe the children who seem to threaten him are not as bad as they seem to be. But on day five it is clear that the boy Manbok has extraordinary powers and can use his eyes to cause damage or even kill people. On the final sixth day, the conflicts mount. It is apparent that the deacon is obsessed and wants to dominate the house and the lives of the children. Eun-Soo follows Manbok into the forest and sees him enter and leave a blue doorway. Eun-Soo opens the door and finds a book illustrated by the children in which he is portrayed as the hero of their story. Once he returns to the house, he pleads with the children to let him leave. Only Young-Hee is sympathetic to him, but there are major clashes with the deacon, and in a series of flashbacks we learn that the children were actually born in 1959, 1960, and 1965 and were raised in this house, which was an orphanage called "House of Happy Children." Along with many other children they were starved, beaten, and raped. Some were even killed. The director of the orphanage resembled the deacon. Through an accident with a television set, Manbok's eyes were electrified so that he developed extraordinary powers with his sight to kill or electrify other people. When the deacon endeavors to slit Eun-Soo's throat, Manbok saves him and destroys the deacon. But when Eun-Soo wants to leave the children, they try to compel him to stay insisting that they do not want to grow up or leave the forest because adults in the outside world are too cruel. They want him to stay with them because they think he is different. Eun-Soo protests and tells them that the world is not so bad and that he will take them with him and protect them. Yet, they refuse to believe him and assert that he is the hero of their story. Finally, he resorts to burning their picture book so he can be released. The next thing he knows he is on the ground near his car. He is dazed from the accident and sees the police on the highway at the scene of the accident.

It appears that Eun-Soo may have dreamt about all the episodes in the forest. However, in the final scene that takes place in his apartment in the city, Eun-Soo is apparently living contentedly with his wife and baby. It is Christmas, and his wife needs some powdered milk. Before he leaves the apartment, he notices a strange book beneath the Christmas tree. It is actually the book drawn by the three children of the forest and shows a final picture of the children in the city. When Eun-Soo leaves the apartment building to get the powdered milk, he sees the profiles of the three children in the distance walking away from him.

Whether Eun-Soo's experiences were real or ethereal, that is, part of a traumatic nightmare, is incidental. What is significant is Pil-Sung's brilliant vision and critical exploration of the brutal treatment of innocent children in our contemporary world where barbarity often blends with civility or exists in high tension with civility. In an interview on the DVD of the film, Pil-Sung states that the director's role is not simply that of a storyteller, but that part of his job is to express a story visually in a different way because we have become a visually focused generation. His illuminating adaptation of "Hansel and Gretel" succeeds because he manages to make every symbol in each frame come alive with the extraordinary colors of the interior that blend with the colors of the forest, facial expressions that always have deeper meanings, and reflections through mirrors and windows that trouble our vision. Nothing and nobody are what they seem except perhaps for Eun-Soo, who, in some ways, is more innocent than the children, who impart lessons to him about child abandonment and abuse just as he is about to have a baby with his girlfriend. Though Pil-Sung's contemporary interpretation and retelling of "Hansel and Gretel" is filled with dread and horror, the film is not a horror film. Rather, it is more a surreal meditation about what we do to children when we bring them into a vicious world and when home can be a savage place.

Tom Thumb: Survival of the Little Person

Like many classical fairy tales, "Tom Thumb" and its diminutive protagonist are much better known than its authors Charles Perrault and the Brothers Grimm, and more than likely most people do not know the plot of the 1697 French text and how closely it is connected to "Hansel and Gretel." Nor do they probably care. Tom Thumb is that cute little guy, who is always in danger because of his diminutive size, but he always manages to avoid disaster through cunning or luck and sometimes both. Nevertheless, it is important to briefly review some of the historical background of the tale type because of its close connection to other tales that deal with child abandonment.

Actually, there are three literary texts connected to widespread oral versions that serve as the "hypotexts" for most of the Tom Thumb films. The first, represented most clearly by Charles Perrault's 1697 version "Little Tom Thumb" ("Le Petit Poucet"), involves child abandonment. A woodcutter and his wife have seven children and are extremely poor. Their youngest child is tiny, does not speak, and is considered somewhat dumb. Because of his size, he is called Little Tom Thumb. When a famine threatens the family with starvation, the parents abandon their children in a forest. Tom Thumb tries to foil their plans but fails. Eventually he leads his brothers to an ogre's house in the forest. The ogre and his wife live there with their seven daughters and pretend to be hospitable. However, little Tom learns that they plan to eat them while they sleep. So, he tells his brothers to take the night caps of the seven daughters so that their parents will mistake who they are in the dark. Consequently, the ogre and his wife eat their own children. Tom and his brothers escape but are pursued by the ogre wearing seven-league boots. When the ogre tires during the chase and falls asleep, Tom Thumb steals the seven-league boots, brings his brothers home, and then returns to the ogress and convinces her to give him all their treasures. Finally, he uses the seven-league boots to carry the treasure back to his family.

While Perrault's literary version bears strong resemblance to the plot of "Hansel and Gretel," the Grimms' tales about Little Tom Thumb are markedly different and stem from another folk-tale tradition that basically celebrates the cunning and courage of the little guy, who uses his wits to survive when he separates from his parents. The Grimms published two versions in their edition of *Children's and Household Tales*, "Thumbling" and "Thumbling's Travels," which basically have the same plot. In the first one, a poor farmer and his wife are childless and wish to have a child even if it is no bigger than a thumb. Their wish comes true, and Thumbling is the joy of their lives and helps them in unusual ways. However, two strangers see him and want to buy him so they can exhibit him in cities for money. At first the farmer refuses, but Thumbling convinces him to take the money. Soon after he escapes from the strangers by hiding in a mouse hole, and then his real adventures begin. He outwits robbers and exposes their crime; he is swallowed by a cow whom he causes to be slaughtered. Finally, a hungry wolf gobbles him into his belly, and since he is still starving, Thumbling leads him to his parents' home where the father kills the wolf and rescues his son. Then Thumbling declares he is home to stay.

In "Thumbling's Travels," Thumbling is born into a tailor's family and decides that he wants to see the world. His father gives him a darning needle as a sword, and off he goes to work as an apprentice and then joins some robbers whom he helps by stealing money from a king. After this accomplishment he works as an apprentice and then is swallowed by a cow from whom he escapes only to be gobbled up by a fox. Finally, he leads the fox to his home where Thumbling's father agrees to give the fox all the chickens it can eat if the fox lets Thumbling go. The tale concludes with the narrator remarking that the son's life is worth more than all the chickens in the barnyard.

Both of the Grimms' versions were widely disseminated in Europe during the eighteenth and nineteenth centuries in many different forms and are connected to the travels of young men, often apprentices, who had to leave their homes to find work and often became exploited and involved in crimes of various kinds. Their tiny size indicates their lack of power and social status, but the small heroes always have great wits and manage to return home, a place of security, much wiser through their experiences. Unlike Perrault's tale, which deals with child abandonment due to poverty and famine, the tale type of Thumbling is similar to many other tale types in which a young man goes out into the world to prove himself and generally does *not* return home. He will more than often obtain wealth and a wife and begin to build his own home under better circumstances.

Predictably, most of the cinematic versions about Tom Thumb that stem from the Perrault hypotext have been produced in France. Beginning in 1909 with the Spanish director Segondo de Chomón's short silent film *Little Tom Thumb*, almost all cinematic versions have been adaptations of the Perrault text. De Chomón's work was followed by Louis Feuillade's *Little Tom Thumb* (1912) and Robert Boudrioz's *Little Tom Thumb* (1920). All three films show the influence of Georges Méliès' stop-motion techniques and comic interpretation. Almost all live-action and animated films dealing with the Perrault version do not diverge greatly from the plot of the text. There are two films, however, that are original interpretations of the Perrault narrative and explore the causes of poverty and abandonment in greater depth than the run-of-the-mill adaptations—Michel Boisrond's *Tom Thumb* (1972) and Olivier Dahan's *Tom Thumb* (2001).

Boisrond, who worked as an assistant with Jean Cocteau early in his career, gives the tale a poetic if not melodramatic touch by adding an adolescent love story to the plot. Moreover, he uses vivid colors and characters throughout the film that are reminiscent of Victorian illustrated fairy-tale books. To contrast the poverty of the poor woodcutter's family, Boisrond introduces a king and queen living in a magnificent palace. Their only concern is the welfare of their young graceful daughter Rosemonde, whereas the woodcutter must labor to nourish seven growing boys. Every day he delivers wood to the castle and barely earns enough to support his wife and sons. One day Rosemonde's dearest toy, a paper mâché blue butterfly, is carried off by a wind into the forest, and the king orders his men to search for it. They fail in their mission, but Tom Thumb finds it and secretly brings it back to the princess in the night. Rosemonde is taken by the kind boy and hopes to see him again, especially because she has no contact with the outside world. However, a famine seeps into the land, and Tom Thumb's parents decide to abandon their sons in the forest, where, unknown to them, an ogre lives with his seven nasty, greedy daughters. Here the film follows the Perrault text, but Boisrond emphasizes the savagery not only of the ogre but also of his daughters, who are eventually eaten by the ogre. Tom uses his wits, steals the seven-league boots, and not only does he save his brothers, but he also rescues the Princess Rosemonde from the ogre. In true sentimental form, the film brings about a reconciliation of rich and poor at the end. Though Boisrond sweetens the tale with the love story of Rosemonde and Tom Thumb, he also creates class conflict by revealing how frivolous the king and queen are. The young people in the film become the moral arbiters who awaken the adults to the dire consequences of poverty.

Dahan, too, employs child protagonists as moral arbiters, but avoids the melodrama and senti- mentality of the love story. His film, which takes place during the religious wars of the fifteenth and sixteenth centuries, begins with the voiceover of an adult Tom Thumb narrating his past adventures. The first scene shows how Tom Thumb is picked on by his four older brothers and scolded by his father. The family lives in squalid conditions in a clearing near the forest. When Tom Thumb, who is about eight or nine, is sent to search for wood, he comes upon a mysterious young girl wearing a cape, who is about the same age. They are immediately attracted to each other, and she gives him a charm to wear around his neck to protect him and then disappears. It is apparent that they have an unusual bond, and that she will reappear in his life. But first, he and his family will be savagely attacked by a gruesome band of soldiers who ransack their house and take all their supplies. Not able to feed their children anymore, the parents decide to abandon their sons in the forest. Here Dahan follows the Perrault text and has the parents abandon them twice, but he deviates from the Perrault narrative by depicting how the peasants are at the mercy of both sides in a merciless battle. Moreover, when the children become lost in the woods, they are threatened by vicious wolves, and Dahan heightens the feeling of desperation by setting the scenes in a stark, ravaged forest with barren trees and a fiery red background. Eventually, Tom Thumb spots a light that leads them to a gigantic temple-like mansion with bizarre sculptures. The boys knock on the large door, and a beautiful young woman dressed in black opens and tries to persuade them to run away. However, they are too hungry to listen to her, and she lets them in.

Again, Dahan follows the Perrault narrative and has a vicious, scowling ogre suddenly appear and dominate the young woman. He finds the boys and orders them to dine with his daughters. It will be their last meal because he intends to eat them in the morning. Surprisingly, one of the daughters turns out to be Rose, Tom Thumb's friend, and she resists the ogre's bellowed commands. It is clear that she does not want to become an ogress. In fact, Rose saves Tom Thumb and his brothers after the ogre eats his own daughters. She leads the boys into the forest pursued by the ogre wearing seven-league boots. Tom Thumb manages to trick him so that he falls off a cliff. Then he puts on the seven-league boots and flies through the air over a battlefield filled with corpses. He stops to gather a message for the queen, and after he brings it to her, the war is ended. Tom Thumb is rewarded and embraced by his parents and brothers.

Though the film, intended for a family audience, ends on a traditional happy-end note, the majority of the scenes depict ruthless and wanton killing, not only because of the war but because the general barbarous conditions under which the people are living. It is a dog-eat-dog world, and it is difficult to conceive of kindness and generosity. Yet, in the eyes of Tom Thumb and Rose and through their perspective and behavior, the film conveys a sense of the dignity and integrity that children possess even when abandoned and abused. The parents and Tom Thumb's siblings learn from him and his relationship with Rose. The images of brutality are not downplayed throughout the film which only makes the beauty of the survival of the young more striking.

Whereas Tom Thumb in the Perrault cinematic discourse is celebrated for his admirable courage and cunning, the films that are somewhat connected to the Grimms' texts tend to emphasize the comic exploits of Tom Thumb. There have been a host of cartoons such as Ub Iwerks' *Tom Thumb* (1936), Burt Gillett's *The Adventures of Tom Thumb, Jr.* (1940), Chuck Jones' *Tom Thumb in Trouble* (1940), and Sid Marcus' *Tom Thumb's Brother* (1941) that have portrayed the little protagonist in preposterous situations which enable him to expose the foibles of his stronger opponents. Two feature films, George Pal's *Tom Thumb* (1958) and Dave Borthwick's *The Secret Adventures of Tom Thumb* (1993), best exemplify the adaptations made by directors to represent current ways tiny people have used to avoid the pitfalls of life.

Pal's family musical is notable for its banal if not insipid interpretation of the Grimms' "Thumbling," just as Pal diminished the lives of the poor brothers in his 1962 film, *The Wonderful World of the Brothers Grimm*, which is anything but wonderful. In the case of *Tom Thumb*, Pal begins with Charles Perrault's tale, "The Three Wishes." Jonathan, a well-dressed and neat woodcutter, is about to chop down a tree when the charming young Queen of the Forest appears and grants him three wishes if he spares the tree. When he returns home, he and his wife Anna have an argument causing his nose to turn into a sausage. They waste their wishes just so Jonathan can have his nose re-transformed. However, the merciful queen grants them an extra wish and allows the childless couple to adopt a five-inch young man whom they name Tom. Once he appears in the form of the dancing and singing Russ Tamblyn, the fun begins. That is, the film becomes your conventional boring musical. Tom dances and sings in the nursery and town fair with Pal's puppetoons that he made famous in stop-motion animated shorts between 1940 and 1946. He is duped by two loveable crooks played by the hilarious British comic actors Terry Thomas and Peter Sellers and then organizes their capture. He helps a lamentable town musician win the hand of the Queen of the Forest. In the end, like many films made during the Cold-War 1950s, the harmonious ending in which rich and poor joyously celebrate a homecoming is as artificial as Pal's reading of fairy tales.

In contrast—and perhaps as a spoof of Pal's film—Dave Borthwick's *The Secret Adventures of Tom Thumb*, supposedly created by the Bolex Brothers (perhaps a reference to the Brothers Grimm), is a brilliant somewhat gruesome adaptation of "Thumbling." The word "bollix" is the plural of ballock (testis) and is used as a verb meaning to throw into disorder or to bungle. And certainly Borthwick as the fictional Bolex Brothers throws the Grimms' tale of Tom Thumb into complete disorder, perhaps reflecting on the pestilence that is threatening the real world. Similar to the work of Pal and Harryhausen, Borthwick uses clay puppets and stop-motion animation to tell his story, but he also has his live actors move as if they were clay puppets, and when they talk, they basically grunt, moan, wheeze, scream, and bark. Their speech is unintelligible, but the actions of the puppets, miniature people, and the large humans are clear. The first scene which takes place in a weird artificial insemination factory portrays a mishap that causes a woman to give birth to a child in a dilapidated apartment filled with mechanical insects in a slum neighborhood. The insects

Figure 51
Dave Borthwick,
*The Secret Adventures
of Tom Thumb*

pervade every scene. While the woman moans in her bed, her unshaven and uncouth husband drinks in the next room. Finally, when she gives birth, she presents him with a tiny naked and bald clay child with blue eyes that resembles E. T. They name him Tom Thumb. No sooner is he born than two slickly dressed men break into the apartment, kill the mother, and take Tom to a laboratory where all kinds of animals and humans are locked in cages or are enduring torturous experiments by anonymous human scientists. The place is filled with suffering mutants. With the help of a mechanical lizard, Tom manages to escape through a sewerage drain into a junkyard or dumpyard, where miniature clay people, fearful and anxious, have built a village. Bewildered, Tom does not know what to do. Fortunately, Jack the Giant Killer, a valiant clay figure, becomes his guardian. He protects Tom from scavengers, drunks, and scientists. Meanwhile, Tom's despondent father is depicted in a sleazy tavern, mourning over the loss of wife and son. After the scavengers destroy the miniature village in the junkyard, Jack shoots two of them with his bow and arrow, and together with Tom, he returns to the laboratory and causes an emergency shutdown. The final frame shows a clean-shaven father and Tom's mother holding an unidentified newly-born baby in a white blanket. They are standing against a flowery wallpapered wall with insects crawling about the place. Mother and father are smiling.

Borthwick's ingenious film, which is filled with mechanical monstrosities, broken-down human beings, and sympathetic miniature clay people, mocks the traditional fairy tale of Tom Thumb, and at the same time it generates compassion for the little people caught in a highly technological world in which ruthless experimentations of all kinds appear to be common and appear to have created a dark and pestilent society. The little people or children like Tom Thumb have fear written on their faces, and they lead lives of bitter survival. One is compelled to ask whether Borthwick's vision of the plight of children is a contemporary critique of our present world, or whether he is envisioning what is yet to come. Whatever the case may be, his vision is bleak, and Tom Thumb's chances, not to mention the chances for all children, to show his courage and cunning and to triumph over obstacles have become extremely limited.

Piping For Another World

On the other hand, the cinematic discourse about the chances for children to march to their own beat, that is, to the beat of a savior like the Pied Piper, is clearly optimistic, even if adults are held in disrepute. Interestingly, he was never mentioned in the first reports about the children who disappeared from Hamelin. The earliest source of the legend about the Pied Piper is a stained-glass inscription in about 1300 that read: "On the day of John and Paul 130 children in Hamelin went to Calvary and were brought through all kinds of danger to the Koppen mountain and lost." About 150 years later, the monk Heinrich of Herford recorded this event in the Latin *Lüneburg Manuscript*, in which he stated that a thirty-year-old man came and led the children from the town of Hamelin playing a flute. The next record we have about this event was a 1553 diary written in German by Hans Zeitlos, the mayor of Bamberg, and it was followed by a similar short version in 1556 by the theologian Jobus Fincelius. Up until this time, rats had never been mentioned in any of the accounts, and it was only in 1565 in the *Family Chronicles* of Count Froben Christof of Swabia that rats enter the picture and are linked to the children of Hamelin and a pied piper dressed in a colored garment.

There are numerous other sources in Hamelin itself such as the front of a house erected in 1602/03 that has the stone engraving: "In the year 1284 on the Feast of Saints John and Paul, the 26th of June, 130 children were led astray by a pied piper and led out to Calvary by the Koppen where they all disappeared." Another house built in 1610 bears the engraving: "In the year of Our Lord, 1284, 130 children from Hamelin, in the custody of a piper, were led out to the Koppen, and there they disappeared." Again no rats, but they appeared in other versions and eventually became standard fare in the Pied Piper Legend by the time the Brothers Grimm wrote their own in 1816:

The Children of Hamelin

In the year 1284 a peculiar man appeared in Hamelin. He wore a bright multi-colored coat, and this is why he was allegedly called Brightman. He said he was a ratcatcher and promised to free the town of all the mice and rats for a certain amount of money. The townspeople reached an agreement with him and guaranteed to pay him a particular sum for his work. Thereupon, the ratcatcher pulled out a little pipe and began blowing. All at once, the rats and mice came crawling out of the houses and gathered around him. When he thought there were none left in the homes, he started walking out of the town followed by the entire pack. After reaching the Weser River, he took off his clothes and went into the water. All the animals followed, and when they plunged into the river, they drowned.

Once the townspeople were freed from their plague, however, they regretted that they had promised to pay the man and refused to give him any money. Instead, they made up all sorts of excuses so that he went away angry and bitter. On the 26 of June, the feast of St. John and St. Paul, at seven o'clock in the morning, or at noon according to other people, he reappeared, now in the form of a hunter with a terrifying face and a strange red hat, and he began playing his pipe in all the streets of the town. This time there were no rats and mice that immediately appeared. Instead, the children, boys and girls from four and up, came running in large numbers, including the grown-up daughter of the mayor. The entire flock followed him, and he led them out of the town to a mountain, where they all disappeared together. A nanny had seen all this from a distance, for she had been drawn there with a child in her arms, then turned around, and brought the news back to the town. The parents ran in crowds through the gates and searched for their children with heavy hearts. The mothers were miserable and shrieked and wept. Messengers were sent at once by sea and land all around the region to inquire whether the children, or even only a few of them, had been seen, but everything was in vain. Altogether 130 children had been lost. Two are said to have returned somewhat later, but one of them was blind and the other deaf so that the blind child was not able to show the place where the piper had taken the children and could only tell about it, while the deaf child could show the place but had heard nothing. A little boy had run along with just a shirt and had turned around to fetch his jacket, thereby escaping the misfortune that had befallen the others, for when he had run back to join them, the others had already disappeared into the hole in the side of the hill that is still shown today.

The street on which the children ran through the gate to leave the town was called the Street of Silence even in the eighteenth century (as it is still called) because no dancing or music is allowed there. Indeed, when a bride is brought to the church with music, the musicians must stop playing the instruments when they reach this street. The mountain near Hamelin, where the children disappeared, is called Poppenberg, and on the left and right two stones have been erected in the form of a cross. Some say that the children were led through a cave and came out on the other side in Siebenbürgen.

The townspeople of Hamelin documented this event in the town records and took care to note the year and day of the loss of their children. According to Seyfried it was the 22nd of June not the 26th of June that is given in the town records. The following lines are inscribed on the town hall:

> In the year 1284 A.D.
> 130 children born in Hamelin

were led out of our town
by a piper and lost in the mountain.

And on the new town gate, one can read:

Centum ter denos cum magnus ab urbe puellos
duxerat ante annos CCLXXII condita porta fuit.

In the year 1572 the mayor had the story painted on the church windows with the appropriate inscription that has become unreadable for the most part. There is also a coin with the inscription on it.

What is going on here? How do we begin interpreting this evidence and examine all the tales, poems, and documents that eventually culminated in the famous poem by Robert Browning "The Pied Piper of Hamelin" (1842), which itself was based on a 1605 English version by Richard Verstegan?

Most scholars agree that two different tale types merged and blended by 1565. The first concerns the actual incident of a mass emigration by children in 1284. Some historians believe that the children might have actually been lured away from Hamelin long before the year 1284 to take part in the Children's Crusade of 1212, while others think that the legend concerns a plague or epidemic in 1284, and it was death that carried off the children. Perhaps the best explanation concerns the social and economic situation of the town at the end of the thirteenth century: due to the lack of jobs and poverty, the young people of Hamelin did not have much of a future, and there are documents which reveal that a professional recruiter, looking for people to colonize German parts of Eastern Europe, came to Hamelin between 1250 and 1285, and convinced a large group of young people into resettling in the East. Whatever the case may be, it is apparent that the townspeople concealed the reasons why so many young people left Hamelin and, out of shame, invented stories to make it seem that "children" were taken away from them through magic or a demonic figure.

As the story developed and spread, storytellers embellished it with the second tale type, which concerned plagues and ratcatchers, and turned the narrative into a quasi wonder tale or fairy tale. Due to the diseases carried by rats, a real profession of ratcatchers developed during the Middle Ages, and as in all professions—shoemakers, tailors, soldiers, spinners—stories circulated among and about these people and their craft. Therefore, at one point in the oral tradition, a storyteller made the piper into a ratcatcher, and new fairy-tale elements were added to the legend of the strange mass exodus from Hamelin that made the tale more wondrous than it had ever been.

Though we still cannot be absolutely certain about the actual incident today, we do know that something traumatic and significant happened in the town of Hamelin in or around 1284. It was of such magnitude and mystery that the tale has been spread through the oral tradition, print, illustration, and painting from the sixteenth to the twentieth century when many filmmakers have sought to explore the mystery while commenting on how we value children, or whether we value children enough to protect them from diseases, reptiles, and mysterious outside forces.

The cinematic discourse is rich and vast and does not always focus on the "tragic" or "justifiable" abduction of the children. For instance, the animated cartoons experiment in most unusual ways with the characters and the plot. Surprisingly, the 1933 Disney production of *The Pied Piper*, directed by Wilfred Jackson, has strong political echoes of the Great Depression and a critique of greedy townspeople. Not only does the mayor deceive the pied piper, but he does so with all the people in the town in a colorful cartoon filled with music and a sprightly piper, who stands up to the hypocritical inhabitants of Hamelin, calls them dishonest, and promises to "pay" them back. In the closing scene he leads all the children, including the lame boy, to a utopian joyland, where they do not seem to be bothered by separating from their parents. In *Pied Piper Porky* (1939), directed by Robert Clampett, Porky Pig boasts in his usual stuttering manner how he has driven all the rats from Hamelin, but he is confronted with one ornery leftover rat, whom he tries to catch with the help of a cat. As usual, he is outwitted in chase scenes until the rat beats up the cat and breaks Porky Pig's horn. Many cartoons tend to portray blundering cats who have no luck in chasing mice or rats from a town. In Lou Lilly's *Playing the Pied Piper* (1941), a foolish pied piper cat tries to catch a mouse by reading a self-help book about how to be a pied piper in ten easy lessons. Of course, he fails. In Friz Freleng's *The Pied Piper of Guadelupe* (1961) Sylvester the Cat takes flute lessons to learn how to drive out cats in the town of Guadalupe, but Speedy Gonzales frustrates his efforts and drives him crazy in typical hilarious chase scenes. In Don Christensen's *The Pied Piper Puss* (1980) Tom the Cat is hired by a store owner to get rid of two mice and is also mocked in chase scenes that lead to his demise.

In other cartoons, cats play a negligible role. For instance, in *The Pied Piper from Space* (1978), directed by Ray Patterson and Carl Urbano, children are abducted from earth by aliens, and super friends such as Batman, Robin, Superman, and Wonder Woman must come to their rescue. Some cartoons make use of motifs from "The Pied Piper" to celebrate the exploits of famous protagonists of popular culture. The ghostbusters must get rid of obnoxious ghosts in *The Pied Piper of Manhattan* (1997) to bring calm to the city. In *The Pied Piper of Hamelin* (1981), produced by the Cosgrove Studios in England, Mark Hall uses clay puppets and stop-motion to retell Robert Browning's poem. The settings of the Middle Ages, the vicious rats, and the frightened townspeople are depicted with exquisite detail, and the final scenes are filled with gloom. However, there is no gloom in *It's The Pied Piper, Charlie Brown* (2000), in which Snoopy plays a concertina to lead mischievous soccer-playing mice from the streets of his neighborhood. Neither is there gloom in episode 510 of *The Muppet Show* (1981), in which the renowned flautist, Jean-Pierre Rampal, helps a village of rats chase away nasty boys and girls who are devouring and destroying their homes. While all the cartoons tend to adapt and "fracture" the traditional narrative, the 1960 episode of *The Pied Piper* in the Rocky and Bullwinkle show is the most outrageous. At the beginning we are introduced to a young man, who studies for five years because he wants to become a traveling minstrel. Once he completes his studies, however, nobody likes his music, and since he manages only to drive rats from towns with an instrument he calls the flatt, he becomes an exterminator. When a king who dislikes his mother-in-law hears about his skill, he decides to hire him to get rid of the dominating woman. However, she falls in love with his music, and they fall in love with each other. In the end, the king is driven out of his very own kingdom.

Most of the animated films are technically well-made, but they rarely touch on the controversial themes of child abuse and abandonment in a serious way. However, Jirí Barta, the brilliant Czech director, does not hesitate to probe the dark side of "The Pied Piper" in his stop-motion animated film, *Krysar* (1985). Children do not appear in harrowing adaptation, nor are they abducted. They are behind the scenes, so to speak. Barta is more concerned with revealing the materialism of the entire populace of a medieval town. Rich and poor alike are absorbed by making money. They bargain bitterly with one another and fight over money, or they literally make money, that is, stamp and hoard coins. They are all wasteful and corrupt, no matter what their social class is. In short, they are infected by petty greed not by rats. There is no reference to Hamelin in particular as the designated town, for Barta has sought to create a universal parable about the pestilence of money. Of course, one could draw a parallel with the political sickness and contamination of so-called "socialist" Czechoslovakia in 1985, when he produced the film. Yet, his film is even more pertinent today when avarice, exploitation, and ruthless competition have globally undermined the basic ethical behavior of people.

Barta has been strongly influenced by the expressionist films of the 1920s and also by the work of his Czech compatriot Jan Svankmajer and the Russian Yori Norstein. In *Krysar*, which means "ratcatcher" in Czech, he creates a slanted, deformed town on a mountain surrounded by a desolate landscape as his predominant set. The opening scene features mechanical wheels that click and clack setting the town in motion. Sculpted wooden figures appear—all the characters and sets were hand-carved—and they begin to engage themselves in their daily activities in stop-motion. Barta employs the animation of real food and live rats throughout the film and uses different angles, montage, close-ups, and dim lighting to create a deformed world that is bringing about its own decay. As the crafts people and tradesmen begin negotiating with one another, and as the pompous councilors, all men, meet to eat and drink and make decisions and rich people adorn themselves in jewels, rats begin to appear. One is beaten to a bloody death on a street. Blood oozes from the rat, and the savage behavior of the people forecast the savagery that is to come. An ox is slaughtered, and his blood is carried to the councilors to drink. People speak in gibberish. They grunt and groan and order each other about rather than communicate. The more they neglect their surroundings, the more the rats take over the town, and every nook and cranny becomes occupied by the rats. The only hope for the town is an outsider, the strange piper, a puppet made of dark wood, wearing a hood that covers deep-set eyes and a beard. He is tall and upright and bears a slight resemblance to Jesus Christ. But he is not a religious savior and demands 1,000 gold coins from the helpless councilmen to rid the town of rats. As he leads the rats through the streets of the town playing his flute, he prevents an innocent young woman named Agnes, a puppet made of light wood, very different from all the other darker figures, from being molested by an insidious jeweler who wants to marry her. After all the rats drown in a river that is overlooked by a poor fisherman, the piper returns to Agnes and sits in a garden with her. As they rest, the entire landscape around the town is transformed into a radiant forest with brightly colored flowers. The background music becomes more melodic. Hope is in the air. Then the piper goes to collect his fee and is given a mere black button while the councilmen gorge themselves like gluttons at a feast. About the same time that the piper storms from the town hall, the jeweler, now drunk, returns to Agnes with some friends, and they rape and kill her. The piper discovers her too late to save her. The next morning he climbs to the highest tower of the town and prevents the sun from rising. Then he takes out his flute and plays a morbid tune that causes all the townspeople to change into rats and scatter to the edge of the river where they plunge to

Figure 52
Jiří Barta,
Krysar

their deaths. The fisherman leaves his boat and walks to the point where the piper is standing. However, the piper disappears, and his cloak flies off and is carried away by the wind. The fisherman enters the deserted town and finds a child in a cradle. To protect the child's innocence, the fisherman carries the baby away from the town.

Though Barta has stated that he wanted to leave audiences with a vision of small hope,[161] his film is more a devastating critique of the darkness that has encompassed the world. The pulsating feeling generated by the wooden puppets who mangle each other and base all their actions on greed and consumption is one of imminent doom. Similar to Kafka's story "Metamorphosis," the people are transformed into vermin. Unlike Kafka's arbitrary transformation of Gregor Samsa into an insect that lives in an absurd world, however, the people of the town are deservedly transformed into rats, and the world is not absurd. It is a world of people who are so malevolent that children cannot grow up in their environment, and the only child born there must be carried off so that it can be humanely nurtured.

The fact that children do not appear in Barta's film emphasizes their significance all the more. The children are missing from the very beginning because they cannot develop into decent human beings in a corrupt society. They cannot be used to forgive abusive and hypocritical parents. In contrast, many live-action films exploit the role of the children to bring about reconciliation with their parents who must learn to act on their behalf with more responsibility. Two idiotically didactic American films from the Cold War era are *The Pied Piper of Hamelin* (1957) and *The Clown and the Kids* (1967). Billed as a TV special starring Van Johnson in the dual role of pied piper and teacher, *The Pied Piper* is a typical musical in which the actors are forced to sing dripping sentimental songs and to speak in rhymed iambic verse. The crooner Van Johnson is in love with the greedy mayor's daughter, and he leads the opposition in the town to save the children so that they can be educated with good morals. Nobody is harmed or disappears in this film where images of artificial happiness and reconciliation conceal the many contradictions of how children were being raised in America during the 1950s. In *The Clown and the Kids*, another half-baked musical which was filmed in Bulgaria, the focus is on the evil Mr. Scrag, who tyrannizes a village of East Europeans, who speak with thick Slavic accents. A circus troupe run by the famous American clown Emmett Kelly gets lost and lands in Scragville. Of course they speak and sing with cheerful American accents and are carrying democratic ways with their acts. When nobody attends the first circus performance, Kelly and his son and daughter become suspicious. When they learn how Scrag has more or less imprisoned the children, they set out to free them through their songs, dance, and acrobatic tricks. Kelly becomes the Pied Piper, who organizes the children to fight the villainous police and their dictator. In the end, "democracy" wins the day, and the villagers and their children are emancipated. However, democracy consists of kitsch, stereotypes, and poor acting that marks the film as one of the most insipid adaptations of the Pied Piper narrative.

Three other live-action films based on novels merit more serious comment than the banal American musicals. Interestingly, all three were produced outside America. The first one, *The Pied Piper* (1942) is adapted from Nevil Shute's novel, *Pied Piper*, published the same year that the film was produced, and it stars the inimitable Monty Woolley, whose marvelous transformation into an altruistic piper is the center of the film. (Incidentally, the novel was adapted again for a British TV film *Crossing to Freedom* in 1992 with Peter O'Toole playing the major role.) In the 1942 film, which takes place in 1940 right before World War II erupts, an English gentleman named John Sydney Howard takes a fishing vacation in France. When the Germans invade and occupy France more quickly than anticipated, Howard is caught in northern France, and he is asked to take several French children with him back to England. Though he dislikes children, he agrees, and as he spends more time with them, he grows very fond of them and is willing to make sacrifices for them. At one point Howard wants to smuggle the group of children on a fishing boat and get them to England.

Figure 53
Jacques Demy,
The Pied Piper

However, he is caught by a German officer, who, much to Howard's surprise, allows him safe passage providing that he also take his niece, who has a Jewish mother and has been orphaned, with him.

Here the pied piper is at first a reluctant hero, who gradually comes to appreciate the "value" of children. Also the children are reluctantly leaving their homes, not able to realize where they are going, what safety means, and why they must flee. Filmed in black and white without much melodrama, the film has a "documentary" feeling of authenticity and avoids the stereotypical representation of Germans as Nazis. The focal point shifts from the abduction of children to punish adults in "The Pied Piper" to the growing awareness of an elderly man that he is more obligated to children than he realizes and that he must guide them to a land where they will have the opportunity to survive in desperate times.

This awareness permeates the French director Jacques Demy's *The Pied Piper* (1972), which takes place in northern Germany during the Black Plague of 1349. Demy, who worked with the great French animator of fairy tales, Paul Grimault, and was also influenced by Jean Cocteau, broke with his usual surrealistic style and flowery music to create a more historically realistic picture of life in the late Middle Ages. The film is a serious critique and condemnation of the nobility and the church. However, the film fails because Demy chose Donovan, a popular Scottish folk singer during the 1960s, but one without any acting talent, to play the blasé pied piper, who joins a group of traveling actors who land in the corrupt town of Hamelin as the Black Plague rages throughout Europe. To Demy's credit, his film is a fascinating failure because he endeavors to paint a huge canvas of corruption and pestilence and suffering. The burgermeister of the town has arranged a marriage of his young daughter, barely twelve, with Franz, the malevolent son of the baron, who is primarily interested in the dowry to increase his army so that he can start another war. The burgermeister wants to marry into the nobility, and his wife Frau Poppenick wants to bed Franz. Meanwhile, the baron has drained money through taxes and bribes to build a gigantic cathedral in the middle of the town to honor him and bring about his salvation. The sycophantic priests, all dressed in red which makes them appear more like pandering devils than devout servants of God, egg on the baron so that they can profit from the new cathedral. There is no money left for anyone in the town, and the peasants and craftspeople suffer the most. When the rats carrying the plague invade the town, the only hope for salvation is in the Jew Melius, an alchemist/doctor, who is trying to create an antidote. But he is dismissed as a heretic and burned at the stake. The piper, who manages to lead the rats from the city, is betrayed by the burgermeister, and he merrily leads the children out of the city over a hill. Finally, the traveling actors, who signify decency and hope, leave for greener pastures. Like

Barta's grim portrayal of the townspeople of Hamelin, Demy's gesture of hope at the end of the film is feeble. This is a film that was made during the Vietnam War and student struggles in the West to oppose the corruption of governments and churches, and perhaps Demy sought to draw a parallel with the plague and religious wars of the fourteenth and fifteenth centuries. Pestilence has, however, deep roots, and takes different forms as the cinematic discourse about the pied piper continues to show.

In the other cinematic live-action adaptation of "The Pied Piper," this time of a novel by Russell Banks, *The Sweet Hereafter*, published in 1991, the Canadian director Atom Egoyan took many liberties with the plot of the novel by adding numerous references to "The Pied Piper" with Banks' approval. Banks based his novel on an incident that happened in Alton, Texas, on September 21, 1981, when a Dr. Pepper truck crashed into a Mission school bus. Twenty-one children were killed and sixty injured. Numerous lawyers rushed to Alton to file suits to make as much money for the families of the victims and for themselves. Ethics charges were filed against some of the lawyers, and though all the families received payments, the money won brought trouble to many of the people involved.

Banks re-set the accident in his novel to a small town in upstate New York. An opportunist city lawyer named Mitchell Stevens arrives soon after the bus accident to convince parents of the dead and injured children to sue for damages. It is not clear how the accident happened, and Banks employs multiple first-person narratives to shed light on the people of this area and their different reactions to the tragedy. While the lawyer is trying to convince the townspeople to sue so that he can make a good deal of money, he is also trying to deal with his own daughter, a drug addict, who has recently tested positive for AIDS. Eventually, there is a court trial, and everything depends on the testimony of Nicole Burnell, a partially paralyzed fifteen-year-old student, who was sitting at the front of the bus. She lies and testifies that the bus driver was speeding. Consequently, nobody will be able to profit from the accident. And nobody, except her father, knows why she is lying, but it is clear that she wants to prevent him from profiting from the accident because of his incestuous involvement with her.

Egoyan once again shifted the setting of the town, this time to British Columbia and made subtle changes in the plot that recall the important themes of child abandonment and adult guilt in "The Pied Piper." At one point before the accident, Nicole Burnell, who is played movingly by Sarah Polley, reads "The Pied Piper" to some of the children killed in the accident. In the film, Nicole is happy, appears to have a bright career ahead of her as a singer, and is apparently mesmerized by her father, a perverse pied piper, who has led her astray. After the accident, she is completely paralyzed from the waist down, and barely speaks. Traumatized, she seems to identify with the lame boy who was left behind in "The Pied Piper." In this instance, Nicole may be wishing that she had died with the others in crash. Clearly, she refuses to be complicit with the lawyer and her father.

Figure 54
Atom Egoyan,
The Sweet Hereafter

Egoyan uses flashbacks and multiple perspectives to reconstruct the accident as a kind of documentary so that the audience can serve as a jury. The camera is not partial to any one perspective, nor does it condemn the father or the lawyer. Everyone is trapped by previous behavior that is exposed by the accident. In particular, the incest that was undetected and remains undetectable is associated with a virus or disease that spreads through the lawyer, who clearly wants everyone, including himself, to profit from the misfortune of the children. Nicole is unwilling to speak about the incest, but she is also unwilling to let the town benefit from irresponsible behavior. This is a sad but brilliant adaptation of "The Pied Piper," and Egoyan's treatment of incest as a repressed disease that has many manifestations is subtle and bears witness to the way that adults keep silent and rationalize their powerful grip on the future of children.

The Shame of Incest

There is, of course, a very long history of incest in literature and culture of the western world that can be clearly traced back to the Greek and Roman myths, in particular to the antics of the male gods such as Jupiter and Zeus. Though a taboo, incest has been more common than we realize and remains a social problem that is rarely addressed in public, despite more accounts about it and about pedophilia in the last forty years.

In the western world the theme of incest took on significance in folklore and literature during the eleventh century. By the thirteenth century a group of manuscripts dealing with incest and the sanctity of women were produced, and these manuscripts were eventually catalogued by scholars as the Constance Saga. They include: Matthew Paris's "The Life of Offa I" in *Chronica Majora* (late twelfth and early thirteenth centuries), *Mai and Beafor* (c.1257–1259), written by an anonymous layman in Austrian Bavarian dialect, Philipe de Remi's French romance *La Manekine* (c.1270), and Jan Enike's rhymed story in *Weltbuch* (Universal Chronicle) written in the thirteenth century. The basic plot of these manuscripts concerns a wealthy king, a widower, who desires to marry his daughter so that he will have an heir; the daughter refuses and is either cast out to sea or driven away after some kind of physical mutilation such as cutting off her hands; the princess, who is beautiful, is discovered by a foreign king either on the shores of his realm or in the forest; they marry, but she is slandered (often by her mother-in-law) and made to appear undignified in the eyes of the king; once again, she is driven away, wanders, and finds refuge in the realm of a powerful king or pope, who protects her; her husband, the king, discovers his wrongdoing, repents, searches for his wife, and is reconciled with her.

Numerous oral tales, manuscripts, and chapbooks dealing with this topic circulated in the late Middle Ages and influenced the "incest" fairy tales of Straparola, Basile, Perrault, and the Grimms. For instance there is a story in Chaucer's *Canterbury Tales*, a version printed in Ser Giovanni Fiorentino's *Il Pecorone* (1385) as "Dionigia and the King of England," and the fifteenth-century verse romance of *Belle Hélène de Constantinople* that contributed to the formation of a fairy-tale discourse. The father's incestuous desire has always been depicted as shameful and sinful, and the second half of the story, the transformation of the princess into a mutilated person or squalid, animal-like servant, has parallels with the Cinderella tales. However, for the most part the heroine is a princess, and the plot revolves around her fall from and return to royalty. Her purity and integrity are tested, and she proves through a ring or shoe test that she is worthy of her rank. Depending on the attitude of the writer, the incestuous father is punished or forgiven. Sometimes he is just forgotten, as if it would be too shameful to recall the crime that eventually leads to the happiness of a persecuted princess.

In the literary tradition, the most well-known narrative in the fairy-tale discourse is Perrault's verse adaptation, "Donkey-Skin," which he wrote in 1697, about the same time that he was involved in a public debate in Paris about the role of women. Perrault argued for more rights for women, and many of his tales reflect his support of their cause. In his version of "Donkey-Skin," he has the most powerful king in the world (an obvious reference to King Louis XIV) promise his dying gorgeous wife that he would never marry another woman unless she is more beautiful, accomplished, and wiser than she is. After a short period of mourning, he decides to move on with his life, but the only woman who equals his dead wife is his daughter. After he approaches her and proposes marriage, she seeks out her fairy godmother for advice. The fairy tells her to stall her father and to ask him to provide her with three dresses with the colors of the sky, moon, and sun at different times. The king succeeds, and so the princess must ask for the skin of the magical donkey that constantly fills her father's purse with gold coins. Even here the father grants her wish and demands to be married to her. Consequently, the fairy tells her to wear the donkey-skin as a disguise and set out for foreign lands. She also gives the princess a magic wand that enables her to take her chest of jewels, clothes, and toilet articles with her and use them whenever she needs them. Eventually, the princess, now called Donkey-Skin, finds a job as scullion on a farm where she must clean out the pig troughs and wash clothes. In secret she sometimes adorns herself with her beautiful clothes, and the prince accidentally sees her and is so struck by love that he falls sick and cannot recuperate unless Donkey-Skin makes a cake for him. She acquiesces and plants a golden ring in the cake. When the prince discovers it, he declares to his parents that he will marry only the woman whose finger fits the ring. The last to try is Donkey-Skin, and once the finger fits her finger, she reappears as a marvelous princess, and once the wedding takes place, her father arrives, and we are told that he has cleansed himself of the criminal and odious urges of his heart.

Perrault concluded his narrative by writing:

The tale of Donkey-Skin is hard to believe,
But as long as there are children on this earth,
With mothers and grandmothers who continue to give birth,
This tale will always be told and surely well-received.

To a certain extent, this may be true, but the fact is, "Donkey-Skin" is not as well known as Perrault's other classical fairy tales, and it has not been as widely distributed as much as his other tales. Incest does not make for a good subject for children, not to mention adults, and very few writers and filmmakers have dared to touch the topic.

Jacques Demy has been one of the few filmmakers courageous enough to approach the theme of incest. However, like his filmic recreation of "The Pied Piper," his *Donkey Skin* (1970) is a curious and tantalizing failure because it is unclear at the end of the film whether or not Demy winks at the serious nature of incest. Perhaps the best way to describe Demy's film is simply to call it a camp fairy-tale film that mocks the notion of incest and invites the audience to enjoy all the sexual innuendoes and romantic melodrama of the tale. The threat of incest is to be taken lightly.

Following in the wake of his success in *The Umbrellas of Cherburg* (1964) and *The Young Girls of Rochefort* (1967), Demy uses sweet melodic tunes, songs, and dance in idyllic settings. He colors the people of the castles and palaces with pastel shades, predominantly blue and red, and fills them with statues of other fairy tales such as "The White Cat" by Mme d'Aulnoy and "Puss in Boots" by Perrault. The handsome king of the blue realm is played by Jean Marais, notable for his performance in Cocteau's *Beauty and the Beast* (1946), and his daughter is the young exquisite actress Catherine Deneuve, who is obliged to mouth saccharine words that drip with hyperbolic sentiments. As if this is not bad enough, the princess appears to be so attached to her father that she is willing to acquiesce in his offer of marriage. Her sprightly fairy godmother, played by the charming actress Delphine Seyrig, must appear to give her a lesson in sex education. It is also hinted at this time that the fairy is having some kind of dalliance with the king. Once the girl learns her lesson, Demy follows the traditional plot of Perrault's tale and banishes the princess, now called Donkey Skin, to work for mean peasants, who delight in singing nasty songs about her. Soon after the prince (Jacques Perrin) discovers her by chance, her fortune is made, and we are treated to dream scenes of romance and lush scenes of pomposity in the prince's palace, where extravagance and elegance are prized. The princess shows no signs of being traumatized, and she willingly joins in the comedy of manners, which ends with a great surprise. Just as the nuptials are being celebrated in the enormous garden behind the prince's castle and dignitaries from all over the world are arriving, a helicopter sweeps down and lands near the young couple. Out jump Donkey Skin's father and her fairy godmother. All is forgiven with hugs and kisses. The fairy godmother has married the king, but there is one last glance by the king that indicates his lechery has not abated.

We know from Demy's *Pied Piper* that he is critical of corruption, greed, and exploitation, which he represents as perverse. However, *Donkey Skin* leaves the question of incest open. He seems to ask if abnormal sexual behavior is a crime. Certainly, French attitudes toward sex are different from those of other cultures. The French are known to be more laissez-faire than people raised in other cultures. Or are they? Was Demy mocking or critiquing this laissez-faire attitude? Whatever the case may be, the ending of the film returns the surreal tale of incest to the tale of its real persistence.

Other filmmakers such as Nadezhda Koscheverova and Steve Barron have endeavored to deal with the persistence of incest and to continue the cinematic discourse of "Donkey-Skin" with mixed results. Koscheverova directed a Russian *Donkey Skin* (1982) for family audiences with a direct reference to Perrault's narrative but essentially bowdlerized the tale by eliminating incest from the plot. The film is a frivolous comedy that begins with a court poet stepping out of a portrait in an art gallery at midnight. He tells the other figures in paintings that come to life a tale about a king who sends his magic donkey into the forest to die after it stops producing gold coins. About the same time this happens, his wife gives birth to a daughter, Theresa, and dies soon after. Then he remarries an ambitious queen, who wants Theresa to marry a very wealthy old man when she is about twenty. But Theresa is in love with Prince Jacques and runs away. With the help of a fairy who gives her a donkey-skin and magic ring, she manages to survive many adventures, saves Jacques from robbers, and marries him even though she must prove that she heroically rescued him. About the only positive aspect of the film is the portrayal of an active, smart, and gifted heroine. Otherwise, though the acting is more than competent, the plot, the jokes, and the mocking of the court are stale conventions of the Russian fairy-tale film industry. The question of incest and its consequences for women are glossed over.

Barron's film, *Sapsorrow* (1988), part of Jim Henson's remarkable TV series *The Storyteller*, is based on a screenplay written by the gifted director Anthony Minghella, who adapted "Donkey-Skin" in a most original way by borrowing motifs from the closely related "Cinderella" tale type and a German folk tale, probably the Grimms' "All Fur." Instead of one daughter, there are three. The two eldest are homely and petty, while the youngest is beautiful and kind, moreover she loves animals that inhabit her room. A widower for many years, the king decides to marry when he realizes that his daughters who have reached the age of marriage will soon be leaving his palace and he does not want to be lonely. However, he will only remarry if he finds a woman whose finger fits his dead wife's marriage ring. Many women try on the ring but fail. The king does not lust after his beautiful daughter. It is only by accident that she tries on the ring that fits her finger. Because it is the law of the land, he regretfully must marry her, but his daughter hides in her room and demands three dresses from him. As time passes, she is helped by the animals that cover her with feathers and fur. Eventually, wearing a straggly coat of feathers and fur, she escapes to the forest and makes her way to another kingdom, where she charms a haughty prince and eventually marries him by trying on a golden slipper to prove that she is the young woman whom he loves.

Typical of the style and production of all the films in the *Storyteller* series, *Sapsorrow* is narrated by an eccentric storyteller played by John Hurt sitting by a fire with a fluffy and ornery puppet dog by his side. Often the dog contradicts the storyteller, and often they both enter into the action of the story that is being told. Barron and Henson are fond of this perfectly timed estrangement effect, and they also use skewed frames, montage, diverse angles, shadows in frames, windows, and silhouettes to surprise and alter if not expand the perspective of audiences. Their depiction of an unwilling father who resists marrying his daughter is complicated by his decision to bow to the authority of the law of the land. Donkey-Skin, more aligned with the laws of nature, rebels against her father and also teaches her future husband what it means to be demeaned. There are no fairy godmothers. The young princess determines her own destiny with the help of the animals whom she has treated kindly. Though she forgives her nasty sisters, her father has died by the time she marries the prince. The incest is not pardoned. Barron's *Sapsorrow* is one of the more unique family films that openly deals with the shame of incest that most filmmakers of fairy tales are unwilling to address.

The Entangled Juniper Tree

Of course, incest is a very delicate issue and demands a careful and sensitive approach by filmmakers. Therefore, many have not been willing to deal with this subject, especially by adapting "Donkey-Skin"-type tales. On the other hand, as we have seen, filmmakers have not shied away from treating other topics that concern the abuse of children. Fairy-tale discourses about the violation of children were initiated in the cinema almost as soon as moving pictures were invented and were closely bound to the oral and literary traditions that carried these stories—and still are. Almost all the classical fairy tales have a clear cinematic discourse that can be traced to the beginning of the twentieth century, while other less popular tales, which may raise highly sensitive issues, such as the murder of non-biological children by step-parents, have rarely been adapted for the cinema while they are still maintained by word of mouth and print. Every now and then, however, a singular tale will emerge and be adapted by filmmakers. This is the case with the Grimms' "The Juniper Tree," which recounts the bloody murder of a little boy by a stepmother, who wants her biological daughter Marlene to inherit all the family's money. This tale is extremely important in folklore because it is only one of two printed in dialect in the Grimms' collection and contains motifs that may hark back several thousands of years. The tale begins with a childless woman, who wishes for a child as white as snow and as red as blood under a juniper tree. She eats its berries. When she gives birth to a baby boy, she dies. The father remarries, and her new wife gives birth to a girl named Marlene. The stepmother mistreats the son and kills him by slamming the lid of a chest of apples to cut off his head. She places the blame on her innocent daughter, cooks the boy in a stew, and serves it to the father. Marlene, who is distraught, collects the bones of her half-brother, and places them beneath the juniper tree. The bones disappear, and a magical bird flies off and sings a song to a goldsmith, shoemaker, and miller.

> My mother, she killed me.
> My father, he ate me.
> My sister, Marlene, she made sure to see
> my bones were all gathered together,
> bound nicely in silk, as neat as can be,
> and laid beneath the juniper tree.
> *Tweet, tweet*! What a lovely bird I am![162]

He receives a gold necklace from the goldsmith, red shoes from the shoemaker, and a millstone from the miller. When the bird returns to his home, he perches on a branch of the juniper tree and sings his song. As the bird sings, the father goes outside, and the bird drops the gold chain as a gift. Next, the sister Marlene appears and receives the red shoes from the bird. Finally, the stepmother comes out of the house only to be crushed by the millstone as punishment for her crime. Then the bird is transformed into the little brother and goes into the house with his father and sister.

In almost all the cultures of the western world where the juniper tree grows, its berries have been considered to contain magical properties. They have been used as cures for all kinds of diseases, plagues, arthritis, venereal diseases, toothaches, and colitis. The wood is thought to protect homes, boats, and stables from demons and fires. In Iceland, it is said that if the branches of the juniper tree and the rowan are taken into a house, they will cause a fire. Perhaps this why Nietzchka Keene filmed her extraordinary adaptation of "The Juniper Tree" in Iceland.

Indeed, Iceland was perfect for the location of Keene's *The Juniper Tree* (1990) for many other reasons. As Pauline Greenhill and Anne Brydon note,

> Keene uses the Icelandic landscape to underscore the mood of melancholia and otherness. The treeless expanse dwarfs the characters. For European and North American viewers, the absence of a middistant wood emphasizes the difference between the vastness of sky and land and the isolation and frailty of the individuals who bridge the space between. The film's black and white images reinforce this melancholic aspect.[163]

Unlike the Grimms' tale, Keene's film takes place some time in the late Middle Ages and might have taken place anywhere. It has a dreamlike desolate atmosphere, and due to the hills made of lava and lack of vegetation, it appears as if this film signals the end of the world. Nevertheless, there are definite clues, such as the persecution of witches that indicate the occurrences are connected to the late Middle Ages. This historical connection and the setting immediately distinguish the film from the Grimms' tale. Moreover, instead of pointing the finger at the criminality of the stepmother and punishing her for her crime, Keene's film is a radical re-interpretation of the stepmother's actions and demands a more nuanced reading of infanticide, especially when it is caused by women.

Clearly, Keene's film is partial to the perspective of the young girl Margit who has special powers of seeing. She and her older sister Katja have fled their homeland because their mother was burned at the stake for being a witch. They find refuge in a barren region where a farmer named Jonah is living with his young son Jonas (about ten or eleven years old), whose mother died in childbirth. Desperate for a safe place to live, Katja decides to seduce Jonah, often using magic spells, and to win the favor of Jonas. Under the eyes and constant watching of Margit, Katja succeeds in sleeping with Jonah and becoming pregnant. But she fails to win the affection of Jonas, who accuses her of being a witch. He clings to the memory of his dead mother who appears to him in visions, and Katja eventually taunts him to jump off a cliff to see if the dead mother will protect him. After his death, Katja cuts off Jonas's thumbs. She places one of them into his mouth and sews it shut so that he will not be able to tell anybody what happened. Then she throws his body into a river. Later she places the other thumb in a stew which is eaten by Jonah and Katja. Margit steals the thumb and buries it in Jonas's mother's grave, where a tree grows and a raven appears. Then Margit tells Jonah that Katja killed Jonas, even though she did not mean to. Once the pregnant Katja is exposed, she rides off with all the horses, but instead of feeling relieved, Jonah mourns her loss and follows her a few days later to bring her back. At the end of the film, Margit is left alone, and she tells a tale about two children whose father was a human and mother, a bird. After the children fly off with the mother, they return from the land of the birds to find that their father has remarried and does not recognize them, and the children are abandoned.

Although the film and its narrative are disjointed and very slow, and although the acting is somewhat flat with Icelandic actors speaking English with different English accents, there is a poetic surrealist quality about it that endows it with the quality of a melancholy meditation about home.

Figure 55
Nietzchka Keene,
The Juniper Tree

The initial and closing frames of the film are highly significant. At the beginning Jonas is pictured at the meager grave of his mother, alone and despondent. Right after this image, we see Katja and Margit walking through a stony field. They come across a stream in which they discover a dead young woman whose hands are tied behind her back. She, too, may have been declared a witch and murdered. Katja tells her younger sister that they can never return home and must seek a new home far away where nobody knows anything about their past. In the closing frame of the film, Margit is left alone, and in the distance Jonah disappears over a hill in pursuit of Katja.

The loneliness of Margit, who continually has visions of her lost mother throughout the film, is stark. In the course of the film she loses a half-brother, stepfather, and her sister. Keene questions whether we can ever find home and humane attachment. The communication between all the members of the patched-up family is sparse, and their beliefs are a mixture of Christian religion and pagan superstition. Their common goal or raison d'être appears to be survival. Yet, we are compelled to ask what the meaning of life is if its telos is basically survival. Keene's adaptation of "The Juniper Tree" may leave us with a greater understanding of why women are driven to commit certain atrocities that involve infanticide, but it also leaves us without much hope.

Fortunately, not all the fairy-tale films that engage in a discourse about child abuse and abandonment are as pessimistic as Keene's *The Juniper Tree*, but the better films do seek to touch a sensitive chord in audiences that raises questions about adult responsibility for creating unfavorable conditions for the development of children. The numerous filmic versions of "Hansel and Gretel," "Tom Thumb," "The Pied Piper," and "Donkey-Skin" deal primarily with impoverished children or young persecuted women who are exploited and victimized. For the most part, they are films of hope projecting possibilities for alternative ways of living, but it is often a hope that serves to rationalize the incapacity of modern societies to cope with the inequalities that make life merely a matter of survival for the majority of people. Sometimes, films with no hope are more honest and hopeful than those with rosy endings.

11

Choosing the Right Mate:
Why Beasts and Frogs Make for Ideal Husbands

As we all know full well, the beast and the frog almost always get their women. Their stories are engraved in our hearts and minds. Two of the most popular fairy tales in the world, "Beauty and the Beast" and "The Frog Prince," have developed regular narrative schemes which have outlined the rules of courtship and mating that have evolved in different countries over thousands of years. In the field of folklore these tales have been categorized as tale type ATU 425, "The Search for the Lost Husband,"[164] which is a misleading title for a group of tales with subsets that demonstrate how women are more or less coerced into relationships with bestial men. Indeed, men set the rules of mating games in which they woo and copulate with young women to reproduce for their own gain. Marriage is often incidental. Men also set (and continue to set) the narrative schemes that rationalize the manner in which they use power to teach women proper lessons and to dominate them, or if not dominate then persuade them to accommodate themselves to male rules and regulations. The subsets of ATU 425 have titles such as "The Animal as Bridegroom," "The Son of the Witch," "Beauty and the Beast," "The Vanished Husband," "The Enchanted Husband Sings a Lullaby," "The Snake as Bridegroom," and "The Insulted Bridegroom Disenchanted." The focus is always on the male protagonist as some sort of enchanted animal or reptile, who seeks to appropriate an "appropriate" wife. What the titles do not tell, however, is that these tale types involve a young woman, who is generally forced or obliged by her father or parents to sleep with and wed a revolting bestial male.

Let us consider some of the plots of these beast/bridegroom oral tales that eventually laid the groundwork through literature, opera, theater, and dance for the cinematic discourse of "Beauty and the Beast" and "The Frog Prince." These plots can be found throughout the world in different variants, and they all pertain to mating rituals.

Some of the better known narratives can be schematized as follows:

1) The youngest and most beautiful daughter of a king/merchant requests a flower or bird when he goes on a journey. He finds the flower/bird in the garden of a ferocious beast, and in exchange for robbing the garden, he must promise his daughter to the beast. He tries to send someone else to the beast, but soon the obedient, kind daughter agrees to go to the beast to save her father's life. Eventually, her dedication to the beast lifts an enchantment, and the beast is transformed into a handsome prince.

2) A childless couple (generally aristocrats) wishes for a child no matter what species it may be. Their wish is granted by a fairy, spirit, or higher power, and the wife gives birth to a donkey, viper, fish, pig, hedgehog, frog, bird, snake, tiger, or some sort of repulsive mixed beast. Loved and cultivated by the couple, the beast demands a wife when he grows up. He devours or kills false brides until he finds the one willing to comply with his wishes without question. They marry, and due to her curiosity, she discovers that her husband is a beast during the day and human at night, and she breaks a prohibition to be silent about his transformation. Consequently, he vanishes and she is in despair. Once she receives some counsel from a wise woman or helpers, she pursues her husband and must perform three difficult tasks to win him back in human form.

3) A young girl's future is determined from birth by fate or some higher power: she must marry an animal bridegroom when the time comes for her to wed. Though she may try to avoid her fate, she eventually agrees to live with him in his castle. Curious, she discovers that he becomes handsome at night when he sheds his animal or reptile skin. When she reveals his secret by listening to relatives and/or by burning his animal/reptile skin, he disappears and she must embark on a quest (often in iron shoes) to find him. To complete her quest, she needs the help of the sun, moon, wind, and stars or the assistance of animal helpers, hermits, or wise women. Sometimes she finds her husband married to another woman. She must undergo three tests to show that she is the true bride.

4) A young beautiful woman bathes in the sea. While she is swimming or bathing, a serpent (seal, dragon, or sea monster) steals her clothes. He refuses to return them unless she marries him. She accompanies him to his underwater castle where she gives birth to two children. However, she wants to visit her parents to show them her children. The serpent demands that she complete three difficult tasks often involving spinning and working in iron shoes. Finally, the serpent gives her permission to visit her parents for three days providing that she does not disclose anything about him. But his children tell his relatives about the serpent and his magic. The relatives summon and kill him. When the woman returns to the underworld, she learns that her husband is dead and punishes her children by having them turned into trees.

5) A young princess (sometimes the youngest of three princesses) goes to a well for water, or she goes with a golden ball or some other toy. She encounters a frog/toad and has some difficulties. The frog helps her by giving her water or retrieving a golden ball. She promises to be his friend and allow him to eat and drink with her and to sleep in her bed. She runs off to avoid keeping the promise. Her father forces her to keep her promise when the frog appears. When the princess takes him into her room, she smashes him against the wall or she lets him sleep three nights in her bed. After he is smashed, or after three nights in the bed, he turns into a handsome prince. Sometimes the frog asks the princess to decapitate him, and he turns into a handsome prince.

6) In manifold versions of the tale known as "Amor and Psyche" or "Cupid and Psyche," a beautiful young woman, often the youngest of three sisters, marries a supernatural bridegroom. She does this because: she is given away by her father to appease supernatural gods; the bridegroom wins her in a contest; she accidentally finds her way to his subterranean realm by pulling up a root; the supernatural bridegroom, son of a powerful goddess or witch, is attracted to her. Once they are married, the young woman becomes curious about her lover's identity and breaks a prohibition by revealing to other people (her sisters or other members of her family) that he is supernatural—an animal during the day and a handsome prince at night, or she looks at him when she is not supposed to do so. Before the husband vanishes, he leaves her with some article (iron shoes, feather, ring). She must go on a quest/journey of repentance to find her husband. During the quest, she must complete onerous tasks to prove that she is the true and faithful bride and deserves her husband.

There are other related types of beast/bridegroom tales that can be found throughout the world, and despite the variants, they all represent metaphorically the manner in which young women have been selected for mating. That is, the tales form a large, rich and varied discourse about the selection of mates and how choice is played out to favor the male bridegrooms. But the conventions of mate selection have not remained static and fixed. The principles of mate selection and the arrangements have been altered greatly, especially in the last four hundred years, and the male-dominated conventions have become modified by social and political movements. Of course, the challenges to the manner in which the lives of women are determined by the rules of mating and marriage depend on the relative freedoms won in different cultures so that they can make their own choices. In this respect, it is interesting to note that the cinematic discourse about the principles of mate selection that has become more conflicted has taken place largely in the western world as evidenced by films based on "Beauty and the Beast" and on "The Frog Prince." Yet, even in the "Beauty and Beast" and "Frog Prince" films there are still strong remnants of antiquated views regarding gender roles and the demands placed on women to make sacrifices for daddy and beast.

Sources of Beauty and the Beast Films

Most scholars generally agree that the *literary* development of the children's fairy tale "Beauty and the Beast," conceived by Madame Le Prince de Beaumont in 1756 as part of *Magasin des Enfans*, translated into English in 1761 as *The Young Missses Magazine Containing Dialogues between a Governess and Several Young Ladies of Quality, Her Scholars*, owes its origins to the Roman writer Apuleius, who published the tale of *Cupid and Psyche* in *The Golden Ass* in the middle of the second century AD. It is also clear that the oral folk tale type ATU 425A, the beast/bridegroom, played a major role in the literary development. There were various beast/bridegroom tales in oral circulation even before Apuleius wrote his famous version of "Cupid and Psyche." By the middle of the seventeenth century, the Cupid and Psyche tradition was revived in France with a separate publication of Apuleius' tale in 1648 and led La Fontaine to write his long story *Amours de Psyche et de Cupidon* (1669) and Corneille and Molière to produce their tragédie–ballet *Psyché* (1671). The focus in La Fontaine's narrative and the play by Molière and Corneille is on the unfortunate curiosity of Psyche. Her desire to know who her lover is almost destroys Cupid, and she must pay for her "crime" before she is reunited with Cupid. These two versions do not alter the main plot of Apuleius' tale and project an image of women who are either too curious (Psyche) or vengeful (Venus), and their lives must ultimately be ordered by Jove.

The allegiance to the classical Latin model and to Corneille and Molière was broken and transformed by Madame d'Aulnoy, who was evidently familiar with different types of beast/bridegroom folk tales and was literally obsessed by the theme of Psyche and Cupid and reworked it or mentioned it in several fairy tales: "Le Mouton" ("The Ram," 1697), "La Grenouille bienfaisante" ("The Beneficent Frog," 1698), and "Serpentin Vert" ("The Green Serpent," 1697), "Gracieuse et Percinet" ("Gracieuse and Percinet," 1697), and "Le Prince Lutin" ("Prince Lutin," 1697). The two most important versions are "The Ram" and "The Green Serpent," and it is worthwhile examining some of the basic changes in the motifs and plot that break radically from the male literary tradition of Psyche and Cupid. In "The Ram," the heroine is actually punished by a relentless fairy. Based on the King Lear motif, this tale has Merveilleuse, the youngest daughter of a king, compelled to flee the court because her father believes mistakenly that she has insulted him. She eventually encounters a prince who has been transformed into a ram by a wicked fairy, and she is gradually charmed by his courteous manners and decides to wait five years until his enchantment will be over to marry him. However, she misses her father and two sisters, and through the ram's kind intervention she is able to visit them twice. The second time, however, she forgets about returning to the ram, who dies because of her neglect.

In "The Green Serpent," the heroine Laidronette acts differently. She runs away from home because she is ashamed of her ugliness. Upon encountering a prince, who, as usual, has been transformed into a serpent by a wicked fairy, she is at first horrified. Gradually, after spending some time in his kingdom of the Pagodes, who are exquisite little people that attend to her every wish, she becomes enamored of him and promises not to see him and to marry him in two years when his bewitchment will end. However, even though she reads the story of Psyche and Cupid, she breaks her promise and gazes upon him. This breach of promise enables the wicked fairy Magotine to punish her, and only after Laidronette performs three near-impossible tasks helped by the Fairy Protectrice is she able to transform herself into the beautiful Princess Discrète and the green serpent back into a handsome prince. Their love for each other eventually persuades the wicked fairy Magotine to mend her ways and reward them with the kingdom of Pagodaland.

The issue at hand in both fairy tales is fidelity and sincerity, or the qualities that make for tenderness, a topic of interest to women at that time, for they were beginning to rebel against the arranged marriages or marriages of convenience. Interestingly, in d'Aulnoy's two tales, the focus of the discourse is on the two princesses, who break their promises and learn that they will cause havoc and destruction if they do not keep their word. On the other hand, the men have been punished because they refused to marry old and ugly fairies and wanted a more natural love. In other words, d'Aulnoy sets conditions for both men and women that demand sincerity of feeling and constancy, if they are to achieve true and happy love. Her tales may have had an influence on Jean-Paul Bignon's "Zeineb" (1714). They certainly were known by Madame Gabrielle de Villeneuve, who published her highly unique version of "Beauty and the Beast" in *La Jeune Amériquaine et les contes marins* in 1740, and it became the classic model for most of the "Beauty and the Beast" versions that followed in the eighteenth century. Indeed, it served as the basis for Madame Le Prince de Beaumont's most famous tale in 1756, which, in turn, provided the material for Countess de Genlis' dramatic adaptation, *The Beauty and the Monster*, in 1785 and for Jean-François Marmontel's libretto for the opera *Zemir et Azor* by André Modeste Grétry in 1788. Most significant by this time is the fact that Mme de Villeneuve wrote a tale of over 200 pages (the length depends on which edition one reads) and was addressing a mixed audience of bourgeois and aristocratic adult readers. The social function of the fairy tale had changed: its basis was no longer the salon and the games that had been played there. Rather, the literary fairy tale's major reference point was another literary tale or an oral tale and was intended to amuse and instruct the isolated reader, or perhaps a reader who read aloud in a social situation.

Like d'Aulnoy, de Villeneuve was concerned with the self-realization of a young woman, and like the lesson preached by d'Aulnoy, de Villeneuve's message for women is ambivalent. While all the rules and codes in her fairy tale are set by women—there are numerous parallel stories that involve a fairy kingdom and the laws of the fairies—Beauty is praised most for her submissiveness, docility, and earnestness. In de Villeneuve's version, she does not break her vow to the Beast. Rather she is steadfast and sees through the machinations of her five sisters in time for her to return to her beloved Beast. Then, after she saves him, and he is transformed into a charming prince, she is ready to sacrifice herself again by giving up her claim to him because she is merely bourgeois while he is a true nobleman. Her fairy protector, however, debates with the prince's mother, who has arrived on the scene, and argues that Beauty's virtues are worth more than her class ranking. Eventually, though the fairy wins the debate, we learn that Beauty is really a princess, who had been raised by her supposed merchant father to escape death by enemies to her real father, a king.

With de Villeneuve's projection of Beauty, the person as an embodiment of the virtue "self-denial," the ground was prepared for a children's version of the Beauty and the Beast tale, and Mme Le Prince de Beaumont did an excellent job of condensing and altering the tale in 1756 to address a group of young misses, who were supposed to learn how to become ladies and that virtue meant denying themselves. In effect, the code of the tale was to delude them into believing that they would be realizing their goals in life by denying themselves.

By the time the Grimms wrote their version of "The Singing, Springing Lark," which they had heard from Henrietta Dorothea Wild in 1813, there were hundreds if not thousands of oral and literary versions that incorporated motifs from the oral beast/bridegroom cycle and the literary tradition of "Cupid and Psyche" and "Beauty and the Beast." For instance, even before the publication of the Grimms' tale, Charles Lamb wrote the long poem, *Beauty and the Beast: or a Rough Outside with a Gentle Heart* (1811), and there were important versions by Ludwig Bechstein, Walter Crane, and Andrew Lang in the nineteenth century. The proliferation of these tales up the present has been strengthened by Jean Cocteau's classical film *La Belle et la Bête* (1946) and later by the Walt Disney Corporation's production of *Beauty and the Beast* (1993).[165] While Cocteau and the Disney Corporation have suggested that self-denial has great rewards for women, more recent films such as the *Shrek* quartet have contested that idea and propose that fairy tales can offer other possibilities for fulfilling desire and for mate selection—not only for women but for men. Whatever the case may be, the filmic discourse of "Beauty and the Beast" has revealed optional choices for audiences tired of viewing how women tame themselves while taming beasts.

The Cocteau and Disney Classics

Though there were several early silent "Beauty and the Beast" films directed by Percy Stow, Albert Capellani, and Guy Newall as well as cartoons by Herbert Dawley and Friz Freleng, it was not until Jean Cocteau conceived and produced his famous, if not classical, *La Belle et la Bête* in 1946 that "Beauty and the Beast" began making its mark in the fairy-tale filmic discourse. In fact, Cocteau's recreation of "Beauty and the Beast," which was at first dismissed by film critics and neglected by audiences, gradually became such an important cult film that it influenced numerous directors up to the present and has received more attention from scholars and researchers in the fields of literature and film than any other fairy-tale film with the possible exception of Disney's *Snow White*. While some of the interpretations and analyses of Cocteau's *Beauty and the Beast* are somewhat contrived and forced, most of them, taken together, form a kaleidoscopic view of a film filled with such ambivalence that it has engendered many different approaches to discover Cocteau's "ultimate" secret meaning in creating the film.

For instance, Rebecca Pauly describes how Cocteau appropriated literary sources in recreating "Beauty and the Beast";[166] Susan Hayward reports about the importance of the film in postwar France;[167] Michael Popkin claims that the film concerns the life and death of a poet;[168] David Galef describes how Cocteau used the camera to create a sense of magic;[169] Susan Hayward, Naomi Greene, Dennis DeNitto, Sylvia Bryant, and Jerry Griswold are concerned with Cocteau's homosexuality and study issues related to masochism, male desire, and homoerotic love in the film.[170] While all these essays contribute to some understanding of Cocteau, his intentions, hidden psychological meanings, and the historical significance of his film, none of the essays deal with the key theme and pattern of the film that emanated from folklore: desire and mate selection. If they do so, they only touch upon it and thus overlook why the film has continued, I believe, to attract viewers and critics. The only critic who has treated the issue of mate selection and its roots in folklore is Thomas Koebner, who has written a comprehensive essay that also situates the importance of Cocteau's classic in film history.[171] But before discussing some of the points raised by Koebner, I want to re-evaluate the changes that Cocteau made to his hypotext, Mme Le Prince de Beaumont's "Beauty and the Beast," and how he plays with and alters the pattern of mate selection and desire that are at the root of the beast/bridegroom tales.

As I have already mentioned, Mme Le Prince de Beaumont's tale was expressly written for young girls, and her narrative gushes with didacticism. Le Prince de Beaumont had a great talent for killing the magic of ambivalence in fairy tales. Though well-intentioned, she was also too moralistic and sought to establish a pattern of exemplary behavior for girls (mainly from the upper classes) so that their beautiful modest behavior would attract and win a prince. In my essay on "Beauty and the Beast" in *Fairy Tale as Myth/Myth as Fairy Tale*, I pointed out that there was a shift in the social function of the literary fairy tale as it began to be scripted for children: it was to instruct in an amusing way and was now received by children of the upper classes in the home where lessons were taught by private tutors or by governesses. Moreover, some of the fairy tales were evidently used in schools or in schooling the children of the upper classes. That boys were to be treated differently from girls is apparent from the structure and contents of Mme de Beaumont's book, or in other words, "Beauty and the Beast" originated as a sex-specific tale intended to inculcate a sense of good manners in little girls. What is this sense of good manners? The sense to: 1) sacrifice one's life for the mistakes of one's father; 2) learn to love an ugly beast–man if he is kind and has manners; 3) keep one's pledge to a beast, no matter what the consequences may be. When confronted by her sisters, who accuse her for not being concerned about her father who is sentenced to death for picking a rose, Beauty responds: "Why should I lament my father's death when he is not going to perish? Since the monster is willing to accept one of his daughters, I intend to offer myself to placate his fury, and I feel very fortunate to be in a position to save my father and prove my affection for him."[172] Beauty is selfless, and perhaps that is why she has no name. She is nameless. All girls are supposed to become "beauties," i.e., selfless and nameless. There is a false power attributed to Beauty as a virtue. By sacrificing oneself, it is demonstrated, the powers that be, here the fairies, will reward her with a perfect husband. The most important thing is to learn to obey and worship one's father (authority) and to fulfill one's promises even though they are made under duress. Ugliness is associated with bad manners like those of her sisters. The beast is not ugly because his manners are perfect. Beauty and the Beast are suited for one another because they live according to the code of civility. They subscribe to prescriptions that maintain the power of an elite class and patriarchal rule.[173]

For Cocteau this pattern of submission actually constituted a horror story, and it had to be transformed. Some critics have even called "Beauty and the Beast" a horror film citing scenes of the Beast threatening Beauty's father, or the blood-drenched Beast frightening Beauty in his palace, to prove their point. And there is something to their point: Cocteau shows the horrific underbelly of courting and the mating process and transforms the happy end of Le Prince de Beaumont's conventional fairy tale into a mock celestial flight toward happiness. There is no wedding. Beauty's father and daughters are totally out of the picture. Who knows what will happen to Beauty, who obviously was disappointed when she beheld a dandy prince after the Beast died.

All the fascinating changes Cocteau made in the Le Prince de Beaumont story reflect Cocteau's questioning of "true" heterosexual love. His introduction of a figure like Avenant into the tale was thus brilliant, for he is not only the counterpart to the Beast, his rival, and represents raw desire, but he also is the man whom Beauty actually desires. One need only look at the close-ups of her gaze when she talks with him and speaks about him. The only reason that she rejects him is because of her attachment to her father. When she is living with the Beast, she tells him of her love for Avenant, who courts her throughout the film. Interestingly, he is not the Prince Charming type. Rather, he appears more to be a decadent member of the middle class, who spends his time with Ludovic, Beauty's gambling brother, who squanders the family's wealth. At the same time, Avenant wants "nobly" to take her away from her miserable existence, and when she returns home from the Beast's palace, he declares her love for her and wants to kill the beast to save her. He believes that she is under some sort of magic spell.

Beauty never denies her love for Avenant and tells him so, and she also explains that though she loves the Beast, she loves him in a different way, for she always views him as an animal. When she returns to save the Beast, it is not because she is in love with him but because she wants to be faithful to a friend, whom she knows will die if she does not keep her promise. Unlike Le Prince de Beaumont's story, she fails, and yet, her gesture does produce a "reward"—the dandy prince. The close shot of her face reflects her surprise and disappointment. She is confused when she sees a prince who resembles Avenant, and it is hard for her to believe that the prince had once been the Beast. She, like the audience, must suspend belief, because everything has become magical. There is nothing real left in the film. A story that began with a realistic portrayal of a country mansion in ruin and the pettiness and pretensions of a declassé family ends in another world where a beautiful prince is transporting a bourgeois Beauty to his heavenly kingdom.

Cocteau's other brilliant idea was to create two distinct worlds: the decayed rural home of Beauty where she works like a slave for her father, and the mysterious enchanted world of the Beast, where she is treated like a queen. Beauty's life is indeed impoverished, for her fate depends on the mercantile dealings of her father, who becomes a pauper, on the gambling of her brother, and on the greed of a money-lender. She is demure and passive in this drab world. Once she enters the bizarre realm of the Beast, where statues come to life in charming gardens, arms with torches extend themselves from the walls of a lavish palace, glamorous clothes and jewels appear from nowhere, she becomes more active and assertive. As the Beast tells her, everything is at her command, and he even entrusts her with his most prized magic possessions: the mirror, the glove, the golden key, the horse named Magnifique, and the ring. Beauty is empowered in a world in which a beast tries to tame himself and to treat her with courtly manners. His realm is a surrealistic world of dream and possibility. But it is an ephemeral world that can only be glimpsed if one suspends skepticism about fairy-tale myths.

There are many other changes that Cocteau made, but the two I have discussed are the most important because they totally reshape the literary text and shift the fairy-tale discourse about desire and mate selection. In the traditional beast/bridegroom fairy tales, Beauty is assigned one and only one suitor. She has no choice. In Cocteau's film, she is at least offered some choice. Even if she is somewhat confused at the end, she chooses to go with the prince. The confusion stems from the fact that there are two rivals who court Beauty, Avenant and the Beast, and neither one is successful, unless one grants that the Beast was always the dandy prince and becomes a "cleaned-up" Avenant. This does not make much sense because, when Avenant dies, he becomes the Beast, punished perhaps for not believing in magic. Cocteau's ending is much too ironic and ambivalent to be taken seriously as an ideal union or a happy heterosexual coupling.

While his film, I believe, undermines its hyptotext, Le Prince de Beaumont's "Beauty and the Beast," it also has a political utopian aspect to it. As we know from his own remarks in the introduction to the film and in his diaries, Cocteau intended the film to offer some hope after the devastation of World War II and France's shame and complicity in the spread of "bestial" Nazism. Without drawing an allegory, it seems clear to me that the two realms depicted in the film are images of France's lamentable past and France's possible future with innocent Beauty caught between them. The drab merchant's decrepit mansion, the immoral behavior of family and friends that cause the old merchant to suffer and become ill, the shots of the rural estate that is falling apart, the opportunism of Beauty's sisters, brother, and Avenant—all these elements of the film are to be contrasted with a magical realm where a beast is trying to become noble, where inanimate objects come to life and treat Beauty with kindness and respect, where Beauty's every wish is granted, and where she learns that the drudgery of her life, her serfdom, can be overcome. She and the prince transcend both worlds at the end of the film, and this ending seems fitting because, though the prince says he is taking her to his realm, they are really flying off to no place, the real meaning of utopia.

Figure 56
Jean Cocteau,
Beauty and the Beast

Koebner's essay touches on many of the points that I have raised above and comes to a more critical conclusion about the hope that the ending seems to promise, and his analysis needs to be taken into consideration. He states that Cocteau did not intend to make a fairy-tale film but to make a film with fairy-tale effects, and he discusses how Cocteau borrowed many of Georges Méliès' tricks such as dissolves, stop-motion, and animated objects to achieve those effects. But Cocteau, a modernist, went beyond Méliès in his use of lighting, music, and, of course, characterization. While Méliès used surrealist backdrops and openly displayed their artificiality, Cocteau's blending of black-and-white light, his electronic music, quick changes from close-ups to distant shots, and mirror reflections all contributed to transforming the unreal into credible real and haunting images. Moreover, as Koebner points out, Cocteau employed a plot with a double structure that traced the fates of his two main protagonists. (Actually, one could even argue that there is a triple structure if one includes Avenant.) What is most important, however, in Koebner's essay is his demonstration of Cocteau's skepticism with regard to the canonical fairy tale that accounts paradoxically for its great success as a fairy-tale film.

Koebner maintains that Cocteau used all the magical effects of lighting, music, design, costume, movement, and animation to create a disturbingly uncanny atmosphere.

In his fairy-tale film Cocteau was not concerned to develop a cartoon broadsheet for children or naive spectators. Rather, he wanted to tell a sad romance about the "Other," from a certain critical distance, that is a story about a different being or species, perhaps even an allegory dealing with a hidden and forbidden existence that almost seems to have an ending pasted on from *The Threepenny Opera*. The rescue that becomes the flight into the heavens excludes the well-worn paths of fairy-tale interpretation. What remains are beauty and despair, the beauty of Beauty and the despair of the Beast. Neither one can help each other. If beauty could perhaps earlier still be understood as a blessed quality, as a divine gift, as a distinguished quality that one had not asked for, but is accredited to the person as a benefit—the shameless selection of the beautiful lady over others as it has been the custom in fairy tales—Cocteau's film differs and shows beauty to be ineffectual or only an ephemeral moment, in which a lighted sculpture becomes visible, a second, in which a woman dressed in a glamorous costume of a past time turns away from a window through which light streams. These are moments of a "lighted happiness" that will not succeed in brightening the gloom. . . . Beauty loses her true admirer and the inconsolable Beast, his life. The chord of reconciliation at the end is an ironical masquerade, a compromise between customary thinking and truth. They soar off into nothingness, for this communion between the prince and the daughter of a bourgeois merchant, between man and woman, between baying beast and untouchable Madonna is only a chimera.[174]

While I agree with Koebner's incisive analysis of how Cocteau's film undoes and undermines the traditional fairy-tale schemata, the film remains a fairy-tale film despite Koebner's view to the contrary. What is significant about Cocteau's approach is that he has created a fairy-tale film that questions itself and questions the artificial fairy-tale thinking that Disney and others had begun to promulgate in the 1930s. Cocteau seriously intended to expose the hollow myths and fairy tales with which we tend to guide our lives and have become staples in the culture industry. To transform our lives into fairy tales was, as I stated earlier, a horror for Cocteau, and he would have been horrified by how the Disney Corporation stole many of his ideas and inventions to restore the initial impulses of Le Prince de Beaumont's "Beauty and the Beast" and to re-transform the story back into a didactic fairy-tale film that pretends to offer hope for feminists and enlightened beasts while blithely concealing its reactionary ideological meanings. In the meantime, the Disney *Beauty and the Beast* has already reached classical status as a best-selling commodity in our world of joyful consumerism, and it is now time to turn our attention to those ingredients that have made this film so successful.

Of course, when one discusses the Disney Corporation's *Beauty and the Beast,* one must now regard it as a trilogy and bear in mind that there is a Broadway musical and numerous other products that have made the initial film a small business of its own. The original film appeared in 1991 and sprouted two vapid "midquels," *Beauty and the Beast: The Enchanted Christmas* (1997) and *Beauty and the Beast: Belle's Magical World* (1998), both direct-to-video films. A midquel means that the story takes part during the time of the original *Beauty and the Beast,* but what it really means is that the Disney Corporation wanted to get rid of the garbage and leftovers that it had in its studios. These two films are not worth discussing, but since the 1991 film has captivated audiences and critics alike and has reached classical status, it is important to devote a few pages to questioning why it is so successful.

Although Le Prince de Beaumont's story is credited by the Disney Corporation as the hypotext for the film, this is outrageous because it is apparent that most of the plot and characters are copied from or influenced by Cocteau's film. If Le Prince de Beaumont stamps the Disney film in any way, it is in the manner in which it appears to want to further the independence of young women while encouraging them to play the mating game according to male rules and to serve the interests of a male hierarchy. What is frightening about the Disney film is the manner in which it artistically and technically accomplishes this feat by reshaping Cocteau and by using the same stale Broadway/ Hollywood musical structures.

Let us briefly examine what Gary Trousdale and Kirk Wise, the directors, orchestrated to deplete the Cocteau film. Clearly, the addition of Gaston as the Beast's rival was taken from the Cocteau film as were the animated objects that come to life. But these are minimal borrowings in a film that inventively transforms both Cocteau and Le Prince de Beaumont. In fact, the changes are immense: the Disney film begins with a prologue captured in stained glass that explains why the cruel prince was transformed into a beast because he did not help a fairy disguised as a beggar; Belle, an only child, is portrayed in the very first sequence as a young intellectual, who wants to leave her provincial surroundings because she is not free to develop the way she wants; Gaston and the villagers are

Figure 57
Gary Trousdale/Kirk Wise,
Beauty and the Beast

depicted as lower-class boobs, who have no regard for the finer things in life; Maurice, Belle's father, is an eccentric inventor, who is a loveable comic figure; the Beast is not frightening, rather is a regal lion, who means well and must learn how to express his tender feelings, and all his former servants transformed into articles still worship him and do their best to encourage the "coupling" of beauty and beast. The final scene which recalls the struggle of the witch in *Snow White* to escape the dwarfs is a typical Hollywood ending that features the male rescuing his sweetheart and dying in her arms. In this case, however, since there is magic afloat and since the traditional story demands it, boy and girl are transformed into prince and princess, and they dance to the admiration of the prince's servants and the villagers who have learned what their proper places are.

Critics and audiences have raved about this film—the use of traditional and computer animation, the charming songs and dances, the comic characters, the colorful backdrops—and some have even lauded its "feminist" ideology. But what passes as "feminist" and new is really the same old, same old. Aside from strongly suggesting that the age-old, folkloric mate selection be kept alive—women will benefit by sacrificing themselves and gain a rugged hero with fit genes to protect themselves and that book-loving young women's primary role is to tame uncivilized men—the film contains a strong elitist ideology and mocks people from the lower classes, unless they are loyal servants in the Beast's palace. In a typical Disney film from *Snow White* through *The Princess and the Frog*, the protagonists are, or always become rulers, and the people and creatures from the lower classes dutifully pay homage to the rulers, whose bloodlines decree that they should govern and live in luxury. Sometimes meritocracy plays a role. But there is never any suggestion that (as in many folk and fairy tales) radical reformation of structured behavior and civil norms is needed if a profound transformation is to occur.

In almost all the animated Disney fairy-tale films the notion of happiness is perverted. Implied in the Disney *Beauty and the Beast* is that if the ruling classes are happy, then everyone will be happy. Of course, the ruling classes must be taught manners and ethics sometimes—as in the case of present-day politics in practically every country of the world —but they know better than the masses how to arrange the affairs of the world so that everyone supposedly will profit. But who is to profit from constant stale diversions and amusing films that keep repeating the same message with the same regular narrative patterns and banal tunes?

The European Legacy

There is an acute difference between European and American "Beauty and the Beast" films that reveal conflicting attitudes and perspectives in the fairy-tale discourse. The aesthetics of the films and approaches to folk and fairy tales are also different. These differences can be seen in some Russian, Czech, and British beast/bridegroom films that have not been widely disseminated in the West. In general, they offer alternative views toward the process of courting and gender roles, albeit with some nationalistic biases, and they indicate how adaptation and recreation can offer new possibilities for interpreting age-old customs.

There are three interesting Russian films based on "Beauty and the Beast", all made during the Cold War: *The Little Scarlet Flower*[175] (*Alenki zwetotschek*, 1952) directed by Lev Atamanov; *Finist, the Bright Falcon* (*Finist, jasni sokol*, 1975) directed by Gennadi Vasilyev; and *The Scarlet Flower* (*Alenki zwetotschek*, 1978) directed by Irina Povolotskaya. Of the three films, *Finist* is by far the most egregious example of Soviet ideological propaganda intended for family audiences and can be dealt with briefly because it is so trite and poorly made. Based on twelfth- and thirteenth-century legends about the attacks by the Tatar hordes, the film depicts how a blond-haired, blue-eyed hero with extraordinary powers, guided by a hawk, defends the Russian peasants and their soil. At one point he rescues the beautiful maiden, Alyonushka, and she falls head over heels in love with him. However, the evil leader of the Tartars, Kartaus, orders his eccentric wizard to transform Finist into a gigantic frightening beast, and once a beast without a voice, Finist cannot help the peasants or the good Russian soldiers who protect a settlement. Only Alyonushka, who has woven a wedding cloak, recognizes that the beast is really the true Russian hero, Finist, and she throws the magic wedding cloak over him so that he becomes human again. However, there are more battles and episodes, and Alyonushka must rescue Finist a second time before the Tartars are finally overcome. Of course, they will marry in traditional Russian peasant costumes. Although the film is intended to be both comic and romantic and inspire patriotic feelings in Russian viewers, it is more boring and banal than inspirational. All the characters are stereotypes; the plot is predictable; the acting is stilted; the sets are cardboard and resemble picture postcards of medieval festivals. It is true that Alyonushka is depicted as an independent young peasant woman, who selects her mate, but there is something suspiciously racial and Aryan about this Soviet film in which Russian blood and soil are championed above the dark enemies. This fairy-tale film celebrates xenophobic attitudes and paranoia while pretending to exemplify the spirit of the Russian folk.

Some of these attitudes "creep" into the two filmic renditions of Sergey Aksakov's nineteenth-century fairy tale "The Scarlet Flower," but these films are much more artistic; they avoid blatant dogma and propaganda and adapt the tale in highly innovative ways. Aksakov (1791–1859), a conservative and classical writer known for his semi-autobiographical works, published "The Scarlet Flower" in *Childhood Years of Grandson Bagrov* (1858), and it is important to summarize the plot because it served as the hypotext for both Atamanov's and Povolotskaya's films.[176]

Akaskov's narrative recounts the adventures of a wealthy merchant in a certain realm, in a certain land. Before embarking on a voyage across the sea, he asks his three lovely daughters what kinds of gifts they would like him to bring them upon his return. The eldest would like a golden crown set with precious stones that can turn the dark of night into the light of day; the middle daughter wishes for a mirror of Eastern crystal that will make her look young and increase her beauty; the youngest daughter, her father's favorite, wants the little scarlet flower, which is supposed to be the most beautiful thing in the world. Since the father knows how to obtain the crown and the mirror, he does not consider these gifts difficult to find. He is, however, perplexed by the scarlet flower, but promises to find it. After he sails off to distant realms, he acquires the crown and mirror and also earns a great deal of gold for his wares. On his way home, however, he must journey over land and is robbed by infidels. In order to save his life, he flees into a forest and is led by a strange light to a marvelous palace made out of beautiful crystal. After he spends the night in the castle, he enters the verdant gardens and is drawn to the scarlet flower. As soon as he picks it, a monster appears and tells him he must die unless one of his daughters is willing to come of her own free choice and live with him, for he is lonely and wants company. The merchant has three days to make up his mind at home, and if none of the daughters will replace him, he must return and be killed. The monster gives him a ring to travel home, and once he is at home, all his lost treasures arrive. The daughters are happy, but when they learn about his fate, only the youngest is willing to go and live with the Beast of the Forest and the Denizen of the Deep. She feels that it is her duty. Soon after she arrives, she returns the flower to its proper place. The monster tells her that he is her slave and that he will fulfill her every wish. He is unwilling to reveal himself because of his terrible appearance. He has a wild voice and is described as follows: "His arms were crooked, he had the talons of a wild beast, the legs of a horse, and great camel humps before and behind; he was covered in hair from head to foot, he had a boar's tusk sticking out of his mouth, a nose curved like an eagle's beak, and the eyes of an owl." (This description of the beast, who is generally only vaguely described in most versions, is one of the most graphic ones in the beast/bridegroom cycle of tales.) The merchant's daughter is dismayed and frightened. But she comes to trust and respect him and enjoy his conversation, and soon she becomes accustomed to his looks. When she has a dream that her father is dying, the monster gives her the magic ring and tells her to visit her family for three days and three nights. If she does not return at the end of the third day, he will die. The merchant's daughter is happy and spends three days and nights with her family, but the sisters are jealous and change the clocks so that she will not return to the beast at the right time. Indeed, he is dead when she arrives. When she declares her love for him, however, lightning strikes, and she faints. After she awakes, she is sitting on a golden throne with a prince next to her and her family kneeling around them. She learns that the prince had been abducted as a little boy by a wicked witch who had been angered by his father. Out of revenge he was transformed into a beast for thirty years and his only hope for salvation was a maiden willing to love him for the kindness of his heart. No sooner does the prince tell his story than the merchant gives his blessing, and the young couple is wed.

There are strong religious overtones in this tale, and it is apparent that the heathens and the witch represent foes of Christianity. The merchant is always referred to as an honest man. The youngest sister is not exploited by her sisters at the beginning. Later they become envious. The merchant embarks on his trip and is successful until he is robbed. The beast does not need to be tamed or to be made civil. He demonstrates that he has a good heart, and it is through this good heart that he courts the merchant's daughter.

Atamanov's animated adaptation of 1952 remains close to Aksakov's narrative, but he does make many significant imaginative changes that affect the meaning of the original tale. In contrast to the American animated tradition of the 1950s, this forty-two-minute Russian film has practically no songs, comic characters, or talking animals. The depiction of the characters is in keeping with socialist realism. Every gesture and expression of the characters has a deep meaning in a social context, and the workers in the port city are portrayed as noble people. The decor, costumes, and sets are all carefully drawn and designed to resemble medieval and Russian conditions. Atamanov and his animators make brilliant use of turquoise and bronze colors and shades of red and create an atmosphere of local color. There is an appeal to a "heroic" Russian folk spirit throughout the film. The simple line drawings and colors are mixed and glitter when the merchant, who is on his return voyage with a rich cargo, is thrown overboard during a storm and lands on an enchanted island. The focus and emphasis in the film is on "natural love." That is, once the youngest daughter is on the island, she shows a great affection for the animals, thrives in nature, and insists on wearing her traditional Russian costume. For his part, the Beast tells her that they are equals; he needs her as a companion to overcome his loneliness. They are drawn to each other naturally, and later, when it seems that she has returned too late to save his life, she declares her love for him with the scarlet flower in her hand. The flower magically reattaches itself to the stem in the soil, and the entire island glistens. The final frames depict the tiny Russian port city with a rainbow over it and bells ringing.

Figure 58
Lev Atamanov,
*The Little Scarlet
Flower*

Though this is clearly a *Russian* film that honors hearth, soil, simplicity, kindness, and honesty, it is not didactic, nor does it preach a political agenda. The tender love that blossoms between a prince and a daughter of the merchant class breaks the hierarchy of social class. The marriage is not in a regal palace, but in a non-pretentious town. It is obvious that the conventions of courting and mating in the film reflect changes in the Soviet Union of the 1950s that gave more freedom to women.

But the film that makes a much more intriguing and critical comment on such changes is Povolotskaya's 1977 live-action *The Scarlet Flower*. It should be noted from the beginning that both the director, Povolotskaya and the screenwriter, Ryazantseva, are women—a rarity in fairy-tale filmmaking—and that the feminine or feminist perspective is very strong in this film. Moreover, though Povolotskaya and Ryazantseva began by adapting Aksakov's tale, they kept changing the screenplay throughout the production of the film so much that the final outcome is a tantalizing surrealistic if not impressionistic version of an amalgam of beast/bridegroom tales.

Unlike Atamanov's film, this version of "The Scarlet Flower" begins in a rural somewhat primitive village. Even before the title is flashed on the screen, we see Alyona, the merchant's youngest daughter, in bed having a dream and hearing a voice saying: "I'll die without you." Then there is a flashing image of a baroque palace. These introductory frames fade away, and we next see a bustling small settlement somewhere in the country. Preparations are being made for the merchant's trip to sell his wares. There is a good deal of commotion. Alyona cannot be found. She has hidden herself in her father's covered wagon because she wants to help and protect him. It is clear that she is a fiery young woman, and when she is found, she makes a strange request for a scarlet flower before her father departs. Her sisters have already asked for a crown and a mirror. The merchant is accompanied by a young peasant boy, and they travel over a rugged road through verdant forests and difficult terrain. The scenes of the journey are interrupted by shots of a luxurious baroque palace with a long hall lined with portraits and gilt furniture. At times we see a beautiful older woman dressed in a magnificent gown. A portrait of this elegant woman at a younger age also appears from time to time as does an old servant dressed in old-fashioned attire, who does the woman's bidding. An enchantress, she is completely mysterious, and the film provides only clues about her mysterious being that never resolve her mystery. But, what we do learn is sufficient to provide a frame for the narrative of the film.

In the distant past, this lady was a princess who loved a prince and gave him the gift of a scarlet flower that she always wore in her hair. However, the prince laughed at her and said that anyone truly in love had to give more than a flower. She must give her entire heart. Insulted, the enchantress transformed him into a beast. He becomes a "tree beast" covered by foliage and can only return to his human form if a maiden grows to love him despite his ugly beast form. Fragments of this story are revealed during the merchant's journey as the merchant is lured to the palace by the enchantress's servant, who uses disguises and magic and enables the merchant to obtain gifts for his two older daughters. In the meantime the enchantress haunts a palace of decadent splendor and appears to be waiting for something to happen. The merchant is led over a sea to the palace after he abandons his wagon and, though he is treated well in the baroque setting, he is toyed with and trapped in a labyrinth by the enchantress, who does not seem to have a heart. While desperately seeking a way out of the baroque palace, he is led into the gardens where he is attracted by the glow of the scarlet flower. Once he picks it for his daughter, he is threatened by the beast.

While Povolotskaya follows the broad outlines of Aksakov's narrative and depicts how Alyona decides to save her father and goes to the palace by using the magic ring, she also transforms the narrative into a spiritual quest using impressionist images of the gardens, palace, forest, and villages that are interwoven throughout the film. Landscapes, costumes, rooms, and buildings are "painted" with different hues of red. The natural beauty of the forest and gardens are contrasted with the artificial and exaggerated decor of the palace. The enchantress watches and observes Alyona and the beast as they develop a friendship outside in nature that turns into love because of their kind hearts and gracious behavior. Meanwhile the enchantress spies on them with a telescope. She speaks to Alyona and tries to warn her and encourages her to flee the palace and gardens forever. However, the tenderness and gentleness of the beast win her heart. His transformation, however, is not the end of the film.

Like Cocteau, Povolotskaya brilliantly adds two new characters, the enchantress and her servant, to enrich and deepen the film. Just as Avenant became the beast's rival, the enchantress is Alyona's rival. The arrogant, if not cynical, enchantress does not believe in a natural and tender love, and though she may not actively vie for the beast's heart, she wants to exact revenge and prove that no heart is generous enough to love an ugly beast. It is she, however, who is "transformed" at the end of the film when she decides to leave the palace forever and gets into a rowboat followed by her servant, who is moved by her and does not want to abandon her. There is a certain irony at the end of the film, but it is not like Cocteau's irony that questions the essence of fairy tales, mating, and coupling; rather, it is an irony that exposes the arrogance and decadence of royalty and celebrates the hope of young love. And all this hope is not expressed through socialist realism but through experimental surrealism. The creative Povolotskaya abandons traditional narrative and insists on retelling conservative stories from a kaleidoscopic perspective that undermines traditional male views that lure young women into submission.

Unfortunately, a Czech film made in the year after Povolotskaya made hers returns to traditional storytelling. This is not to say that Juraj Herz's film *Beauty and the Beast* (1978) does not have unusual features, or that its production qualities are meager. In fact, the opening scenes that depict vultures flying in the sky and several wagons loaded with goods are striking. The tired and angry men appear to be lost in a muddy terrain; a desperate woman wants to stop. As they plunge into a desolate forest, the camera flashes to a village where the peasants are preparing for a large, festive party. It is being organized by a wealthy merchant, who has three beautiful daughters. The two eldest are hoping to choose an eligible bachelor to marry. Julie, the youngest daughter, who resembles her dead mother, declares she will never marry, for she wants to be close to her father. In the meantime, the wagons crash into a ravine, and the men are killed by a strange beast that viciously attacks them; he claws the woman to death.

This realistic, happy and harrowing beginning includes two contrasting events, which seem to have no connection and are intended to stir the curiosity of viewers. The contrast, however, is quickly resolved: the wagons belong to the wealthy merchant, and he was going to use the money from the successful sale of his goods to offer rich suitors a dowry for his daughters. Instead, he is ruined and must sell all his furniture and property including the portrait of his dead wife, which he takes with him on his horse to a nearby town. On his way, his horse dies, and he must carry the painting through a forest where he becomes lost, finds his way to a palace in ruins, picks a flower for Julie, and the rest is history.

Herz used Gabrielle-Suzanne de Villeneuve's version of "Beauty and the Beast," a theatrical adaptation by the Czech playwright Cesky Krumlov, and Cocteau's work to create his own "horror" film, but it is not Cocteau's ironic horror. In each and every shot of the Beast, Herz stresses the gruesome features of the monstrous protagonist—his beak, sharp talons, dark wings, ferocious glare, snarling voice. He is torn by an evil inner voice that urges him to kill Julia or to kill himself. We never learn why the Beast has been transformed, only that he is driven by evil urges that he must overcome if he is to become human. It is Julie who eventually saves him. She dreams of him in his handsome human form (the influence of de Villeneuve) and remains true to him out of her own free will. Herz's depiction of the torn Beast is also reminiscent of Cocteau's Beast. But the ending recalls some of the worst traditional endings in the beast/bridegroom films: transformed into a regally dressed prince, the former Beast carries Julie in his arms through a hidden door into a baroque palace, where we expect they will live happily ever after. The horror of the film is in its portrayal of anticipated happiness.

But there is no happiness at the end of the kitsch fantasy film *Blood of Beasts* (2003) directed by David Lister and filmed in some remote region of South Africa. This is a most unusual and original adaptation of "Beauty and the Beast," and it is a shame that the screenplay is mediocre and corny, that the acting falls flat, and the sets resemble the horror rides of amusement parks into a darkened realm where ghouls, skeletons, and torture chambers are more titillating than frightening. The story takes place in some Viking medieval past. Freya, the beautiful daughter of King Thorsson, refuses to marry a creepy warrior named Sven, even though the king demands that she must do so after he travels to a mysterious island, which should be part of his domain. However, it is ruled by an awesome beast, who captures the king, while the cowardly Sven escapes. Consequently, Freya sets sail for the island to free her father and take his place. While on the island, she learns that the beast is actually Agna, her former lover, who has been cursed by Odin. (Incidentally, the beast is one of the most comic beasts in film history. The poor actor who plays the role must wear a moth-infected bear skin and show his painted face through the jaws of the bear and speak in a low rough voice and growl.) They return to King Thorsson's realm, and Agna fights for the right to wed the brave Freya. In the midst of the duel, Freya leaps to protect Agna, and is unfortunately killed by Sven, who is then slain by Agna. The film ends with Freya's funeral. Though she represents a new type of heroine—a daughter who rebels against her father, and fights for her right to decide whom she will wed—it is difficult to weep at her funeral. Well-intentioned though the film may be, it defeats its purpose by presenting us with comic-book pulp.

Happy Fairy-Tale Films as Horrific Films/Horror Fairy-Tale Films as Carnivalesques

For the most part the American film industry has been happy to maintain what I ironically call the "horrific representation" of happiness that basically reaffirms fixed gender roles with slight touches of feminism and male benevolence: good women as self-denying, kind, and spiritually strong who mate with men whom they can shape; good men as stumbling beasts who need women to help them find the path to true love and tolerance. These charming happy fairy-tale films are offensive and scary because of the earnestness and seriousness with which they purport to show how true love works and how women in particular should conduct themselves in the mating game—how submissive they should be to their father and how devoted they should be to their father's replacement, the beast, that noble figure, who seems to be cursed for no good reason. There are a series of commercial films made for the big screen, television, and the video market that basically employ new images to map out an old path to happiness, even if the female beauties appear to have freer choice in choosing their bestial princes. The most egregious of these happy fairy-tale films that appear to overcome horror while concealing the horrific mendacious pattern that allegedly leads to genuine love and marriage are Roger Vadim's *Beauty and the Beast* (1983), a Faerie Tale Theatre production; Eugene Marner's *Beauty and the Beast* (1986), a Cannon Studio production; Ron Koslow's TV series *Beauty and the Beast* (1987–1990); and Brian Brough's *Beauty and the Beast: A Latter-Day Tale* (2007). All these self-help films are basically variations on the same theme: how to help attractive, seemingly strong women realize that appearances are deceiving and that happiness in wedlock is within their grasp if they understand the goodness of good-hearted men. The kindest thing one can say about Vadim's infantile version of "Beauty and the Beast," which apes Cocteau's film, is that he adds a bit of humor to the story while changing Avenant into a bumbling aristocrat named Jacques and the father into an angry man who tries to prevent Beauty from returning to the Beast, played by Klaus Kinski, who speaks with a crude German accent and is the spitting image of Cocteau's Beast. Typical of the Faerie Tale Theatre productions, the film is a star-studded vehicle for celebrities like Kinski, Susan Sarendon, Anjelica Huston, and Stephen Elliott. But all their talents cannot help this film, which degenerates horrifically into happiness when Beauty calls herself a monster and rescues the Beast through self-sacrifice. The same thing can be said of the Cannon musical version, except that it is enlivened by songs, dances, and dreams. In this film, an eclectic mix of the Villeneuve story, images from Cocteau's film, and sentimental Broadway lyrics, Beauty must learn to see with her heart and declare that she loves and will marry the Beast before he can be transformed into a royal prince. She appears somewhat confused at the end when she sees the handsome prince. This may be due to the fact that the Beast mask is not hideous but has some appeal: the beast resembles a noble lion with an attractive mane and rugged features. Who knows, but this image may have been copied by Ron Koslow for his TV series and later re-transformed into the Disney lion-like Beast?

In many respects it was the handsome striking Beast in Koslow's "Beauty and the Beast" series that captured the minds and imaginations of American viewers for over two years from 1987 to 1990. Set in New York City, this hour-long telecast began with a wealthy Manhattan woman named Catherine who is raped by thugs and left for dead. Fortunately, a strange monstrous creature from the underworld named Vincent saves her. This noble, if not magnificent, beast lives with his benevolent and patriarchal father in a maze of subway tunnels with other marginalized people who are more humane than the inhabitants of the upper world of New York. Through Vincent's tender care, Catherine recuperates, and though she returns to this upper world to work as an assistant district attorney, a stronger and more socially conscious woman than she was before the rape, she is totally in love with Vincent, and the episodes of the TV series involve their constant saving and savoring one another in a platonic relationship that only becomes sensually fulfilled toward the end of the programming when the series was declared dead in 1990. Though there were positive aspects of this modernization of the traditional *Beauty and the Beast*, such as the independent woman who is not crippled by an Oedipal tie to her father, and the sensitive, alien male, who tries to understand the woman's soul, the plots of each episode were contrived and followed the prescribed criminal-adventure stories that depicted the triumph of the noble heroine and hero at the end of each hour.

Both Beauty and the Beast remain static characters after the first episode: they are idealized as uncommon protagonists bound to each other through mental telepathy of love in mysterious ways. Yet, it is the lion-like Vincent, a modern-day Richard the lion-hearted, who represents the better of the two worlds and sets the higher ideals that cannot be met in the real streets of New York. It is Catherine who must be attracted to this other realm, who must realize how shallow her life was, and who acts to meet the expectations that she sees in Vincent's gaze. Consequently, despite the "feminist" touch-up of Beauty in this TV series, the basic plot of submission/domination is merely re-formed to make the contemporary beautiful working-woman less aware of her bonds.

Times have greatly changed since Koslow adapted "Beauty and the Beast" to take place in the mean streets and sewers of "heathen" New York. Christian filmmakers have entered the fairy-tale discourse and produced two religious contemporary remakes of "Beauty and the Beast," in which angry men find their way back to God through the pure love and kindness of the good Christianized Beauty. For instance, in *Beauty and the Beast: A Latter-Day Tale*, filmed in the Colorado mountains, Eric Landry, a wealthy business consultant, turns away from God after his wife's unfortunate death and begins to treat people in a bestial manner until the young devout Belle Watson comes to work for him to make up for her father's actions. Her dedicated and devoted work, not to mention her good looks, brings him back to God, and their happiness is blessed by his power of holy love. Nothing more needs to be said about the horrific message of this film except that its contrived representation of pristine Christian family life and love are out of touch with reality.

There was and still is a strong conservative religious and social concept of love and courting in Le Prince de Beaumont's "Beauty and the Beast," and many filmmakers, beginning with Cocteau, have struggled to transform it so that it might be made more relevant for the many diverse ways in which women and men select their mates. Perhaps the most effective mode of adaptation in this particular cinematic discourse has been the carnivalesque. I am referring to Mikhail Bakhtin's concept which he developed in *Rabelais and his World*.[177] Bakhtin drew from the European practices of carnival—turning the world upside down, mocking of authority, sensual displays of liberty, sumptuous feasting, and breaking conventions—to discuss how various Renaissance writers employed these modes of social behavior in their writing. By leveling hierarchies and arbitrary regulation, many Renaissance writers, according to Bakhtin, intimated that a transformation and regeneration of society was possible. Though his focus was on a particular period of time, Bakhtin's notions of the carnivalesque have been adapted and applied to the critical writing styles of artists from other epochs up through the twenty-first century. Carnivalesque implies *devastating and brazen* satire, parody, critique, and anti-authoritarianism; it also brings with it a utopian sense of humor, for whatever forms of acting and thinking it opposes and destroys will also give rise to great hope for a more meaningful and satisfying form of life. There is an explosive quality to the carnivalesque that can be found in different kinds of films. As we have seen, fairy-tale cartoons depend on the carnivalesque, but there are also long animated and live-action fairy-tale films that possess qualities of the carnivalesque. This is the case with *Shrek* and *No Such Thing*. (2001).

Ironically, the animated *Shrek* films, which are related to the beast/bridegroom folklore tradition but appear to have nothing to do with reality, are more connected to real mundane issues of courting and mate selection than the so-called realistic Christian films. Of the four *Shrek* films, the first is the most significant, and I want to discuss it at length. But before I do, a word or two about William Steig's picture book is necessary.

Steig generally wrote and illustrated books for children between the ages of five and ten, and like the best illustrators, his work is so ironic and provocative that there are always many levels to his stories. But no matter what he created, it was filled with optimism. As he stated in an interview with Anita Silvey, "the child is the hope of humanity. If they [children] are going to change the world, they have to start off optimistically. I wouldn't consider writing a depressing book for children."[178] This is a moral stance that pervades all his masterful stories such as *Sylvester and the Magic Pebble* (1969), *The Amazing Bone* (1976), *Abel's Island* (1976), *Doctor De Soto* (1982), *Brave Irene* (1986), *Grownups Get to Do All the Driving* (1995), and *The Toy Brother* (1996). It is a moral stance, it should be stressed, that is backed by gentle irony, and this humor appeals to readers from five to ninety. After all, Steig began his career as a cartoonist for *Judge* and became one of the leading artists for *The New Yorker*. Only late in his career did he begin illustrating books for young readers. His work was always provocative—almost childlike with heavy black lines and pastel colors and characters that appeared to come off the colorful streets of the Bronx where he grew up. Steig was influenced by the Grimms' fairy tales, Charlie Chaplin's movies, the Katzenjammer Kids, the opera *Hansel and Gretel*, and *Pinocchio*,[179] and his works bear witness to these influences. They are notable for their slapstick scenes, vaudeville characters, and unpredictable plots that lead readers in directions that they might not have anticipated.

While *Shrek!* (1990) is not one of his complex works, it is perhaps the best example of how the fairy tale of "Beauty and the Beast" has been fractured and continually transformed, indicating its radical potential in our digital age, especially with the production and success of the 2001 digitally animated film. Since very few reviewers of the film have paid attention to the book *Shrek!*—not to mention book reviewers—I should like to summarize the plot briefly and comment on the morality of the tale before turning to a discussion of the significance of the film.

Steig's *Shrek!* is very different in tone and style from the film. The title is based on a Yiddish expression that means "horror" or "terror," not fear as some reviewers have said. *Schrecken* in German and Yiddish means to scare, terrify, or horrify, and the ogre Shrek on the cover of Steig's book is a scary figure. He has a green face with protruding ears and a bald head with a pointed top. His face is spotted with black stubble; his eyes are red; his nose large and round; and his teeth sharp and crooked. He is tall and barrel-chested. His fingernails on his green hands are long. He wears a multi-colored violet tunic with a belt around his midriff and striped pants. The color combinations change at times throughout the book, but not his features and character.

> His mother was ugly and his father was ugly, but Shrek was uglier than the two of them put together. By the time he toddled, Shrek could spit a flame of full ninety-nine yards and vent smoke from either ear. With just a look he cowed the reptiles in the swamp. Any snake dumb enough to bite him instantly got convulsions and died.[180]

One day Shrek's parents kick him out of the swamp and send him into the world to do damage. So the entire question of evil—What is evil? Who causes evil?—is relativized from the very beginning. The anti-hero retains power and questions what heroism is about. Along the way he encounters a witch, who tells his fortune: he will be taken to a knight by a donkey, and after conquering the knight, he will marry a princess who is even uglier than he is. Wherever he goes, every living creature flees because he is so repulsive. When he comes upon a dragon, he knocks it unconscious. Then he has a dream in which children hug and kiss him, and such a paradisaical vision—not unlike a scene in Oscar Wilde's "The Unhappy Giant"—is a nightmare for him. He wakes to meet the donkey that takes him to the nutty knight who guards the entrance to the crazy castle where the repulsive princess waits. After he defeats the knight, he has the real test of his life: he enters a room filled with mirrors, and for the first time he learns what fear is when he sees how hideous he is. At the same time, this recognition raises his self-esteem, and he is "happier than ever to be exactly what he is." Once he has passed this test, so to say, he has a "romantic" meeting with the ugly princess:

Said Shrek: "Your horny warts, your rosy wens,
              Like Slimy bogs and fusty fens,
              Thrill me."

Said the princess:	"Your lumpy nose, your pointy head,	
	Your wicked eyes, so livid red,	
	Just kill me."	

Said Shrek:	"Oh, ghastly you,	I could go on,
	With lips of blue,	I know you know
	Your ruddy eyes	The reason why
	With carmine sties	I love you so—
	Enchant me.	You're so ugh-ly!"

Said the princess:	"Your nose is so harry,
	Oh let us not tarry,
	Your look is so scary,
	I think we should marry."[181]

Indeed, they do marry, and they are married by the dragon, who looks more like an alligator in a green robe, and Steig comments: "And they lived horribly ever after, scaring the socks off all who fell afoul of them."[182]

This mock fairy tale plays with all the conventions of the traditional folk and fairy tale to provoke readers to consider the relative nature of evil and beauty. Instead of a handsome prince or a gifted third son, there is an outsider from the swamps, ugly and stinking, who wins a repulsive princess by overcoming fear of himself. The tale is obviously a parody of the Grimms' "The Young Man Who Went out in Search of Fear" and a reversal of Le Prince de Beaumont's "Beauty and the Beast," but it is also more than that, for Steig levels the playing field for people considered to be despicable and evil. Shrek represents the outsider, the marginalized, the Other, who could be any of the oppressed minorities in America. He may even come from the streets of the Bronx, and the humor of the tale is clearly identifiable as New York Jewish humor. What was once a European folk tale has through Steig's soft watercolor images and brazen irreverent language becomes a contemporary literary fairy tale that thrives on playfulness, topsy-turvy scenes, and skepticism. This is a fairy tale that radically explodes fairy-tale expectations and fulfills them at the same time: the utopian hope for tolerance and difference is affirmed in an unlikely marriage sanctified by a dragon. The ogre and his wife will continue to frighten people, but they will be happy to do so in the name of relative morality that questions the bias of conventionality associated with evil.

Some of this utopian spirit pervades the film. However, for the most part, the screenplay, written by Ted Elliott, Terry Rossio, Joe Stillman, and Roger Schulman (along with twenty-seven dialogue writers and story artists) is much more sarcastic. The film's most severe critic, Michael Atkinson of the *Village Voice*, describes it as follows:

> *Shrek* is not in essence a cartoon—it's an Umberto Eco-style hypercinema, stuck between being drawn and being photographed as Disney's Celebration U.S.A. is stuck between life and entertainment. Spectacle this is—like a Grucci blastoff, impressive for having been manu-factured—but *Shrek* is at the same time witheringly cynical. Desperately avoiding the risk of even a half-second of boredom, the movie is wall-to-wall-window-to-door noise, babbling, and jokes (the first minute sees the first fart gag), and demographically it's a hard-sell shotgun spray.[183]

Atkinson, who goes on to disparage the film because its co-producer Jeffrey Katzenberg of Dreamworks allegedly used the film to take revenge on Michael Eisner, head of the Disney Corporation, and could not restrain his spite, is so vehement in his criticism that he cannot grasp the radical nature of the film and its many positive features. In fact, though there may be some weaknesses to the film, it is exactly what Eliza Dresang would hold up as a radical exemplary work of art for children in a digital age.

Radical in plot, radical in technique, *Shrek* is an unusual film because it opens up questions about the conflict within the culture industry with regard to who is going to control the realm of animation and amusement for the young. To make their point, the creators of the film were obliged to transform Steig's storyline and moral and political purpose. Let us recall the film's plot.

Shrek, who is a powerful ogre, lives like a hermit in a swamp, and he likes his privacy. In the past the outside world had rejected him because of his ugliness, and he is content to live alone and to take an occasional mud shower. All of a sudden, however, fairy-tale characters such as the Seven Dwarfs, Sleeping Beauty, and the Three Little Pigs, begin invading his privacy. They have all been banished from Lord Farquaad's kingdom of Duloc because the king despises fantasy or anything that is out of the ordinary. Shrek decides to seek out Farquaad and to demand that the "squatters" or refugees be allowed to return to Duloc, and along the way, he meets a bumbling, talkative, good-natured donkey, who admires him and becomes his sidekick. When they arrive in Duloc, depicted as a sanitized Disney world in perfect symmetry, Shrek wins a contest of powerful knights in front of Farquaad, who is a tiny man with a big head, and the king agrees to take back the fairy-tale characters if Shrek will rescue the princess Fiona, guarded by a monstrous dragon. Farquaad has been told by his magic mirror that he must marry a princess to have a perfect kingdom, and in a parody of the TV program "The Dating Game," he chooses Fiona. So, one beast is pitted against another beast. Shrek is not interested in courting anyone, and Farquaad only wants to wed Fiona to fulfill his plans of establishing a perfect kingdom, not for love.

Once Shrek agrees, he sets off to conquer the dragon, who falls in love with Donkey, and there is a fight-and-escape scene that mocks some of the famous episodes in the Disney films *Snow White*, *Sleeping Beauty*, and *Beauty and the Beast*, while at the same time heightening the suspense. Shrek and Donkey escape with Fiona, and to his surprise Shrek discovers that the smart Fiona not only knows karate and other techniques, but that she has a mysterious secret. The viewers of the film learn before Shrek that Fiona is enchanted, and at night she turns into an ugly princess, just as repulsive as Shrek. Her secret and their love for one another is not consummated until the very end, when Shrek's quest is fulfilled and Farquaad is exposed as a petty tyrant and overturned. Fiona's enchantment also ends, but she remains ugly and goes off to live with Shrek in the swamp.

The artificial Disney world of Duloc versus the natural beauty of the swamp, conformists versus outsiders, conventionality versus unconventionality, the tyranny of symmetry and homogenization versus the freedom of asymmetry and heterogeneity—these are some of the conflicts in the film that represent a real struggle within the film industry of cultural production. One of the "moral" questions that *Shrek* raises is: must we continue to stuff the brains of our children with sentimental stereotyped films produced by the Disney Corporation which, for over sixty-five years, has dominated animation and mass-mediated fairy tales? Isn't there something immoral about the way the messages of the Disney Corporation have been transmitted and controlled? Do we ever think enough about the tyranny of the Disney kingdom? Are the Disney aesthetics concerning beauty and ugliness questionable?

Certainly, numerous books on Disney films, the Disney Corporation, and Disney himself have been published in the last twenty years that have sought to convince us that there is something else possible more meaningful and more enjoyable in the realm of entertainment.[184] So it is not as if there have not been "Disney" skeptics and critics. What is especially significant about *Shrek* is that it goes beyond the Disney animated fairy-tale films—and beyond Steig—to show through stunning digital animation how the world, art, and institutions can be depicted differently and be directed in a more humane manner. The three-dimensional scenes, the color schemes, the voiceovers, the language, and yes, the devastating critique of the Grimms and Disney point to experimentation that

Figure 59
Hal Hartley,
No Such Thing

furthers more tolerance and compassion in a technological world that often seems devoid of humanity. What is also significant is that "the shrek" of Shrek, that is, the horror of the beast, is transformed in such a way that we are led to question xenophobia and so-called norms of beauty and ugliness. Two ugly creatures unite at the end of the film and still live at the borders of society. They have come together because of their otherness and because they have developed feelings of mutual respect. This is a far cry from the perfect union dreamed up by Le Prince de Beaumont and it is a far cry from the perfect union that Farquaad desired. Ultimately, *Shrek* uses various strains of the carnivalesque to explode standard notions of the fairy tale and normative standards of beauty, proper mating behavior, femininity, and masculinity. The freakiness of *Shrek* is a delightful and hopeful anticipation of a de-Disneyfied world.

To a certain extent, this is also true about the freakiness in Hal Hartley's *No Such Thing* (2001). This cynical film is a flawed carnivalesque experiment to use the "Beauty and the Beast" story to utter a tirade against all the evils of the world through the mouth of a monster who cannot die: the corrupt mass media corporations, the secret military experiments, the abuse of medical technology, the narcissism of the yuppie generation, and the arrogance of people in power. Hartley portrays a young, innocent newsroom assistant, played by the talented Sarah Polley, who convinces a tyrannical TV boss, played by the equally talented Helen Mirren, to fly to Iceland, where her boyfriend and other members of a TV crew had been torn apart by a hideous monster. On her way, her plane crashes in the ocean, and she is the only survivor. Through a miracle of modern medicine and technology, she recovers from a long difficult operation in Reykjavik. Afterward, she makes a journey to the wastelands of Iceland and encounters a flame-throwing monster with a green face and horns who, due to some kind of mutation, cannot die. He is fed up with the world and needs the help of a mad scientist (controlled by the military) to leave the world. Beatrice is not afraid of him and decides to help him. They fly off to New York, where she is acclaimed as a celebrity. Caught up in fame, she forgets her mission to help the monster and becomes a "degenerate" socialite. However, she sobers up when she learns how the monster is being maltreated. With the help of friends, she returns to Iceland with the monster and the mad scientist, and she organizes the monster's death that releases him from the inhumanity of humanity. Or, Beauty saves the Beast from the tortures of savage civilization.

This film can only be taken somewhat seriously if one views it as a comic book or graphic novel. Hartley clearly wanted the characters to play their roles as if they were flat stereotypes in a predictable science-fiction adventure. None of them shows real emotion; they are all like cardboard figures on the back of a cereal box. The hyperbolic tirades of the monster are ludicrous. The tyrannical actions of the boss of the TV network are wooden. Even Beatrice the beauty's descent into decadent society is contrived. The difficulty with Hartley's endeavor to transform the "Beauty and the Beast" plot into a carnivalesque social and political critique is that it lacks humor. There is no joy in the role reversals and the mockery of contemporary politics. The film takes us on a listless and pointless voyage.

Rearranging Arranged Marriages in the Beast/Bridegroom Tales

One of the most important subtexts in the evolution of the beast/bridegroom tales from the oral through the literary to film is that of arranged marriages. Clearly, by the time that the French women writers of the late seventeenth and early eighteenth centuries began writing their fascinating fairy tales about beauties and beasts, they were rebelling against or at the very least questioning arranged marriages and marriages of convenience. Metaphorically, the Beast represented the older, ugly man to whom a young girl/woman was betrothed through a contract. The father's trip and encounter with the beast is a form of contact/contract. Beauty's stay in the Beast's magnificent palace is the period of time she needs to become accustomed to the ugliness and old age of her alien husband. Her reward is the miraculous illusion or self-delusion: the Beast as prince with tons of money and a magnificent realm to boot.

The theme of marriages of convenience has been the topic of hundreds if not thousands of stories, novels, poems, plays, operas, and musicals. So, it is not by chance that there are numerous films about arranged marriages in which a strict father orders a daughter to marry someone from a wealthy family, or films in which marriage makers are employed to find the right mate. Other films feature blind dates arranged by friends or relatives, or mail-order and email brides. All the films reflect how courting and mating customs have changed in different countries and how cultural norms play a powerful role in the way wives and husbands are chosen. Some of the better known films are: *Beyond the Rocks* (1922), *Fiddler on the Roof* (1971), *Effi Brest* (1974), *Castaway* (1987), *The Piano* (1993), and *Birthday Girl* (2002).

It would be extremely difficult to sort out which films about arranged marriages intentionally or unintentionally drew upon the beast/bridegroom tradition to represent how mate selection has been represented in the cinema. Therefore, I want to conclude this part about "Beauty and the Beast" films to discuss only one very recent film, *Brick Lane* (2007), because I believe that it encapsulates some of the problematic aspects of mating, arranged marriages, and love in a sublime manner without directly referring to the "Beauty and the Beast" tradition.

Based on a novel by Monica Ali, the film begins in a Bangladesh village in the 1980s with seventeen-year-old Nazneen and her sister running carefree through the fields. At one point they talk about marrying a king who rescues them from a tower. However, their dreams are smashed when their mother unexpectedly commits suicide. In the aftermath, Nazneen's father decides to send her to London to marry an educated older man because he wants to cut down on the mouths that he must feed. Desolate, Nazneen obeys her father and embarks for England. The film fast forwards sixteen years to Brick Lane, where Nazneen is living in a London council flat in the East-End borough of Tower Hamlets, heavily populated by Pakistanis and Indians. She has two young daughters about fourteen and ten, and her husband Chanu is a monstrous fat man, pompous and insecure, who is always trying to look at the bright side of things from their drab flat. It is obvious that the silent Nazneen is not in love with him and barely tolerates his presence. Her life is spent mainly by shopping for food, looking after her daughters, and cooking for her family. The only time she ventures outside is to shop or accompany her husband on an errand. She appears to be a passive victim or prisoner, who bears her fate with stoicism and dignity. She is frequently pictured looking through lace-covered windows into the courtyard and longing for more contact in her life. All this changes when her husband loses his job and she acquires a sewing machine so that she can compensate for his loss of revenue. Without knowing it, this acquisition is a declaration of independence. She reveals her inner desires and needs through letter writing to her sister and through a stream of consciousness in a voiceover narrative. Soon, Nazneen falls in love with a handsome young delivery man named Karim, who becomes active in the Muslim community's efforts to fight against discrimination. Feeling more and more liberated through this affair, she, too, attends the meetings, and her husband becomes aware of her liaison. When the attack on the World Trade Center takes place on September 11, 2001, her husband decides that it is too dangerous to stay in London because of the racism and attacks on Muslims. In the meantime, Karim turns more radical in his politics and neglects Nazneen, who does not want to leave London, nor do her daughters. However, as they pack to go to Bangladesh, a wish that Nazneen had cherished for years, she sees how tender and sensitive her husband is, despite his awkward social behavior. She also realizes that she is not in love with Karim. As she is about to yield to her husband's decision to return to Bangladesh, her oldest daughter protests, insisting that London is their home and that Nazneen is not being true to herself. In the end, her husband sadly sets off for Bangladesh by himself, leaving Nazneen with her daughters playing in the snow-covered courtyard of the housing estate.

Though there is never any explicit reference to "Beauty and the Beast," there are clear parallels that one can draw between the film and the tale—and more important, transformations of the plot and characters that suggest how complicated mate selection has become even when the traditional strictures are still in place. Once the father arranges for Nazneen's marriage, he disappears from the scene and his influence is no longer felt. In contrast, Nazneen has a loving relationship with her sister and depends on her through letters to keep her dreams alive. The "beast" in the film, Nazneen's repulsive husband, suffers greatly from an inferiority complex and is himself alienated in the London setting. He is transformed in the end, not into a handsome charming prince, but into a more sympathetic caring individual who can no longer endure his loneliness and marginalization in London. Karim, the rival in the film, is no Avenant, nor is he Nazneen's savior. He helps to raise Nazneen's awareness about her situation, but it is she who decides that she does not want either beast or prince. In some respects, she fulfills what is implied in the ending of Cocteau's film without irony.

Kissing Frogs May No Longer Work

If the trajectory of the "Beauty and the Beast" films in the twenty-first century appears to be heading away from the fulfillment of the demands of the father and the desires of the beast, the same can be said about the "Frog Prince" films. This is not to say, however, that the power of beasts and frogs are dwindling. Rather, the manner in which men and women court throughout the world has undergone immense changes that make it more difficult for fathers (and complicit mothers) to determine the appropriate husbands for their daughters, and for men to lure and subdue women psychologically and physically so that they will agree to wed them. The resilient feminist movement continues to alter the relations within the mating process and within the family. The "Frog Prince" films attest to this social and political change.

In my essay, "What Makes a Repulsive Frog So Appealing: Applying Memetics to Folk and Fairy Tales,"[185] I traced the development of the tale type catalogued by folklorists as ATU 440: "Frog King" or "Iron Henry," related to the Beast/Bridegroom narratives, from oral versions up through present-day films to show how this tale type has spread memetically over centuries to stick in our brains, and I discussed iconic representations in literature, cartoons, music, poems, and all sorts of cultural artifacts. As in the "Beauty and Beast" filmic discourse, there are different perspectives on what constitutes proper courting and mating. The emphasis is somewhat different in the "Frog Prince" films, for the major question has become whether the princess is smart or stupid to kiss a frog who has more or less forced his way into her palace/home and manages to gain the support of her father so that he can sleep with her. Since the plot is fairly straightforward, the story does not lend itself to feature films, and those long live-action films that have been made tend to be more conservative in their outlook than the short ones, especially the cartoons.

For instance, even though there are amusing antics in Jim Henson's *Tales from Muppetland: The Frog Prince* (1972) and Eric Idle's *The Tale of the Frog Prince* (1982), produced by the Faerie Tale Theatre, the frog is transformed into a likeable prince and the princess learns that kindness to kind reptiles pays an ample reward. Both films mock the original fairy tale, but the ideological underpinnings of the films are not much different from the Grimms' tale, in which a prince and happiness are promised to each and every girl who learns to overcome her fear of the phallic-looking frog and adapt to male commands. This same message is also conveyed in Tom Davenport's Appalachian version, *The Frog Prince* (1981), which, despite a change in decor, basically follows the plot of the Grimms' tale as does David Kaplan's short, black-and-white experimental film, *The Frog King* (1994). In this version, the teenage princess is repelled by the slimy phallic appearance of the frog. However, her decrepit old parents, a farmer couple, compel her to comply with the frog's desires. Kaplan ends his film with an ironic shot of the parents, who are content that their daughter is mating with the frog turned prince, even though it does not seem that she is enjoying herself.

The more interesting "Frog Prince" long feature films tend to be more inventive and pay homage to feminism even if they always strive for a sentimental ending. Jackson Hunsicker directed an unusual musical, *The Frog Prince* (1987), for Cannon Studio, in which marriage is not the goal of the princess, nor is courting central to the action. Instead, we have a singing and dancing, non-erotic twelve-year-old princess named Zora (Aileen Quinn) and her nasty beautiful elder sister named Henrietta (Helen Hunt), who are vying to be declared a genuine princess in their uncle's court. (Their parents are dead.) Zora loses her golden ball in a well. An enchanted lonely prince named Ribbit wearing a frog's mask returns the ball in exchange for a promise of friendship. Indeed, he teaches her how to dress and dance so she can win the court's favor. However, he is caught by Henrietta and stuffed down a dry well. With the help from a friend, Zora discovers this misdeed, saves the frog, and is anointed a true princess at the end of the film. Ribbit has been transformed into a human after receiving a peck on the cheek from Zora, and they innocently dance before a well-wishing court of aristocrats.

Zora is the epitome of the virginal sweet singer of the Disney tradition of fairy tales and looks like Disney's Snow White, but she is not as dumb and passive. Zora wins the hearts of everyone in the palace and Ribbit because of her acts of kindness. Poor Helen Hunt is obliged to act the role of the stereotypical vain and deceitful sister. The film is intended for children and infantilized minds of adults. In short, the film is silly and predictable and the characters one-dimensional.

This is not the case with two East European films. Walter Beck directed a DEFA production, *The Frog King* (1987), which is one of the more interesting Grimm adaptations from the former East Germany. The traditional plot is made more substantial and expanded in interesting ways; the excellent acting does not patronize children; the sets are unique. While the DEFA fairy-tale films always sought to appeal to family audiences, they did not want to dumb down their audiences. In this version of "The Frog Prince," the father is kind and caring; his youngest daughter, called Henriette (an allusion to the Grimms' tale, in which the faithful servant is called Heinrich or Henry), pouts and tries to avoid her obligations to a tiny puppet frog after she makes a promise to allow him to drink from her cup, eat from her plate, and sleep in her bed. Once she throws him against the wall in a fit of anger, she smiles when he turns into a most rugged and handsome prince. Insisting on a kiss, the prince abruptly refuses and departs for a place unknown because she did not keep her promises and was too arrogant. Her father sends out messengers to try to find him and learns that he has gone to the end of the world. Against her father's wishes, Henriette decides to redeem herself by traveling to the end of the world and show her integrity. Disguised as a young boy named Heinrich, she finds her way to the dark and gloomy castle where the prince is condemned to live and she manages to drink from his cup, eat from his plate, and sleep in his bed. When the prince recognizes her and her valor, he returns to her palace to marry her. There are no songs or comic antics in this version of "The Frog Prince," which focuses more on the independence and cleverness of a young girl than on her submission to her father and the wish for Prince Charming. There are subtle and ironic touches throughout the film, particularly when Henriette is pictured as a boy and bribing a cook and servant so she can attend the prince. In fact, the entire film can be viewed as a series of ironic transformations that enable a young girl to come into her own.

This theme is also emphasized in the Czech film, *The Frog Prince* (1991), directed by Juraj Herz after Czechoslovakia had become independent from the Soviet Union, but the film is in keeping with earlier fairy-tale adaptations; it borrows heavily from the great Czech cult film *Three Wishes for Cinderella* (1973). Herz's princess is the youngest daughter of a king who has already married off two of his daughters, and she must also wed within a year to save the realm from a curse. The difficulty is that she is a feisty tomboy and very unconventional, and her intended suitor is an arrogant, conceited young man, who insults a fairy. Disguised as a man, the princess demonstrates that she can shoot better than the prince and also ride a horse more competently. After a series of adventures and mistaken identities, the bold princess gradually falls in love with the prince, but he is tricked into kissing another woman and is punished by the fairy, who changes him into a frog because he has hurt the princess. Of course she eventually loses her small golden ball in his pond and must promise him that he can have a kiss and sleep in his bed. When she gives him a kiss, she faints and finds the repentant prince before her eyes. Together they save the kingdom by marrying. Filmed as a Shakespearean comedy, both the prince and princess need taming, or at least their energetic playful urges must be directed toward each other and toward accepting the responsible roles they must play to prevent the kingdom from being destroyed by the curse. The film gently mocks the conventions of the court. The camera focuses on the princess's zest for life and her free spirit, which is never crushed. Like *Three Wishes for Cinderella*, the film contains a critique of the traditional Grimms' fairy tale by stressing the active role played by the princess in determining her fate. It is also possible to view the film as a political allegory in which a kingdom (Czechoslovakia) is rescued from the curse that would have had the realm ruled by a beast. Such an interpretation might stretch a viewer's imagination. Nevertheless, there are clear signs that the film is an expression of joyful liberation.

In contrast to the Czech film, the American made-for-TV film *Prince Charming* (2001), directed by Allan Arkush, calls for a return to a firm belief in sentimental love and marriage. And once again we have a Shakespearean-like comedy with all sorts of mistaken identities and subplots. The setting is England in 1500, and young Prince John of Arkan is obliged to marry a princess from another realm to end years of the Tulip Wars. However, Prince John cannot keep his sword in his pants, and he is constantly rescuing damsels in distress only to seduce them. In fact, he runs off and copulates in a church tower with a luscious peasant woman on the day of his wedding. For this mistake he and his squire are transformed into frogs for eternity unless the prince can find a princess who will kiss him. Once he is transformed into a prince, however, he has five days to marry the princess and must remain true to her. Five hundred years pass, and Sir John and his squire are accidentally picked up as frogs by an American in England and transported to New York City. By chance, they make their home in Central Park, which they consider a forest, and Prince John is accidentally kissed by a vain actress playing different aristocratic roles in Shakespeare in the Park. He and the squire reassume their natural forms, and John soon falls in love with a young woman named Kate, who drives a horse and buggy in Central Park. It is only by demonstrating that he can keep his sword in his pants and

Figure 60
Allan Arkush,
Prince Charming

be true to Kate that John, despite the curse, can retain his human shape. Given the sentimental tradition of American TV films, *Prince Charming* unfortunately demonstrates that sweet somewhat independent girls like Kate can eventually learn to trust boyish playboys like John. What is needed is a bit of patience and belief in true love, for most frogs, despite their warts, can become princes.

This is also the message in the very latest Disney animated feature, *The Princess and the Frog* (2009). Despite the vibrant and original music of Randy Newman that runs throughout the film, the story is stale and filled with stereotypes and a typical Disney happy ending. The plot could be taken from any mediocre live-action love story: Tiana, a young black woman, daughter of a seamstress, wants to start a restaurant in New Orleans during the 1920s to honor her dead father's dream. She works two jobs and is the epitome of the Protestant work ethic, while her rich white friend Charlotte, daughter of the wealthiest man in town, Big Daddy La Bouff, is a giddy, spoiled brat, who dreams of marrying the playboy Prince Naveen. However, he is turned into a frog by the voodoo doctor Facilier as is Tiana by accident. Then, in keeping with his sinister ways, Facilier transforms Prince Naveen's butler Buford to impersonate the prince so that Buford can marry Charlotte and Facilier can take possession of Big Daddy's soul and money. In the meantime, Tiana and the prince must take a journey as frogs to obtain help from Mama Odie, a rotund, powerful witch of the Bayou swamp. Along the way they fall in love and learn some moral lessons: all work and no play makes Tiana too straight, and only love can free her from her obsession. On the other hand, the prince must learn that all play and no work and love will cause him to lose the person he comes to cherish most. Of course, there are some bumps along the road, that is, along the swamp, when they return to New Orleans and defeat the sinister Dr. Facilier. The film critic in the Minneapolis *Star Tribune* noted: "There's nothing wrong with the film, except the feeling that there's not quite enough in it. This is a film that colors inside the lines beautifully, but never thinks outside the box."[186]

Much ado was made in the world-wide media about the Disney animators' coloring a black princess inside the box, but the Disney Corporation is so far behind the times that, though it will make a huge amount of money by seeming to break the color line, this film will do nothing to change animation and especially fairy-tale films. As usual, the characters are flat and stereotypes.

Charlotte is a male sexist depiction of a spoiled rich daughter of a stereotypical Big Daddy, fat and boisterous. The African American villain, Dr. Facilier, is also a pale imitation of sleazy con men, while the prince's butler has been depicted as a bungling Englishman hundreds of times. Whether black, brown, white, pink, or yellow, Disney animators have never learned to shape the prince and princess-to-be other than as clean-cut dolls, who are motivated by love. In the corporate view of love and mating, everybody must be pristine and sincere, but not everybody becomes a prince or princess at the end. One must merit promotion to royalty by adhering to the Protestant ethic, and courting is a process that brings out the qualities of good, kind rulers. In the end, it is no surprise that Tiana opens her restaurant with her prince at her side. This is what her Daddy had in mind for her from the beginning, and she proves herself to be Daddy's good girl.

All the narratives of the five feature films that I have discussed are interesting because of the manner in which they arrange and rearrange the plot of the well-known Grimms' fairy tale to comment on contemporary beliefs, customs, and practices with regard to courting and mating. Each one reveals the influence of the western feminist movement to a degree, although we should bear in mind that all the films were directed and filmed by men, offering a sympathetic view of men. The cartoon tradition, also dominated by men, tends, however, to be more radical in reflecting how the beast/bridegroom might be changed.

For instance, there are two provocative fractured fairy tales from the Rocky and Bullwinkle Show that turn the "Frog Prince" narrative upside down. In *The Frog Prince* (1960) there are too many witches in a kingdom who have turned all the princes into frogs. So a desperate little witch finds a frog and transforms him into a prince. Since all the princes are frogs, a desperate princess marries this prince, even though he insists that he is a frog. But after they are married, the prince is re-transformed into a frog, and the princess is frustrated until she, too, becomes a frog. In another fractured fairy-tale film, *The Enchanted Frog* (1961), there are three frogs living happily in a pond until one of them named Filbert grows to be five feet tall and thinks he is now a prince. He leaves the pond to find a princess, but only finds unhappiness and returns to his mother and brother because you can take the frog out of a pond, but you cannot take the pond out of a frog.

These fractured fairy-tale films are somewhat tame when compared with the very short *Frog Prince* (2008), which appeared in Seth MacFarlane's Cavalcade of Cartoon Comedy on the Internet. In this version a beautiful princess comes across a talking frog sitting on a tadpole in a pond. She tells him that he must be a prince. The frog replies that she should give him a kiss to find out. However, he does not turn into a prince when she kisses him, and he says that she has to touch the underside of his penis to find out whether he is truly a prince. She does this, but again he does not change. She accuses him of being a pervert, and the frog replies that he never told her he was a prince. She storms off, and another princess comes by and expects him to change into a prince, but he brushes her off by telling her that she must make a load on his back. This raunchy cartoon explodes and ridicules in a blunt manner the false notions that women have of frogs who are capable of turning into princes. Another cartoon, *The Frog Prince* (2006), which appeared on YouTube and was made from the Sims2 video game by Vicala, mocks the classical tale from another perspective. No words are spoken in this cartoon. We only hear the music of Harry James's song "Prince Charming." The characters are life-like computer-animated figures. A tall frog dressed in a suit enters a princess's garden and with a glittering ring begs the hesitating princess to marry him. Suddenly, they are under a marriage bower in the garden. The frog prince leans over and kisses her. In the next frame they are in their underclothes sitting on a sofa in her mansion. The frog is still in a frog in underpants. She enters the bedroom and waits for him. He goes outside and changes into a knight in shining armor and joins her in the bed. Pleasantly surprised, the princess has intercourse with him. The next day, they are once again in the living room, and the "prince" dressed in jeans and a sports shirt watching a boxing match on a flat TV screen. The princess is mad. He shows himself to be a lazy parasite. So, she kicks him out of her mansion and banishes him. The last frame of the cartoon informs us: "And she lived happily ever after."

In the cartoon world of frog princes and princesses, conventional mating and marriages are next to impossible. Women have increasingly set the conditions under which they want to cohabit a living space with another person, whether it be with a man or another woman. The formulas developed through the beast/bridegroom tales are no longer functioning effectively, and this has spurred many filmmakers to rearrange characters, plots, and motifs to suggest alternatives to the traditional mating games. That is unless one is a filmmaker who adheres to the Disney formula.

12
Andersen's Cinematic Legacy:
Trivialization and Innovation

I'm Hans Christian Andersen, I've many a tale to tell.
And though I'm a cobbler, I'd say I tell them rather well.
I'll mend your shoes and I'll fix your boots when I have a moment free,
When I'm not otherwise occupied as a purple duck,
or a mountain side, or a quarter after three.
I'm Hans Christian Andersen, that's me!

Samuel Goldwyn Production, *Hans Christian Andersen*
Song composed by Frank Loesser and sung by Danny Kaye

For many people, young and old, who have grown up viewing the classic RKO film *Hans Christian Andersen*, produced in 1952 and starring the inimitable Danny Kaye, it is difficult to know who Hans Christian Andersen actually is and what really is significant about his tales. Like Andersen's own autobiography, *The Fairy Tale of My Life*, which he wrote to conceal many uncomfortable facets of his life, there is very little truth in this charming film, which distorts not only his life but also the meaning of many of the tales. Yet, the powerful impact of *Hans Christian Andersen* is such that people continue to believe Andersen was a happy-go-lucky cobbler, unlucky in love, who sought to entertain children with his delightful storytelling. The problem with this rosy image of a highly neurotic man, who was afraid to love and had only occasional contact with children, is that it belies the profound and disturbing contribution that Andersen made to the fairy-tale tradition throughout the world.

But it is not just the 1952 cinematic version of Andersen's life that minimizes and trivializes Andersen's significance as fairy-tale writer, it is also such films as the *The Little Mermaid*, produced by the Walt Disney corporation in 1989. This film marked the resurgence of the Disney studio in the field of animated fairy-tale films while unfortunately simplifying the complex meaning of Andersen's fairy tale. Yet, it is not only the Disney Corporation that has appropriated and transformed the meaning of Andersen's tales to serve its own interests. There are many other directors and film studios that have used and/or exploited Andersen's tales simply to make money off his name, not to explore their complex meanings. At the same time, there are also some film-makers who have improved upon the original tales or developed themes in extraordinary ways that open new vistas on the contradictory aspects of Andersen's stories. In the twentieth and twenty-first centuries the film adaptations of the classical tales by Andersen (as well as those by the Brothers Grimm and Charles Perrault) have become better known than the classical texts, which, in comparison, have virtually lost their meanings due to the fact that the films have replaced them. As I have already emphasized, comparison of the film adaptations with the original classical texts can be hazardous. Clearly, we cannot fix the "original" significance of an Andersen fairy tale. In fact, we cannot determine the "authentic" meaning of any fairy tale. Nor do we know anything about Andersen's "true" intentions. At best, we can only study the structure, linguistic usage, prevalent themes, tendentious meanings, and ideology of Andersen's tales in a socio-historical context to understand how they formed dispositions toward a reception, and how the reception reveals attitudes and tastes of reading audiences during his time and in other socio-historical contexts. Here it is significant to note that Andersen's tales were more or less canonized while he was still alive, and this canonization also set the grounds for tendentious readings, that is, they predisposed readers to a consensual reception that has continued throughout the twentieth century and into the twenty-first.

Andersen did his very best to try to control the reception of his tales. Vain and talented as he was, he wanted history to remember him as a serious artist, a genius, who created tales that adults would ponder and read in awe because of their unusual meanings. He never intended for history to record his fame primarily as a writer of fairy tales for children, for he wrote numerous novels, plays, poems, and essays. He would probably be disappointed and astounded to see what Hollywood and Disney have made out of his life and tales. But he would also probably be more intrigued by the European cinematic interpretations that probe his tales with greater imagination than the American filmmakers.

But fairy-tale films based on Andersen's texts cannot be judged by speculation of what he might have thought or on how close or far the films are based on the printed word. As artistic works in their own right, the films demand to be appreciated and understood as recreations and representations that reflect upon Andersen's works while drawing primarily upon attitudes, tastes, customs, and tendencies in our own times. Fairy-tale films based on Andersen's tales add a new dimension to his stories and inadvertently comment on his role as a writer and the function of fairy tales in the period from 1945 to the present. Their point of departure is always a reading of an Andersen text, at the very least, a familiarity of the text, and an appropriation of the text as the basis for the film. The point of departure is also a parting of the ways, a taking apart the text, breaking it down, to reform and reshape it through a medium that will amplify its meaning in many ways: a new script based on the ideas of the screenplay writer; actual images of the setting, clothes, and articles in the story invented and designed by many hands; full-fledged personalities of the characters portrayed by actors with unique talents; perspectives on the action determined by the camera angle and perspective of the director of the film; color and music that provide atmosphere; animated drawings created by numerous artists who are responsible for the designation of character and setting; voiceovers by actors whose abilities to speak in particular ways enliven apparent unreal characters. A fairy-tale film based on an Andersen fairy tale is never solely concerned with the Andersen text except as a point of departure to explore new cultural meanings and technical inventions, to experiment with aesthetical design, and to provide entertainment for a mass public.

There are questions that we must ask, however, about the point of departure. For instance, why do the director and producer choose an Andersen fairy tale for the basis of their film? How seriously do they and their crews examine and interpret Andersen's work? That is, are they using his name and fame to promote their film as a commodity to make money? Do they intend to explore and elaborate on Andersen's text to shed new light on its meaning? Do they intend to add something new to our cultural knowledge of Andersen and his fairy tales, and do they succeed? Do they reduce Andersen's fairy tale to an appropriate self-censored film for family audiences that infantilizes children? How are they contributing to the general development of the fairy-tale film whether they are live-action productions or animated films?

These are all important questions because Andersen's cultural heritage is being determined, especially in America, more by the cinematic adaptation and interpretation of his tales than by his texts or collections of his tales. This is not to argue that his tales are not being read today, but it is a fact that people, young and old, are reading less and less, and even their reading will be influenced by movies and TV. If Andersen is studied at all, it is at our universities, and even there, he has not been as widely examined as Perrault, the Grimms, and other fairy-tale writers. Nevertheless, there appears to be a discursive struggle over his heritage and the meaning of his tales through cinematic adaptation. On the one side, there is the American viewpoint that tends toward a commodification and trivialization of his tales; on the other side, the Europeans, especially in Russia, France, Czechoslovakia, Denmark, and Germany, offer a different and more serious ideological view of Andersen's tales based on artistic innovation. It is important not to exaggerate this dichotomy or even to create a dichotomy, for there are American films that are unusual artistic endeavors and artificial European films made for the market of the culture industry. Yet, there are clear differences between European approaches to fairy-tale films for children and adults and those produced in America. It is also obvious that the control of the distribution of the films has played and will continue to play an important role with regard to who will win the struggle over Andersen's heritage. Most people are unaware that there is a struggle, and yet it has existed ever since his works were translated and distributed in other countries.

The appropriation of Andersen's fairy tales and stories was something he both desired and feared, for he realized that his fame might shadow his real self and contribute to what he felt was a general misunderstanding of his poetic genius during his lifetime. He articulated this fear clearly in his brilliant tale "The Shadow," which served as the basis for an extraordinary animated film, *H. C. Andersen's The Long Shadow* (1998), directed by Jannik Hastrup, which I shall discuss later. Today the shadow is not caused so much by critics but by the tendencies of the American culture industry to commodify anything it can get its paws on. Andersen's tales appear to the American public largely through a Disney or entertainment lens—as commodities to be consumed for enjoyment offered by a quaint Danish writer. Disney has overshadowed Andersen. There is an ethical problem in such adaptation that I shall discuss at the end of this chapter. But first I want to outline the discourse of cinematic appropriation as a struggle over Andersen's legacy before talking about ethics.

There are only a select number of Andersen tales that have been adapted for the cinema and TV in the North America and Europe, and I want to analyze film adaptations of "The Little Mermaid," "The Princess on the Pea," "The Swineherd," "The Nightingale," "The Emperor's New Clothes," and "The Snow Queen" to reflect upon our predisposition to commemorate Andersen's fame in the twenty-first century, more than 200 years after his birth. (Of course, two series of animated films were produced in 2004 and 2005 to commemorate the 200th birthday of Andersen in Denmark: *The Fairytayler* directed by Jørgen Lerdam, and *Hans Christian Andersen's Fairy Tales* directed by Jorgen Bing. Neither of these charming series has been widely distributed in Europe or North America.)

Many of the Andersen films that I shall examine are not well known in the US and UK, and yet these "unknown" films inform the popular image and reception of Andersen in English-speaking countries. That is, the public is rarely informed about them.

The Little Mermaid

Published in 1837, "The Little Mermaid," one of Andersen's most popular tales, has been adapted for film and television more than any of his other works with the possible exception of "The Snow

Queen." This popularity may, in fact, have a great deal to do with the long history of the European fascination with mermaids, often associated with sirens and water sprites. Myths, legends, and folk tales recounting the formidable power of mermaids can be traced back to Greek and Roman antiquity. Generally speaking, they have always been regarded as dangerous due to their beauty and the seductive voices that they use to lure seamen to disaster and death. At the same time, many folk tales and legends feature mermaids who are more humane and long to possess a Christian soul. The classic example of this type of tale is Friedrich de la Motte Fouqué's *Undine* (1811), in which a water sprite falls in love with a knight and can only marry him if she possesses a soul. After she makes a great sacrifice for the knight, Undine marries him only to be betrayed. Andersen knew Fouqué's story and was clearly influenced by it. However, Andersen transformed the tale into a Christian miracle narrative that was intended to celebrate the power of Christian salvation.

In Denmark, most Andersen scholars now accept the view proposed by James Massengale that

> "The Little Mermaid" concerns a miracle, rather than a simple matter of unrequited love and suicide which is followed by a bit of authorial "structuring invocation". This is not to say that there are no valid critical methods around that would deny the miracle issue. That would be silly. But it is no longer the case that those who accept Andersen's use of an integrally positioned and functionally necessary miracle will find themselves in an isolated periphery.[187]

By exploring the narrative from the perspective of the Mermaid's behavior and desires, Massengale demonstrates convincingly that the young fifteen-year-old protagonist has been strongly influenced by her grandmother. She learns that she must suffer to gain a position in the upper world and that she can never gain an immortal soul. Her grandmother explains: "'We can live until we are three hundred years old; but when we die, we become the foam on the ocean. We cannot even bury our loved ones. We do not have immortal souls. When we die, we shall never rise again.'"[188] Disappointed, the Mermaid responds, "'Why do I not have an immortal soul! . . . I would give all my three hundred years of life for one day as a human being if, afterward, I should be allowed to live in the heavenly world'".

Although the Mermaid has fallen in love with the prince, it is not so much the young man whom she desires but rather a Christian soul. Therefore, her task is twofold: she must learn what the mermen laws require so that she can barter her voice to become human; she must learn the Christian principles of compliance with the laws of God based on compassion, charity, and self-sacrifice so that she can obtain a soul. Her story is not a coming of age story. It is a Christian conversion story based on a miracle: the pagan girl learns all about Christian love and devotion. Instead of dying at the end of the fairy tale, the Mermaid miraculously becomes a daughter of the air, and the daughters, just like her grandmother, provide her with new rules of Christian instruction:

> Mermaids have no immortal soul and can never have one, unless they can obtain the love of a human being. Their chance of obtaining eternal life depends upon others. We, daughters of the air, have not received an eternal soul either; but we can win one by good deeds. We fly to the warm countries, where the heavy air of the plague rests, and blow cool winds to spread it. We carry the smell of flowers that refresh and heal the sick. If for three hundred years we earnestly try to do what is good, we obtain an immortal soul and can take part in the eternal happiness of man. You, little mermaid, have tried with all your heart to do the same. You have suffered and borne your suffering bravely; and that is why you are now among us, the spirits of the air. Do your good deeds and in three hundred years an immortal soul will be yours.[189]

It is important to recall that the prince never learns that it was the Mermaid who saved him. Nor does he fall in love with her. He is struck by her devotion, and it is her devotion to him that entails self-sacrifice and brings about her own miraculous salvation. There is some debate among Danish scholars as to whether the salvation is Catholic or Lutheran. But as Massengale points out, this debate is somewhat irrelevant because Andersen really invents his own peculiar, mystical Christian salvation. What is more relevant is the manner in which Andersen stylized the legendary material to make it acceptable for bourgeois households in Denmark, especially for children, who were to learn about virtuous behavior.

Virtuous behavior in an Andersen tale almost always requires self-submission: the dialogues are exchanges about power relations; the omniscient narrator, while often ironic, rationalizes the behavior of protagonists who alter their lives to be dominated or become a member of the dominant class; the ideology underlines the principles of divine providence and faith in higher powers often represented by a Christian God. But "The Little Mermaid" is not only about Christian obedience, virtue, and salvation. It is, from a feminist perspective, a misogynist tale about dampening the sexual curiosity of a young female, who wants to explore other worlds.[190] The Mermaid must learn her proper place in the order of things, and it is apparently improper for her to pursue a young man, to express her sexual drives, and to change her social position. It is not by chance that Andersen has her tongue cut out, and she feels as if her legs were piercing her like swords when she walks. Once she turns human, she enters a world totally dominated by male desire and has no choice but to commit suicide. She realizes that she will never fit into a world that does not accept her devotion, and murdering the prince will not bring her any satisfaction. The contrived miracle is nothing but a false compensation for a young woman, who has lost hope in life and cannot fulfill her desires. The tragedy of depression due to social oppression runs through western literature up to the present, and the hidden theme of female suicide in fairy tales has been amply explored openly in Anne Sexton's *Transformations*, a collection of provocative poetical retellings of the Grimms' tales. Sexton, who committed suicide, depicts bitter and tragic struggles of female protagonists who seek to break out of the confines of bourgeois domestic life depicted as a prison and coffin. Andersen pre-dated Sexton by over 130 years, but he concealed his sadomasochism in tales that involved notions of self-effacement and punitive attitudes toward women. Yet, they are clearly elaborated in "The Little Mermaid," which can also be interpreted as a commentary about art and the artist.

If we understand the Mermaid metaphorically as representing the artist, Andersen also asks how the artist can articulate his desires and needs as well as his love of beauty in a public realm governed by patronage. This question is raised most poignantly in "The Nightingale," but "The Little Mermaid" prefigures that tale and outlines the dilemma of an artist, totally dependent on a prince who does not and cannot appreciate what she has to offer. Whereas the nightingale as singer survives and comes to an agreement with the emperor, the artist in "The Little Mermaid" loses her voice and cannot express why she is vital for the prince's life. She is miserable as a mime. She cannot dance without feeling pain. She cannot sing. At the court she is a mere ornament whose essence cannot be truly valued. She had deluded herself into believing that she could attract the king through her art. What is there for her to do but to kill herself, thereby creating an artistic tragedy? Self-denial and abnegation constitute the suffering that prompts some of Andersen's great masterpieces. His suffering and self-denial formed a well of experience to which he returned time and again to exploit and explain that he deserved more recognition than he was granted.

Far be it from the Disney Studios, however, to produce a film about suicide and abnegation for family audiences in 1989. *The Little Mermaid*, directed by Robert Clements and John Musker, is a coming-of-age story about a feisty "American" mermaid, who pouts and pushes until she gets her way: she is the charming, adorable, spoiled and talented princess, Daddy's pet, who demonstrates that she deserves to move up into the real world by dint of her perseverance and silence. Ariel must learn to channel her sexual desires and suffer for a man before she can win him as a prize—and make no doubt about it, Eric, the prince, is a prize catch, viewed by the eyes of Americans young and old. There is nothing Danish or European about the Disney film, for Ariel and Eric are depicted as your typical American teenagers, and the film resembles more a Broadway and Hollywood musical than it does the serious, religious fairy tale written by Andersen. In fact, the Disney film is an eternal-return-of-the-same romance about girl meets boy, girl falls for boy, boy falls for girl, evil forces prevent the virtuous youngsters from consummating their love, but love triumphs over evil, and the couple will live happily ever after. This is a formula that Walt Disney developed with music and color animation in the early 1930s. As I have already shown, *Snow White and the Seven Dwarfs* (1937) laid down the prescribed formula: Snow White and the prince fall in love through a song in the first scene of the film; an older woman as witch/queen despises Snow White and wants to eliminate her so that she can become the most powerful and beautiful queen in the land; Snow White's curiosity almost causes her death; the dwarfs defeat the witch; the prince revives Snow White. In *The Little Mermaid* the formula is almost exactly the same: Ariel spies the prince and falls in love with him; Ursula the sea witch hates her and her father and wants to destroy them and take over their kingdom; Ariel's curiosity and desire to be part of another world almost causes her death as well as her father's; the prince saves Ariel by piercing the witch with the phallic bow of his ship; thanks to him Ariel is re-transformed from mermaid into a beautiful bride.

In many respects Disney's *The Little Mermaid* was the quintessential *American* film to close out a decade that had been largely determined by Hollywood spectacle and the reign of Ronald Reagan. The 1970s had been a decade of instability, violence, social upheaval, and the rise of mass movements for social reform. The 1980s began turning back the clock through self-healing, self-absorption, and the reintroduction of conservative values and practices. By 1989, even though the unromantic George Bush was in power, America was back in the romance mode of spectacle, entertainment, delusion, and anesthesia, and a film for the family, especially a Disney film, that might deal with religion, suicide, and death would not only have been a commercial failure and turn away audiences, it would have been "sinful" and not in keeping with Disney corporate practices.

The Little Mermaid was indeed a success because it was true to the conventional Disney form and formula of animated fairy-tale films, and it is certainly not without its artistic merits. The songs are catchy; the humor, witty; the animation, effective. Ariel is a spunky heroine, who speaks and acts like a good white, middle-class heroine of the 1980s. It is true that she sacrifices her voice and fins for the love of a man, but it should be noted that this gesture can be read as an acceptance of the Other, an overcoming of xenophobia, a celebration of her curiosity. Though she marries a prince who has a similar background to hers, Eric is not a member of the merfolk, and Ariel goes against her father's wishes when she pursues him. In other words, we have a mixed marriage in the end, another acceptance of the Other. Finally, as Laura Sells argues to temper the feminist critique of the film, "even though Ariel has been complicit in the death of Ursula, and the destined alliance with patriarchy is fulfilled, I remain hopeful. After all, Ariel enters the white male system with her voice—a stolen, flying voice that erupted amidst patriarchal language, a voice no longer innocent because it resided for a time in the dark continent that is the Medusa's home."[191]

Sells wrote these comments before the "Little Mermaid" sequels appeared and more than likely her hope for Ariel has been disappointed. Ariel's temporary non-conformist behavior was basically a selling point in the Disney film; her rebellion was never to be taken seriously because she was destined from the beginning to wed the perfect partner and form a charming couple that would beget not a only a baby, but a TV series of *The Little Mermaid* (1992–1994), and two sequels, *The Little Mermaid II: The Return to the Sea* (2000) and *The Little Mermaid III: Ariel's Beginning* (2008). The underlying principle of the Disney corporate production of films is to seek topics that will sell the same message in slightly different packaging to advertise the brand name of their products. The first sequel is basically a repeat of the first film, but much duller. This film should have been titled: "Return to the Fold." It concerns little Melody, the twelve-year-old daughter, spawned by Ariel and Eric. They try to keep her away from the sea because she was threatened by the witch Morgana,

Ursula's sister, when she was a baby. Yet, Melody has a natural inclination for the water, rebels against her mother, and is duped by Morgana, who pretends to support her rebellion and appears to be a mother substitute. Melody steals the magic scepter of her grandfather, King Triton, for Morgana, who tricks her. Once Morgana has the scepter, all hell breaks loose. Melody realizes that she has caused a great deal of destruction by her irresponsible actions. Therefore, she steals the scepter back from Morgana, who becomes imprisoned in ice for the rest of her life. Melody is then reconciled with her parents, and they will undoubtedly live happily ever after.

The trite story involves a traditional mother–daughter conflict: Ariel is overly protective, and Melody does not understand why her mother wants to keep her from the sea. Her anger is misdirected at Ariel and therefore she must learn the error of her ways. So the film's simple message is about corrective behavior: the daughter must learn to trust her mother; the mother must learn to trust her daughter. All's well that ends well. On a positive note, the film offers a critique of the "me-generation" of the 1990s, an antidote to the narcissism of the young. However, serious questions about social attitudes and political power struggles are rarely treated with depth in Disney fairy-tale films, especially the Andersen adaptations. Whereas Andersen's tale is disturbing and ambivalent about the meaning of happiness, the Disney films about the Little Mermaid are sentimental, romantic, and one-dimensional. In the second sequel, we are offered a foundation myth which deals with Ariel's early years and how she came into conflict with her father, Triton, who banned music in his undersea realm Atlantica after the death of his wife. Eventually, after Ariel is almost killed, Triton becomes remorseful and saves his daughter from another witch through the power of music so he can become happy again. Happiness is there for the grabbing. One just needs will power (and perhaps a little help from rich and powerful dads and granddads). In all three "Mermaid" animated films, there is also an interesting hidden motif that is played down (or under) and needs to be explored because of its significance in most of the Disney and American fairy-tale films. It is the question of male hegemony: Triton appears in all the Disney "Little Mermaid" films as a powerful, benevolent ruler, who is gentle and uses his phallic scepter for the good of the multi-colored merfolk. His reign is always threatened by dark female witch figures, Ursula, Morgana and Marina, who are projected as slithery octopuses with tentacles grabbing for power, or a conniving evil governess. What are we to make of this black-and-white image of the gender power struggle? What are we to make out of the contrast between the dark witches and the white fairy heroines Ariel and Melody, who are lovely, innocent, and sweet? The harmonious endings of all three films suggest that we, the audience, are not to think any more about evil associated with women and blackness, just as long as the magic scepter is in Triton's hands.

The dramatic conflict between the kind king Triton and the wicked sea witches Ursula and Morgana is totally lacking in the Faerie Tale Theatre production, *The Little Mermaid* (1987), directed by Robert Iscove. So are the humor and the music. Iscove's *Little Mermaid*, is one of the least stimulating of the live-action films in the Faerie Tale series. In fact, it is downright tedious. Unlike the Disney adaptation of the Andersen tale, this film sticks fairly close to the original narrative, though it drops the Christian themes and motifs. The story is told by Neptune, the little mermaid's father, and the girl is anything but little: she is called Pearl and turns twenty-one at the beginning of story. After a brief celebration of her birthday, she is allowed to rise to the top of the ocean for twenty-four hours. During this time she falls in love with a sailor prince named Andrew, saves his life, and returns to the bottom of the ocean, where she visits an outspoken, wry sea witch, who gives her legs. But she also takes away her voice and tells Pearl that she will turn into sea foam unless the prince falls in love with her and marries her. When she returns to land as a human, Pearl discovers that the prince, who is fond of her like a little pet or sister, is in love with Princess Amelia. In fact, he marries her, and Pearl's sisters are despondent because she will have to become sea foam. However, Pearl's sisters surface with a knife and encourage her to kill the prince so she can regain her mermaid form. Pearl resists and turns into a sea spirit, not sea foam. Neptune, the omniscient narrator, appears to believe that this is a grand accomplishment of some sort, and the film ends on a bittersweet note and a view of the ocean.

The tragedy of the film has nothing to do with the mermaid's fate but with the tedium and meaninglessness of the adaptation. Pearl has no personality whatsoever, and her rebellion is virtually placid. The sea witch played by the well-known comic actress Karen Black endeavors to add some spark to the film, but her American slang and corny jokes fall flat. It is a trademark of the Duvall fairy-tale films that the characters often speak with British, American, Irish, and regional accents in the same setting; they are supposed to be cute and comic, but add very little to the characterization of the particular people and detract from the action and meaning of the film. One is supposed to suspend one's imagination while watching a fairy-tale film, but the suspension cannot work if art is banal. The prince, who is depicted as the typical Prince Charming, is too virtuous to be true, and though there is some dramatic tension between Princess Amelia and Pearl, the acting is so predictable that few spectators can be moved by the Pearl's death after the marriage of Amelia and Andrew.

There are other American adaptations of "The Little Mermaid" that follow the same schemes of the Disney and Duvall versions and are not worth reviewing because they are so imitative. The difficulties that most of these films have are related to their effort to make Andersen's tales appropriate for the children and the family "market" while introducing new elements that will draw people to "consume" the films. Appropriate generally means simplistic and moralistic. The morals of the American fairy-tale films tend to be clear and easy to grasp, and there can never be real tragedy or exploration of sexuality and politics. Though European films often follow the same pattern, there are some important exceptions, especially because the European directors often add complex philosophical and ideological aspects to their films. Nor were they always produced to pander to a commercial market. In some cases, they were actually conceived to develop a political critique of totalitarian states while avoiding censorship.

One of most intriguing cinematic adaptations of Andersen's "The Little Mermaid" is the Russian director Vladimir Bychkov's *Rusalochka* (1976). Set in the nineteenth century, the film begins in a large coach traveling through the countryside. A man with a top hat and beard who resembles

Figure 61
Vladimir Bychkov,
The Little Mermaid

Andersen in his forties gazes at a young woman, blonde and fragile, who is evidently disturbed by something. To cheer her up, the traveler/Andersen tells her an unusual version of "The Little Mermaid," in which he assumes the role of Sulpicius, a poet, and the young woman, the role of the mermaid.

The traveler/Andersen sets his story in the late medieval period; the landscape is barren and rough, and the stone dwellings and castle are solid but not particularly beautiful or splendid. A foreign ship is off at sea, and the birthday of the prince is being celebrated. He gazes into the sea and notices the mermaid, who bedazzles him, and it appears that the sailors are also bewitched. The ship runs aground on rocks, and the ship must be abandoned. The mermaid saves the prince and deposits him on the beach in a safe place. The princess of the kingdom, who is a very cold and opportunistic person, happens to come by with her ladies-in-waiting, and they bring the prince back to her castle.

The mermaid, struck by love, wants to see the prince again and manages to swim up to the moat of the castle. When some men see her, they want to harm her because mermaids are associated with the devil. She avoids them and encounters the poet Sulpicius, to whom she reveals her love for the prince. In turn, he warns her to avoid the people of the village and return to the sea. However, she is so desperately in love that Sulpicius promises to help her. He fetches a witch, who is an innkeeper, and the witch gives her legs and takes away her hair. She tells her that she will die from love if the prince marries some one else. The only way she can be saved is if some man sacrifices his life for her.

What is interesting in this story is that the mermaid retains her voice, and whenever she is confronted and questioned about her intentions and identity, she always tells the truth. Thus she is persecuted constantly as an outsider, a stranger, who cannot adjust to the intolerant populace and the artificiality of court life. Sulpicius manages to save her time and again, but the prince, who becomes involved in a duel with an insidious prince over the hand of the cold princess, does not have much integrity, and ignores the mermaid's love. Even when he learns that the haughty princess has been deceitful, he still feels he must honor the chivalric code and marry her. This marriage will kill the mermaid, who tries to overcome her sadness and despondency by dancing on his wedding night. The next day, a masked man challenges the prince to a duel on behalf of the mermaid, and the prince kills him. When the mask is taken off the man, we see that it is Sulpicius who has sacrificed his life to save the mermaid, who turns into an immortal dream. Then the story returns to the coach with the traveler/Andersen and the young woman, who appears to have regained her composure, and the coach travels on.

Bychkov packs this film with several important interrelated themes. The major one concerns identity. Throughout the film, even though her form changes, the mermaid guards the integrity of her feelings that are sincere and candid. She wards off the cruelty of the superstitious soldiers and peasants and cannot be corrupted by the court society. Her innocence is protected by the poet Sulpicius, who grasps the danger of her situation and protects her until he realizes that he can only save her by sacrificing his own life. As the figure of ineffable innocence and honesty, the mermaid's identity cannot be determined by other people who want to brand her as siren, witch, devil, pet, angel, and so on. Her actions speak for her character, and her character reveals the ugly sides of a society that is hollow and barbaric. The social codes of the court and the religious beliefs are exposed by the mermaid, who in some ways is almost a Christ figure, for she remains gentle and compassionate throughout her adventures in a world that is foreign to her. If Sulpicius represents the power of art, then the film appears to argue that its function is to save integrity and truth during a time of social and political degeneration.

Unlike the American cinematic versions of "The Little Mermaid," Bychkov's film takes Andersen's tale more seriously philosophically and ideologically to explore issues of class struggle, identity, love, and religion in innovative ways. In fact, the film also seeks to make a comment on the poetics of Andersen, the storyteller. Unlike the Faerie Tale Theatre film, in which Neptune does not play a role in the action and benignly blesses his daughter, the narrator Andersen becomes immersed in the tale he narrates: the storyteller tells his tale out of compassion for his listener, and it is his love for her that spurs the story, which is intended to strike a chord in her heart. Art is not designed for consumption, but to arouse the feelings of the audience, to inspire people to contemplate their ontological situation. It is also very personal, as was Andersen's art. But the Russian director is not so much interested in capturing Andersen's "true" personal situation as artist, but to address the personal and political in his own times. If Soviet society in the 1970s was unfeeling, bigoted, and censored, artists had to be clever storytellers, and they often used fairy-tale materials to reflect deeply upon the hypocrisy of the state and what effect its policies had on the people.

The very same year that Bychkov produced his film, the Czech director Karel Kachnya created another live-action version with the usual title *The Little Mermaid* which differed greatly from the Russian work and also from Andersen's tale. Kachnya's focus is on the relationship between the king of the seas and his sixth daughter. More than the first half of the film is a poetic portrayal of the underworld realm ruled by a king who despises the human world because of the wars and murders that humans commit and because they harm the creatures of the seas. The king is especially close to his youngest daughter, who reminds him of his dead wife. He intends to have her inherit the throne when he dies. Kachnya captures the tenderness of their relationship and the gentle nature of the people in the underworld. Yet, when the king causes a shipwreck during a celebration beneath the sea, his daughter saves a prince and falls in love with him. As a result of her longing for the prince, she gives her beautiful voice to a sea witch to become human and to join the prince's court. Sentenced to silence, however, she cannot tell the prince that she was the woman who saved him.

Kachnya basically follows the plot in Andersen's tale from this point on, but he does make a few changes. The prince is a young ruler who does not believe in material wealth and has plans to build dams and cultivate his realm. He falls in love with the little mermaid, and only at the last moment, when he is obliged to visit the kingdom of Saragossa, does he meet the princess who accidentally found him on the beach after the mermaid had saved him. He feels more drawn to her than to the mermaid and marries her. Unfortunately, the mermaid can only return to her father's realm if she kills the prince and princess. In the end she refuses and dies a tragic death.

This is not a sentimental love story; rather, it is a narrative about a young woman trapped between two worlds. Kachnya frequently depicts the majestic quality of the sea, its power and beauty. The mermaid's father is not a wrathful king. He is saddened by the loss of his daughter. The prince's feelings for the mermaid are sincere, and he does not betray her when he marries the princess, because he had confessed to the mermaid that he wanted to wed the woman whom he thought saved him. It is the mermaid's silence that condemns her to death. To speak freely was, however, not just a problem for the mermaid, but it had become a major problem in Czechoslovakia during the 1970s, and the mermaid's dilemma was more than likely understood by Czech audiences to have been shared by them.

The Princess on the Pea

Another remarkable Russian fairy-tale film produced in 1976 was Boris Rytsarev's *The Princess on the Pea*, which makes use of four different fairy tales by Andersen. "The Princess on the Pea" (1835) was one of Andersen's first tales; it is very short, brisk, and ironic. The narrator informs us that there was once a prince who wanted to marry a real princess. He travels the whole world looking for one without success. So he returns home, sad and despondent, and evidently withdraws from society because he does not appear again until the very end of the story. In the meantime, a "real" princess arrives one night during a storm. The king himself lets her into the palace. He and his wife do not

Figure 62
Boris Rytsarev,
The Princess on the Pea

believe she is a real princess. They give her a test by placing a pea beneath twenty mattresses to see how sensitive she is. She passes the test by informing them that she was not able to sleep the entire night and is black and blue all over. The prince marries her, and the pea is placed in the royal museum. The narrator comments that we can go and see it if it hasn't been stolen and exclaims, "Now that was a real story!"[192]

What is real is associated with true, authentic, and pure. It may be also associated with blood. As we know, there is a strong essentialist streak in many of Andersen's stories. One character is often brilliant, handsome, and genial and born into nobility as is the case with the ugly duckling. The prince plays a very minor role in the tale, and the irony is that he could have found what he sought if he had just remained at home. Andersen's delightful tale is somewhat simplistic and simple, but it has served as the frame for more profound elaboration.

Rytsarev's film is one of the more original and imaginative explorations of "The Princess on the Pea." He introduces three other Andersen tales ("The Swineherd," "The Traveling Companion," and "The Most Incredible") into the frame by having the king send the prince out into the world the morning after the "real" princess arrives during a nocturnal storm. The king and queen, not very wealthy, had become desperate about finding the right princess for their son and had even placed a sign in front of their castle: "Princess Wanted." They are unaware that the young woman who had arrived during the night was truly a princess. This is why the prince sets off on his travels before he can get to know her.

Rytsarev transforms Andersen's fairy tale into a story about the education of a young prince in three stages. His first stop is at a castle where he views a beautiful but arrogant princess, who values artificiality over natural beauty. The prince exchanges roles with a swineherd to win her affection, but he only learns how supercilious she is and repays her arrogance by humiliating her. The second stop is at a castle where another beautiful princess forces her suitors to guess the answer to three riddles if they want to marry her. If they fail, they are beheaded. The prince discovers that she is in love with a troll, but the princess is afraid to admit this to her father. It is the troll who provides the princess with the riddles so they can get rid of her suitors and continue to meet in secret. However, the prince reveals their secret and actually brings about their union. His third stop is at a kingdom where a princess promises to wed the artist who produces the most superb work of art in her honor. The prince manages to create a magnificent rose in a luminous vase, but all at once a brutal knight arrives and mocks his art by destroying it. The princess is awed by the knight's macho behavior and is delighted to be swept off her feet by him. There is nothing left for the prince to do but to return forlorn to his castle. To his surprise he sees that the princess, whom he does not believe is a princess, is still there and has won the affection of his mother and father. Since he has grown during his journey, he is also able to see how honest, genuine, and natural she is, especially compared with the princesses he has met. Finally, his mother and father try the pea test to see whether she is truly a princess. Of course, she passes the test. Later a merchant purchases the pea and places it in a museum.

The question of authenticity is central for Rytsarev. The pea test is incidental and only verifies what everyone already knows: the princess is a genuine person. There is no value placed on royalty or blood. On the contrary, all the aristocrats are frauds and duplicitous. The vision of the prince and his parents must be corrected to appreciate values such as sincerity, modesty, honesty, and so on. On each one of the encounters during his journey the prince learns to see that beauty and social rank can be deceptive. Rytsarev's sets and costumes are created to emphasize the difference between artificial spectacle and the beauty of simplicity. The prince is constantly placed in a position of an outsider looking into and beneath the veneer of beauty represented by the princess. Moreover, Rytsarev brings out different perspectives with regard to authenticity by drawing on three other Andersen tales and exploring their meanings in unusual ways, thereby enabling us to see how Andersen himself was constantly seeking to establish what constitutes the nature of authentic art, a theme that is most productively treated in "The Nightingale."

In Andersen's "The Princess on the Pea," sensitivity was the standard by which one was to judge "realness" or authenticity. In Rytsarev's film, however, there are many more standards, for the prince as critic is educated first to dismiss artificiality, deception, and pretension. His eyes are opened, and by virtue of insight, he can begin to determine what constitutes beauty. The princess he chooses is physically not the most beautiful of women, but she is the most natural; there is nothing deceptive or pretentious about her. She is disarming because she is so forthright and reveals the extraordinary in the ordinary. This was a key artistic principle in Andersen's style that Rytsarev develops, for it is through the prince's eyes that spectators come to appreciate the beauty of natural simplicity and candor.

In the Faerie Tale Theatre production, *The Princess and the Pea* (1984), directed by Tony Bill, there is a similar attempt to explore the meaning of authenticity, but the slapstick humor, mixed accents, and stupid sexism undermine the defense of simplicity and gentleness. Nevertheless, the frame of the story is interesting: a custodian in a nineteenth-century museum explains to a bungling married couple the significance of a pea in a glass case by telling the story of "The Princess and the Pea." The custodian becomes the royal fool, and the man and wife become the pompous king and queen, who are also vain and superficial. Their son, played by the British actor Tom Conti, is not much better: he is naïve, spoiled, and ignorant. As a pampered prince, who has never grown up, all he wants is a pet for a friend. The court fool must convince him that at his age a wife might be better than an animal. Therefore, the prince asks his parents to provide a wife, and they agree to find one providing that she is a real princess. By coincidence a princess, played by Liza Minnelli with an American accent and verve, appears out of a storm and she is admitted into the castle by the prince who hides her in the fool's room to keep an ordinary girl out of the sight of his parents, for he does not believe she is a real princess. One of the first things she does is to clean the fool's room to show she has the talents of a good housewife. Then she gives the prince sound advice each time that he is introduced to prospective brides who are either pretentious or opportunistic. Finally, he realizes he is in love with the gentle, sincere princess, whom he has been concealing. Once she is submitted to the pea test she passes, to his pleasant surprise, and they marry, although one must wonder why she would wed such a self-absorbed, simple-minded man.

The answer, of course, is that the director and actors are just having fun with the tale, creating entertainment for audiences who are not supposed to think about the complex nature of authenticity. A good, clean-cut girl as pet for the prince provides the answer to his boredom, a girl whom he will be able to control because she is so malleable. If one of the dominant messages in the classical fairy tales from the seventeenth century to the twentieth century was the domestication of beautiful girls who were celebrated for their compliance, then this 1984 cinematic version does not reflect much about the transformation of women's roles in society. According to the film, the "authentic" princess is the authentic house cleaner and pet, who knows her proper place.

The Swineherd

This message is also prominent in the West German filmmaker Herbert Fredersdorf's adaptation of "The Swineherd," one of Andersen's most successful satiric fairy tales, which also deals with the question of authenticity. In his brief narrative, a poor prince courts a supercilious princess and sends her a beautiful rose and a nightingale with a marvelous voice. However, she rejects them because they are real. So the prince disguises himself as a swineherd and captivates her with a marvelous pot that plays divine music. She must pay the prince ten kisses for the pot. Then he creates a rattle that plays all the waltzes and dances of the world. Again she ardently desires to possess the rattle, but the prince now demands a hundred kisses, which, after hesitating, she eventually agrees to give him. This time her father, the emperor, catches them in the act, and he banishes her from the empire. As for the prince, he declares, "I have come to despise you. . . . You did not want an honest prince. You did not appreciate the rose or the nightingale, but you could kiss a swineherd for the sake of a toy. Farewell!" He closes the door to the kingdom, and the princess is left with nothing.

As usual, Andersen criticizes the upper class for its artificial values. To be more precise, he uses a female figure as he did in "The Little Mermaid" and "The Red Shoes" to embody superficiality and fickleness. The overt sexist portrayal was common in Andersen's times and can be found in the fairy tales of other writers such as "King Thrushbeard" by the Brothers Grimm, who often subscribed to the motto: shrews must be tamed, and even innocent girls must be taught brutal lessons. In Andersen, females are often tamed as well as humiliated and tortured. In "The Swineherd," he punishes the princess severely because she has no aesthetic appreciation and enjoys petty, worthless objects. There can be no redemption for her.

In contrast, Fredersdorf has some compassion for the princess. After all, he created this film shortly after the end of World War II, and he apparently wanted to produce a fairy-tale film for family audiences that radiated with forgiveness and harmony. His changes to the plot are minor but significant. He adds a court jester named Hick to the cast of characters, and this fool intercedes on behalf of Prince Honestheart, who works as a swineherd at the palace of Princess Rosemouth after she rejects his beautiful gifts. Indeed, the new swineherd makes a great impression on her and her father when he cleans up the pigsty and is always clean-cut himself. As in Andersen's tale, he invents two toys that enchant her, and after the king discovers their kissing act, he banishes her. However, the prince knows that she, too, has a good heart and must only learn a lesson in humiliation. So he informs the king who he really is through Hick the jester. The princess is led to believe that she must marry the swineherd and succumbs to her fate. Yet in this cinematic version of Andersen's tale, her fate is a royal reward: she marries the prince, and the king ironically remarks in the end: "Such a good swineherd I'll never be able to find."

While there is a great deal of irony in the film thanks to an intrusive narrator, who is also corny and foolish, the storyline basically follows the traditional plot of sentimental romance. There is no question in the film about authentic versus false art. The major question pertains to the transformation of a spoiled princess. In this regard, Fredersdorf, who produced other fairy-tale films during this time, follows a tendency in West German filmmaking to produce happy-end films that would not disturb postwar audiences, especially children. Conflict was to be avoided or sugar-coated, and reconciliation of differences was to be fostered. It was also important to put women in their proper place, especially since many had worked in factories or had joined the workforce during World War II and had become independent. While Andersen punished women for forgetting their proper roles in his fairy tales, the German Fredersdorf uses Andersen to slap them on their wrists and promise them a better future. Their authentic role calls for submission to both father and husband.

The Nightingale

Another Faerie Tale Theatre production that deals with authenticity is *The Nightingale* (1983), starring Mick Jagger and Barbara Hershey, narrated by Shelley Duvall, and directed by Ivan Passer. Andersen's tale is perhaps one of his most profound meditations on the nature of art and patronage. The mighty Chinese emperor goes through a learning process and realizes that the pure and natural music of the nightingale is more valuable for his well-being than a beautifully ornamented mechanical bird that has no feeling for his life and becomes useless when it breaks down. The quality of authentic art for Andersen depends on the freedom granted the artist in the patronage system. The nightingale produces magnificent music that enthralls the Emperor and the court out of genuine affection for the Emperor, who will die if he cannot hear such soothing music, that is, pleasurable art that is an erotic life force and provides meaning in life. Art from an ordinary-looking bird can only endure if there is mutual affection and respect.

This is the basic message of Passer's *The Nightingale*, but there are some additional flourishes added to the plot that make this film one of the more unique and successful productions in the Faerie Tale Theatre series. The major protagonist in the film is not the Emperor of Cathay or the nightingale, but the kitchen maid. It is she who discovers the nightingale in the forest while she is looking for a root that will heal her sick grandmother. When the Emperor hears about the exquisite nightingale, it is she who leads the courtiers to bring the bird back from the forest to their ruler. Finally, after the nightingale is banished by the austere Emperor and he is about to die, it is the kitchen maid who pleads with the nightingale in the forest to return to the court and save the Emperor's life. In the end it is the Emperor's discovery of the kitchen maid's heroic actions that brings him happiness and makes him realize how false and pretentious his court and courtiers are.

Passer's cinematic adaptation of "The Nightingale" remains close to the text. The Oriental setting and costumes are lavish, and they are contrasted with the more natural setting outside the palace and in the forest. The courtiers are much too foppish throughout the film, and the Emperor appears to bathe in their flattery. His seclusion from the outside world has apparently contributed to his narrow appreciation of beauty. Once again, in keeping with Andersen, it is the simplicity of art, the extraordinary nature of the ordinary that is virtuous because it can heal the soul and make one aware of what is essential in life.

This is also the message of the famous Czech film, *The Emperor's Nightingale* (1948), directed by Jirí Trnka and Jirí Brdecka, who also wrote the screenplay. Trnka was one of the foremost puppeteers and illustrators in Europe, and the design, setting, and puppets for this live-action/animated film are highly imaginative, as is the plot. The story is set in contemporary Czechoslovakia, that is, the late 1940s, and a rich boy in a sailor suit is to celebrate his birthday in a huge mansion. However, instead of being happy, he is sad because his parents are not present, and he is prohibited from leaving the grounds by a huge steel fence and wall that surrounds the property. A little girl about the same age, perhaps nine or ten, wants to play ball with him, but he cannot leave the grounds, and she cannot enter through the fence. The celebration of the boy's birthday is a disaster, and in the evening, he has a dream about the Chinese Emperor. At this point, the animation begins, and we are transported to China where the Emperor leads an extremely regimented life that suffocates him. It is not until a little girl brings him a nightingale that he begins to breathe and feel free. It is thanks to her music and the friendship of the little bird that the Emperor begins to break with custom and routine to lead a more spontaneous and natural life. When the boy awakens the next morning, he immediately realizes the meaning of the dream, gets dressed, and runs outside. The film ends with a shot of him climbing over the fence to join the girl, who leads him into the nearby woods.

Trnka and Brdecka created this film immediately following World War II, when Czechoslovakia was undergoing massive social and political changes. Therefore, the emphasis in this film is not so much on the authenticity of art, but how art can emancipate people from senseless tradition, strictures, and regimentation. Both the boy and the Emperor are incarcerated; they yearn for a different kind of life. It is through the dream sequences for the boy and through the music and companionship of the bird for the Emperor that they come to the realization that they have it within themselves to transform their lives. What makes this film especially effective and poetic is that no words are spoken. The action is narrated by a storyteller—and it is interesting to note that in the English version of 1951, the narrator is the brilliant actor Boris Karloff—there is unusual lyrical music throughout the film. Unlike many live-action/animated films, there is no romance, no sentimentality. Rather, Andersen's tale is used to explore psychologically the suffering of an abandoned child, and how the imaginative power of art can work therapeutically to overcome depression brought about by containment and restrictions.

The Emperor's New Clothes

Clearly, Andersen's own tales have a substantial psychological dimension, and if it were not for his peculiar therapeutic artwork, the creation of tales for his well-being, he himself might have died from the suffering he endured. So it is not so much the artist's giving of himself to a patron in the hope of gaining a proper estimation of his creative talents—although this is important—that is crucial for Andersen's survival, but it is more what his art brought to himself so that he could maintain a vital equilibrium. Andersen's anger at a pretentious and indifferent upper class that lacked sensitivity for art, especially for his particular kind of art, had to be channeled in such a way that he would not become self-destructive. This is most clear in the short poignant tale "The Emperor's New Clothes," which is not only an exposure of the foibles of the aristocracy but also a critique of their aesthetic taste and false art. Unlike the Chinese emperor in "The Nightingale," the emperor in this tale is consumed by his fondness for new clothes. In fact, clothes are his fetish, for he has an outfit for every hour of the day. Clothes make the person is obviously his motto, and therefore he is easy prey when the swindlers arrive and announce that they can weave a marvelous and beautiful cloth that "had the strange quality of being invisible to anyone who was unfit for his office or unforgivably stupid."[193] The duping of the emperor and his courtiers is nothing more than the expression of Andersen's critique of the Danish aristocracy, easily swindled by artists, who know nothing about the true nature of art. The swindlers know a great deal about fashion and fetishism. They know how to market useless wares. They know all about the gullibility of people who presume to be connoisseurs. Andersen once again raises the question about what constitutes authentic art and its appreciation, and his narrative has a bittersweet taste of revenge at the end. The emperor, though he knows that he has been exposed, maintains the pretense and walks even more proudly to finish the procession. It is an open question as to whether the emperor has learned anything or will change. Certainly, he will become wiser in the future. Andersen's tale, which is not a fairy tale per se, is a satirical presentation of a pompous and narcissistic emperor, surrounded by sycophants. He is literally undressed so that he will expose himself as a fraud. What is interesting is that the swindlers serve truth, and we never learn what happens to them. Do we need deceivers to learn the truth about decadent and deceptive emperors? Or, do we need childlike honesty? Will the emperor be toppled by the people after they learn the truth? The tale raises just as many questions as it answers and remains open-ended—an attack, an interrogation, an exposure.

The open end allows for many possible interpretations and interesting possibilities for artists who have sought to adapt the tale. The American film versions of Andersen's story have been more drawn to the character of the swindlers and have tended to emphasize the comic aspect of the emperor's exposure to the truth that he wants to keep from himself. Moreover, some have added romance to the plot, totally changing the signification of Andersen's story. Instead of a tale about decadent rule and the tasteless aesthetics of a king, who is consumed by his own "beauty," the films, with one exception, minimize the effects that the ruler has on the people of his kingdom and generally makes light of the greed and hypocrisy of the emperor. The "heroes" of the tale are the swindlers, who are warm-hearted rascals and are appealing because they use their cunning to survive and rob the rich.

The first American rendition of "The Emperor's New Clothes" was an ABC television special in 1972 that capitalized on Danny Kaye's fame as Hans Christian Andersen. This version was filmed in a small town in Denmark with Kaye as the narrator dragging children about the town and speaking to an American TV audience about the quaintness of the Danish village. At one point he gathers the children around him, just as he had done in the film *Hans Christian Andersen*, and after donning the top hat of a swindler, he explains that it is part of a story that he begins to tell, one that is performed by puppets in cel animation and animagic as he narrates it. Unlike Andersen's tale, the major characters are the swindlers Marmaduke (voiced by Kaye) and his companion Musty (Alan Swift), who decide to seek the reward of one million grinklens by making extraordinary new clothes for the Emperor Klonkenlocker (Cyril Ritchard). Little do they know that the court jester Jaspar (Robert McFadden) has been robbing the emperor and intends to marry his daughter Princess Klonkenlocker (Imogene Coca), who has another preferred suitor. In this version the questions of art and authenticity are secondary to those of greed and justice. The swindlers are basically good-hearted souls; the emperor, a good-natured misguided ruler; and the jester, a conniving thief. Nothing is what it seems to be, and ironically the swindlers must correct the vision of the emperor and his subjects so that they can set everything right.

The puppetry in this film is superb. The movement is fluid, and the expressions are synchronized perfectly to make the behavior of the puppets credible; the costumes are colorful, and voiceovers by the actors lend depth to the personalities of the characters. The element of play is maintained throughout the film: Kaye is playing with the audience and the children in the film; the puppets are playing at being real people; the swindlers play at deceiving the emperor. If at times Kaye himself borders on being too sweet and infantile, he does not cross the line into meaningless humor. It is the gentle Kaye who tells a gentle romantic version of "The Emperor's New Clothes" that becomes the essential message of this film.

The 1987 Cannon production *The Emperor's New Clothes*, directed by David Irving, endeavors to create the same kind of gentle entertainment in a live-action film but ultimately fails. In 1986–1987 the producers Menahem Golan and Yoram Globus hurriedly made six fairy-tale films called Cannon Movie Tales evidently to try to compete with Shelley Duvall's Faerie Tale Theatre. For the most part, the results are disastrous. Though some of the films have unique and original elements, they all follow the same formula, which calls for a combination of the Disney and Hollywood musicals with sentimental plots that add very little to our understanding of the original fairy tales, and, if anything, make them seem trite.

It appears that Irving may have been familiar with the ABC television version of "The Emperor's New Clothes." The emperor, played by the inimitable comedian Sid Caesar, is obsessed by clothes, and he wants to have a splendid garment made for himself to celebrate the forthcoming wedding of his daughter Gilda, who is being forced to marry an insipid, ugly prince named Prince Nino because of his wealth. The two swindlers, a cunning rogue named Henry and his handsome nephew Nicholas, arrive and deceive the emperor and his foppish courtiers by promising to make a garment spun from his own jewels. Those who are not worthy of their station will not be able to see the new clothes. As they are making a gown out of thin air that the emperor and his advisors pretend to see so as not to reveal their unworthiness. Gilda falls in love with the charming Nicholas and conspires with the swindlers to avoid marriage with Prince Nino. In the end, Gilda elopes with Nicholas. The roguish Henry escapes but foolishly loses the jewels he has stolen. The emperor is exposed, but he is none the wiser, for it appears he will continue to be a slave to his clothes fetish.

The acting in the film is ludicrous, and if there is any meaning to the adaptation, it is lost in the slapstick comedy. In fact, the Andersen tale appears to be simply a vehicle for actors to clown about in a traditional romantic comedy, which celebrates how true love can triumph despite a father's stupidity, greedy courtiers, and crafty statesmen. The quality of the film, which has extravagant settings and costumes, is so poor that it does not even reach the level of camp because it is so predictable and boring. Perhaps it can be considered an achievement to transform an Andersen fairy tale into a boring film that reflects little upon the tale and reflects poorly on the marketing policy of its producers.

In contrast to the Cannon movie, the Faerie Tale Theatre production of *The Emperor's New Clothes* (1984), directed by Peter Medak, is unusually creative and raises some important social and political questions. The costumes and sets in this production are designed to bring out the difference between the social classes: the king and his court wear lavish clothes in baroque parlors, while the lower classes are dressed in tattered clothes as are the two swindlers, Morty (Art Carney) and Bo (Alan Arkin). But before the two hucksters are introduced, we are treated to a highly comic spectacle of the emperor (Dick Shawn), who admires himself in mirrors and then treats his subjects to a mock fashion show. He strolls up and down a platform to the applause of his court and the people, whom he has taxed to support his extravagance. Soon thereafter the scene switches to Morty and Bo on the outskirts of the city. They speak in slang with New York accents, and Morty tells Bo that he wants to quit the fraud business, settle down, and set up a duck farm. All these plans are put on the back burner when they enter the town and learn of the emperor's fetish for clothes. Bo convinces Morty to pull off one more swindle before they become "honest."

The plot of the film follows the Andersen story closely from this point on with one major exception: Morty and Bo encounter an innkeeper, who reveals how she might lose her inn and how heavily the people of the land are being taxed. In fact, conditions are so bad that the army consists of only one preposterous soldier, and the people have very little to eat. Consequently, Morty decides to take the emperor for all he is worth and to give the money and jewels to the innkeeper to share with the people. When the emperor is exposed by a little boy and driven from the town, Morty and

Figure 63
Peter Medak,
*The Emperor's
New Clothes*

Bo make off with enough gold to start a duck farm. Soon thereafter the emperor returns to the kingdom, and having learned his lesson, he holds court in modest attire and begins to give money to the needy.

Although the ending with the transformation of the emperor appears to be tagged on, the changes made to Andersen's tale in this film, which is enriched by the stellar performances of Shawn, Arkin, and Carney, provide more substance to the tale. Whereas Andersen never reveals the impact of the Emperor's extravagance on the people, Medak's film shows the poverty of the people, who are highly critical of the Emperor. While Andersen was concerned with the authenticity of art and sought to convince the aristocracy that there was virtue in honesty and simplicity, Medak shifts the focus to questions of government, social injustice, and reform—questions that were appropriate during the Reagan regime in America throughout the 1980s, for Reagan's inner government was stylized as a Hollywood court.

The Snow Queen

The focus on art and pretention in "The Emperor's New Clothes" is not of major concern in Andersen's famously misread tale, "The Snow Queen." Rather it is the abuse of children and the role that religion should play in their lives. "The Snow Queen" begins with a brilliant and humorous prologue tale that explains how evil came to the world and why little Kai is kidnapped and placed at the mercy of evil forces. The narrator tells the reader that the most evil troll in the world had once invented a huge mirror that had the power of making anything good or beautiful seem horrid in its reflection, and anything evil and worthless appear good and worthy. The trolls decide to carry the mirror to heaven to mock God and the angels, but on the way they drop the gigantic mirror so that it shatters into millions and billions of pieces. The result is that when any one of the splinters enters a person's eyes, he will only see the flaws of the world and the faults of the people. If a splinter enters a person's heart, the heart turns to ice. All this, of course, pleases the devil.

After this prologue, the narrator introduces us to the playmates Kai and Gerda, who are about ten years old. They listen to stories by an old grandmother, and at one point she tells them about the Snow Queen, who can turn hearts to ice. That same night Kai believes that he has seen the Snow Queen outside his window. During the summer, Kai and Gerda play together in a rose garden, and they sing a song that will become a refrain throughout the tale:

> In the valley where the roses be
> There the child Jesus you will see.[194]

Soon thereafter two splinters strike Kai in his eye and heart, and his behavior begins to change. He becomes nasty and stops playing with Gerda. That winter, he is kidnapped by the Snow Queen, who carries him off to her realm in the North. The following spring Gerda decides to go in pursuit of Kai, and her story of travails is well known. At first she is delayed by a good witch in her flower garden. Once she leaves this place she is helped by a crow and prince and princess and given a coach to travel to the Snow Queen's palace. However, the coach is attacked by ruthless robbers who kill everyone except Gerda. Fortunately, a robber girl takes a liking to her and gives Gerda a reindeer, mittens, and boots to continue on her quest to save Kai. After a Lapp woman aids her, Gerda goes to the Finnish woman near the Snow Queen's palace, and the reindeer expects her to give Gerda magic powers. But the Finnish woman explains to him,

> I can't give her any more power than she already has! Don't you understand how great it is? Don't you see how men and animals must serve her; how else could she have come so far, walking on her bare feet? But she must never learn of her power; it is in her heart, for she is a

sweet and innocent child. If she herself cannot get into the Snow Queen's palace and free Kai from the glass splinters in his heart, how can we help her?[195]

So the reindeer carries Gerda to the Snow Queen's garden, and leaves her. When Gerda says her prayers,

> a whole legion of little angels stood around her. They threw their spears at the snow monsters, and they splintered into hundreds of pieces. Little Gerda walked on unafraid, and the angels caressed her little feet and hands so she did not feel the cold.[196]

Once she finds Kai and weeps on his breast, her tears melt the ice and glass splinters in him, and she sings their psalm:

> Our roses bloom and fade away,
> Our infant Lord abides always.
> May we be blessed his face to see
> And ever little children be.[197]

Released from the spell of the Snow Queen, Kai rejoices, and together with Gerda they travel back to their city. As soon as they step through the doorway of the grandmother's apartment, however, they realize that they have grown up. The grandmother is sitting in the sunshine and reading aloud from her Bible: "*Whosoever shall not receive the Kingdom of Heaven as a little child shall not enter therein.*"[198] Gerda and Kai now understand the meaning of the psalm and sit and bask in the warmth of the summer day.

"The Snow Queen" ends simply with the triumph of good over evil, and it depicts the child protagonists as adults who remain children at heart and devoted to a Christian stricture. In many ways, the tale is a baptismal ritual: Gerda and Kai must prove that they have expunged the evil in their bodies before they will be accepted in the kingdom of God. All children must prove their "innocence," if they want to be saved. Gerda is, of course, innocence incarnate, and she is one of the few female figures in Andersen's works who does not become contaminated. Moreover, she is much more active than most, perhaps because she is protected by angels. Andersen imagines that children can be infected by evil forces associated with a real devil, who holds them in his power. He also associates evil with cold reason that opposes basic good instincts. The Snow Queen's palace is on the "lake of the Mirror of Reason," and Kai is playing the "Game of Reason," when Gerda finds him. He can only learn to spell "Eternity" after Gerda arrives and frees his heart. It is faith that children must learn to trust not reason, and it is blind trust in Christian faith that Andersen relentlessly preached in most of his fairy tales for children and adults. To be sure, his Christian faith was mystical and mixed with notions of divine intelligence. What is interesting is that most contemporary films and their audiences do not have an inkling of Andersen's overly religious and manipulative sentiments with regard to children in "The Snow Queen." Almost all the filmic adaptations struggle with how to save the story from Andersen's preaching, and I want to consider some of the better versions and explore how they have interrogated the text to find a different mode of rescuing Kai, that is, rescuing him from Andersen's pathetic approach. Since I have already discussed the Russian director Lev Atamanov's *The Snow Queen* (1957), I shall concentrate on the works by Martin Gates, Päivi Hartzell, David Wu, and Julian Gibbs all with the same title but very different approaches: animated comedy, horror, melodrama, and musical fantasy.

Each feature-length "Snow Queen" film that I shall be examining discards Andersen's religious emphasis to focus on the human qualities that young people need to live in a world threatened by a power monger. Why this threat is always posed in the form of a terrifyingly beautiful woman is open to question. For Andersen it is obvious that he had a "woman" problem, that is, he was so afraid of women and sex that he wanted to keep them in place in his stories. Filmmakers, whether male or female, seem to have accepted Andersen's starting point without questioning it. But they have all done away with Andersen's faith in intelligent design that places humans in the hands of God. They are literally in their own hands.

In the highly comic neatly drawn animated *Snow Queen* (1995) directed by Martin Gates, there are numerous changes that liven the action and transform the plot in unusual ways. The film begins with a grandmother reading "The Snow Queen" to a very young girl while her older brother and sister, Tom and Ellie, about twelve and ten, are playing with a puzzle nearby. The grandmother stops reading to send them to bed. Tom announces that he doesn't believe in such a thing as a Snow Queen. A talking cuddly sparrow named Pete, dressed in winter clothes and seated outside the window enjoys the story and is disappointed that the grandmother has stopped in the middle of it. The scene then switches to the North Pole where three adorable but clumsy trolls with lower-class British accents are trying to finish a flying machine for the Snow Queen. She wants them to carry a gigantic mirror to a spot where she can divert the sun so that the earth will freeze over and she can rule the world with her atrocious bats. However, the trolls are so incompetent that when they place the mirror on a large piece of ice, it falls to earth, cracks, and sends splinters of glass flying through the air. The bats retrieve all but two that enter Tom's heart. As a result, the Snow Queen kidnaps Tom so that he can reassemble all the pieces of the glass mirror as in a puzzle. Then she will kill him and take over the world.

When Ellie learns that the Snow Queen has captured Tom, she sets off accompanied by the funny sparrow as sidekick. All of Ellie's adventures with the witch, the silly prince and princess, and the robbers are delightful interludes on her quest. They depict her fortitude. They are also mixed with scenes of the Snow Queen urging Tom to finish the puzzle and the trolls trying to persuade Tom not to complete his task. In the end Ellie has the help of a timid reindeer and Frida the Lap Woman, who creates a magic potion that will dissolve the glass shards in Tom's heart. Together, brother and sister overcome the Snow Queen, who is frozen into a statue. But even as the brother and sister along with the sparrow are carried back to their home, Frida warns that the Snow Queen is not dead and could return in the future.

Normally, this would be the cue that alerts us that a sequel to this fine animated film has been planned. But fortunately there has not been a sequel, for the film stands on its own as realistic "statement" about the nature of evil in the world today. Gates also reinforces the traditional fairy-tale narrative about the necessity of cooperation to overcome abusive power. In many fairy tales, the protagonist or protagonists need the assistance of helpful agents to complete their tasks/quests. Here we have the sparrow, magic reindeer, an indigenous wise woman, and the trolls who must all do their part to help Ellie rescue Tom. There is nothing glitzy in this animated film and yet it sparkles with an unusual approach to a humorless tale.

Hartzell's fabulous film *The Snow Queen* (1986) is perhaps even more sparkling and is the most innovative filmic interpretation of Andersen's story that I have seen. The Finnish director turns the didactic tale into a lush nightmare with Gerda seemingly caught like Alice in an absurd and threatening wonderland. The film begins with a voiceover informing the audience that a green crystal, which had fallen from the crown of darkness, lies buried in the ice somewhere in an Arctic region. In order to retrieve it, the Snow Queen needs a human who can wield a black sword to smash the ice. Once the crystal is in her hands, the queen can restore it to the crown and place it on her head. If she succeeds, she will become the uncontested ruler of the world, turn everything completely dark, and stop time from moving.

Soon after we hear this introduction, we are transported to a beautiful summer beach where Gerda and Kai are playing and discover a music box with a tiny ballerina and three golden buttons. They are pictured running through the beautiful dunes, obviously delirious to be in each other's company and enjoying the early bloom of adolescence. The next scene moves us quickly to winter. It is evening, and Gerda and Kai are asleep. Then Kai gets out of bed, goes to the window, and is lured by the Snow Queen into her sled as she drives by. She is gorgeous and entrances Kai. Gerda awakes with tears. Spring arrives, but she is clearly sad while her friends play in the warm weather. Only by chance does she come upon one of the golden buttons that had been discarded by the Snow Queen and realizes that Kai is still alive. She boards a strange row boat adorned with white veils and drifts down a river until she comes to a dock where a sinister lonely witch wants to possess her. This is actually the beginning of a transformation on two levels—an erotic awakening leading toward womanhood, and the realization that she is prey or a sexual object and must put her dolls behind her.

There is very little dialogue in Hartzell's film. The music shifts from classical to hard rock. Each scene is elaborately and extravagantly staged. Some of the shots of the mountains, icy landscapes, and castles are breathtaking. The colors are symbolically dazzling. Gerda is dressed in a bright yellow dress and carries a doll with her wherever she goes. And wherever she goes, she is menaced first by the witch who wants to petrify her as a ballerina, then the frivolous prince and princess want her for a playmate. Finally, the robbers take sadistic pleasure in torturing her. Gerda is not given any help or hints on her journey to find Kai. Images of Kai, especially images of the beach scene, inspire her to continue on her quest, and she keeps finding the golden buttons that eventually lead her to the good sorceress of the north who finally explains why Kai had been kidnapped. He is to smash the ice with a black sword and will be killed by the Snow Queen after he serves this function. Only with the help of the three golden buttons and her own courage will she be able to rescue Kai. In the end, however, it is Kai who defeats the Snow Queen when he is touched to the heart by Gerda's courage.

Hartzell's secular re-interpretation of Andersen's overtly religious tale deepens, I believe, its significance. Clearly, it is the deep love that Gerda and Kai feel for each other that enables them to overcome the ruthless Snow Queen, not some faith in God. And clearly the Snow Queen represents the evil of tyranny and also the petrifying danger of those forces that threaten to deaden nature. At the end of the film, Gerda and Kai return to the beach and bury the music box and the three buttons. It is as though they have both passed through a stage in their development and can now move on in springtime. But it is because of their faith in themselves, not in any supernatural power, that they triumph over horrific predators.

Whereas Hartzell made a great effort to create a story without place and time and thereby creating an aura of pure fantasy, David Lu did anything but in creating his three-hour Hallmark TV

Figure 64
Päivi Hartzell,
The Snow Queen

melodrama. This film takes place in the American northwest during the late nineteenth century, and the Andersen narrative is totally Americanized—in every sense of the term. The film begins merrily with a small band playing music on the ice while people listen and skate. A mother says goodbye to her nine-year-old daughter Gerda and rides off (we never know why) into the woods where the Snow Queen creates a winter storm and kills her. In the meantime, the leader of the band named Wolfgang stops playing when he sees the white horse returning without its rider, his wife. A search party eventually finds the dead woman. Blackout. The film skips nine years, and Wolfgang, who owns a large cabin-like hotel in the town, has become a solemn man, and his beautiful daughter Gerda floats about like a melancholy fragile leaf. Enter Kai, a strapping young farmer who is hired as a bell boy. Despite the disapproving glare of Wolfgang, Kai courts Gerda until she emerges from her long mourning for her lost mother. As usual, however, there must be an obstacle or mis-understanding in every American kitsch love film, and in this film it is embodied by the sexy actress Bridget Fonda, who is always dressed in glamorous white. She has already caused Kai to turn mean by inadvertently breaking a mirror created by the devil. One of the glass splinters has landed in Kai's eye, and she needs him to repair the mirror. Once he kisses her three times, she will have the final piece, kill him, and take charge of the world.

Wu may have borrowed the mirror idea from Martin Gates, but he embellishes it by having the three other seasons, spring, summer, and fall, represented by three other "witches," who try to manipulate Gerda, who sets out to free the kidnapped Kai. Meanwhile, Kai struggles to keep the memory of Gerda alive in the Snow Queen's icy palace, which resembles the cozy hotel, and he is guarded by a gigantic talking polar bear, who is in love with the Snow Queen and totally devoted to her. In the end, Gerda's love for Kai frees him, and the Snow Queen is knocked unconscious. In one of the most bizarre and stupid scenes of the film, the polar bear picks up the Snow Queen and is transformed into a handsome prince. Then he winks at Gerda and Kai and carries off the Queen in his arms. The ice dissolves and the palace becomes the hotel. The sad Wolfgang turns into a happy father. The final scene returns us to the frozen lake where Wolfgang leads his merry band and Kai and Gerda embrace.

Whether Andersen would have turned over in his grave if he had seen this interpretation of his tale is questionable. It is certainly a well-made American melodrama in the Disney tradition, even if it is live-action and boring at points. It has all the "feel-good" elements of a Hollywood narrative: young girl's loss of mother, sad father and daughter, young pull-yourself-up-by-the bootstraps hero, highly erotic villainess, valiant black-and-white struggle between the erotic force of evil and the pure and honest American soul, reconciliation between father and suitor for his daughter's hand, happy

Figure 65
Julian Gibbs,
The Snow Queen

ending. Theses changes to Andersen's story are radical, but they add very little new insight into the meaning of his tale and only reinforce the conventional filmmaking in Hollywood.

The major change made by Julian Gibbs in his short BBC film *The Snow Queen* (2005) involves Kai, who is a homeless boy taken in by Gerda and her mother. They become fast friends, but one night he opens the window as the Snow Queen causes a storm. A splinter of ice hits his eye, and he is transformed into a mean boy at the mercy of the Snow Queen. Once he is lured into her sled, the film traces the traditional quest of Gerda, this time led by a raven. What makes the film interesting is the music composed by Paul Joyce, who had written a set of operatic songs based on Andersen's tales that were first performed in 2003 with a narrator and the London Symphony orchestra. The film privileges the songs, and the dialogue is kept to a minimum. In this regard, the acting is particularly good since the plot is basically told through the expressions and gestures of the actors in scenes that are extremely well choreographed and designed. The film is only fifty-six minutes long, and Gibbs condenses the plot and centers it around Gerda's power of love. Once again, faith, angels, and God have little to do in this version. It is never clear why the evil Queen wants to kidnap Kai—a weakness in this film—but the queen is certainly terrifyingly beautiful and wicked. Gibbs' version undoubtedly wanted to address the theme of child abandonment and homelessness, but it unfortunately becomes more of a moody fairy-tale film and a vehicle for the music. Perhaps if Gibbs had pursued the theme of homelessness, he might have created a more compelling film. Of course, Andersen had already created a very disturbing tale, "The Little Match Girl," about this topic. It drips with Christian morality, and very few filmmakers, with the exception of Michael Sporn as we shall see, have dared to adapt this tale. Adapting Andersen is a tricky affair.

Ethics and Adaptation

The film adaptations of Andersen's tales raise some interesting ethical questions with regard to his legacy. For instance, is it ethical to produce a film that not only warps Andersen's intentions as a serious writer, but also overshadows his work and his life to such an extent that he and his tales are literally obfuscated and erased? This is certainly the case in such films as the RKO *Hans Christian Andersen* (1952) and the Disney *The Little Mermaid* (1989). But what has ethics to do with free artistic expression? Haven't artists always taken their material from the past, altered it, appropriated it, and reproduced it in keeping with their interests and the expectations of their audiences? Isn't such adaptation their prerogative and right? Is there a politically correct way to reproduce Andersen's stories for the cinema and TV? Can ethics lead to censorship?

I raise these questions because they are relevant for understanding the struggle over Andersen's legacy in English-speaking countries, especially the US and UK, and especially because they reflect upon the cultural wars in America. The authenticity of art that Andersen so valiantly and desperately sought to defend against the artificial and instrumental interests of the upper classes and intelligentsia in his own time is in play when it comes to determining whether the Andersen's struggles as an artist have a chance to be understood. The difference between his day and our own is that his legacy, and hence the distinction between authentic and artificial art, is mediated through a powerful culture industry that marginalizes all serious endeavors to comprehend artworks and artists of the past and their historical significance. The culture industry not only participates in a public sphere in which critical discourse takes place, but it helps create it and sets the parameters of what can be discussed and distributed.

One of the more immoral tendencies within the American culture industry concerns the exploitation of children, children's needs, and children's expectations, and the deception of the public at large fostered by films that pretend to speak truths and record history, even when they announce that the film is fiction. Perhaps one should use the word amorality when referring to the culture industry because the corporations that control it are virtually without morals, and their bottom line for judging the quality of their films and TV shows is profit. Since the moral standards that the film industry and TV conglomerates pretend to uphold are so shallow and contradictory, and since even religion has become a commodity, there can be no question of ethics and morals in regard to the making of fairy-tale films, whether they are made for educational purposes or pure entertainment. The culture industry markets ethics and is immune to ethical questions that are bothersome like fleas. And yet, there still are and must be ethical questions, otherwise art itself would not be meaningful, and the humanities would be insignificant. In America the cultural wars call for ethical questions that challenge and judge the amoral assumptions of all cultural producers, especially those who operate and hold power in the culture industry.

In Andersen's case, it is vital, I think, for the survival of the humanities and historical culture that contemporary audiences gain a more palpable sense of how disturbed he was by social class discrimination and the rigid norms of propriety and religion of his own time. His disturbance should be our own. I say should because there is a kind of moral imperative in culture that informs our humanity. We all want to be treated as we treat others, and to treat a writer and his works as if they were simply commodities and means to make profit can be considered immoral and unethical. There is something perverse in the fraudulent representation of the works and life of an artist who gave his life to art and to his people.

Here it is important to note that there is a split image of Andersen between scholars and the general public in the US and the UK, not to mention in Denmark. Ever since Elias Bredsdorff's superb biography, *Hans Christian Andersen*, appeared in 1975,[199] critics and specialists have been familiar with the sad facts of Andersen's life and his diverse production as a writer. But even with the very recent biography, *Hans Christian Andersen: A New Life*, written by Jens Andersen and published in 2003 in Denmark and 2005 in English translation,[200] the general public has very little notion of his complex character. As Diane Crone Frank and Jeffrey Frank have written in their highly informative introduction to the translation of his tales,

> beyond Scandinavia Andersen has generally been regarded not as a literary genius but as a quaint nineteenth-century writer of charming stories. Nothing contributed more to this view than *Hans Christian Andersen*, the 1952 Danny Kaye film. Although it had almost nothing to do with the real Andersen—and, to be fair, never claimed to—the movie helped to make an idealized version of the writer's life as familiar as his fairy tales, almost an extension of them.[201]

Jackie Wullschlager's thorough biography, *Hans Christian Andersen: The Life of a Storyteller*[202] has also revealed how troubled a person Andersen was, although she spends much too much time trying to prove his homosexuality, something denied by Bredsdorff and the Franks. One need only read Andersen's tales to see the dark side of his rosy public image that the mass media and popular culture have created.

There cannot be a correct, ethical prescription of how to represent Andersen and his tales in film. Yet there are tendencies in the films that enable us to see how sincere and serious the producers are with regard to Andersen's legacy. The more critical and curious they are of Andersen and his works, in my opinion, the more they are just and creative in their own recreations. The more they are disturbed by the very same things that disturbed Andersen, the more potential they have in passing on Andersen's legacy and remaining "truthful" to it, that is, exploring and recalling his pain and suffering and contradictions. This is, I believe, the ethical responsibility of artists when they appropriate another artist's work.

I want to close by briefly discussing three examples of ethical and unethical appropriation in the fairy-tale film industry because they have a bearing on Andersen's legacy. One example,

Michael Sporn's animated Andersen films, is directly related to Andersen's tales; the second, Jannik Hastrup's *H. C. Andersen's The Long Shadow* (1998) is a stunning animated biographical film that captures the inner turmoil of Andersen's life; and the third, *Finding Neverland* (2004), the live-action film about J. M. Barrie's life, is indirectly related to the portrayal of Andersen's life and directly related to all the inane films that do a disservice to complex fairy-tale writers such as the 1954 RKO depiction of Andersen, George Pal's kitschy *The Wonderful World of the Brothers Grimm* (1962), and Terry Gilliam's moronic *The Brothers Grimm* (2005).

From 1990 to 1992 Michael Sporn, an American animator, adapted three of Andersen's fairy tales, "The Nightingale," "The Red Shoes," and "The Little Match Girl" for Italtoons Corporation, and they are currently distributed by Weston Woods Studios, an educational company. The films, all about twenty-five minutes long and created for children between five and ten, have been shown on HBO, but for the most part they have not received wide public attention, and they can be considered marginal cultural products of the culture industry—all the more reason that they deserve our attention, because Sporn's films written by Maxine Fisher are profound interpretations of Andersen's stories that transcend age designation and keep alive Andersen's legacy. They all use voiceover and colorful still sets as backdrops, and naively ink-drawn characters who come alive because they are so unpretentious and resemble the simple and found art of children.

Two of Sporn's films are particularly important because they transform motifs from Andersen's tales to deal with contemporary social problems. Both take place in New York City, and the music and dialogue capture the rhythms and atmosphere of present-day urban life. In *The Red Shoes*, Sporn depicts the warm friendship of two little black girls, Lisa and Jenny, and how they almost drift apart because of a change in their economic situation. The story is narrated by Ozzie Davis as a shoemaker who lives in a poor section of New York. Lisa and Jenny often visit him, and he describes their lives and how both love to dance and play and enjoy each other's company. One day Lisa's family wins the lottery, and they move to another part of the city. Now that she is rich, Lisa ignores Jenny until they meet at a ballet about red shoes. The spoiled Lisa ignores Jenny, but later she returns to her own neighborhood and steals some red shoes that the shoemaker had been making for Jenny. Guilt-ridden, Lisa finds that the red shoes have magic and bring her back to the old neighborhood and help her restore her friendship with Jenny.

In *The Little Match Girl*, Sporn depicts a homeless girl, Angela, who sets out to sell matches on New Year's Eve 1999 to help her family living in an abandoned subway station on Eighteenth Street. She meets a stray dog named Albert who becomes her companion, and together they try to sell matches in vain at Times Square. The night is bitter cold, and they withdraw to a vacant lot where Angela lights three matches. Each time she does this, she has imaginary experiences that reveal how the rich neglect the poor and starving people in New York City. Nothing appears to help her, and when she tries to make her way back to the subway station, she gets caught in a snowstorm, and it seems that she is dead when people find her at Union Square the next morning. However, she miraculously recovers, thanks to Albert, and the rich people gathered around her (all reminiscent of those in the dream episodes) begin to help her and her family.

Sporn's films are obviously much more uplifting than Andersen's original tales. But his optimism does not betray Andersen's original stories because of his moral and ethical concern in Andersen and his subject matter. In fact, his films enrich the tales with new artistic details that relate to contemporary society, and they critique them ideologically by focusing on the intrepid nature of the little girls rather than on the power of some divine spirit. At the same time, they are social comments on conditions of poverty in New York that have specific meaning and can also be applied to the conditions of impoverished children throughout the world. What distinguishes Sporn's films from Andersen's stories is that he envisions hope for change in the present, whereas Andersen promises rewards for suffering children in a heavenly paradise.

Sporn's films are tendentious in that they purposely pick up tendencies in Andersen's tales to express some of the same social concerns that Andersen wanted to address. His critical spirit is maintained, and even some of his faults are revealed. Most important, he is taken seriously.

And, of course, if there is any filmmaker who has taken Andersen seriously and creatively dealt with his great talent and contradictions, it is the gifted Danish director Jannik Hastrup, whose animated film, *H.C. Andersen's The Long Shadow* (1998), is, by far, the most insightful portrayal of Andersen's life using the fairy tale of "The Shadow" to shed some light on Andersen. It is a shame that this astounding film has not been distributed in the US and the UK and is not available in English on DVD. It is somewhat ironical that it has been obfuscated by films that diminish Andersen's talents and life. But before turning to Hastrup's film, a word or two must be said about Andersen's "The Shadow."

In "The Shadow" (1847), Andersen clearly sought to confront some demons through an ironic tale about a philosopher's shadow that separates itself from its owner and becomes immensely rich and successful. When it becomes a person in its own right and returns to visit its owner, the scholar,[203] the shadow puts the philosopher in his place when he explains that it was poetry that made a human being out of him. Not only does the shadow become humanlike, but he gains power over other people through his ability to see evil. Ironically, the shadow's sinister talents allow him to improve his fortunes, whereas the philosopher, who can only write about the beautiful and the good, becomes poor and neglected. Eventually the philosopher is obliged to travel with his former shadow—the shadow now as master, and the master as shadow. When the shadow deceives a princess to win her hand in marriage, the philosopher threatens to reveal the truth about him. The crafty shadow, however, convinces the princess that the philosopher himself is a deranged shadow, and she decides to have him killed to end his misery.

Andersen ingeniously reworks the folk motif of Adelbert Chamisso's *Peter Schlemihl* (*Peter Schlemihls wundersame Geschichte*, 1814), in which a young man sells his shadow to the devil to become rich; and he also explores the Hegelian notion of master–servant in a fascinating way. The shadow–servant, who is closer to the material conditions of life than the intellectual owner of his services, is able to take advantage of what he sees and experiences—the basic conditions of social life—to overthrow his master; whereas the master, who has been able to experience reality only through the mediation of his shadow, is too idealistic to defend himself. From a philosophical viewpoint Andersen questions the idea of autonomous identity; from a psychological viewpoint he studies the manifestations of a split personality, a version of the *doppelgänger* motif common in nineteenth-century literature. The ironic reversal of roles appears at first to be a harmless joke, but

Figure 66
Jannik Hastrup,
*H. C. Andersen's
The Long Shadow*

Andersen convincingly depicts how the subconscious can subdue both conscience and consciousness. The final effect is a chilling picture of those dark and irrational undercurrents in human experience that continue to surface no matter how people try to repress them.

There is also another significant aspect to the "chilling effect" of the tale that pertains to the ethical role of the artist and art. Clayton Koelb points to this feature in his insightful essay, "The Rhetoric of Ethical Engagement":

> There is no doubt that "The Shadow" operates on one level at least as a melancholy allegory of the relationship between an artist and his work of art. Andersen takes the traditional notion that an artist's works are his "offspring," capable of living on after he is dead, and turns upon it an almost Freudian suspicion. The more successful a work of art is, the more it puts its creator in the shade. . . . That Andersen cast in the role of protagonist a transparent double of himself adds to the grim irony of the parable.[204]

In essence, the story reveals a process by which an author becomes eclipsed and eliminated by his very own works. There is thus a "shady" side to artistic production, for the artworks that survive the artist may do damage by revealing secrets that harm people and the artist himself.

Hastrup expands upon this theme by portraying a feeble Andersen on his deathbed with many of the characters from his tales emerging from the sea and the port city of Copenhagen to gather around his bed. Their presence sends him into a reverie about his life and provides the means for Hastrup to set the scene for a fairy-tale biography that contradicts Andersen's own autobiography, *The Fairy Tale of My Life* (1847). Hastrup begins by showing the young Andersen, about ten years old, who saves an ugly duckling from being beaten. This wonderful duck named Emma will then accompany Andersen as a pet throughout the film. Then Andersen is shown being picked upon by other boys in the town where he was a marginal figure and strange because of his desire to be a writer and actor. Finally, we see his close relationship to his mother, a washerwoman, who believes in his talent and sends him as a raw teenager to Copenhagen. Finally, before his trip, Hastrup introduces Andersen's unruly, nasty shadow, who often gets Andersen in trouble by splitting from him and embarrassing him.

Hastrup is a marvelous animator. He uses ink drawings and watercolors to paint backdrops and characters with sharp angular features, very much in keeping with the early UPA style. He weaves other scenes and introduces other characters into the film with great imagination. For instance, he creates a dapper but malicious devil dressed in a top hat and suit who takes advantage of Andersen's worried mother. He shows Andersen's fear of sex and women in a brothel, and his love for the Swedish nightingale Jenny Lind. Most of all, he captures Andersen's loneliness and his disputes with himself by having his shadow interfere with his ambition to become a famous writer. Andersen has only the duck as a devoted companion who believes in him. But Andersen is not a pathetic figure. Hastrup has a great sympathy for the storyteller. Rather, he is so embarrassingly dedicated to his art that he commits faux pas wherever he goes until he retreats in isolation. Meanwhile, his shadow separates from him and enjoys the fame that Andersen has garnered in the outside world. As the dying Andersen continues to dream about his past, the shadow returns to get rid of Andersen. And in scenes reminiscent of "The Shadow," Hastrup shows how the shadow triumphs over the great storyteller and has him committed to an insane asylum while he takes Andersen's place in the real world.

Despite this nightmarish end to Hastrup's Andersen, he awakes to gaze at the fairy-tale characters who surround him. They assure him that he need not fear death, for his tales will become immortal. The devil comes to take away the shadow. The duck is beside him. The camera fades from Andersen's room and focuses once more on the city of Copenhagen. Hastrup's tale is done, and it is a film that does justice to Andersen's remarkable works and painful life.

This cannot be said for the "immoral" work of Marc Forster in the film *Finding Neverland* (2004), based on Allen Knee's play. Though this film has been widely praised in the American media, it is, like the 1952 film *Hans Christian Andersen*, a good example of how a literary and personal legacy can be destroyed and twisted in a spectacle that creates a false illusion about the significance of a major Scottish writer. I choose here to write about Barrie and not about Andersen because this twenty-first-century film is the most recent example of the unethical way some so-called writers of children's literature are presented in the public sphere—presented in such a way that thousands if not millions of viewers will come to accept the fictive Barrie as the real one.

Some brief facts: J. M. Barrie was a very short man, barely five feet tall, who became involved with the Llewelyn Davies family as early as 1897 when there were only three Davies boys aged four, three, and one. From the time of this meeting in a London park until the time of Sylvia Llewelyn Davies' death in 1910, Barrie intruded into the Davies' affairs so much that Sylvia's husband Arthur resented him and tried to keep him out of their family. But Barrie persisted, and ironically, when Arthur and Sylvia unfortunately died within a few years of each other, he became the foster father of the boys more by force than by the will of Sylvia. His play, *Peter Pan, or the Boy Who Would Not Grow Up*, was never intended for children, and it always had the backing of the American producer Charles Frohman. There were no children from the children's hospital at the first performance. Barrie, who was impotent, married and divorced probably because of problems with his own sexuality (not unlike Andersen), and had a very strange relationship to the Davies boys that bordered on pedophilia.

In *Finding Neverland*, all these facts are twisted into a tear-jerking love story between Sylvia and Barrie, who are played by celebrity stars Kate Winslet and Johnny Depp. Instead of the troubled, intrusive Barrie, the film depicts a noble, dedicated, sensitive writer. Astonishingly, Barrie's wife and Sylvia's mother are shown to mistreat and misunderstand Barrie, and he must live down the suspicions of a society that thinks he spends too much time with Sylvia's boys. According to the film, Barrie dotes on the boys and Sylvia because he simply cares for them. There is not the slightest lascivious or lustful sign in Depp's portrayal of Barrie. It is as if he were a good-natured uncle and as if the love he shared with Sylvia, if there was such a love, was totally innocent. Yet, we know that Barrie was a very calculating and manipulative individual. His *Peter Pan* play was never performed in Sylvia's parlor in 1904 when she and her husband were very much alive, and Peter Davies, the eldest son, who supposedly became the man of the family, grew up to hold Barrie in contempt.

What are we to make of the romantic portrait of Barrie in Forster's film and Knee's play? Certainly, they have a right, as all artists do, to sweeten, change, alter, and remake an artist and his work.[205] But it is clear that they have done Barrie and themselves a disservice by not treating him with more critical analysis based on a more accurate account of history. An embellished Barrie is an ugly Barrie, as is the case in the depiction of Andersen in *Hans Christian Andersen*. In fact, the handsome Barrie becomes more listless and boring in their treatment, for he was a very troubled writer, difficult to portray because of his mood swings just like Hans Christian Andersen, whose legacy does not need to be turned into a myth. On the contrary, the myths and fairy tales spread about Barrie deserve to be questioned so that we can grasp how and why it is he came to produce works that have caught our imagination and still play an enormous role in western culture.

This is also true about Andersen, and why I have drawn a comparison with Barrie. If we recall his image in the RKO film *Hans Christian Andersen*, it is practically impossible to catch a glimpse of who Andersen was and why he wrote. His history was for the most part repressed by the film, which cruelly overshadows the trials and tribulations of his life. His legacy can be better sensed in the film adaptations of his works. But here, too, only traces of Andersen's original impetus can be found in the films based on his tales during the last sixty years. Fortunately, the field of cultural production is still open enough that there are competing versions of what his work means and how his life should be played out. Given the significance of the mass media, especially of film, in the twenty-first century, let us hope that his legacy will not succumb to immoral trivialization. After all, he knew and strongly represented a viewpoint that we should never forget: the making and marketing of art poses an ethical problem.

III

13
Adapting Fairy-Tale Novels

The overpowering impact of *The Wizard of Oz* on film adaptation of other children's fantasy novels, however, has only been treated superficially. Since the 1939 release of the MGM film, a number of filmmakers have attempted to recreate its popularity (and eventual monetary success) when adapting other works of fantasy to the screen. In creating these adaptations, Hollywood has recast sometimes very different literary fantasies as new versions of *The Wizard of Oz*. In general, these adaptations, based on stories that were groundbreaking and highly original, have been artistic failures.

Joel Chaston, "The 'Ozification' of American
Children's Fantasy Films"[206]

The last level of metaphor in the *Alice* books is this: that life, viewed rationally and without illusion, appears to be a nonsense tale told by an idiot mathematician. At the heart of things science finds only a mad never-ending quadrille of Mock Turtle Waves and Gryphon Particles. For a moment the waves and particles dance in grotesque, inconceivably complex patterns capable of reflecting on their own absurdity. . . . This vision of the monstrous mindlessness of the cosmos ("Off with its head!") can be grim and disturbing, as it is in Kafka and the Book of Job, or lighthearted comedy, as in *Alice* or Chesterton's *The Man Who Was Thursday*. . . It is a vision that can lead to despair and suicide, to the laughter that closes Jean Paul Sartre's story "The Wall," to the humanist's resolve to carry on bravely in the face of ultimate darkness. Curiously, it can also suggest the wild hypothesis that there may be a light behind the darkness.

Martin Gardner, *The Annotated Alice*[207]

The question of fidelity is not entirely irrelevant when discussing filmic adaptations of fairy-tale novels, because there is generally a particular and known hypotext that serves as reference point for the director and audience alike. Sometimes the film "begs" for comparison with the text. That is, the filmmaker chooses to make a film because the subject matter is already known and popular. The fairy-tale novel may have been a touchstone in the director's youth, and the filmmaker may want to share a childhood experience. Along with his co-workers, the director often counts on shared experiences and on the popularity of the fairy-tale novel to attract audiences that want to see whether the film has been true to the novel, whether the creative director has enhanced the novel by fleshing it out and elaborating on aspects that are not entirely evident in a reading of the hypotext, or whether the filmmaker and staff have ruined the novel by misinterpreting it and misrepresenting it. In the minds of viewers, fidelity to the text is a credible standard for evaluating a filmic adaptation. Yet, fidelity will always be a slippery slope on which to evaluate the success of a filmic adaptation. Each viewer has his or her own "true" interpretation of a novel, and no director in the world will ever come close to this truth.

Filmmakers are, therefore, on firmer ground when they disregard notions of a literal interpretation and endeavor to provide a new reading of the fairy-tale novel by re-creating it with the techniques and moving images of film. They are fully aware that they are implicated in a cultural discourse about a particular fairy-tale novel and that they are staking out a claim *not* to present the most truthful interpretation of the work in moving pictures but its most innovative and imaginative representation. This representation is historically stamped. It is valid in and for its time, and if it has highly unusual artistic qualities, it may transcend its time and eventually be considered somewhat typical, original, classical, or canonical in the cultural discourse about the hypotext. It may also generate future recreations that indicate it is time to re-visit the fairy-tale novel, to look deeper and differently into its substance.

Many fairy-tale novels such as *Alice in Wonderland*, *Pinocchio*, *Peter Pan*, and *The Wonderful Wizard of Oz* are considered "national treasures" or classics that are regarded as works of mythic proportion, for they allegedly reveal something significantly profound about the national character of a country. But the national heritage has not prevented "foreign" filmmakers from adapting the narratives and providing a view from the outside that exposes hidden meanings or turns the novel into a means for interpreting entirely different social realities. Such may be the case with Jan Svankmajer's film *Alice* (1988), made in Czechoslovakia to address Czech and not only Czech living conditions, and, certainly, Disney did this with his interpretation of Collodi's *Pinocchio*, transforming the puppet into a clean-cut all-American boy, while Russian filmmakers have taken Aleksey Tolstoy's *The Golden Key*, a literary adaptation of *Pinocchio*, and produced remarkable live-action and animated versions of Tolstoy's work for the screen to comment on the ideology of growing up in the Soviet Union. There is also the case of the Japanese filmmaker, Taiji Yabushita, who created the first feature-length animated film in Japan based on the Chinese classic *The Legend of Madame White Snake*, which grew from song and legend in the medieval period to novel and opera in China in the twentieth century. Yabushita envisioned the Japanese film in 1958 as a gesture of peace and reconciliation with other Asian countries.

Intentions, interpretations, and reception do not always coincide with one another and cannot be accurately correlated. What is clear, however, is that just as there have been numerous cultural discourses about individual short fairy tales that evolved and were spread from oral storytelling through print to the electronic means of communication, there have been fascinating ways in which print fairy-tale novels have generated filmic discourses that keep challenging viewers to see and read anew. In this chapter, I want to focus on several important texts to explore how they have been interrogated and re-represented by various filmmakers. The novels are: L. Frank Baum's *The Wonderful Wizard of Oz* (1900), Carlo Collodi's *The Adventures of Pinocchio* (1883), Lewis Carroll's *Alice's Adventures in Wonderland* (1865), and James Barrie's *Peter and Wendy* (1911). I shall deal only with a few examples from each filmic discourse, adaptations that, I believe, represent unusual and typical approaches to the novels. These fairy-tale novels are remarkably similar even if they have distinct and specific histories: 1) they all rose to prominence during the late nineteenth and early twentieth centuries when nation-states were seeking to draw clear lines about national identity, culture, and heritage; 2) they all introduce issues of otherness and queerness; alternate life styles and worlds are explored that appear to counter the trend toward nationalism, or at least, complicate national determination; 3) they all involve young protagonists, who take miraculous journeys and are transformed through their adventures; all of the protagonists have helpers who assist them in their quest for self-identity or challenge conventional identity; 4) the plot of all the texts and films follows the traditional outlines of the fairy tale's scheme of departure from home, transformation through unusual adventures, and resolution; the narrative structure recalls the plot of the novel of education or *Bildungsroman*; the search for home is a utopian struggle to know oneself and what it takes to move forward to a just society that is not known but intuited; 5) the narrative of each film constitutes a kind of socializing process that makes a statement about what it means to be a proper child or young person; and 6) the manipulation of young protagonists borders on pedophilia and voyeurism by the filmmakers and co-workers, and at the same time, they genuinely want to make a statement about the problematic aspects of acculturation and the civilizing process and seek approval by children and parents.

L. Frank Baum's Utopian Wish for a Better Life: Oz Denied

In my book, *Fairy Tale as Myth/Myth as Fairy Tale*, I remarked that L. Frank Baum's conception of Oz is not just any utopia.[208] It is a specific American utopia, which may appear to be a contradiction in terms, for a utopia is no place. But Oz *is* a place and space in the American imagination, and as such, it embodies that which is missing, lacking, absent in America. Oz is the counterpart to the crude reality of the golden age in America, a possibility that has never been realized except in the imagination of writers such as Baum and his heirs. It is in constant need of revision, review, and reconstruction because social and material conditions in America keep changing, and our utopian longings and projections have responded to the changes and keep persisting in Oz images that filmmakers have created to depict what Americans lack—and not only Americans.

To ground our understanding of Baum's Oz, there are certain facts we must bear in mind that are not always on the minds of viewers.

1) Baum did not write just one novel about Dorothy and Oz, but fourteen from 1900 to 1919 to demonstrate Dorothy's growing social awareness and alienation from America where it is impossible to realize one's dreams. Consequently, she decides to leave America for good by the sixth novel, *The Emerald City of Oz* (1910), in which Baum outlined the utopian aspects of Oz:

> No disease of any sort was ever known among the Ozites, and so no one ever died unless he met with an accident that prevented him from living. This happened very seldom, indeed. There were no poor people in the Land of Oz, because there was no such thing as money, and all property of every sort belonged to the Ruler. The people were her children, and she cared for them. Each person was given freely by his neighbors whatever he required for his use, which is as much as any one may reasonably desire. Some tilled the lands and raised great crops of grain, which was divided equally among the entire population, so that all had enough. There were many tailors and dressmakers and shoemakers and the like, who made things that any who desired them might wear. Likewise there were jewelers who made ornaments for the person, which pleased and beautified the people, and these ornaments also were free to those who asked for them. Each man and woman, no matter what he or she produced for the good of the community, was supplied by the neighbors with food and clothing and a house and furniture and ornaments and games. If by chance the supply ever ran short, more was taken

from the great storehouses of the Ruler, which were afterward filled up again when there was more of any article than the people needed.

Every one worked half the time and played half the time, and the people enjoyed the work as much as they did the play, because it is good to be occupied and to have something to do. There were no cruel overseers set to watch them, and no one to rebuke them or to find fault with them. So each one was proud to do all he could for his friends and neighbors, and was glad when they would accept the things he produced.[209]

In other words, Dorothy's quest for home cannot be realized in Kansas or anywhere else in America. Home is a futuristic concept for Baum, and thus, Dorothy "drags" Aunt Em and Uncle Henry to Oz to realize her utopian wishes. Oz is constantly embattled in the late fairy-tale novels because enemies such as the witch Mombi and the Nome King want to destroy the utopian land.

2) Baum himself tried to realize Oz as utopia in three films and failed. In 1914 he established the Oz Film Manufacturing Company, which produced three feature-length films: *The Patchwork Girl of Oz* (1914), *His Majesty, The Scarecrow of Oz* (1914), and *The Magic Cloak of Oz* (1914). Baum wrote the screenplays for all three films, and although some outstanding actors must have enjoyed playing goofy characters, the films were silly renditions of Baum's adaptations of his own materials. The plots reveal Baum's fondness for queerness and otherness, but nothing more; the films are tied by sappy and sloppy happy ends. Dorothy plays a negligible role if any, and the unusual utopian spirit of Oz is grounded.

3) This is also the case with the other "major" endeavor to adapt the Oz books before the classical 1939 MGM production. In 1925 Larry Semon, the great comic actor, filmed *The Wonderful Wizard of Oz* and also starred in it as the Scarecrow, farmhand, and toymaker. However, Semon transformed his screenplay and vision of Oz into a slapstick comedy that also features Oliver Hardy of Laurel and Hardy fame as the Tin Woodman, and the African American actor Spencer Bell as a stereotypical black worker and the Cowardly Lion. The thin plot involves Dorothy, eighteen years old and more than ripe for marriage. She is told that she is the long-lost princess of Oz and is intended to marry Prince Kynd. Just as she learns this, she and her companions are swept by a tornado to Oz, where the evil Prince Kruel and his Ambassador Wikked try to prevent Dorothy from reigning in Oz. But most of the focus is on the comic antics of Semon and his buddies. In the end, Dorothy and Prince Kynd manage to flee Oz on an airplane. Indeed, Oz is stripped of all its utopian implications.

Interestingly, by 1929 America as utopia, land of the free and melting pot suffered a severe blow by the Great Depression, and it was not coincidental that, during the years of the Depression, the cinematic version of *The Wonderful Wizard of Oz* was conceived and completed by 1939, and that many of its co-creators were associated with socialist and left-wing causes.[210] Oz was resurrected out of the misery of the 1930s, an alternate vision of America, a mirror that reflected America's disgrace and promise. Somewhere over the rainbow there was a land we all dream of, and ironically it was realized through the cooperative efforts of numerous people and marked as fantasy. But, in fact, the fantasy was the real, materialist outcome of the needs of individuals who in a group effort wanted to mark what was missing in American society.

Oz as a hopeful measure of lack in America. The film did not have an immediate impact as political critique. That is, it was a success, but a moderate success. It had to wait for 1956 before it became a national success and political monument of America's failure to live up to its myth. Interestingly, it was disseminated through television and had a powerful effect as cinematic fantasy during the 1950s was stamped by the McCarthy inquisitions, the Rosenberg trial, the Korean War. Then as now, Oz was what America was not. Oz as national iconic representation was truth denied, reality unfulfilled. Both film and book formed a utopian constellation, a reference point, by the beginning of the 1960s, one that fortunately has not gone away and compels us to return time and again to question our national character and identity.

Of course, one may take issue with my short narrative of how Oz came into being as an American myth, that is, how it has not come into being or been fulfilled in reality. As utopian icon, Oz has stood and stands for many things, and it is always important to clarify as much as one can what Oz is as a reference point or the icon of a hypotext:

1) Is the utopian icon the Oz of Baum's first book, *The Wonderful Wizard of Oz*?
2) Is it the sum of all fourteen Oz books?
3) Is it the Oz of the MGM film of 1939?
4) Is it a mix of the MGM film and Baum's books?
5) Is Oz really a symbol of escape fantasy?
6) Is the utopianism of Oz subversive and harmful to children as some librarians asserted during the 1950s?
7) What is the difference between Alice's Wonderland, Peter Pan's Neverland and Dorothy's Oz?
8) Is there really something peculiarly American about Oz?
9) Does Dorothy really change in Oz?
10) Do tolerance and acceptance of Otherness stamp the utopian quality of Oz?

It is impossible to answer all these questions without writing a long and thorough study about the reception history of the novel and the film. But we can ascertain to a great extent how the film dealt with the themes of utopianism, identity, and otherness. First, we must remember that the black-and-white monochrome beginning and end must be contrasted to the Technicolor of the Oz dream sequence. In other words, just as Baum painted Kansas as drab and gray, so did the creators of the film version. Of course, they also softened Baum's image by making the farm and surroundings less hostile and forbidding. Nevertheless, the environment cannot be equated with a paradise. Dorothy feels threatened. Miss Gulch, the richest woman in the country, is about to exterminate Dorothy's dog Toto, and Aunt Em and Uncle Henry cannot stop her. There is, in fact, no resistance to the tyrant, who has the law on her side. The picture that we have of Kansas and farm life in the film's frame prologue has nothing to do with a pastoral paradise. Aunt Em and Uncle Henry have introduced incubators into the farm, and it is obvious that they are receptive to the age of mechanization. They are so consumed by their work that Dorothy is ignored and told to keep out of trouble. All this leads Judy Garland as Dorothy to sing her now famous song;

Somewhere, over the rainbow, way up high,
There's a land that I heard of once in a lullaby.
Somewhere, over the rainbow, skies are blue,
And the dreams that you dare to dream really do
come true.

Someday I'll wish upon a star
And wake up where the clouds are far behind me,
Where troubles melt like lemon drops,
Away above the chimney tops
That's where you'll find me.

Somewhere over the rainbow, bluebirds fly,
Birds fly over the rainbow,
Why then, oh why can't I? [211]

It is clear from her original distressed situation and this song that Dorothy *desires* to leave Kansas, where she is bored, neglected, and threatened. If there is a paradise, it is conceived out of her utopian longing, and it is way beyond Kansas. It is something that Dorothy realizes that she must find or create, and in the film, she runs away from home to do this. The only reason she returns to the drab house at the beginning of the film is because Professor Marvel guilt trips her into feeling sorry about Aunt Em. This emotional blackmail sends Dorothy back to the farm where she is knocked unconscious by the cyclone hitting the house.

Unlike Baum's novel, in which Dorothy is actually carried to a real place named Oz, the film depicts Dorothy dreaming of her experiences in Oz. To a certain extent, this dream is unnecessary because Dorothy had already found the brains, courage, and heart to return home to face the circumstances of the tumultuous farm life in Kansas. Therefore, the dream merely reconfirms the self-confidence that she has already demonstrated. In the dream sequences Dorothy always has it in her through the ruby/silver shoes to go home whenever she wants. She just does not recognize it. But she does need to be "recharged," that is, she needs the encouragement of fantasy and dreams to survive home. As a child figure in both the novels and the film, she has a clear identity as moral arbiter. It is through her innocent eye that we perceive Kansas and Oz, and it is through her moral actions that home is defined.

The episodes with the bizarre characters, the Munchkins, the Scarecrow, the Tin Woodsman, the Cowardly Lion, the Wizard, and the witches in the film are necessary to emphasize her perseverance and grit as a "true" American girl, who can combat difficult situations in depressed times. As Joel Chaston comments,

> That *The Wizard of Oz* is so overtly goal-oriented, with its heroine coping with a series of setbacks to achieve ultimate happiness, is one of the reasons for its success. Moreover, inasmuch as character consistency and well-defined motivation are important features of the classical film, Dorothy's wish to return home represents a way of unifying and controlling the fantasy elements that might otherwise subvert the film's progress toward the accomplishment of her goal. Her unswerving desire to go home provides a frame of reference for interpreting the otherwise disparate characters and adventures she meets while in Oz.[212]

When Dorothy does make it home, that is, when she wakes up, nothing has changed in Kansas. Her dream of Oz is not taken seriously by her aunt and uncle and the farmhands because they know reality and are simply glad that Dorothy has survived. They are all survivors, and Dorothy is glad to be home. Though she asserts that "there's no place like home,"[213] she is more reconciled to home because of her experiences in the utopia of Oz.

Neither the film nor the novel celebrates America as home or America as utopia. On the contrary, it is Oz as symbol of wish-fulfillment dreams, as the symbolical embodiment of the longing for a better life, as the utopian realm in which justice is attained that is the key icon of the film and novel. Dorothy, who is more meek than strong, cannot rid Kansas of rich tyrants like Miss Gulch and the bankers, who hold the mortgage to the farm of Uncle Henry and Aunt Em. Kansas will remain stark, and Dorothy must and does face up to this fact because she wants the love of Aunt Em and Uncle Henry and needs their recognition as moral arbiter. However, only through experiencing the strange utopia of Oz, learning about aliens and other ways of behaving and living, does Kansas become bearable.

Philosophically speaking, the return home is a move forward to what has been repressed and never fulfilled. The pattern in most traditional fairy tales—and *The Wizard of Oz* is a fairy tale as novel and film—involves the reconstitution of home on a new plane, and this accounts for the power of its appeal to both children and adults. Phrased another way, if there is a mythic appeal in *The Wizard of Oz* as film and novel to Americans, it is due to the glimpse that we all receive of a utopian counterpart to America, what America could become but has not become. The MGM film provides a glimpse of utopia but regresses in the end to compromise the promise of utopia. Good Dorothy is the good girl who always returns to the family.

Baum himself sensed the failure of the promise of America to become paradise, and this is the reason that he kept sending Dorothy back to Oz over the course of fourteen novels and eventually had her remain (with Aunt Em and Uncle Henry) in Oz, safe from the capitalist bankers and Eastern businessmen in America. And, throughout the past century, Americans keep returning to the Oz material not because of the American myth but because of the promises that America as a nation has failed to keep. Oz is the utopia that challenges the myth of America as land of the free and brave.

The political implications of Oz as utopia, already repressed in the MGM film, have not always been realized in the adaptations of the various Oz books nor are they explicit in the popular veneration of Baum's Oz materials. But I believe that the significance in the particular way Americans have received and worked with Baum's utopian vision of Oz is connected to the gaps that we feel in our lives, to political and social deprivation that keep us wishing for home in Oz, which often becomes an experimental "other" land in which we work through conflicts that pertain to our real situation.

After the establishment of the MGM film in 1939 as the definitive cinematic representation and recreation of Baum's *The Wonderful Wizard of Oz*, it has been difficult for other filmmakers to compete with it. They tend to copy it, and there have been over twenty different national and international endeavors to adapt Baum's work since 1960. That is, one could argue that many of the endeavors are based on the MGM film of 1939 as well as Baum's first novel, and that American filmmakers have conceived their Oz as utopian icon to comment on both the MGM film and on Baum's work. More importantly, their images of Oz are always related to what is missing in post-1945 America. For the most part, the American films have generally relied on celebrity actors to play the major roles of Dorothy, the Wizard, Scarecrow, Lion, and Tin Woodsman in an endeavor to transcend the brilliant performances of Judy Garland, Frank Morgan, Ray Bolger, Bert Lahr, and Jack Haley. But the performance of stars cannot substitute for a narrative that demands a substantial and unique revision of Oz, and most of the films fail to evoke the spirit of Oz as utopia; they merely recall Oz as an idle fantasy. However, these flawed fairy-tale films are significant because they attempt to recall what is missing in life and signify that even idle fantasy has a serious implication—the loss of a genuine utopian spirit, for Oz seems to have become shallow.

There are five feature-length films spanning five decades that I want briefly to discuss: *Journey Back to Oz* (1974), *The Wiz* (1978), *Return to Oz* (1985), *The Muppets Wizard of Oz* (2005), and *Tin Man* (2007). It should be mentioned that the filmic adaptation of the Oz books was delayed somewhat because of copyright issues. When some of the works were finally declared to be in the public domain, Shirley Temple included a frivolous version, *The Land of Oz* (1960), in her TV series *Shirley Temple's Storybook*.

Frivolity stamps the first two feature-length films that introduce regressive notions of Oz as another society that is actually worse than America, and Dorothy as heroine must save Oz from destruction. *Journey back to Oz*, an animated film based loosely on Baum's second novel *The Marvelous Land of Oz* (1904), was begun in 1964 by Hal Sutherland and Filmation Studio and was not completed (due to financial problems) until 1972, when it was released in the UK and two years later in America. To compensate for its mediocre hand-drawn animation, thin plot and characterization, and boring pop music, the producers hired major stars to do the voiceovers: Liza Minnelli, daughter of Judy Garland, was the voice of Dorothy Gale, and she was assisted by such celebrities as Ethel Merman, Milton Berle, Mickey Rooney, Danny Thomas, Margaret Hamilton, and Risë Stevens. However, nothing could save this film from destroying Baum's notions of otherness and utopia. Dorothy, a polite, pale character of about ten, still believes in Oz after her return to Kansas and is criticized by her Aunt Em for being delusional. However, when a cyclone comes, Dorothy is knocked unconscious and sent back with Toto, her faithful dog, to Oz, which is dominated now by Queen Mombi and her vicious green elephants. With the help of Pumpkinhead and Woodenhead, two new characters, and the intervention of Glinda, the good witch of the north, she defeats Mombi, when the witch's own elephants trample her to death, and then Dorothy re-installs the Scarecrow as king of Oz. In the end, Glinda tells Dorothy that the greatest magic in the world is love and faith, and she sends her back to Kansas in a cyclone.

In contrast to all the depictions of Kansas in books and films, Sutherland has Kansas portrayed as an idyllic farmland and assigns Liza Minnelli the task of singing a sentimental song about her sad feeling for home. Perversely, Kansas becomes her utopia, and she never comes of age or develops a greater social awareness as moral arbiter. Instead, Dorothy remains static, and the cinematic representation of Oz as utopia is strangely an undesirable place that Dorothy will never want to visit again.

To a certain extent, this is also the case in *The Wiz*. Once again we have a film stuffed with celebrities who try their best to rescue a poor screenplay and stereotypical Broadway staging. This version of *The Wizard of Oz* is an adaptation of an adaptation, namely the 1975 Broadway musical, and features an African-American cast with some of the finest entertainers in the business: Diana Ross, Michael Jackson, Lena Horne, Nipsey Russell, and Richard Pryor. In addition, the film was directed by Sidney Lumet, one of the more socially active directors in Hollywood. Yet, their talents could not help a narrative based largely on a sequence of musical interludes and dance numbers strung together by a weak plot that repeats the message of returning home and regression.

Dorothy, played one-dimensionally by Diana Ross, is a timid school teacher living in Harlem with her aunt and uncle, who try to encourage her to come out of herself and move up in the world. During a snowstorm at Thanksgiving, Dorothy runs out to save Toto and finds herself in Oz, which resembles a strange modernistic New York with opulently designed scenes in the underworld, garbage dumps, subways, and factories. Dorothy lands on Evermean, the Wicked Witch of the East, and is considered a hero. She is given silver slippers by Miss One, the Good Witch of the North, and instructed to follow the yellow brick road to the Emerald City, where the Wiz will help her return to Harlem. She dances and sings her way to the Wiz and then later to Evilene, the Wicked Witch of the West, who is the head of a motorcycle gang and heads a sweatshop in the sewers. When Dorothy accidentally kills Evilene and frees all the workers, she exposes the Wiz as a con man and can return to Harlem by clicking her silver heels three times, for she is no longer timid.

If Lumet intended to make some kind of political statement with this film, he utterly failed, and he also painted Oz as a place from which one would want to escape and never visit again. Life in Harlem is cozy and neat, and there is no sense that there are any problems in Harlem, New York, or America in the 1970s. Even if Dorothy has overcome her timidity in Oz, there is no indication in the film that she has developed great insight about herself or society, but she has certainly learned how to sing and dance. Ironically, in a Disney film, in which one would expect to see frivolity and the celebration of celebrity, the opposite is true in *Return to Oz*, a live-action/animated film, one of the more subtle and original interpretations of two Baum novels, *The Marvelous Land of Oz* (1904) and *Ozma of Oz* (1907). Directed by Walter Murch, this chilling film begins with Aunt Em taking Dorothy to a clinic run by a "con-man" Dr. Worley to receive electro-shock therapy. Aunt Em is concerned that Dorothy has wild dreams, still believes in Oz, and claims to have found an Oz key in the hen yard. Abandoned in the clinic by Aunt Em, Dorothy hears strange noises from the basement and encounters a mysterious girl who reveals that Dr. Worley's treatment has driven many patients insane. This girl helps Dorothy escape the clutches of a sinister nurse, and together they flee the clinic during a lightening storm. Soon after they dive into a tumultuous river, they are separated.

It seems that the other girl drowns, but Dorothy is eventually swept ashore and finds herself in Oz with her favorite hen Billina, who can now talk.

Together with Billina, she makes her way across the Deadly Desert and finds that the Emerald City is in ruins and all the people have been turned into stone, including the Tin Woodsman and the Cowardly Lion. All the glittering emeralds are missing. Vicious Wheelers, who are humanoids with wheels for their hands and feet, threaten her. Tik-Tok, a clockwork robot, who is also the royal army of Oz, saves her. When she enters the palace, she finds that the witch Mombi, who has many different heads and sides to her, is now queen and locks her up because she wants to wear Dorothy's head as well. In captivity, Dorothy discovers Jack Pumpkinhead and Gump, a green-nosed moose, and with their help, she, Billina, and Tik-Tok fly to the Nome King's mountain to free the Scarecrow and return the Emerald City to its former glory.

Once they confront the powerful Nome King, who can transform himself into anything and is depicted as a craggy shape-shifting rock, Dorothy and her friends must complete several tasks before the Nome King will allow things to return to the way they were. He has imprisoned the Scarecrow and stolen all the emeralds and the ruby glass slippers because he thinks they rightfully belong to him. To his dismay, Dorothy succeeds, and the Nome King retracts his offer and wants to eat her and her companions. However, Billina drops an egg down his throat, and because eggs are poison to Nomes, he dies, and everyone and everything is liberated in Oz. The witch Mombi is put into a cage, and the Scarecrow becomes ruler of Emerald City, which glitters once again. Dorothy says she would like to live in Oz and in Kansas at the same time, but since she cannot do so, she decides return to Kansas because she does not want to hurt Aunt Em and Uncle Henry. Before she does, however, the mysterious girl who had helped her appears as Princess Ozma, the rightful ruler of Oz, and she helps her return to Kansas. Once there Dorothy learns that Dr. Worley had died when the lightening set his clinic on fire, and Nurse Wilson, who looks like Mombi, is carted off by the police. When looking into her mirror at home, Dorothy sees Ozma looking back at her and knows that her experiences in Oz were not a dream. There is an indication that she will return to Oz at some time in the future.

Dorothy was played by the gifted young actress Fairuza Balk, who was about ten years old at the time of the production, and she convincingly portrayed a young girl who never panics even when she is in desperate situations. Her confidence, it seems, stems from her belief in herself and Oz. This is a young person who has already been to Oz and has been tested. She is already filled with Oz's utopian spirit. Her return to Oz may (or may not) be due to the mysterious calling of Ozma. Whatever the case may be, she is brought back to Oz because the utopian city had been ruined by ominous and vicious people. Murch's film thrives on picturing the danger to humane people and characters who want to re-animate a utopian land that has been turned into stone. The lavish sets include a barren endless desert, a verdant forest, talking rocks, a crystal palace, and dark caverns in the Nome's mountain. Murch and his animators invented a cuddly tin clock-like robot as Tik-Tok and realistic puppets for Billina and the moose's heads; they used marvelous techniques of claymation to enable rocks to speak and the Nome king to change his shape. There is no singing in this film, only a young girl who takes very odd characters and objects in her stride, as she struggles to restore the vision that had endowed her with her remarkable qualities. *Return to Oz*, if I dare recall, was produced well after John Kennedy's call for a New Frontier in America had been trampled by the life styles of Americans during the narcissistic and greedy 1980s. Dorothy's return to Oz seems to me somewhat like a vaccination boost at a time when the spirit of Oz seemed to have been diminished. Dorothy has not broken contact with Oz. She is determined not to forget that her experiences in Oz were real, and she has been marked differently by her encounters in a strange realm.

In the twenty-first century it has been difficult to keep the spirit of Oz alive, especially during the criminal Bush years. But American television made two endeavors to re-capture and represent Oz, one a dismal failure, and the other a mixed but popular success. The dismal failure was *The Muppets Wizard of Oz* (2005), which followed the Jim Henson Company's by now stale routine of gently mocking a fairy tale by having the Muppets star along with live actors in a parody of the fairy-tale novel. In this case, two of the celebrity performers were Ashanti and Queen Latifah, who tried their best to mix with the Muppets in a boring repetition of *The Wizard of Oz*, but the Muppets were better actors. Ashanti stiffly plays a teenage waitress who detests the provinciality of Kansas, aspires to be a singer, and wants to audition for the Muppets' new show "Star Hunt," despite her Aunt Em's objections. A cyclone whisks her off to Oz, where she meets the usual companions played by the Muppets, and after defeating the Wicked Witch of the West, played by Miss Piggy, she eventually becomes a singer. However, Dorothy has come to realize that family is more important than a career, and she returns to the people she loves in Kansas. Of course, Kermit the Frog is waiting for her and offers her a contract to sing in the Muppets' show.

Not only is the storyline banal, but the jokes are infantile. Once again, Oz is not a particularly marvelous utopia, and America turns out to be the place where she will make a name for herself. Dorothy is merely set on becoming a celebrity and has no moral or ethical backbone. Everything in the film is too pat and predictable, and if the film has a message, it basically seeks to demonstrate how Oz has become irrelevant, while fame and individualism are celebrated.

This is not the case in *Tin Man* (2007), a five-hour TV mini series, directed by a British film-maker, Nick Willing, who spent his childhood in Portugal, where he read *The Wizard of Oz* and acknowledged that he was aware of the responsibility of adapting and interpreting the fairy-tale novel as an "outsider." Fortunately, he had an excellent screenplay written by Craig Van Sickle and Steven Long Mitchell with which to work. Moreover, the film marked a great departure from most other adaptations because Oz was transformed into a science fiction realm called the O.Z., which stands for the Outer Zone. Due to the length of the series (approximately 270 minutes), the plot is arbitrarily complicated by complex characters with unique and odd qualities and backgrounds, and all sorts of computerized creatures and machines. As in a science fiction novel, the film has numerous subplots that can be confusing, and consequently I want to focus on the main thread of the film to provide an idea of how unusual the film is.

The Dorothy in *Tin Man* is called DG, and she is about twenty years old and works as a waitress in a small Kansas town. As usual, she dislikes her surroundings and does not feel that she fits into the Kansas farm life. She actually has good reasons for feeling this way because, unknown to her, she is a princess of the O.Z., and her name DG stands for Dorothy Gale. Her parents sent her out of

Figure 67
Nick Willing,
Tin Man

the O.Z. under the protection of two androids, whom she mistakenly believes to be her parents, to protect her because her older sister Azkadellia wants to kill her. (She actually killed her once but DG was revived by their mother, who lost her reign and super powers by doing this.) Azkadellia has become a vicious and potent witch, has separated her parents, and rules the O.Z.; she desires to get rid of DG so that there will be no question about her legitimate claim to the throne. So, she sends Nazi-like soldiers, dressed in black leather coats throughout the film, just as she is always dressed in a sexy black futuristic outfit, to murder DG in Kansas. However, they inadvertently chase her into a cyclone that dispatches DG to the O.Z. Once there she meets Glitch, formerly a great nobleman, whose brain has been removed by Azkadellia; Wyatt Cain, once a policeman, who has joined the resistance against Azkadellia and seeks revenge because his wife was murdered by Azkadellia's henchmen; and Raw, who looks like the cowardly lion but is actually a cowardly visionary. They join forces to help DG find the Mystic Man in Central City so that DG can learn why she was banished from the O.Z., why her sister hates her so much, and where her parents are. (Her companions have other quests that parallel hers.) Along the way there are numerous skirmishes with the Nazi Longcoats and the dracula-like wombats. They all learn that Azkadellia wants to darken and destroy the O.Z. by obtaining the Emerald of the Eclipse, and only DG knows where it is and needs to refresh her memory of the past to find it. As she does this while playing hide and seek with Azkadellia's soldiers, she remembers that she had been very close to Azkadellia when they were children, but she had accidentally caused Azkadellia's body to be possessed by an ancient witch while they were playing in a cave. From that point on, the evil witch controlled Azkadellia and sought to destroy the O.Z. by manipulating her. Once DG recalls this, her quest becomes a double one: to save the O.Z. from being destroyed and to rescue her sister from the evil witch within her. Just as it seems that the witch will be victorious, DG manages to extend her hand to Azkadellia, and their spiritual reunion drives the witch from her body. The witch melts; the sisters join their parents and watch two suns rise from behind the moon and cast light on the O.Z.

The charm of this power-packed adventure/horror film, which recalls the *Indiana Jones* films and many other popular Hollywood adventure films, emanates from the seriousness and sincerity with which the actors play their roles. Also its comic aspects are dependent on the straight acting. Each character has an urgent mission, including Katherine Robertson, who plays the possessed Azkadellia. There is a deliciousness in the way she heightens her evil acts. Moreover, the sets and special effects bring out the bravado and nobility of the heroes' cause: forests and cabins that resemble scenes from the Wild West; sleek, silver towering castles that emerge in deserts; work camps that seem to be slave labor camps; underground market and amusement streets that resemble Western towns or big city entertainment quarters; gruesome mechanical runners that have deadly jaws; and frightening machines of torture. We never learn how the O.Z. was ruled, what the laws were like, and how the people lived before Azkadellia's wicked reign, but we are led to believe that life was more peaceful, idyllic, and democratic before Azkadellia seized power. We learn that DG and her family are related to Dorothy Gale and that Dorothy actually emerges from a tomb to give DG the Emerald of the Eclipse. Most important, we learn that DG has no intention of returning to Kansas. The O.Z. is her home, and once it is illuminated again, she recognizes where she belongs and what she desires. Unlike all other Oz adaptations, this film concerns the pursuit of identity of a confused young woman, who intuits that she is not what she seems to be. Bewilderment is her constant condition just as viewers are constantly bewildered.

Though filled with kitsch scenes, the film is a serious endeavor to deal with knowing and dreaming. In each episode DG learns something new about herself and how to imagine and re-imagine to forge a new identity. In a DVD interview, Willing stated that all films are fantasies, and that we all have our greatest dreams within us. Films can lead us to recognize that we already have the qualities that are represented on the screen. To view is to know, and DG comes to know that she is other than she was, but this otherness was always part of her. Somehow it had to be brought out, and indeed *Tin Man* is a science-fiction/fairy-tale film, which fosters hope that we can embody our dreams. To do so, the feisty heroine remains in the O.Z. and leaves Kansas far behind her.

Alice and the Absurdity of Home and Utopia

In creating Dorothy and Oz, L. Frank Baum reported that he had read Lewis Carroll's *Alice's Adventures in Wonderland* and was somewhat influenced by it. However, the influences were minimal, for the two fairy-tale novels have totally different plots and perspectives. For instance, there is not the slightest trace of utopianism in Carroll's work, nor does Alice want to return home. Instead, it is a grim tale about a ten-year-old girl who basically tries to make sense out of the absurdity of life, in particular, of life in the Victorian world, which resembles the Kafkaesque world of *The Trial*.

The bare plot of Carroll's novel is deceptively simple, and Will Brooker has aptly summarized how most films adapt it in his informative chapter on *Alice* adaptations in *Alice's Adventures: Lewis Carroll in Popular Culture*:

> We are introduced to Alice in the real world, with either an older sister or other adult characters. She follows a White Rabbit into some form of tunnel or hole, and entering Wonderland finds a small door she wishes to get through. She drinks a magic potion that shrinks her, and then eats a magic cake. Animals swim in a pool of tears. The Rabbit mistakes her for his maid, Mary Ann, and sends her to his house, where she makes herself big again, then small again as the animals try to evict her from the house. She leaves the house and encounters a Caterpillar who asks "Who are you?" She joins a Mad Tea Party, and meets the Queen of Hearts with her court; they play croquet. There is a trial culminating from the dream.[214]

As early as 1903, this basic structure was followed in Cecil Hepworth and Percy Stow's short silent film and in W. W. Young's exquisite feature film, *Alice in Wonderland*, in 1915. Young's adaptation shows the most innovation because the characters in Alice's dream are anticipated in her real experiences on an American farm, and the literal interpretation of the novel is enlivened by superb acting and unusual costumes and sets. The clear intention of this film and most of the adaptations that follow is to enliven and picture the novel through film as faithfully as one can. This is, indeed, a laudable goal, but the "literal" films tend to restrain experimentation and diminish the profound and complex themes of Carroll's novels that are closely connected to our so-called postmodern condition. Citing Gilles Deleuze on Carroll's works, Claudia Springer remarks:

> The *Alice* texts represent for Deleuze freedom from static, rule-bound conventions that words and phrases have accrued over time. In *Wonderland* and *Through the Looking Glass*, language is free to make new associations, paradoxical ones, that bask in semiotic spontaneity. Alice is continually disoriented, unable to cling to a conventional understanding of temporal and spatial relations or logic. . . . It can thus be argued that the Alice texts are prophetic, foreshadowing the features of postmodernism that would become commonplace during the latter half of the next century. Alice is bombarded by rapid-fire constantly changing language that escapes meaning, the same sort of language that now dominates the discourses of advertising in our consumer society. She also experiences the confusion now frequently inspired by circuitous and labyrinthine postmodern architecture and by the MTV-style fast-paced manipulation of space, time, and logic.[215]

If both *Alice in Wonderland* and *Through the Looking Glass* are particularly relevant to our liquid and globalized postmodern world, as Springer believes they are—and I agree with her—they are also deceptively "emancipatory" because they also contain misogynistic and oppressive elements. As Springer remarks,

> Alice's frustration [the real Alice Liddell, who was often mistaken for the fictional Alice while in New York] might well speak for any number of women thrust into the muse who have seen their public images transformed beyond their control by male artists. The Alice books simply heighten the typical erasure of female subjectivity by making Alice's loss of identity explicit. Although the Alice books are usually read as charming children's stories, it is possible to interpret them as exercises in terror for their young protagonist/victim.[216]

In the filmic discourse about *Alice in Wonderland*, the tendency is to emphasize the charm rather than the terror. More important than charm or terror, I believe, is the manner in which Alice, similar to Dorothy, is used in filmic adaptations to confront the onrush of postmodern conditions. To explore the different approaches to the "perplexed" Alice, who is not a moral arbiter, I want to discuss Dallas Bower's *Alice in Wonderland* (1949), the Disney *Alice in Wonderland* (1951), Jonathan Miller's *Alice in Wonderland* (1966), Jan Svankmajer's *Alice* (*Neco z Alenky*, 1988), Nick Willing's *Alice in Wonderland* (1999), and Tim Burton's *Alice in Wonderland* (2010).

Bower's *Alice in Wonderland* has an interesting history to it. Produced by Lou Bunin (1905–1994), a superb puppeteer who also directed the animation, the film was more or less dismissed in the United States and the United Kingdom when it was released in France in 1949. Walt Disney, worried about how Bower's and Bunin's film might detract from his own forthcoming production in 1951, began a lawsuit that hindered its distribution in America, and in the UK it was censored because the film ridiculed the queen of England. Bunin might have expected such difficulties. Early in his career, he had worked in Mexico City with the great socialist painter Diego Rivera in 1926 and had created political puppets for theaters and various films including an anti-fascist cartoon, *Bury the Axis*, in 1943. While working for MGM during the 1940s, Bunin was fired because of his

Figure 68
Dallas Bower,
Alice in Wonderland

left-wing politics and went to England, where he worked on *Alice in Wonderland*, only to see it denigrated and "blacklisted" by the American and British press in partial collusion with Disney. It is a shame because the film is clearly an interesting, political and artistic, collaborative effort that explores the relations of oppression in the *Alice* novel. Bunin worked with Bower and the writers Edward Eliscu, Albert Lewin, and Henry Myers to create the film, and though it is difficult to know how much of a role he played in adapting Carroll's novel, and how much credit he deserves, he produced a minor gem.

The frame of the film announces the politics of the film and is based partially on events in Carroll's life as the real mathematics professor Charles Dodgson at Oxford. Dallas begins the film with a pedantic professor scurrying like the White Rabbit to the Dean, Henry George Liddell of Christ Church College. He wants Dodgson dismissed and sent elsewhere because of the young professor's scandalous literary works. Meanwhile Dodgson is in the garden trying to photograph the three beautiful Liddell daughters dressed in Chinese costumes. Everything and everybody is in motion because Queen Victoria is about to visit Oxford and to be honored at a tea party. The queen, who arrives in a carriage, is depicted as arrogant and ignorant. The king is pictured as a demure tagalong, while Dodgson is a polite rebel against tradition. The three Liddell sisters are ordered to stay in their rooms because they might upset the decorum of the reception. Dodgson tries in vain to intervene on their behalf. The most he manages is to steal a cherry tart to bring to Alice as consolation. Later, he takes all three girls rowing on the nearby river and tells them a tale with Alice as the protagonist, while she falls asleep as he is talking. From this point on, she plunges as a live actress down a rabbit hole into the animated portion of the film and engages with the marvelous creatures of Wonderland.

Alice's adventures in this Wonderland are played out like a Gilbert and Sullivan opera in stop-motion animation that is brilliantly conceived. Bunin's puppets, based on the original illustrations of John Tenniel, are not cute but peculiar and odd, and they fit into stark landscapes that have a surreal quality. When the creatures break out into song, the verses are taken from Carroll's book and add to Alice's confusion. Her pursuit of the White Rabbit is most important because it eventually turns into a pursuit of Alice herself in two ways: Alice loses her identity and must find it; the White Rabbit wants her head chopped off because she is insolent. The characterization of the White Rabbit is most unusual and transforms Carroll's novel into an investigation of political collusion in an arbitrary authoritarian regime. We learn early that the White Rabbit had come from the working classes and had learned to adapt to the queen's regime to become a "gentleman," that is, a toady. At one point, when he catches the Knave of Hearts eating one of the queen's tarts, he takes one himself and tells the knave not to worry because he will incriminate Alice. From that point on, he wants to hunt her. When they finally meet at the queen's croquet game, he seizes the opportunity to accuse Alice of stealing the tart. Alice denies this accusation and seems to be supported by the Knave of Hearts, who declares that Alice is telling the truth, but it is he who is really Alice, and Alice is the Knave of Hearts. Everything is turned upside down as it has been throughout Alice's adventures, and she is wakened by one of her sisters. Dodgson tells her that he has finished his story as they arrive at the shore, and that she was not listening just dreaming. However, Alice insists that her dream was real and pursues Dodgson and her sisters who move ahead of her as if they were entering some rabbit hole.

The politics of Alice's adventures mesh in Wonderland with the politics in Oxford. Each one of the animated creatures bears a resemblance to the characters in the frame story. For instance, the White Rabbit is the conformist, finicky professor, Queen Victoria, the queen of Wonderland, and so on. Alice herself is a mixture of Dodgson and Alice Liddell, or what Lewis Carroll would like Alice to become—feisty, inventive, assertive, and perceptive. While Alice is indeed confused at times, she enjoys all the oddities of Wonderland except for the queen and the White Rabbit. She has no intention of leaving Wonderland, and the ending of the film is subtly ambivalent, for Alice appears to be pursuing her imagination.

Alice is played by the British actress Carol Marsh, and she is clearly in her twenties, but she manages to perform the role of a young girl without acting infantile. There is also a hint or two that Dodgson, about thirty, has more than a tutorial interest in her. But the manipulative courting of Dodgson does not lead to a romance. Instead, Alice has no interest in him or love. She is more intrigued by Wonderland, where she uncovers the machinations of the queen and exposes the obsequiousness and deviousness of many of her subjects. If Alice learns anything in this filmic adaptation, it is that her longing to meet Queen Victoria and her "incarceration" in her room while the Queen was in Oxford, were disappointments that enabled her to grasp the relations that produce oppression.

This is not the case in the Disney 1951 production of *Alice in Wonderland*, which had three directors who "obsequiously" followed the Disney formula of adapting a fairy-tale work and transforming it into an irrelevant Hollywood musical that has more fluff than substance. Moreover, the film is so stupidly pedantic that it takes the life out of all the comic antics and song and dance routines. At the beginning, Alice is pictured sitting in a tree with her cat Dinah and ignoring the history lesson that her prim and proper governess is reading to her. The governess is annoyed that Alice is not paying attention, and Alice responds by saying that a book without pictures is dull. The governess states that this is nonsense. Soon after, Alice breaks out into a song about a Wonderland: "If I had a world of my own, everything would be nonsense." And she gets her wish right after the song.

Without any transition, Alice sees the White Rabbit and pursues him down the rabbit hole. Her adventures in Wonderland, however, are quite different from those more meaningful ones in Bower's film and may be one of many reasons why Disney wanted Bower's film blocked in America. Though the animation is slick and appealing, and though the directors introduced other hilarious characters and scenes from Carroll's *Through the Looking Glass*, the narrative turns into a series of lessons for Alice, who suffers humiliation after humiliation and becomes utterly despondent in the Tulgey Wood, a dark and dreary forest, where she weeps and wishes to go home. The Cheshire Cat, a smiling sadist, opens a tree and points the way to the queen's castle, for it is only through the queen that she can learn how to get home. However, Alice is accused once again of upsetting the queen and placed on trial. She rebuts the queen and calls her a tyrant. The film ends with the queen and her followers chasing Alice, who is wakened by her governess and asked to recite her lessons. Alice can only recite some babble, but the governess forgives her and they march home to tea.

As Chaston has remarked in his essay on the "Ozification" of many Hollywood fantasy films,[217] the Disney production is a classic example of how numerous screenplays are geared to represent a young girl experiencing an unusual other world only to long for the conventional and regressive image of home. The Disney adaptation is truly infantile in almost every sense of the word: it has silly slapstick humor that bleaches the complex enigmas of Carroll's work; features a helpless blonde girl who does not learn to help herself; draws papier-mâché, cuddly one-dimensional creatures that are more decorative than intriguing and complex. There is little to redeem this interpretation of Carroll's works, even though the directors intended to give the film a modern look. Instead, they produced a repeat of the Snow White recipe without romantic love, which, in their hands, would have only added icing to a tasteless sponge cake.

There is no icing or "Ozification" in Jonathan Miller's stark black-and-white 1966 adaptation of *Alice in Wonderland*, which might aptly be titled "Alice in Wasteland," for Alice's adventures are set in moldy ornamented Victorian homes and churches, dry and dull forests, and on rocky beaches. Rather than taking part in all the incidents of her dream, Alice is a stoic observer. Detached and alienated from her surroundings and barely interacting with the characters she meets, Alice is more like a sleepwalker, somewhat dazed but meditating on what it means to change in a repulsive world. As Miller himself has written,

> I recognized that I could only succeed with *Alice* if the film realized the characteristically disjunctive grammar of dream. The strange juxtaposition of elements in a scene that never strike us as odd when we are dreaming, should occur as almost passing details in a film. When visualizing the law court in *Alice* we furnished it with lodges and stage boxes in which spectators could be seen hastily dressing, casually shaving or having Christmas dinner, as the trial proceeded. As Alice runs through the garden on her flight from the White Rabbit's house she was shown passing an enameled bath-tub in which a naked man is carefully washing himself. These items are normal in every respect except the context in which they appear before the eye. . . . Apart from the way that things are inappropriately juxtaposed in the same scene, dreams are characterized by the way one scene gives way to the next without any of the transitions that lend ordinary narrative text its coherence.[218]

The abrupt dream sequences begin soon after Alice is groomed by a maid before a mirror in a tiny, well-ordered Victorian home. Her older sister watches and is obviously displeased that she must spend an afternoon with Alice. Nothing is said as they depart for a spot on a hill, where the sister sits down without a word and begins reading. Alice has brought nothing with her. So, she lies back and begins to dream, and during the dream, she narrates everything that happens to her and speaks at times to herself in an inner dialogue. Every now and then, she speaks to the caricatures of the typical Victorian people whom she meets. But for the most part, she remains the outsider, contemplating what is happening to her as she changes sizes and observes the absurd behavior of adults. (Kafka's *The Trial* resonates throughout the film.) Alice's face is expressionless for the most part. She does not show her emotions, nor does she participate much in the bizarre rituals that she witnesses. When called as a witness by the queen during the trial of the knave who stole the queen's tarts, she denounces the trial, which is held in an utterly chaotic and bizarre church, and wakes up as the queen screeches. Alice is not disturbed at all by her dream. She sits for a moment, contemplating the dream, and says to herself, "The things that I have seen, I can see no more."

Figure 69
Jonathan Miller,
Alice in Wonderland

This ambivalent remark could mean that she has put her childhood behind her, or that she simply can no longer visualize what she has seen. When she arises and moves with her silent sister toward their home, we are left with a black-and-white exposure of a girl who does not reveal her feelings and is not upset by the absurd behavior of the adults whom she has encountered in her dream. Miller's interpretation of Carroll's fairy-tale novel is both a bleak critique of the Victorian and modern worlds at the same time. As Scott Thill has perceptively remarked about Miller's work,

> In his assured hands, *Alice in Wonderland* is not merely a fantastical tale of caterpillars, mice, and bloodthirsty queens looking to cut off some heads, but rather a journey of self-realization and maturation for a young British girl locked in a Victorian nightmare filled with, to paraphrase de Saint-Exupery's similarly structured *The Little Prince*, adults executing matters of "consequence" that mean, like Footman says, nothing at all in the scheme of things. As Miller explains it, "Once you take the animal heads off, you begin to see what it's all about. A small child, surrounded by hurrying, worried people, thinking 'Is that what being grown up is like?'"The fact that they make no sense, are trapped—like the Mad Hatter, played with sparkling annoyance by Peter Cook—by time, dance about the meaningless caucuses until they're utterly spent, fuss over keeping their children prim and proper right before they go outdoors and play, and conduct ludicrous proceedings—such as in the King and Queen's court—when what they really want to do is to behead each other, doesn't jibe with the supposed air of solemnity, importance, and meaning that inflates everything they do.[219]

It is really unclear whether Alice matures in Miller's account of Alice's adventures. I am inclined to believe that she has become more resistant to the forces that act upon her, more solemn. In this regard, she resembles many young girls in the 1960s, not just in the Victorian period, contemplating a web woven of inconsistencies and contradictions that constitute the environment in which they were compelled to grow up.

Svankmajer's Alice is similar to Miller's in that she narrates her dream and really does not change much during her adventures. She, too, is much more the observer than a participant in a dream. If she learns anything, it is to resist the tyrannical rants and acts of the queen. But that is where the similarity between the two Alice films ends. Svankmajer's *Alice* is a narrated dream of a trip into Wonderland that resembles a horror house ride in a motley amusement park that is falling apart. His film is bleak, grotesque, and macabre without any kind of resolution. Alice, who is a bored ten-year-old, dreams a nightmare that ends as a surreal extension of the nightmare. The frame of the movie begins with a naturalistic picture of Alice and her sister leaving a dismal house in the country and walking to a nearby brook. The older sister sits down and reads and wants nothing to do with Alice by her side. Alice lays back and pictures herself in a room with toys and other strange objects. Before the title had been shown in the film, Alice's lips had informed us that "You must close your eyes, or else you won't see anything." Thus the dream of her adventures is illumination. And the dream as nightmare ends *not* with Alice returning to the side of her sister near the brook, but to the decrepit room of objects that have played a role in her dream. Alice says nothing. She gazes. The camera follows her gaze around the room, focusing on inanimate toys and objects that had been in the dream, and her surreal awakening is heightened by the broken glass case in which a large stuffed rabbit had been placed. He had initiated the sequence of events in Alice's nightmare by breaking out of the case and leading her to the queen. A revolting white rabbit with sharp buck teeth, he had spent a good deal of his time in the "adventures" replacing his stuffing of sawdust that kept falling out of his stomach and licking the sawdust off his pocket watch. He was not a friendly rabbit, and he turned out to be the queen's executioner, and when ordered by the queen, he used scissors to cut off the heads of animate and inanimate creatures. He is missing at the end of the film as Alice sits on the floor with cards spread on and around her lap and two dolls sitting by her side. It seems that

Alice returns from the nightmare of her dreams to the nightmare of her reality. As she gazes at the broken case, her lips declare, "He's late as usual. I think I'll cut off his head."

Michael O'Pray has remarked,

> Svankmajer has consistently returned to the theme of childhood, especially in *Jabberwocky*, *Down to the Cellar*, and *Alice*. His obsession with marionettes, puppets and primitive folk tales also relates to childhood and its forms of representation—tales of the imagination while often use fear, horror and anxiety. He has remarked that "I have never viewed my childhood as something that I have left behind me." . . . For Svankmajer, his exploration of childhood is part of a type of paranoiac-critical method, whereby his own highly personal associations stemming from childhood and what he sees as its natural ally—dream life—actively construct the films in which such projections are given shape.[220]

Svankmajer's film technique is crucial for understanding his depiction of Alice as an artist/writer, who gives shape to her dream and her real environment. Just as the filmmaker Svankmajer arranges objects, including puppets, dolls, apple cores, mousetraps, beetles, socks, skeletons, and animates them to become characters in his film about Alice's anxieties, Alice becomes his mouthpiece, literally and figuratively, as her lips are shown commenting on the episodes. She more or less takes charge of the filming of her dream, and in this respect, she is a very different Alice than all the other filmic Alices. Dirk de Bruyn has commented,

> gone is Carroll's vision of Alice as a perfect English upperclass girl, who through her refinement and her bossy natural superiority protects herself from this topsy-turvy world. Svankmajer's world, here as in his other films, is more inherently fearful, where everyday objects, the tools of our comfort, are capable of turning on us. It is a world that an 'innocent' Alice negotiates, sifts through, inspects.[221]

Alice has not made any kind of passage through childhood to adulthood. The various episodes from Carroll's fairy-tale novel that Svankmajer adapts with his puppets and extraordinarily animated found objects, refuse, bones, tools, and plants do not form a logical, goal-oriented plot. Instead, these encounters recall occurrences in real everyday life that a child, any child, experiences with a certain dread and wonder. Svankmajer's Alice narrates her way through these encounters to become the "executor" of her life. Perhaps, "executive" might be a better term, for she is not a killer, but she will give the orders that will determine the course of her life. Svankmajer tries to shed the pedophilic tendencies and the male gaze by having to contend with the camera's eye. The result is a most unusual exploration of drab conditions and a surrealist film that pays homage to the imagination of young girls.

Unfortunately, despite all its glitz and cameo appearances of famous movie stars such as Martin Short, Peter Ustinov, Miranda Richardson, Ben Kingsley, Whoopie Goldberg, and Gene Wilder, Nick Willing's 1999 adaptation, influenced by both Miller's and Svankmajer's films, is a travesty of the imagination and the childhood of young girls. It is a spectacle for the sake of spectacle based on a stupid plot-line: the film begins with an anxious Alice being groomed for a song recital that she is expected to deliver at her parents' garden party—a scene that recalls Miller's opening frame—and as her hair is being combed, the camera moves outside the large Victorian mansion to introduce us to the very odd guests, who will soon populate Alice's dream. And, indeed, Alice will have a dream once she is taken into the garden and runs away into a nearby forest because she dreads performing before the lavishly dressed and peculiar people, who act with extravagant manners.

The film is really all about extravagance. Willing is infatuated with showing off his imagination rather than with exploring Carroll's novel or recreating an unusual interpretation, for all he wants to depict in each episode is Alice learning to conquer her anxiety so that she will sing for her supper.

This is a very pathetic message in a film inflated by ridiculous performers making themselves look ridiculous. Whoopie Goldberg plays a Cheshire Cat with a smiling-ass grin; Ben Kingsley, a weird caterpillar, puffs a hookah pompously on top of a mushroom; Miranda Richardson is irritating as a shrill, wooden queen; Robbie Coltrane and George Wendt look like fat balloons and act like infants as Tweedledee and Tweedledum; Gene Wilder, as Mock Turtle, is an endearing and cuddly performer; and Christopher Lloyd is a bumbling White Knight. Many of the characters are taken from *Through the Looking Glass*, only so that they can play a role in building Alice's confidence and can add a bit of flavor to the didactic plot. In the end, Alice awakes beneath an apple tree—the ripeness of the apples is supposed to suggest something—and she bravely returns to the party and sings a song of her own choice instead of "Cherry Ripe." Viewers are expected to feel that Alice has finally matured and feels confident in life. But film adaptations that simplify very complex and profound novels with a banal message can never convince audiences to respond happily to the filmmaker's directions, even if the actors have done so. In this case, Willing has violated a novel that he claims to love, and he paradoxically violates Alice as well by making her into an obedient and innocent young girl, who thrives on pep talks from silly creatures.

In Tim Burton's delightfully bizarre *Alice in Wonderland* (2010), his Alice does not need pep talks. Rather she runs away from pep talks by people who want to encourage her to marry a dim-witted, pretentious aristocrat. Burton's Alice is nineteen years old and fortunately has a mind of her own as well as a great imagination, which she has clearly inherited from her father. The film begins with a six-year-old Alice talking to her merchant father, who has wild dreams of opening trade routes to the Pacific. She clearly admires him and needs his love and affection before going to bed because she has been troubled by nightmares about a weird kingdom. Her father tucks her in bed and jokingly tells her that she's bonkers and all the best people are bonkers.

Unfortunately, Alice's father dies before she reaches puberty, and it is because her mother has fallen on hard times that she has arranged a marriage for Alice against the girl's will. She is obviously more interested in money than Alice's welfare. But since Alice is indeed a bit bonkers in the positive sense of the word, she runs off into the nearby forest just as her unctuous suitor is officially proposing to her at a lavish garden party. As usual, she falls down a rabbit hole, but this time she arrives in "queerland," not wonderland. Indeed, Burton queers the narrative of *Alice in Wonderland* by crossing genders, mixing sexual identity, and creating all sorts of bizarre animated characters who remind us that there is no such thing as normal, whether in reality or in our imaginations. Burton introduces characters from both *Alice in the Wonderland* and *Through the Looking Glass* to spice up the plot, and many of the characters resemble those she had met at the garden party. Whereas most *Alice* films are coming-of-age narratives, Burton's film differs in that his Alice is on a quest to determine whether she should marry the prig who has proposed to her. She must also prove that she is the Alice who had one time visited "queerland," for the queers need her to fight against the tyrannical Red Queen, who is destroying their lives. And of course Alice eventually becomes the champion of the queers, defeats the Red Queen, who is a malicious dragon, and returns to the garden party to reject her flabbergasted suitor.

Burton's film is lavish—the images of the castles and the forests are gorgeous and stunning. The plants and characters are unique and exotic, and all the characters act with exaggerated mannerist gestures and hyperbole. Interestingly, Alice is never overwhelmed by anyone or anything because she has been there before, and she believes that she is in a dream that she needs to control. Throughout the dream sequences, Alice keeps saying that this is my dream, and I can decide who appears and what happens. But she cannot always do that. Either her unconscious imagination or psyche gets the better of her, or Burton imposes arbitrary obstacles so that Alice cannot live the dream that she wants to dream. In other words, there is a battle over the narrative—and Burton asks: Can we control our dreams? Can a young woman write her own narrative? Can we humans who have become caricatures of humans in today's society of the spectacle in which commercials, advertisements, and other media influences invade our lives, determine the plot and narrative of our lives?

Unfortunately, Burton was financed by the Disney Corporation, and his film does not explore the profound questions that it raises. The film is a mish-mash of Burton and Disney. It has a dark, macabre side, but it eventually dissipates into a Hollywood sentimental film with a traditional battle scene at the end that one finds in *Peter Pan, Narnia*, or *Harry Potter* films, not to mention *The Lord of the Rings*—glorious battle for the sake of spectacular battle. Despite the extravagant color and characters, Burton's film is too black and white. In other words, the dichotomy between evil and good is so apparent that it becomes artificial if not superficial.

What saves the film is Burton's depiction of a strong-willed young woman. Even here, however, there are massive contradictions. From the beginning, Burton's Alice has an inquisitive and critical mind. Her trip down the rabbit hole only reinforces her independent spirit. This girl is not the typical Disney heroine. She is not overwhelmingly beautiful or cute, more Tomboy than petite comatose princess. She is not looking for a mate but for herself. She is valiant in battle when need be. She has a sense of humor. But there is the contradiction in the end when she decides to stay well within the safety of her upper-class society by making a deal with the man who took over her father's business. Her "vision" is to colonize China through trade! In other words, she will probably become a rich business woman and live off the Chinese in the late nineteenth century. Of course, children (and adult) viewers will not think about the consequences of her decision. They will see an empowered young lady determined to follow in her father's footsteps. All power to patriarchy in the end! Will Brooker makes a very significant comment about the absence of sexual elements in the filmic adaptations of *Alice in Wonderland*:

> This absence even from the adaptations that explore *Alice* as a sometimes brutal, sometimes frightening expression of the unconscious is surprising when we remember the extent to which the idea of Carroll as some form of paedophile—repressed obsessive, shy lover of Liddell girls, troubled deviant—recurred in newspaper stories, biographies, and novels like *Still She Haunts Me* and *Automated Alice*. Given that this image of Carroll is so pervasive, we might have expected an "adult" adaptation of the book that Alice Liddell inspired to have incorporated some hint of the Wonderland denizens seducing, falling in love with, or preying sexually on the heroine.[222]

Alice appears to be an icon of innocent childhood, and there appears to be a taboo about "molesting" innocent icons such as Dorothy, Alice, Pinocchio, and Peter Pan. Yet, one must wonder why writers and artists are infatuated by these young characters and use them implicitly and explicitly to represent their own sexual desires, maturation, and development of social cognition. It is as if they want to put childhood behind them, when childhood persists throughout their lives. The Alice filmic adaptations provide substantial evidence that we will always cope with childhood even as we grow older, but that there are aspects of childhood that we repress as we represent them in images.

Pinocchio and the Carving of a Young Boy

While the figure of Carroll's Alice, as icon of innocent childhood, has been pampered, bullied, and bewildered but never touched in most of the filmic adaptations, Carlo Collodi's Pinocchio, another icon of childhood, has generally been manhandled and beaten into his identity. This may be due to Collodi's very different perspective on childhood and boys. In his fairy-tale novel he combined folklore and literary fairy-tale traditions to reflect upon the situation of illiterate, playful, *poor* boys during the latter half of the nineteenth century in Italy. He never wrote simply for an audience of young readers. His work was intended to appeal to children and adults alike and to suggest a mode of educating young boys, especially when they did not seem fit to be educated.

Read as a type of *Bildungsroman* or fairy-tale novel of development, *Pinocchio* can be interpreted positively as a representation of how peasant boys, when given a chance, can assume responsibility for themselves and their families and become industrious members of society. After all, Pinocchio is literally carved out of wood—out of an inanimate substance—and turns miraculously into a human boy who becomes responsible for the welfare of his poor father. This theme of education or development, however, is very complex, for Collodi had not initially planned to allow Pinocchio to develop. In fact, he intended to end the series printed in *Il giornale per i bambini* at Chapter 15 in which Pinocchio is left hanging on an oak tree, ostensibly dead. Yet, when this episode appeared in the November 10, 1881 issue of the newspaper with the "finale" printed at the end, there was such a storm of protest from readers young and old that Collodi was forced to resume Pinocchio's adventures in the February 16, 1882 issue of the newspaper. In other words, Collodi was forced to "develop" or "educate" his wooden protagonist despite his initial pessimistic perspective. Therefore, if the development of a piece of carved wood as a young boy is the central theme of *Pinocchio*, it is a theme that the author ironically questioned from the very beginning of the adventures, just as he questioned the optimistic structure of the fairy tale. This questioning accounts for the tension of skepticism and optimism in the novel. Moreover, the very structure of all the episodes also contributes to the tension because they were never intended to culminate in a novel, just as Pinocchio was never intended to become human.

Collodi conceived each chapter for the newspaper so as to keep his readers interested in the strange fate of a "live" piece of magic wood that is turned into a puppet. He did this with wry humor and suspense. Though the specific events are not predictable, all the episodes have the same plan: each begins with a strange situation that leads to a near tragedy and borders on the ridiculous. However, since Collodi created a topsy-turvy fairy-tale world that faintly resembled Tuscany but constantly changed shape, anything is possible. Moreover, Collodi mischievously plays with readers by leaving them "hanging" in suspense at the end of each chapter. In fact, each episode is a predicament. And one predicament leads to the next. No chapter is ever finished, and even the end of the book can be considered "unfinished," for it is uncertain what lies ahead of Pinocchio after he turns human. He is still a boy. He has very little money. He is not educated. There is no indication that he will prosper as in a traditional fairy tale, even though he has developed a sense of responsibility and compassion. Pinocchio has survived boyhood and has been civilized to take the next step into manhood—and it is unclear where this step may lead.

Given the unfinished business of Pinocchio's development, Collodi's major and constant question throughout this fairy-tale novel of education is whether it is indeed worthwhile becoming "civilized." It is a question that Mark Twain was asking about the same time when he wrote *The Adventures of Huckleberry Finn*, and in some ways Huck Finn is the American version of Pinocchio, for both boys are brutally exposed to the hypocrisy of society and yet compelled to adapt to the values and standards that will allegedly enable them to succeed. Huck refuses civilization in the end while Pinocchio appears to have made peace with law and order.

Yet ultimately, Collodi asks us to reflect critically about how this socialization has come about, and if we consider how the "innocent" piece of wood, whose vices consist in his playfulness and naïvety, is treated by the people and social forces around him, then there is something almost "tragic" to the way he is beaten and lulled into submission. From the beginning, Pinocchio's destiny is stamped by the fact that Geppetto carves him into a boy puppet because he wants to make money, using the puppet as his meal ticket. Simply put, his father "gives birth" to him because, in his old age, he wants to earn a living through him. Geppetto has no interest in learning who his son is and what his desires are. His son is an investment in his own future. This is not to imply that Geppetto is an uncaring father, but his relationship to Pinocchio is ambivalent because of his initial "desire" to create a puppet that will know how to dance, fence, and turn somersaults so that he can earn a crust of bread and a glass of wine. In other words, Pinocchio is supposed to please him, and Geppetto literally holds the strings to the puppet's fate in his hands. In Chapter 7, after Pinocchio has lost his feet, Geppetto at first refuses to make new feet for him until Pinocchio says, "I promise you, father, that I'll learn a trade and be the comfort and staff of your old age."[223] Geppetto complies with Pinocchio's wish, and the puppet shows his gratitude by expressing his desire to go to school. In addition, he is extremely moved when Geppetto then sells his own coat to purchase a spelling-book required for school. Collodi comments: "And although Pinocchio was very good-humored boy, even he became sad, because poverty, when it is true poverty, is understood by everyone—even by children."[224]

On the one hand, Pinocchio wants to be and is socialized to please his father; on the other, he cannot control his natural instincts to explore the world and to seek pleasure. Caught in a predicament—to please his father means to deny his own pleasures—Pinocchio as a poor illiterate peasant boy must learn the "ups and downs of the world," as Geppetto puts it; that is, he must be physically subdued and put in his place so that he functions properly as an industrious worker, curbed of his rebellious instincts. Collodi clearly demonstrates in a very specific class analysis that poor Italian boys of this period had very little choice if they wanted to advance in life. Using Pinocchio as a symbolic figure, Collodi torments and punishes the puppet each time Pinocchio veers from the norm of acceptable behavior. Among his punishments are the loss of legs through burning; the expansion of his nose as a consequence of lying; the hanging from an oak tree; imprisonment for four months; being caught in a trap and used by a farmer as a watchdog; being caught in a net and almost fried as a fish by the Green Fisherman; the transformation into a donkey; being compelled to work in a circus; being drowned to escape skinning; and being swallowed by a gigantic shark.

These forms of punishment in the novel are, of course, so preposterous that readers can take delight and laugh at the events. At the same time, the laughter is mixed with relief that the readers do not have to undergo such tortures. Besides, the laughter is instructive, for readers learn what to avoid through Pinocchio's mistakes and they learn how to attain dignity. It is this attainment of self-dignity as a human being that is most crucial at the end of Pinocchio's adventures. As in most fairy-tale narratives, Pinocchio is obliged to fulfill specific tasks to gain his reward, and two are primary: first Pinocchio must rescue his father Geppetto, and second he must keep his promises to the Blue Fairy by showing that he can be obedient, honest, and industrious. No matter how much he suffers, he perseveres and earns the recognition of the Blue Fairy. He is also able to distinguish between good and bad, between ridiculous puppet and responsible boy behavior. In this regard, Collodi's narrative is a fairy-tale novel of development that makes a sober statement, despite its humor and grotesque scenes.

For readers of Collodi's time, who were largely from the middle and educated classes, *Pinocchio* represented a warning to mischievous scamps and set a model of proper behavior. For Collodi himself, one can speculate that he viewed *Pinocchio* in part as representing the difficulties he himself had experienced and had had to overcome in order to be accepted in Florentine society of his time, a perspective that other readers from the lower classes may have shared. For today's readers, Collodi's *Pinocchio* may come as a surprise, for most will probably be shocked to find that the novel is not the same as the Disney film which they have probably seen before reading Collodi's original work. They will realize that Collodi let his imagination run wild more than Disney did, and that he developed his puppet in more extraordinary ways. Indeed, thanks to Collodi's wild imagination, we have a rich commentary on what it meant to develop as a peasant boy in Italian society of the nineteenth century. But more important, perhaps, his fairy-tale novel transcends history and continues to raise questions about how we "civilize" children in uncivilized times.

It is important, however, to bear in mind that Collodi's name in English-speaking countries has been effaced by Disney, who became the alleged creator of *Pinocchio* and substantially changed the meaning of the novel through his film.[225] More than likely, Disney is still considered the author of *Pinocchio* the world over. Yet, even when it came to making the film, Disney was never the "real" originator. The idea for adapting Pinocchio came early in 1937 from Norm Ferguson, a member of the studio staff, and Disney became enthusiastic about the possible project after he read Collodi's fairy-tale novel. His main concern, however, was to find a way to utilize the newly developed multiplane camera and to introduce innovative techniques in animation.[226] Work began on the production in 1937, but was stopped for a brief period because Disney was not satisfied with the early results of the animators. The original Collodi storyline was proving to be too complex to streamline, and it was not until Disney saw Yasha Frank's musical *Pinocchio: A Musical Legend* in June of 1937, as Richard Wunderlich and Thomas Morrissey have argued, that Disney embraced the idea of the film wholeheartedly:

> Disney consciously created a story line different from Frank's but took the new image of Pinocchio and Geppetto from Frank. Disney's decision was deliberate and well thought out. Furthermore, Disney was clearly conscientious in his endeavor to know Collodi's tale. Not only did he acquire the Italian original and various editions and adaptations of the translations, but—perhaps to be sure of the material—he also contracted for his own translation.[227]

Key for Disney in reshaping Frank's musical and the Collodi material was to make the relationship between father and son more harmonious and tender, to "Americanize" the representation of boyhood itself, and to simplify the plot so that Disney's personal moral code of success based on conforming to the dictates of good behavior and diligence could be transmitted through song, dance, and rounded images of tranquility. Richard Schickel remarks that

> one must suspect that Disney found in this story elements of autobiography, since he had himself been a child denied the normal prerogatives of boyhood. It is certainly possible that at least some portion of his drive for success was a compensation for his failure to find the father who had, in the psychological sense, been lost to him since childhood. . . . such an interpretation suggests why *Pinocchio* is the darkest in hue of all Disney's pictures and the one which, despite its humor, is the most consistently terrifying. The menacing whips that crack over the heads of the boys are turned into donkeys after their taste of the sybaritic life and may have their origin in his recurrent nightmare of punishment for failure to deliver his newspapers. And, of course, one suspects the dream of winning the neglectful father's approval by a heroic act—such as rescuing him from a living death in the whale's maw—must have occurred to Disney at some point in his unhappy youth.[228]

It is obviously somewhat misleading (and yet compelling) to identify Disney with Pinocchio and his father with Geppetto, for we know that numerous hands played a role in designing the characters and storyline of the film under Disney's supervision.[229] But this is all the more reason to focus on the image of the boy Pinocchio and how he is socialized to represent "the American boy." If Disney and his staff worked together on projecting what it takes to be a good boy—or what Douglas Street insightfully calls a pipsqueak in contrast to Collodi's picaro[230]—then this figure represents a product of a particular group of American male artists reflecting on what it takes to be a good boy and son in their society. To this extent, the father–son relationship and boyhood as depicted in the pictures, edited, and projected on the screen represent more than just Disney's wish fulfillments and desires. As model characters Geppetto and Pinocchio are idealistic projections, corrections to the reality of boyhood in America, but one wonders whether such correct relations and behavior in the Disney remake of Collodi are as exemplary as they seem. After all, they suggest the benefits of conformity and the nullification of individual experimentation with reality to gain a sense of one's particular drives and identity vis à vis social demands.

In Disney's streamline reduction of the Collodi novel, he shifted the role of the cricket, ignominiously killed by Pinocchio in the Italian version, to that of moral conscience. In fact, Jiminy Cricket is the major character in Disney's film. It is he who frames and narrates the story; his voice becomes the authentic fairy-tale voice. His moral conscience is imposed on Pinocchio and the audience at the same time. He is like the sympathetic vaudeville clown, charming and naïve, who wins over the audience through his comic routine numbers that always have him stumbling but landing on his feet. From the beginning we know that he will triumph because he has already survived his adventures with Pinocchio and lives to tell that wishes can come true. His omniscient voice of narrator is a soothing, didactic one that will explain what one has to do to transform oneself from an inexperienced foolish puppet to a good little human boy. The difficulty with his story is that Pinocchio the puppet is uninteresting if not boring, and that Jiminy Cricket must provide the spark and excitement in the story.

This story was superbly condensed by Disney and his collaborators. If we study its structure based on a triad of adventures—three is the fairy-tale lucky number—we can see that the tale is carefully constructed to follow the classical form. After the initial birth of the hero, he is obliged to depart, ostensibly to go to school, but in reality this departure marks the beginning of three adventures of conflict and escape: 1) Pinocchio's servitude in the marionette theater and escape from Stromboli; 2) the trip to Pleasure Island where Pinocchio is semi-transformed into a donkey and the escape via sea to the mainland; and 3) the search for Pinocchio's father and escape from the whale. At the end, Pinocchio is rewarded for his unselfish act (saving his father at sea) by rising from the dead and becoming a real boy. Pinocchio is safe at home, and his conscience Jiminy Cricket is rewarded for work well done.

This straightforward, simple storyline is enhanced by the extraordinary camera work that relied on the multiplane camera to zoom in and out and provide depth in all the key scenes of the village, theater, Pleasure Island, the whale, and the sea. The song-and-dance scenes reinforce the didactic lessons in an amusing manner, while the creation of minor characters such as Figaro the cat and Cleo the goldfish add a light touch to the action that often borders on the tragic. Here, of course, Stromboli, the rogues Honest John and Kitty, the Lord of Pleasure Island, and Monstro are remarkable creations of villainy who symbolically represent the "evil father." If Schickel is correct in assuming that there are autobiographical undertones in this film, then more must be made out of the evil father, who indeed may have been closer to Disney's real father than Geppetto. Taken together as aspects of the "bad father," the sinister figures represent dishonesty, exploitation for profit, and greed, whereas Geppetto is sincerity, nurturing love, and sacrifice. One could even argue that there is something "motherly" or feminine about him. But truly, in this all-male cast of characters—the fairy and the fish remain in the background of the action—Pinocchio must learn to choose which male models to follow or to disregard. He comes into the social world magically like Casper Hauser or the Wolf Child, an innocent, a natural creature, who must learn how to speak, and as he learns how to speak, to identify words with things and actions with moral implications. Without a conscience to guide him, he would be lost.

It is the voice of conscience that makes the Disney film so fascinating and complex. Few critics have paid attention to the fact that, while Jiminy Cricket is the narrator of the story, it is the fairy who holds power and intervenes to reward and punish according to the code of bravery, truth, and unselfishness. She is the supreme nurturer and judge who literally pulls all the strings to safeguard Pinocchio's future. She intervenes to settle the strife among sons and fathers or, at the very least, to point Pinocchio in the right direction so he can succeed in his endeavors to become a "real boy," which is his goal. We should also note, in typical Hollywood tradition, returning home is linked to his boyhood identity.

The maternal soothing voice of the fairy is reinforced by the gentle voice of the cricket, who is not only a friend but also a father figure. In fact, the organized forces of fairy/cricket/clockmaker and their voices merge and form the model parent for Pinocchio, who is reborn at the end of the film to reenter the world as a finished product that will not make any mistakes. Pinocchio is the perfect charming good boy when he awakes on his bed, but he is almost too perfect to be true. Like a doll that has been mass produced and ready to be taken home from the shelf of a store, he is the dream toy that Geppetto has wished for, prefabricated by the fairy's instructions and endowed with a moral conscience also supplied by the fairy.

This is the irony at the end of Disney's *Pinocchio*: the unreal puppet who was believable becomes a boy who is too real to be true. Disney and his collaborators produce before our eyes the making of a perfect "American" boy. Though the film appears to take place in Tyrol—the father speaks with a German accent and the village and scenery are reminiscent of Tyrol and northern Italy—the voice and mannerisms of Pinocchio are clearly more American than European. It is almost as if the Old World is giving birth to something newer and more honest than decadent Europe. But what is new in *Pinocchio* is really old, for Disney's boy is carved out to be obedient, diligent, and honest, not "bad" virtues in themselves, but in the context of the story, these virtues constitute a masochistic character. Like many "gifted" children, Pinocchio will aim to please and repress his desires and wishes to make sure that his father is first and foremost happy. Such a boy is easily manipulated for the good of the country, the good of the corporation, and the good of the Disney studio.

In the course of the development of filmic fairy-tale discourse during the twentieth century, *Pinocchio* is pivotal because it became just as much a reference point for filmmakers who wanted to adapt Collodi's novel as the novel itself. Directors sought to rectify the image of Pinocchio represented by Disney, reclaim Collodi's image through a semi-literal adaptation of the novel, or totally re-create a new Pinocchio, who might reflect the transformation of boyhood in modern times. The adaptations are numerous, and, I want to discuss six of them that illustrate different approaches to the icon of Pinocchio that involve questions of boyhood and the father/son relationship: Alexandr Ptushko's *The Golden Key* (1939), Ray Goossens' *Pinocchio in Outer Space* (1965), Walter Beck's *Turlis Abenteuer* (*The Adventures of Turli*, 1967), Luigi Comincini's *Le avventure di Pinocchio* (*The Adventures of Pinocchio*, 1972), Michael Anderson's *The New Adventures of Pinocchio* (1999), and Daniel Robichaud's *Pinocchio 3000* (2004).

In Chapter 5 I already examined a Russian animated adaptation of *Pinocchio* by Ivanov-Vano that was produced in 1958 and based on Aleksey Tolstoy's 1935 fairy-tale novel *The Golden Key*. I also mentioned that Ivanov-Vano's film was greatly influenced by the classic black-and-white live-action/animated *The Golden Key* directed by the brilliant Alexandr Ptushko, made two years before Disney's film. Since Ptushko's film was more of an adaptation of Tolstoy's work and since Tolstoy wrote the screenplay for his film, it would be unfair to compare his work with Disney's. However, I do want to comment that, despite the difficult conditions under which Ptushko worked and the inferior technology he used at that time, his film is much more innovative and fascinating than Disney's in almost every respect.[231]

Ptushko uses black-and-white film to his advantage and creates a neo-realistic mystery with splendid hand-carved puppets that interact with humans on a daily basis and eventually rebel against the tyrant Karabas Barbaras to determine their own destiny. The action takes place in a small Italian village on a seacoast, and Carlo, a craftsman, plays the organ in the town square and sings a lovely, haunting melody that will be heard in different variations throughout the film. At one point Duremar, a fisherman and the village fool, pesters him. The village seems idyllic and peaceful until the circus arrives in a grand parade with Karabas on top of a float. He is a huge portly man with a long black beard and sings a strident song announcing the events. The puppets are on a merry-go-round behind him. Soon after, Karabas is pictured in one of the circus wagons where he has dragged Duremar, who will serve as his accomplice throughout the film. While Karabas reveals that he has the golden key and is looking for entrance to an enormous treasure somewhere in the town, a live black poodle named Artemon overhears their conversation and runs off. (Artemon will play a key role as Buratino's helper in many of the forthcoming incidents.) The scene then shifts to the courtyard of Carlo's neighbor, a woodcutter, who is having difficulty chopping a magic log that squeaks and frightens him. Carlo arrives and is intrigued by the log that bops him on the head. Carlo has an argument with his friend, and they fight like cocks, imitated by puppet cocks. Then they make peace, and Carlo cradles the log like a baby and brings it home with him. Once in his own confines, Carlo begins to carve and speak to the log kindly until he finishes making a foot-tall boy called Buratino. The wooden boy has a pointed nose, indicating that he is born as a liar or trickster, and a cap; otherwise, he is not really dressed up. He is what he is: a wooden puppet that moves by itself and speaks with a squeaky voice. When Carlo runs to get some food, he is almost eaten by a rat until Carlo returns to save him. Buratino has had his first encounter in a "rat-eat-rat" world. Protected by a kind father, he will soon go off and learn much more about this world. Lively and curious, he is not afraid.

The scene then quickly shifts to the circus stalls and market place, and two other tiny beggar puppets, the cat and fox, are pictured trying to steal fruit from a stand. The cat is a female named Alicia, and the fox, a male named Basilio. The crowd interacts with them as though they were human, and by this time viewers of the film have come to accept all the creatures, objects, and puppets as real. That is, Ptushko, long before magic realism and following in the long footsteps of E. T. A. Hoffmann, transforms everyday realism gradually into a surrealistic space in which everything has a life of its own and is involved in social relations. As in all fairy tales, the teller/director does not endeavor to persuade the audience to suspend belief or to create a distinction between real and unreal. Ptushko's fairy-tale film is an exploration of real and unreal borders, and he wants to uncover the magic in everyday life. Like Méliès, Ptushko is a great magician, and as director, he infuses Tolstoy's screenplay, which is different from his novel, with extraordinary puppets, live animals, and humans that feel an urgent need to be free.

Unlike the film, Tolstoy's novel gives a greater role to Alicia the Cat and Basilio the Fox and does not include the comic character Duremar and the corrupt police. It ends with a grand performance by the liberated puppets, who have all abandoned Caracas's theater, and the tyrant is left sitting in a puddle. In contrast, Ptushko's film, which involves numerous episodes of conflicts with Karabas, Duremar, and the police, concludes with Buratino, Carlo, and all their friends fleeing through a secret door opened by the golden key to an underground cavern. The "treasure" in the cavern does not consist of gold and jewels as Karabas thinks; it is a gigantic storybook. Meanwhile, Karabas tries unsuccessfully to break through the secret door and ends up with his beard caught in the door. Soon he hears a commotion outside. Duremar and the police cut off his beard to free him from the door, and they rush outside to see Carlo, Buratino, and the puppets performing a play with the magic storybook serving as a backdrop. When Karabas threateningly approaches them, a schooner pictured in the book emerges and turns into a real gigantic schooner that lands in the village square. The captain of the ship, who looks like an Artic explorer, descends and invites Carlo, Buratino, the poodle, and all the puppets on board. When Karabas tries to board, the captain knocks him down into a dirty puddle. Then the schooner slowly flies off to the wonderful land of the free with all the villagers rejoicing for them and singing the lovely song that began the film.

Though Tolstoy's novel and play, written in 1935, tended to be didactic and pointed to the USSR as a kind of utopia, and though the moral education experienced by Buratino was to transform him into a good communist citizen, there is very little didacticism in the film. Buratino's qualities of curiosity, liveliness, and cunning are not tamed; instead, they are channeled more toward helping others. Moreover, he learns what oppression is and how to oppose it. He and his friends do *not* remain in their homeland, as Buratino does in the novel. They fly off to an unknown utopian land, and although some critics have commented that this utopia is associated with the USSR, the ending is much more ambivalent. We must remember that a great deal had transpired between 1935, when the novel was published, and 1939, when the film appeared.[232] The Moscow Show Trials, hundreds if not thousands of executions, greater police control, and general depression created a gloomy atmosphere in Russia, and the people were treated like the puppets in the film. To what extent Ptushko and Tolstoy, not known to be dissidents, were critiquing Stalin, who could have been likened to Karabas, and Stalinism in general, is not clear. Nor is it clear whether the Russian spectators viewed the film as a critique of conditions in the Soviet Union. Nevertheless, it is clear that Buratino grows up in a society in which corruption and oppression are rampant, and it is clear that he and his companions are glad to abandon this society in quest of greater freedom. Unlike Disney's pampered Pinocchio, who becomes a joiner, Buratino learns through hard knocks that a long nose helps one's curiosity, that obedience is *not* beneficial to his compatriots, that school is unnecessary, and that mutual respect, cooperation, and kindness are blocks of quality that build character.

In contrast to the Russian Pinocchio films, one of the first American animated films to follow Disney's film, Ray Goossens' *Pinocchio in Outer Space* (1965), did not intend to copy Disney by producing a kind of sequel. In this adaptation, which is basically an infantile story similar to many simplistic TV science-fiction cartoons for kiddies, the Blue Fairy has punished Pinocchio and transformed him back into a wooden puppet because he had returned to his old nasty habits and had become a scamp. The only way he can become human again is by doing something good. Of course, he manages to do something extraordinary by saving interplanetary travel. He joins with Nurtle the Twurtle in his spaceship, and together they capture a rogue flying whale. In the end, he returns to the earth to his weeping father Geppetto, and since he has shown that he can be a good boy, the pretty Blue Fairy flies down from her star in the skies and makes him human again.

This film, which was produced by Norm Prescott, who had inspired Disney's film, repeats the same banal message of many commercial adaptations of Collodi's novel. Despite the unusual science-fiction set, the film keeps hammering the usual didactic message: Pinocchio can only be truly good if he listens to his father and attends school. It is a very strange message because even when he is bad and is a puppet, Pinocchio does not appear to be a rebel or particularly wayward. Good actually means becoming a celebrity and saving the world. In other words, to please the fairy and his father, he must become heroic and even more of a pure goody-goody than he is. To the extent that Goossens' approach to boyhood in his film makes no endeavor to grasp where boys are at and what childhood is in the 1960s, the direction of this animated work with very mediocre line drawings is an insult to boyhood.

And perhaps one could say the same for the East German film, *The Adventures of Turli* (1967), directed by Walter Beck. The approach is slightly different from that taken by Goossens insofar as Beck used marionettes with live actors. However, the result is the same. Here an old craftsman named Kasimir receives a large log from a little boy as a gift, and he carves a puppet, which he names Arturo after his best friend, the director of a puppet show. As in the traditional Pinocchio adaptations, Kasimir wants Turli to go to school and become a good boy. And, as in the more conventional films, the marionette falls into bad company. In this case the cat and fox are played by adult actors, and since this is a "socialist" film, the villain is a businessman, who transforms delinquent children into donkeys and sells them all over the world. Turli as a boring marionette goes through the paces of being robbed by the cat and fox, almost changed into a jackass, and swallowed by a whale. In the end, a plump fairy with a child dressed in an absurd costume as poodle save the day, and Turli is changed into a human boy. The last scenes depict him in a traditional Prussian schoolroom, nice and obedient, a model for the East German regime's educational programs.

There is a strange history to this slight film. The American filmmaker Ron Merk bought the rights to this film in 1968 and dubbed and distributed it. In an interview that appeared in Kiddiematinee, he remarked:

> It did absolutely fantastic business. No one could have guessed the kinds of grosses we would see. The kiddie matinees played Saturday and Sunday, usually the early afternoon, for one or two shows. The film opened in New York, in February of 1969, in 69 theaters. The first weekend's gross was $101,000. . . . It is to this day, the most successful kiddie matinee film ever.[233]

The success may have had something to do with the popular title *Pinocchio*, which may have misled viewers to think that they were going to watch the Disney film. But I am also inclined to think that the overly didactic message and benign depiction of childhood intended for East German children was just as acceptable in the United States as it was in East Germany. Boys are led to believe that they can "glide" through childhood simply by obeying fathers, who are always kind, and by being good and attending school.

Only the Italians could rectify the misleading interpretations of Collodi's novel—and here I am not referring to Roberto Benigni's recent sentimental and disastrous 2002 adaptation, *Pinocchio*, but to Luigi Comincini's earlier 1972 film, *Le avventure di Pinocchio* (*The Adventures of Pinocchio*), which featured superb performances by Nino Manfredi and Gina Lollobrigida. However, it is not so much the marvelous acting by the entire cast that make the film one of the more interesting representations of boyhood, but Comincini's interpretation of Collodi's fairy-tale novel, the realistic sets of the film, the wry, gentle humor, and the use of animation.

Figure 70
Luigi Cominicini,
*The Adventures
of Pinocchio*

Comincini's film begins during a very hard winter that strikes an impoverished Tuscan village in the nineteenth century. The roads and streets are muddy; the buildings are somewhat dilapidated. Everyone is cold and hungry. Geppetto looks unkempt and famished. After his friend Master Cherry gives him a magical talking log that causes a funny quarrel between the two, Geppetto returns to his squalid one-room habitat and carves an unattractive puppet as his son because he is very lonely in his old age and wants company. Hanging on a bare wall in the room is a picture of his dead wife, the attractive Gina Lollobrigida, with whom he has conversations every now and then. After Geppetto has finished carving the bare-boned puppet, he dresses it with a plain linen cloth and goes to sleep. During the night, the beautiful Blue Fairy (Geppetto's dead wife) appears and transforms the puppet into a human boy. She warns him that she will re-transform him into a wooden puppet if he does not behave, go to school, and help Geppetto in his old age. She tells him that Geppetto had always wished for a son. Pinocchio promises, and the next morning, Geppetto is stunned and exceedingly happy to find a real boy instead of a puppet.

The insertion of the Blue Fairy into the narrative at the very beginning is a brilliant idea, for she will appear throughout the film to change the human Pinocchio into a wooden puppet each time the boy misbehaves. And this Pinocchio is a persistent delinquent. From the very beginning, he takes advantage of the kind Geppetto and orders him to obtain food and clothing. He even causes his arrest by the police. Pinocchio is unlikable and unruly. He is a survivor who essentially thinks more about himself than anything else. Geppetto is a patient father, willing to sacrifice everything for his son to make sure that he has a bright future. The irony of the film is that there is no guarantee Pinocchio's future will be bright because he does not fundamentally change. Nor do the conditions under which they live.

Comincini pictures Pinocchio enduring the same travails that Collodi described in his book: captured by the puppetmaster, exploited and robbed by the cat and fox, forced to work as a watchdog by a peasant, transformed into a donkey and cast into the sea, swallowed by a shark. Comincini also shows the intervention of the Blue Fairy, who constantly forgives Pinocchio in scenes that are almost like Catholic confessionals. At times she appears to be the Virgin Mary, and the film suffers from a patriarchal view of the role of the mother as mild mediator between humans and God.[234] Indeed, there is something very Catholic about this film that portrays Pinocchio as a constant "sinner" in need of constant pardon. But Comincini reminds us that Pinocchio is normal, not really a sinner. He is an illiterate peasant boy, who has very little chance of advancing in a brutal society. The shots of the Tuscan villages and countryside do not bring out their beauty but their rugged nature, and the peasants tend to be rude and crude. In the final scene, after Pinocchio and Geppetto are saved from the shark's jaws by the large tuna fish and brought to shore, Pinocchio is in rags and Geppetto is feeble and exhausted. The boy jumps along the shore, and when he spies a house in the distance, he starts running toward it while his father calls out to him to wait. With a gesture of indulgence, he hastens after his son.

If we recall, Collodi's novel ends on a sentimental note with Geppetto and Pinocchio in a cozy home. While still wooden and sick, Pinocchio is visited by the Blue Fairy in a dream and pardoned for his actions because he has learned to be good. Geppetto concludes the novel by telling him that all the good changes are his doing: "Because when children go from bad to good, they have the power of making things turn on a bright new look inside within their families too."[235] In the film, nothing is cozy from beginning to end. Pinocchio as a self-indulged boy remains spoiled and the apple of his father's eye. There is something about this indulgence that has nothing to do with boyhood in nineteenth-century Italy but more to do with late-twentieth-century attitudes towards boys, especially in Italy. The turn toward indulgence and guilty fathers marks a change in western attitudes toward children.

The majority of Pinocchio films in the 1990s and early part of the twenty-first century tend to reverse the emphasis of the novel and demonstrate that fathers must first learn to be good before their sons do. Of course, the films do this with different twists, and unfortunately most of them are too predictable and didactic despite their originality. For instance, *The Adventures of Pinocchio* (1996) directed by Steve Barron and *The New Adventures of Pinocchio* (1999) as sequel directed by Michael Anderson focus more on Geppetto's foibles as father than the good puppet Pinocchio's behavior. The common links between the two films are the screenplay writer Sherry Mills and the actors Martin Landau (Geppetto), and Udo Kier (Lorenzini). There is also an inside joke that runs between the films: the villain is the sinister puppetmaster Lorenzini, the real name of Carlo Collodi, which was a pseudonym. It is as though Lorenzini himself is ironically being accused for inventing Collodi and for wanting to "eat" and destroy little boys. In the first film, he changes three times and becomes: a puppetmaster, who exploits puppets; owner of the Valley of Fun, who turns boys into donkeys and sells them; and a monstrous whale, who eats humans. In the sequel, he returns in drag as Madame Laflamme, owner of a carnival, who delights in eating humans turned into fish and wants to become a huge success as puppetmaster by turning Geppetto and Pinocchio into puppets under his control. Though Pinocchio does make a few mistakes in both films, he is essentially a good kid, whose major fault lies in his desire to become a performer or entrepreneur. Geppetto is the one who makes major mistakes, and the conflict in both films is between the two fathers Lorenzini and Geppetto, who are implicitly accused of manipulating the boy for their own selfish interests. Both films were made in different parts of Europe, and the actors speak English with many different accents and tend to be hyperbolic. In fact, the films have many "camp" elements with Lorenzini dressed in drag and a dwarf performed by a puppet cricket. The Jim Henson's Creature Shop provided the puppetry for both films, but the unusual wooden characters could not save the films from turning into sentimental shows that turn neglectful fathers into "good" fathers.

This same message can be traced in two other twenty-first-century adaptations of *Pinocchio*: *Geppetto* (2000), directed by Tom Moore, and *Pinocchio 3000* (2004), directed by Louis Duet. Though different in approach and technique, they both could be titled "Father Wars." *Geppetto* is an American TV musical that stars Drew Cary as a helpless father, Geppetto, a lonely, single toymaker, who complains (in song, of course) that parents do not know how to treat their children. During the evening, he will be given his chance by the comic, playful Blue Fairy played by Julia Louis-Dreyfuss, who brings his puppet to life. However, Geppetto fails utterly as a father, and the film consists of a series of musical numbers in which Geppetto tries to win back the love of his puppet son and protect him from the evil puppetmaster Stromboli. In keeping with true sentimental Hollywood plots, father and son reunite, and Geppetto will live happily ever after because he has learned a lesson from his son.

The Canadian/French/Spanish animated film, *Pinocchio 3000*, appears to take an entirely different look at Collodi's fairy-tale novel and the father/father conflict by setting the story in the distant future. Yet, the result is very much the same. In this film, Scamboli, the mayor of Scamboville, wants to transform the city into the perfect stream-lined technological city without a trace of nature. He is a single father, who will do anything for his petite blonde daughter Marlene, except change his plans to dominate the city. Marlene has an "ecological" heart and dislikes the changes that her father has brought about in Scamboville. But Scamboli's real opponent is Geppetto a master computer scientist, who invents robots of all kinds and brings the robot Pinocchio to life. When he does this, Cyberina, the Blue Fairy, who is voiced by the well-known actress Whoopi Goldberg and resembles her, appears and promises to help Pinocchio become a real boy if he learns to distinguish between right and wrong. This task can certainly bewilder a young boy who is surrounded by speedy automatons, speaking doors, burly robots, and zooming spaceships. Moreover, he must learn to dance and sing pop songs and mediate between Scamboli and Geppetto. When he inadvertently helps Scamboli devise a plan to change all the children into robots because they irritate him, Pinocchio joins with the feisty Marlene to upset Scamboli's evil manouvers. In the end, the two youngsters subvert Scamboli's plans, and Scamboli is turned into a robot himself while his city becomes green again. Though the computer-animated film is slick, glitzy, and colorful, the basic theme is thin, predictable, and banal. The trend in most commercial films intended for young people and their families is to empower children through the actions of boys and girls who know better than their parents and can fix the world. Such quick-fix films that want to undo the entanglement and sterilization of life caused by their parents may be well-meaning, but they run the risk of simplifying the real dangers caused by their parents. Collodi's novel succeeded because he had a profound interest in illiterate boys raised under semi-barbaric conditions in a biased class society and he spoke to their concerns, wondering whether it was possible to become civilized in a society with little civility.

The Great Refusal: Peter Pan's Romantic Gesture

James Barrie wrote stories about Peter Pan in the 1890s and produced the play, *Peter Pan*, in 1904. He continued to doctor and revise the play, until he published the full text in 1928. Yet, there is a sense that he had wanted to provide definitive closure of the story earlier with the publication of the prose novel *Peter and Wendy* in 1911: Peter goes on living in this work while Wendy dies. And even though Wendy dies, her daughter and their daughters return to the immortal Peter. He will never be without her and her offspring, just as we are never without some version of *Peter Pan*.

The "definitive" novel is the most complicated and sophisticated of all the versions of *Peter Pan*. Although it may have been directed in part at young readers, *Peter and Wendy* is clearly a testament to Sylvia Llewellyn, the mother of the four Davies boys, whom Barrie adopted, and it was written primarily for adults. It is *not* fiction for children. There are just too many in-jokes, asides, allusions, and intrusions made with the wink of an eye for children to grasp what is fully occurring throughout the novel. Not that adult readers can entirely comprehend the meaning of Peter and Neverland, but it is apparent that the narrator of the novel is sharing his story with adults and, given his intimate knowledge of children and their world—something he tends to lord over his readers— he has made it his mission to explain children to adults:

> I don't know whether you have ever seen a map of a person's mind. Doctors sometimes draw maps of other parts of you, and your own map can become intensely interesting, but catch them trying to draw a map of a child's mind, which is not only confused, but keeps going round all the time. There are zigzag lines on it, just like your temperature on a card, and these are probably roads in the island; for the Neverland is always more or less an island with astonishing splashes of colour here and there, and coral reefs and rakish-looking craft in the offing, and savages and lonely lairs, and gnomes who are mostly tailors, and caves through which a river runs, and princes with six elder brothers, and a hut fast going to decay, and one very small old lady with a hooked nose.[236]

After commenting that each child has a Neverland which has its own unique qualities, the narrator continues:

> On the whole the Neverlands have a family resemblance, and if they stood still in a row you could say of them that they have each other's nose, and so forth. On these magic shores children at play are for ever breaching their coracles. We too have been there; we can still hear the sound of the surf, though we shall land no more.[237]

Paradoxically, it is the impossibility of conveying the fantastic experiences that Barrie himself thought possible to capture or recapture through the invention of an omniscient narrator, who takes delight in playing with his readers and imparting his vast knowledge about children. This reading experience that Barrie offers to adults is in direct contrast to the experience that he had already provided them in his drama. Whereas the play, which can be equally enjoyed by children and adults, is demonstrative and filled with action that needs no real explanation, the novel, which is difficult for young readers to enjoy and at times ponderous, is explanatory and serves as a commentary to the play, with which, Barrie had to assume, most readers were familiar and still are.

Peter and Wendy is thus an anti-fairy tale and seeks to explicate mystery where fairy tales simply display magic and mystery. It is a self-help book written by a doctoring author for those adults who have lost touch with their imagination and need to regain it through a reintroduction to children's imaginative play. It is a prosaic novel intended to rekindle the light of a possible childhood experience that the narrator wants to preserve for eternity, or at least, as long as he lives. Otherwise, he would not tell it and explain to us so many details about the figment of his conceived notion of children's imaginations.

In her brilliant analysis of the Peter Pan writings as a cultural phenomenon, Jacqueline Rose maintains that

> what Barrie's *Peter and Wendy* demonstrates too clearly for comfort is that language is not innocence (word and thing), but rather a taking of sides (one word against the other). In *Peter and Wendy*, the line between the narrator and his characters is not neat and/or invisible; it is marked out as a division, not to say opposition, or even war.[238]

Rose argues that the narrator is never sure and assumes different roles as servant, author, and child. Moreover, Barrie himself as author was trying to bring together two different strands of children's fiction that collided with one another in his novel: the adventure story for boys and the domestic and fairy story for girls. Barrie was unable to weave these strands together satisfactorily. Rather he revealed more about the impossibility of defining children and childhood than he realized.

> *Peter and Wendy* was . . . the response to a demand for a "classic," the definitive written text for children. Something definitive is, however, exactly what Barrie's text failed to provide—either inside the book (the sliding of the narrator) or outside the book (all the other, more simple, versions which were to follow).[239]

Rose's claim—that it is impossible to define children and childhood or write the definitive text about children—is truer than even she realizes, for Peter Pan as icon has shape-shifted and been shaped at various times to symbolize many different things about children just like Dorothy, Alice, and Pinocchio have been arbitrarily transformed to comment on children and how we do our best to civilize them. Nevertheless, there is one gesture that remains firm: Peter's refusal to return to civilization and lead a "normal" life in which the imagination is diminished. The debate in all sorts of art forms and media is whether this refusal is justifiable, regressive, irresponsible, neurotic, or characteristic of the author's psychological difficulties. Peter Pan has often been cited as the perfect model for *puer aeternus*, the eternal youth, who is the god of divine youth, vegetation, and resurrection in Ovid's *Metamorphoses*. Linked also to Pan and Dionysus, Peter Pan has given rise to psychological studies such as Dan Kiley's *The Peter Pan Syndrome: Men Who Have Never Grown* (1983) and Ann Yeoman's *Now or Neverland: Peter Pan and the Myth of Eternal Youth* (1998).[240] For the most part, critics have argued that it is necessary for men to leave childhood and Peter Pan behind them, while some psychiatrists like Adam Phillips argue that we never leave childhood behind us, nor should we. At one point in his important book, *The Beast in the Nursery: On Curiosity and Other Appetites*, he quotes Norman Brown's *Life Against Death*:

Our repressed desires are not just for delight, but specifically for delight in the fulfillment of the life of our own bodies. Children, at the stage of early infancy which Freud thinks critical, are unable to distinguish between their souls and their bodies; in Freudian terminology, they are their own ideal. . . . Freud of course neither advocates nor thinks possible a return to a state of innocence; he is simply saying that childhood remains man's indestructible goal.

Then Phillips comments:

Freud is not saying that we are really children, but that the sensual intensities of childhood cannot be abolished, that our ideals are transformed versions of childhood pleasures. That the values and ambitions—the representations—of the adult are an obscured picture of the passions and conflicts and curiosities of childhood. . . . Looking forward, as Brown spells out, is a paradoxical form of looking back. The future is where one retrieves the pleasures, the bodily pleasures of the past. And to be distracted from one's preoccupation as a child (and as an adult), Freud intimates, is a subtle and insidious form of humiliation.[241]

Peter Pan experienced humiliation as a baby when he was locked out of his nursery, and at the end of all the different Peter Pan works he refuses to be humiliated again. In this respect he is not a figure of regression, but a figure of protest. He does not symbolize a return to childhood. He is childhood, but a childhood that is not compromised and remains an ideal. He is content in Neverland and does not want to abandon it. In this regard, Peter and Neverland appeal to children and adults alike because, I believe, we sense how our present civilizing process continually humiliates us and tarnishes the ideals of childhood. We know deep down that to move forward in life means preserving those youthful ideals in a struggle with arbitrary and unjust social norms and passing those ideals on to our young.

The filmic adaptations of Barrie's conception of Peter, based on his play and novel, question whether it is possible or worthwhile to keep childhood and the ideals of childhood alive. Almost all follow the same plotlines of Barrie's 1904 play and 1911 novel: Peter loses his shadow in the nursery of the Darling children; he takes Wendy and her brothers to Neverland; Tinker Bell becomes jealous and almost causes Wendy's death; Wendy becomes the "mother" of the lost children; Peter rescues Tiger Lily, the Indian, from Hook and the pirates; Tinker Bell almost dies to save Peter Pan from being poisoned by Hook; Peter appeals to the world to believe in fairies so that Tinker Bell may continue to live; Peter fights and defeats Captain Hook and the pirates so that Wendy and her brothers can return home; Wendy tries to convince Peter to come and stay in the real world, but he refuses. In the novel, *Peter and Wendy*, Peter returns time and again to take Wendy's children and grandchildren to Neverland so that their imaginations and souls can be rejuvenated. He remains immortal, however, not because he is static and a symbol of infantilism, but because he represents the constant resurgence of lost ideals that refuse to be humiliated.

Most Peter Pan films consciously or subconsciously celebrate Peter's choice to remain in Neverland, but in some interpretations he is not the major protagonist, nor does his depiction necessarily represent a profound understanding of childhood. There are two threads that run through the Peter Pan filmic adaptations that show how complicated Peter Pan is as icon, and I want to trace both of them as part of a Peter Pan discourse. Here it should be noted that there are very few Peter Pan films because Walt Disney bought the rights to film *Peter Pan* from the Great Ormond Street Hospital in London as early as 1939.[242] Barrie had donated the rights to the hospital in 1928, and the hospital watched over them like a censoring hawk, just as Disney guarded its acquisition and prevented the production of other competing films. The censorship and control of rights abated somewhat in 1987 when the Peter Pan materials became part of the public domain in some countries and allowed other filmmakers to use Peter Pan materials.[243] It was not until 2008 that the hospital lost control of rights to Peter Pan products and thus could no longer act as a censor, nor could Disney.[244]

The first cinematic thread that depended on the hospital authorizing permission is a series of TV musical films based closely on Barrie's play, and they include *Peter Pan* (1960), directed by Vincent Donahue and starring Mary Martin as Peter, and *Peter Pan* (2000), directed by Glenn Casale and Gary Halvorson and starring Cathy Rigby.[245] Both films are adaptations of the same Broadway musical in which Sandy Duncan, a well-known actress, also played Peter. Numerous other leading female performers have assumed the role of Peter in a tradition that Barrie himself sponsored, but their lively acting and singing have never been able to add much depth to the play. They are essentially caricatures of Barrie's drama with the focus on tour-de-force performances and special effects. The emphasis is placed on harmony, belief in fairies, and saving the imagination. Whereas Barrie's play was not explicitly written for a children's or even family audience, the musicals cater to children. Childhood is sacred and innocent. Nothing is ever made of a young woman dressed as a young boy, and the idea that Peter as a female actress might actually develop a crush on Wendy or vice versa has always been tightly repressed on stage and in films. Indeed, there is no probing of the Peter Pan material; it is used as a vehicle for high-flying actors who always appear to be thrilled to return home to mom and dad, even if it means leaving Peter and the joys of adventure far behind them.

In contrast, the second thread that runs through the Peter Pan materials is fascinating because it is not explicit. But there is a remarkable change: Wendy becomes the focus of the camera's eye, and eroticism and romance mingle in the plot only to be mangled in endings that celebrate male benevolence and practicality. In one film, it is not Wendy, but Peter as an older man, who must recover his youth. The pertinent films in this case are: Herbert Brenon's *Peter Pan* (1924), the Disney *Peter Pan* (1953), Steven Spielberg's *Hook* (1991), and P. J. Hogan's *Peter Pan* (2003).

Though Brenon's black-and-white silent film was intended to be a grand melodrama and to celebrate America as home sweet home, it is, from a contemporary viewpoint, a hilarious comedy with dark undertones. Brenon's wife Betty played an attractive Peter, and Mary Brian played Wendy as an equally attractive teenager, who cannot keep her hands off Peter. The setting of the film is an *American* home, and the family is upper middle class, very gentile. Peter is real, not a figment of the imagination, for it is Mrs. Darling who discovers his shadow at the beginning of the film, and at the end it is Mrs. Darling who agrees to allow Peter to return every year and bring Wendy back to Neverland for a week to do spring housecleaning. Boxed between the frames of the narrative, the action consists of Wendy's efforts to have Peter reciprocate the love she feels for him, her disappointment when she is rejected, and her resignation at the end of the film. Even then, just before Peter departs from the window, she embraces and kisses him, and Peter winces and tears himself from her to fly back to Neverland. Whether the wince is connected to a refusal to admit lesbian love or a puritanical refusal to enjoy erotic love, it is difficult to say because the play has some other themes running through it.

At various times, Peter declares that he is eternal youth, joy, and a small hero like Napoleon. (How he knows about Napoleon is beyond me!) Finally, he becomes the boy who refuses to become the president of the United States. The patriotic theme is introduced a few times during the course of the play. Michael Darling, Wendy's youngest brother, warns the Lost Boys that they will be dealt with severely if they don't act like American gentlemen and treat Wendy accordingly. In the final scenes on the pirate ship the Darling brothers refuse to join the pirates because Hook declares that he will not be faithful to the stars and stripes. Wendy tells her brothers and the Lost Boys that she has a message from their real mothers who want them to die like American men. The boys respond by singing "My country 'tis of thee, sweet land of liberty." After Hook is defeated, Peter lowers the pirate flag and replaces it with the American flag. He flies them home in a ship as American captain.

Finally, after he has closed the window to prevent Wendy and her brothers from re-entering their nursery, he hears Mrs. Darling playing "Home Sweet Home" on the piano, changes his mind about blocking Wendy and her brothers from entering the nursery, and opens the window so that there can be a family reunion and celebration of America as home. But Brenon appears to contradict this theme in the very final frame when Peter declares that he does not want to grow up, turn into a man, work, and become president. Viewed today, the contradictions and Americanization of Peter Pan are comic, but they also reveal tensions and profound meanings in the Peter Pan materials that other filmmakers were also to glean and explore—but always with kid gloves and extraordinary care.

In his astute and comprehensive essay about the Disney *Peter Pan*, Donald Crafton remarks,

> The protagonist of Barrie's play was a boy who wouldn't grow up; that of Disney's film is a girl who did grow up, rather suddenly, in the space of a couple of hours of dreaming. During her allegorical fantasy she has arrived at a new erotic awareness, presumably coupled with an awareness of her sexually mature body, and she has acquired what was at that time being called an "integrated" personality, combining her mother nurturing tenderness with her father's pragmatism and awareness of temporality. Immediately upon awakening, she tells her parents that she's ready to grow up, and the cloud-ship of youthful imagination begins to vaporize. The dream is over, but not its interpretation. . . . *Peter Pan* is a work by adults which aims at instructing other adults in ways to make children more like adults. . . . Beyond these general instructions about youth, the film also yields two somewhat more veiled lessons, that menstruation is normal and part of the maturation process, and that it is good because it means the woman is ready for motherhood.[246]

Like Brenon's American *Peter Pan*, Disney's version is marked by American puritanical culture and the prudish time period in which it was produced. Crafton perceptively points out that the plot of the film is related very much to films about teenagers in the 1950s and attitudes toward menstruation. The life-like animated figures are wholesome, innocent, and fun-loving—both in the Darlings' home and in Neverland. But Wendy is showing signs of puberty, and thus, father/Hook does not want her telling stories anymore to her brothers or sleeping in the same room with them. The dream sequence that follows father's commands is a major departure from most adaptations of Barrie's Peter Pan materials: it is clearly Wendy's dream that paradoxically puts an end to all her dreams, for she recognizes that father is always right when she awakes. She must become practical and forget all about Peter Pan and Neverland. Though her father relents and does not banish her from the nursery, it is only a matter of time that she will leave it for good. It is implied that she has learned to abandon "childish nonsense."

The Disney film took a long time to be conceived and realized.[247] And though it is one of the studio's better animated productions—more concise narrative, less slapstick, more complex characterization, less glitzy scenes—it is also filled with some negative scenes such as the racist portrayal of Native Americans, and it eliminates the important appeal to the audience to believe in fairies and the imagination by having Tinker Bell save Peter from a bomb explosion—shades of the cold war and fear of the atomic bomb—and fly with him to the pirate ship to rescue Wendy and the Lost Boys. It is as if they have an important practical task to complete before Wendy can return home with the boys. The final battle scene that involves the defeat of the father is not a triumph for Wendy, for though she wins in the symbolical order of things, she loses in reality when she returns to accept the patriarchal order. Whatever erotic inclinations that were expressed in the dream are now repressed and contained. Disney's film is a film that wants to put an end to fairy tales and the imagination.

Spielberg's *Hook* is not much better. It is a convoluted film about a pirate-like father named Peter Banning, a corporate lawyer so consumed by making ruthless deals and tons of money that he neglects his wife and children and forgets he is the real Peter Pan. It is only when he takes a trip to London to celebrate the expansion of Wendy Darling's orphanage that he is compelled to remember who he is. Wendy is *the* Wendy Darling of Barrie's work. She is now old, a grandmother, and she had once helped Peter find a home in America after he had decided to leave Neverland. So, we have the Americanized Peter Pan, played by the gifted Robin Williams, returning to London to revisit Wendy, played by the talented Maggie Smith. Peter's starved-for-affection children continue to be starved in London, where they are kidnapped by the debonair Captain Hook, played by the comic Dustin Hoffman, who threatens to kill them until the feisty Tinker Bell, played by the cute Julie Roberts, bops Peter on the head and takes him back to Neverland, where he must rejuvenate, become fit, and fight Hook to claim leadership of the Lost Boys and regain the respect and love of his children. Of course, Peter does all this, and he even wins the love of Tinker Bell, but resists temptation to consummate this relationship because he is true to his good wife.

This could have been a short and succinct interesting film, but there are so many stupid jousts, unnecessary sub-plots, and sentimental scenes held together by a weak, didactic theme that the film becomes boring. The lesson we are taught is that Peter Pan must learn how to have fun in life and not devote himself to "pirating" the way that Hook does. All he needs is a dose of Neverland again, and he will become a changed man—more sensitive and humane. This is pure Hollywood melodrama and has nothing to do with Barrie's deliberation about the problematic socialization of children and troubled childhood. It has nothing to do with the exploitation and devastation of childhood by corporate America, and why children are lost and flounder. It is a "flighty" film about "fun," an American film about American adulthood in an era when ambitious rich fathers are allegedly more devoted to their careers than to their families. Consequently, poor rich kids are "fatherless," and according to Spielberg, fathers need to become true fathers by learning how to have fun in life. That is, they need to become Peter Pans or at least recognize the Peter Pan within themselves. This simplistic formula for change and the depiction of Neverland as an American theme park diminishes the figure of Peter Pan as defender of children who refuse to join the civilizing process, and who have good reasons for rejecting society, but this film never bothers to ask why nor how Peter became the arrogant lawyer he was. Perhaps, he was having too much "fun"?

Hook does not exactly fit the second thread of films that focus more on Wendy than on Peter Pan, but like the "Wendy films," it exposes some hidden themes that Barrie never addressed. In Spielberg's case, he unwittingly reveals that fun in Neverland is not a sufficient alternative for children starved for love. On the other hand, love is all that counts in the Australian director P. J. Hogan's *Peter Pan*, which was filmed in Australia and New Zealand. There are no holds barred in the romantic relationship between Wendy and Peter. From the first moment that Peter arrives in the nursery to hear Wendy tell tales about his adventures, she is stricken by love, and Peter himself apparently has greater feelings for Wendy that exceed her role as a mother for the Lost Boys. There are constant close-ups of the two teenagers bursting into puberty throughout the film. And, of course, a very sexy and sprightly Tinker Bell is driven crazy with jealousy. But she cannot stop Wendy from becoming mother to the lost children and quasi wife to Peter. At one point, after Peter frees Tiger Lily and John and Michael from the pirates, Peter and Wendy indulge themselves in a romantic fairy dance, and Wendy is so head over heels in love with Peter that she pressures Peter to confess his "true" feelings for her. However, Peter is so totally naïve about sex and his feelings that he becomes annoyed with Wendy and tells her to return home if she is not happy as mother in Neverland. Instead—in a major change—Wendy decides to co-mingle with the pirates and becomes known as Red-handed Jill, hoping to make Peter jealous. The ruse fails. Then Hook makes Wendy and the Lost Boys his prisoners. Tinker Bell drinks the poison intended for Peter, who pleads with the sleeping children, the Darlings, and the pirates to believe in fairies so that Tinker Bell will not die. Of course, she lives to join Peter in a battle on the pirate's ship. At one point, Peter almost dies

Figure 71
P. J. Hogan, *Peter Pan*

in his duel with Hook, but Wendy kisses him and revives his spirits. In the end, Wendy returns to London with her brothers, and there is a parting-is-such-sweet-sorrow scene between Peter and Wendy.

Though the acting is passable, and though the special effects (a computerized crocodile, flying characters, dancing on clouds, and mechanized fight scenes) are enjoyable, the film is overbearing in its endeavor to transform Barrie's Peter Pan materials into a Romeo and Juliet film about star-crossed lovers, in which the teenagers do not die. Since the film also wants to be a blockbuster, it chooses fluff and decoration over substance, and there cannot be a serious exploration of love between two "alienated" youngsters who thirst for a genuine relationship—at least, Wendy does, and this is a film about Wendy.

From 1990 to 2004, Régis Loisel, a French artist, produced six volumes of a graphic novel with the overall title *Peter Pan*. The action takes place in Victorian England and reads like a dark Dickensian novel. Peter is a destitute working-class boy, beaten by his alcoholic mother, who is a prostitute and casts him out on the streets in Whitechapel, where Jack the Ripper is still committing his crimes. Peter, who does not have a last name, has only one friend, the elderly Mr. Kundall, who tells him wonderful tales and knows all about Peter's past. The desperate Peter knows nothing except that he does not want to grow up in such a brutal, sordid society. He is pictured as a sad and depressed boy without much chance for happiness. At one point, a fairy named Clochette appears and takes Peter to Neverland to save the inhabitants from Capitaine Crochet and the pirates who want to steal a treasure that they think is located in Neverland. The creatures of the island are mermaids, fairies, elves, dwarfs, centaurs, and the great god Pan himself. All the creatures of the imagination have fled to Neverland because nobody believes in them anymore. It is there that Peter, who flies back and forth to London, eventually bringing friends from an orphanage with him, finds his destiny. Without realizing it, Peter has been on a journey and quest of self-discovery. He has two sides to him, morbid and hopeful, and is helped by Pan to understand the essence of nature and the wonder of the imagination. When Pan dies, Peter takes the name Pan to distinguish himself and forge a new identity. He realizes that he must defend the imagination against Crochet, but he also senses that he shares some of the same traits with the pirate. Indeed, he discovers toward the end of the series of graphic novels that Crochet is his father. To preserve his integrity and the integrity of the imagination, Peter must overcome the cynical pirate and take a new approach to life which means that he will always remain in Neverland that has aspects of a utopia.

Loisel is a brilliant graphic artist and writer. The colored images of London and Neverland are drawn with great attention to historical detail and with great innovation. The characters are all subtly individualized and shown in startling new relations to one another. There is an intelligence at work throughout the six volumes that makes it eminently clear why it is reasonable to refuse to grow up and commit oneself to be a member of an atrocious society. Peter's story is the tale of a homeless boy, whose "history" is paralleled today by millions of young boys and girls throughout the world.

I mention Loisel's graphic novels because they break the censorship of the Great Ormond Street Hospital and the Disney social code. They reveal the underside of innocence and the dark side of philanthropy. That is, Loisel rebels against corporate censors that have prevented many artists from exploring the Peter Pan materials and showing how humiliation, rage, poverty, and the abuse of children are central to Barrie's works. Loisel indicates that there is something eminently wrong in a society when self-appointed legislators of morality obfuscate the causes of immorality to which they contribute. There is something wrong when filmmakers must adhere to social codes that they do not write and make compromises with institutions that determine how artworks should be shaped.

All this is not to say that filmmakers have colluded with corporations to avoid dealing realistically and honestly with the troubles of children and the problems of childhood. After all, children and childhood have always been a significant topic in all the arts, and there have always been stark and realistic portrayals of childhood and persistent critiques about the "rightful" presentation of children. The desire to cultivate and honor children has led to an obsession with childhood that continues to take on new contours with every new generation in every society in the world. The future of civilization, so we tend to believe, depends on the "proper" way we educate and acculturate children. Consequently, imagining children in different contexts and creating images of children in films have become a "norm" in all sorts of media; the moving pictures rationalize ideological perspectives of adults bent on integrating into or excluding them from the camera's eye and the screen.

In the movie industry, there has been and will always be conflicts among filmmakers with regard to the representation of children and childhood, a topic that I discuss at length in the final chapter. Fairy-tale films have played an enormous role in portraying children's problematic existences—children from every social class, ethnicity, and creed. Aside from the filmic adaptations of fairy-tale novels that I have discussed, there are other important films that contribute to the cultural discourse about childhood such as several different versions of Astrid Lindgren's *Pippi Longstocking* (Per Gunvalll's *Pippi Longstocking*, 1949; Michael Schaack and Clive Smith's *Pippi Longstocking*, 1969; Ken Annakin's *The New Adventures of Pippi Longstocking*, 1988); Robert Stevenson's *Mary Poppins* (1964); and two adaptations of Michael Ende's works: Wolfgang Petersen's *Neverending Story* (*Die unendliche Geschichte*, 1984) and Johannes Schaaf's *Momo* (1986). They are all—and there are many more—recreations and remakes that need serious study, for they reveal that as we adapt to social and political changes, we can never hold on to the "truths" of these fairy-tale novels just as we can never hold on to the elusive truths and ideals of childhood.

14

Between Slave Language and Utopian Optimism: Neglected Fairy-Tale Films of Central and Eastern Europe

In order to position Russian cartoons between California and the Kremlin, we nonetheless have to define the relationship of mermaids, garrulous rabbits, and wizened wizards to the official aesthetic theory of the Soviet Union, socialist realism. How real, for example were tales of medieval magic and mystery? . . . All of these real (or unreal) emphases allow us to suggest that animation was so successful in mapping the huge empty domain between Marx and Disney that it in fact came to represent and promote a different type of socialist selfhood, a new type of protagonist and person. These novel heroes of Soviet cartoons were massively popular across the biggest country in the world for decades, but have garnered no scholarly attention.

David MacFadyen, *Yellow Crocodiles and Blue Oranges:*
Russian Animated Film Since World War II[248]

While it has often been observed that British audiences respond well to Czech films because of some indefinable similarity in the sense of humour, this fails to explain the much wider appeal of Czech comedy, which has become almost synonymous with the ways in which Czech cinema has been perceived.

Peter Hames, *Czech and Slovak Cinema: Theme and Tradition*[249]

Yet Czech animation has "got something," a something which has won it a good deal of acclaim. Perhaps a large part of it is Czech humor, which differs markedly from American and British humor. Czech humor is often satirical; but when it is not satirical, it tends to be whimsical, even a bit sentimental. . . . an even more basic quality is optimism which we might expect, but do often find in American counterparts.

Harriet Polt, "The Czechoslovak Animated Film"[250]

In the so-called free, democratic West we have not been totally free to view the abundant production of fairy-tale films produced in Central and Eastern Europe during the twentieth century. In fact, most western film critics and general viewers are unaware of the significant cultural role that the fairy-tale film, live-action and animation, has played in Central and Eastern European countries[251] on large and small screens. It is only within the last twenty years that these films have become more available for viewing on video tapes and DVDs and through YouTube, but we must keep in mind that millions of Central and Eastern European children and adults were and are still exposed to these films, and they have enjoyed them throughout their lives. Some of the fairy-tale works even managed to sneak out of Central and Eastern Europe to become cult films such as Václav Vorlícek's *Three Wishes for Cinderella* (1973). But most have been excluded, neglected, censored, poorly dubbed, or blocked.

The reasons for the exclusion of Central and Eastern European fairy-tale films in the West are due to World War II, the Cold War, monopoly control of distribution by western competitors, interference and censorship by the state-run movie industries in Central and Eastern Europe, different cultural tastes and priorities, and high costs of dubbing, subtitles, and film editing. There has not been a conspiracy to keep Central and Eastern European fairy-tale films from challenging or "subverting" western films. One can only shake one's head sadly and acknowledge that we have been deprived of a cultural exchange that would have enriched East and West and hope that there will now be a real free exchange and that the "new" globalization of culture will *not* lead to the domination of the fairy-tale market by American commercial interests.

It has only been recently that scholars in the UK, USA, and Germany have begun producing detailed analyses of the Central and Eastern European films produced between 1919 and the present. Several excellent studies have appeared in the last twenty years. To cite a few: Daniel Goulding, ed. *Post New Wave Cinema in the Soviet Union and Eastern Europe* (1989); Thomas Slater, ed., *Handbook of Soviet and East European Films and Filmmakers* (1993); Peter Hames, ed., *The Cinema of Central Europe* (2004); David MacFadyen, *Yellow Crocodiles and Blue Oranges: Russian Animated Film Since World War II* (2005); Mark Haltof, *Historical Dictionary of Polish Cinema* (2007); Birgit Beumers, ed. *The Cinema of Russia and the Former Soviet Union* (2007); Peter Hames, *Czech and Slovak Cinema: Theme and Tradition* (2009), and Birgit Beumers, *A History of Russian Cinema* (2009).[252] However, with the exception of MacFadyen's study, these books pay scant attention to fairy-tale films, live-action and animation, despite the fact that these films were highly innovative and extremely popular in Central and Eastern European countries throughout the twentieth century. It is only within the past decade that some western scholars such as Dieter Wiedermann, Birgit Beumers, Alexander Prokhorov, Marina Balina, and Alfrun Kliems have written informative and insightful essays about the significance of fairy-tale films in Central and Eastern Europe.[253]

Since it would be an immense, if not impossible, task to cover the remarkable production of fairy-tale films in Central and Eastern Europe from 1919 to the present, I want to focus on some examples from Russia, the former Czechoslovakia, and the former East Germany indicative of their particular endeavors to create fairy-tale films that differ from the Disney models. I have already discussed some of these works in previous chapters. Wherever I can, I shall draw parallels with fairy-tale films from other Central and Eastern European countries that are related to the works in Russia, Czechoslovakia, and East Germany.[254]

Slave Language and Subversive Images of Russian Fairy-Tale Films

Bertolt Brecht, the sly "communist" playwright and founder of the Berliner Ensemble, loved to talk about the necessity of using slave language (*Sklavensprache*) in hard times, a term used by Lenin before the October Revolution of 1918 to disguise his radical intentions.[255] This term is better known in Russia as Aesopian language. As the astute literary critic Hans Mayer explains, during Brecht's exile from Germany from 1933 to 1948, the dramatist (and other artists) had to learn a special type of writing while contending with an oppressive regime:

> making the contradictions and points of disagreement sharp and visible through a language that seemingly meant consent. However, this way was possible only when one found readers, listeners, and spectators who showed understanding and were of the same frame of mind. All of Brecht's texts composed in slave language demand this dialectical cooperation and thinking of his audience.[256]

Ironically, even after 1948 when he returned to "socialist" East Germany, Brecht had to keep using slave language. In the case of the Soviet Union, there is also a certain irony in how Lenin's slave or Aesopian language played itself out, for as Lenin took over the reins of government and began speaking more dictatorially and was followed by Stalin and his henchmen and apparatchiks, the Russians had to learn how to employ slave language and soon became linguistic and artistic masters of dissent through complicity. Dissent took many forms of subterfuge, and a genre that served writers, artists, and filmmakers well was the fairy tale because of its metaphorically ambivalent language. But even the seemingly harmless fairy tale had a difficult time in the early stages of the Soviet Union. As Marina Balina explains, the fairy tale was seen as a bourgeois corrupting force in the 1920s, and the debates about its value in the new communist state led to the 1928 book *Why We Are Against the Fairy Tale*, with contributions by many different authors.

> The genre's form and structure were perceived as "directly opposed to the task of fostering communist values," and therefore, "even if [the tale] did contain revolutionary content" (Rybnikov), it was considered "bourgeois" by its very nature. Fairy-tale features such as magic, fantasy, animism, and anthropomorphism—all devices that compose the essence of the genre—were condemned as "idealism." Just as "bourgeois" culture was supposed to have disappeared after the October Revolution, so the fairy-tale tradition should have been eliminated from the new Soviet literature.[257]

However, this viewpoint began to change in the 1930s when Maxim Gorky gave a speech at the 1934 First Soviet Writers' Congress and brought about (with the support of many other writers) the rehabilitation of folklore and fairy tales by stressing the optimism of the tales, the extraordinary qualities of the common hero, the role that the fairy tale played in struggles against oppression, and their roots in the folk.[258] With the founding of the state-run cartoon and animation studio Soyuzmultfilm in 1936, fairy-tales became a main staple of films produced for children and adults up through 1989, and in the 1970s more live-action fairy-tale films began to be produced and were widely distributed in the Soviet Union and Central Europe. Among the significant directors of animation and live-action fairy-tale films are Mikhail Tsekhanovsky (1899–1975), Valentina Brumberg (1899–1975), Zinaida Brumberg (1900–1983), Ivan Ivanov-Vano (1900–1987), Alexandr Ptushko (1900–1973), Nadezhda Kosheverova (1902–1989), Vera Tsekhanovskaia (1902–1967),Vasili Zhuravlyov (1904–), Lev Atamanov (1905–1987), Alexander Rou (1906–1973), Ivan Aksenchuk (1918–), Vladimir Bychkov (1929–), Boris Rytsarev (1930–1996), Irina Povolotskaya (1937–), Gennadi Vasilyev (1940–1999), Garri Bardin (1941–), and Yuri Norstein (1941–).

Although these directors and animators worked in different styles and used diverse methods in adapting fairy tales, there are certain common features that mark their works: 1) given the centralization of film production and the control by state authorities, the filmmakers were all familiar with each other's works; 2) they were highly aware of the cultural policies of the state and what might be censored; 3) they were well-funded from 1936 to 1989; and 4) they all were attracted to the fairy tale because the genre allowed them a certain amount of artistic and ideological freedom that live-action or documentary films, which had to follow the principles of socialist realism more closely, did not afford them.

Given the symbolical nature of fairy tales and the metaphorical images of the films that contained a great deal of ambivalence, filmmakers did not have to reveal their "true" political perspectives. In fact, many were adherents of the Communist Party, some were dissidents, and others apolitical. Soviet audiences were also free to view the films as critiques of the Soviet state, tongue-in-cheek celebrations of socialism, or exemplary uses of folklore that spoke to the needs and wishes of the Russian people. The filmmaker's disposition was always protected by the "slave" language and images of the films just as the spectator could read political conformity or deviance into the films. From a contemporary non-Russian perspective, however, there are some unusual common denominators in the fairy-tale films, universal motifs that transcend the social and political context of the times in which the films were produced: resistance to oppression, exemplary protagonists from the lower classes, pride in the folklore of the common people, and utopian optimism. These motifs were woven into the narratives of the films in innovative and conventional ways, and I want to discuss several different types of Russian fairy-tale films that represent conventional conformity and also a sophisticated use of slave language, which has not totally lost its socio-political function. (It should be noted, of course, that I have already analyzed many other Russian fairy-tale films in other chapters.)

The Stone Flower (1946)

After directing one of the first stop-motion animation films in the world, *The New Gulliver* in 1935 and the brilliant animated/live-action film, *The Golden Key*, based on Collodi's *Pinocchio* and Aleksey Tolstoy's novel in 1938, right before the outbreak of World War II, Alexandr Ptushko turned primarily to live-action films and produced an important fairy-tale film right after the war, *The Stone Flower* (1946). This film was not significant because of the artwork, although some of the color shots of the forest, the wedding celebration, and the underground caverns are stunning; it was significant because it set the political parameters in which most filmmakers would have to work during the Stalinist postwar years. The basic principles can easily be summarized: 1) If fairy tales were to be adapted and produced in the Soviet Union, they would have to be *new* kinds of fairy tales based on folklore of the people and the works of progressive writers; 2) class antagonism and oppression of the folk by wealthy if not ignorant parasites had to be depicted; 3) the protagonists had to stem from the lower classes; 4) artworks were not to be sponsored by the wealthy and shown privately, they were to be seen in public by everyone, and 5) children were to listen to the deeply rooted folk tales told by wise men and to follow the examples of the protagonists that these wise men presented.

All of these principles are embodied in the plot and action of Ptushko's film based on Pavel Bazhov's fairy tale, "The Malachite Box." Though many of the characters in the film come close to being stereotypes and caricatures, Ptushko, a remarkable director, breathed life into them just like his protagonist, the young stone carver Danilo makes his artworks come to life. In keeping with socialist pedagogical principles, Ptushko begins the film with a group of peasant children seeking out a wise but blunt old man at a campfire that serves as the frame of the film. The profound hoary storyteller proceeds to tell them the tale about Danilo, his bride Katinka, and the Mistress of the Copper Mountain that takes place in the Ural Mountains at the end of the nineteenth century, when feudal conditions prevailed. As he tells the tale, moving images unfold before the eyes of the children, and in some respects, the storyteller paints pictures that show the hard life of the peasants and factory workers on the one hand, and on the other, they also glamorize the customs of the peasants and their cooperative spirit. This is the wonderful contradiction of the film: Ptushko critiques art for art's sake and yet is carried away by his own art and imagination by filming elaborate and fantastic pastoral scenes, folk rituals with splendid costumes and song, and glistening mystical caverns.

Danilo, the hero of the film, who prefers to play his pipe in the forest, learns about familial and social responsibility when he saves his grandfather from a flogging by a landowner's overseer. Indeed, he is constantly humiliated by the wealthy landowner, who controls the region. Yet, soon Danilo manages to become the favorite apprentice of the greatest stone carver in the Ural mountains and learns to master the art of the craft. As his fame spreads, he becomes obsessed by his own art, and though he is engaged to the beautiful and sincere Katinka, he decides to abandon her on their wedding night to serve the Mistress of the Copper Mountain, an enigmatic enchantress, and become the supreme sculptor in the country. As he works in seclusion in the caverns, he realizes, however, that there is no joy to his work, and he decides to return to Katinka, who has become a sculptress in her own right, and to dedicate his art to the common people—all this with the blessing of the enchantress, who was only testing him. His union with Katinka, who is not afraid to confront the Mistress of the Copper Mountain, is like a return to Mother Russia, who is forgiving, loving, and caring.

At the end of the film, the camera returns to the campsite where a young boy tells the venerable storyteller that he wants to become just like Danilo. This pedantic point, a concession to the Soviet authorities, and a previous shot of Danilo and Katinka moving hand-in-hand toward a sunrise, come close to ruining the film that is saved by a good dose of humor running throughout the scenes and superb camerawork. Most of all, *The Stone Flower* is significant because, in its time, it raised numerous questions about the artist's responsibility to depict class antagonisms as they were, to use his or her art to benefit the people rather than exploitative landowners, and to employ fairy tales to educate the young. Ptushko may have conceded too much to Communist Party principles, but there is a certain intriguing ambivalence if one considers that Danilo's refusal to be narcissistic and to serve the ruling classes can be read as a rejection of art in the service of communist state officials.

The Frog Princess (1954), A Walnut Switch (1955), Cipollino (1961)

Whereas Ptushko introduced some ambivalence in his support of socialism, the animated fairy-tale films tended to serve the precepts of socialist realism and didactic socialist pedagogy. Mikhail and Vera Tsekhanovsky's *The Frog Princess* and Ivan Aksenchuk's *The Walnut Switch*, also known as *Witch and Switch*, are examples of the numerous conventional adaptations of fairy tales that celebrated Russian nationalism, socialist heroism, and collective action, while Dezhkin's delightful *Cipollino* reveals a deft subversive touch by celebrating a cunning boy and his friends who undermine political oppression.

The Tsekhanovskys adapted a well-known European folk tale, which has many different versions. One of the more popular ones can be found in the important collection of Alexander Afanas'ev, *Russian Fairy Tales*,[259] and is related to the beast/bridegroom tale type ATU 425A. However, they drew upon other Russian folk motifs and characters and portrayed the protagonists as true Russian heroes. In their version, Vasilissa the beautiful, who is close to nature, is kidnapped by Kaschei the immortal demon, who loves gold and destroys nature by turning it into gold and diamonds. Vasilissa is transformed into a frog because she refuses to marry him and must remain a frog three years and three days before she can regain her human shape. In the meantime, a Russian king orders his three sons to shoot their arrows to find their brides. Wherever their arrows land, they must wed the nearest maiden. The youngest son Prince Ivan's arrow lands next to Vasilissa as frog. Ashamed of her looks, Ivan must nevertheless marry her. When she proves to have magic powers that demonstrate his choice of a bride is better than that of his brothers, he no longer cares about how she looks. At one point, he burns her frog skin not realizing that it is too early in her enchantment to do this, and thus she must return to Kaschei, who transforms her into a gold statue. Ivan learns

Figure 72
Mikhail and Vera
Tsekhanovsky,
The Frog Princess

about her fate and goes on a quest to rescue her. He meets an old man, who gives him advice and then helps a bear, a wolf, an eagle, and a fish in the forest. They will later help him. Most important, he encounters the famous Russian witch Baba Yaga, who reveals how he can defeat Kaschei. In the final battle scene of the film, he is assisted by the animals, conquers the demonic Kaschei, and flies back with Vasilissa to his realm where the forests that had been turned into gold become natural once more.

Success in *The Frog Princess* can only come about through collective action as is the case in Aksenchuk's *The Walnut Switch*, which has a faint resemblance to "Hansel and Gretel." Two children, Anna and Mischa, are sent into the woods to gather mushrooms and are warned by their mother not to go near the Black Oak and to beware Griselda the witch. However, Mischa, a sweet-looking boy, is lured into the dark woods by the witch who can assume many different forms. Once she captures him, she flies back to her castle and intends to eat the boy. Anna discovers that her younger brother is lost and tries to find him. In the middle of the forest, she finds a dying tree and learns that Griselda wants to destroy the forest and take over the land. Anna kills a worm that is poisoning the tree and brings it back to life. As a reward, the tree gives her a magic wand that can make anything grow either small or big. She is also told where to find Mischa, and she sets out to rescue him. Along the way, she is helped by a crow, a gentle giant, and some mice. Anna is cunning and brave, as is Mischa. In the end, Griselda is overcome, and the brother and sister return home to their mother as if nothing much had happened in the forest.

Both *The Frog Princess* and *The Walnut Switch* reek with sweetness and are depicted as perfect models of Soviet childhood. Similar to the realistic style used by Disney, the human characters are all drawn as realistically as possible and are adorned in quaint Russian costumes. Though there is some humor in the films, the fluid narrative structure is seriously goal-oriented: 1) a greedy demon/witch captures an innocent young person; 2) a brave hero/heroine goes on a quest to save their bride/friend; 3) three or more animals/helpers provide gifts for the hero/heroine; 4) order is restored, and the admirable qualities of the hero/heroine are on display for viewers to imitate.

Cipollino, Dezhkin's short animated film, which appeared at the beginning of the 1960s, follows the same pattern but with some remarkable changes. Based on a novella by Gianni Rodari, the foremost writer of children's books in Italy during the twentieth century, who happened to be an

Italian communist, it takes a different perspective on collective action. Rodari published *Cipollino* (1951) soon after World War II, and it contained strong anti-fascist tendencies. In fact, there is an implied critique of Mussolini and his henchmen—a critique that could also apply to Stalin.

All the characters in this film are vegetables and fruit. The hero is a sprightly young onion, Cipollino, a shoeshine boy, who accidentally steps on the toe of Prince Lemon. Since he is threatened with imprisonment, despite the slight crime, his father confesses to the crime and is dragged to prison. At the same time, a working-class pumpkin builds a tiny house on Prince Lemon's property, and Signor Tomato, chief of the police, has him arrested. Both the pumpkin and old-man onion are locked up in a prison that resembles a fascist dungeon. Cipollino is informed of the arrests, and the clever boy joins with a cute radish girl and a spindly cactus, who works in Prince Lemon's garden, to free the men. The remainder of the film consists of escapes and chases in which Prince Lemon and his family consisting of two cherries as countesses and a cherry nephew are ridiculed.

Although Dezhkin stresses the theme of collective action and exemplary behavior of a young boy, his film differs from the fairy-tale films directed by the Tschanovskys and Aksenchuk in that there is a revolution not a reordering of society: the oppressors are chased from the garden village. Moreover, Dezhkin breaks with the tenets of social realism. His anthropomorphized vegetable and fruit characters are more like comic-strip characters than real plants, and the village and background images are not related to Russia. However, the political oppression can easily be associated with life in a police state similar to the Soviet Union. Slave language is clearly at work in this film.

Puss in Boots (1957)

During the 1950s, most filmmakers of fairy-tale films did not challenge Soviet policies of socialist realism even when they adapted western fairy tales written by Charles Perrault, the Brothers Grimm, and Hans Christian Andersen. Alexander Rou, one of the foremost Russian directors of fairy-tale films, provided an exemplary model with *Puss in Boots*, which was intended to be a parody of an effete and corrupt seventeenth-century French royal court, but which turned out to be a silly, infantile, and somewhat didactic film intended to amuse young audiences.

To his credit, Rou, a prolific and popular director of fairy-tale films, did not offer a literal inter-pretation of "Puss in Boots." Rather, he imaginatively recreated the context by setting the frame of the film in the present. Ljuba, a contemporary teenager, lies sick in bed, and her grandfather and doctor are anxious because she does not seem to get better. Some of her friends, who belong to the communist pioneer youth group, visit her to rehearse a play based on "Puss in Boots," and two nasty neighbors burst into the room with Ljuba's cat, angry because the animal had wandered into their apartment. They cause a commotion, and the grandfather ushers everyone from the room so that Ljuba can sleep. Of course, she dreams her own version of "Puss in Boots," filled with everyone introduced in the frame narrative; they all assume roles in her seventeenth-century baroque fantasy. Rou cleverly designs the setting as a chess castle, and the characters are chess pieces and speak in rhymed verse. He also makes major changes in the plot. Ljuba acts the role as a sick princess. Her grandfather becomes a king who offers a reward for anyone who can cure his daughter. A minister named Crivello and a lady-in-waiting named Dvulice, the neighbors, are poisoning the princess with horror tales. Vanja, the miller's son, arrives with his magic cat to cure her. However, she is kidnapped by the powerful witch, Pique Dame, who is in league with the sinister minister and lady-in-waiting. In the end, Vanja and his cat kill the witch and rescue the princess, who is to wed Vanja as a reward. The film ends with Ljuba rising with joy the next morning because she has been cured by the therapeutic dream.

The exaggerated mannerist acting and the extravagant theme-park sets are wasted in this film. The obvious message—the curing of a princess by a peasant boy who is natural and pure—becomes lost in the numerous comic scenes and special effects. While other directors successfully re-created western fairy tales in unique "socialist" ways, Rou merely went through the motions of adaptation to create a hackneyed version of a seventeenth-century tale that is much more profound than he realized.

The Tale of Time Lost (1964)

The tendency in live-action fairy tale films to draw parallels with the present can be seen in one of Ptushko's films of the 1960s. *The Tale of Time Lost*, based on a screenplay by Yevgeni Schwartz, one of the foremost writers of fairy-tale plays in the Soviet Union, takes a unique approach to transforming the traditional fairy tale into a contemporary realistic fairy-tale film. Set in a large metropolitan Russian city, the film concerns Peter, a lazy, carefree boy of about ten, who shirks responsibilities and plays hooky from school. Little does he know that four "evil" old sorcerers, two men and two women, are planning to steal wasted time from boys and girls like Peter so that they can become young again while the children become old. These sorcerers are depicted as eccentric fools, who constantly bungle their endeavors to cause trouble in the city. The entire film is cast in the mold of the comic silent films of Chaplin and Buster Keaton. Sight gags and commotion are employed throughout, and as usual, Ptushko mixes puppets and animation into the live action. Four children, including Peter, are bewitched without realizing they have become old and continue to behave as children. Meanwhile, the four mean sorcerers who have turned young begin causing trouble among school children. As an old man, Peter stumbles upon the underground hideout of the sorcerers and provides the cuckoo in the cuckoo clock with water. Due to this kindness, the cuckoo reveals the magic incantation that will help him and his friends become young again and make the sorcerers disappear. Once Peter gathers together the three other children and they race back to the clock in a comic chase scene, everything is restored to order, and a voiceover announces to young spectators about the importance of work before pleasure.

This ending turns a film that had interesting potential as a political farce—the four sorcerers could have represented secret police agents—into a didactic educational film. It is surprising because Schwartz was known to have dissident inclinations and wrote many plays and screenplays that were more subtle. Here he and Ptushko sincerely attack laziness, procrastination, and the lack of values in Russian society. But it is questionable in *The Tale of Time Lost* as to whether they are speaking in the name of the state or in the name of Aesopian artists.

How Ivanushka the Fool Traveled in Search of Wonder (1976)

Fortunately, fairy-tale films were somewhat less "educational" in the 1970s, and some of the better live-action productions were based on Russian folklore and were not overly didactic. Nadezhda Kosheverova's film is a good example of a composite adaptation of tales about Ivan or Ivanushka, who is generally the third maltreated son in a family or a simpleton, but a simpleton who is either wiser than one thinks or has more cunning than others. In Kosheverova's film, Ivanushka is portrayed as a deeply sensitive, honest, and forthright peasant, who touches the hearts of other people because of his kindness and decency. Based on motifs from different Russian folk tales, *How Ivanushka the Fool Traveled in Search of Wonder* is a tender and comic film that takes place largely in the scenic countryside and reveals how Ivanushka brings out the best in people. When Nastenaka, the charming and sincere daughter of the rich landowner Marko, falls heads over heels in love with him, Marko wants him poisoned because he thinks Ivanushka wants his money. He sends an old lady to poison him, but Ivanushka thwarts her attempt. In the meantime, Nastenaka thinks that

Ivanushka was killed and becomes so traumatized that she can no longer have feelings for anyone. Only a miracle can save her. So, Ivanushka goes on a quest and visits the bizarre witch Baba Yaga, who tells him what he must do to save Nastenaka. After many exploits, he encounters the great sorcerer Lukomor, who, after 500 years of performing miracles and magic, wants to commit suicide because he has lost faith in humanity: people use his miracles to exploit others and to seek their own profit. Yet, when he encounters the altruist Ivanushka and sees his honesty and modesty, he regains his faith in humans. Moreover, he provides Ivanushka with a magic slate that enables him to return to Nastenaka and enable her to regain her true feelings. In the end, they embrace and walk arm in arm into the fields with Ivanushka's faithful horse.

Although there are stereotypical farcical scenes that mock the landowner and a king with his retinue, and although the film glamorizes the humanity of Ivanushka, the fool, who knows he isn't a fool, *How Ivanushka the Fool Traveled in Search of Wonder* does not succumb to blatant didacticism. It is an amusing folk film, well-acted and in keeping with the messages and humor of traditional Russian tales.

Tale of Tales (1978)

Traditional is not an adjective that one can use when discussing Yuri Norstein's animated films. Long considered one of the greatest contemporary Russian animators, Norstein worked with other directors such as Ivanov-Vano on animated films during the 1960s and 1970s and produced several short, startling folk-tale films of his own such as *Fox and Rabbit* (1975), *Heron and Crane* (1975), and *Hedgehog in Fog* (1975). His major accomplishment thus far is *Tale of Tales*, which really should be titled "The Neverending Tale," for it is a fairy-tale film about the persistence of human beings and all living creatures to forge their way in a life filled with wrecks and wars. It is a wondrous film filled solely with images, music, and sounds that are seemingly not related to one another and yet recur with renewed vigor and deeper significance each time they occur.[260] They are sparked by the free association of the animator prompting viewers to appreciate signal moments of on-going struggles.

Figure 73
Yuri Norstein,
Tale of Tales

It may be misleading to "categorize" *Tale of Tales* as a fairy-tale film because it is so experimental and breaks with traditional narrative sequence. However, the images tend to include and comprehend fairy-tale motifs in such a unique way that, I believe, the film becomes a virtual fairy tale with an emphasis on relativity and metaphorical transformation: it estranges the contemporary world and transforms it into haunting nostalgic pictures that offer traces of hope for the future.

Tale of Tales begins with a voiceover Russian lullaby:

> Baby, baby, rock-a-bye
> On the edge you mustn't lie
> Or the little grey wolf will come
> And will nip you on the tum
> Tug you off into the wood
> Underneath the willow-root.

In the film, the lullaby is translated as follows:

> Lullaby, lullaby,
> Hush, little baby,
> Don't you cry,
> Or the little wolf will hear.
> The wolf is always near.
> Sleep tight, baby,
> And be good,
> Or he'll take you
> To the dark and scary woods.

Originally, the film was titled *The Little Grey Wolf*, but Norstein was compelled by the Soviet film authorities to change it because the title was allegedly too scary. This is strange since the film was not made for children. What is significant is that, despite the change, this fairy-tale film is all about a little grey wolf and the world turned upside down in Chagallian images, how the wolf manages to find a home with a baby that he snatches, and how the lullaby is subverted and transformed into a fairy tale of hope.

A good deal has been written about Norstein's scrupulous and innovative artistic techniques.[261] Norstein uses cutout figures made of small pieces of celluloid which he animates, and he works on a multiplane camera which he designed himself. In fact, he was involved in every aspect of the film—lighting, camera movements, reflections, and development of the film. Aside from choosing the music—Bach, Mozart, and tango music by Jerzy Petersburski—he collaborated on the screenplay with Ludmilla Petrushevskaya, but he improvised so much that only a fifth of the script was used. Therefore, the images of the film, largely drawn in black and brown, evoke numerous references, and the startling juxtapositions of arbitrary creatures recall paintings by surrealists, especially by Chagall. For instance, Norstein paints cutouts dancing on roofs, or a bull playing jump rope with a little girl and a penguin observing their play. He also uses photo montage in scenes with junk and dilapidated cars and a scene with a campfire.

The key character in the film is undoubtedly the wolf, who is a gentle and kind observer throughout the film and who, at the end, takes the baby, a white paper manuscript from the top of a desk that turns into a swaddled baby, runs into the forest, and seemingly protects it in a cradle while ironically singing and humming the Russian lullaby about the danger of the grey wolf. Following the scene with the wolf next to the cradle, Norstein returns to the images at the beginning of the film: a baby sucking on a mother's breast, a glittering tree and wet glistening apple and closes with images of snow, the dilapidated house, and a bridge. One hears the whistle of trains, and then tango music; the final image is that of a lamp post that dims and goes out.

Many critics have viewed Norstein's film as a series of autobiographical ruminations about his childhood, war, hardship, and survival. And certainly, the film is marked by his experiences. On the other hand, this limits the accomplishment of Norstein's work, for it is a lullaby transformed into a fairy-tale film. The tender expressions of the nurturing wolf, who looks like a little lost pup, indicate that the Russian lullaby lies and belongs to a Russian tradition that can no longer be trusted. And perhaps the Russian "family" cannot be trusted with its own children. After all, we have images of Russian soldiers drafted, sent to war to die for the fatherland, and their wives and families abandoned. We have images of waste, junk, and dilapidation. The tiny wolf experiences all this, and unlike wolves in lullabies and fairy tales, he steals the baby to save it. There is no telling what will happen. Life will go on. Tales will be told. The wolf will keep humming against lullabies and happy fairy-tale endings.

Obviously, one can interpret Norstein's *Tale of Tales* in many other ways. Historically, as an experimental animated fairy-tale film, Norstein set an example for Eastern and Central European animators that dedication to one's art and maintaining one's integrity could also serve the larger public. The metaphorical transformation of lullaby and fairy-tale motifs that explore the depths of experience in a world filled with havoc has seldom been reflected as sharply in a fairy-tale film such as *Tale of Tales*. Fortunately, it has served to encourage other Eastern and Central European filmmakers to follow his example.

The Rider on the Golden Horse (1980)

However, we must bear in mind that *Tale of Tales* was an exception, and that most of the live-action and animated fairy tales produced in the 1980s and 1990s after Norstein's accomplishment remained conventional if not banal. One brief example is sufficient to show how filmmakers complied with official directives bent on celebrating Russian heroism and nationalism. The example in this case was also produced to show Soviet multiculturalism. Vasili Zhuravlyov's *The Rider on the Golden Horse* takes place in Bashkiria now known as the Republic of Bashkortosan in the southern Urals. Two young people from different Bashkirian tribes celebrate an arranged marriage but fall deeply in love with one another. This union infuriates an evil sorcerer, who wants complete control over the region. He separates the two lovers and sends a stone monster and other ridiculous villains to create animosity between the Bashkirian tribes. In the end, the young hero, who is absurdly strong—similar to a superhero—defeats the sorcerer and a witch. The tribes are united after a spectacular battle for the sake of battle scenes that resemble some of the worst Hollywood warrior films including *Narnia* and *The Lord of the Rings*. Aside from seeking to promote understanding for Turkic people and a notion of solidarity among Soviet republics, the film glorifies the young Bashkirian hero and his comrades while stereotyping the villains and most of the villagers in traditional costumes. In general the film represents fakelore instead of folklore and is indicative of many of the fairy-tale films that dutifully painted a pretty picture of peasants while harsh Soviet policies of forced collectivization radically imposed living and working conditions that the farmers opposed. The optimism of the film is so phony and sentimental that it is hard to believe that anyone could have taken it seriously. It is a disgrace to the other more serious attempts of Russian filmmakers to understand Russian folklore through film.

Wry and Conventional Czech Fairy-Tale films

One of Brecht's famous plays, *Schweik in the Second World War* (*Schweyk im Zweiten Weltkrieg*, 1943) based on Czech writer Jaroslav Hašek's famous novel, *The Good Soldier Švejk* (1923) is about World War I and a common soldier who is always tricking his superiors while seeming to consent to their commands. Brecht's play is always cited as a superb example of the dramatist's use of slave language as a means to subvert totalitarian oppression. Indeed, Brecht may have touched upon an unusual cultural trait developed by the Czechs. As Peter Hames notes,

> *The Good Soldier Švejk* is arguably the best known of all Czech novels. Initially based on Hasek's experience of the Austrian army in 1915, its anarchistic and apparently idiotic hero was clearly a Czech making fun of his masters. Its effective use of irony and satire as a weapon was something that became "engrained in the Czech psychology and artistic imagination". ... It has been alleged that many Czechs know passages of the novel by heart but others have come to see its idiotic hero as characteristic of the stupidities of bureaucratic rule under communism.[262]

Of course, not all Czech films are light-hearted and biting subversive comedies, but comic slave language does play a major role in Czech fairy-tale films. The Czech film industry began its development in the 1920s,[263] but aside from some short animated films produced late in the 1930s and during the 1940s, there was very little interest in producing either animated or live-action fairy-tale films. However, once the industry became nationalized in 1945, film studios were established in Prague and Bratislava, and there were some strong signs of interest in animated fairy-tale films by Jiří Trnka, Karel Zeman, and many other animators and puppeteers. That interest was not encouraged when the communists took over Czechoslovakia in 1948 and socialist realism was promoted. However, the Czechs were never great believers in doctrinaire approaches to art, and during the 1950s and 1960s, Czech filmmakers continued to produce innovative animated and live-action fairy-tale films that were filled with slave language. What was essential for all filmmakers was the funding supplied by the nationalized industry that gave Czech producers and directors adequate funds that enabled them to experiment in all genres of film and led to the so-called New Wave in the 1960s. However, this wave was crushed and controlled after the suppression of the Prague Spring in 1968. Numerous filmmakers were imprisoned, left the country, or were not able to find employment. Yet, fairy-tale films continued to be produced, some in conformity to the ideology of the Communist Party and some still in resistance. Indeed, there were a fair number of subversive fairy-tale films, mainly live-action, that were produced from 1968 to 1989 because the metaphorical images and language of the fairy tales enabled the filmmakers to disguise their critiques of the state, create ambivalent messages, and convey their dissent through satire. After the Velvet Revolution in 1989, the film industry became privatized, and though fairy-tale films continue to be produced, they are dependent on the commercial interests of US, Anglo-American, and international corporations. In addition, numerous fairy-tale films are made for television or the DVD market.

Since I have already dealt with some of the major animated fairy-tale films by Trnka, Zeman, Jan Svankmajer, and Jiří Barta in previous chapters,[264] I want to discuss important live-action films by Vojtech Jasný (1925–), Borivoj Zeman (1912–1991), Oldrich Lipský (1924–1986), Juraj Herz (1934–), and Václav Vorlícek (1930–). These directors and others have produced well over fifty live-action fairy-tale films during the past sixty years. As in the Soviet Union, there has been a tendency to rediscover and adapt national folk tales, especially those written or collected by Karel Erben and Božena Nemcová, to foster the cultural heritage of the Czechs and Slovaks. In addition, Czech filmmakers have adapted many of the tales by Charles Perrault, the Brothers Grimm, and Hans Christian Andersen and have recreated them in unusual ways—always with a critical eye to history and to conditions in modern Czechoslovakia.

Schweik as Clown in Jasný's *Cassandra Cat*

One of the most innovative directors of the New Wave of the 1960s in Czechoslovakia was Vojtech Jasný,[265] and he created one of the most experimental fairy-tale films in 1963, *Cassandra Cat*, which did not see its like until Jan Svankmajer began producing his marvelous fairy-tale films in the 1980s and 1990s. He was fortunate in having the assistance of two superb screenplay writers, Jirí Brdecka and Jan Werich, and a great cast of actors including Werich (Mr. Oliva/magician), Vlastimil Vásáryova (Robert the school teacher), Jirí Sovák (school principal), and Emilia Vasáryová (Diana, circus performer). Along with a gifted crew of artists and technicians, they produced a haunting surreal and melancholic film that illuminated the frustrations and dreams of the Czech people in the postwar period.

Jasný made great use of the *doppelgänger* motif and Brecht's estrangement effect. Werich plays Mr. Oliva, the narrator of the film, and the magician in the circus troupe that enters the town and mesmerizes the townspeople. The film begins with Mr. Oliva opening a small window in a bell tower overlooking the enormous town square, and he speaks directly to the audience and warns spectators that they might not believe what they are about to see, but he asserts that everything happened as he will tell and show. He then peers through a tiny microscopic telescope at the people below him, some in the square, some in their homes, and comments that they are not who they seem to be. Of course, nor is the slippery Mr. Oliva, a master of Schweikian slave language, the person he appears to be, and we shall never know who he is.

Once Mr. Oliva finishes his commentary, the scene switches quickly to the town square where the school principal, who is also a leading taxidermist, shoots a beautiful bird that he wants for his collection. Many of the townspeople are upset by this cruel act, but he justifies his actions, claiming that he has a permit to shoot animals and that the town is famous for its taxidermy museum. In the very next scene, we are brought to the school where the principal is trying to fondle the breasts of his secretary, the school teacher Robert's wife, while Robert is teaching art to third graders and trying to free their imaginations. Mr. Oliva soon appears to pose for the children, and he tells them a fantastic story about how he fell in love with a beautiful acrobat named Diana, who had a magic cat named Mokol, who wore magic glasses and could see and bring out the true character of the

Figure 74
Vojtech Jasný,
Cassandra Cat

people around them, their deceitful and also their kind behavior. The children are captivated by the tale, and Mr. Oliva keeps them in suspense by relating how he followed Diana everywhere, but was never able to realize his love for her.

With the introduction of this tale, Jasný sets the scene for the major action of the film. Within hours a travelling circus arrives in the town square. Not only do the exquisite Diana and her spectacled cat Mokol perform that evening, but also Mr. Oliva's double, the magician, directs the pantomime shows by conjuring white figures against a black background that parody most of the well-known townspeople, who grimace and laugh uneasily, as they watch. All of a sudden, Mokol takes off his spectacles, and the audience panics when they begin to see each other in colors that the magician had painted in the form of roses: the petty people are blue; the swindlers and hypocrites, yellow; the lovers, red. Exposed, all the people begin gyrating and erupt into a bizarre modern dance that reveals all their foibles, contradictions, and desires. This amazing scene, which lasts about ten minutes, resembles an orgy, accompanied by unusual cacophonic jazz music composed by Svatopluk Havelka. During this "illumination," the innocent children observe and are shocked by their parents.

Much later that night, Mr. Oliva, who watched the bedlam from a statue above the square, takes Mokol, replaces his spectacles, and sets the cat free. At the same time, Robert, who has fallen in love with Diana, seeks her out and in several dreamlike scenes takes a boat ride with her, drinks wine by a lake, and is returned to the town with her in a hay wagon driven by Oliva. Now, however, the principal wants order restored in the town and organizes a hunting party to capture, kill, and stuff Mokol. The children find the cat first. They hesitate to bring it to the principal, but they do so when he promises to treat Mokol well. Once the children discover that he actually wants to kill and stuff the cat, they rebel, and Robert is caught in the middle because he is afraid to lose his job. However, the children have more courage than he does. They draw and paint pictures of Mokol and paste them all over the town. After they regain Mokol, they disappear with the cat. The townspeople are frantic when they cannot find their children and hold a meeting in the square where they confess their "sins" of lies and cheating. Their language resembles the false language of communist self-criticism. Nevertheless, the children are persuaded by Robert, the only sincere person in the town, to return to their parents and bring Mokol back to Diana. They had been hiding in the bell tower with Mr. Oliva and the cat. When the circus troupe departs, Robert runs after the little van but cannot catch it. As he turns around at the town gate, he sees the children running toward him and realizes that he must dedicate himself to them. The final frame is a shot of Mr. Oliva up in the bell tower. He appears to want to explain everything to the audience and comment. Then he just closes the window, and the film ends.

Jasný uses different colored lenses throughout the film so that the entire film has a kaleidoscopic effect; colors blend, separate, are shaped and lose their shapes, and the projected reality of the film is turned into a fairy tale that directs the way that actors and audience learn to see contradictions and ambivalence. The storyteller, Oliva, is the master of the narrative, and he employs ironic slave language and images to contend with "official reality." Official reality is the public sphere that is sustained by the false and manipulative behavior of the townspeople. Nobody wants to admit that the town is constrained and under the control of immoral authorities until the magic cat demonstrates how sinister and devious they are. Yet, the film is not just an exposé of the pettiness of small townspeople, it is also an wry optimistic film about hope. The children are depicted as lively, inquisitive, and creative. They sense that there is something about art that can free them and can enable them to grasp and enjoy their world. They seize the opportunity to transform their parents and the town.

Jasný was one of the first European directors to experiment with fairy-tale motifs in live-action films, and his work, anticipated by Méliès at the beginning of the twentieth century, renewed and reinvigorated the print and oral tradition of telling fairy tales to confront the illusions of social reality. The juxtapositions and jump-cut scenes, the eerie and comforting music, and the mysterious phenomena that open up inner disturbances—these are some of the elements of modern fairy-tale films that Jasný developed to illuminate the conflicts and contradictions of social life that have yet to be resolved. Despite the bitter sarcasm, that is, the sardonic critique of the unrelenting lies of petty bureaucrats, Jasný's film shows how the fairy tale can convey profound sentiments of joy even when love remains unfulfilled.

The Sentimental Optimism of Borivoj Zeman

Borivoj Zeman, brother of the remarkable animator Karel Zeman, was the most famous director of live-action fairy-tale films in the 1950s, but unlike his brother's highly experimental and unusual films, Borivoj was the master of the well-made, high kitsch, communist fairy-tale film. He directed three live-action fairy-tale films, *The Proud Princess* (1952), *Once Upon a Time, There Was a King* (1955), and *The Incredibly Sad Princess* (1968), which are all sentimental romantic versions of well-known Czech and European tales that celebrate humane qualities of the folk while indicating that inept and/or corrupt rulers can be reformed. For instance, *The Proud Princess*, which is perhaps the most popular fairy-tale film ever produced in Czechoslovakia, is based on a tale written by Nemcová and is generally categorized by folklorists as ATU 900, King Thrushbeard. Variants of this tale can be found throughout the world, and it carries with it strong sexist implications. A haughty beautiful princess refuses to wed any of the suitors who come to court her. She ridicules them by giving them insulting names. The one whom she calls Thrushbeard or Grizzly Beard decides to punish her. He disguises himself as a gardener or beggar, wins entrance into her apartments, and seduces her. Once she becomes pregnant, she is forced to travel with him to his domain. He maintains his disguise and maltreats and humiliates her along the way. Shakespeare gave this treatment a name—the taming of the shrew. In the end, when she gives birth to a baby and is fully tamed, her tormenter reveals that he is King Thrushbeard, and they will live happily ever after.

Zeman modified the plot by introducing a major figure, the vain princess's father, as a bungling king who cannot manage his kingdom or his daughter, Princess Maruska. Zeman also sweetened the tale with burlesque humor. Nor does the princess suffer much torment. The young King Miroslav, who comes to court Princess Maruska and is rejected, decides to change her ways with the help of a singing flower. He disguises himself as a gardener, and once he cures her of her mean and capricious ways, they must flee the castle because her father plays into the hands of sinister ministers. The princess continues to think that the young king is really a gardener, and while they live among the peasants, she develops respect and appreciation for the hard-working lower classes. Of course, the ministers are overthrown, and the young king and princess celebrate a grand marriage with music at the end of the film. Though well-acted, this black-and-white film is too one-dimensional in its portrayal of the transformation of the princess and idealization of the peasants. If it were not for the humor—brisk and witty depictions of the old king being deceived and his daughter tricked by the good prince—the film would have been a disaster. As it is, it foreshadows many of the romantic Hollywood fairy-tale films like *Ever After* or the conventional fairy-tale films made by Cannon or Faerie Tale Theatre. Zeman obviously thought that communism could win the hearts of the Czechs and Slavs through cheerful and wacky films that embellish fairy tales and make the aristocratic life seem ridiculous.

His other well-known film, *Once Upon a Time, There Was a King*, focuses on the antics of a plump, ignorant, and autocratic king, a widower, who has three beautiful daughters. Since he is tired of ruling his tiny kingdom, where all the courtiers echo his every word and are as pompous as he is, he decides to wed his daughters to three different princes, all fops, and to offer his kingdom to the daughter who loves him the most. He becomes despondent when his favorite daughter, Princess

Maruska, who prefers the simple life to court life, responds à la King Lear that she loves him more than salt. He commands her to leave the palace before she has a chance to explain that salt is more of a necessity for people than gold. (Indeed, salt is highly esteemed in Czech society even today.) In his fury, the king ignorantly seeks to destroy all the salt in the kingdom. Meanwhile, Maruska wanders into the forest, where she meets first a fisherman, with whom she falls in love, and second, an old herb gatherer, who is a wise sorceress and endows her with the magic power of invisibility. Most of the film focuses on the comical king with a good heart and a slow-witted brain and exposes the frivolous way he treats the peasants and everyone around him. Slapstick prevails, and in the end, not only do all three of his daughters marry peasants, but even he weds a feisty peasant widow, who had the courage to criticize the way he disparaged salt and maltreated the people in his kingdom.

The humor in this film is constituted by bizarre sarcasm, outrageous sentimentality, and blind optimism. Once again Zeman adapted a Nemcová fairy tale, "Salt over Gold" ("Sul nad zlato"), and drained it of any serious critique of the ruling classes by portraying the aristocrats as harmless buffoons. Though it is possible to infer that Zeman was being somewhat subversive by prompting viewers to draw a parallel between the communist leadership in Czechoslovakia and the foolish king and his retinue in the fairy-tale film, it seems that the film is more an apology for the communist dictatorship that supposedly has a soft heart and only needs to be reformed. In general, this sort of comic fairy-tale film also served (and still serves) as an escape and safety valve that released tension and diverted audiences that faced grim realities.

Lipský's Farces

Another director, prone to slapstick, who dabbled in fairy-tale films, was Oldrich Lipský. In 1972 he directed a children's film, *Six Bears and a Clown*, that mocked the Czech authorities. It is not exactly a fairy-tale film, but it includes many motifs from the Cockcaigne/Cuccagna tradition of folk tales—the world turned upside down. In this instance it is a school that is turned inside out. A popular clown loses his job and his live bears at a circus because of a corrupt deal between two circus directors. The children who love him and his act help him find a job as cook at their school, and once the clown arrives, there is nothing but bedlam. The principal, school inspector, custodian, and circus directors are constantly outwitted and fooled by the clown, a chimpanzee, the bears, and the children. In the end, the clown is re-installed at the circus to the children's delight. This film resembles the Marx Brothers' *Night at the Circus* and reveals Lipský's fondness for the absurd, that is, for making the world of officialdom look absurd.

His other important fairy-tale film is *Three Veterans* (1983), which was very popular in Czechoslovakia in the 1980s. And rightly so. Here he teamed with the famous actor and writer Jan Werich to create a bizarre political fairy tale about the adventures of three veterans in the aftermath of a war that takes place in Europe some time about the beginning of the twentieth century. A general steps over bodies on a ravaged battlefield and awards medals to an infantryman named Pankrac, a cook named Servac, and a cavalryman named Bimbac. Though they seem to be worn out, they ride off in a carriage and get drunk to celebrate the end of the war. Along the way they meet a beggar, also a veteran, playing an organ, and he warns them that they will become just like he is. They ignore him, and in the next scene we see them hungry and downcast at a campfire in a forest. During the evening each one of them is wakened by an elf, and each one is given a gift: a red top hat that will conjure up anything, food or objects; a small purse that supplies endless amounts of gold coins; a small harp that can produce large numbers of strong men and soldiers. The elves only ask them to provide joy for the elves and to use the gifts wisely. The three veterans transform themselves into elegant gentlemen and ride off in a carriage. However, when Bimbac, who still thinks of himself as a patriotic soldier, wants to create battle scenes in front of children on a poor peasant's field, the other two veterans become worried and decide that he needs a wife to pacify him. So, they ride off to a fly-infested tiny dilapidated kingdom, Monte Alba, where everyone carries fly swatters. Everyone is poor and corrupt, and at first they treat the foreigners (the veterans) in a friendly fashion. It is obvious that though everyone is dressed in Oriental costumes, this realm is a microcosmic representation of Czechoslovakia. Nothing works. The officials want bribes. The villagers are deceitful. The veterans are duped by the king and his beautiful daughter, Bosanna, who steals the three magic gifts. Moreover, her father wants them executed, and in a marvelous chase scene through the village, the three veterans barely escape with their lives and return to their country.

Once they have collected themselves, the veterans seek out the nose tree where the elves generally meet, and they are granted a reprieve. The elves shower them with small delicious apples that make any nose grow and small pears that return the nose to its normal shape. Then the elves transport them back to Monte Alba disguised as wizened doctors from the Orient. Once they manage to get Princess Bosanna to eat some of the apples, her nose grows so large that it turns into an enormous tube that travels throughout Central Europe up to Potsdam. Along the way it is honored as visiting royalty, while the poor woman is in torment. Her father saves her by returning the top hat, the purse, and the harp to the veterans. In turn they dash back to their country and resume their decadent life by celebrating and becoming drunk. In his happy stupor, Bimbac wants to conjure another battle with the harp, while Pankrac wants to block it. They almost start a horrendous war in front of children, but the elves fly over them as birds and prevent the calamity. That evening, they are pictured around a campfire, and the elves appear to scold them for abusing the gifts and inciting war. The next morning the three veterans are pictured with an organ next to a lake. They begin to sing a song of peace and dance. Children with joyous faces come to join them as three birds fly in a V-shape over them.

Though this anti-war fairy-tale film ends on a didactic optimistic note, it is largely a hilarious farce, extremely well-acted, which uses slave language brilliantly to poke fun at the Czech government after the disaster of 1968. Many of the people who worked on this film were known dissidents, and they relied on slapstick, in-jokes, and absurdity to portray how moth-eaten the Czech regime had become by the early 1980s. Of course, the film can be enjoyed simply as a nonsensical fairy-tale film. Nevertheless, the political overtones remain, especially with regard to patriotism and nationalism.

Some of the small touches are brilliant: the peasant border guard wants packages of Camel cigarettes as a bribe; everyone in the kingdom of Monte Alba carries a fly swatter and swats flies all the time because the spiders are not doing their job; one of the veterans disguises himself as a chimney sweep to "clean up" things, so to speak; the nose appears to be a gigantic penis envied by every country in which it appears; the king shows off ancestors that are stuffed in a hall. As Andrew Horton has written,

> *Tri veterani* is a pleasing antidote to the simplistic fairy-tales of Disney. Unlike in their American counterparts, no Czech fairy-tale would ever forget to have some bite to it and *Tri veterani* is full of sharp satire and social commentary in a way that Disney could never dare attempt. The characters have more depth; the heroes have their faults and villains are, in their own way, loveable.[266]

Herz's Fondness for Horror

Unlike Zeman and Lipský, the Slovak director Juraj Herz added horror motifs and dark features to his adaptations of fairy-tales that were tempered by irony. Herz, who survived the Ravensburg concentration camp during World War II and was plagued by the censors in Czechoslovakia, became one of the most prolific and versatile Czech/Slovak filmmakers in the postwar period.[267] He directed over thirty films for the big screen and television in many different genres including mystery, burlesque, and horror. Four were feature fairy-tale films: *Beauty and the Beast* (1978), *The Galoshes of Happiness* (1986), *The Frog King* (1990), and *The Emperor's New Clothes* (1994). Since I have already discussed three of the films in previous chapters, I want to focus here on *The Galoshes of Happiness*, which was made in Czechoslovakia just before Herz was about to emigrate to West Germany.

The film is based on Hans Christian Andersen's "The Galoshes of Fortune" (1838), which can be considered one of the first science-fiction fairy tales in European literature. It consists of time-travel episodes in which people come upon "lucky" galoshes that transport them in time and compel them to consider whether they are satisfied in their present condition. The galoshes are somewhat related to the folk motif of the seven-league boots that enable people to travel great distances in a matter of seconds. However, seven-league boots are rarely used to carry a protagonist to the past or future, as the galoshes do in Andersen's tale, which was not written for children and is one of his more successful serious interrogations of fate. It begins with two fairies dressed as maids attending their mistresses at a big party. One is called Good Fortune and the other Sorrow. It is Good Fortune's birthday, and she decides to give human beings a present of magic galoshes that will enable them to be transported to any place in seconds so that they will find happiness. However, Sorrow does not believe that the galoshes will help human beings and that they will bless the moment that they get rid of the galoshes. Several episodes follow that demonstrate how unlucky the people are when they put on the galoshes, and ironically, it is Sorrow who saves a young man from death at the end and then disappears.

While just as ironic as Andersen, Herz is more optimistic and makes major changes in the plot which ends with a young fairy giving up immortality to live with a young artistic student. He starts his film in the evening with two powerful older fairies, Sestana and Starost, meeting on the rooftops of a nineteenth-century city. They are joined by an apprentice fairy named Mina. It is the last night of Carnival, and they will be attending a masked ball in the city. When they enter the attic of a boarding house, Sestana decides to transform a pair of old boots into magic galoshes that will grant the person who wears them anything he wishes. Starost believes that the wishes and galoshes will only make the person unhappy. They make a bet about the outcome. In the meantime, the pert Mina has begun flirting with a poor student in the boarding house and would like to see him win the galoshes and happiness.

During the rest of a dark rainy night, the three fairies will be transported by an easy-going coachman to a masked ball, an opera, and a park filmed with sumptuous color. The men who accidentally come upon the galoshes are a councilman, lampman, a doctor/professor's assistant, and a police clerk. Throughout the night they will have horrific experiences—the councilman is transported back to the medieval period and almost killed for being Satan; the lampman is transformed into a gambling lieutenant with large debts and appears to be killed by a brutal, swindling captain, the assistant has a facelift and is drawn into an opera that becomes surreal; the police clerk wishes to be a bird and is turned into a parrot in the cage of some wealthy snobs who have attended the ball and the opera. Throughout the night, Mina tries her best to bestow the galoshes on the poor student whom she loves, even though she may lose her immortality if she falls completely in love with him. Finally, when he does obtain the galoshes, he is put to a riddle test by a court made up of the wealthy people who have been scorning him. When he fails to solve the third riddle, he is to be executed. However, he is saved when he guesses that the happiest place in the world is death. He is saved because the two older fairies have pity on him and revive him for Mina. In the final scene, the two fairies return to their carriages on the rooftops of the city and separate in good spirits.

It is possible to read the film autobiographically, for Herz was about to separate from Czechoslovakia while making the film, and there is a sense of trials and new beginnings throughout the film. (Incidentally, he returned to Prague several years later.) Yet, *The Galoshes of Happiness* transcends autobiography and also Andersen's tale. Herz, who disliked making political films, returns to a theme raised by Lipský's *The Three Veterans*, namely, how would you change your life if you were granted wishes by the fates or fairies? Would life be any different, and would you possibly waste the wishes? Herz adroitly exposes the empty lives of the supercilious aristocrats, officials, and military while also showing the petty manners of the middle class. He does not judge the decadent lives they lead. Rather, he embellishes and exaggerates their manners, garments, and dialogues that conceal their swindles. The fairies observe the trouble that they cause these people with glee. Of course Mina, in her youthful exuberance, is concerned by the poor student. Herz will not have her disappointed, and though he is not afraid to depict horrific dangers, he has that profound Czech zest for life. His fairy-tale film about lucky galoshes bursts with zest and is one of the better artistic films made in the 1980s.

Master Magician Vorlícek

Among the post-1948 Czech fairy-tale filmmakers, Vorlícek has been the most prolific but not the most artistic. Although he won fame as the director of the popular *Three Wishes for Cinderella* in 1973, a remarkable film, which I have discussed in the chapter on "Cinderella" films, and has produced over ten live-action fairy-tale films and two very popular TV fairy-tale series, *Arabela* (1979) and *Arabela Returns* (1993), Vorlícek tends toward commercializing fairy tales and transforming them into kitschy or glamorous soap operas. His very first film, *Saxana—The Maiden on the Broomstick* (1971) is a good example of how he banalized some fairy tales.

The film begins in a school for witches, and Saxana, a sassy but not very bright adolescent witch, who wears a red wig and sexy black dress that reveals much leg, decides to leave the realm of the witches and vampires for the human world after she is left back in school. She is followed by a janitor vamp, who is to keep an eye on her. In the human world she befriends Jan, the teenage son of a zoo director, who eventually helps her find a wench's ear, an idiomatic term for a special herb that will enable Saxana to remain among humans forever. For most of the time in this predictable film, she accidentally changes school teachers into rabbits and doctors into cows because she does not know how to use spells properly. Three revolting boys who promise to help her find a wench's ear taunt and betray her, and she turns them into teddy bears. In the end, as expected, she finds the herb, and both she and the janitor vamp remain among the humans.

Not only is the plot stupid and the acting stilted, but Vorlícek drains the magic out of this contemporary fairy tale and makes it into a grade B film, which recalls the fairy-tale films produced by Zeman and Lipský that light-heartedly satirize law and order, schools, and other social institutions. There is absolutely no subtlety in this film and some others of Vorlícek's works that drip with sentimentality. In fairness to Vorlícek he did improve his techniques after this *Saxana*, and in the Arabela TV series of 1979 and 1993, he was more creative in the manner in which he depicted the contrasts between the fairy-tale and human worlds. Both series hinge on events that turn the worlds inside out. In *Arabela*, a storyteller named Honzik Majer is kidnapped by the evil magician Rumburak and taken to the fairy-tale world, where he accidentally shoots and kills the wolf. From that point on, Little Red Riding Hood is compelled to try to eat her grandmother and the hunter. Arabela, daughter of the fairy-tale king Hyacinth, is expected to resolve the chaos caused by this event. Naturally she marries Honzik in the end. In *Arabela Returns*, Arabela and Honzik have been married ten years and are living in the human world. Rumburak wants revenge and causes the pregnant Arabela to give birth to two grandfathers instead of twin babies. In the fairy-tale realm, the magician causes a giant to devour all the fairy-tale figures he can find. Arabela and Honzik fly back and forth between the worlds to restore balance. In both series, Vorlícek cleverly raises questions about storytelling and stock characters. The comic aspects appeal to the Czech and Slovak fondness for slapstick and preposterous behavior and action. Interestingly, the second series, which is much longer than the first, reflects the massive changes that occurred in Czechoslovakia in 1979, and gave rise to the Republic of Slovakia and the Czech Republic. The dizziness of such rapid transformations is captured in the two grandfathers and the two different worlds. It is only through looking at real social conditions through the lens of bizarre fairy tales, Vorlícek seems to say, that one can step back and assess the turmoil of the 1990s. In this regard, Vorlícek shows how well he has overcome the quirks of commercializing fairy tales for contemporary audiences.

Ever since 1989, Vorlícek has made fairy-tale films with international funding and has tried to speak to a broader audience. In the process, his films have become more slick and bombastic. Nevertheless, there are many direct and indirect references to the changing conditions in the former Czechoslovakia, and he has demonstrated a great mastery of special effects.

One of his best fairy-tale films is *The Queen of the Lake* (1999), which concerns a sinister middle-aged queen, who wants to marry a young prince named Victor, so that she can unite two kingdoms and become the most powerful ruler of the world. Unfortunately for Victor, his father wants to compel his son to marry the queen because of her wealth and power. Yet, he does not know that this vicious queen, who lives in an underwater castle, has kidnapped seven younger princesses and turned them into mute ballerinas and swans so that they cannot compete for Prince Victor. She also has had children kidnapped and forces them to pluck pearls from the oysters in the nearby ocean to increase her wealth. However, one of the princesses named Odetta escapes and flies off as a swan. She is mistakenly shot from the sky by Prince Victor's servant, but fortunately she survives, and Victor falls in love with her. Meanwhile, the queen sends her unctuous counselor to recapture her and takes sadistic delight in punishing the beautiful princess. Victor goes on a quest to find her, and with the help of magic water given to him by an old man and also assistance from a kind old witch, he is able to free Odetta, the children, and the princesses. The queen is turned to stone at the edge of the lake while all the families of the princesses gather in a verdant meadow to celebrate their disenchantment.

Shot in baroque palaces and exquisite studio settings, Vorlícek's film oozes with fairy-tale motifs, characters, and atmosphere. He draws upon stories by the Grimms and Andersen in which a young maiden is either transformed into a swan or becomes mute. The princesses dance to the music of Tchaikovsky's *Swan Lake*. A friendly dwarf instructs the ballerinas and tries to help them. The old witch is an adorable cunning woman dressed in rags who swims about as a fish and seeks to rescue her old husband. A gigantic fish with frightening sharp teeth swims in an underground dungeon and devours the queen's prisoners. Amidst all the chaos, Victor's father learns that uniting his kingdom with the evil queen's realm is not a very good idea, and the match with Princess Odetta's family will be much better. If Vorlícek was thinking about the separation of the Czech and Slovak republics and the formation of new alliances in Central Europe, it is difficult to say. But it is clear from the production style of the film that Vorlícek wants to standardize the classical fairy-tale narrative to amuse audiences in the West and East.

The Rise of the DEFA Fairy-Tale Film

No sooner did World War II come to a close than explanations were urgently sought to explain why the Germans had committed atrocious, if not barbarous acts. After all Germany had always been regarded as one of the more enlightened and humanistic nations in Europe since the early nineteenth century, when the Grimms among many other great Romantic writers endeavored to unite the German principalities and bring about constitutional monarchy. Given the importance that fairy tales played in the German socialization process, particularly the Grimms' tales, it was somewhat ironic that the occupation forces, led by the British, briefly banned the publication of fairy tales in 1945.[268] According to the military authorities, the brutality in the fairy tales was partially responsible for generating attitudes that led to the acceptance of the Nazis and their monstrous crimes. Moreover, the tales allegedly gave children a false impression of the world that made them susceptible to lies and irrationalism.

The decision by the occupation forces led the Germans themselves to debate the value of fairy tales,[269] and it should be noted that the Grimms' tales were practically synonymous with the general use of the term *Märchen* (folk tale). That is, the Grimms' collection, especially during the Nazi regime, had been become identical with a German national tradition and character, as if all the Grimms' tales were "pure" German and belonged to the German cultural tradition. Therefore, unless a distinction was made in the discussions about fairy tales and folk tales after 1945, it was always understood that one meant the Grimms' tales. They ruled the realm of this genre, and thus they were also held partially responsible for what had happened during the German Reich.

Although the ban against publishing fairy tales was lifted by 1946, the discussion about their brutality and connection to Nazism continued into the early 1950s in both East and West Germany. There were two general arguments in this debate: 1) the Grimms' tales had conditioned German children to accept brutal acts and prepared them for a savage regime; 2) the tales had nothing to do with the barbarism of the Nazis; rather, the cruelty of the Nazis had to be understood in light of traditional German authoritarianism and socio-economic factors. The controversy over the Grimms' tales was never resolved, largely because the viewpoints expressed could not be documented and because very little research had been done about the effects of fairy tales on children and adults. However, the debate about the Grimms' tales set the tone for their reception in both Germanies, where there were, once upon a time, two distinctive Grimm traditions in the Federal Republic of Germany (FRG) and the German Democratic Republic (GDR).

In fact, the overall reception of the Grimms' tales in the postwar period is a complex one, and there are numerous factors that must be taken into consideration such as: 1) the customary attitude of the German people toward the Grimms' tales as part of their cultural legacy; 2) the policies of publishers and the government; 3) the use of the Grimms' tales at home and in schools, libraries and the mass media; 4) the influence of scholarly and critical works on the Grimms by academics, psychologists, and folklorists; 5) the differences in the reception of the Grimms' tales by children and adults as well as gender differences; and 6) the references to the Grimms' tales in advertisements, commercials, feature films, and cartoons.

The postwar debate about the harmful effects of the Grimms' tales was always tied in the GDR to questions about the cultural heritage. That is, once the communists solidified their power in 1949, all literature considered bourgeois was to be evaluated and appropriated in a dialectical sense to further the nation's progress toward genuine socialism and eventually communism.[270] The Grimms' tales were rather easy to appropriate since they were considered part of the oral folk tradition and thus depicted how people from the lower classes overcame oppression and fought to improve their lot. Two early scholarly works of the 1950s by Gerhard Kahlo and Waltraut Woeller[271] elaborated this position to show the folk tale's connection to the historical reality of the life experiences of the peasantry. In other words, it was argued that the Grimms' tales and other German folk tales contained positive elements of the class struggle and were part of a grand European tradition that corresponded to the internationalist aspect of communism. Moreover, the tales were considered helpful in developing the moral character of young people, also a basic educational principle in the Soviet Union and Czechoslovakia. As Anneliese Kocialek stated in her work, *Die Bedeutung des Volksmärchens für Unterricht und Erziehung in der Unterstufe der deutschen demokratischen Schule*

(*The Meaning of the Folk Tale for Instruction and Education in the Primary Grades of the German Democratic School*):

> The moral and aesthetic education of pupils through folk tales in the primary levels of the schools in the German Democratic Republic are inseparably fused with one another. The special attributes of the artistic fairy-tale forms make the children more receptive to the moral content and simultaneously provide aesthetic pleasure. The tales of our own people are superbly suited to maintain in our children a love for their homeland, and the tales of other peoples waken in them a respect for their cultural achievements.[272]

Since specific criteria for the moral and political development of the people in the GDR were stringently set by the state and party leadership, the Grimms' tales came under close scrutiny, and beginning in 1952, the early editions of the Grimms' tales all underwent revision so that they conformed to the value system of the state: racist and religious elements were eliminated; violence and brutality were diminished; moral statements were added. It was not until 1955 that the first unabridged complete edition of the Grimms' tales was published, but even after that event, the censorship and/or revision of the Grimms' tales continued. The result was a de-historization of the Grimms' tales due to an endeavor to transform them into "pure" folk tales that could be used for the moral and political elevation of the people. From 1952 to 1975 there were forty-eight different editions of the Grimms' tales published in the GDR[273] with very little criticism of the possible regressive elements in the tales and with changes based on a one-dimensional view of what a folk tale is or should be. The Grimms' tales were considered sacrosanct: perfect for the moral upbringing of children; perfect for making adults aware of the class struggle. It was, in fact, during this period that the most exceptional contributions to the Grimm legacy in East Germany began.

One of the best kept secrets of the Cold War was East Germany's production of marvelous fairy-tale films for children.[274] Fortunately, with the fall of the Berlin Wall, there are very few secrets left, and we now have access to these cinematic treasures created by DEFA (Deutsche Film Aktiengesellschaft), the state film company of the former East Germany. More than twenty-five fairy-tale films were produced from 1950 until 1989, and they emphasize the profound humanitarian aspect of the fairy tales written by the Brothers Grimm and by other writers such as Gisela von Arnim and Wilhelm Hauff, who enriched the European fairy-tale tradition with original works. In addition, DEFA adapted Mongolian, Ugurian, and Arabian fairy tales for the screen in an effort to go beyond the European tradition and introduce children to other cultures that have traditional stories about the valorous deeds of common people.

In contrast to the animation work that is popular in America, the DEFA films, which are now shown throughout Germany and have been distributed through videos and DVDs in America, use live characters in realistic settings that recall the historical background of the fairy tales. But this realism quickly becomes fantastic and magical, and the films, which vary in style because different directors made them, blend imaginative plots with messages that stimulate young viewers to think about social issues that involve greed, vanity, envy, tyranny, racism, exploitation, and hypocrisy. Incidentally, this cinematic fairy-tale project was organized before any similar project in West Germany, not to mention other western countries and the USA.

Originally the DEFA films were looked upon with a certain skepticism by the East German cultural authorities because they did not believe fairy tales were the proper means to convey and promote socialist ideas and morals. However, the filmmakers soon proved the government wrong by transforming and, in many cases, changing the tales into dramatic allegorical depictions of moral dilemmas. In many cases, the films like *The Singing Ringing Tree* (1957), *The Tinderbox* (1959), *Little Redcap* (1959), *Snow White* (1961), *Six Make their Way through the World* (1972), and *Iron Jack* (1988) stress the need for cooperation and mutual respect to defeat evil tyrants and predators. The focus in most of the fairy tales is on the little hero or the oppressed heroine so that young viewers can better identify with the protagonists. Thus, the diminutive young man in *The Brave Little Tailor* (1956), directed by Helmut Spiess, shows how a small person can use his wits to succeed in life. Here success turns out not to be defined by a royal marriage and the acquisition of money. In fact, the tailor chooses a servant as his bride after the king and his haughty daughter leave the kingdom. In *How to Marry a King* (1969), directed by Rainer Simon and based on the Grimms' "The Clever Peasant's Daughter," the young protagonist Marie also demonstrates her cunning in original ways so that she not only marries a king but also teaches him a lesson in justice. In *Who's Afraid of the Devil* (1977), directed by Egon Schlegel, a peasant boy named Jacob luckily avoids a death sentence by the king and then uses his brains to disguise himself, outsmart the devil, and then win the king's daughter for his bride. Finally, in *Gritta von Rattenzuhausebeiuns* (1985), based on a fairy tale written by Bettina and Gisela von Arnim, friends of the Brothers Grimm, a plucky young girl of thirteen prevents the overthrow of a kingdom by a ruthless governor and also helps her father, a misfit inventor, get his feet on the ground.

All the fairy-tale films are filled with learning processes that stimulate critical thinking in young viewers without being overly didactic. Two of the films, *The Blue Light* (1976), directed by Iris Gusner, and *Bearskin* (1986) directed by Walter Beck, depict how young men are mistreated by kings after they have served their countries in war. The discharged soldiers seek their revenge by making pacts with demonic characters, but they learn that friendship, kindness, and generosity are more important than revenge and money. Other characters also come to realize that greed for money can turn them into callous people. Thus, in *The Cold Heart* (1950), Peter Munk, the charcoal burner, almost loses his heart in his striving to become the richest and most powerful man in his village. Only his humility and love for his poor wife save him in the end. In *Rumpelstiltskin* (1960), directed by Christoph Engel, the king who thinks only about gold spun into straw by the miller's daughter realizes that his newborn son is more important to him than all the money in the world.

The lessons to be learned in the DEFA fairy-tale films are not overly preachy. They arise almost magically and often comically from the stories themselves that the screen writers and directors have retold and altered in innovative ways. There is practically no graphic violence in any of these films, and there is an implicit message that any human being is capable of changing for the better. All these positive ideological values, however, are often diminished by kitsch aesthetics and stereotypical characterization in many of the films. Some lack humor and the zest for joy apparent in the Czech fairy-tale films. Yet, it is difficult to generalize about the DEFA films because they changed over time, were created by different directors, and responded to political censorship with slave language.

Commenting on the rise and fall of DEFA in East Germany from 1946–1989, Detlef Kannapin has written:

> That DEFA followed no monolithic aesthetic formula is doubtless the case. It is also beyond question that the contents of DEFA films set new standards in the German cinema landscape both with their tradition of antifascist films and with the tendency to observe attentively the lives of the lower and middle strata of society. DEFA productions were also of great substance as logistical and technical undertakings. But in terms of film aesthetics I can see no specific studio style in evidence. That is, unless one tries to paste together a makeshift DEFA aesthetic out of such traits as the use in conventional films of dream sequences in the style of poetic realism, or the wordiness of rather many DEFA works, or pathos in film—which surely is inadvisable. On the other hand, it should be objectively stated that the aesthetic innovations in the 1960s were hardly able to carry over in the films of the 70s and 80s.[275]

Founded in 1945 under the auspices of the Soviet administration, DEFA's mission was to aid in the re-construction of Germany and to educate the German people in the principles of democracy and humanism. This was a laudable goal, and for the first three or so years it seemed as if those writers, artists, and filmmakers who had progressive socialist leanings might accomplish them. But the internal cultural and political battles in the Soviet zone were won by the Stalinist hard-liners, and many more liberal directors, writers and artists left East Germany during the 1950s to work elsewhere. Nevertheless, those filmmakers who remained in East Germany managed to produce remarkable films—all kinds of fiction films that dealt with the Nazi past, the struggles of the working class and peasantry, adaptations of German classics, educational documentaries, animated shorts, and so on. Special attention was paid to educating the young, and a large number of the films produced by DEFA were live-action fairy tales, numerous animated films, but not many animated fairy-tales. While Kannapin's remarks are true—there was no governing DEFA aesthetic—all the films in the former East Germany were subject to great scrutiny and censorship, and they were obliged in one way or another to abide by principles laid down by the state and Communist Party. These entailed an adherence to anti-fascism, social realism, positive depiction of workers and farmers, that is, the common people as heroes, a socialist appropriation of German history and culture, and basic support of current political policies without any criticism.

As in most of the countries in the Eastern bloc from 1945 to 1989, there were periods of thaws and relative artistic freedom, but every filmmaker worked under the pressure of censorship. Perhaps because of this pressure, and because fairy-tale films allowed relatively more freedom of expression, albeit in metaphors, than other genres, many well-known talented directors and actors gradually chose to participate in the production of live-action fairy-tale films. Consequently, the quality of the acting, music, sets, and special effects was high, even when some of the scripts were banal and didactic. Some films were made in cooperation with the Czech national film company. And like the Czechs, East German filmmakers explored the use of slave language to disguise their frustrations with and disappointment in the East German state leadership and its obsequious position vis-à-vis the Soviet Union. Since I have discussed some of the DEFA fairy-tale films above and in previous chapters, I want to examine in more detail several films that endeavored to combine "correct socialist" principles of education with aesthetic innovation.

The Inspiration of Wilhelm Hauff

During the late 1940s two highly talented directors, Paul Verhoeven (1901–1975) and Wolfgang Staudte (1906–1984), became involved in the DEFA project to develop a series of fairy-tale films, which were not at first directed primarily at children. The most successful and perhaps the most famous early film was *The Little Mook*, produced in 1954, and directed by the talented Wolfgang Staudte, who had already made a name for himself with his films *The Murderers Are Among Us* (*Die Mörder sind unter uns*, 1947) and *The Kaiser's Lackey* (*Der Untertan*, 1953). His fairy-tale film is based on "Der kleine Muck" (1825) by Wilhelm Hauff (1802–1827), and before I turn to the film and its significance, I want to say something about Hauff and his tale.

Though Hauff died at an early age, he was an extremely productive writer, especially toward the end of his life. Born in Stuttgart into a middle-class family, Hauff studied at Tübingen where he received his doctorate in theology in 1824. However, instead of becoming a minister, he began working as a private tutor and a freelance writer. During the next three years, he published three collections of fairy tales, a historical romance, six novellas, parodies, poems, and sketches and became editor of Cotta's well-known newspaper in Stuttgart, *Morgenblatt für gebildete Stände* (*Morning Newspaper for the Educated Classes*). His tales were popular in his own time and have remained fairly popular in German-speaking countries up to the present—that is, among "educated classes," and in many different forms. They have generally been associated with the Biedermeier period, and Hauff has never been considered a progressive writer but more a writer for the morally upright, and some critics have even argued that his ideological perspective is that of a philistine. Certainly, his tales have a "homey" or *gemütlich* quality to them, but Hauff was also a writer who believed in the emancipatory if not subversive quality of the fairy tale. *Little Mook* exhibits both sides of his tendentious writing, and I want to summarize the plot of his story briefly because it differs from the film's scenario.

"Little Mook" is part of a collection of tales called *Die Karawane* (*The Caravan*), which uses a frame to allow different storytellers to recount unusual tales, and this story is told by Muley, a young cheerful merchant, in the first person, who recounts the "history" of little Mook, whom he used to tease and persecute when he was a young boy living in Nicea, his home city. When the merchant's father discovers that Muley is abusing his friend Mook, a tiny misshapen man, he punishes him by spanking him twenty-five times with a stick and then telling a story about Mook's life.

We learn that Mook grew up in Nicea, the son of a poor but respected man, who was ashamed of Mook and never gave him an education. When Mook turns sixteen, his father dies, and the cold-blooded relatives send him out into the world to seek his fortune. After three days the starving Mook arrives in a city where he is taken in by an old woman named Ahazvi, who hires him to look after her cats and dogs. Since the cats play tricks on him and he falls into disfavor with the old witch, he must flee. Thanks to a dog whom he has helped, he manages to take the witch's magic slippers and magic walking stick as his wages. The slippers enable him to fly through the land to be anywhere he wishes; the magic stick leads him to uncover silver and gold. Mook flies to another city, wins a race against the royal messenger thanks to the magic slippers, and replaces him as the king's messenger. However, all the servants and officers at the court become jealous of Mook, who tries to win their friendship by giving them gold that he has discovered through his magic walking stick. Yet they become even more envious and make him seem a traitor in the king's eyes. Mook is arrested, and his slippers and walking stick are taken away from him. The king has mercy on him and banishes Mook, who later discovers some magic figs outside the city. One kind of figs produces donkey ears on a person when the figs are eaten; the other kind gets rid of them. Mook disguises himself, returns to the court, and manages to entice the king and his officers to eat the figs that produce the donkey ears. Then he enters the court as a doctor and promises to get rid of the donkey ears if he can take anything he wants from the king's treasury. Naturally he chooses the slippers and walking stick and removes the donkey ears from everyone except the king. Then he speeds away with the help of the slippers and returns to Nicea where he continues to live as a very rich but isolated and lonely man.

At the conclusion of this story, the merchant reports that he and his friends began treating Mook in a more friendly way when they discovered the truth about the strange old man.

While Hauff's major emphasis in the tale centers on intolerance and on how gold cannot buy friends, he undermines this message when he "rewards" Mook with money. Though he is lonely and mocked by the young, he obviously has connections with the older merchants in the city, for it was he who tells the merchant's father that his son and the other young people are mistreating him. But now is not the time to do a thorough analysis of Hauff's story.

Rather it is time to ask what Staudte made of Hauff's story and why. We must recall that it was 1953, the time of the workers' revolt in the DDR when Staudte began work on the film. Germany was divided and still recovering from the war. In East Germany, there were signs of the war all over. Many children were orphans or had lost a parent. Life was very hard. The people were discontented.

The film *Little Mook* was adapted by Staudte to speak to many different social and political problems in East Germany, if not the world, at that time. The changes that he made are too numerous to note, but I should like to give a skeleton outline of how he and Peter Podehl changed the plot and added many new relevant motifs than enrich and deepen the original fairy tale.

1) First of all, the frame is completely different. At the beginning of the film we see Mook, an old man with a humpback and beard, as a potter, who is sent to deliver some pots and chased by the children of the town who make fun of him and throw things at him calling him a wicked old man. He evades them and finally tricks them into entering a small house. He locks the doors and gets them to listen to his *own* story. (We must ask if is this the persecuted Jew, the Other, the dark-skinned strange old man, who can only achieve peace and tolerance through the art of storytelling.) Once the story is told—and there are several interruptions—Mook wins the sympathy, compassion, and friendship of the children, and he is carried back to work by them. (Is Mook representative of the older persecuted generation in the new German Democratic Republic? Do the rebellious children, the workers, the people, need to hear how the poor leaders of the new German Democratic Republic suffered during the war years so they will work with the older leaders?)

2) In the new Mook's story, we learn that his father was not ashamed of him and tries to get him educated. However, the father dies when Mook is about ten. Mook must flee his greedy relatives and he goes off to seek the merchant's fortune, an idea that his dead father had instilled in him.

3) Mook meets the old witch in the desert and takes the magic slippers and walking stick.

4) Mook arrives in a city ruled by a corrupt and foppish king.

5) Mook beats the royal messenger in a race and drives the noble messenger out of a job, something that Mook did not really want to do.

6) Mook is involved in helping the king's daughter in her romantic relationship with a noble prince from another kingdom. The king's daughter is being forced to marry another villainous prince.

7) This villainous prince wants to influence the king and have him declare war on the noble prince's kingdom.

8) Mook prevents the war with the help of the former royal messenger, who is unemployed.

9) Mook is framed by the evil prince and the corrupt court counselors. He is arrested; the magic slippers and stick are taken from him; he is banished from the court.

10) Mook discovers the magic figs, and with the help of the noble prince and the kind king's daughter, he returns to the court and punishes the king and counselors who grow donkey ears after eating the figs.

11) Mook regains his magic slippers and stick. The noble prince and king's daughter are united. The king regains his natural ears. The evil prince is defeated.

12) Mook goes into the desert and buries the magic stick and slipper because he realizes that they cannot bring him the merchant's fortune or any fortune for that matter. Implied is that it is only through one's *natural* qualities, talents, virtues that some modicum of happiness or fortune can be attained. The children recognize Mook's valor and integrity and form a new "community" with him.

Both ideologically and aesthetically, this film is exemplary in the DEFA production of fairy-tale films. Some general points to consider are: 1) No matter what the final results were, the production teams reworked the fairy tales very carefully and creatively so that they would become appropriate for a socialist humanist heritage and to contribute to the debate about *Kulturerbe* (cultural legacy). Who was to inherit and continue the legacy of the humanities in a divided Germany? 2) The use of real-life characters mixed with artificial sets and magic tricks was a risk that the directors took that was hotly debated. Sometimes the unusual designs and staging were effective—much along the lines of the Brecht's estrangement effect. Sometimes they were kitschy and had an unintended comical effect. When effective, the use of real-life characters enabled the directors to engender a greater range of personalities and deepen the emotional impact of the films. 3) *Little Mook* set a standard in almost all the DEFA films by seeking to convey the perspective of the little person, the oppressed, the exploited, versus the corrupt court, ogres, or greedy materialist people. The "socialist" optimism of the DEFA fairy-tale films and their metaphorical style have a utopian appeal that is in sharp contrast to the socialist realism favored for a long time in the German Democratic Republic.

The Strange Forewarning

One of the last fairy-tale films made before the fall of the wall in 1989, *Iron Hans* (1988), directed by Karl Heinz Lotz, is fascinating because it is an unusual anticipation of the collapse of the totalitarian regime in East Germany and was filled with all sorts of contradictions. It is also a good example of the final phase of the DEFA, Russian, and Czech fairy-tale films, which depended on state funding for a certain freedom while also conforming to state ideology.

In the Grimms' 1850 version of "Iron Hans," there is a king whose forest is inhabited by some mysterious creature who kills all who enter it. For many years nobody ventures into the forest until a stranger arrives and disenchants the forest by capturing a wild man who had been dwelling in a deep pool. This man was as brown as rusty iron—hence his name—and his hair hung over his face down to his knees. The king has the wild man placed in an iron cage in the castle courtyard, gives the key to the cage to the queen, and forbids anyone to open it under the penalty of death. However, one day the king's eight-year-old son loses his golden ball, and it bounces into the cage. So, the wild man tells him that the only way he can regain his ball is by stealing the key from under his mother's pillow and opening the cage. When the boy finally frees the wild man, he is so terrified of his father's wrath that he asks the wild man to take him along. So the wild man carries the boy to a golden spring in the forest and tells him that he must not allow anything to fall into it, otherwise the water will become polluted. The boy's finger, which had gotten stuck while he was freeing the wild man, begins to hurt, and he dips it into the spring. The finger turns to gold as does his hair after the wild man gives him two more chances. Therefore, the boy must leave the forest. However, at this point the wild man reveals his name to the boy and tells him that whenever he needs something, he is to return to the forest and cry out "Iron Hans." The prince covers his golden hair with a little cap and eventually obtains a job as a gardener's helper at another king's castle. One day, while working in the garden, he takes off his cap, and the king's daughter notices his golden hair from her window. She invites him to her room and rewards him for bringing flowers to her. Soon after this, with the help of Iron Hans, who gives him a magnificent steed and knights, the boy helps the king win a war. Disguised in armor, he leads a troop of knights into battle and then disappears quickly, returning the stallion and knights to Iron Hans to resume working as the simple gardener's helper. In order to discover the strange knight's identity, the king holds a tournament. The princess throws out a golden apple three days in a row, and the disguised prince, helped by Iron Hans, who gives him red, white, and black armors and horses, rides off with the prize each time. However, on the third day, the king's men give pursuit and manage to wound him and catch a glimpse of his golden hair, before he escapes. The next day, the princess asks her father to summon the gardener's helper, and she reveals his golden hair. Consequently, he produces the golden apples to show that he was indeed the true hero of the tournament. As a reward, the young man asks to marry the princess, and on the wedding day, his mother and father attend and are filled with joy. During the celebration, Iron Hans suddenly appears, embraces the bridegroom, and says, "I am Iron Hans and was turned into a wild man by a magic spell. But you released me from the spell, and now all the treasures that I possess shall be yours."[276]

In contrast to the Grimms' tale, which has deep roots in a vast European oral tradition, Lotz's film takes great liberties in his adaptation to re-create the tale and clearly and implicitly refer to the contemporary situation in East Germany and Europe. The film begins with a voiceover announcing that once upon a time people lived in harmony with nature, but that this harmony had been destroyed. Immediately thereafter, the film projects images of two different kingdoms: one led by a barbaric king who wantonly kills animals and destroys nature; the other ruled by a wealthy frivolous and pompous monarch, who shirks responsibilities and passes the day by playing infantile games. Since the barbarian king wants free rein in the forest to hunt and kill as he pleases, he sends the Black Hunter to capture Iron Hans, who is the protector of nature. Once he is imprisoned, the king announces that anyone who frees him will be condemned to death. His son Joachim is revolted by his tyrannical father, and consequently he steals the key to the prison from the drunken father, liberates Iron Hans, and flees with him into the forest. Once there, he undergoes an apprenticeship but fails when he accidentally dips his hand into a crystal spring. As punishment, he must leave pristine nature and wear a cap to cover his golden hair. Despite the punishment, Iron Hans promises to help him when he is in need. Iron Hans finds his way to the frivolous king's castle, and with the help of some kind peasants, he finds a job in the royal kitchen. While working, he encounters Princess Ulrike, and they fall in love. Like Prince Joachim, she is critical of her father's ways. Just as their love is about to flourish, the barbarian king sends the Black Hunter to arrange a marriage for him with Princess Ulrike, but she rejects the offer. War is declared, and Prince Joachim must defeat the Black Hunter in the forest to save Ulrike and her father's king. He does this with the help of Iron Hans, who endows him with a golden armor and sword. Once Prince Joachim is victorious, there is a carnavalesque wedding celebration in the heart of the forest.

The plot summary of Lotz's film might make it seem to be just another conventional fairy-tale film. To a certain extent this is true, but the acting and the sets are extremely well done and raise it above the conventional. The barbaric ruler and his knights are appropriately demented, crude, and dangerous; the frivolous king and his followers are suitably foppish and ludicrous. The castles resemble rough medieval worn-down buildings while the restored forest is mysterious and glistening. Typically, Lotz portrays the peasants as kind and robust, connected to nature. What makes this film interesting is Lotz's obvious ecological perspective, for the East German government was not known for its "green" policies, and industry in the German Democratic Republic caused a great deal of pollution. Though Lotz defends nature and the peasant way of life throughout the film, his jump-cut contrasts of the two kingdoms and the final reconciliation, which results in the marriage of Prince Joachim and Princess Ulrike, do not provide an alternative or solution to the problems raised in the film. For instance, neither king is overthrown or killed. Princess Ulrike had at one time declared that she would never marry a cook's assistant, only a prince. Neither she nor Prince Joachim are admirable figures, and if it had not been for Iron Hans, they would not have been successful in preventing Ulrike's marriage to Joachim's father. Both kingdoms, perhaps symbolic of East Germany and the Soviet Union, or East and West Germany, appear forlorn but are declared to be worth saving.

Of course, it may be misleading to read too much ideology and contemporary politics into this fairy-tale film, and yet, the film itself had to subscribe to ideological policies, and no director in East Germany—and in all the counties of the Soviet Bloc—could make a film without thinking somewhat about politics. Clearly, Lotz employed a heavy dose of slave language in the making of *Iron Hans*, but it is not evident what he was subverting or whether he really subverted anything in the making of his fairy-tale film. Today, most of the DEFA fairy-tale films are harmless, but, in my opinion, they along with fairy-tale films from all the Eastern and Central European countries deserve to be recovered and analyzed not as important relics of history but as part of the cultural tradition of the fairy tale in which slave language plays a role that should not be minimalized.

15

Fairy-Tale Films in Dark Times:
Breaking Molds, Seeing the World Anew

The twentieth century began with an explosion and expansion of wars that have continued into the twenty-first century. Endless wars, big and small, on every continent. These wars bring immense darkness with them. Of course, there have always been conflicts and wars ever since humans began creating weapons, whether to survive or to exercise power for domination. But as civilization has "progressed," the wars have become more brutal and barbarian and the effects of efficient weapons and tactics, greater. There is practically no way to prevent these wars, even though most people would prefer not to experience them. Resistance seems almost futile, and if there is recourse, it appears that our only hope is to record and contest war mongers through narratives of many different kinds. To spread tales of resistance. For instance, some time after World War II ended, the great Italian writer Gianni Rodari, who always wrote against the grain, produced a wonderful tale for children called "The War of the Bells":

> Once upon a time there was a war, a great and terrible war that caused many soldiers on both sides to die. We defended our territory, while our enemy fought for their land. We fired on them day and night, and they fired back. But the war was so long that at a certain point we ran out of steel for the missiles and metal for the bayonets and other weapons.
>
> Our commander, the four-star general Bombardi, ordered all the church bells of the country to be taken down from the steeples and to be smelted so that he could build an enormous missile, just one, but large enough to win the war with one single blow.
>
> In order to erect this missile we needed one hundred thousand cranes, and to transport it to the front lines, we needed ninety-seven trains. General Bombardi rubbed his hands with glee and said, "When my missile is fired, our enemies will be blown to smithereens."
>
> Finally the grand moment arrived. The missile was pointed at the enemy, and we filled our ears with cotton because the thunderous roar might burst our ear drums.
>
> General Bombardi ordered, "Fire!"
>
> A soldier pushed a button. And all at once, from one end of the front to the other, a gigantic chiming could be heard:
>
> "*Ding! Dong! Dell!*"
>
> We took the cotton out of our ears so that we could hear better.

"*Ding! Dong! Dell!*" the missile sounded. And a hundred thousand echoes could be heard repeatedly throughout the valleys and mountains.

"*Ding! Dong! Dell!*"

"Fire!" screamed the general a second time. "Fire, damn it!"

The soldier pushed the button another time, and again a joyful concert of bells spread from trench to trench. It seemed that all the bells of our country were chiming. General Bombardi began pulling his hair in rage and continued to pull his hair until there was only one left on his head.

Then there was a moment of silence. And soon, from the other side of the front, came a delightful deafening answer: "*Ding! Dong! Dell!*"

Why this noise? Well, I must tell you that General Nix, the commander of the enemy forces, had also come up with the idea of building an enormous missile with all the church bells of his country.

"*Ding! Dong!*" our missile chimed.

"*Dell!*" responded our enemy's missile. And the soldiers from the two armies leapt from the trenches, ran toward one another, danced and cried out, "The bells, the bells! It's a holiday! Peace! Peace has finally come!"

General Bombardi and General Nix threw up their hands, jumped into their cars, and drove far away. They used up all their gas, but the chimes of the bells are still ringing in their ears even today.[277]

Fairy tales have never shied away from wars and have posed questions about abusive power, injustice, and exploitation. Fairy-tale films, the very best of them, are concerned with profound human struggles and seek to provide a glimpse of light and hope despite the darkness that surrounds their very creation and production. At the very basis of all fairy-tale films is the urge to provide and shed light on conflicts that keep tearing at our souls, not to mention tearing up bodies. The worst of fairy-tale films belong to the society of the spectacle and generate illusions that divert us from what we need most: a bit of illumination and hope. Illumination about the causes of our conflicts, hope that we may enjoy epiphanies that deepen the meaning of our lives. Indeed, the best of fairy-tale films are, in my opinion, all about illumination and hope.

Most books end with some sort of conclusion. Justly so. But I would prefer to end with a beginning—with hope that this book will help initiate more thorough explorations of fairy-tale films that are worth being conserved and woven into the global culture of the humanities. Of course, there is no reason to insist on privileging fairy-tale films in the conflicts of the culture industry except to say that they have been paradoxically excluded from mainstream film and cultural studies while they have probably attracted more audiences than any other film genre. Or, perhaps I should say in keeping with the ideological argument of my book, the vital fairy-tale films have been obfuscated by the banal Disney films and their imitators. The time has come, I think, to view fairy-tale films with another lens and to look for what we have missed in the evolution of fairy tales to recapture traces of hope.

So I close with glimmers of alternatives and new possibilities—with glimpses at several fairy-tale films that I believe have offered illumination and hope at the end of the twentieth century and beginning of the twenty-first century, films with artistic integrity and provocative views about reshaping our world by recreating fairy tales, films that touch our deep need for genuine resilient storytelling, films that ignite imaginative and critical thinking.

The Princess Bride (1987)

If any fairy-tale film burst with unabashed joy onto cinema screens in the latter part of the twentieth century and entranced large audiences and soon became a cult film, it is *The Princess Bride* directed by Carl Reiner and written by William Goldman. Unpretentious and unspectacular, this film is a gentle spoof on true love that turns conventional fairy-tale characters and motifs inside out and is more serious than it seems. There are two kinds of true love in this fairy tale, the love between a grandfather and his grandson, and the love between a farm girl named Buttercup and a farm boy named Westley. And perhaps one could also mention a third love—between friends.

The first love sets the frame of the film. A young boy of about ten, who lives in Chicago—he wears a Chicago Bears sweatshirt and has a Chicago cubs pennant on a wall—is sick in bed. His mother tells him that his grandfather has come to visit him. But the boy would prefer to play with a computer game in bed because, he says, his grandfather will pinch his cheek and bore him. His mother protests, but the grandfather enters and immediately pinches his check with affection and unwraps a present—a book of fairy tales. The grandson is not too pleased. However, the grandfather promises that he will read him a story that has pirates and adventure. The mother leaves, and the grandfather begins to tell a tale about Buttercup and Westley and how they fall in love. The scene shifts from the bedroom to the farm in the hills of some distant country. When Buttercup and Westley kiss, the grandson interrupts the tale and asks his grandfather whether this is a kissing book. It is obvious that the boy dislikes anything to do with love and kissing. The grandfather urges the grandson to be patient and promises that there will be adventures, for Westley, a poor farm boy, wants to depart and seek his fortune before he consummates his love for Buttercup.

At various points throughout the film, the grandson will interrupt and comment on the story, and as he does, he becomes more immersed in it. As he becomes immersed, the audience becomes detached and participates in the grandfather's ruse as narrator, for it is clear that he is improvising and telling a modern mixture of classical tales with a strong dose of Jewish irony. In fact, this is also a film about the use of fairy tales and storytelling in films. The telling of a mock fairy tale is a dialogue intended to cure a sick boy, to provide him with a sense of true love, to incite his curiosity, and to open him up to strange experiences. The filmic narrative succeeds because its message about true love is comically sincere and transparent. It is also a dialogue with the audience, prompted by the storyteller to see through false spectacles and gain a sense about what is genuine.

Reiner benefits from superb matter-of-fact acting. Every ironic line is spoken with conviction. Hyperbole and embellishment are kept to a minimum. Westley ships off for five years and is supposedly killed by the pirate Roberts. In the meantime, Buttercup is in despair and eventually decides to marry Prince Humperdinck, who really wants to kill her to start a war with a neighboring country. Instead of introducing three fairy-tale helpers to assist her, Reiner introduces three scoundrels, the mastermind Vizzini, the swordsman Inigo Montoya, and the giant Fezzik, who kidnap her. However, Westley disguised as a pirate enters the scene and frees her, only to be captured by Humperdinck. Not only is Westley imprisoned, but he is tortured to death. However, thanks to two of the men, whom he had defeated, Montoya and Fezzik, he is taken to the goofy wizard, Miracle Max, who gives Westley a potion that restores him to life. In the end, Westley, though handicapped by the potion that makes him sluggish, and his friends are victorious. Montoya kills the sinister Count Rugen, who has killed his father, while Westley ties up Humperdinck and lets him live to suffer a guilty conscience. Fezzik provides four white horses for the three heroes plus Buttercup to ride off into the sunset, where Buttercup and Westley kiss. The film ends with the grandson remarking that he would not mind hearing another tale like this the next day, even if there is kissing.

Interestingly, there is no marriage or glistening castle in the clouds at the end of this fairy-tale film. And there is no sequel. Throughout the film, Reiner uses fairy-tale motifs, topoi, and functions

Figure 75
Carl Reiner,
The Princess Bride

to inform the audience that everything is made up—everything except the simple sentiments of true love and friendship. The grandfather's calm tongue-in-cheek voice engenders the comic images of the film that tease the viewer and ridicule the violence and mindless celebrations of royalty in conventional fairy-tale films. The dangerous places such as "the cliffs of insanity," "the fireswamp," and "the pit of despair" are parodies of grade-B horror films, and Miracle Max and his loony wife are slapstick characterizations of wizards and witches just as Humperdinck proves to be more a pompous conniver than a cruel and cunning prince.

It has always been difficult to narrate a fairy tale about true love and depict it on film without falling prey to exaggerated sentiments, bombastic scenes in tangled forests and luxurious palaces, glorious ceremonies, and spectacular happy endings that announce the resolution of conflict forever. Many filmmakers have tried to imitate *The Princess Bride* with varying success. For instance, Andy Tennant retold "Cinderella" in *Ever After* (1998) with a certain charming irony, and Matthew Vaughn's *Stardust* (2007), based on a novel by Neil Gaiman, created a film with a strong comic flare that prevented the love story from falling flat and turning into a banal narrative. But neither film succeeded in matching the subtle and subdued gentle narrative of true love in *The Princess Bride*, which calls for endless storytelling of hope and illumination.

Little Otik (2000)

Jan Svankmajer's scintillating fairy-tale film, *Little Otik*, has nothing to do with hope but a great deal to do with illumination. It is perhaps the most perfect film to initiate viewers into the bizarre happenings of the twenty-first century. Not only is it a dark comedy about how the Czechs stumbled into global capitalism that may swallow them alive, but the film digs deep into Czech folklore and transforms a delightful fairy tale into a harrowing filmic critique of voracious consumerism that can be best grasped and fully enjoyed as parody, filled with what Germans might call "gallows humor."

Svankmajer's film is based on the great Czech folklorist Karel Erben's folk tale "The Wooden Baby,"[278] published in 1865. Erben (1811–1870) collected and wrote fairy tales to waken an interest in Czech culture and foster pride in the Czech language and history. "The Wooden Baby" is a short tale about poor peasants, a nameless man and wife, who live on the edge of a village and yearn to have a baby despite their poverty. One day the husband digs up a tree stump shaped like a baby. He trims it until it looks just like a real baby. Then he brings it home and presents it to his wife, who sings a lullaby that apparently gives life to the wooden stump. The woman is overcome with joy, but the baby wants food and vast amounts of it. In fact, the baby turns out to be insatiable and soon eats his "mother" and "father." And the more he devours, the more voracious he becomes. Soon he eats the dairymaid, a wheelbarrow, a peasant with his cart of hay, a swineherd with his pigs, and a shepherd with his sheep. Gigantic, the baby moves into a field of cabbages where he begins digging up the plants. An old woman warns him to stop destroying her cabbages, and when he tries to eat her as well, she strikes him with her hoe and slits open his stomach. Out pop all the people, animals and articles that the now dead baby had swallowed, and the peasant couple never again wishes for a child.

This ironic fairy tale, one that comments subversively on the many stories in which a childless couple is either rewarded with a beautiful baby or a bestial baby that later turns out to be a marvelous individual, attracted the attention of Svankmajer's wife Eva, who had illustrated the story for a children's book publisher and also wanted to make it into an animated film. In an interview with Peter Hames, Svankmajer stated that he stole the story from his wife because he realized that it concerned a highly significant topic—the Faust myth, which is a rebellion against nature and its tragic consequences. The Czech title of *Little Otik* is *Otesánek*, and Svankmajer explains why he chose it:

> The word "Otesánek" itself is a blend consisting of the word to hew (a tree, a stump, a beam) and the diminutive noun-ending "ánek". It's used mostly with words characterising features usually associated with children, like "usmrkánek" (snotty brat) and "mazánek" (mummy's darling). Figuratively, the word "otesánek" is used in Czech to characterise a person who devours and digests everything (not only food).[279]

Indeed, Svankmajer's *Little Otik* is a film about consumption and consumerism on many different levels. It is about a tree stump turned into a baby that devours his parents; it is an inverse if not perverse interpretation of the Cronos myth; it subverts Carlo Collodi's *Pinocchio* by depicting how it is impossible for a piece of wood, that is, a piece of nature, to be tamed and civilized; it is about unrestrained consumerism in post-1989 Czechoslovakia in which consumption is related to cannibalism and barbarianism. Svankmajer has a genial ability as animator and live-action filmmaker to see the grotesque in everyday objects and habits and is able to transform a simple Czech fairy tale into a metaphorical parable that touches, I believe, on how Czech society was made somewhat monstrous after 1989. Moreover, he is able to draw abundant parallels from the microcosmic quakes in Czech society to a dark macrocosmic earthquake that has shaken the world. The absurd behavior of ordinary people becomes extraordinary, and the only sane perspective in the film is that of a little girl about ten, who observes and comprehends what is transpiring while reading the fairy tale "The Wooden Baby" and interpreting the colorful pictures designed by Eva Svankmajer.

Using stop-motion and three-dimensional animation combined with live action, Svankmajer focuses so closely on everyday objects with the camera that reality becomes fantasy and reveals the horrific and bizarre aspects of daily relations. For instance, the film begins with images of a nude baby in different positions and squealing as the credits are flashed on the screen. The baby's large open mouth and the breasts of the mother are shown in close-ups. Once the credits are finished, a beautiful pregnant woman dressed in lush red is shown standing in a doctor's waiting room. Immediately, the camera's gaze is associated with the spectacled gaze of Karel Horak, a man in his early thirties, who is also waiting, along with pregnant women, for his wife to exit the doctor's office. He turns to an open window and looks down onto an open fish market where women are standing in line to purchase fish. The seller scoops a baby out of a water tank with a net, weighs it on a scale, and wraps it in newspaper for a customer. All of a sudden, Karel sees himself at the end of the line, waiting to procure a baby. But the door to the doctor's office opens, and he turns to see his wife,

Bozena, dressed in white, with tears in her eyes. He tries to comfort her as the woman in red watches from a distance. The nurse calls out, "Next!" and the scene quickly switches to a dismal apartment building in an old section of Prague. There is no elevator in this building, and the shoddy staircase and gloomy interior of the building will often be the center of action. A young girl of ten named Alzbetka (Elizabeth) plays with a ball that bounces down the stairs onto the street. She rushes to fetch it and is almost hit by the car driven by Karel. Alzbetka glares at Karel, and as the couple get out of the car, Alzbetka keeps glaring with suspicion. Once they enter the building, she puts the ball beneath her blouse as though she were pregnant.

The scene jumps to a ghastly image of mushy unappetizing soup on the lunch table in Alzbetka's apartment. It looks like dirty swamp water. Her mother, Mrs. Stádlerová, serves her. Her gruff father Frantisek, dressed in a bathrobe, is reading a sports paper. Alzbetka studies a book on sexual dysfunction that she tries to keep away from her father's prying eyes. Her father slaps her for talking about babies insisting that she is too young to know about birth and sex. Crying, Alzbetka leaves the table and complains that she is the only child in the building and wants a friend because she is very possessive. Once in her room, she watches an old woman, who is hoeing in her cabbage patch in the courtyard. Soon after Alzbetka encounters a creepy old pedophile on the stairs, imagines that his fly opens by itself, and reports him to the old woman, who refuses to believe that the man is dangerous. Indeed, he isn't, but danger lurks in this building.

This beginning, a real ordinary day in the life and times of Alzbetka, is portrayed close up as if under a microscope so that we see its surrealistic warts. Typical of magic realism that also recalls the unusual, fairy-tale narrative techniques of E. T. A. Hoffmann up through Kafka, Svankmajer's camera reveals the grotesque features of common people and objects; their uniqueness and also ghastly qualities are recorded by the camera. There is no separation between reality and fantasy. The relations are filled with tension and suspicion. Everyone seems to be spying on someone else.

Karel proceeds to purchase a small cabin in the woods next to the cabin owned by Frantisek, and from this point onward, the old Czech fairy tale takes a firmer grip on reality. Karel pulls out a tree stump from the ground and then carves it into a spindly wooden baby to amuse his wife. However, Bozena is not amused. Instead, she becomes obsessed by the wooden baby, calls it Otik, begins

Figure 76
Jan Svankmajer,
Little Otik

dressing it in baby clothes, and nurses it. Despite the protests of her husband, she pretends to the neighbors to have given birth to a real baby after she has spent a long time in the country. In Prague, she manages to convince most people, except Alzbetka, that the wooden baby is a live baby. She continues to nurture it so much that it does come alive, and from that point on, Otik develops a huge appetite and swallows a postman, social worker, the pedophile, and several other people including Karel and Bozena—all with the help and collaboration of Alzbetka, who hides Otik in the basement of the building.

Unknown to her parents, Alzbetka has read the fairy tale of "The Wooden Baby" and knows and understands the baby's appetite. She also knows that the old woman who owns the cabbage patch may kill Otik and tries to keep him from devouring her cabbages. In the end, however, she fails. Poor Otik will be beaten to death by the old woman. It is almost as if this robust elderly woman represents the old Czech culture that rises up against the voracity of the new generation.

Jan Uhde has remarked,

> Like Norstein, Svankmajer, oblivious to trends and fashions rejects modern animation techniques and technologies. He remains outside the computer animation world, preferring plain, common materials: paper, stone, wood, clay metal, fabric. He is attracted by articles of everyday use, found objects, dolls, figurines and puppets as well as products of the early industrial age: simple mechanisms and devices and early automata manufactured from elemental materials, which to him suggest originality, ingenuity and accomplished crafts-manship—today's *objets d'art*. In more ways than one, the Czech animator is on the opposite end of the spectrum of most of the hi-tech animation dream factories of North America.[280]

In *Little Otik* Svankmajer has created one of his most macabre puppets, a wooden gigantic child with arms and legs like roots and tentacles that swallows tons of food and people alive. Otik's voice resembles the gurgles a baby makes when hungry. The food on Alzbetka's table comes alive, and the figures in the fairy-tale book jump off the page. The constant close-ups of all the people focus on their mouths and lips, and it seems that they continually want to swallow something or some one. Throughout all the misadventures, Alzbetka plays the role of a detective seeking to disclose the secret of Bozana and Karel and to protect the live wooden baby, her only friend, for she is indeed possessive.

In "Dream Works," Marina Warner notes that "though Svankmajer can express himself in many media, the private dreamworld opened up by the screen has become for him a perfect space for improvised play. Like the surrealists—Svankmajer belongs to the last vigorous strand of that movement—he often adopts the viewpoint of a child to re-enchant experience."[281] And he certainly does so in this film. However, she also maintains that he frequently does this to deal with abuse of power. Here the end of the film is frighteningly ambivalent, for Alzbetka, who is constantly abused by her father and isolated in the apartment building, is seeking to save a monstrous wooden baby that has killed innocent people. Yet, we must also remember it is a wooden baby that did not ask to be brought to life, a baby that has no control over its natural voracious appetite. Svankmajer seems to be saying that we had better be careful for what we wish for, for we may be devoured by our own wishes if we are not prepared for the consequences and not prepared to nurture the young in an age of rampant consumerism.

Pan's Labyrinth (2006)

At the very beginning of Guillermo del Toro's disturbing fairy-tale film, *Pan's Labyrinth*, better known in Spanish as *El Laberinto del Fauno* (2006),[282] a pregnant young woman named Carmen is traveling with her eleven-year-old daughter Ofelia in a Bentley limousine. They are being driven through a verdant forest to be with Carmen's fascist husband, Captain Vidal, who is rounding up and killing the last of the guerillas in northern Spain. It is 1944, and the Franco regime has been firmly established. But there are still pockets of resistance in the countryside that the fascists need to "cleanse" and control. At one point during the trip, Carmen takes the book that Ofelia is reading in the limousine and remarks, "Fairy tales? You're too old to be filling your head with such nonsense." Later on, after their arrival at the fascist encampment, Ofelia asks Mercedes, the intrepid maid, who is clandestinely helping the desperate guerillas in the woods, whether she believes in fairies, and Mercedes replies: "No. But when I was a little girl, I did. I believed in a lot of things that I don't believe anymore." Then, toward the end of the film, right before her mother dies, she warns Ofelia, "As you get older, you'll see that life isn't like your fairy tales. The world is a cruel place." She moves to a fireplace carrying a magic mandrake that Ofelia had used to save her pregnant mother and unborn baby brother. "You'll learn that," she says, "even if it hurts." All at once she throws the mandrake into the fire. Ofelia screams "Noooo!" Her mother scolds her: "Ofelia! Magic does not exist! Not for you, me, or anyone else!" The mandrake writhes and squeals in the flames. The mother doubles over in pain and will soon die. Without magic, Ofelia cannot save her mother, and it is questionable whether she can save herself.

These three scenes are crucial for understanding how del Toro uses the fairy tale in *Pan's Labyrinth* to offset and comment on the lurid experiences of innocent people struggling to survive in the dark times of the Franco regime. As we know from history, their resistance to the fascists was noble but futile. Eventually, however, the Spaniards emerged from darkness in the 1980s to appreciate those wondrous essential elements of life that are often unseen and neglected. Like the flower on the tree at the end of del Toro's film, hope was reborn for a short period. But today, we live in dark times once again, even the liberated Spaniards. Fascism has returned in new and ugly forms throughout the world. Perhaps we may emerge from all the wars, torture, lies, arrogance, and sadism one day as the Spaniards managed to do in the 1980s. But will fairy tales help us? Did fairy tales help the anti-fascists in Spain? Can fairy tales provide light and optimism? What good is it to read fairy tales or even view fairy-tale films in times of darkness?

These are some of the questions, I think, that del Toro asks in a chilling film that does not mince words nor delude us about the cruelty in our world. Del Toro wants to penetrate the spectacle of society that glorifies and conceals the pathology and corruption of people in power. He wants us to see life as it is, and he is concerned about how we use our eyes to attain clear vision and recognition. Paradoxically it is the fairy tale—and in this case, the fairy-tale film—that offers a corrective and more "realistic" vision of the world in contrast to the diversionary and myopic manner in which many people see reality.

There is another very early scene in *Pan's Labyrinth* that is a good example of del Toro's emphasis on developing sight and insight through the imagination. Right before Ofelia and her mother arrive at the encampment of the fascists at an old mill, the pregnant Carmen becomes nauseous. The limousine stops. They get out of the car. Carmen throws up. Ofelia walks into the woods and discovers a stone eye that belongs to an old pagan statue. As she re-inserts the eye into the statue's socket, a fairy disguised as a praying mantis appears on top of the statue's head. Ofelia sees it and recognizes it as a fairy. From that point on, this vision, which is really an imaginary projection, changes her life. In fact, she has *real* double vision, unique visionary powers that enable her to see two worlds at the same time, and we watch as she tries to navigate through two worlds, trying to use the characters, symbols, and signs of her imaginary world to survive in a social world destitute of dreams and filled with merciless brutality and viciousness. Tragically, she cannot reconcile these worlds.

Del Toro moves us back and forth between the two worlds with a focus mainly on Ofelia's struggle for reconciliation between the horrors she sees the fascists perpetuate on the local peasants and the arduous tasks of her own fairy-tale world. Though del Toro has conceived his film as telling one complete story with two plots that are inextricable, it is necessary to sort the plots to understand the nature of his unusual fairy tale.

One plot level is simple and recalls all those popular war films about resistance to fascism and tyranny. Carmen has married Captain Vidal, seemingly a pathological brute, but no different from many ordinary fascists who kill people as they please. She had formerly been married to a modest tailor who had been killed. Though beautiful and kind, Carmen has become nothing but a show piece and vessel for Vidal's unborn baby—who he insists will be a son—and now he has summoned her to the forest because he believes a newborn son should be with his father so he can mold the child according to his vision of Spanish manhood. Ofelia, the tailor's daughter, detests her mother's husband and refuses to call him "father." Once she and her mother arrive, Ofelia quickly grasps not only their desperate situation but also the hardships of the peasants and the guerillas. She perceives how Mercedes is collaborating with the village doctor to assist the guerillas, who are the last resistance to fascism. As Ofelia tries to find a way to help her mother and unborn brother, the rebels seek different ways to defeat the fascists. Vidal responds by depriving the peasants, torturing prisoners, and murdering suspicious people. He also sequesters Carmen so that his unborn son will be protected. At one point, he viciously tortures one of the captured guerillas and calls the doctor to keep the prisoner alive. But the doctor disobeys him and ends the young man's misery. In revenge, Vidal kills the doctor, leaving no hope for Carmen, who dies while giving birth to a son. Ofelia tries to save her brother during the guerilla attack on the fascists, but she is trapped by Vidal, who shoots her. After he takes his son, he is captured by the guerillas, and just before he is shot, Mercedes tells him that his name will be wiped from his son's memory.

The second plot involves primarily Ofelia. Her life consists of a series of traumatic events, and she resorts to interpreting them and seeing them as part of a *real* fairy tale. This second plot is introduced to us at the beginning of the film as the actual frame "story," and it is somewhat confusing because Del Toro begins with Ofelia's "miraculous death" while Mercedes hums a lullaby. In fact, Ofelia actually revives to transcend the brutal world without anyone realizing this. The first frame is described in the screenplay written by Del Toro as follows:

> Ext. Labyrinth—Night
> In the foreground, Ofelia—11 years old, skin white as snow, ruby lips and ebony hair—is sprawled on the ground.
> A thick ribbon of blood runs from her nose.
> But—the blood is *flowing backward* into her nostril. Drop by drop, the blood leaps up and disappears.
> Ofelia's pupils dilate—[283]

This brief scene is extremely important for several reasons. Del Toro associates Ofelia with Snow White, a persecuted heroine, who finds refuge with the seven dwarfs in the forest. Ironically, del Toro's Snow White will *not* find refuge in a large lodge in which the atmosphere is gothic and sinister. Instead of living happily with the seven dwarfs as protectors, she will be menaced by the cruel Captain Vidal and be killed by him. However, this first scene reveals that she is alive after her death, and the rest of the film will explain why her blood returns to her and fills her with life.

The fairy tale frames the realistic story about the end of the Spanish Civil War. According to the male voiceover, who narrates the tale and returns at the end of the film to conclude it, and the images that follow the scene of Ofelia returning to life, a princess called Moanna escapes from the underworld to the human world above ground. She forgets who she is in the bright world and suffers from cold, sickness, and pain. She eventually dies. However, the father, the king, knows that she will return in another body, in another place, and at another time, and so he waits. It is apparent in the next few frames that Ofelia is reading this tale or dreaming it as she sits with her mother in the Bentley. Whatever the case may be, she *wills* herself into this tale, and for all intents and purposes, it is she who appropriates the tale and creates it so that she can deal with forces (her mother, Vidal, the end of the Civil War) impinging on her life. What happens in her fairy tale is what provides her with the courage to oppose the real cruelty of monstrous people.

Ofelia sets herself three tasks in her fairy tale that are assigned to her by a mysterious faun, whom she meets in an ancient labyrinth near the lodge. The immense and weird-looking faun, ancient and sphinx-like, is clearly ambiguous as a "trustworthy" creature; he appears to be kind and gentle sometimes and mean and menacing at other times. He is the messenger of the king of the underworld and gives Ofelia tasks to complete one by one. In order for Ofelia to prove to him that she is the true Princess Moanna, who has died and been reborn and is destined to return to the wonderful underworld, she must first obtain a key from a venomous toad and save a tree from dying. Then she must obtain a dagger from an eyeless and hideous monster, who eats children and fairies. Finally, the faun demands that she sacrifice her brother in the labyrinth. After her first encounter with the faun, Ofelia becomes convinced that she is truly the Princess Moanna, and once she receives a blank book from the faun, she fills it with her imaginings. Whatever she experiences in her imagination forms the essence of her strength and courage. It is the fairy tale that enables her to develop the courage to face the darkness of her times.

When Ofelia dies, the blank magic book reveals an image of Ofelia at the magnificent court of the Underworld. Her father the king sits on his throne. Next to him is Ofelia's mother, his queen. Ofelia is wearing a red dress with sparkling red shoes, reminiscent of Dorothy in *The Wizard of Oz*, who conquered the Wicked Witch of the North. Here Ofelia is praised for her final deed of refusing to draw her brother's blood, and celebrated by the entire court. She is reunited with her father and mother. And even though she is dead, her spirit lives on. The narrator tells us that afterwards she reigned with justice in her kingdom for many centuries and that she left small traces of her time on earth like the flower budding on the tree that are visible only to those who know where to look.

Del Toro insists again at the end of the film on the great significance of looking, perceiving, recognizing, and realizing. The images of the fairy tale, even the grotesque and macabre images, are intended to compel us to open our eyes. When Ofelia fails her second test by eating the luscious grapes on the table, she does not see that the monster has awakened and is using his eyes to eat the good fairies and to menace her. It is as if del Toro were telling us that neither the real world nor the fairy-tale world is safe from perversity if we close our eyes, if we are not alert, if we don't maintain a vigilant and imaginative gaze at our own experiences, imagined and real.

Figure 77
Guillermo del Toro,
Pan's Labyrinth

To say the least, del Toro is highly creative and imaginative. He employs different camera angles, zooming and fading from scenes, blending black and white with a spectrum of colors, shifting abruptly from Ofelia's personal story to the struggles of the guerillas. Del Toro has said that he was strongly influenced by Arthur Rackham's famous fairy-tale illustrations, except that del Toro's images and creatures convey a greater sense of dread and Gothic horror. Each scene demands full concentration, for there are small details that reveal how enmeshed the real world is with our unconscious and our daydreams. Vidal's obsession with time is symbolized by his heirloom, the pocket watch, which is connected to the hourglass used to test Ofelia. Time is linked to order, and order to oppression. When Vidal's pocket watch, which belonged to his father, is smashed in the end, it prefigures the end of the fascist heritage. Ofelia's mandrake root which she uses to try to save her mother and her unborn brother recalls the image of the wooden log used by Svankmajer in his disturbing fairy-tale film *Little Otik*. The gnarled log comes alive as a baby, just as the mandrake root resembles and makes sounds as a baby. Its appearance is similar to the gnarled tree that Ofelia saves when she overcomes the poisonous toad that inhabits it. All of del Toro's images are intended to evoke startling associations that make us question our realities.

Del Toro has stated,

I know for a fact that imagination and hope have kept me alive through the roughest times in my life. Reality is brutal and it will kill you, make no mistake about it, but our tales, our creatures and our heroes have a chance to live longer than any of us. Franco suffocated Spain for decades as he tried to fashion it after what he believed to be "good for her." Yet Spain didn't die; she exploded, vibrant and alive, in the 80s. Spain lived the 60s in the 80s and they are still feeling the aftershocks of such a wonderful explosion.[284]

It is of course debatable how much hope fairy-tale films can bring audiences, or whether Spain has fully recovered from the cruelties of Franco's regime. When del Toro speaks about stories that affirm humanism, he is alluding to tales and films that do not eschew politics but dare to depict the gruesome atrocities in life in horrifying detail. When it comes to fairy-tale films, he sets a new standard of honesty and frankness in his depiction of torture, sadism, and fascism. I know only a few fairy-tale films that focus on the indomitable and resilient spirit of courageous human beings to confront the cruel and arrogant forces that appear to be dominating our world today.

The Fall (2006)

Though much more breathtaking and extravagant than *The Princess Bride, Little Otik,* or *Pan's Labyrinth,* Tarsem Singh's *The Fall* continues the strong tradition of immersing children in fairy-tale films and theorizing about storytelling and its effects in fairy-tale films. In this case there is a veritable struggle over ownership of the improvised tale that is projected through astounding images of a little girl's mind. These images were collected by Tarsem and filmed in twenty-four countries over four years, and the plot was taken from the Bulgarian director Zako Heskja's *Yo Ho Ho* (1981), which was more a pirate adventure film than a fairy-film.

There are several intricate narratives and themes woven into Tashem's fabulous film. The first regards the history of stunt men in early silent motion pictures. As the credits are shown, there are black-and-white shots of stunt men performing incredible acts such as jumping off trains, bridges, and horses. Once the credits are finished, we read "once upon a time in Los Angeles." The time is about 1913 or 1914. At the end of the film there are once again black-and-white shots of stuntmen, some of them comic, riding horses and springing on and off cars and trains and crashing through buildings. Some of the shots appear to feature Charlie Chaplin, but Tarshem's film is about a young stuntman named Roy, who takes a precarious jump to impress his girlfriend because she has left him for the star of the silent action film, in which Roy acts as his double. He is now paralyzed lying on his back in a hospital bed and spends most of the film trying to find a way to commit suicide. In the course of the film he makes friends with a young immigrant girl named Alexandria, also a patient, and tells her a preposterous fairy tale to trick her so that she will help him obtain morphine. However, he inadvertently causes her to have an accident that almost leads to her death. In the end she survives, but we never learn what happens to the paralyzed stuntman. Alexandria is told that he recovers and returns to his work, performing amazing stunts in films. But she does not really believe that tale. Stuntmen, it seems, remain anonymous and expendable.

The second plot concerns Alexandria, who is about six. She is an immigrant, probably from Romania, and had been working in an orange grove near Los Angeles until she too had a fall. She broke her arm badly and is recuperating in the same hospital as Roy. Her father had been murdered in Europe, and she lives with her mother, who cannot speak any English and rarely visits her. Alexandria wanders freely about the hospital. She is like a little detective—a curious observer, whom everyone adores. She has already seen a great deal of suffering in her short life, and though she continues to see people in pain and patients who die, she is resilient and hopeful. Most of all, she becomes attached to Roy through his fairy tale and seeks to prevent him from killing himself. In the end, she returns to her mother in the orange grove. She is working again, joyful, but there is no telling what will happen to her.

The third plot involves the battle over storytelling and its meaning, especially the meaning and value of fairy tales. Alexandria accidentally sends a paper message from her second-floor window that arrives on Roy's bed. When she comes to collect it, he begins to tell her about Alexander the Great until the doctors come. He stirs her imagination as primary storyteller. The next day Roy begins to invent a fairy-tale epic about five men stranded on a desolate island, banished by the vicious Governor Odius. The five men are: Otta Benga, a muscular African ex-slave; Luigi, an Italian anarchist and explosive expert; an Indian mystic; Charles Darwin and his monkey Wallace; and the masked Black Bandit, the leader of the gang. They all have good reasons to kill Governor Odius, and over the next week or so, Roy will build his story like Scheherazade, interrupting it at various points to create suspense and to manipulate Alexandria to search for the morphine in the hospital dispensary. He also wants to use the storytelling to provide reasons for his desire to commit suicide. But his telling is not one-sided, nor is he in total control of the narrative. For instance, the masked bandit, who is supposed to be Alexandria's father, speaks with a Romanian accent at the

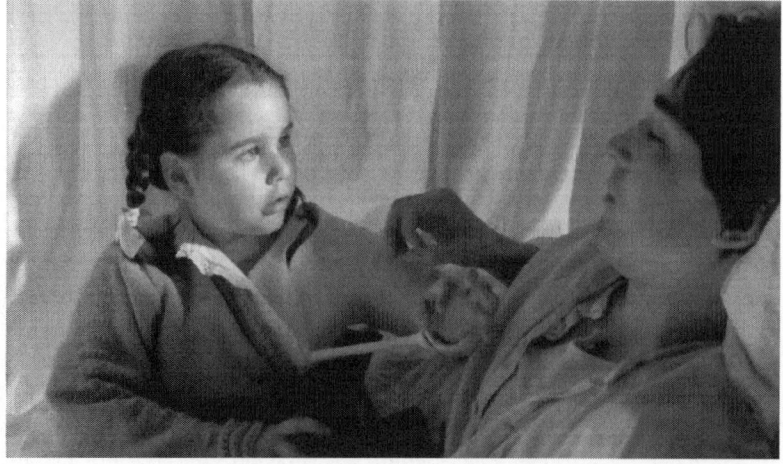

Figure 78
Tarsem Singh,
The Fall

beginning of the tale until Alexandria informs Roy that her father had been murdered. She wants the voice changed. From that point on, the bandit speaks in Roy's own voice and is identified as Roy in Alexandria's imagination. In fact, all the protagonists are associated with people whom Alexandria and Roy encounter in their daily activities. As the tale progresses and Alexandria insists on certain changes, it is clear that Roy must follow her lead to keep her interested. She even enters the tale itself to intercede in behalf of the masked bandit, who wants to rescue a beautiful princess from the treacherous Odious. In reality, this princess is the girlfriend who had deserted Roy while he was a stuntman. Toward the end, the struggle to determine the outcome of the tale becomes intense. Roy is bitter because he has failed to commit suicide, and though he has almost caused Alexandria's death, he wants to conclude the fairy tale by having all the wonderful if somewhat bizarre protagonists killed off one by one in brutal ways. Alexandria sobs and pleads for him to stop. But Roy persists until there is only the masked bandit facing Odious, and it seems that the bandit will die and Odious will make off with the beautiful princess. Alexandria continues to plead, "Let him live! Let him live!" And finally, the masked bandit, who almost drowns in a pool, emerges from the water and knocks out Odious. Shortly after, Odious accidentally kills himself, and the bandit rejects the princess because she had been deceitful and wanted to live with Odius and enjoy his wealth and power.

All three narrative plots are open-ended. We have no idea what will happen to the stuntman Roy, the immigrant Alexandria, and the masked bandit. Yet, all three narratives resound with hope because the stories are visualized through Alexandria's imagination. Some critics have accused Tashem of exoticism and extravagance, shooting scenes in different countries in deserts, oceans, castles, labyrinth gardens, and on mountains. The costumes are stunning; the attention paid to detail, meticulous. The glamorous images flash like glistening jewels and are, at times, over-whelming—even the shots in the colonial-like hospital. Yet, we must remember that the hyperbole of the images correspond to a child's view trying to sort out her mundane reality and grasp Roy's inner turbulence. Interestingly, Roy begins telling tales to Alexandria to help her and to explain the world to her, but by the time the epic fairy-tale is concluded, the storytelling has restored his will to live. In a certain sense, he has become "cured" by Alexandria's zest for life.

Mermaid (2007)

But what is happening to this resilient spirit? Similar to *Pan's Labyrinth*, Anna Melikyan's *Mermaid* leaves us with a feeling that it might be squashed just as it is about to flourish. At least, in the "new" Russia. Her film, based loosely on Hans Christian Andersen's "The Little Mermaid," begins in post-1989 Russia on a sea coast. As the credits run, we see a very large, fat woman meander through bathers on a beach to an isolated rocky spot, where she strips and walks naked into the sea. Once in the sea, she swims happily almost like a porpoise. Meanwhile, a sailor comes by and sits down by her clothes. He is tired and dozes. After a few minutes he slowly opens his eyes and is stunned when this huge woman emerges from the sea, stark naked like an enormous mermaid. He is obviously entranced. What happens next is not shown on the screen, but it is apparent that they will sleep together and produce a daughter, Alisa. The sailor will depart and will never be seen again except in Alisa's dreams.

In the very next scene, we see the shadow of tiny Alisa running at dusk toward the end of a dock, where she stands and blows into the wind as though she had magical powers. She feels that she can make her wishes come true. Then we hear her voice, which will comment on the action throughout the film. She tells us that long ago she had been a fish until her father, a sailor, had come along, and she was born. The scene jumps to a miserable shack on the beach. Alisa is living with her ancient, wrinkled grandmother and her imposing mother. She is about eight or nine years old. She wants to become a ballerina and try out for a position in a dance academy. Her enormous mother comes home from work, disgusted, and refuses to take her to the audition until she learns that a man might be there. They arrive too late. Alisa will never become a ballerina. It is not her destiny.

We shall not learn what her destiny is until much later. But the scene has been set. Her gigantic mother is the embodiment of Mother Russia, poor, single, exhausted and gruff, longing for a man, another "Prince Charming." She does not care about Alisa's welfare. Alisa, perhaps a distant cousin of Lewis Carroll's Alice, is a little fish with boundless energy and dreams. She is emotionally abandoned by her mother and grandmother. All the more reason why she will fight to realize her dreams. All the more reason why she plunges into life. She races when she walks. She desperately wants to change her life. The grandmother is dried-up Russia, infirm and inarticulate, just waiting to die. On the other hand, Alisa wants to leave the provincial town on the Crimean sea coast and surge into new life.

It seems that Melikyan's film will be a fairy-tale allegory that uses Andersen's "Little Mermaid" to comment on the hopeless situation of working-class youth, in particular girls, who find themselves ignored in the "New Russia." However, this is not a simplistic allegory but a complex rethinking of different fairy tales and how they might shed light on the drastic condition of Russian youth looking for possibilities to activate themselves and to grab a bit of happiness. This is an enlightening fairy-tale film, not Andersen's didactic Christian sermon about how a mermaid must sacrifice herself to win the Lord's approval.

Alisa is not the passive little mermaid in Andersen's tale nor the bewildered Alice of Carroll's novel. And she is certainly not the helpless Cinderella type dependent on the aid of animals and fairy godmothers. Melikyan deftly moves the narrative along and depicts Alisa at about seventeen, ready to take charge of her life. She wishes for a powerful storm to blow down her mother's shack so that the family can move to Moscow. When the storm actually arrives, her wish is fulfilled, and her mother finds a job in a supermarket, while Alisa takes on odd jobs while applying to the university. There are also dream scenes in which Alisa keeps her hopes of becoming a ballerina alive. She also dreams about finding her father. Melikyan's close-ups of Alisa's face reveal her determination and feistiness. But she also portrays her humiliation and despair. One of Alisa's jobs entails walking the streets, dressed as a mobile phone or beer mug. She becomes a walking advertisement, detached from the pedestrians and incarcerated in the box-like costume. In fact, she becomes another object on the streets, reified as a fetish. Moscow, like Alisa's wonderland, is an artificial city full of spectacular displays and advertisements that prevent people from establishing humane relationships. Wherever Alisa turns, she encounters images and advertisements that sing out "Winner Takes it All," "Toward Your Desires," "Everything is in Your Hands," "The Driving Force of Your Desires," and "Progress Depends on You."

Moscow has become the capitalist dreamland for the nouveau riche, and it is clear that there is very little space for Alisa. After she thinks that she has caused the death of a student in a car accident because she had wished to gain a position at the university, Alisa becomes mute and does not want to have any more contact with people. She decides to commit suicide, but when she goes to jump off a bridge, she comes upon a young man who throws himself into a river in a suicide attempt before she can do anything. Ironically, she saves him and brings him to his apartment. It turns out that he is a successful advertising con-man, named Sasha, or Alexander, who sells lots on the moon to the nouveau riche. Successful but depressed, this "prince," who is handsome and about thirty, lives off drugs, parties, and big deals in advertising. He also has a beautiful blonde girlfriend, Rita, but he does not want to marry her and merely enjoys her for the sex. In contrast to Rita, Alisa is scrawny, not particularly glamorous, and yet, she glows with spirit like the goldfish in Sasha's apartment. Indebted to her for saving his life, Sasha hires her as his cleaning "woman," and she falls more and more in love with him while he virtually neglects her and considers her somewhat of a pest. He never learns her last name or asks about her, while she silently helps him when he is in a stupor wandering about the city.

Soon after Alisa begins working for Sasha, she dyes her hair green and looks after his favorite goldfish. At one point she goes with him to his studio, and one of Sasha's assistants discovers that she is the perfect model, the moon girl, to advertise the lots on the moon that they are selling. They take numerous photographs of her that they intend to use as billboards. Now Alisa believes that she is drawing closer to Sasha, but when she discovers Rita and Sasha making love, she is crushed and tries in vain to sleep with a student. So, she returns home and has a terrible nightmare about Sasha dying in a plane accident. The next morning, she calls him, but he does not answer because he has had an argument with Rita, and they have broken up. As he is driving to the airport, Alisa calls again and saves his life by telling a preposterous lie about her grandmother's death as her grandmother stares at her. She distracts him so that he has a minor car accident and cannot arrive at the airport. Once her mission is accomplished, she is exuberant and races into the city passing signs, banners, and advertisements that read "Follow Your Star," "The Best Is Possible," "The Future Depends on You," and "You're Special."

In the meantime, Sasha is back in Moscow sitting in a cafe and relating to some friends how lucky he was not to have taken a plane to Volgograd that crashed with another plane. As he is talking, he suddenly realizes how vital Alisa has become in his life and how much he cares for her. While he is talking, he catches a glimpse of her racing by the cafe and chases after her through the streets of Moscow. However, Alisa is too fast as she always was ever since she was a child. She is on her way to her unknown destiny with a broad smile on her face. However, this destiny turns out to be a sports car that runs her over and abruptly ends her life. It was probably driven by one of the carefree and careless nouveau riche drivers, and Alisa's voice comments that her death is nothing unusual because there are over 2,000 car accidents a year in Moscow.

Sasha is still searching for Alisa and bumps into Rita by chance. She asks him whether he has been looking for her. He lies, not wanting to hurt her feelings, and she embraces him. She feels she has won him although he is somewhat distant. As they walk arm in arm down the street, they pass a large billboard with Alisa pictured as the moon girl and then a jump-cut to the final frame of Alisa's smiling face in bright colors. Her hair is green and is blowing in the wind on the Crimean sea coast. She appears to be deliriously happy.

Figure 79
Anna Melikyan,
Mermaid

In a short article, "Glamor Discourse," which was part of a round-table discussion published on the Internet by *ArtMargins*, Bettina Lange remarks that,

> What makes Alisa interesting to the viewer is her individuality. The film is not a chronicle of an upper class soap-opera romance, but tells a story of an individual protagonist who does not neatly fit into role-models and story patterns and who interprets them in her own way. Alisa has the potential for a unique life-story and not just a second-hand media-based identity. It is precisely her raw and unspoiled naturalness that makes her attractive to Sasha and his customers. . . . In Sasha's empty life there are no real values, only virtual ones, like the lots on the moon he is selling. In his world, Alisa is an exotic creature, connected with the sort of real life that he and Rita lost long ago.[285]

All the discussants in the round-table discussion, Lange, Henrike Schmidt, Christine Goelz, Matthias Meindl, Svetlana Sirotinna, and Natascha Drubek-Meyer, agree that the vibrant Alisa assumes the figure of a moral arbiter whose approach to life carries an explicit critique of the uncouth capitalism in contemporary Russia. But they tend to disagree about the ending. Some believe it is tragic and pessimistic, while others argue that Alisa has entered into the lives of Sasha and Rita as their lucky star so that they will be transformed and find a deeper meaning in life and abandon their decadent ways.

Interestingly, the last shots of Alisa's smiling face recall Vanessa's smiling face in Matthew Bright's *Freeway* (1996). It is the face of an indomitable teenage woman, who has resisted all the forces and tendencies in their artificial worlds to embrace the simple joys of life. Despite the treacheries of adults and the machinations of institutions and businesses that prey upon them, Alisa and Vanessa hold onto themselves, that is, they possess inalienable values that they will not exchange to fit into a society that has neglected and abandoned them.

How to Train Your Dragon (2010)

It is not by chance that the most recent computer-animated fairy-tale film is a major anti-war film that features a meek young Viking by the name of Hiccup, who defies his brute father to save a dragon and bring peace to their world. Compared with the blockbuster conventional Disney commercial films, *The Princess and the Frog* (2009) and *Alice in Wonderland* (2010), *How to Train Your Dragon* is aesthetically and ideologically a necessary antidote to these other films that have very little substance and are produced for the sake of spectacle. This is not to say that the DreamWorks studio did not intend to make a great profit from *How to Train Your Dragon*. But it is clear that the directors, Dean DeBlois and Chris Sanders and their colleagues were conscious of producing an alternative to the animated tripe that is produced in Hollywood and elsewhere.

DeBlois and Sanders substantially adapted a 2003 novel by Cressida Cowell, who has written a series of books that involve the eleven-year-old Hiccup, his Viking playmates, and dragons. To their credit, DeBlois and Sanders have recreated the novel with such depth and originality that it can be counted among the more significant works in the filmic fairy-tale tradition of counter dragon-slayer tales. The major literary source for this kind of story is Kenneth Grahame's *The Reluctant Dragon* (1898), which set a model for numerous children's books that have incorporated anti-militaristic and anti-violent messages in comic and serious narratives. In the cinema, aside from the delightful 1941 Disney adaptation of Grahame's *Reluctant Dragon*, there are two other very good animated versions directed in 1981 and 1987 by Sam Weiss and Bridget Appleby plus an unusual film, *The Flight of Dragons* (1982), which is more about a conflict between magic and science than it is about the need to recognize the dragons as other creatures that need understanding.

What makes *How to Train Your Dragon* so exceptional is its sophisticated approach to the question of war and tolerance of other creatures. Though a so-called family film, it does not dumb down audiences with simplistic characters and predictable plots. The hero of the film, Hiccup, has a wry sense of humor and great intellectual powers. Though he is not very athletic and inclined to violence, he wants to please his gargantuan father Stoick, chief of the Vikings, to become a stalwart warrior and protect their village, from the marauding dragons. Only when his special shooting device snares a rare beautiful dragon called a Night Fury and injures it does Hiccup begin to question the war with the dragons and what the beasts are really like. The film's narrative is a narrative of exploration, interrogation, and discovery. By trying to heal and train the Night Fury, which Hiccup calls Toothless, to fly with an artificial tail wing, the boy learns (as does the audience) a great deal about the dragons, their different characteristics, and why they are compelled by a tyrannical monstrous dragon to attack the Vikings and their sheep. Hiccup learns through Toothless, who carries him to the monster dragon's lair, how and why the dragons are driven to fight a war that they really do not want to fight. After Hiccup and Toothless manage to destroy the monster dragon in a scintillating battle scene that involves all the Vikings and dragons, there is a final joyous image of diverse cuddly fierce dragons of every size and color and many different Vikings living in harmony in a land that we shall never know but may still be on our horizon.

The computer animation and special effects are astounding in this film. The thrill of flying several hundred miles an hour on a saddled dragon that looks more like a miniature whale than any kind of fowl or beast is the thrill of freedom. The flights that Hiccup and his friends take are journeys of self-discovery and lead to a realization that the world can become a safe haven if weapons are turned into plows. Everything depends on whether the creative play of children and their talents can be turned from public performances of brute strength and violent killing into public acts of kindness and compassion.

Children and Childhood in Fairy-Tale Films

To be oneself in our current climate of advanced globalized capitalism, one must perform oneself and sell oneself in a public dis-play. Dis-play is the opposite of play, which can be termed the imaginative exploration of the self and environment. Curiosity and spontaneity are the champions of play. Dis-play denigrates, instrumentalizes, and controls autonomous imagination in service of a socio-economic system that tends to extol prostitution as the most desirable and profitable means through which one can and should obtain a function in the system to celebrate oneself as a brand and actually to survive. Learning to dis-play and become a celebrity of sorts is crucial for children who must be schooled early and reconfigured in a rapidly changing civilizing process that depends more and more on spectacle to delude everyone engaged in social relations of the public sphere— and even within the family. Investing in and selling one's child or other people's children has become the primary operating principle of the socialization of children in most capitalist and even non-capitalist societies. If parents do not actually sell their children as brand names, they will buy as much as they can and give as much money as they can so that children will sell themselves. Selling oneself through dis-play and celebration is a necessary condition for attaining a position and wage through the market of every field and institution. It seems to be unavoidable.

Or is it?

In those fairy-tale films of the past twenty years that are worth studying and conserving, there has been an obvious shift in focus on the child and childhood. In discussing the introduction of images of the child in film, Vicky Lebeau remarks,

> Drawing on its origins in still photographs, as well as a diverse history of screen practice, early cinema looks forward to a century in which the image of the child on film—whether still or

moving—would become part of the experience of everyday life. . . . Whether in classic, "world" or contemporary cinemas, children are everywhere on our screens, a ubiquity that turns cinema into an invaluable—in fact, potentially overwhelming—resource for reflecting on the cultural histories of childhood in the twentieth century. But what is the child *for* cinema? What does cinema *want* of the child?[286]

These are short simple questions that demand long complex answers. The general trend has been toward a commodification of the child through all types of films, including the fairy-tale film. The child is displayed as sexual toy, symbol of innocence, evil seed, magically empowered champion, battered and abused victim, sympathetic nerd or outsider, and so on. All too often, despite the sincere concerns of the filmmakers, the child in the film and the child actor end up as images to be exchanged and sold in the culture industry. It is difficult to combat the process of commodification.

Yet, as I have noted above, there appears to be a certain shift in the making of fairy-tale films in which children inside and outside the fairy-tales insist on playing active roles in interpreting and narrating their lives. As fairy-tale figures, they manifest a critical reflection and representation of children seeking to know themselves despite an environment that wants to deny self-knowledge and social awareness. This can be clearly seen in the six films I have discussed at length, *The Princess Bride, Little Otik, Pan's Labyrinth, The Fall, Mermaid,* and *How to Train Your Dragon.* The grandson tries to intervene in the grandfather's storytelling to determine what love means for himself; Alzbetka investigates and wants to change Otik's fairy-tale fate and to combat the older generation; Ofelia makes her life into a fairy tale to resist fascism; Alexandria compels Roy to change the fairy-tale narrative to see the hope in life; Alisa, despite her death, believes in her magic power to save Sasha and change his destiny. Hiccup opposes his martial father and tries to prevent a war with dragons and to defend "otherness." All of these fairy-tale films focus on the child as moral arbiter, who refuses to make compromises with the corrupt if not corroded adult world.

But these films are not the only ones that have been engaged with this theme. In previous chapters I have singled out some other highly important fairy tale films such as Nietzchka Keane's *The Juniper Tree* (1990), Matthew Bright's *Freeway* (1996), Atom Egoyan's *The Sweet Hereafter* (1997), Michel Ocelot's *Kirikou and the Sorceress (Kirikou et la Sorcière,* 1998), Hayao Miyazaki's *Spirited Away (Sen to Chihiro no kamikakushi,* 2001), Christoph Hochhäusler's *This Very Moment (Milchwald: Ein Märchen in Angst und Farbe,* 2003), Yim Pil-Sung's *Hansel and Gretel* (2007), and Catherine Breillat's *Bluebeard (La Barbe Bleue,* 2009). And there are other fairy-tale films which I unfortunately have not discussed but are worth mentioning such as Wolfgang Petersen's *The Neverending Story,* 1984), Mike Newell's *Into the West* (1992), John Sayles's *The Secret of Roan Inish* (1994), Niki Caro's *Whale Rider* (1992), Kin Ji-woon's *A Tale of Two Sisters* (2003), Vilsoni Hereniko's *The Land Has Eyes (Pear ta ma'on maf,* 2004), and Tim Burton's *Charlie and the Chocolate Factory* (2005).

What is crucial in most of these films is the trope of the child trying to cope in a hostile world, writing his or her narrative, or challenging the conventional fairy-tale narrative. None of these films employ fairy-tale narratives to create a false sense of happy end or an empowered child who can obtain anything he or she wants and master the world. For the filmmakers the child dares to investigate the world to illuminate the contradictions that adults foster and to proceed as best as he or she can despite the constant obstacles that they face. Almost all these fairy-tale films are endless stories that do not make false promises. In fact, one of the miraculous features of the more artful fairy-tale films is this innovative aesthetic and ideological gift: fairy-tale films are more realistic than so-called realistic fictional films. By addressing social realities through imaginative metaphors they engage with social realities as storytellers, who are in touch with the mysteries of life, and if we watch these fairy-tale films closely, perhaps a tiny bit of their wisdom will rub off on us.

Endnotes

1 I should also mention the two excellent chapters "Magical Illusion: Fairy Tale film" and "'Happily Ever After': Fairy Tale as Popular Parody" written by the South African scholar Jessica Tiffin in her book, *Marvelous Geometry: Narrative and Metafiction in Modern Fairy Tale* (Detroit: Wayne State University Press, 2009): 179–234.
2 *Le Pouvoir des Contes* (Paris: Casterman, 1981): 153–154.
3 Ibid, 206–209.
4 Sigmund Freud, "The Uncanny," *New Literary History*, 7 (Spring, 1976): 619–645. See also Hélène Cixous, "Fiction and its Phantoms: A Reading of Freud's *Das Unheimliche*," in this same issue, 525–548.
5 Ibid, 634.
6 Ibid, 640.
7 See *The Uses of Enchantment: The Meaning and Importance of Fairy Tales* (New York: Knopf, 1976).
8 See my revised and expanded critique of Bettelheim's book, "On the Use and Abuse of Folk and Fairy Tales with Children: Bruno Bettelheim's Moralistic Magic Wand," in *Breaking the Magic Spell: Radical Theories of Folk and Fairy Tales*, rev. ed. (Lexington, KY: University Press of Kentucky, 2002): 179–205.
9 Freud, "The Uncanny," 630.
10 Ernst Bloch, "Karl Marx and Humanity: The Material of Hope," in *On Karl Marx* (New York: Seabury, 1971): 30–1.
11 Ibid, 44–45.
12 For a detailed discussion of Bloch's essays, see my "Introduction: Toward a Realization of Anticipatory Illumination" in Ernst Bloch, *The Utopian Function of Art and Literature*, trans. Jack Zipes and Frank Mecklenburg (Cambridge, MA: MIT Press, 1988), xi–xliii and my chapter "The Utopian Function of Fairy Tales and Fantasy: Ernst Bloch the Marxist and J.R.R. Tolkien the Catholic," in *Breaking the Magic Spell*, 146–178.
13 Ibid, 133.
14 Ibid, 135.
15 Julie Sanders, *Adaptation and Appropriation* (Abingdon, Oxon: Routledge, 2006): 158.
16 Christine Gudin, "'J'utilise les contes comme un minerai avec lequel j'essaie de faire des bijoux': Entretien avec Michel Ocelot," in *Contes et légendes à l'écran*, Carol Aurouet, ed. (Condé-sur-Noireau: Corlet Éditions Diffusion, 2005): 272.
17 Robert Stam, "The Theory and Practice of Adaptation" in *Literature and Film: A Guide to the Theory and Practice of Film Adaptation*, eds. Robert Stam and Alessandra Raengo (Malden, MA: Blackwell, 2005): 45–46.
18 Tiffin, *Marvelous Geometry*, 7.
19 Kamilla Elliott also provides useful concepts of adaptation: the psychic, ventriloquist, genetic, de(re)composing, incarnational, and trumping. However, they are more applicable to filmic adaptations of novels. See "Literary Film Adaptation and the Form/Content Dilemma," in *Narrative Across Media: The Languages of Storytelling*, ed. Marie-Laure Ryan (Lincoln, NE: University of Nebraska Press, 2004): 220–243.
20 Stam, "The Theory and Practice of Adaptation," 45–46.
21 Walter Ong, *Orality and Literacy: The Technologizing of the Word* (London: Methuen, 1982): 12.
22 Alphonse Daudet, "The Romance of Little Red Riding Hood," in *The Trials and Tribulations of Little Red Riding Hood*, ed. Jack Zipes, 2nd rev. ed. (New York: Routledge, 1993): 160.
23 Adam Phillips, "On Translating a Person" in *Promises, Promises: Essays on Literature and Psychoanalysis* (London: Faber and Faber, 2000): 141.
24 Ibid, 134.
25 Jacques Derrida, "What is a 'Relevant' Translation?" in *The Translation Studies Reader*, ed. Lawrence Venuti, 2nd ed. (New York: Routledge, 2004).
26 Ibid, 443.
27 Paul Ricoeur, *On Translation*, trans. Eileen Brennan, Intro. Richard Kerney (London: Routledge, 2004): 10.
28 Ibid, 10.
29 Ibid, xx.
30 Ibid, xv.

31 David Bordwell, "Neo-Structuralist Narratology and the Functions of Filmic Storytelling," in *Narrative across Media: The Languages of Storytelling*, ed. Marie-Laure Ryan (Lincoln, NE: University of Nebraska Press, 2004): 203–219.

32 Constantine Verevis, "Remaking Film," *Film Studies* 4 (Summer 2004): 87. See also his excellent book that expands upon his theses: *Film Remakes* (Edinburgh: Edinburgh University Press, 2005).

33 See Rick Altman, *Film/Genre* (London: British Film Institute, 1999).

34 Verevis, "Remaking Film," 87.

35 Richard Schickel, *The Disney Version: The Life, Times, Art and Commerce of Walt Disney* (New York: Simon and Schuster, 1968): 296–297.

36 Donald Crafton, "The Last Night in the Nursery: Walt Disney's *Peter Pan*," *The Velvet Light Trap*, 24 (Fall, 1989): 35.

37 Kamilla Elliott, "Literary Film Adaptation and the Form/Content Dilemma," in *Narrative Across Media*, ed. Marie-Laure Ryan, 235.

38 David Bordwell, *Narration in Fiction Film* (Madison, WI: University of Wisconsin Press, 1985): 157. For two other helpful works that deal with different approaches to cinematic narration, see Graeme Turner, *Film as Social Practice*, 3rd ed. (London: Routledge, 1999) and Patrick Keating, "Emotional Curves and Linear Narratives," *Velvet Light Trap* 58 (Fall 2006): 4–15.

39 Guy Debord, *The Society of the Spectacle*, trans. Donald Nicholson-Smith (New York: Zone Books, 1995): 12.

40 Ibid, 19–20.

41 Peter Hames, "Bringing Up Baby: Jan Svankmajer interviewed by Peter Hames," *Sight and Sound* 11.10 (October 2001): 28.

42 Louis Marin, *Utopics: Spatial Play*, trans. Robert A. Vollrath (Atlantic Highlands, NJ: Humanities Press, 1984): 241.

43 Ibid, 246.

44 Norman Klein, *Seven Minutes: The Life and Death of the American Animated Cartoon* (London: Verso, 1993): 27.

45 Ibid, 134.

46 Michael Barrier, *Hollywood Cartoons: American Animation in its Golden Age* (New York: Oxford University Press, 1999): 100.

47 Theodor W. Adorno, *Aesthetic Theory*, trans. Robert Hullot-Kentor (Minneapolis, MN: University of Minnesota Press, 1997): 118–119.

48 Ibid, 119.

49 John Frazer, *Artificially Arranged Scenes: The Films of Georges Méliès* (Boston: G. K. Hall, 1979): 18–19.

50 For more detailed information about Méliès' life, see the following excellent studies: Georges Sadoul, *Georges Méliès* (Paris: Seghers, 1961); Madeleine Malthête-Méliès, *Méliès, l'enchanteur* (Paris: Hachette, 1973); Paul Hammond, *Marvellous Méliès* (London: Gordon Fraser, 1974), and Elizabeth Ezra, *Georges Méliès: The Birth of the Auteur* (Manchester: Manchester University Press, 2000).

51 Hammond, *Marvellous Méliès*, 22.

52 For a thorough discussion of Méliès' involvement in politics and the Dreyfus affair, see Ezra, *Georges Méliès*, 68–74.

53 Norman McLaren, "Homage to Georges Méliès" in *Georges Méliès: First Wizard of Cinema (1896–1913)*, ed. David Shepard (Los Angeles: Flicker Alley, 2008): 4. McLaren's essay is taken from a pamphlet included in a set of five DVDs that contains 173 of Méliès' films.

54 Frazer, *Artificially Arranged Scenes*, 39.

55 See Jean-Jacques Meusy, "How Cinema Became a Cultural Industry: The Big Boom in France between 1905 and 1908," *Film History* 14.3/4 (2002): 418–429.

56 Katherine Singer Kovács, "Georges Méliès and the *Féerie*," *Cinema Journal* 16.1 (Autumn, 1976): 1–2.

57 Paul Ginisty, *La Féerie* (Paris: Louis-Michaud, 1910): 12.

58 See Michele Rak, *Da Cenerentola a Cappuccetto rosso: Breve storia illustrata della fiaba barocca* (Milan: Bruno Mondadori, 2007).

59 Ginisty, *La Féerie*, 96.

60 See David Gies, *Theatre and Politics in Nineteenth-Century Spain: Juan de Grimaldi as Empresario and Government Agent* (Cambridge: Cambridge University Press, 1988).

61 James Robinson Planché, *Recollections and Reflections: A Professional Autobiography*. 2 vols. London: Tinsley, 1872. Vol. 1, 44.

62 See Paul Buczkowski, "J.R. Planché, Fredrick Robson, and the Fairy Extravagance,"*Marvels & Tales* 15.1 (2001): 42–65.

63 Kovács, "Georges Méliès and the *Féerie*," 6.

64 Frazer, *Artificially Arranged Scenes*, 6.

65 Ibid, 220.

66 Ibid, 213.

67 Klein, *Seven Minutes*, 1.

68 Esther Leslie, *Hollywood Flatlands: Animation, Critical Theory and the Avant-Garde* (London: Verso, 2002): vi.

69 For some of the best studies of early animation, see Giannalberto Bendazzi, *Cartoons: One Hundred Years of Cinema Animation*, trans. Anna Taraboletti-Segre (London: John Libbey, 1994); Donald Crafton, *Before Mickey: The Animated Film 1898–1928* (Cambridge, MA: MIT Press, 1982) and "Tricks and Animation" in *The Oxford History of World Cinema*, ed. Geoffrey Nowell-Smith (Oxford: Oxford University Press, 1996): 71–77; Charles Solomon, *The History of Animation: Enchanted Drawings* (New York: Wings Books, 1994); and Paul Wells, *Understanding Animation* (London: Routledge, 1998).

70 (Cambridge, MA: MIT Press, 1982): 11.

71 Terrance R. Lindvall and J. Matthew Melton, "Towards a Post-modern Animated Discourse: Bakhtin, Intertextuality and the Cartoon Carnival," in *A Reader in Animation Studies*, ed. Jayne Pilling (London: John Libbey, 1997): 211.

72 See *Breaking the Magic Spell: Radical Theories of Folk and Fairy Tales* [1979], rev. ed. (Lexington, KY: University Press of Kentucky, 2002); *Fairy Tales and the Art of Subversion: The Classical Genre for Children and the Process of Civilization* [1983], rev. 2nd ed. (New York: Routledge, 2006); *Why Fairy Tales Stick: The Evolution and Relevance of a Genre* (New York: Routledge, 2006).

73 Walter Benjamin, "The Work of Art in the Age of Mechanical Reproduction," in *Illuminations*, trans. Harry Zohn (New York: Harcourt, Brace & World, 1968): 223.

74 Klein, *Seven Minutes*, 32.

75 Mikhail Bakhtin, *Rabelais and His World*, trans. Helen Iswolsky (Bloomington, IN: University of Indiana Press, 1984): 34.

76 Ibid, 94.

77 Adorno, *Aesthetic Theory*, 118–119.

78 Ibid, 119.

79 For a comprehensive study of Disney's early films, see Russsell Merritt and J. B. Kaufman, *Walt in Wonderland: The Silent Films of Walt Disney* (Baltimore: Johns Hopkins University Press, 1993): 14.

80 Solomon, *The History of Animation*, 73.

81 John Grant, *Masters of Animation* (New York: Watson-Guptill Publications, 2001): 84–85.

82 Klein, *Seven Minutes*, 81.

83 Rubinoff also introduced another Fleischer cartoon, *Morning, Noon and Night* (1933).

84 See Klein, *Seven Minutes*, 83–85.

85 Ibid, 163–164.

86 Tex Avery's cartoons are: *Little Walking Hood* (1937), *A Bear's Tale* (1941), *Red Hot Riding Hood* (1943), *Swing Shift Cinderella* (1945), *The Shooting of Dan McGoo* (1945), *Wild and Woolfy* (1945), *Uncle Tom's Cabana* (1947), *Little Rural Riding Hood* (1949); Friz Freleng's films are: *The Trial of Mr. Wolf* (1941), *Little Red Riding Rabbit* (1944), *Little Rodent Riding Hood* (1952), and *Red Riding Hoodwinked* (1955).

87 Gary Morris, "Goosing Mother Goose: The Fairy Tales of Tex Avery," *Bright Lights Film Journal* 22 (September 1998): http://www.brightlightsfilm.com/22/texaverytales.html.

88 Amid Amidi, *Cartoon Modern: Style and Design in Fifties Animation* (San Francisco: Chronicle Books, 2006): 112.

89 Solomon, *The History of Animation*, 52.

90 Klein, *Seven Minutes*, 113.

91 Ibid, 114.

92 Richard Leskosky, "The Reforming Fantasy: Recurrent Theme and Structure in American Studio Cartoons," *The Velvet Light Trap* 24 (Fall, 1989): 53.

93 Amidi, *Cartoon Modern*, 1.

94 Grant, *Masters of Animation*, 178.

95 See William Moritz, "Some Critical Aspects on Lotte Reiniger," *Animation Journal* 5.1 (Fall, 1996): 48–51.

96 Richard Neupert, "Trouble in Watermelon Land: George Pal and the Little Jasper Cartoons," *Film Quarterly* 55.1 (Fall, 2001): 15.

97 Ibid, 18.

98 One of the best studies is: Giannalberto Bendazzi, *Cartoons: One Hundred Years of Cinema Animation*, trans. Anna Taraboletti-Segre (London: John Libbey, 1994). See also Annika Schoemann, *Der deutsche Animationsfilm: Von den Anfängen bis zur Gegenwart, 1909–2001* (Sankt Augustin: Gardez! Verlag, 2003). While Schoemann's focus is on the historical development of German animation, she deals with the broad development of animation in Europe.

99 See Joachim Giera, "Mit Aschenputtel durch die Zeiten: Märchen aus dem DEFA-Trickfilmstudio," in *Die Trick-Fabrik: DEFA-Animationsfilme 1955–1990*, ed. Ralf Schenk and Sabine Scholze (Berlin: Bertz, 2003): 225–262.

100 Paul Wells, *Animation: Genre and Authorship* (London: Wallflower, 2002): 84.

101 For an informative study that covers animated feature films up to 1977, see Bruno Edera, *Full-Length Animated Feature Films*, ed. John Halas (New York: Hastings, 1977).

102 Alexander Prokhorov, "Arresting Development: A Brief History of Soviet Cinema for Children and Adolescents," *Russian Children's Literature and Culture*, ed. Marina Balina and Larissa Rudova (New York: Routledge, 2008): 135–136.

103 Bendazzi, *Cartoons: One Hundred Years of Cinema Animation*, 177.

104 Prokhorov, "Arresting Development," 137.

105 Birgit Beumers, "Comforting Creatures in Children's Cartoons," *Russian Children's Literature and Culture*, ed. Marina Balina and Larissa Rudova (New York: Routledge, 2008): 160.

106 See Hans-Jörg Üther, *The Types of International Folktales: A Classification and Bibliography*, vol. 1 (Ff Communications No. 284. Helsinki: Suomalainen Tiedeakatemia, 2004): 308–313.

107 See Pyotr Yershov, *The Little Humpbacked Horse*, trans. Louis Zellikoff, illustr. Nikolai Kochergin (Moscow: Raduga Publishers, 1957).

108 Marina Balina, Helena Goscilo, and Mark Lipovetsky, eds., *Politicizing Magic: An Anthology of Russian and Soviet Fairy Tales* (Evanston, IL: Northwestern University Press, 2005): 112.

109 Prokhorov, "Arresting Development," 141.

110 This film was dubbed into English with the voices of the British actors Peter Ustinov, Denholm Elliott, Claire Bloom, and Max Adrian. Unfortunately it is has not had a wide distribution in the US and is not well known even though it has had a strong influence on the successful Japanese animator Hayao Miyazaki.

111 Noel Megahey, "Le Roi et L'Oiseau," 22-12-200310:00 at http://www.dvdtimes.co.uk.

112 Jean-Pierre Pagliano, *Paul Grimault*, 2nd ed. (Paris: Dreamland, 1996): 56.

113 Amid Amidi, "Jules-Engel—1001 Arabian Nights (1959)," http://cartoonmodern.blogsome.com/2006/08/25/jules-engel-1001-arabian-nights-1959/.

114 Ward Jenkins, "Twice Upon a Time: The Movie That Time Forgot," http://wardometic.blogspot.com/2007/09/twice-upon-time-movie-that-time-forgot.html.

115 See Paghat the Ratgirl, "Cinematic Adaptations of The Legend of Madame White Snake," http://www.weirdwildream realm.com/f-whitesnake.html.

116 Steven Horn, "Interview with Hayao Miyazaki," http//movies.ign.com/articles/371/371579p1.html.

117 Gudin, "'J'utilise les contes comme un minerai avec lequel j'essaie de faire des bijoux," 268–267.

118 Richard Neupert, "Kirikou and the Animated Figure/Body," *Studies in French Cinema*, 8.1 (2008): 43.

119 Steve Fritz, "A French Master and his New Film," http://www.newsarama.com/film/0903-animated-shorts-michel-ocelot.html.

120 Anneke Smelik, *And the Mirror Cracked: Feminist Cinema and Film Theory* (London: Macmillan, 1998): 185.

121 Sandra Gilbert and Susan Gubar, *The Woman Writer and the Nineteenth-Century Literary Imagination* (New Haven: Yale University Press, 1979); *The Madwoman in the Attic: The Woman Writer and the Nineteenth-Century Literary Imagination* (New Haven: Yale University Press, 2000): 36. Maria Tatar quotes this passage in her fine book, *The Classic Fairy Tales* (New York: Norton, 1999): 74, and her introductory remarks to "Snow White," pp. 74–80, provide important background material for setting it in a historical context.

122 See M. Thomas Inge, " Walt Disney's Snow White and the Seven Dwarfs: Art, Adaptation, and Ideology," *Journal of Popular Film and Television* 32.3 (Fall 2004): 132–142, and Scott Simmon and Martin Marks, "Snow White (1916)," *Treasures from American Film Archives: 50 Preserved Films* (San Francisco: National Film Preservation Foundation, 2000): 103–107.

123 Klein, *Seven Minutes*, 83.

124 See Richard Hollis and Brian Sibley, *Walt Disney's Snow White and the Seven Dwarfs and the Making of the Classic Film* (New York: Simon and Schuster, 1987).

125 Klein, *Seven Minutes*, 195.

126 "Interview: Picha (Blanche Neige, La Suite)," *Excessif,* http://www.dvdrama.com/news-18632-interview-picha-blanche-neige-1.

127 Mark Harman, ed. *Robert Walser Rediscovered: Stories, Fairy-Tale Plays, and Critical Responses* (Hanover, NH: University Press of New England, 1985): 104–105. The play, *Snow White*, pp. 101–135, was translated by Walter Arndt.

128 Ibid, 133–134.

129 Angela Carter, *The Sadeian Woman: An Exercise in Cultural History* (London: Virago Press, 1979): 6.

130 Jacques Malthête and Laurent Mannoni, *L'Œuvre de Georges Méliès* (Paris: Éditions de La Martinière, 2008): 117–118.

131 Rob Craig, "Red Riding Hood and the Monsters," http://www.kgordonmurray.com/f09.html, 6–7.

132 See Sandra Beckett, *Red Riding Hood for All Ages: A Fairy-Tale Icon in Cross-Cultural Contexts* (Detroit: Wayne State University Press, 2008): 62–74.

133 Angela Carter, *The Curious Room: Plays, Film Scripts and an Opera* (London: Chatto & Windus, 1996): 187.

134 Ibid, 141.

135 Ibid, 243.

136 Ibid, 244.

137 Charlotte Crofts, "Curiously Downbeat Hybrid or Radical Retelling?: Neil Jordan's and Angela Carter's *The Company of Wolves*," in Deborah Cartmell, I. Q. Hunter, Heidi Kaye, and Imelda Whelehan, eds., *Sisterhoods: Across the Literature/Media Divide* (London: Pluto Press, 1998): 57–58.

138 James Berardinelli, "Freeway," 1996. http://reelviews.net/movies/f/freeway.html.

139 Philip Lewis, *Seeing Through the Mother Goose Tales: Visual Turns in the Writings of Charles Perrault* (Stanford: Stanford University Press, 1996).

140 See Ute Heidmann, "La Barbe bleue palimpseste," *Poetique* (April 2008): 162–182 and "Comment faire un conte moderne avec un conte ancien? Perrault en dialogue avec Apulée," *Littérature* 153 (March 2009): 19–35.

141 See Lewis, *Seeing Through the Mother Goose Tales*.

142 Jack Zipes, "The Male Key to Bluebeard's Secret," in *Why Fairy Tales Stick: The Evolution and Relevance of a Genre* (New York: Routledge, 2006): 155–193.

143 For some informative comments about English filmic adaptations, see Casie Hermansson, *Bluebeard: A Reader's Guide to the English Tradition* (Jackson, MI: University Press of Mississippi, 2009): 144–178.

144 Patricia Hutchins, "A Clay Blue Beard (1938)," in *Science is Fiction: The Films of Jean Painlevé*, eds. Andy Masaki Bellows and Marina McDougall (Cambridge, MA: MIT Press, 2000): 141.

145 Maria Tatar, *Secrets Beyond the Door: The Story of Bluebeard and his Wives* (Princeton, NJ: Princeton University Press, 2004): 90–91.

146 Erik Ulman, "Edgar G. Ulmer," *Senses of Cinema*, http://www.sensesofcinema.com/contents/directors/03/ulmer.html.

147 Chris Kirkham, "Bluebeard (1972): A Euro-trashy Review," http://alansmithee.5u.com/junkdrawer/danning/blue beard/ bluebeard.html.

148 Mark Shivas, "An Interview with Claude Chabrol," http://home.comecast.net/~chabrol/Chabrol-interviews.html.

149 See Vladimir Propp, *La fiaba russa*, ed. Franca Crestani (Milan: Einaudi, 1990): 191–279. An English translation of *The Russian Folktale* by Sibelan Forrester will be published by Wayne State University Press in 2011.

150 See Alan Dundes, ed., *Cinderella: A Folklore Casebook* (New York: Garland, 1982). See also Marian Emily Roalfe Cox, *Cinderella: Three Hundred and Forty-Five Variants of Cinderella, Catskin, and Cap o'Rushes, Abstracted and Tabulated with a Discussion of Medieval Analogues, and Notes* [1893], Intro. Andrew Lang (Nendeln, Liechtenstein: Kraus Reprint,

1967); Nai-tung Ting, *The Cinderella Cycle in China and Indo-China* (Helsinki: Suomalainen Tiedeakatemia, 1974); and Anne Birgitte Booth, *The Cinderella Cycle* (New York: Arno Press, 1980).

151 Charles Perrault, "Cinderella or the Glass Slipper," in *Beauties, Beasts and Enchantments: Classic French Fairy Tales*, ed. Jack Zipes (New York: Meridian, 1989): 25.

152 Jacob and Wilhelm Grimm, *The Complete Fairy Tales of the Brothers Grimm*, ed. Jack Zipes, 3rd ed. (New York: Bantam, 2003): 79.

153 For a comprehensive analysis of the film's production, see Susan Ohmer, "'That Rags to Riches Stuff': Disney's Cinderella and the Cultural Space of Animation," *Film History* 5 (1993): 231–249.

154 Christy Williams, "The Shoe Fits: *Ever After* and the Pursuit of a Feminist Cinderella," in Pauline Greenhill and Sidney Eve Matrix, eds., *Fairy Tale Film and Cinematic Folklore: Fantastic Voyages, Monstrous Dreams, and Wonderful Visions* (Logan, UT: Utah State University Press, 2010): 99–115.

155 For an informative article, which deals mainly with *Working Girl* and *Pretty Woman*, see Wuming Zhao, "Cinderella in Eighties' Hollywood," *CineMagaziNet* 1 (Autumn, 1996): 1–18. http://www.cmn.hs.h.kyoto-u.ac.jp.

156 Vera Dika, "A Feminist Fairy Tale," *Art in America* (April 1987): 31.

157 See my essay "Hansel and Gretel: On Translating Abandonment, Fear, and Hunger," in *Why Fairy Tales Stick*, 195–222.

158 Engelbert Humperdinck and Adelheid Wette, *Hänsel und Gretel*, ed. Wolfram Humperdinck (Stuttgart: Reclam, 1952) 46–7. My translation.

159 See my essay, "The Rationalization of Abandonment and Abuse in Fairy Tales: The Case of Hansel and Gretel," in my book, *Happily Ever After: Fairy Tales, Children, and the Culture Industry* (New York: Routledge, 1997): 39–60.

160 See "The Children in the Wood," in Joseph Jacobs, *English Fairy Tales and More English Fairy Tales*, ed. Donald Haase (Santa Barbara, CA: ABC-CLIO, 2002): 264–269.

161 See Phil Ballard, "Magic against Materialism: Czech Animator Jiří Barta Interviewed," *Kinoeye* 3.9 (September 15, 2003): 1–6.

162 Jacob and Wilhelm Grimm, *The Complete Fairy Tales of the Brothers Grimm*, 161–162.

163 Pauline Greenhill and Anne Brydon, "Mourning Mothers and Seeing Siblings: Feminism and Place in *The Juniper Tree*," in Pauline Greenhill and Sidney Eve Matrix, eds., *Fairy Tale Film and Cinematic Folklore: Fantastic Voyages, Monstrous Dreams, and Wonderful Visions* (Logan, UT: Utah State University Press, 2010): 125. This excellent essay provides important background information on the making of the film and emphasizes its feminist aspects.

164 Hans-Jörg Uther, *The Types of International Folktales*, 247–269.

165 There have also been two interesting studies that have endeavored to trace and explain the popular dissemination of the "Beauty and Beast" tales. See Betsy Hearne, *Beauty and the Beast: Visions and Revisions of an Old Tale* (Chicago: University of Chicago Press, 1989) and Jerry Griswold, *The Meanings of Beauty & the Beast: A Handbook* (Toronto: Broadview Press, 2004).

166 Rebecca Pauly, "*Beauty and the Beast*: From Fable to Film," *Literature/Film Quarterly* 17.2 (1989): 84–90.

167 Susan Hayward, "*La Belle et la Bête*," *History Today* 46.7 (July 1996): 127–136.

168 Michael Popkin, "Cocteau's *Beauty and the Beast*: The Poet as Monster," *Literature/Film Quarterly* 10.2 (1982): 100–109.

169 David Galef, "A Sense of Magic: Reality and Illusion in Cocteau's *Beauty and the Beast*," *Literature/Film Quarterly* 12.2 (1984): 96–106.

170 Susan Hayward, "Gender Politics—Cocteau's Belle is Not that Bête: Jean Cocteau's *La Belle et la Bête* (1946)," *French Film: Texts and Contexts*, eds. Susan Hayward and Ginette Vincendeau (London: Routledge, 1990): 1127–1136; Naomi Greene, "Deadly Statues: Eros in the Films of Jean Cocteau," *French Review* 61.6 (May 1988): 890–898; Dennis DeNitto "Jean Cocteau's *Beauty and the Beast*," *American Imago* 33.2 (Summer 1976): 123–154; Sylvia Bryant "Reconstructing Oedipus through 'Beauty and the Beast'," *Criticism* 31.4 (Fall, 1989): 439–453; Jerry Griswold, "Films," in *The Meanings of "Beauty and the Beast": A Handbook* (Toronto: Broadview Press, 2004): 231–252.

171 Thomas Koebner, "'Märchenhaft, aber kein Märchen.' Jean Cocteau's film *La belle et la Bête* (1946) in *"Daß gepflegt werde der feste Buchstab": Festschift für Heinz Rölleke*, eds. Lothar Bluhm and Achim Hölter (Trier: Wissenschaftlicher Verlag Trier, 2001): 337–352.

172 "Beauty and the Beast" in *Beauties, Beasts and Enchantment*, 237.

173 Jack Zipes, *Fairy Tale as Myth/Myth as Fairy Tale* (Lexington, KY: University Press of Kentucky, 1994): 32–33.

174 Koebner, "Märchenhaft, aber kein Märchen,'" 350.

175 This film is also known under the title *The Little Red Flower*.

176 For the complete text, see Sergej Aksakov, *The Little Scarlet Flower*, trans. James Riordan, illustr. Marina Topaz (Moscow: Progress, 1976).

177 Mikhail Bakhtin, *Rabelais and his World*, trans. Helene Iswolsky (Bloomington, IN: Indiana University Press, 1984).

178 Anita Silvey, ed., *Children's Books and Their Creators* (Boston: Houghton Mifflin, 1995): 626.

179 Ibid, 262–263.

180 William Steig, *Shrek!* (New York: Farrar, Straus, Giroux, 1998): unpaginated.

181 Ibid, unpaginated.

182 Ibid, unpaginated.

183 Michael Atkinson, "Manic Regression," *Village Voice* (May 16–22, 2001).

184 By far the best book on Disney is Steven Watts, *The Magic Kingdom: Walt Disney and the American Way of Life* (Boston: Houghton Mifflin, 1997). See also Richard Schickel, *The Disney Version* (New York: Simon and Schuster, 1968); Elizabeth Bell, Lynda Haas, and Laura Sells, eds., *From Mouse to Mermaid: The Politics of Film, Gender, and Culture* (Bloomington: Indiana University Press, 1995); Carl Hiassen, *Team Rodent: How Disney Devours the World* (New York:

Ballantine, 1998); and Henry A. Giroux, *The Mouse That Roared: Disney and the End of Innocence* (Lanham, MD: Rowman & Littlefield, 1990).

185 Jack Zipes, "What Makes a Repulsive Frog So Appealing: Applying Memetics to Folk and Fairy Tales," in *Relentless Progress: The Reconfiguration of Children's Literature, Fairy Tales, and Storytelling.* New York: Routledge, 2009: 87–120.

186 Colin Covert, "A Ribbet-ing Return: Disney Gets Back into Old School Animation with its First Black Princess," *Star Tribune* (December 11, 2009): E11.

187 James Massengale, "The Miracle and a Miracle in the Life of a Mermaid," in *Hans Christian Andersen: A Poet in Time*, eds. Johann de Mylius, Aage Jørgensen, and Viggo Hjønager Pedersen (Odense: Odense University Press, 1999): 555.

188 Hans Christian Andersen, *The Complete Fairy Tales and Stories*, trans. Erik Haugaard (New York: Doubleday, 1974): 66.

189 Ibid, 75–76.

190 See Roberta Trites, "Disney's Sub/version of *The Little Mermaid*," *Journal of Popular Television and Film* 18 (1990/91): 145–159.

191 Laura Sells, "'Where Do the Mermaids Stand?' Voice and Body in *The Little Mermaid*," in *From Mouse to Mermaid*, 185.

192 Andersen, *The Complete Fairy Tales and Stories*, 20.

193 Ibid, 77.

194 Ibid, 237.

195 Ibid, 257.

196 Ibid, 258.

197 Ibid, 261.

198 Ibid, 262.

199 See Elias Bredsdorff, *Hans Christian Andersen: The Story of His Life and Work, 1805–75* (London: Phaidon, 1975).

200 See Jens Andersen, *Andersen – En biografi.* 2 vols. Copenhagen: Gyldendal, 2003 and *Hans Christian Andersen: A New Life*, trans. Tiina Nunnally (New York: Overlook Duckworth, 2005).

201 Diane Crone Frank and Jeffrey Frank, *The Stories of Hans Christian Andersen* (Boston: Houghton Mifflin, 2003): 2–3.

202 See Jackie Wullschlager, *Hans Christian Andersen: The Life of a Storyteller* (London: Penguin, 2000).

203 In Danish, Andersen uses the term "lærde mand" or "learned man," which can be translated as either philosopher or scholar. But this man can also be interpreted as the traditional poet, who does not write poetry out of emotion but slavishly follows the rules of classical forms. Therefore, the so-called classical poetry as true, beautiful, and good is regarded by Andersen as divorced from poetic inspiration. From this perspective the learned man is a slave of dead values, and the shadow is a manipulative destroyer of this slave and does not have any values at all. Genuine poetry, that stems from inspiration and is a force of life, is absent in this pessimistic story that reveals how traditionalism can turn on itself and bring about its own destruction.

204 Clayton Koelb, "The Rhetoric of Ethical Engagements," in *Inventions of Reading: Rhetoric and the Literary Imagination* (Ithaca: Cornell University Press, 1988): 219.

205 For an interesting review of *Finding Neverland*, which more or less defends the film as a good "weepie," see Anthony Lane, "Lost Boys: Why J. M. Barrie created Peter Pan," *The NewYorker* (November 12, 2004): 98–103. While Lane recognizes that there may be huge distortions in the film, when he remarks, "Depp [the actor playing J. M. Barrie] resembles Barrie in no way, except in his slenderness of form," he completely avoids the ethical question of such a misleading sentimental writer, even when he calls Barrie a wounded creature whose works are painful to read.

206 Joel Chaston, "The 'Ozification' of American Children's Fantasy Films: *The Blue Bird*, *Alice in Wonderland*, and *Jumanji*," *Children's Literature Association Quarterly* 22.1 (1997): 13.

207 Lewis Carroll, *The Annotated Alice: Alice Adventures in Wonderland/Through the Looking Glass*, ed. Martin Gardner (New York: New American Library, 1960): 15.

208 See Jack Zipes, "Oz as American Myth," in *Fairy Tale as Myth/*, 119–138.

209 L. Frank Baum, *The Wonderful World of Oz: The Wizard of Oz, The Emerald City of Oz, Glinda of Oz*, ed. Jack Zipes (New York: Penguin, 1998): 122.

210 See Aljean Harmetz, *The Making of the Wizard of Oz* (New York: Knopf, 1978).

211 Noel Langley, Florence Ryerson, and Edgar Allan Woolf, *The Wizard of Oz: The Screenplay*, ed. Michael Patrick Hearn (New York: Delta, 1989): 39–40.

212 Chaston, "The 'Ozification' of American Children's Fantasy Films," 14.

213 Ibid, p. 132.

214 Will Brooker, *Alice's Adventures: Lewis Carroll in Popular Culture* (New York: Continuum, 2004): 203.

215 Claudia Springer, "The Seduction of the Surface: From *Alice* to *Crash*," *Feminist Media Studies* 1.2 (2001): 199.

216 Ibid, 207–208.

217 See Chaston, "The Ozification of American Children's Fantasy Films," 13–20.

218 Jonathan Miller, *Subsequent Performances* (London: Faber & Faber, 1986): 241–42.

219 Scott Thill, "Jonathan Miller's *Alice in Wonderland* (1966) on DVD," *Bright Lights Film Journal*, http;//www.brightlightsfilm.com/42/alice.htm.

220 Michael O'Pray,"Jan Svankmajer: A Mannerist Surrealist," in Peter Hames, ed., *The Cinema of Jan Svankmajer: Dark Alchemy*, 2nd ed. (London: Wallflower Press, 2008): 64–65.

221 Dirk de Bruyn, "Chasing Rabbits out of the Hat and into the Shedding of Childhood," *Senses of Cinema* 20 (May/June 2002): http//:www.archive.sensesofcinema.com/contents/cteq/02/20/alice.html.

222 Brooker, *Alice's Adventures*, 226.

223 Carlo Collodi, *The Adventures of Pinocchio: Story of a Puppet*, ed, and trans. Nicolas Lorenzini. Bilingual ed. (Berkeley: University of California Press, 1986): 131. There are two other dependable, modern translations with informative introductions: Carlo Collodi, *The Adventures of Pinocchio*, ed. and trans. Ann Lawson Lucas (Oxford: Oxford University Press, 1996) and Carlo Collodi, *The Adventures of Pinocchio: Story of a Puppet*, ed. and trans. Nancy Canepa (South Royalton, VT: Steerforth Press, 2002).

224 Collodi, *The Adventures of Pinocchio* (1986), 135.

225 See Richard Wunderlich and Thomas Morrissey, *Pinocchio Goes Postmodern: Perils of a Puppet in the United States* (New York: Routledge, 2002).

226 See Leonard Mosley, *Disney's World* (New York: Stein and Day, 1985): 177: "This would be a breakthrough film for all of them, he said, in which all the lessons and new techniques they had learned from *Snow White* would be implemented and perfected, and all the mistakes they had made in earlier films would be rectified. 'What I will be looking for in this production will be color and dimension and wonderful effects of a kind that has never been seen in animated movies before,' he said. 'It will be the costliest cartoon film ever made, but we've got the money in the bank (which was true at the moment)—and damn the expense. Because *Pinocchio* is going to be the biggest challenge in the history of animation.'"

227 Richard Wunderlich and Thomas J. Morrisey, "The Desecration of *Pinocchio* in the United States," *The Horn Book Magazine* 58 (April 1982): 211.

228 Richard Schickel, *The Disney Version: The Life, Times, Art and Commerce of Walt Disney* (New York: Simon and Schuster, 1968): 232–233.

229 The supervising directors were Ben Sharpsteen and Hamilton Luske. Sequence directors: Bill Roberts, Norman Ferguson, Jack Kinney, Wilfred Jackson, and T. Hee. Animation directors: Fred Moore, Franklin Thomas, Milton Kahl, Vladimir Tytla, Ward Kimball, Arthur Babbitt, Eric Larson, Wolfgang Reithmann. Story adaptation: Ted Sears, Otto Englander, Webb Smith, William Cottrell, Joseph Sabo, Erdman Penner, Aurelius Battaglia. Music and lyrics: Leigh Harline, Ned Washington, and Paul J. Smith.

230 Douglas Street, "*Pinocchio*—From Picaro to Pipsqueak," in *Children's Novels and the Movies*, ed. Douglas Street (New York: Frederick Ungar, 1983): 47–57.

231 For a full description and background of the film, see "The Golden Key," *Kiddiematinee.com*, http://kiddiematinee.com/g-goldenkey.html. Much of the information was provided by Marc Berezin.

232 For an excellent discussion of the historical background of Ptushko's film, see Marina Balina, "Sowjetische Magie: Die subversive Macht des Märchens," in *Filme der Kindheit/Kindheit im Film in Nord-, Mittel- und Osteuropa*, eds. Christine Goelz, Karin Hoff, Anja Tippner, Vol. 66 (Frankfurt am Main: Kinder-und Jugendkultur-literatur-medien, 2010): 182–199.

233 "An Interview with Ron Merk," *Kiddiematinee.com*, http:www.kiddiematinee.com/ron_merk.html.

234 See lesson 9 of Rebecca West's, "The Persistent Puppet: Pinocchio's Heirs in Fiction and Film," *Fathom Archive*, The University of Chicago Library: Digital Collections. http://fathom.lib.uchicago.edu/2/72810000/.

235 Collodi, *The Adventures of Pinocchio* (1986), 461.

236 J. M. Barrie, *Peter Pan: Peter and Wendy and Peter Pan in Kensington Gardens*, ed. Jack Zipes (New York: Penguin, 2004): 9.

237 Ibid, 9.

238 Jacqueline Rose, *The Case of Peter Pan or The Impossibility of Children's Fiction*, 2nd ed. (Philadelphia: University of Pennsylvania Press, 1992): 72–73.

239 Ibid, 85.

240 See Dan Kiley, *The Peter Pan Syndrome: Men Who Have Never Grown Up* (New York: Dodd, Mead, 1983) and Ann Yeoman, *Now or Neverland: Peter Pan and the Myth of Eternal Youth* (Toronto: Inner City Books, 1998).

241 Adam Phillips, *The Beast in the Nursery: On Curiosity and Other Appetites* (New York: Pantheon, 1998): 134–135.

242 See Neal Gabler, *Walt Disney: The Triumph of the American Imagination* (New York: Random House, 2006): 490.

243 The copyright laws in the United States are different from those in the UK and Europe. The rights to the name and play were not in the public domain in America until 1987. In the UK and Europe, they became free in 2008. Since the play and Peter Pan's name as trademark provided a steady and large income for the Great Ormond Street Hospital, this institution has zealously guarded the rights and also acted as a moral censor and arbiter.

244 See Matthew Rimmer, "Never Neverland: Peter Pan and Perpetual Copyright," *InCite* (December 2004), http//www.alia.org.au/publishing/incite/2004/12/copyright.html and Katie Allen, "Never ends for Peter Pan," *Guardian* (December 28, 2007) http//:www. guardian.co.uk/business/2007/dec/28/gtormondst.

245 For an informative account of the TV productions of *Peter Pan*, see Theresa Jones, "Peter and Me (or How I Learned to Fly): Network Television Broadcasts of *Peter Pan*," in *Second Star to the Right: Peter Pan in the Popular Imagination*, eds. Allison Kavey and Lester Friedman (New Brunswick, NJ: Rutgers University Press, 2009): 243–264.

246 Donald Crafton, "The Last Night in the Nursery: Walt Disney's *Peter Pan*," *The Velvet Light Trap* 24 (Fall 1989): 46. This essay is by far the most illuminating one on *Peter Pan* that I have read. Another stimulating piece is Tim Brayton's "Disney Animation: When You Leave the World Behind," *Agony & Ecstasy* (November 11, 2009): http://antagonie.blogspot.com/2009_11_01_archive.html. He writes "*Peter Pan* is actually first and above all the story of Wendy Darling, at least in Disney's telling. . . . The primary dramatic conflict is certainly not between Peter and Hook—we are watching what is clearly defined as only the final stage in a months- or even years-long contest between them—but between Wendy's desire to stay young and innocent, and her increasing awareness of what it means to be an adult."

247 For a thorough discussion of the development and dissemination of the film, see Susan Ohmer, "Disney's *Peter Pan*: Gender, Fantasy, and Industrial Production," in *Second Star to the Right*, 151–187.

248   David MacFadyen, *Yellow Crocodiles and Blue Oranges: Russian Animated Film Since World War II* (Montreal: McGill-Queen's University Press, 2005): xix.

249   Peter Hames, *Czech and Slovak Cinema: Theme and Tradition* (Edinburgh: Edinburgh University Press, 2009): 32.

250   Harriet Polt, "The Czechoslovak Animated Film," *Film Quarterly* 17.3 (Spring, 1964): 40.

251   In *The Cinema of Central Europe* (London: Wallflower Press, 2004), Peter Hames discusses the problem of defining Central Europe and Eastern Europe. "For most practical purposes (for example, from the perspective of the European Union, the World Bank, and US foreign policy) the countries considered in this book—the Czech Republic, Hungary, Poland and Slovakia—are considered Central European. However, from those of the Western media and in popular perception, they remain 'East European' and they are described in a number of academic contexts as 'East Central European'," p. 1. For my purposes, I shall use the general term Central and Eastern Europe and shall include the former East Germany and all the Eastern European countries that were part of the Soviet Bloc.

252   There are a few interesting works that preceded these books. See Antoine Liehm, *Closely Watched Trains: The Czechoslovak Experience* (White Plains, NY: International Arts and Sciences Press, 1974); Mira Liehm and Antoine Liehm, *The Most Important Art: Eastern European Film After 1945* (Berkeley, CA: University of California Press, 1977); David Paul, ed., *Politics, Art and Commitment in the East European Cinema* (New York: St. Martin's Press, 1983).

253   See Dieter Wiedermann, "Der DEFA-Kinderfilm zwischen pädagogischem Auftrag und künstlerischem Anliegen," in *Zwischen Marx und Muck: DEFA-Filme für Kinder*, eds. Ingelore König, Dieter Wiedemann, and Lothar Wolf (Berlin: Henschel 1996): 21–31; Birgit Beumers, "Comforting Creatures in Children's Cartoons," in *Russian Children's Literature and Culture*, eds. Marina Balina and Larissa Rudova (New York: Routledge, 2008): 153–172; Alexander Prokhorov, "Arresting Development," 129–152; Marina Balina, "Sowjetische Magie: die subversive Macht des Märchens," in *Filme der Kindheit/Kindheit im Film in Nord-, Mittel- und Osteuropa*, eds. Christine Goelz, Karin Hoff, Anja Tippner, vol. 66 (Frankfurt am Main: Kinder-und Jugendkultur-literatur-medien, 2010): 182–199; Alfrun Kliems, "Die slowakische Frau Holle und der deutsche Gevatter Tod: Todeskonzeptionen im Märchenfilm und ihre kulturellen Bezüge," in *Filme der Kindheit im Film in Nord-, Mittel- und Osteuropa*, eds. Christine Goelz, Karin Hoff, Anja Tippner, vol. 66 (Frankfurt am Main: Kinder-und Jugendkultur-literatur-medien, 2010): 165–182.

254   Part of the reason why I have limited this chapter to Russia, Czechoslovakia, and East Germany is due to my limitations in Eastern European languages and the availability of the films. I have a good command of German, French, Italian, and Spanish, and since most of the films produced in Central and Eastern Europe have not been dubbed or produced with subtitles, I have had to make use of films, primarily videocassettes and DVDs, in languages that I understand. It should also be said that Russia, Czechoslovakia, and East Germany were most productive among the Eastern European countries in the field of fairy-tale films.

255   See Kristin Wardetzy's important essay, "Sklavensprache: Märchen und Fabeln in repressiven Gesellschaftssystemen," in *Kinder—Lesen—Literatur*, eds. Monika Plath and Gerd Mannhaupt (Baltmannsweiler: Schneider, 2008): 179–193. She addresses the use of slave language primarily in East Germany but also in some other cultures.

256   Hans Mayer, *Steppenwolf and Everyman*, trans. Jack Zipes (New York: Thomas Y. Crowell, 1971): 125.

257   Marina Balina, "Fairy Tales of Socialist Realism," in *Politicizing Magic: An Anthology of Russian and Soviet Fairy Tales*, Marina Balina, Helena Goscilo, and Mark Lipovetsky, eds. (Evanston: IL: Northwestern University Press, 2005): 107.

258   Ibid, 107–109. See also Felix Oinas, "The Political Uses and Themes of Folklore in the Soviet Union," in *Folklore, Nationalism and Politics*, ed. Felix Oinas (Columbus, OH: Slavica, 1978): 77–97.

259   Alexsandr Afanas'ev, "The Frog Princess," *Russian Fairy Tales* (New York: Pantheon, 2945): 119–124.

260   For two of the more interesting interpretations of the film, see Clare Kitson, *Yuri Norstein and Tale of Tales* (Eastleigh, UK: John Libbey, 2005) and David MacFadyen, "Skazka Skazkok/Tale of Tales," in *The Cinema of Russia and the Former Soviet Union*, ed. Birgit Beumers (London: Wallflower Press, 2007): 183–192.

261   In particular, see Maureen Furniss, *Art in Motion: Animation Aesthetics*, rev. ed. (Eastleigh, UK: John Libbey, 2007): 45–47.

262   Hames, *Czech and Slovak Cinema*, 34.

263   Ibid, 1–31.

264   See also the chapter on animation in Hames, *Czech and Slovak Cinema*, 188–205, and Polt, "The Czechoslovak Animated Film," 31–40.

265   For an informative account of his life and work, see Antinine Liehm, *Closely Watched Trains: The Czechoslovak Experience* (White Plains, NY: International arts and Sciences Press, 1974): 123–138.

266   Andrew James Horton, "A Czech Fairy-tale on Tour: Oldrich Lipsky's *Tri veterani*," *Kinoeye* 0.13 (December 21, 1998); http://www.ce-review.org/kinoeye/kinoeye13old3.html.

267   See Daniel Bird, "The Grotesque in Juraj Herz's Czech Films," *Kinoeye* 2.1 (January 7, 2002): http//www.kinoeye.org/02/01bird01.php and Ivana Kosulipvá, "Drowning the Bad Times: Juraj Herz Interviewed," *Kinoeye* 2.1 (January 7, 2002): http//www.kinoeye.org/02/01bird01.php.

268   Ulrike Bastian, *Die "Kinder- und Hausmärchen" der Brüder Grimm in der literaturpädagogischen Diskussion des 19. und 20. Jahrhunderts* (Frankfurt am Main: Haag & Herchen, 1981): 186.

269   Cf. Johannes Langfeldt, "Märchen und Pädagogik," *Pädagogische Rundschau* 2 (1940): 521–525; W. Gong, "Vorschule der Grausamkeit?" *Der Tagespiegel* (February 7, 1947); Gerhard Boettger, "Das Gute und Böse im Märchen," *Lehrerrundbrief* 3 (1948): 290–291; Werner Lenartz, "Von der erzieherischen Kraft des Märchens," *Pädagogische Rundschau* 2 (1948): 330–336; Wolfgang Petzet, "Verteidigung des Märchens gegen seine Verleumder," *Prisma* 1 (1947): 3, 11.

270   See Wolfgang Steinitz, "Das deutsche Volksmärchen: Ein wichtiger Teil nationales Kulturerbes," *Neues Deutschland* (November 17, 1951): 19.

271 See Gerhard Kahlo, *Die Wahrheit des Märchens: Grundsätzliche Betrachtung* (Halle: Niemeyer, 1954) and Waltraut Woeller, *Der soziale Gehalt und die soziale Funktion der deutschen Volksmärchen* (Berlin: Habilitations-Schrift der Humboldt-Universität zu Berlin, 1955).

272 Anneliese Kocialek, *Die Bedeutung der Volksmärchen für Unterricht und Erziehung in der Unterstufe der deutschen demokratischen Schule* (Dissertation: Humboldt-Universität, Berlin, 1951): 183.

273 Cf. Isa Bennung, *Das deutsche Märchen als Kinderliteratur: Eine Untersuchung von den Anfängen bis zur Entwicklung in der DDR*, doctoral dissertation (Halle: Martin-Luther-Universität, 1975): 292, and Bastian, *Die "Kinder- und Hausmärchen" der Brüder Grimm*, 225.

274 See Ingelore König, Dieter Wiedemann, and Lothar Wolf, eds. *Märchen: Arbeiten mit DEFA-Kinderfilmen* (Munich: KoPäd, 1998).

275 Detlef Kannapin, "Gibt es eine spezifische DEFA-Ästhetik?" in *apropos: Film 2000: Das Jahrbuch der DEFA-Stiftung*, eds. Ralf Schenk and Erika Richter (Berlin: Das Neuxe Berlin, 2000): 64. Translation by Barton Byg in Barton Byg and Betheny Moore, eds., *Moving Images of East Germany: Past and Future of DEFA Film* (Washington, DC: American Institute for Contemporary German Studies, 2002): 16–17.

276 Grimms *The Complete Fairy Tales of the Brothers Grimm*, 449.

277 This tale is a more literal translation of the adaptation of Rodari's tale, "The Missiles of Peace," which I included in my book, *Speaking Out: Storytelling and Creative Drama for Children* (New York: Routledge, 2004): 156–160.

278 See Karel Erben, "The Wooden Baby," *Tales from Bohemia*, trans. Vera Gissing, illustr. Artus Scheiner (London: MacDonald, 1969): 33–40.

279 Peter Hames, "Interview with Jan Svankmajer," *The Cinema of Jan Svankmajer: Dark Alchemy*, ed. Peter Hames, 2nd ed. (London: Wallflower Press, 2008): 130.

280 Jan Uhde, "Jan Svankmajer: Genius Loci as a Source of Surrealist Inspiration," in *The Unsilvered Screen: Surrealism on Film*, eds. Graeme Harper and Rob Stone (London: Wallflower Press, 2007): 62.

281 Marina Warner, "Dream Works," *Guardian* (June 16, 2007).

282 The screenplay was written by del Toro.

283 See the official website that offers an English translation of the screenplay: www.panslabyrinth.com/downloads/PanslabyrinthEnglishScreenplay/pdf.

284 "The Making of Pan's Labyrinth," http://www.moviesonline.ca/movienews_10978.html. (April 29, 2009).http://www.artmargins.com/index.php/bettina-lange-glamor-discourse.

285 Bettina Lange, "Glamor Discourse," *ArtMargins: Contemporary Central and East European Visual Culture* (April 29, 2009).http://www.artmargins.com/index.php/bettina-lange-glamor-discourse. The other insightful articles that form the roundtable discussion are: Henrike Schmidt, "Happy End," Christine Goelz, "A Modern Fairy Tale," Matthias Meindl and Svetlana Sirotinna, "Theodor Adorno, Fairy Tales, and 'Rusalka'," and Natascha Drubek-Meyer, "A Little Mermaid in the World of Russian Advertising."

286 Vicky Lebeau, *Childhood and Cinema* (London: Reaktion Books, 2008): 11–12.

Bibliography

Fairy tales and fiction

Afanas'ev, Aleksandr. *Russian Fairy Tales*. Trans. Norman Guterman. New York: Pantheon, 1945.

Aksakov, Sergej. *The Little Scarlet Flower*. Trans. James Riordan. Illustr. Marina Topaz. Moscow: Progress, 1976.

The All About Story Book. Illustrated by John B. Gruelle, Thelma Gooch and Other Famous Artists. New York: Cupples & Leon, 1929.

Andersen, Hans Christian. *The Complete Fairy Tales and Stories*. Trans. Erik Christian Haugaard. New York: Doubleday, 1974.

——. *The Stories of Hans Christian Andersen*. Trans. Diane Crone Frank and Jeffrey Frank. Boston: Houghton Mifflin, 2003.

——. *Fairy Tales*. Trans. Tiina Nunnally. Ed. Jackie Wullschlager. New York: Viking, 2004.

——. *Fairy Tales*. Trans. Marte Hvam Hult. Ed. Jack Zipes. New York: Barnes & Noble Classics, 2007.

Anthony, Edward and Joseph Anthony. *The Fairies Up-to-Date*. Illustr. Jean DeBosschère. London: Thornton Butterworth, 1923.

Auerbach, Marjorie. *King Lavra and the Barber*. New York: Knopf, 1964.

Balina, Marina, Helena Goscilo, and Mark Lipovetsky, eds. *Politicizing Magic: An Anthology of Russian and Soviet Fairy Tales*. Evanston: IL: Northwestern University Press, 2005.

Barrie, J. M. *Peter Pan, or The Boy Who Would not Grow Up*. Ed. Andrew Birkin. Illustr. Paula Rego. London: The Folio Society, 1992.

——. *Peter Pan: Peter and Wendy and Peter Pan in Kensington Gardens*. Ed. Jack Zipes. New York: Penguin, 2004.

Baum, L. Frank. *The Wonderful World of Oz: The Wizard of Oz, The Emerald City of Oz, Glinda of Oz*. Ed. Jack Zipes. New York: Penguin, 1998.

Bayley, F. W. N. *Nursery Tales*. London. W. S. Orr, 1846.

——. *Puss in Boots, Robinson Crusoe, Cinderella*. London: W. S. Orr, 1846.

Broun, Heywood. *The Fifty-first Dragon* [1921]. Illustr. Ed Emberley. Englewood Cliffs, NJ: Prentice-Hall, 1968.

Carroll, Lewis. *The Annotated Alice: Alice's Adventures in Wonderland & Through the Looking Glass*. Ed. Martin Gardner. Illustr. John Tenniel. New York: New American Library, 1974.

Carryl, Guy Wetmore. *Grimm Tales Made Gay*. Illustr. Albert Levering. New York: Houghton Mifflin, 1902.

Carter, Angela. *The Curious Room: Plays, Film Scripts and an Opera*. Ed. Mark Bell. London: Chatto & Windus, 1996.

Collodi, Carlo. *The Adventures of Pinocchio: Story of a Puppet*. Ed. and Trans. Nicolas Perella. Bilingual Ed. Berkeley: University of California Press, 1986.

——. *The Adventures of Pinocchio*. Ed. and Trans. Ann Lawson Lucas. Oxford: Oxford University Press, 1996.

——. *The Adventures of Pinocchio: Story of a Puppet*. South Royalton, VT: Steerforth Press, 2002.

Darton, F. J. Harvey, Ed. *The Surprising Adventures of Baron Munchausen*. London: Navarre Society, 1930.

Erben, Karel J. *Tales from Bohemia*. Trans. Vera Gissing. Illustr. Artus Scheiner. London: MacDonald, 1969.

Grimm, Jacob and Wilhelm. *The Complete Fairy Tales of the Brothers Grimm*. Ed. and Trans. Jack Zipes. 3rd Ed. New York: Bantam: 2003.

Gross, Milt. *Nize Baby*. New York: George H. Doran, 1926.

Harman, Mark, ed. *Robert Walser: Rediscovered: Stories, Fairy-Tale Plays, and Critical Responses*. Hanover, NH: University Press of New England, 1985.

Hearne, Betsy, ed. *Beauties and Beasts*. Phoenix: Oryx Press, 1993.

Jacobs, A. J. *Fractured Fairy Tales*. New York: Bantam, 1997.

Jacobs, Joseph. *English Fairy Tales and More English Fairy Tales*. Ed. Donald Haase. Santa Barbara, CA: ABC-CLIO, 2002.

Laboulaye, Édouard. *Last Fairy Tales*. Trans. Mary L. Booth. New York: Harper & Brothers, 1884.

Loisel, Régis. *Peter Pan: Londres*. Issy-les-Molineaux (Hauts-de-Seine): Vents d'Ouest, 1990.

——. *Peter Pan: Opikanoba*. Issy-les-Molineaux (Hauts-de-Seine): Vents d'Ouest, 1992.

——. *Peter Pan: Tempête*. Issy-les-Molineaux (Hauts-de-Seine): Vents d'Ouest, 1994.

——. *Peter Pan: Mains rouges*. Issy-les-Molineaux (Hauts-de-Seine): Vents d'Ouest, 1996.

——. *Peter Pan: Crochet*. Issy-les-Molineaux (Hauts-de-Seine): Vents d'Ouest, 2001.

——. *Peter Pan: Destins*. Issy-les-Molineaux (Hauts-de-Seine): Vents d'Ouest, 2004.

Minghella, Anthony. *Jim Henson's The Storyteller*. Illustr. Darcy May. New York: Knopf, 1991.

Qingge, Zhao. *The Legend of the White Snake*. Trans. Paul White. Beijing: New World Press, 1998.

Rodari, Gianni. *Il romanzo di Cipollinio*. Rome: Edizioni della Cultura Soziala, 1951.

Selznick, Brian. *The Invention of Hugo Cabret*. New York: Scholastic, 2007.

Sexton, Anne. *Transformations*. Boston: Houghton Mifflin, 1971.

Steig, William. *Shrek!* New York: Farrar, Straus, Giroux, 1998.

Tatar, Maria, ed. *The Classic Fairy Tales*. New York: Norton, 1999.

Tolstoy, Aleksey. *The Golden Key, or The Adventures of Buratino*. Trans. Eric Hartley. London: Hutchinson's Books for Young People, 1947.

Yershov, Pyotr. *The Little Humpbacked Horse*. Trans. Louis Zellikoff. Illustr. Nikolai Kochergin. Moscow: Raduga Publishers, 1957.

Zipes, Jack, ed. and trans. *Beauties, Beasts and Enchantment: Classic French Fairy Tales*. New York: Meridian, 1989.

——. *Spells of Enchantment: The Wondrous Fairy Tales of Western Culture*. New York: Viking, 1991.

————, ed. *The Trials and Tribulations of Little Red Riding Hood*, 2nd Rev. Ed. New York: Routledge, 1993.

Critical works

Adorno, Theodor W. *Aesthetic Theory*. Trans. and Ed. Robert Hullot-Kentor. Minneapolis, MN: University of Minnesota Press, 1997.

Allan, Seán and John Sanford, eds. *DEFA: East German Cinema 1946–1992*. New York: Berghahn, 1999.

Allen, Katie. "Never ends for Peter Pan." *Guardian* (December 28, 2007). http//:www. guardian.co.uk/ business/2007/dec/28/gtormondst.

Altman, Rick. *Film/Genre*. London: British Film Institute, 1999.

Andersen, Jens. *Andersen – En biografi*. 2 vols. Copenhagen: Gyldendal, 2003.

——. *Hans Christian Andersen: A New Life*. Trans. Tiina Nunnally. New York: Overlook Duckworth, 2005.

Anwell, Maggie. "Lolita Meets the Werewolf: The Company of Wolves." In *The Female Gaze: Women as Viewers of Popular Culture*. Eds. Lorraine Gamman and Margaret Marshment. London: Women's Press, 1988. 76–85.

Armitt, Lucy. "The Fragile Frames of *The Bloody Chamber*." In *The Infernal Desires of Angela Carter: Fiction, Femininity, Feminism*. Eds. Joseph Bristow and Trev Lynn Broughton. London: Longman, 1997. 88–99.

Aurouet, Carole, ed. *Contes et légendes à l'écran*. Condé-sur-Noireau: Corlet Éditions Diffusion, 2005.

Avery, Gillian. "The Cult of Peter Pan." *Word & Image* 2.2 (April–June 1986): 173–185.

Aycock, Wendell and Michael Schoenecke, ed. *Film and Literature: A Comparative Approach to Adaptation*. Lubbock, TX: Texas Tech University Press, 1988.

Bacchilega, Cristina and John Rieder. "Mixing It Up: Generic Complexity and Gender Ideology in Early Twenty-First-Century Fairy Tale Films." In *Fairy Tale Film and Cinematic Folklore: Fantastic Voyages, Monstrous Dreams, and Wonderful Visions*. Eds. Pauline Greenhill and Sidney Eve Matrix. Logan, UT: Utah State University Press, 2010. 23–41.

Bakhtin, Mikhail. *Rabelais and his World*. Trans. Helene Iswolsky. Bloomington, IN: Indiana University Press, 1984.

Balázs, Béla. *Theory of the Film: Character and Growth of a New Art*. Trans. Edith Bone. New York: Dover, 1970.

Balina, Maria. "Sowjetische Magie: die subversive Macht des Märchens." In *Filme der Kindheit/Kindheit im Film in Nord-, Mittel- und Osteuropa*. Eds. Christine Goelz, Karin Hoff, Anja Tippner. Vol. 66. Frankfurt am Main: Kinder-und Jugendkultur-literatur-medien, 2010. 182–199.

Balina, Maria and Larissa Rudova, eds. *Russian Children's Literature and Culture*. New York: Routledge, 2008.

Balio, Tino. *Grand Design: Hollywood as a Modern Business Enterprise 1930–1939*. Berkeley, CA: University of California Press, 1993.

Ballard, Phil. "Magic against Materialism: Czech Animator Jirí Barta Interviewed." *Kinoeye* 3.9 (September 15, 2003): 1–6.

Barzilai, Shuli. "Reading 'Snow White': The Mother's Story." *Signs* 15.3 (1990): 515–534.

Bastide, Bernard. "Présence de Perrault dans le cinéma français des premiers temps." In Carole Aurouet *Contes et légendes à l'écran*. Condé-sur-Noireau: Corlet Éditions Diffusion, 2005. 24–33.

Bazalgette, Cary, and David Buckingham, eds. *In Front of the Children: Screen Entertainment and Young Audiences*. London: British Film Institute, 1993.

Beckett, Sandra. *Red Riding Hood for all Ages: A Fairy-Tale Icon in Cross-Cultural Context*. Detroit: Wayne State University Press, 2008.

Bell, Elizabeth, Lynda Haas, and Laura Sells, eds. *From Mouse to Mermaid: The Politics of Film, Gender and Culture*. Bloomington, IN: University of Indiana Press, 1995.

Berardinelli, James, "Freeway, 1996." http://reelviews.net/ movies/f/freeway.html.

Berezin, Marc. "The Golden Key," *Kiddiematinee.com*. http://kiddiematinee.com/g-goldenkey.html.

Berger, Eberhard and Joachim Giera, eds. *77 Märchenfilme: Ein Filmführer für jung und alt*. Berlin: Henschel, 1990.

Bettelheim, Bruno. *The Uses of Enchantment: The Meaning and Importance of Fairy Tales*. New York: Knopf, 1976.

Beumers, Birgit, ed. *The Cinema of Russia and the Former Soviet Union*. London: Wallflower Press, 2007.

——. "Comforting Creatures in Children"s Cartoons." In *Russian Children's Literature and Culture*. Ed. Marina Balina and Larissa Rudova. New York: Routledge, 2008. 153–172.

——. *A History of Russian Cinema*. Oxford: Berg, 2009.

Billman, Carol. "'I've seen the Movie'; Oz Revisited." In *Children's Novels and the Movies*. Ed. Douglas Street. New York: Ungar, 1983. 92–100.

Bird, Daniel. "The Grotesque in Juraj Herz's Czech Films," *Kinoeye* 2.1 (January 7, 2002): http//www.kinoeye.org/ 02/01bird01/php.

Blackford, Holly. "PC Pinocchios: Parents, Children, and the Metamorphosis Tradition in Science Fiction." In *Folklore/Cinema: Popular Film as Vernacular Culture*. Ed. Sharon R. Sherman and Mikel J. Koven. Logan, UT: Utah State University Press, 2007. 74–92.

Bloch, Ernst. *On Karl Marx*. New York: Seabury, 1971.

——. *The Utopian Function of Art and Literature*. Trans. Jack Zipes and Frank Mecklenburg. Cambridge, MA: MIT Press, 1988.

Bock, Hans-Michael. "East Germany: The DEFA Story." In *The Oxford History of World Cinema*. Ed. Geoffrey Nowell-Smith. Oxford: Oxford University Press, 1996. 627–639.

Booth, Anne Birgitte. *The Cinderella Cycle*. New York: Arno Press, 1980.

Bordwell, David. *Narration in the Fiction Film*. Madison, WI: University of Wisconsin Press, 1985.

——. "Neo-Structuralist Narratology and the Functions of Filmic Storytelling." In *Narrative Across Media: The Languages of Storytelling*. Ed. Marie-Laure Ryan. Lincoln, NE: University of Nebraska Press, 2004. 203–219.

——. *The Way Hollywood Tells It: Story and Style in Modern Movies*. Berkeley: CA: University of California Press, 2006.

Bordwell, David and Kristin Thompson. *Film Art*. 7th ed. New York: McGraw-Hill, 2004.

Bourdieu, Pierre. *The Field of Cultural Production*. Trans. Randal Johnson. New York: Columbia University Press, 1993.

Bowser, Eileen. *The Transformation of Cinema, 1907–1915*. Berkeley, CA: University of California Press, 1990.

Boyd, Brian. *On the Origins of Stories: Evolution, Cognition, and Fiction*. Cambridge, MA: Harvard University Press, 2009.

Bredsdorff, Elias. *Hans Christian Andersen: The Story of His Life and Work, 1805–75*. London: Phaidon, 1975.

Bristow, Joseph and Trev Lynn Broughton, eds. *The Infernal Desires of Angela Carter: Fiction, Femininity, Feminism*. London: Longman, 1997.

Brooker, Will. *Alice's Adventures: Lewis Carroll in Popular Culture*. New York: Continuum, 2004.

Bryant, Sylvia. "Re-Constructing Oedipus through 'Beauty and the Beast'." *Criticism: A Quarterly for Literature and the Arts* 31.4 (Fall 1989): 439–453.

Buczkowski, Paul. "J.R. Planché, Fredrick Robson, and the Fairy Extravagance." *Marvels & Tales* 15.1 (2001): 42–65.

Byg, Barton. "Introduction: Reassessing DEFA Today." In *Moving Images of East Germany: Past and Future of DEFA Film*. Eds. Barton Byg and Betheny Moore. Washington, DC: American Institute for Contemporary German Studies, 2002. 1–23.

Byg, Barton and Betheny Moore, eds. *Moving Images of East Germany: Past and Future of DEFA Film*. Washington, DC: American Institute for Contemporary German Studies, 2002.

Card, Claudia. "Pinocchio." In *From Mouse to Mermaid: The Politics of Film, Gender, and Culture*. Eds. Elizabeth Bell, Lynda Haas, and Laura Sells. Bloomington, IN: Indiana University Press, 1995. 62–71.

Caronlowins, E. "Fairy-Tale Films: Capturing the Youth Market." *Revue du Cinema* 401 (1985): 45–63.

Carter, Angela. *The Sadeian Woman: An Exercise in Cultural History*. London: Virago Press, 1979.

Cartmell, Deborah and Imelda Whelehan, eds. *The Cambridge Companion to Literature on Screen*. Cambridge: Cambridge University Press, 1997.

——. *Adaptations: From Text to Screen, Screen to Text*. London: Routledge, 1999.

Cartmell, Deborah, I. Q. Hunter, Heidi Kaye, and Imelda Whelehan, eds. *Sisterhoods: Across the Literature/Media Divide*. London: Pluto Press, 1998.

Chaston, Joel. "The 'Ozification' of American Children's Fantasy films: *The Blue Bird*, *Alice in Wonderland*, and *Jumanji*." *Children's Literature Association Quarterly* 22.1 (1997): 13–20.

Chodorow, Nancy. *The Reproduction of Mothering: Psychoanalysis and the Sociology of Gender*. Berkeley, CA: University of California Press, 1978.

Cixous, Helene. "Fiction and its Phantoms: A Reading of Freud's *Das Unheimliche*." *New Literary History* 7 (Spring, 1976): 525–548.

Clerc, Jeanne-Marie and Monique Carcaud-Macaire. *L'adaptation cinématographique et littéraire*. Paris: Klinsieck, 2004.

Cohen, Paula Marantz. *Silent Film and the Triumph of the American Myth*. New York: Oxford University Press, 2001.

Cox, Marian Emily Roalfe. *Cinderella: Three Hundred and Forty-Five Variants of Cinderella, Catskin, and Cap o'Rushes, Abstracted and Tabulated with a Discussion of Medieval Analogues, and Notes* [1893]. Intro. Andrew Lang. Nendeln, Liechtenstein: Kraus Reprint, 1967.

Crafton, Donald. *The Talkies: American Cinema's Transition to Sound, 1926–1931*. Berkeley, CA: University of California Press, 1997.

Craig, Rob. "Red Riding Hood and the Monsters," http://www.kgordonmurray.com/f09.html, 1–20.

Crofts, Charlotte. "Curiously Downbeat Hybrid or Radical Retelling?: Neil Jordan's and Angela Carter's *The Company of Wolves*." In *Sisterhoods: Across the Literature/Media Divide*. Eds. Deborah Cartmell, I. Q. Hunter, Heidi Kaye, and Imelda Whelehan. London: Pluto Press, 1998. 48–63.

——. *Anagrams of Desire: Angela Carter's Writing for Radio, Film and Television*. Manchester: Manchester University Press, 2003.

Davenport, Tom and Gary Carden. *From the Brothers Grimm: A Contemporary Retelling of American Folktales and Classic Stories*. Fort Atkinson, Wisconsin: Highsmith Press, 1992.

Davis, Jo Ann, ed. *The Classic Russian Fairy Tale Film Collection*. Sherman Oaks, CA: Multi Entertainment Holdings, 1991.

Debord, Guy. *Society of the Spectacle*. Trans. Donald Nicholson-Smith. New York: Zone Books, 1995.

Denby, David. "No Kids' Stuff: 'Shrek the Third' and 'Paprika.'" *The New Yorker* (May 28, 2007): 86–87.

DeNitto, Dennis. "Jean Cocteau's *Beauty and the Beast*." *American Imago* 33.2 (Summer 1976): 123–154.

DeNitto, Dennis and William Herman. *Film and the Critical Eye*. New York: Macmillan, 1975.

Deppman, Jed, Daniel Ferrar, and Michael Gordon, eds. *Genetic Criticism: Texts and Avant-textes*. Philadelphia: University of Pennsylvania Press, 2004.

Derrida, Jacques. "What Is a 'Relevant' Translation?" In *The Translation Studies Reader*. Ed. Lawrence Venuti. 2nd Ed. New York: Routledge, 2004.

Deslandes, Jacques. *Le Boulevard du Cinéme à l'époque de Georges Méliès*. Paris: Les Éditions du Cerf, 1963.

Dika, Vera. "A Feminist Fairy Tale." *Art in America* (April 1987): 31–33.

Doughty, Amie. *Folktales Retold: A Critical Overview of Stories Updated for Children*. Jefferson, NC: McFarland, 2006.

Drubek-Meyer, Natascha. "A Little Mermaid in the World of Russian Advertising." *ArtMargins: Contemporary Central and East European Visual Culture* (April 29, 2009): http://www.artmargins.com/index.php/natascha-drubek-meyer-a-little-mermaid-in-the-world-of-Russian-advertising.

Dumont, Renaud. *De l'écrit à l'écran: Réflexions sur l'adaption cinématographique*. Paris: L'Harmattan, 2007.

Dundes, Alan, ed. *Cinderella: A Folklore Casebook*. New York: Garland, 1982.

Elliott, Kamilla. "Literary Film Adaptation and the Form/Content Dilemma." In *Narrative across Media: The Languages of Storytelling*. Ed. Marie-Laure Ryan.

Lincoln, NE: University of Nebraska Press, 2004. 220–243.

Elsaesser, Thomas, ed. *Early Cinema: Space, Frame, Narrative.* London: British Film Institute, 1990.

Elsaesser, Thomas and Malte Hagener. *Filmtheorie zur Einführung.* Hamburg: Junius, 2007.

Elsaesser, Thomas and Michael Wedel. "Defining DEFA's Historical Imaginary: The Films of Konrad Wolf." *NGC* 82 (Winter 2001): 3–24.

Erens, Patricia. "Twice Told Tales." *The Film Center Gazette,* 17 (July 1988): 2.

Fanning, Deidre. "The Shelley and Ted Show." *Forbes* 145 (February 5, 1990): 172–174.

Fell, John, ed. *Film Before Griffith.* Berkeley, CA: University of California Press, 1983.

Fischlin, Daniel. "Queer Margins: Cocteau, *La Belle et la bête,* and the Jewish differend." *Textual Practice* 12.1 (Spring 1998): 69–88.

Frank, Diane Crone and Jeffrey Frank. *The Stories of Hans Christian Andersen.* Boston: Houghton Mifflin, 2003.

Franz, Kurt, ed. *Märchenwelten: Das Volksmärchen aus der Sicht verschiedener Fachdisziplinen.* Baltmannsweiler: Schneider, 2003.

Franz, Kurt and Walter Kahn. *Märchen—Kinder-Medien: Beiträge zur medialen Adaption von Märchen zum didaktischen Umgang.* Baltmannsweiler: Schneider, 2000.

Freud, Sigmund. "The Uncanny," *New Literary History,* 7 (Spring, 1976): 619–645.

Friedrich, Andreas, ed. *Fantasy- und Märchenfilm.* Stuttgart: Philipp Reclam, 2003.

Frow, John. *Genre.* New York: Routledge, 2005.

Galef, David. "A Sense of Magic: Reality and Illusion in Cocteau's *Beauty and the Beast." Literature/Film Quarterly* 12.2 (1984): 96–106.

Gamman, Lorraine and Margaret Marshment, eds. *The Female Gaze: Women as Viewers of Popular Culture.* London: Women's Press, 1988.

Gies, David. *Theatre and Politics in Nineteenth-Century Spain: Juan de Grimaldi as Empresario and Government Agent.* Cambridge: Cambridge University Press, 1988.

Gilbert, Sandra and Susan Gubar. *The Woman Writer and the Nineteenth-Century Literary Imagination.* New Haven: Yale University Press, 1979.

——. *The Madwoman in the Attic: The Woman Writer and the Nineteenth Century Literary Imagination.* 2nd Rev. Ed. New Haven: Yale University Press, 2000.

Ginisty, Paul. *La Féerie.* Paris: Louis-Michaud, 1910.

Gjovaag, Eric. "The Outer Limits: Sci Fi Channel's *Tin Man* Updates *The Wizard of Oz." The Baum Bugle,* 51.3 (2007): 25–30.

Goelz, Christine. "A Modern Fairy Tale." *ArtMargins: Contemporary Central and East European Visual Culture* (April 29, 2009): http://www.artmargins.com/index.php/christine-goelz-a-modern-fairy-tale.

Goelz, Christine, Karin Hoff, Anja Tippner, eds. *Filme der Kindheit/Kindheit im Film in Nord-, Mittel- und Osteuropa.* Vol. 66. Frankfurt am Main: Kinder-und Jugendkultur-, literatur,-medien, Frankfurt am Main, 2010.

Goldstein, Diane, Sylvia Ann Grider, and Jeannie Banks Thomas. *Haunting Experiences: Ghosts in Contemporary Folklore.* Logan, UT: Utah State University Press, 2007.

Goulding, Daniel, ed. *Post New Wave Cinema in the Soviet Union and Eastern Europe.* Bloomington, IN: Indiana University Press, 1989.

Greene, Naomi. "Deadly Statues: Eros in the Films of Jean Cocteau." *French Review* 61.6 (May 1988): 890–898.

Greenhill, Pauline and Sidney Eve Matrix, eds. *Fairy Tale Film and Cinematic Folklore: Fantastic Voyages, Monstrous Dreams, and Wonderful Visions.* Logan, UT: Utah State University Press, 2010.

Greenhill, Pauline and Anne Brydon. "Mourning Mothers and Seeing Siblings: Feminism and Place in *The Juniper Tree.*" In *Fairy Tale Film and Cinematic Folklore: Fantastic Voyages, Monstrous Dreams, and Wonderful Visions.* Eds Pauline Greenhill and Sidney Eve Matrix. Logan, UT: Utah State University Press, 2010. 116–135.

Greenhill, Pauline and Steven Kohm. "Little Red Riding Hood and the Pedophile in Film: *Freeway, Hard Candy,* and *The Woodsman." Jeunesse: Young People, Texts, Culture* 1.2 (2009): 35–65.

Griswold, Jerry. *The Meanings of Beauty & the Beast: A Handbook.* Toronto: Broadview Press, 2004.

Haase, Donald P. "Gold into Straw: Fairy-Tale Movies for Children and the Culture Industry." *The Lion and the Unicorn* 12.2 (1988).

——. ed. *The Greenwood Encyclopedia of Folktales and Fairy Tales.* Westport, CN: Greenwood Press, 2008.

Halthof, Mark. *Historical Dictionary of Polish Cinema.* Lanham, MD: Scarecrow Press, 2007.

Hames, Peter. "Czechoslovakia: After the Spring." In *Post New Wave Cinema in the Soviet Union and Eastern Europe.* Ed. Daniel J. Goulding. Bloomington, IN: Indiana University Press, 1989. 102–142.

——. "Czech Cinema: From State Industry to Competition." Special Issue of *Canadian Slavonic Papers* 42.1–2 (2000): 63–85.

————, ed. *The Cinema of Central Europe.* London: Wallflower Press, 2004.

——. "A Business Like Any Other: Czech Cinema since the Velvet Revolution," *Viniculture* (2006): http://www.kinokultura.com/specials/4/hames.shtml.

——. *Czech and Slovak Cinema: Theme and Tradition.* Edinburgh: Edinburgh University Press, 2009.

Häntsche, Hellmuth, ed. . . . *und ich grüße die Schwalben: Der Kinderfilm in europäischen Ländern.* Berlin: Henschelverlag, 1985.

Harper, Graeme and Rob Stone, eds. *The Unsoldered Screen: Surrealism on Film.* London: Wallflower Press, 2007. 60–71.

Hastings, A. Waller, "Moral Simplification in Disney's *The Little Mermaid." The Lion and the Unicorn,* 17.1 (1993).

Hayward, Susan. "Gender Politics – Cocteau's Belle is Not That Bête: Jean Cocteau *La Belle et la Bête* (1946)." In *French Film: Textes and Contextes.* Ed. Susan Hayward and Dinette Vincentia. 2nd Ed. London: Routledge, 2000. 127–136.

——. "*La Belle et La Bête*: What Cocteau's Film Fable Tells Us about Society, Politics, Gender and Sexual Identity in Post-War France." *History Today* 46 (July 1996): 43–48.

Hearne, Betsy. *Beauty and the Beast: Visions and Revisions of an Old Tale.* Chicago: University of Chicago Press, 1989.

Heidmann, Ute. "La Barbe bleue palimpseste." *Poetique* (April 2008): 162–182.

——. "Comment faire un conte moderne avec un conte ancien? Perrault en dialogue avec Apulée." *Littérature* 153 (March 2009): 19–35.

Hermansson, Casie. *Bluebeard: A Reader's Guide to the English Tradition.* Jackson, MI: University Press of Mississippi, 2009.

Höfig, Willi. "Märchen als Vorlage für Film und Hörspiel." In *Märchen in unserer Zeit: Zu Erscheinungsformen eines populären Erzählgenres*. Ed. Hans-Jörg Uther. Munich: Diederichs, 1990. 39–55.

Hoggard, Lynn. "Writing with the Ink of Light: Jean Cocteau's *Beauty and the Beast*." In *Film and Literature: A Comparative Approach to Adaptation*. Ed. Wendell Aycock and Michael Schoenecke. Lubbock, TX: Texas Tech University Press, 1988. 123–134.

Holloway, Ronald. "The Short Film in Eastern Europe: Art and Politics of Cartoons and Puppets." In *Politics, Art, and Commitment in East European Cinema*. Ed. David W. Paul. London: Macmillan, 1983. 225–251.

Horton, Andrew James. "A Czech Fairy-tale on Tour." *Central Europe Review* 0.13 (December 21, 1998): http//www.ce-review.org/kinoeye/kinoeye13old3.html.

Hughes, Alex and James Williams, eds. *Gender and French Cinema*. Oxford: Berg, 2001.

d'Humières, Catherine, ed. *D'un Conte à l'autre, d'une génération à l'autre*. Clermont-Ferrand: Presses Universitaires Blaise Pascal, 2008.

Hutcheon, Linda. *A Theory of Adaptation*. New York: Routledge, 2006.

Hutchings, David. "Enchantress Shelley Duvall Creates a Magic Garden in her Faerie Tale Theatre for TV." *People Weekly* 20 (September 12, 1983): 58–60.

Hutchins, Patricia. "A Clay Blue Beard (1938)." In *Science Is Fiction: The Films of Jean Painlevé*. Eds. Andy Masaki Bellows and Marina McDougall. Cambridge, MA: MIT Press, 2000. 141.

Jacobs, Lewis. *Introduction to the Art of the Movies*. New York: Noonday, 1962.

——. ed. *The Emergence of Film Art: The Evolution and Development of the Motion Picture as an art from 1900 to the Present*. 2nd Ed. New York: Norton, 1979.

——. "George Méliès : Artificially Arranged Scenes." In *The Emergence of Film Art*. Ed. Lewis Jacobs. 2nd Ed. New York: Norton, 1979. 10–19.

Jean, Georges. *Le Pouvoir des Contes*. Paris: Casterman, 1981.

Jones, Theresa. "Peter and Me (or How I Learned to Fly): Network Television Broadcasts of *Peter Pan*." In *Second Star to the Right: Peter Pan in the Popular Imagination*. Eds. Allison Kavey and Lester Friedman. New Brunswick, NJ: Rutgers University Press, 2009. 243–264.

Kahlo, Gerhard. *Die Wahrheit des Märchens: Grundsätzliche Betrachtung*. Halle: Niemeyer, 1954.

Kannapin, Detlef. "Gibt es eine spezifische DEFA-Ästhetik?" In *apropos: Film 2000: Das Jahrbuch der DEFA-Stiftung*. Eds. Ralf Schenk and Erika Richter. Berlin: Das Neue Berlin, 2000. 142–164.

Kavey, Allison and Lester Friedman, eds. *Second Star to the Right: Peter Pan in the Popular Imagination*. New Brunswick, NJ: Rutgers University Press, 2009.

Keating, Patrick. "Emotional Curves and Linear Narratives." *The Velvet Light Trap* 58 (Fall, 2006): 4–15.

Kiley, Dan. *The Peter Pan Syndrome: Men Who Have Never Grown Up*. New York: Dodd, Mead, 1983.

Kirkham, Chris."Bluebeard (1972): A Euro-trashy Review," http://alansmithee.5u.com/junkdrawer/danning/bluebeard/bluebeard.html.

Knight, Arthur. *The Liveliest Art*. New York: Macmillan, 1957.

Koebner, Thomas. "'Märchenhaft, aber kein Märchen.' Jean Cocteau's Film *La belle et la Bête* (1946). In *"Daß gepflegt werde der feste Buchstab": Festschrift für Heinz*

Rölleke. Eds. Lothar Bluhm and Achim Hölter. Trier: Wissenschaftlicher Verlag Trier, 2001. 337–352.

Koelb, Clayton. *Inventions of Reading: Rhetoric and the Literary Imagination*. Ithaca: Cornell University Press, 1988.

König, Ingelore, Dieter Wiedemann, and Lothar Wolf. *Märchen: Arbeiten mit DEFA-Kinderfilmen*. Munich: KoPäd, 1998.

Kosolicová, Ivana. "The Morality of Horror: Jirí Barta's Krysar." *Kinoeye* 2.1 (January 7, 2002): http//www.kino eye. org/02/01bird01/php.

——. "Drowning the Bad Times: Juraj Herz Interviewed." *Kinoeye* 2.1 (January 7, 2002): http//www.kinoeye.org/02/01bird01/php.

Koven, Mikel J. "Folklore Studies and Popular Film and Television: A Necessary Critical Survey." *Journal of American Folklore* 116.460 (2003): 176–195.

Lakoff, George and Mark Johnson. *Metaphors We Live By*. 2nd Ed. Chicago: University of Chicago Press, 2003.

Lane, Anthony. "Lost Boys: Why J. M. Barrie Created Peter Pan." *The New Yorker* (November 22, 2004): 98–103.

Lange, Bettina. "Glamor Discourse." *ArtMargins: Contemporary Central and East European Visual Culture* (April 29, 2009). http://www.artmargins.com/index.php/bettina-lange-glamor-discourse.

Langley, Noel, Florence Ryerson, and Edgar Allan Woolf. *The Wizard of Oz: The Screenplay*. Ed. Michael Patrick Hearn. New York: Delta, 1989.

Larvors, Mariette. "Les Paradis de l'Illusion: Les Contes de Perrault au Cinéma." *Marvels & Tales* 5.2 (December 1991): 264–287.

Lebeau, Vicky. *Childhood and Cinema*. London: Reakton, 2008.

Leitch, Thomas. *Film Adaptation and Its Discontents: From Gone with the Wind to The Passion of Christ*. Baltimore: Johns Hopkins University Press, 2007.

Lescarmontier, Jeanine. *Paul Grimault: Traits de mémoire*. Preface by Jean-Pierre Pagliano. Paris: Seuil, 1991.

Lewis, Philip. *Seeing Through the Mother Goose Tales: Visual Turns in the Writings of Charles Perrault*. Stanford: Stanford University Press, 1996.

Liehm, Antoine. *Closely Watched Trains: The Czechoslovak Experience*. White Plains, NY: International Arts and Sciences Press, 1974.

Liehm, Mira and Antoine Liehm. *The Most Important Art: Eastern European Film After 1945*. Berkeley, CA: University of California Press, 1977.

Lim, Bliss Cua. "Serial Time: Bluebeard in Stepford." In *Literature and Film: A Guide to the Theory and Practice of Film Adaptation*. Eds. Robert Stam and Alessandra Raengo. Malden, MA: Blackwell, 2005. 163–190.

Liptay, Fabienne. *WunderWelten. Märchen im Film* (Flimstudien 26). Remschied: Gardez, 2004.

Loevy, Diana. "Inside the House That Henson Built." *Channels* 8 (March 1988): 52–53.

Londré, Fleicia Hardison. *The History of World Theater: From the English Restoration to the Present*. New York: Continuum, 1991.

MacFadyen, David. "*Moscow Does Not Believe in Tears*: From Oscar to Consolation Prize." *Studies in Russian and Soviet Cinema* 1.1 (2007): 45–67.

McCormick, John. *Popular Theatres of Nineteenth-Century France*. London: Routledge, 1993.

McGowan, Raymond. "Jean Cocteau and *Beauty and the Beast*." *New Orleans Review* (Winter, 1981): 106–108.

Maries, Michel. *Le Cinéma Muet*. Paris: Cahiers du Cinéma, 2005.

Marin, Louis. *Utopics: Spatial Play.* Trans. Robert A. Vollrath. Atlantic Highlands, NJ: Humanities Press, 1984.

Massengale, James. "The Miracle and a Miracle in the Life of a Mermaid." In *Hans Christian Andersen: A Poet in Time.* Eds. Johan de Mylius, Aage Jørgensen, and Viggo Hjørager Pedersen. Odense: Odense University Press, 1999. 555–576.

Mayer, Hans. *Steppenwolf and Everyman.* Trans. Jack Zipes. New York: Thomas Y. Crowell, 1971.

Meindl, Matthias and Svetlana Sirotinna. "Theodor Adorno, Fairy Tales, and Russia." *ArtMargins: Contemporary Central and East European Visual Culture* (April 29, 2009): http://www.artmargins.com/index.php/matthias-meindl-and-svetlana-sirotinina-theodor-adorno-fairy-tales-and-qrusalkaq.

Meisel, Martin. *Realizations: Narrative, Pictorial, and Theatrical Arts in Nineteenth-Century England.* Princeton: Princeton University Press, 1983.

Meraklis, Michael. "Däumling und Menschenfresser." In *Enzyklopädie des Märchens.* Vol. 23. Ed. Kurt Ranke (Berlin: de Gruyter, 1981): 359–365.

Meusy, Jean-Jacques. "How Cinema Became a Cultural Industry: The Big Boom in France between 1905 and 1908." *Film History* 14.3/4 (2002): 418–429.

Miller, Jonathan. *Subsequent Performances.* London: Faber & Faber, 1986.

"Miss Piggy Went to Market and $150 Million Came Home. Interview with Jim Henson." *American Film* XV (November, 1989): 18–21.

Mitchell, W. J. T. *What Do Pictures Want? The Lives and Loves of Images.* Chicago: University of Chicago Press, 2005.

———. *Picture Theory.* Chicago: University of Chicago Press, 1994.

Mitchell, W. J. T., ed. *The Language of Images.* Chicago: University of Chicago Press, 1980.

———. ed. *On Narrative.* Chicago: University of Chicago Press, 1981.

Mitrokhina, Xenia. "The Land of Oz in the Land of the Soviets." *Children's Literature Association Quarterly* 21.4 (1996–97): 183–188.

Moi, Toril. "Appropriating Bourdieu: Feminist Theory and Pierre Bourdieu's Sociology of Culture." *New Literary History* 22 (1991): 1017–1049.

Morris, Tim. *You're Only Young Twice: Children's Literature and Film.* Urbana, IL: University of Illinois Press, 2000.

Mulvey, Laura. "Visual Pleasure and Narrative Cinema." (1975). Rpt in *Movies and Methods Volume II.* Ed. Bill Nichols. Berkeley, CA: University of California Press, 1985.

Nathan, George Jean. *The Popular Theatre.* New York: Knopf, 1918.

Nathanson, Paul. *Over the Rainbow: The Wizard of Oz as a Secular Myth of America.* Albany: State University of New York Press, 1991.

Nichols, Bill, ed. *Movies and Methods.* Vol. II. Berkeley, CA: University of California Press, 1985.

Niemeyer, Christine. *Idéologie dans les films de contes de fées de la DEFA (1946–1989).* Master II Recherche. Université de Nantes, 2006.

Nowell-Smith, Geoffrey, ed. *The Oxford History of World Cinema.* Oxford: Oxford University Press, 1996.

Ohmer, Susan. "Disney's *Peter Pan*: Gender, Fantasy, and Industrial Production." In *Second Star to the Right: Peter Pan in the Popular Imagination.* Eds. Allison Kavey and Lester Friedman. New Brunswick, NJ: Rutgers University Press, 2009. 151–187.

Oinas, Felix. "The Political Uses and Themes of Folklore in the Soviet Union." In *Folklore, Nationalism and Politics.* Ed. Felix Oinas. Columbus, OH: Ohio Slavica, 1978. 77–97.

———. *Essays on Russian Folklore and Mythology,* Columbus, OH: Slavica Publishers, 1984.

Ong, Walter. *Orality and Literacy: The Technologizing of the Word.* London: Methuen, 1982.

Ostmeier, Dorothea. "Magic Realities Reconsidered: *Ever After.*" *Mosaic* 42.4 (2009): 113–129.

Palacio, Jean de. *Les Perversions du merveilleux: Ma Mère l'Oye au tournant du siècle.* Paris: Séguier, 1993.

Pape, Walter. "Däumling." In *Enzyklopädie des Märchens.* Vol. 23. Ed. Kurt Ranke (Berlin: de Gruyter, 1981): 350–360.

Paul, David, ed. *Politics, Art and Commitment in the East European Cinema.* New York: St. Martin's Press, 1983.

Pauly, Rebecca. "Beauty and the Beast: From Fable to Film." *Film Quarterly* 17.2 (1989): 84–90.

Peterson, Mark Allen. "From Jinn to Genies: Intertextuality, Media, and the Making of Global Folklore." In *Folklore/Cinema: Popular Film as Vernacular Culture.* Eds. Sharon R. Sherman and Mikel J. Koven. Logan, UT: Utah State University Press, 2007. 93–112.

Phillips, Adam. *The Beast in the Nursery: On Curiosity and Other Appetites.* New York: Pantheon, 1998.

———. "On Translating a Person." In *Promises, Promises: Essays on Literature and Psychoanalysis* (London: Faber and Faber, 2000): 125–147.

Planché, James Robinson. *Recollections and Reflections: A Professional Autobiography.* 2 vols. London: Tinsley, 1872.

Plath, Monika and Gerd Mannhaupt, eds. *Kinder—Lesen—Literatur.* Baltmannsweiler: Schneider, 2008.

Polan, Dana. "A Brechtian Cinema: Towards a Politics of Self-Reflexive Film." In *Movies and Methods.* Ed. Bill Nichols. Vol. II. Berkeley, CA: University of California Press, 1985.

Popkin, Michael. "Cocteau's *Beauty and the Beast*: The Poet as Monster." *Literature/Film Quarterly* 10.2 (1982): 100–109.

Prokhorov, Alexander. "Arresting Development: A Brief History of Soviet Cinema for Children and Adolescents." In *Russian Children's Literature and Culture.* Eds. Marina Balina and Larissa Rudova. New York: Routledge, 2008. 129–152.

Propp, Vladimir. *Morphology of the Folktale.* Eds. Louis Wagner and Alan Dundes. Trans. Laurence Scott. 2nd Rev. Ed. Austin: University of Texas Press, 1968.

———. *La fiaba russa.* Ed. Franca Crestani. Milan: Einaudi, 1990.

———. *The Russian Folktale.* Trans. Sibelan Forrester. Detroit: Wayne State University Press, 2011.

Rak, Michele. *Da Cenerentola a Cappuccetto rosso: breve storia illustrata della fiaba barocca.* Milan: Bruno Mondadori, 2007.

Ricoeur, Paul. *On Translation.* Trans. Eileen Brennan. London: Routledge, 2004.

Rimmer, Matthew. "Never Neverland: Peter Pan and Perpetual Copyright." *InCite.* (December 2004), http//www.alia.org.au/publishing/incite/2004/12/copyright.html.

Robinson, Chris. *Unsung Heroes of Animation.* Bloomington, IN: Indiana University Press, 2006.

Rodowick, D. N. *The Difficulty of Difference*. New York: Routledge, 1991.

Rollin, Lucy, ed. *The Antic Art: Enhancing Children's Literary Experiences Through Film and Video*. Fort Atkinson, WI: Highsmith Press, 1993.

Rooth, Anna Birgitte. *The Cinderella Cycle*. New York: Arno Press, 1980.

Rose, Jacqueline. *The Case of Peter Pan or The Impossibility of Children's Fiction*. 2nd Ed. Philadelphia: University of Pennsylvania Press, 1992.

Ross, Deborah. "Home by Tea-time: Fear of Imagination in Disney's *Alice in Wonderland*." In *Classics in Film and Fiction*. Eds. Deborah Cartwell, I.Q. Hunter, Heidi Kaye, and Imelda Whelehan. London: Pluto Press, 2000. 207–227.

Rothman, Andrea. "The Henson Kids Carry On." *Business Week*, 3198 (February 4, 1991): 72–73.

Ryan, Marie-Laure, ed. *Narrative across Media: The Languages of Storytelling*. Lincoln, NE: University of Nebraska Press, 2004.

Sanders, Julie. *Adaptation and Appropriation*. Abingdon, Oxon: Routledge, 2006.

Schenk, Ralf, ed. *Das zweite Leben der Filmstadt Babelsberg: DEFA-Spielfilme 1946–1992*. Berlin: Henschel, 1994.

Schmidt, Henrike. "Happy End." *ArtMargins: Contemporary Central and East European Visual Culture* (April 29, 2009): http://www.artmargins.com/index.php/henrike-schmidt-happy-end.

Scruton, Roger. *Beauty*. Oxford: Oxford University Press, 2009.

Sells, Laura. "'Where Do the Mermaids Stand?' Voice and Body in *The Little Mermaid*." In *From Mouse to Mermaid: The Politics of Film, Gender, and Culture*. Eds. Elizabeth Bell, Lynda Haas, and Laura Sells. Bloomington, IN: Indiana University Press, 1995. 175–192.

Sheaffer-Jones, Caroline. "Fixing the Gaze: Jean Cocteau's *La Belle et la Bête*." *Romanic Review* 93 (2002): 361–374.

Sheets, Robin Ann. "Pornography, Fairy Tales, and Feminism: Angela Carter's 'The Bloody Chamber.'" *Journal of the History of Sexuality* 1.4 (1991): 633–657.

Sherman, Sharon R. and Mikel J. Koven, eds. *Folklore/Cinema: Popular Film as Vernacular Culture*. Logan, UT: Utah State University Press, 2007.

Shivas, Mark. "An Interview with Claude Chabrol." http://home.comecast.net/~chabrol/Chabrol-interviews.html.

Silverman, Kaja. "Masochism and Male Subjectivity." *Camera Obscura*, 17 (May 1988): 31–66.

Silvey, Anita, ed. *Children's Books and Their Creators*. Boston, MA: Houghton Mifflin, 1995.

Simmon, Scott and Martin Maks, eds. *Treasures from American Film Archives: 50 Preserved Films*. San Francisco: National Film Preservation Foundation, 2000.

Slater, Thomas, ed. *Handbook of Soviet and East European Films and Filmmakers*. Westport, CT: Greenwood Press, 1992.

Smelik, Anneke. *And the Mirror Cracked: Feminist Cinema and Film Theory*. London: Macmillan Press, 1998.

Smith, Kevin Paul. *The Postmodern Fairytale: Folkloric Intertexts in Contemporary Fiction*. Basingstoke/New York: Palgrave, 2007.

Sobchack, Vivian. "The Fantastic." In *The Oxford History of World Cinema*. Ed. Geoffrey Nowell-Smith. Oxford: Oxford University Press, 1996. 312–321.

Springer, Claudia. The Seduction of the Surface: From *Alice* to *Crash*." *Feminist Media Studies* 1.2 (2001): 197–213.

Stabile, Carole and Mark Hanson. *Prime Time Animation*. London: Routledge, 2003.

Stam, Robert. *Literature through Film*. Malden, MA: Blackwell, 2005.

Stam, Robert and Alessandra Raengo, eds. *Literature and Film: A Guide to the Theory and Practice of Film Adaptation*. Malden, MA: Blackwell, 2005.

Steiner, Wendy. "Pictorial Narrativity." In *Narrative across Media: The Languages of Storytelling*. Ed. Marie-Laure Ryan. Lincoln, NE: University of Nebraska Press, 2004. 145–177.

Stephens, John and Robyn McCallum. "Utopia, Dystopia, and Cultural Controversy in *Ever After* and the Grimm Brothers' 'Snow White.'" *Marvels & Tales* 16.2 (2002): 201–213.

Street, Douglas, ed. *Children's Novels and the Movies*. New York: Ungar, 1983.

Sugarman, Sally. "Whose Woods are These Anyhow?: Children, Fairy Tales and the Media." *The Antic Art: Enhancing Children's Literary Experiences Through Film and Video*. Ed. Lucy Rollin. Fort Atkinson, WI: Highsmith Press, 141–151.

Susina, Jan. *The Place of Lewis Carroll in Children's Literature*. New York: Routledge, 2009.

Swartz, Mark Evan. *Oz Before the Rainbow: L. Frank Baum's The Wonderful Wizard of Oz on Stage and Screen to 1939*. Baltimore: Johns Hopkins University Press, 2000.

Tatar, Maria. *Secrets Beyond the Door: The Story of Bluebeard and his Wives*. Princeton, NJ: Princeton University Press, 2004.

Theweleit, Klaus. *Male Fantasies, Volume 1: Women, Floods, Bodies, History*. Minneapolis, Minnesota, 1989; *Male Fantasies, Volume 2: Psychoanalyzing the White Terror*. Minneapolis, Minnesota, 1989.

Thill, Scott. "Jonathan Miller's *Alice in Wonderland* (1966) on DVD." *Bright Lights film Journal*. http://www.brightlightsfilm.com/42/alice.html.

Thompson, Kristin. *Storytelling in the New Hollywood: Understanding Classical Narrative Technique*. Cambridge, MA: Harvard University Press, 1999.

Tiffin, Jessica. *Marvelous Geometry: Narrative and Metafiction in Modern Fairy Tale*. Detroit: Wayne State University Press, 2009.

Ting, Nai-tung. *The Cinderella Cycle in China and Indo-China*. Helsinki: Suomalainen Tiedeakatemia, 1974.

Trites, Roberta. "Disney's Sub/version of *The Little Mermaid*." *Journal of Popular Television and Film* 18 (1990/91): 145–159.

Turner, Graeme. *Film as Social Practice*. 3rd Ed. London: Routledge, 1999.

Ulman, Erik. "Edgar G. Ulmer" *Senses of Cinema*. http://www.sensesofcinema.com/contents/directors/03/ulmer.html.

Uther, Hans-Jörg. *The Types of International Folktales: A Classification and Bibliography*. 3 vols. Ff Communications No. 284. Helsinki: Suomalainen Tiedeakatemia, 2004.

———. *Handbuch zu den "Kinder- und Hausmärchen" der Brüder Grimm*. Berlin: Walter de Gruyter, 2008.

Vaugeois, Gérard, ed. *La Belle et la Bête*. Paris: Balland, 1975.

Velinger, Jan. "Film and TV Fairy Tales—An Essential Part of Czech Christmas." http//www.radio.cz/en/article/111626.

Venuti, Lawrence, ed. *The Translation Studies Reader*. 2nd Ed. New York: Routledge, 2004.

Verevis, Constantine. "Remaking Film." *Film Studies* 4 (Summer 2004): 87–103.

——. *Film Remakes*. Edinburgh: Edinburgh University Press, 2005.

Vimenet, Pascal, ed. *Cahier de notes sur . . . Le Roi et l'Oiseau*. Paris: Centre national de la Cinématographique, c. 1992.

Vogler, Christopher. *The Writer Journey: Mythic Structure for Storytellers and Screenwriters*. Studio City, CA: Michael Wiese Productions, 1992.

Von Gunden, Kenneth. *Flights of Fancy: The Great Fantasy Films*. Jefferson, North Carolina: McFarland, 1989.

Wardetzky, Kristin. "Sklavensprache: Märchen und Fabeln in repressiven Gesellschaftssystemen." In *Kinder— Lesen—Literatur*. Eds. Monika Plath und Gerd Mannhaupt. Baltmannsweiler: Schneider, 2008. 179–193.

Warner, Marina. *Cinema and the Realms of Enchantment: Lectures, Seminars, and Essays*. London: British Film Institute, 1993.

——. "Dream Works." *Guardian* (June 16, 2007). http://.guardian.co.uk/film/2007/jun/16/film.

West, Rebecca. "The Persistent Puppet: Pinocchio's Heirs in Contemporary Fiction and Film." *Fathom Archive*. The University of Chicago Library: Digital Collections. http://fathom.lib.uchicago.edu/2/728/10000/.

Wheatley, Catherine. "Behind the Door." *Sound & Sight* 20.8 (2010): 38–42.

White, Donna R. "Labyrinth: Jim Henson's 'Game' of Children's Literature and Film." In *The Antic Art: Enhancing Children's Literary Experiences Through Film and Video*. Ed. Lucy Rollin. Fort Atkinson, WI: Highsmith Press, 1993. 117–129.

Williams, Alan. *Republic of Images: A History of French Filmmaking*. Cambridge, MA: Harvard University Press, 1992.

Williams, Christy. "The Shoe Fits: *Ever After* and the Pursuit of a Feminist Cinderella." In *Fairy Tale Film and Cinematic Folklore: Fantastic Voyages, Monstrous Dreams, and Wonderful Visions*. Eds. Pauline Greenhill and Sidney Eve Matrix. Logan, UT: Utah State University Press, 2010. 99-115.

Woeller, Waltraut. *Der soziale Gehalt und die soziale Funktion der deutschen Volksmärchen*. Berlin: Habilitations-Schrift der Humboldt-Universität zu Berlin, 1955.

Wojcik-Andrews, Ian. "The Politics of Children's Films." *The Antic Art: Enhancing Children's Literary Experiences Through Film and Video*. Ed. Lucy Rollin. Fort Atkinson, WI: Highsmith Press, 1993. 217–129.

——. *Children Films: History, Ideology, Pedagogy, Theory*. New York: Garland, 2000.

Woolery, George W. *Children's Television, the First Thirty-Five Years, 1946–1981*. Metuchen: Scarecrow Press, 1983–1985.

Worley, Alec. *Empires of the Imagination: A Critical Survey of Fantasy Cinema from Georges Méliès to The Lord of the Rings*. Jefferson, NC: McFarland, 2005.

Wullschlager, Jackie. *Hans Christian Andersen: The Life of a Storyteller*. London: Penguin, 2000.

Wunderlich, Richard and Thomas Morrissey. "The Desecration of Pinocchio in the United States." *The Horn Book Magazine* 58 (April 1982): 205–212.

——. *Pinocchio Goes Postmodern: Perils of a Puppet in the United States*. New York: Routledge, 2002.

Yeoman, Ann. *Now or Neverland: Peter Pan and the Myth of Eternal Youth*. Toronto: Inner City Books, 1998.

Zhao, Wuming. "Cinderella in Eighties' Hollywood."

CineMagaziNet 1 (Autumn, 1996): 1–18. http://www.cmn.hs.h.kyoto-u.ac.jp.

Zipes, Jack. "Once Upon a Time Beyond Disney: Contemporary Fairy Tale Films for Children." In *In Front of the Children*. Eds. Cary Bazalgette and David Buckingham. London: British Film Institute, 1993. 109–126.

——. *Fairy Tale as Myth/Myth as Fairy Tale*. Lexington, KY: University Press of Kentucky, 1994.

——. *Happily Ever After: Fairy Tales, Children and the Culture Industry*. New York: Routledge, 1997.

——. *Breaking the Magic Spell: Radical Theories of Folk and Fairy Tales* [1979]. Rev. Ed. Lexington, KY: University Press of Kentucky, 2002.

——. *Hans Christian Andersen: The Misunderstood Storyteller*. New York: Routledge, 2005.

——. *Why Fairy Tales Stick: The Evolution and Relevance of a Genre*. New York: Routledge, 2006.

——. *Fairy Tales and the Art of Subversion: The Classical Genre for Children and the Process of Civilization* [1983]. Rev. 2nd Ed. New York: Routledge, 2006.

Zvonkine, Eugénie. "The Structure of the Fairy Tale in Kira Muratova's *The Sentimental Policeman*." *Studies in Russian and Soviet Cinema* 1.2 (2007) 131–145.

Animation

Amidi, Amid. "Jules-Engel—1001 Arabian Nights (1959)." http://cartoonmodern.blogsome.com/2006/08/25/jules-engel-1001-arabian-nights-1959/html.

——. *Cartoon Modern: Style and Design in Fifties Animation*. San Francisco: Chronicle Books, 2006.

Barrier, Michael. *Hollywood Cartoon: American Animation in its Golden Age*. New York: Oxford University Press, 1999.

Beckerman, Howard. *Animation: The Whole Story*. Rev. Ed. New York: Allworth Press, 2003.

Bendazzi, Giannalberto. *Le Film d'Animation*. Trans. Genvie Vidal. Grenoble: La Pens Sauvage, 1985.

——. *Cartoons: One Hundred Years of Cinema Animation*. Trans. Anna Taraboletti-Segre. London: John Libbey, 1994.

Bensevová, Marie. "Tchécoslovaquie une histoire animée." In *Le cinéma d'animation*. Eds. Pascal Vimenet and Michel Roudevitch. Condé-sur-Noireau: Corlet, 1989. 134–140.

Beumers, Birgit. "Comforting Creatures in Children's Cartoons." In *Russian Children's Literature and Culture*. Eds. Marina Balina and Larissa Rudova. New York: Routledge, 2008. 153–172.

"The Big Bad Wolf." *Fortune* X (November 1934): 88–95, 142–48.

Blanchard, Gérard. *Histoire de la bande dessinée*. Verviers, Belgium: Marabout Université, 1969.

Brown, Steven, ed. *Cinema Anime*. New York: Palgrave, 2006.

Canemaker, John, ed. *Storytelling in Animation: The Art of the Animated Image*. Vol. 2. Los Angeles: The American Film Institute, 1988.

Cayla, Véronique, ed. *Du Praxinoscope au cellulo: Un demi-siècle d'animation en France (1892–1948)*. Paris: CNC, 2007.

Cholodenko, Alan, ed. *The Illusion of Life: Essays on Animation*. Sydney: Power Publications in Association with the Australian Film Commission, 1991.

Chunovic, Louis. *The Rocky and Bullwinkle Book*. New York: Bantam Books, 1996.

Covert, Colin. "A Ribbet-ing Return: Disney Gets Back into Old-School Animation with its First Black Princess." *Star Tribune* (December 11, 2009): E-1, E11.

Crafton, Donald. *Before Mickey: The Animated Film 1898–1928*. Cambridge: MIT Press, 1982.

——. *Emile Cohl, Caricature and Film*. Princeton: Princeton University Press, 1990.

——. "The View from Termite Terrace: Caricature and Parody in Warner Bros Animation." *Film History* 5 (1993): 204–230.

——. "Tricks and Animation." In *The Oxford History of World Cinema*. Ed. Geoffrey Nowell-Smith. Oxford: Oxford University Press, 1996. 71–77.

Culhane, Shamus. *Animation: From Script to Screen*. New York: St. Martin's Press, 1988.

Edera, Bruno. *Full-length Animated Feature Films*. London: Focal Press, 1977.

Floquet, Pierre, ed. *CinémAnimationS*. Condé-sur-Noireau, France: Corlet, 2007.

Friedrich, Andreas, ed. *Animationsfilm*. Philipp Reclam: Stuttgart, 2007.

Furniss, Maureen. *Art in Motion: Animation Aesthetics* [1998]. Eastleigh, UK: John Libbey, 2007.

——, ed. *Animation—Art and Industry*. New Barnet, UK: John Libbey, 2009.

Génin, Bernard. *Le cinema d'animation. Dessin animé—marionettes—images de synthése*. Paris: Editions Cahiers du cinéma, 2003.

Giera, Joachim. "Mit Aschenputtel durch die Zeiten: Märchen aus dem DEFA-Trickfilmstudio." In *Die Trick-Fabrik: DEFA-Animationsfilme 1955–1990*. Ed. Ralf Schenk and Sabine Scholze. Berlin: Bertz, 2003. 225–262.

Gifford, Denis. *American Animated Films: The Silent Era, 1897–1929*. Jefferson, NC: McFarland, 1990.

Goldmark, Daniel. *Tunes for Toons: Music and the Hollywood Cartoon*. Berkeley, CA: University of California Press, 2005.

Grant, John. *Masters of Animation*. New York: Watson-Guptill, 2001.

Holman, L. Bruce. *Puppet Animation in the Cinema: History and Technique*. South Brunswick and New York: A. S. Barnes, 1975.

"Interview: Picha (Blanche Neige, La Suite)." *Excessif*. http://www.dvdrama.com/news-18632-interview-picha-blanche-neige-1.

Jenkins, Ward. "Twice Upon a Time: The Movie That Time Forgot." http://wardometic.blogspot.com/2007/09/twice- upon-time-movie-that-time-forgot.html.

Kantrowitz, Barbara. "Fractured Fairy Tales. *Newsweek* 112 (July 18, 1988): 64.

Kaufman, J. B. "Before Snow White." *Film History* 5 (1993): 158–175.

Klein, Norman M. *Seven Minutes: The Life and Death of the American Animated Cartoon*. London: Verso, 1993.

Kozlenko, William. "The Animated Cartoon and Walt Disney." In *The Emergence of Film Art: The Evolution and Development of the Motion Picture as an Art from 1900 to the Present*. Ed. Lewis Jacobs. 2nd Ed. New York: Norton, 1979. 246–253.

Lenburg, Jeff. *The Encyclopedia of Animated Cartoons*. New York: Facts on File, 1991.

——. *Who's Who in Animated Cartoons*. New York: Applause Theatre & Cinema Books, 2006.

Leskosky, Richard. "The Reforming Fantasy: Recurrent Theme and Structure in American Cartoons." *The Velvet Light Trap* 24 (Fall 1989): 53–66.

Leslie, Esther. *Hollywood Flatlands: Animation, Critical Theory and the Avantgarde*. London: Verso, 2004.

Lichtenstein, Manfred, ed. *Animationsfilm sozialistischer Länder*. Berlin: Staatliches Filmarchiv der DDR, 1978.

Lindvall, Terrance and J. Matthew Melton, "Towards a Post-Modern Animated Discourse: Bakhtin, Inter-textuality and the Cartoon Carnival." In *A Reader in Animation Studies*. Ed. Jayne Pilling. London: John Libbey, 1997. 203–220.

Lucci, Gabriele. *Le Cinéma d'animation*. Trans. Claire Mulkai. Paris: Hazan, 2006.

Lulow, Kalia. "Fractured Fairy Tales." *Connoisseur* 214 (November 1984): 54–55.

MacFadyen, David. *Yellow Crocodiles and Blue Oranges: Russian Animated Film Since World War Two*. Montreal: McGill-Queen's University Press, 2005.

Matlin, Leonard. *Of Mice and Magic: A History of American Animated Cartoons*. New York: NAL, 1980.

Merritt, Karen. "The Little Girl/Little Mother Trans-formation: The American Evolution of 'Snow White and the Seven Dwarfs.'" In *Storytelling in Animation: The Art of the Animated Image*. Ed. John Canemaker. Los Angeles: The American Film Institute, 1988. 105–121.

Moritz, William. "Animation." In *The Oxford History of World Cinema*. Ed. Geoffrey Nowell-Smith. Oxford: Oxford University Press, 1996. 267–275.

——. "Animation in the Post-Industrial Era." In *The Oxford History of World Cinema*. Ed. Geoffrey Nowell-Smith. Oxford: Oxford University Press, 1996. 551–557.

——. "Narrative Strategies for Resistance and Protest in Eastern European Animation." In *A Reader in Animation Studies*. Ed. Jayne Pilling. Sydney, Australia: John Libbey, 1997. 38–47.

——. "Resistance and Subversion in Animated Films of the Nazi Era: The Case of Hans Fischerkoesen." In *A Reader in Animation Studies*. Ed. Jayne Pilling. Sydney, Australia: John Libbey, 1997. 228–240.

Napier, Susan. *Anime: From Akira to Howl's Moving Castle*. Rev. Ed. New York: Palgrave, 2005.

Neupert, Richard. "Trouble in Watermelon Land: George Pal and the Little Jasper Cartoons." *Film Quarterly* 55.1 (Fall, 2001): 14–26.

Ohmer, Susan. "'That Rags to Riches Stuff': Disney's Cinderella and the Cultural Space of Animation." *Film History* 5 (1993): 231–249.

Paghat the Ratgirl. "Cinematic Adaptations of The Legend of Madame White Snake." http://www.weirdwildream realm.com/f-whitesnake.html.

Peary, Danny and Gerald Peary, eds. *The American Animated Cartoon*. New York: Dutton, 1980.

Pilling, Jayne, ed. *A Reader in Animation Studies*. Sydney, Australia: John Libbey, 1997.

——. *Animation: 2D and Beyond*. East Sussex, UK: RotoVision, 2001.

Polt, Harriet. "The Czechoslovak Animated Film." *Film Quarterly* 17.3 (1964): 31–40.

Poniewozik, James. "The End of Fairy Tales? How Shrek and Friends have Changed Children's Stories." *Time Magazine* (May 21, 2007): 83–85.

Rabinovitz, Lauren. "Animation, Postmodernism, and MTV." *The Velvet Light Trap* 24 (1989): 99–112.

Russett, Robert and Cecile Starr. *Experimental Animation: Origins of a New Art*. Rev. Ed. New York: De Capo Press, 1976.

Schenk, Ralf and Sabine Scholze, eds. *Die Trick-Fabrik: DEFA-Animationsfilme 1955–1990*. Berlin: Bertz, 2003.

Schneider, Steve. *That's All Folks! The Art of Warner Brothers Animation.* London: Aurum Press, 1991.

Schoemann, Anna. *Der deutsche Animationsfilm: Von den Anfängen bis zur Gegenwart 1909–2001.* Sankt Augustin: Gardez! Verlag, 2003.

Scott, Keith. *The Moose That Roared: The Story of Jay Ward, Bill Scott, a Flying Squirrel, and a Talking Moose.* New York: St. Martin's Press, 2000.

Shull, Michael S. and David E. Witt. *Doing Their Bit: Wartime American Animated Short Films, 1939–1945.* 2nd Ed. Jefferson, NC: McFarland, 2004.

Small, Edward and Eugene Levinson. "Toward a Theory of Animation." *The Velvet Light Trap* 24 (Fall, 1989): 67–74.

Smoodin, Eric Loren. *Animating Culture: Hollywood Cartoons from the Sound Era.* New Brunswick, NJ: Rutgers University Press, 1993.

Solis, Santiago. "Snow White and the Seven 'Dwarfs'— Queercripped." *Hypatia* 22.1 (2007): 114–131.

Solomon, Charles. "Bad Girls Finish First in Memory of Disney Fans." *Milwaukee Journal,* TV Section (August 17, 1980): 28.

——, ed. *The Art of the Animated Image.* Los Angeles: The American Film Institute, 1987.

——. *Enchanted Drawings: The History of Animation.* Rev. Ed. New York: Wings Books, 1994.

Vimenet, Pascal and Michel Roudevitch, eds. *Le cinéma d'animation.* Condé-sur-Noireau: Corlet, 1989.

Wells, Paul. *Understanding Animation.* London: Routledge, 1998.

——. *Animation: Genre and Authorship.* London: Wallflower, 2002.

——. *The Animated Bestiary: Animals, Cartoons, and Culture.* New Brunswick, NJ: Rutgers University Press, 2009.

Whitehead, Mark. *Animation.* Harpenden, UK: Pocket Essentials, 2004.

Wollery, George W. *Animated TV Specials: The Complete Directory to the First Twenty-Five Years, 1962–1987.* Metuchen: Scarecrow Press, 1989.

Directors/Producers

Tex Avery

Adamson, Joe. *Tex Avery: King of Cartoons.* New York: Da Capo Press, 1987.

Benayoun, Robert. *Le mystère Tex Avery.* Paris: Seuil, 1988.

Brion, Patrick. *Tex Avery.* Paris: Chène, 1984.

Gaines, Jane. "The Show Girl and the Wolf." *Cinema Journal* 20/1 (Fall 1980): 53–67.

Morris, Gary. "Goosing Mother Goose: The Fairy Tales of Tex Avery." *Bright Lights Film Journal* 22 (September 1998): http://www.brightlightsfilm.com/22/texaveryyales.html.

Place-Verghnes, Floriane. *Tex Avery: A Unique Legacy (1942–1955).* Eastleigh, UK: John Libbey, 2006.

Scheib, Ronnie. "Tex Arcana: The Cartoons of Tex Avery." In *The American Animated Cartoon: A Critical Anthology.* Eds. Gerald and Danny Peary. New York: E. P. Dutton, 1980. 110–127.

Jacques Demy

Vienne-Villacampa, Maïté. "'Il était *encore* une fois': Jacques Demy l'enchanteur." In *Contes et légendes à l'écran.* Ed. Carole Aurouet. Condé-sur-Noireau: Corlet Éditions Diffusion, 2005. 118–128.

Walt Disney

Allan, Robin. *Walt Disney and Europe: European Influences on the Animated Feature Films of Walt Disney.* London: John Libbey, 1999.

Addison, Erin. "Saving Other Women from Other Men: Disney's *Aladdin.*" *Camera Obscura* 11.1/31 (1993): 4–25.

Ayres, Brenda, ed. *Decolonizing Disney's Magic Kingdom.* New York: Peter Lang, 2003.

Barr, Marleen. "Biology is not Destiny, Biology is Fantasy: *Cinderella,* or the Dream Disney's 'Impossible'/Possible Race Relations Dream." In *Fantasy Girls: Gender in the New Universe of Science fiction and Fantasy Television.* Ed. Elyce Rae Helford. Lanham, MD: Rowman & Little Field, 2000. 187–199.

Bell, Elizabeth, Lynda Haas, and Laura Sells, eds. *From Mouse to Mermaid: The Politics of Film, Gender, and Culture.* Bloomington: Indiana University Press, 1995.

Brayton, Tim. "Disney Animation: When You Leave the World Behind." *Agony & Ecstasy* (November 11, 2009). http://antagonie.blogspot.com/2009_11_01_archive.html.

Bryman, Alan. *Disney and His Worlds.* London: Routledge, 1995.

——. *The Disneyization of Society.* London: Sage, 2004.

Byrne, Eleanor and Martin McQuillan. *Deconstructing Disney.* London: Pluto, 1999.

Crafton, Donald. "The Last Night in the Nursery: Walt Disney's *Peter Pan.*" *The Velvet Light Trap* 24 (Fall 1989): 35–52.

Craven, Allison. "Beauty and the Belles: Discourses of Feminism and Femininity in Disneyland." *European Journal of Women's Studies* 9.2 (2002): 123–142.

Davis, Amy. "The Dark Prince and Dream Women: Walt Disney and Mid-Twentieth Century American Feminism." *Historical Journal of Film, Radio, and Television* 25.2 (June 2005): 213–230.

——. *Good Girls and Wicked Witches: Women in Disney's Feature Animation.* Eastleigh, UK: John Libbey, 2006.

Do Rozario, Rebecca-Anne. "The Princess and the Magic Kingdom: Beyond Nostalgia, the Function of the Disney Princess." *Women's Studies in Communication* 27.1 (2004): 34–59.

Dorfman, Ariel and Armand Mattelart. *How to Read Donald Duck: Imperialist Ideology in the Disney Comic.* Trans. David Kunzle. New York: International General, 1975.

Eliot, Marc. *Walt Disney: Hollywood's Dark Prince.* New York: Birch Lane Press, 1993.

Felperin, Leslie. "The Thief of Buena Vista: Disney's *Aladdin* and Orientalism." In *A Reader in Animation Studies.* Ed. Jayne Pilling. Sydney, Australia: John Libbey, 1997. 137–142.

Gabler, Neal. *Walt Disney: The Triumph of the American Imagination.* New York: Random House, 2006.

Giroux, Henry A. *The Mouse That Roared: Disney and the End of Innocence.* Lanham, MD: Rowman & Littlefield, 1990.

Hansen, Miriam. "Of Mice and Ducks: Benjamin and Adorno on Disney." *South Atlantic Quarterly* 92.1 (1993): 227–249.

Hiassen, Carl. *Team Rodent: How Disney Devours the World.* New York: Ballantine, 1998.

Hoerrner, Keisha. "Gender Roles in Disney Films: Analyzing Behaviors from Snow White to Simba." *Women's Studies in Communication* 19.2 (1996): 213–228.

Hollis, Richard and Brian Sibley. *Walt Disney's Snow White and the Seven Dwarfs and the Making of the Classic Film.* New York: Simon and Schuster, 1987.

Inge, M. Thomas. "Walt Disney's *Snow White and the Seven Dwarfs*: Art, Adaptation, and Ideology." *Journal of Popular Film & Television* 32.3 (Fall 2004): 132–142.

Kinney, Jack. *Walt Disney and Assorted Other Characters: An Unauthorized Account of the Early Years at Disney.* New York: Harmony Books, 1988.

Krause, Martin and Linda Witkowski. *Walt Disney's Snow White and the Seven Dwarfs an Art in its Making.* New York: Hyperion/Indiana Museum of Art, 1994.

Maltin, Leonard. *The Disney Films.* 3rd Ed. New York: Hyperion, 1995.

Merritt, Russell and J. B. Kaufman. *Walt Disney's Silly Symphonies: A Companion to the Classic Cartoon Series.* Gemona, Italy: La Cineteca del Friuli, 2006.

Mosley, Leonard. *Disney's World.* New York: Stein and Day, 1985.

"Mouse and Man." *Time* XXX (December 27, 1937): 19–21.

Murphy, Patrick. "'The Whole Wide World was Scrubbed Clean': The Androcentric Animation of Denatured Disney." In *From Mouse to Mermaid: The Politics of Film, Gender and Culture.* Eds. Elizabeth Bell, Lynda Haas, and Laura Sells. Bloomington, IN: Indiana University Press. 125–136.

Ohmer, Susan. "'That Rags to Riches Stuff': Disney's Cinderella and the Cultural Space of Animation." *Film History* 5 (1993): 231–249.

Schickel, Richard. *The Disney Version: The Life, Times, Art and Commerce of Walt Disney.* New York: Simon and Schuster, 1968.

Seldes, Gilbert. "Disney and Others." In *Introduction to the Art of the Movies.* Ed. Lewis Jacobs. New York: Farrar, Straus & Giroux, 1960. 170–173. (First published in *The New Republic,* June 8, 1932.)

Sells, Laura. "'Where Do the Mermaids Stand?' Voice and Body in *The Little Mermaid.*" In *From Mouse to Mermaid: The Politics of Film, Gender, and Culture.* Eds. Elizabeth Bell, Lynda Haas, and Laura Sells. Bloomington, IN: Indiana University Press, 1995. 175–192.

Shortsleeve, Kevin. "The Wonderful World of the Depression: Disney, Despotism, and the 1930s. Or, Why Disney Scares Us." *The Lion and the Unicorn,* 28 (January 2004): 1–30.

Stone, Kaye F. "Things Walt Disney Never Told Us." *Journal of American Folklore,* 88.347 (1975): 42–50.

Street, Douglas. "Pinocchio — From Picaro to Pipsqueak." In *Children's Novels and the Movies.* Ed. Douglas Street. New York: Frederick Ungar, 1983. 47–57.

Thomas, Bob. *Disney's Art of Animation: From Mickey Mouse to Beauty and the Beast.* New York: Hyperion, 1991.

Trites, Roberta. "Disney's Sub/version of *The Little Mermaid.*" *Journal of Popular Television and Film* 18 (1990/91): 145–159.

Watts, Steven. *The Magic Kingdom: Walt Disney and the American Way of Life*: New York: Houghton Mifflin, 1997.

Wasko, Janet. *Understanding Disney: The Manufacture of Fantasy.* Cambridge: Polity Press, 2001.

White, Timothy and J. E. Winn. "Disney, Animation, and Money: The Reception of Disney's *Aladdin* in South-East Asia." *Kinema* (Spring 1995).

Max Fleischer

Fleischer, Richard. *Out of the Inkwell: Max Fleischer and the Animation Revolution.* Lexington, KY: University Press of Kentucky, 2005.

Paul Grimault

Megahey, Noel. "Le Roi et L'Oiseau," 22-12-200310:00 at http://www.dvdtimes.co.uk.

Pagliano, Jean-Pierre. *Paul Grimault.* Paris: Lherminier, 1986.

———. *Paul Grimault.* Paris: Dreamland, 1996.

Ray Harryhausen

Harryhausen, Ray and Tony Dalton. *The Art of Ray Harryhausen.* New York: Billboard Books, 2006.

Georges Méliès

Association Les Amis de Georges Méliès. *158 Scénarios de films disparus de Georges Méliès.* Paris: Jean Gaulier, 1986.

Bessy, Maurice and Duca Lo. *Georges Méliès Mage.* Paris: Pauvert, 1961.

Bretèque, François de la. "Les contes de Georges Méliès." In *Contes et légendes à l'écran.* Ed. Carole Aurouet. Condé-sur-Noireau: Corlet Éditions Diffusion, 2005. 62–71.

Deslandes, Jacques. *Le Boulevard du cinéma à l'époque de Georges Méliès.* Paris: Éditions du Cert, 1963.

Ezra, Elizabeth. *Georges Méliès: The Birth of the Auteur.* Manchester: Manchester University Press, 2000.

Fischer, Lucy. "The Lady Vanishes: Women, Magic and the Movies." In *Film Before Griffith.* Ed. John Fell. Berkeley, CA: University of California Press, 1983. 339–366.

Frazer, John. *Artificially Arranged Scenes.* Boston: G. K. Hall, 1979.

Hammond, Paul. *Marvellous Méliès.* London: Gordon Fraser, 1974.

Jenn, Pierre. *Georges Méliès cinéaste.* Paris: Albatros, 1984.

Kessler, Frank, ed. *Georges Méliès Magier der Filmkunst.* Basel/Frankfurt am Main: Stromefeld, 1993.

Kovács, Katherine Singer. "Georges Méliès and the Féerie." *Cinema Journal* 16.1 (Fall, 1976): 1–13.

McKlaren, Norman. "Homage to Georges Méliès." In *Georges Méliès: First Wizard of Cinema (1896–1913).* Ed. David Shepard. Los Angeles: Flicker Alley, 2008. 3–5.

Malthête, Jacques and Laurent Mannoni, *L'Œuvre de Georges Méliès.* Paris: Éditions de La Martinière, 2008.

Malthête, Jacques and Michel Marie, eds. *Georges Méliès, l'illusioniste fin de siècle.* Actes du colloque de Cerisy-la-Salle. Paris: Presses d la Sorbonne Nouvelle, 1996.

Malthête-Méliès, Madeleine. *Méliès l'enchanteur.* Paris: Hachette, 1973.

O'Donoghue, Darragh. "Georges Méliès." *Senses of Cinema* at http://www.sensesof cinema.com/contents/directors/04/melies.html. 1–15.

Philippe, Claude-Jean, ed. *Méliès ou le génie de la surprise.* Paris: Centre national de la Cinématographie, 2005.

Robinson, David. "Georges Méliès." In *Cinema: A Critical Dictionary.* Ed. Richard Roud. Vol. 2. London: Secker and Warburg, 1980.

———. *Georges Méliès: Father of Film Fantasy.* London: Museum of the Moving Image, 1993.

Sadoul, Georges. *Georges Méliès.* Paris: Seghers, 1961.

Shepard, David, ed. *Georges Méliès: First Wizard of Cinema (1896–1913).* Los Angeles: Flicker Alley, 2008.

Usai, Paolo Cherchi. *Georges Méliès.* Rome: La Nuova Italia, 1983.

Hayao Miyazaki

Cavallaro, Dani. *The Anime Art of Hayao Miyazaki.* Jefferson, NC: McFarland, 2006.

Horn, Steven. "Interview with Hayao Miyazaki," http//movies.ign.com/articles/371/371579p1.html.

McCarthy, Helen. *Hayao Miyazaki: Master of Japanese Animation.* Berkeley, CA: Stone Press, 1999.

Miyazaki, Hayao. *Starting Point: 1979–1996.* Trans. Beth Cary and Frederick Schodt. San Francisco: VIZ Media, 2009.

Odell, Colin and Michelle Le Blanc. *Studio Ghibli: The Films of Hayao Miyazaki and Isao Takahata.* Harpenden: Kamara, 2009.

Kenji Mizoguchi

Zernik, Clélia. "Onirisme et réalisme du conte chez Mizoguchi." In *Contes et légendes à l'écran.* Carole Aurouet. Condé-sur-Noireau: Corlet Éditions Diffusion, 2005. 146–155.

Yuri Norstein

Kitson, Clare. *Yuri Norstein and Tale of Tales.* Eastleigh: John Libbey, 2005.

MacFadyen, David. "Skazka Skazok/Tale of Tales." In *Russia and the Former Soviet Union.* Ed. Birgit Beumers. London: Wallflower Press, 2007. 183–192.

Michel Ocelot

Fritz, Steve. "A French Master and his New Film." http://www.newsarama.com/film/0903-animated-shorts-michel-ocelot.html.

Gudin, Christine. "La genèse des contes de Michel Ocelot." In *Contes et légendes à l'écran.* Carole Aurouet. Condé-sur-Noireau: Corlet Éditions Diffusion, 2005. 24–33.

———. "'J'utilise les contes comme un minerai avec lequel j'essaie de faire des bijoux': Entretien avec Michel Ocelot." In *Contes et légendes à l'écran.* Carole Aurouet. Condé-sur-Noireau: Corlet Éditions Diffusion, 2005. 267–274.

Neupert, Richard. "Kirikou and the Animated Figure/Body." *Studies in French Cinema.* 8.1 (2008): 41–56.

Ocelot, Michel. *Tout sur Kirikou.* Paris: Seuil, 1998.

Jean Painlevé

Masaki, Andy and Marina McDougall with Brigitte Berg, eds. *Science is Fiction: The Films of Jean Painlevé.* Trans. Jeanine Herman. Cambridge, MA: MIT Press, 2000.

Lotte Reiniger

Mortiz, William. "Some Critical Perspectives on Lotte Reiniger." *Animation Journal* 5.1 (Fall 1996): 40–51.

Reiniger, Lotte. *Shadow Theatres and Shadow Films.* London: B. T. Batsford, 1970.

Strobel, Christel and Hans Strobel. *Lotte Reiniger: Materialien zu ihren Märchen- und Musikfilmen.* Duisburg: Atlas Film + Av, 1988.

White, Eric Walter. *Walking Shadows: An Essay on Lotte Reiniger's Silhouette Films.* London: Hogarth, 1931.

Jan Svankmajer

De Bruyn, Dirk. "Re-animating the Lost Objects of Childhood and Everyday: Jan Svankmajer." *Senses of Cinema* 14 (June, 2001): http//:www.archive.sensesof cinema.com/contents/cteq/01/14.html.

———. "Chasing Rabbits out of the Hat and into the Shedding of Childhood (*Alice*). *Senses of Cinema* 20 (May/June, 2002): http//:www.archive.sensesofcinema.com/contents/cteq/02/20/alice.html.

Furniss, Maureen. "Adapting Alice: Two Contexts." *Art and Design,* 12 (1997): 10–13.

Hames, Peter. "Bringing Up Baby: Jan Svankmajer interviewed by Peter Hames," *Sight and Sound* 11.10 (October 2001): 26–28.

———, ed. *The Cinema of Jan Svankmajer: Dark Alchemy.* 2nd Ed. London: Wallflower Press, 2008.

O'Pray, Michael. "Jan Svankmajer: A Mannerist Surrealist." In *The Cinema of Jan Svankmajer: Dark Alchemy.* 2nd Ed. Ed. Peter Hames. London: Wallflower Press, 2008. 64–65.

Reid, Tina-Louise. "*Neco z Alenky* (*Alice*)." In *The Cinema of Central Europe.* Ed. Peter Hames. London: Wallflower Press, 2004): 215–233.

———. "Jan Svankmajer: Genius Loci as a Source of Surrealist Inspiration." In *The Unsilvered Screen: Surrealism on Film.* Eds. Graeme Harper and Rob Stone. London: Wallflower Press, 2007. 60–71.

Svankmajera, Eva. *Anima Animus Animation.* Prague: Slovart, 1997.

Svankmajerova, Eva & Jan Svankmajer. *De bouche à bouche.* Paris: Éditions de l'œil, 2002.

Uhde, Jan. "The Film World of Jan Svankmajer." *Cross Currents* 8 (1989): 195–208.

———. "Jan Svankmajer: The Prodigious Animator from Prague." *Kinema* 2 (1994): 30–41.

Wells, Paul. "Body Consciousness in the Films of Jan Svankmajer." In *A Reader in Animation Studies.* Ed. Jayne Pilling. Sydney, Australia: John Libbey, 1997. 177–194.

Filmography

The filmography has been divided into the following sections:

Silent Films
Feature Animated Films
American Cartoons
DEFA Shorts and Cartoons
Animated Shorts
Live-Action Fairy-Tale Films
Directors and Producers
Canonical Fairy-Tale Films
Studios, Series, Selected Countries

I have listed the films in each section either chronologically or alphabetically, and in some cases, a film might appear in two sections. However, I have tried to avoid double listing. For instance, none of the canonical fairy-tale films are noted in the "Feature Animated Films" nor under "Live-Action Fairy-Tale Films." There are many excellent directors and producers of fairy-tale films whom I have not listed in the section "Directors and Producers," which had to be kept to a small size. However, I have listed their films. There may be errors and omissions in the filmography. For the most part, I consider this a first "stab" at trying to compile a comprehensive list.

Silent Films

The Devil's Castle (*Le Manoir du diable*, 1896/97)
Director: Georges Méliès

Blue Beard (*Barbe-bleue*, 1897)
Studio: Lumière

Cinderella and the Fairy Godmother (1898)
Director: George Albert Smith

Cinderella (*Cendrillon*, 1899)
Director: Georges Méliès

The Philosopher's Stone (*La Pierre philosophale*, 1899)
Director: Georges Méliès

The Rajah's Dream, or The Betwitched Wood (*Le Rêve du Radjah ou la Forêt enchantée*, 1900)
Director: Georges Méliès

The Sorcerer, the Prince, and the Good Fairy (*Le Sorcier, le Prince et le Bon Génie*, 1900)
Director: Georges Méliès

Coppelia, the Animated Doll (*Coppélia ou la Poupée animée*, 1900)
Director: Georges Méliès

Little Red Riding Hood (*Le Petit Chaperon rouge*, 1900/01)
Director: Georges Méliès

The Sorceress's Home (*Chez la sorcière*, 1901)
Director: Georges Méliès

Bluebeard (*Barbe-Bleue*, 1901)
Director: Georges Méliès

Little Tom Thumb (*Le petit Poucet*, 1901)
Studio: Pathé

The Dwarf and the Giant (*Nain et Géant*, 1901/02)
Director: Georges Méliès

The Enchanted Basket (*La Corbeille enchantée*, 1902/03)
Director: Georges Méliès

The Little Match Seller (1902)
Director: James Williamson

Jack and the Beanstalk (1902)
Director: Edwin S. Porter

Sleeping Beauty (*La Belle au bois dormant*, 1902)
Director: Lucien Nonguet, Ferdinand Zecca

Ali Baba and the Forty Thieves (*Ali Baba et les quarantes voleurs*, 1902)
Director: Ferdinand Zecca

Little Tom Thumb (*Le Petit Poucet*, 1903)
Director: Sigmund Lubin

Puss in Boots (*Le chat botté*, 1903)
Director: Lucien Nonguet, Ferdinand Zecca

Alice in Wonderland (1903)
Director: Percy Stow

The Enchanted Well (*Le Puits fantastique*, 1903)
Director: Georges Méliès

The Sorcerer's Revenge (*Le Sorcier*, 1903)
Director: Georges Méliès

The Kingdom of the Fairies (*Le Royaume des fées*, 1903)
Director: Georges Méliès

The Enchanter Alcofribas (*L'Enchanteur Alcofribas*, 1903)
Director: Georges Méliès

The Magic Lantern (*La Lanterne magique*, 1903)
Director: Georges Méliès

Little Tom Thumb (*Le peitit Poucet*, 1905)
Director: V. Lorant-Heilbronn

The Palace of the One Thousand and One Nights (*Le Palais des mille et une nuits*, 1905)
Director: Georges Méliès

The Dollmaker's Daughter (1906)
Director: Lewin Fitzhamon

Aladdin and the Marvelous Lamp (*Aladdin et la lampe merveilleuse*, 1906)
Director: Albert Capellani, Segundo de Chomon

Jack the Chimney-Sweeper (*Jack le ramoneur*, 1906)
Director: Georges Méliès

The Fairy Carabosse or The Fatal Dagger (*La Fée Carabosse ou le Poignard fatal*, 1906)
Director: Georges Méliès

Blue Beard (*Barbe-bleue*, 1907)
Director: Étienne Arnaud

Sleeping Beauty (*La Belle au bois dormant*, 1907)
Studio: Lux

Cinderella, or the Marvelous Slipper (*Cendrillon ou la pantoufle merveilleuse*, 1907)
Director: Albert Capellani

The Pied Piper (1907)
Director: Percy Stow

Cinderella (1907)
Director: Lewis Fitzhannon

Beauty and the Beast (*La Belle et la bête*, 1908)
Director: Lucien Nonguet

Little Tom Thumb (*Le petit Poucet*, 1908)
Director: Albert Capellani

Donkey Skin (*Peau d'âne*, 1908)
Director: Albert Capellani

The Devil's Boots (*Les bottes du diable*, 1908)
Director: Étienne Arnaud

The Two Fairies (*Les deux fées*, 1908)
Director: Étienne Arnaud

Riquet with the Tuft (*Riquet à la houppe*, 1908)
Director: Albert Capellani

Sleeping Beauty (*La belle aus bois dormant*, 1908)
Director: Albert Capellani/Lucien Nonguet

A Modern Cinderella (1908)
Director: Percy Stowe

The Grandmother's Tale and the Child's Dream (*Conte de la grand-mère et Rêve de l'enfant*, 1908)
Director: Georges Méliès

The Marvelous Fountain (*La Fontaine merveilleuse*, 1908)
Director: Georges Méliès

The Marvelous Cobweb (*La Toile d'araignée merveilleuse*, 1908)
Director: Georges Méliès

The Fairy Libellule, or The Enchanted Lake (*La Fée Libellule ou le Lac enchanté*, 1908)
Director: Georges Méliès

The Spirit of the Clocks, or The Son of the Bell-Ringer (*Le Génie des cloches ou le Fils du sonneur*, 1908)
Director: Georges Méliès

The Good Shepherdess and the Wicked Princess (*La Bonne Bergère et la Mauvaise Princesse*, 1908)
Director: Georges Méliès

Donkey Skin (*Peau d'âne*, 1908)
Director: Albert Capellani

Hansel and Gretel (1909)
Director: J. Searle Dawley

Cinderella's Shoe (*Le soulier de Cendrillon*, 1909)
Director: Gérard Bourgeois

Little Tom Thumb (*Le petit Poucet*, 1909)
Director: Segundo de Chomon

Bluebeard (1909)
Director: J. Searle Dawley

Little Snow White (*La Petite Blanche-Neige*, 1910)
Anonymous

Cinderella's Cousin (*Le Cousin de Cendrillon*, 1910)
Director: Léonce Perret

Alice's Adventures in Wonderland (1910)
Director: Edwin S. Porter

A Modern Cinderella (1910)
Director: J. Stuart Blackton

The Wonderful Wizard of Oz (1910)
Director: Otis Turner

Little Red Riding Hood (1911)
Director: James Kirkwood, George Loane Tucker

Little Red Riding Hood (1911)
Director: A. E. Coleby

A Modern Cinderella (1911)
Director: J. Searle Dawley

Cinderella (1911)
Director: George Nichols

The Hallucinations of Baron Munchausen (*Les Hallucinations du baron de Münchausen*, 1911)
Director: Georges Méliès

Pied Piper of Hamelin (1911)
Director: Theodore Merston

Pinocchio (1911)
Director: Giulio Antamoro

Sammy Opheus; or The Pied Piper of the Jungle (1912)
Director: Colin Campbell

The Shadow of the Sea (*Der Schatten des Meeres*, 1912)
Director: Curt Stark

Little Tom Thumb (*Le petit Poucet, 1912*)
Director: Georges André Lacroix

Tom Thumb (*Le petit Poucet*, 1912)
Director: Louis Feuillade

Cinderella, or The Marvelous Slipper (*Cendrillon ou la Pantoufle merveilleuse*, 1912)
Director: Georges Méliès

The Knight of the Snows (*Le Chevalier des Neiges*, 1912)
Director: Georges Méliès

A Cowgirl Cinderella (1912)
Producer: David Horsely

Cinderella (*Cendrillon ou La petite pantouffe de verre*, 1912)
Director: Georges Méliès

Cinderella (1912)
Director: Colin Campbell

Cinderella (1912)
Director: Arthur Melbourne Cooper

Cinderella (1912)
Director: Arthur Cooper

Lord Browning and Cinderella (1912)
Director: Van Dyke Brooke

When Lillian was Little Red Riding Hood (1913)
Director: Colin Campbell

The Student of Prague (*Der Student von Prag*, 1913)
Director: Stellen Rye

A Princess of Baghdad (1913)
Director: Charles Gaskill

A Modern Cinderella (*Cenerentola*, 1913)
Director: Eleuterio Rodolfi

Cinderella's Gloves (1913)
Anonymous

A Southern Cinderella (1913)
Director: Burton King

Cinderella and the Boob (1913)
Director: Dell Henderson

A Reluctant Cinderella (1913)
Director: C. J. Williams

The Pied Piper of Hamelin (1913)
Director: George Lessey

An Awkward Cinderella (1914)
Director: Otis Turner

Mr. Cinderella (1914)
Director: Eugene Moore

Cinderella (1914)
Director: James Kirkwood

Monsieur Bluebeard (1914)
Director: Charles Giblyn

The Legend of Snow White (1914)
Screenplay: T. O. Eltonhead

His Majesty, the Scarecrow of Oz (1914)
Director: L. Frank Baum

The Patchwork Girl of Oz (1914)
Director: J. Farrell MacDonald

The Magic Cloak of Oz (1914)
Director: J. Farrell MacDonald

Alice in Wonderland, (1915)
Director: W. W. Young

The Tales of Hoffmann (*Hoffmanns Erzählungen*, 1915)
Director: Richard Oswald

Rumpelstiltskin (1915)
Director: Raymond West

Snow White (*Schneewittchen*, 1915)
Educational Pictures

Snow White (1916)
Director: J. Searle Dawley

Snow White (1916)
Director: Charles Weston

A Daughter of the Gods (1916)
Director: Herbert Brenon

Undine (1916)
Director: Henry Otto

Cinderella (*Aschenbrödel*, 1916)
Director: Urban Gad

A Cripple Creek Cinderella (1916)
Director: Ulysses Davis

Jack and the Beanstalk (1917)
Director: Chester and Sydney Franklin

The Babes in the Wood (1917)
Director: Chester and Sydney Franklin

Aladdin and the Wonderful Lamp (1917)
Director: Chester and Sydney Franklin

The Seven Swans (1917)
Director: J. Searle Dawley

The Cinderella Man (1917)
Director: George Sloan Tucker

A Modern Cinderella (1917)
Director: John Adolfi

A Kentucky Cinderella (1917)
Director: Rupert Julian

A Studio Cinderella (1917)
Director: Matt Moore

Cinderella and the Magic Slipper (1917)
Director: Guy McDonell

Puss in Boots (1917)
Studio: Peter Pan Company

Ali Baba and the Forty Thieves (1918)
Director: Chester and Sydney Franklin

Queen of the Sea (1918)
Director: John G. Adolfi

The Bluebird (1918)
Director: Maurice Tourneur

Little Red Riding Hood (1918)
Director: Otis Thayer

The Star Prince (1918)
Director: Madeline Brandis

The Ratcatcher of Hamelin (*Der Rattenfänger von Hameln*, 1918)
Director: Paul Wegener

Little Red Riding Hood (1918)
Director: Otis Thayer

Daddy Long Legs (1919)
Director: Marshall Neilan

The Emperor's New Clothes (*Novoye platye korolya*, 1919)
Director: Yuri Zhelyabuzhsky

Cinderella Cinders (1920)
Director: Frederick Ireland

A Kitchen Cinderella (1920)
Director: Malcolm St. Clair

The Irish Cinderella (c. 1920)
Anonymous

Tom Thumb (*Le petit Poucet*, 1920)
Director: Robert Boudrioz

Cinderella's Twin (1921)
Director: Dallas Fitzgerald

A Rural Cinderella (1921)
Director: Erle Kenton

Cinderella of the Hills (1921)
Director: Howard Mitchell

Tired Death (*Der müde Tod*, 1921)
Director: Fritz Lang

Bluebeard, Jr. (1922)
Director: Scott R. Dunlap

Landru, the Bluebeard of Paris (*Landru, der Blaubart von Paris*, 1922)
Director: Hans Otto

A Lowland Cinderella (1922)
Director: Sidney Morgan

Cinderella (1922)
Director: Walt Disney

<u>*Puss in Boots*</u> (1922)
Director: Walt Disney

Cinderella (Aschenputtel, 1922)
Director: Lotte Reininger

Little Red Riding Hood (1922)
Director: Walt Disney

Sleeping Beauty (*Dornröschen*, 1922)
Director: Lotte Reiniger

Little Red Riding Hood (1922)
Director: Alfred J. Goulding, Al Herman

Little Red Riding Hood (1922)
Director: Anson Dyer

Little Red Riding Hood (*Cervená Karkulla*, 1922)
Director: Svatopluk Innemann

Hansel and Gretel (1923)
Director: Alfred J. Goulding

The Lost Shoe (*Der verlorene Schuh*, 1923)
Director: Ludwig Berger

A Kick for Cinderella (1924)
Director: Bud Fisher

Cinderella (1924)
Director: Herbert Dawley

Sleeping Beauty (1924)
Director: Herbert Dawley

The Comediennes (1924)
Anonymous

The Wonderful Wizard of Oz (1924)
Director: Larry Semon

Peter Pan (1924)
Director: Herbert Brenon

Tattercoats (1924)
Director: Herbert M. Dawley

The Thief of Baghdad (1924)
Director: Douglas Fairbanks

Alice the Piper (1924)
Director: Walt Disney

The Pied Piper (1924)
Director: Walter Lantz

Pied Piper Malone (1924)
Director: Alfred Green

Cinderella (1925)
Director: Walter Lantz

A Kiss for Cinderella (1925)
Director: Herbert Brenon

Big Red Riding Hood (1925)
Director: Leo McCarey

Little Red Riding Hood (1925)
Director: Walter Lantz

The Student of Prague (*Der student von Prag*, 1926)
Director: Heinrich Galeen

Ella Cinders (1926)
Director: Alfred E. Green

Mr. Cinderella (1926)
Director: Norman Taurog

The Pied Piper of Hamelin (1926)
Director: Frank Tilley

A Bowery Cinderella (1927)
Director: Burton King

The Patsy (1928)
Director: King Vidor

The Bush Cinderella (1928)
Director: Rudall Hayward

Cinderella (1930)
Director: Manny Gould, Ben Harrison

Little Red Riding Hood (1930)
Director: Alberto Calvacanti

Feature Animated Films

(The films in this section are arranged alphabetically not chronologically as in most of the sections.)

The Adventures of Buratino (*Priklyucheniya Buratino*, 1960), also known as *Pinocchio and the Golden Key*
Director: Ivan Ivanov-Vano, Dimitriy Babichenko, Mikhail Botov

Aladdin (1992)
Director: John Musker/Ron Clements

Alakazam the Great (*Saiyu-ki*, 1960)
Director: Taiji Yabushita, Daisaku Shirakawa, Osamu Tezuka

The Arabian Nights: The Adventures of Sinbad (*Arabian naito: Shindobaddo no bôken*, 1962)
Director: Taiji Yabushita, Yoshio Kuroda

Azur et Asmar (2007)
Director: Michel Ocelot

Blood Tea and Red String (2006)
Director: Christiane Cegavske

The Book of the Dead (2005)
Director: Kihachiro Kawamoto

The Boy Who Wanted to Be a Bear (*Drengen der ville gore det unmulige*, 2002)
Director: Jannik Hastrup

Castle in the Sky (*Tenkû no shiro Rapyuta*, 1986)
Director: Hiyao Miyazaki

The Castle of Cagliostro (*Rupan sansei: Kariosutoro no shiro*, 1979)
Director: Hayao Miyazaki

The Curious Adventures of Mr. Wonderbird (*La Bergère et le Ramoneur*, 1952)
Director: Paul Grimault

The Dog, the General, and the Birds (*Le Chien, le général et les oiseaux* (2003)
Director: Francis Nielsen

The Emperor's Nightingale (*Cirasuv Slavik*, 1948)
Director: Jirí Trnka, Jirí Brdecka (animation)
Director: Milos Makovec (live-action scenes)

The Fabulous Baron Munchausen (*Baron Prásil*, 1961)
Director: Karel Zeman

Faeries (2005)
Director: Gary Hurst

Gandahar (also known as *Light Years*, 1988)
Director: René Laloux

The Golden Antelope (*Zolotaya antilopa*, 1954)
Director: Lev Atamanov

The Golden Rooster (*Skaska o zolotom petushke*, 1967)
Director: Aleksandra Snezhko-Blotskaya

Happily Never After (2006)
Director: Paul Bolger

The Hobbit (1977)
Director: Jules Bass, Arthur Rankin Jr.

Hoppity Goes to Town (1941)
Director: Dave Fleischer

How to Train Your Dragon (2010)
Director: Dean DeBlois, Chris Sanders

The Humpbacked Horse (*Konyok-gorbunok*, 1947/1976), also known as *Ivan and his Magic Pony*
Director: Ivan Ivanov-Vano, Boris Butakov

Jin-Roh: The Wolf Brigade (1999)
Director: Hiroyuki Okiura

The King and Mr. Bird (*Le Roi et l'Oiseau*, 1979)
Director: Paul Grimault

Kirikou and the Sorceress (*Kirikou et la* Sorcière, 1998)
Director: Michel Ocelot

Kirikou and the Wild Beasts (*Kirikou et les bêtes sauvages*, 2006)
Director: Michel Ocelot, Bénédicte Galup

The Last Petal (*Poslednu Lepestok*, 1977)
Director: Roman Kachanov

The Last Unicorn (1982)
Director: Jules Bass, Arthur Rankin Jr.

The Legend of Kawa the Blacksmith (*Efsaneya Kawaye Asinger*, 2008)
Director: Havi Ibrahim, Stuart Palmer

The Littlest Warrior (*Anju to zushio-maru*, 1961)
Director: Taiji Yabushita, Yugo Serikawa

Magic Boy (*Shônen Sarutobi Sasuke*, 1959)
Director: Taiji Yabushita, Akira Daikubara

The Magic Carpet (*Kakhardakan gorg*, 1948)
Director: Lev Amanatov

Momo (2001)
Director: Enzo D'Alò

My Beautiful Girl Mari (*Mari iyagi*, 2002)
Director: Seong-Kang Lee

My Father's Dragon (*Elmer no boken*, 1997)
Director: Masami Hata

The Mystery of the Third Planet (*Tayna tretey planety*, 1981), also known as *Alice and the Mystery of the Third Planet*
Director: Roman Kachanov

Opopomoz (2003)
Director: Enzo D'Alò

Ponyo (*Gake no ue no Ponyo*, 2008)
Director: Hayao Miyazaki

Prince Bajaja (*Bajaja*, 1950)
Director: Jirí Trnka

The Prince, the Swan and the Czar Sultan (*Skazka o tsare Salta*, 1984)
Director: Ivan Ivanov-Vano, Lev Milchin

The Princess and the Goblin (1992)
Director: József Gémes

Princess Mononoke (*Mononoke-hime*, 1997)
Director: Hayao Miyazaki

Raggedy Ann and Raggedy Andy (1941)
Director: Dave Fleischer

The Scarlet Flower (*Alenki zwetotschek*, 1952), also known as *Beauty and the Beast*
Director: Lev Atamanov

The Secret of Kells (2009)
Director: Tomm Moore, Nora Twomey

Shrek (2001)
Director: Andrew Adamson, Vicky Jenson

Shrek 2 (2004)
Director: Andrew Adamson, Kelly Asbury, Conrad Vernon

Shrek the Third (2007)
Director: Chris Miller and Raman Hui

Shrek Forever After (2010)
Director: Mike Mitchell

Sita Sings the Blues (2008)
Director: Nina Paley

The Snow Maiden (*Snegurochka*, 1952)
Director: Ivan Ivanova-Vano

The Sorcerer's Apprentice (*Carodejuv ucen*, 1978), also known as *Krabat*
Director: Karel Zeman

Spirited Away (Sen to Chihiro no kamikakushi, 2001)
Director: Hayao Miyazaki

The Tale of the White Serpent (*Hakujaden*, 1958)
Director: Taiji Yabushita, Kazuhiko Okabe

The Tale about Tszar Saltan (*Skaza o Care Saltane*, 1943)
Director: Zinaida Brumberg, T. Basmanova, Valentina Brumberg

The Tale of the White Serpent (*Hakujaden*, 1958)
Director: Taiji Yabushita, Kazuhiko Okabe

Taro the Dragon Boy (*Tatsu no ko Tarô*, 1979)
Director: Kiriro Urayama, Peter Fernandez (English version)

A Thousand and One Nights (*Pohádky tisíce a jedné noci*, 1974)
Director: Karel Zeman

Twelve Months (*12 mesyatsev*, 1956)
Director: Ivan Ivanov-Vano, Mikhail Botov

Twice Upon a Time (1983)
Director: John Korty, Charles Swenson

The Wild Swans (*Dikie lebedi*, 1963)
Director: Vera Tsekhanovskaya, Mikhail Tsekhanovsky

Wizards (1977)
Director: Ralph Bakshi

Young Jack and the Witch (*Shônen Jakku to Mahô-tsukai*, 1967)
Director: Taiji Yabushita

1001 Arabian Nights (1959)
Director: Jack Kinney

American Cartoons

The Columbia/Screen Gems Cartoons

Cinderella (1930)
Director: Manny Gould, Ben Harrison

Tom Thumb's Brother (1941)
Director: Sid Marcus

Playing the Pied Piper (1941)
Director: Louie Lilly

Red Riding Hood Rides Again (1941)
Director: Sid Marcus

Wolf Chases Pigs (1942)
Director: Frank Tashlin, John Hubley

Cinderella Goes to a Party (1942)
Director: Bob Wickersham

Willoughby's Magic Hat (1943)
Director: Bob Wickersham, Ub Iwerks

Duty and the Beast (1943)
Director: Alec Geiss

Walt Disney Studio: Laugh-O-Grams and Silly Symphonies

Little Red Riding Hood (1922)
Director: Walt Disney

The Four Musicians of Bremen (1922)
Director: Walt Disney

Jack and the Beanstalk (1922)
Director: Walt Disney

Goldie Locks and the Three Bears (1922)
Director: Walt Disney

Puss in Boots (1922)
Director: Walt Disney

Cinderella (1922)
Director: Walt Disney

The Merry Dwarfs (1929)
Director: Walt Disney

The Ugly Duckling (1931)
Director: Wilfried Jackson

Babes in the Woods (1932)
Director: Burt Gillett

Three Little Pigs (1933)
Director: Burt Gillett

The Pied Piper (1933)
Director: Wilfried Jackson

Giantland (1933)
Director: Burt Gillett

The Big Bad Wolf (1934)
Director: Burt Gillett

The Flying Mouse (1934)
Director: David Hand

The Golden Touch (1935)
Director: Walt Disney

Three Little Wolves (1936)
Director: David Hand

The Brave Little Tailor (1938)
Director: Burt Gillett

The Ugly Duckling (1939)
Director: Jack Cutting

Famous Studios

The Mite Makes Right (1948)
Director: Bill Tytla

Max and Dave Fleischer Cartoons

Mother Goose Land (1925)
Director: Dave Fleischer

Jack and the Beanstalk (1931)
Director: Dave Fleischer

Dizzy Red Riding Hood (1931)
Director: Dave Fleischer

Parade of the Wooden Soldiers (1933)
Director: Dave Fleischer

Betty Boop's Hallowe'en Party (1933)
Director: Dave Fleischer

Snow White (1933)
Director: Dave Fleischer

Betty in Blunderland (1934)
Director: Dave Fleischer

Poor Cinderella (1934)
Director: Dave Fleischer

Little Dutch Mill (1934)
Director: Dave Fleischer

Betty Boop and the Little King (1936)
Director: Dave Fleischer

Popeye the Sailor Meets Sinbad the Sailor (1936)
Director: Dave Fleischer

Popeye the Sailor Meets Ali Baba's Forty Thieves (1937)
Director: Dave Fleischer

Popeye the Sailor Meets Aladdin and his Wonderful Lamp (1937)
Director: Dave Fleischer

The Wizard of Ants (1941)
Director: Dave Fleischer

Hoppity Goes to Town (1941)
Director: Dave Fleischer

Fractured Fairy-Tales from the Rocky and Bullwinkle Show

These films were telecast in 1959 and 1961–1964.

Goldilocks
Jack and the Beanstalk
Rapunzel
The Fisherman's Wishes
Puss and Boots
The Brave Little Tailor
Rumpelstiltskin
The Princess and the Pea
Beauty and the Beast
Sweet Little Beet
Dick Whittington
Tom Thumb
The Elves and the Shoemaker
Cinderella
Snow White
Sir Galahad
King Midas
Pinocchio
Little Red Riding Hood
Sleeping Beauty
Hansel and Gretel
Cinderella Returns
Snow White, Inc.
Jack and the Beanstalk
The Pied Piper
Puss in Boots
Leaping Beauty
Tom Thumb, also known as *Tiny Tom*
Slipping Beauty
Aladdin's Lamp

Rumpelstiltskin Returns
The Enchanted Fish
The Frog Prince
The Pied Piper
Prince Darling
The Ugly Duckling
Son of Rumpelstiltskin
Beauty and Her Beast
The Golden Goose
The Enchanted Frog
The Goose and the Golden Egg
Riding Hoods Anonymous
The Shoemaker and the Elves
Speeding Beauty
The Three Piggs
Goldilocks and the Three Bears
Son of Beauty and the Beast
Androcles and the Lion
The Fisherman and His Wife
The Princess and The Goblins
Snow White Meets Rapunzel
The Little Princess
Thom Tum
Slow White and Nose Red
Prince Hyacinth and the Dear Little Princess
The Giant and the Beanstalk
The Enchanted Fly
Felicia and the Pot of Pinks
Hans Clinker
The Witch's Broom
Son of King Midas
The Magic Chicken
Aladdin and His Lump
The Enchanted Gnat
Milo and the Thirteen Helmets
The Prince and the Popper
Booty and the Beast
Little Fred Riding Hood
Goldilocks
The Ugly Almond Duckling
John's Ogre Wife
The Absent-Minded King
The Mysterious Castle
The Little Tinker
The Tale of a Frog
The Teeth of Baghdad
Little Man in the Tub
Red White
Cutie and the Beast
The Flying Carpet
The Count and the Bird
The Tale of a King
Sweeping Beauty
The Wishing Hat
Son of Snow White
Jack B. Nimble
Potter's Luck
The Magic Lichee Nut
The King and the Witch
The Seven Chickens
A Youth Who Set Out to Learn What Fear Was

Ub Iwerks Cartoons

Jack and the Beanstalk (1933)
Director: Ub Iwerks, Shamus Culhane, Al Eugster

The Brave Tin Soldier (1934)
Director: Ub Iwerks

Puss in Boots (1934)
Director: Ub Iwerks

Aladdin and his Wonderful Lamp (1934)
Director: Ub Iwerks

Brementown Musicians (1935)
Director: Ub Iwerks

Sinbad the Sailor (1935)
Director: Ub Iwerks

Balloonland, or The Pincushion Man (1935)
Director: Ub Iwerks

Ali Baba (1936)
Director: Ub Iwerks

Tom Thumb (1936)
Director: Ub Iwerks

Dick Whittington's Cat (1936)
Director: Ub Iwerks

Walter Lantz Cartoons

Wolf, Wolf (1934)
Gingerbread Boy (1934)
Dizzy Dwarf (1934)
Jolly Little Elves (1934)
The Sleeping Princess (1939)
Director: Burt Gillett

The Pied Piper of Basin Street (1945)
Director: James Culhane

Witch Crafty (1955)
Director: Paul J. Smith.

Red Riding Hoodlum (1957)
Director: Paul J. Smith

His Better Elf (1958)
Director: Paul J. Smith

Little Woody Riding Hood (1962)
Director: Paul J. Smith

Rough Riding Hood (1966)
Director: Sid Marcus

Woody and the Beanstalk (1966)
Director: Paul J. Smith.

The Genie with the Light Touch (1972)
Director: Paul J. Smith

MGM Cartoons

The Chinese Nightingale (1935)
Director: Rudolf Ising

Puss N'Toots (1942)
Director: William Hanna, Joseph Barbera

Red Hot Riding Hood (1943)
Director: Tex Avery

Swing Shift Cinderella (1945)
Director: Tex Avery

Little Rural Riding Hood (1949)
Director: Tex Avery

Paramount/Famous Studios Cartoons

Puss 'N Boots (1954)
Director: Seymour Kneitel

Little Audrey Riding Hood (1955)
Director: Seymour Kneitel

Baggin' the Dragon (1966)
Director: Howard Post

From Nags to Witches (1966)
Director: Howard Post

The Stuck-Up Wolf (1967)
Director: Shamus Culhane

Pathé Frères

A Kick for Cinderella (1916/1924)
Director: Bud Fisher

Terrytoons

Aladdin's Lamp (1931)
The Forty Thieves (1931)
Bluebeard's Brother (1932)
Cinderella (1933)
King Zilch (1933)
A Gypsy Fiddler (1933)
Beanstalk Jack (1933)
A Modern Red Riding Hood (1935)
Aladdin's Lamp (1935)
A Wolf in Cheap Clothing (1936)
String Bean Jack (1938)
Director: John Foster

Wolf's Side of the Story (1938)
Director: Connie Rasinski

The Glass Slipper (1938)
Director: Mannie Davis

Aladdin's Lamp (1943)
Director: Eddie Donnelly

The Frog and the Princess (1944)
Director: Eddie Donnelly

Wolf! Wolf! (1944)
Director: Eddie Donnelly

A Wolf's Tale (1944)
Director: Connie Rasinski

Mother Goose Nightmare (1945)
Director: Connie Rasinski

The Wicked Wolf (1946)
Director: Mannie Davis

Beanstalk Jack (1946)
Director: Eddie Donnelly

Crying Wolf (1947)
Director: Connie Rasinski

Aladdin's Lamp (1947)
Director: Eddie Donnelly

The Wolf's Pardon (1947)
Director: Eddie Donnelly

The Witch's Cat (1948)
Director: Mannie Davis

Magic Slipper (1948)
Director: Mannie Davis

Hansel and Gretel (1952)
Director: Connie Rasinski

Tall Tale Teller (1954)
Director: Connie Rasinski

Reformed Wolf (1954)
Director: Connie Rasinksi

UPA Cartoons

Georgie and the Dragon (1951)
Director: Robert "Bobe" Cannon

The Wonder Gloves (1951)
Director: Robert "Bobe" Cannon

The Emperor's New Clothes (1953)
Director: Ted Parmelee

The Unicorn in the Garden (1953)
Director: William T. Hurtz

The Fifty-First Dragon (1954)
Director: Peter Burness

Riding Hood Magoo (1961)
Director: Grant Simmons

Prince Charming Magoo (1961)
Director: Brad Case

Goldilocks Magoo (1961)
Director: Brad Case

Magoo and the Beanstalk (1961)
Director: Steve Clark

Van Beuren Cartoons

Red Riding Hood (1931)
Director: John Foster, Harry Bailey

Cinderella Blues (1931)
Director: John Foster, Harry Bailey

Fairyland Follies (1931)
Director: John Foster, Harry Dailey

Bold King Cole (1936)
Director: Burt Gillett

The Goose That Laid the Golden Egg (1936)
Director: Burt Gillett, Tom Palmer

Warner Brothers Cartoons

Beauty and the Beast (1934)
Director: Friz Freleng

The Miller's Daughter (1934)
Director: Friz Freleng

Fish Tales (1936)
Director: Jack King

Little Red Walking Hood (1937)
Director: Tex Avery

Cinderella Meets Fella (1938)
Director: Tex Avery

Pied Piper Porky (1939)
Director: Robert Clampett

Ali Baba Bound (1940)
Director: Robert Clampett

The Bear's Tale (1940)
Director: Tex Avery

Tom Thumb in Trouble (1940)
Director: Chuck Jones

The Sheepish Wolf (1942)
Director: Friz Freleng

Coal Black and De Sebben Dwarfs (1942)
Director: Robert Clampett

Jack-Wabbit and the Beanstalk (1943)
Director: Friz Freleng

Puss'n Booty (1943)
Director: Frank Tashlin

Little Red Riding Rabbit (1944)
Director: Friz Freleng

Little Red Rodent Hood (1952)
Director: Friz Freleng

The Turn-Tale Wolf (1952)
Director: Robert McKimson

Red Riding Hoodwinked (1955)
Director: Friz Freleng

Three Little Bops (1957)
Director: Friz Freleng

DEFA Shorts and Cartoons

Mother Holle (*Frau Holle*, 1953)
Director: Johannes Hempel

The Bremen Town Musicians (*Die Bremer Stadtmusikanten*, 1955)
Director: Bruno Böttge

King Thrushbeard (*König Drosselbart*, 1956)
Director: Bruno Böttge

The Emperor's New Clothes (*Des Kaisers neue Kleider*, 1957)
Director: Herbert Schulz

Princess Springwater (*Princessin Springwasser*, 1957)
Director: Bruno Böttge

The Magic Barrel (*Das Zauberfaß*, 1957)
Director: Herbert Schulz

The Story about the Five Brothers (*Die Geschichte von den fünf Brüdern*, 1957)
Director: Kurt Weiler

The Wish Ring (*Der Wunschring*, 1958)
Director: Bruno Böttge

Jorinde and Joringel (*Jorinde und Joringel*, 1958)
Director: Johannes Hempel

Tom Thumb's Adventures (*Däumelinchens Abenteuer*, 1959)
Director: Christl Wiemer

Six Make their Way through the World (*Sechse kommen durche die ganze Welt*, 1959)
Director: Lothar Barke

Brave Hans (*Vom mutigen Hans*, 1959)
Director: Klaus and Katja Georgi

Rumpelstiltskin (*Rumpelstilzchen*, 1960)
Director: Bruno Böttge

The Princess on the Pea (*Die Prinzessin auf der Erbse*, 1960)
Director: Katja Georgi

The Clever Farmer's Daughter (*Die kluge Bauerntochter*, 1961)
Director: Wolgang Bergner

The Golden Marksman (*Das Märchen vom goldenen Schützen*, 1963)
Director: Bruno Böttge

The Swineherd (*Der Schweinehirt*, 1963)
Director: Monnika Anderson

The Tinderbox (*Zündhölzer*, 1963)
Director: Katja Georgi

The Brave Little Tailor (*Der tapfere Schniderlein*, 1964)
Director: Kurt Weiler

Master Thief (*Der Meisterdieb*, 1966)
Director: Jörg d'Bomba

Sleeping Beauty (*Dornröschen*, 1968)
Director: Katja Georgi

Puss in Boots (*Der gestiefelte Kater*, 1968)
Director: Monika Anderson

The Boy Who Went Out to Learn about Fear (*Von einem, der auszog, das Gruseln zu lernen*, 1970)
Director: Rudolf Schraps

Spindel, Loom, and Needle (*Spindel, Weberschiffchen und Nadel*, 1974)
Director: Katja Georgi

The Princess and the Goatherd (*Die Prinzessin und der Ziegenhirt*, 1975)
Director: Bruno Böttge

Hansel and Gretel (*Hänsel und Gretel*, 1976)
Director: Katja Georgi

Little Red Riding Hood (*Rotkäppchen*, 1977)
Director: Otto Sacher

The Jungle Fairy Tale (*Urwaldmärchen*, 1978)
Director: Katja Georgi

"Little Zaches," Named Zinober (*"Klein Zaches", genannt Zinober*, 1979)
Director: Ina Rarisch

Rapunzel (1982)
Director: Christl Wiemer

The Ugly Duckling (*Das häßliche junge Entlein*, 1982)
Director: Ina Rarisch

Cinderella (*Aschenputtel*, 1984)
Director: Horst Tappert

The Story about Caliph Stork (*Die Geschichte vom Kalif Storch*, 1984)
Director: Kurt Weiler

The Dwarf Nose (*Zwerg Nase*, 1986)
Director: Katja Georgi

The Truth about the Frog King (*Die Wahrheit um den Froschkönig*, 1986)
Director: Siegelinde Hamacher

The Goose Maiden (*Die Gänsemagd*, 1987)
Director: Horst Tappert

Sleeping Beauty was a Beautiful Child (*Dornröschen war ein schönes Kind*, 1988)
Director: Katja Georgi

The Myrtle Maiden (*Das Myrtenfräulein*, 1989)
Director: Klaus Georgi

Animated Shorts

(The films in this section are arranged alphabetically not chronologically as in most of the sections.)

About the Cruel Stepmother (*Pro Zluyu Machehu*, 1966)
Director: Zinaida Brumberg, Valentina Brumberg

The Animals and the People of Petrov (*Zviratka a petrovsti*, 1946)
Director: Jirí Trnka

Beauty and the Beast (*Die Schöne und das Tier*, 1976)
Director: Katja Georgi

The Boy Who Went Out to Learn about Fear (*Von einem, der auszog, das Gruseln zu lernen*, 1935)
Director: Ferdinand Diehl

A Brave Little Tailor (*Hrabryj Portnyazhka*, 1964)
Director: Zinaida Brumberg, Valentina Brumberg

The Bremen Town Musicians (*Die Bremer Stadtmusikanten*, 1935)
Director: Ferdinand Diehl

The Bremen Town Musicians (*Die Bremer Stadtmusikanten*, 1935–1938)
Director: Kurt Stordel

Calif Storch (*Kaliftorch*, 1929)
Director: Ferdinand Diehl

A Capricious Princess (*Kapriznaya Princessa*, 1969)
Director: Zinaida Brumberg, Valentina Brumberg

The Cat in Boots (*Kot v Sapogah*, 1968)
Director: Zinaida Brumberg, Valentina Brumberg

Cheburashka (1971)
Director: Roman Kachanov

The City Mouse and the Country Mouse (*Le rat de ville et le rat des champs*, 1926)
Director: Ladislav Starewich

The Cloud in Love (*Vlyublennoe Oblako*, 1959)
Director: Anatoly Karanovich, Roman Kachanov

The Coat of the Old Woman (*Le Manteau de la Vieille Dame*, 2000)
Director: Michel Ocelot

The Cruel Queen and the Showman of Story (*La Reine Cruelle et le Montreur de Fabulo*, 2000)
Director: Michel Ocelot

The Cybernetic Grandmother (*Kyberneticka babicka*, 1962)
Director: Jirí Trnka

The Dancing Frog (1989)
Director: Michael Sporn

The Demon (1972)
Director: Kihachiro Kawamoto

The Devil's Mill (*Certuv mlyn*, 1949)
Director: Jirí Trnka

Dojoji Temple (1976)
Director: Kihachiro Kawamoto

Fig Boy (*Le Garçon des Figues*, 2000)
Director: Michel Ocelot

The Flower with Seven Colors (*Cvetik-Semicvetik*, 1948)
Director: Mikhail Tsekhanovsky

The Frog Princess (*Carevna-Lyagushka*, 1954)
Director: Mikhail Tsekhanovsky

Fulfillment of a Wish, also known as *Wishes Come True* (*Ispolenie Zhelanij*, 1957)
Director: Valentina Brumberg, Zinaida Brumberg

A Girl in the Jungle (*Devochka v Dzhunglyah*, 1956)
Director: Mikhail Tsekhanovsky, Vera Tsekhanovskia

The Golden Fish (*O ziate rybce*, 1951)
Director: Jirí Trnka

Granpa Planted a Beet (*Zasadil dedek repu*, 1945)
Director: Jirí Trnka

Hansel and Gretel (*Hänsel und Gretel*, 1935–1938)
Director: Kurt Stordel

Hansel and Gretel (1951)
Director: Ray Harryhausen

The Inheritance of the Magician Bakhram (*Nasledstvo Volshebnika Bakhrama*, 1975)
Director: Roman Kachanov

Ivashka and Baba-Yaga (*Ivashko i Baba-Yaga*, 1938)
Director: Valentina Brumberg, Zinaida Brumberg

King Midas (1953)
Director: Ray Harryhausen

The Last Petal (*Poslednij Lepestok*, 1977)
Director: Roman Kachanov

Legend of the Forest (1987)
Director: Tezuka Osamu

The Lion Who Became Old (*Le lion devenu vieux*, 1932)
Director: Ladislav Starewich

The Little Match Girl (1999)
Director: Michael Sporn

Little Red Riding Hood (*Krasnaya Shapochka*, 1937)
Director: Valentina Brumberg, Zinaida Brumberg

Little Red Riding Hood (1949)
Director: Ray Harryhausen

The Magic Flute (*La Flûte magique*, 1946)
Director: Paul Grimault

A Magic Wand (*Volshebnaya Palochka*, 1972)
Director: Zinaida Brumberg, Valentina Brumberg

Mermaid (1964)
Director: Tezuka Osamu

Mike Mulligan and his Steam Shovel (1990)
Director: Michael Sporn

A Miraculous Bell (*Chudesnyjkokol'Chik*, 1949)
Director: Zinaida Brumberg, Valentina Brumberg

The Myrtle Maiden (*Das Myrtenfräulein*, 1989)
Director: Katja Georgi

The Night before Christmas (*Noch' Pered Rozhdestvom*, 1951)
Director: Valentina Brumberg, Zinaida Brumberg

Nightingale (1999)
Director: Michael Sporn

Novice (*Novichok*, 1961)
Director: Roman Kachanov

An Old Man and the Crane (*Starik i Zhuravl*, 1958)
Director: Anatoly Karanovich, Roman Kachanov

Once Upon a Time There were Three Sisters (*Es waren einmal drei Schwestern . . .*, 1983) also knowns as *Silberwasser* (East Germany)
Director: Katja Georgi

The Princess on the Pea (*Die Prinzessin auf der Erbse*, 1960)
Director: Katja Georgi

Puss in Boots (*Der gestiefelte Kater*, 1935–1938)
Director: Kurt Stordel

Puss in Boots (*Der gestiefelte Kater*, 1940)
Director: Ferdinand Diehl

Rapunzel (1951)
Director: Ray Harryhausen

Red Riding Hood and the Wolf (*Rotkäppchen und der Wolf*, 1945)
Director: Kurt Stordel

The Red Shoes (1990)
Director: Michael Sporn

The Reluctant Dragon (1981)
Director: Sam Weiss

The Reluctant Dragon (1987)
Director: Bridget Appleby

The Scarecrow (*L'Épouventail*, 1943)
Director: Paul Grimault

The Seven Ravens (*Die sieben Raben*, 1937)
Director: Ferdinand Diehl

Sinbad the Sailor (*Sinbad-Morehod*, 1944)
Director: Zinaida Brumberg, Valentina Brumberg

Sleeping Beauty (*Dornröschen*, 1943)
Director: Ferdinand Diehl

Sleeping Beauty (*Dornröschen*, 1935–1938)
Director: Kurt Stordel

Sleeping Betty (2007)
Director: Claude Cloutier

The Spring-Man and the SS (*Perak a SS*, 1946)
Director: Jirí Trnka

Table Be Covered (*Tischlein Deck Dich*, 1936)
Director: Ferdinand Diehl

The Tale about Chapayev (*Skaz o Chapaeve*, 1958)
Director: Mikhail Tsekhanovsky, Vera Tsekhanovskaia

The Tale about the Fisherman and the Fish (*Skazka o Rybake i Rybke*, 1950)
Director: Mikhail Tsekhanovsky

The Tale about the Soldier (*Skazka o Soldate*, 1948)
Director: Zinaida Brumberg, Valentina Brumberg

The Tortoise and the Hare (1953/2002)
Director: Ray Harryhausen

The Witch (*La Sorcière*, 2000)
Director: Michel Ocelot

The Wolf and the Seven Kids (*Der Wolf und die sieben Geisslein*, 1939)
Director: Ferdinand Diehl

Wow, A Talking Fish! (*Ukh ty, goviryashchaya ryba!*, 1983)
Director: Robert Sahkyants

Live-Action Fairy-Tale Films

(The films in this section are arranged alphabetically not chronologically as in most of the sections.)

The Adventures of Pinocchio (*Le avventure di Pinocchio*, 1947)
Director: Giannetto Guardone

Angels and Insects (1995)
Director: Philip Haas

Arabela (Arabela, 1979–1981), TV series also known as *The Fairy-Tale Bride*
Director: Václav Vorlícek

Arabela Returns (*Arabela se vraci*, 1993)
Director: Václav Vorlícek

Artifical Intelligence: A.I. (2001)
Director: Steven Spielberg

The Big Bad Wolf (*Der Wolf und die sieben jungen Geißlein*, 1957)
Director: Peter Podehl

The Blue Bird (1918)
Director: Maurice Tourneur

The Blue Bird (1940)
Director: Walter Lang

The Blue Bird (1976)
Director: George Cukor

The Chant of Steppes (*Bouzkachi, le chant des steppes*, 2009)
Director: Jacques Debs

Charlie and the Chocolate Factory (2005)
Director: Tim Burton

The Dark Crystal
Director: Jim Henson, Frank Oz

The Donkey, the Table and the Stick (*Tischlein, deck dich*, 1956)
Director: Jürgen von Alten

The Dumb Augustine (*Die Dumme Augustine*, 1991)
Director: Juraj Herz

The Emperor's New Clothes (*Císarovy nové Saty*, 1994)
Director: Juraj Herz

The Fabulous Baron Munchausen (*Baron Prásil*, 1961)
Director: Karel Zeman

The Fall (2006)
Director: Tarsem Singh

The Fast Runner (2002)
Director: Zacharias Kunuk

The Firebird (*Ptak ohnivak/Der Feuervogel*, 1997)
Director: Václav Vorlícek

The Golden Age (*L'age d'or*, 1930)
Director: Luis Buñuel

The Golden Goose (*Die goldene Gans*, 1964)
Director: Siegfried Hartmann

The Golden Key (1938)
Director: Alexandr Ptuschko

The Golden Voyage of Sinbad (1974)
Director: Gordon Hessler

The Incredibly Sad Princess (*Sílene Smutná Princezná*, 1968)
Director: Borivoj Zeman

Into the West (1992)
Director: Mike Newell

Into the Woods (1990)
Director: Stephen Sondheim, James Lapine

Ivashka and Baba-Yaga (*Ivashko i Baba-Yaga*, 1938)
Director: Valentina Brumberg, Zinaida Brumberg

Jack and the Beanstalk (2010)
Director: Gary Tunnicliffe

The Juniper Tree (1990)
Director: Nietzchka Keane

The King without a Heart (*Kunigas jolla ei ollut sydäntä*, 1982)
Director: Päivi Hartzell, Liisa Helminen

Labyrinth (1986)
Director: Jim Henson

The Lady in the Water (2006)
Director: M. Night Shymalan

The Land Has Eyes (*Pear ta ma'on maf*, 2004)
Director: Vilsoni Hereniko

Little Otik (*Otes ek*, 2000)
Director: Jan Svankmajer

The Magic Door (2007)
Director: Paul Matthews

The Magic Galoshes (*Galose Stastia*, 1986)
Director: Juraj Herz

The Magic Sword (1962)
Director: Bert Gordon

Mermaid (*Rusalka*, 2007)
Director: Anna Melikyan

Miracolo a Milano (1951)
Director: Vittorio de Sica

Mischief in Wonderland (*Aufruhr in Schlaraffenland*, 1957)
Director: Otto Meyer

More Than a Miracle (*C'era una volta*, 1966)
Director: Francesco Rosi

Mother Holly (*Frau Holle*, 1951)
Director: Peter Podehl

The Neverending Story (*Die unendliche Geschichte*, 1984)
Director: Wolfgang Petersen

Once Upon a Time, There Was a King (*Byl jednou jeden král . . .*, 1955)
Director: Borivoj Zeman

Ondine (2009)
Director: Neil Jordan

Pan's Labyinth (*El labertino del fauno*, 2006)
Director: Guillermo del Toro

The Piano Tuner of Earthquakes (2006)
Director: The Quay Brothers

Possession (2002)
Director: Neil LaBute

The Prince and the Evening Star (*Princ a Vecernice*, 1978)
Director: Václav Vorlícek

The Princess Bride (1987)
Director: Rob Reiner

The Princess with the Golden Star (*Princezna se zlatou hvezdou na cele*, 1959)
Director: Martin Fric

The Promise (*Wu ji*, 2005)
Director: Kaige Chen

The Proud Princess (*Pysná Princezna*, 1952)
Director: Borivoj Zeman

The Red Shoes (1948)
Director: Michael Powerll and Emeric Pressburger

Rumpelstiltskin (1995)
Director: Mark Jones

Sadko (1953), also known as *The Magic Voyage of Sinbad*
Director: Alexandr Ptuschko

Sampo (1959)
Director: Alexandr Ptuschko

The Saragossa Manuscript (*Rekopis znaleziony w Saragossie*, 1965)
Director: Wojciech Has

Saxana—The Maiden on the Broomstick (*Dívka na kostéti*, 1971)
Director: Václav Vorlícek

The Sea Queen (*Jezerní Královna/Die Seekönigin*, 1998)
Director: Václav Vorlícek

The Secret of Roan Inish (1994)
Director: John Sayles

Sinbad and the Eye of the Tiger (1977)
Director: Sam Wanamaker

The Seventh Voyage of Sinbad (1958)
Director: Nathan Juran

Snow White and Rose Red (*Schneeweißchen und Rosenrot*, 1979)
Director: Siegfried Hartmann

The Sorcerer's Apprentice (2002)
Director: David Lister

The Sorcerer's Apprentice (2010)
Director: Jon Turtletaub

Splash (1984)
Director: Ron Howard

Stardust (2007)
Director: Matthew Vaughn

The Stone Flower (1946)
Director: Alexandr Ptuschko

The Sweet Hereafter (1997)
Director: Atom Egoyan

A Tale of Time Lost (1964)
Director: Alexandr Ptuschko

A Tale of Tsar Saltan (1966)
Director: Alexandr Ptuschko

A Tale of Two Sisters (2003)
Director: Kim Ji-Woon

The Tales of Hoffmann (1951)
Director: Michael Powell, Emeric Pressburger

Three Wishes for Cinderella (Tri orísky pro Popelku, 1973)
Director: Václav Vorlícek

A Thousand and One Nights (*Pohádky tisíce a jedné noci*, 1974)
Director: Karel Zeman

Tomas and the Falcon King (*Král sokulu/Tomas und der Falkenkönig*, 2000)
Director: Václav Vorlícek

The Village (2005)
Director: M. Night Shymalan

Waking Sleeping Beauty (*Jak se budi Princezny*, 1977)
Director: Václav Vorlícek

Whale Rider (1992)
Director: Niki Caro

The Wild Swans (*Dikie Lebedi*, 1962)
Director: Mikhail Tsekhanovsky, Vera Tsekhanovskaya

The Witches (1990)
Director: Nicolas Roeg

The Wonderful World of the Brothers Grimm (1962)
Director: George Pal, Henry Levin

Yo Ho Ho (1981)
Director: Zako Heskija

Directors and Producers

Ivan Aksenchuk (1918–1999)

The Mermaid (*Rusalochka*, 1968)

Lev Atamanov (1905–1981)

The Magic Carpet (*Kakhardakan gorg*, 1948)
The Yellow Story (*Zheltyj Aist*, 1950)
The Scarlet Flower (*Alenki zwetotschek*, 1952), also known as *Beauty and the Beast*
The Golden Antelope (*Zolotaya antilopa*, 1954)
The Snow Queen (*Snezhyaya koroleva*, 1957)
The Shepherd and the Chimney Sweep (*Pastushka i Trubochist*, 1965)

Tex Avery (1908–1980)

Little Red Walking Hood (1937)
Cinderella Meets Fella (1938)
The Bear's Tale (1940)
Red Hot Riding Hood (1943)
Swing Shift Cinderella (1945)
The Shooting of Dan McGoo (1945)
Wild and Woolfy (1945)
Uncle Tom's Cabana (1947)
Little Rural Riding Hood (1949)

Gari Bardin (1941–)

The Grey Wolf and Little Red Riding Hood (*Seryy Volk end Krasnaya Shapochka*, 1995)

The Grey-Bearded Lion (1995)
Puss in Boots (*Kot v sapogakh*, 1995)

Jirí Barta (1948–)

The Pied Piper of Hamelin (1985)

Walter Beck (1929–)

King Thrushbeard (*König Drosselbart*, 1965)
The Adventures of Turli (*Turlis Abenteuer*, 1967)
Sleeping Beauty (*Dornröschen*, 1971)
The Prince Beyond the Seven Seas (*Der Prinz hinter den sieben Meeren*, 1982)
Bearskin (*Bärenhäuter*, 1986)
The Frog King (*Der Froschkönig*, 1988)

Valentina Brumberg (1899–1975) and Zinaida Brumberg (1900–1983)

Little Red Riding Hood (*Krasnaya Shapochka*, 1937)
Ivashka and Baba-Yaga (*Ivashko i Baba-Yaga*, 1938)
The Cat in Boots (*Kot v Sapogah*, 1938)
The Tale about Tszar Saltan (*Skaza o Care Saltane*, 1943)
Sinbad the Sailor (*Sinbad-Morehod*, 1944)
The Tale about the Soldier (*Skazka o Soldate*, 1948)
A Miraculous Bell (*Chudesnyjkokol'Chik*, 1949)
The Night before Christmas (*Noch' Pered Rozhdestvom*, 1951)
Fulfillment of a Wish, also known as *Wishes Come True* (*Ispolenie Zhelanij*, 1957)
A Brave Little Tailor (*Hrabryj Portnyazhka*, 1964)
About the Cruel Stepmother (*Pro Zluyu Machehu*, 1966)
The Cat in Boots (*Kot v Sapogah*, 1968)
A Capricious Princess (*Kapriznaya Princessa*, 1969)
A Magic Wand (*Volshebnaya Palochka*, 1972)

Tim Burton (1958–)

Hansel and Gretel (1982)
Aladdin and his Wonderful Lamp (1986)
Edward Scissorhands (1990)
Sleepy Hollow (1999)
Charlie and the Chocolate Factory (2005)
The Corpse Bride (2005)
Alice in Wonderland (2010)

Enzo D'Alò (1953–)

Momo (2001)
Opopomoz (2003)

Tom Davenport (1939–)

Hansel and Gretel: An Appalachian Version (1975)
Rapunzel, Rapunzel (1979)
The Frog King (1981)
Bristlelip (1982)
Bearskin, or The Man Who Didn't Wash for Seven Years (1982)
The Goose Girl (1983)
Jack and the Dentist's Daughter (1984)
Soldier Jack, or The Man Who Caught Death in a Sack (1988)
Ashpet (1989)
Mutzmag: An Appalachian Folktale (1992)
Willa: An American Snow White (1996)

Jacques Demy (1931–1990)

Donkey Skin (*Peau d' âne*, 1970)
The Pied Piper (1972)

Ferdinand Diehl (1901–1992), Paul Diehl (1886–1976), and Hermann Diehl (1906–1983)

The following films were directed by Ferdinand Diehl with the assistance of his brothers Paul and Hermann:

Calif Storch (*Klaif Storch*, 1929)
The Bremen Town Musicians (*Die Bremer Stadtmusikanten*, 1935)
The Boy Who Went Out to Learn about Fear (*Von einem, der auszog, das Gruseln zu lernen*, 1935)
Table Be Covered (*Tischlein Deck Dich*, 1936)
The Seven Ravens (*Die sieben Raben*, 1937)
The Wolf and the Seven Kids (*Der Wolf und die sieben Geisslein*, 1939)
Puss in Boots (*Der gestiefelte Kater*, 1940)
Sleeping Beauty (*Dornröschen*, 1943)

Walt Disney (1901–1966)

Little Red Riding Hood (1922)
The Four Musicians of Bremen (1922)
Jack and the Beanstalk (1922)
Goldie Locks and the Three Bears (1922)
Puss in Boots (1922)
Cinderella (1922)
The Merry Dwarfs (1929)
The Golden Touch (1935)

Animated Feature Films by the Disney Studio

Snow White and the Seven Dwarfs (1937)
Director: David Hand

Pinocchio (1940)
Director: Ben Sharpstein and Hamilton Luske

The Reluctant Dragon (1941)
Director: Hamilton Luske, Alfred Werker

Cinderella (1950)
Director: Wilfred Jackson, Hamilton Luske, Clyde Geronimi

Alice in Wonderland (1951)
Director: Clyde Geronimi, Hamilton Luske, Wilfred Jackson

Peter Pan (1953)
Director: Wilfred Jackson

Sleeping Beauty (1959)
Director: Clyde Geronimi

The Little Mermaid (1989)
Director: Ron Clements, John Musker

Beauty and the Beast (1991)
Director: Gary Trousdale, Kirk Wise

Aladdin (1992)
Director: John Musker/Ron Clements

Beauty and Beast: The Enchanted Christmas (1997)
Director: Andy Knight

Belle's Magical World (1998)
Director: Cullen Blaine, Daniel de la Vega, Barbara Dourmashkin, Dale Kase, Bob Kline, Burt Medall, Mitch Rochon

Mulan (1998)
Director: Tony Bancroft, Barry Cook

The Emperor's New Groove (2000)
Director: Mark Dindal

The Little Mermaid II: The Return to the Sea (2000)
Director: Jim Kamerud and Brian Smith

The Little Mermaid III: Ariel's Beginning (2008)
Director: Peggy Holmes

The Princess and the Frog (2009)
Director: Ron Clements, John Musker

Disney Live-Action Films with Animation

The Reluctant Dragon (1941)
Director: Alfred Werker, Hamilton Luske

Mary Poppins (1964)
Director: Robert Stevenson

Pete's Dragon (1977)
Director: Don Chaffey

Enchanted (2007)
Director: Kevin Lima

Sydney Franklin (1893–1972) and Chester Franklin (1890–1954)

Alice in Wonderland (1915)
Aladdin and the Magic Lamp (1917)
The Babes in the Woods (1917)
Jack and the Beanstalk (1917)

Friz Freleng (1905–1995)

Beauty and the Beast (1934)
The Miller's Daughter (1934)
Jack-Wabbit and the Beanstalk (1943)
Little Red Riding Rabbit (1943)
Red Riding Hoodwinked (1955)
The Trial of Mr. Wolf (1941)
Little Red Riding Rabbit (1944)

Terry Gilliam (1940–)

Jabberwocky (1977)
The Adventures of Baron Munchausen (1988)
The Brothers Grimm (2005)

Paul Grimault (1905–1994)

The Scarecrow (*L'épouvantail*, 1943)
The Magic Flute (*La flûte magique*, 1946)
The Little Soldier (*Le petit soldat*, 1947)
The Curious Adventures of Mr. Wonderbird (*La Bergère et le Ramoneur*, 1952)
The King and Mr. Bird (*Le Roi et l'Oiseau*, 1979)

Ray Harryhausen (1920–)

Little Red Riding Hood (1949)
Rapunzel (1951)
Hansel and Gretel (1951)
King Midas (1953)
The Tortoise and the Hare (1953/2002)
The Seventh Voyage of Sinbad (1958)
Director: Nathan Juran
Animation and Special Effects: Ray Harryhausen

The Golden Voyage of Sinbad (1974)
Director: Gordon Hessler
Animation: Ray Harryhausen

Sinbad and the Eye of the Tiger (1977)
Director: Sam Wanamaker
Animation: Ray Harryhausen

Jim Henson (1936–1990)

The Dark Crystal (1982)
Director: Jim Henson, Frank Oz

Labyrinth (1986)
Director: Jim Henson

Jim Henson Studio

Muppet Babies

Snow White and the Seven Muppets (1985)
Director: Jeffrey Scott

Beauty and the Schnoz (1988)
Director: Hank Saroyan

The Pig Who Would Be Queen (1988)
Director: Hank Saroyan

Slipping Beauty (1988)
Director: Hank Saroyan

Puss 'n Boots 'n Babies (1989)
Director: Hank Saroyan

Kermit Pan (1989)
Director: Hank Saroyan

Muppet Classic Theater (1994)

The Three Little Pigs
King Midas
Rumpelstiltskin
The Boy Who Cried Wolf
The Elves & the Shoemaker
The Emperor's New Clothes

Jim Henson's The Storyteller

The Soldier and Death (1987)
Director: Jim Henson

Fearnot (1987)
Director: Steve Barron

The Luck Child (1987)
Director: Jon Amiel

A Short Story (1987)
Director: Charles Sturridge

Hans My Hedgehog (1987)
Director: Steve Barron

The Three Ravens (1987)
Director: Paul Weiland

Sapsorrow (1987)
Director: Steve Barron

The Heartless Giant (1987)
Director: Jim Henson

The True Bride (1987)
Director Peter Smith

Juraj Herz (1934–)

Beauty and the Beast (*Panna a netvor*, 1978)
The Magic Galoshes (*Galose Stastia*, 1986)
The Frog Prince (*Zabí král*, 1991)
The Dumb Augustine (*Die Dumme Augustine*, 1991)
The Emperor's New Clothes (*Císarovy nové Saty*, 1994)

Ivan Ivanov-Vano (1900–1987)

The Humpbacked Horse (*Konyok-gorbunok*, 1947/1976), also known as *Ivan and his Magic Pony*
Director: Ivan Ivanov-Vano, Boris Butakov

The Snow Maiden (*Snegurochka*, 1952)
Twelve Months (*12 mesyatsev*, 1956)
Director: Ivan Ivanov-Vano, Mikhail Botov

The Adventures of Buratino (*Priklyucheniya Buratino*, 1960), also known as *Pinocchio and the Golden Key*
Director: Ivan Ivanov-Vano, Dimitriy Babichenko, Mikhail Botov

The Prince, the Swan and the Czar Sultan (*Skazka o tsare Salta*, 1984)
Director: Ivan Ivanov-Vano, Lev Milchin

Ub Iwerks (1901–1971)

During the 1930s Iwerks directed and produced numerous cartoons for Celebrity Productions. Here is a selected list:

Jack and the Beanstalk (1933)
The Brave Tin Soldier (1934)
Puss in Boots (1934)
Aladdin and his Wonderful Lamp (1934)
The Headless Horseman (1934)
The Valiant Tailor (1934)
Bremen Town Musicians (1935)
Sinbad the Sailor (1935)
The Three Bears (1935)
Ali Baba (1936)
Tom Thumb (1936)
Dick Whittington's Cat (1936)

Roman Kachanov (1921–1993)

An Old Man and the Crane (*Starik i Zhuravl*, 1958)
Director: Anatoly Karanovich, Roman Kachanov

The Cloud in Love (*Vlyublennoe Oblako*, 1959)
Director: Anatoly Karanovich, Roman Kachanov

Novice (*Novichok*, 1961)
Cheburashka (1971)
The Inheritance of the Magician Bakhram (*Nasledstvo Volshebnika Bahrama*, 1975)
The Last Petal (*Poslednij Lepestok*, 1977)

David Kaplan (1972–)

The Frog King (1994)
Little Red Riding Hood (1997)
Year of the Fish (2007)

Ernst Lubitsch (1892–1947)

The Oyster Princess (*Die Austernprinzessin*, 1919)
The Doll (*Die Puppe*, 1919)
One Arabian Night (*Sumurun*, 1920)
Bluebeard's Eighth Wife (1938)

Georges Méliès (1861–1938)

The Devil's Castle (*Le Manoir du diable*, 1896/97)
Cinderella (*Cendrillon*, 1899)
The Philosopher's Stone (*La Pierre philosophale*, 1899)
The Rajah's Dream, or The Betwitched Wood (*Le Rêve du Radjah ou la Forêt enchantée*, 1900)
The Sorcerer, the Prince, and the Good Fairy (*Le Sorcier, le Prince et le Bon Génie*, 1900)
Coppelia, the Animated Doll (*Coppélia ou la Poupée animée*, 1900)
Little Red Riding Hood (*Le Petit Chaperon rouge*, 1900/01)
The Sorceress's Home (*Chez la sorcière*, 1901)
Bluebeard (*Barbe-Bleue*, 1901)
The Dwarf and the Giant (*Nain et Géant*, 1901/02)
The Enchanted Basket (*La Corbeille enchantée*, 1902/03)
The Enchanted Well (*Le Puits fantastique*, 1903)
The Sorcerer's Revenge (*Le Sorcier*, 1903)
The Kingdom of the Fairies (*Le Royaume des fées*, 1903)
The Enchanter Alcofribas (*L'Enchanteur Alcofribas*, 1903)
The Magic Lantern (*La Lanterne magique*, 1903)
The Palace of the One Thousand and One Nights (*Le Palais des mille et une nuits*, 1905)
Jack the Chimney-Sweeper (*Jack le ramoneur*, 1906)
The Fairy Carabosse or The Fatal Dagger (*La Fée Carabosse ou le Poignard fatal*, 1906)
The Grandmother's Tale and the Child's Dream (*Conte de la grand-mère et Rêve de l'enfant*, 1908)
The Marvelous Fountain (*La Fontaine merveilleuse*, 1908)
The Marvelous Cobweb (*La Toile d'araignée merveilleuse*, 1908)
The Fairy Libellule or The Enchanted Lake (*La Fée Libellule ou le Lac enchanté*, 1908)
The Spirit of the Clocks or The Son of the Bell-Ringer (*Le Génie des cloches ou le Fils du sonneur*, 1908)
The Good Shepherdess and the Wicked Princess (*La Bonne Bergère et la Mauvaise Princesse*, 1908)
The Hallucinations of Baron Munchausen (*Les Hallucinations du baron de Münchausen*, 1911)
Cinderella or The Marvelous Slipper (*Cendrillon ou la Pantoufle merveilleuse*, 1912)
The Knight of the Snows (*Le Chevalier des Neiges*, 1912)

Hayao Miyazaki (1941–)

The Castle of Cagliostro (*Rupan sansei: Kariosutoro no shiro*, 1979)
Nausicaa: Of the Valley of the Wind (*Kaze no tani no Naushika*, 1984)
Castle in the Sky (*Tenkû no shiro Rapyuta*, 1986)
Kiki's Delivery Service (*Majo no takkyûbin*, 1989)
Porco Rosso (*Kurenai no buta*, 1992)
Princess Mononoke (*Mononoke-hime*, 1997)
Spirited Away (*Sen to Chihiro no kamikakushi*, 2001)
Howl's Moving Castle (*Hauru no ugoku shiro*, 2004)
Ponyo (*Gake no ue no Ponyo*, 2008)

Yori Norstein (1934–)

Tale of Tales (1978)

Michel Ocelot (1943–)

Kirikou and the Sorceress (*Kirikou et la Sorcière*, 1998)
Princes et Princesses (2000)
Includes: *The Princess of Diamonds* (*La Princesse des Diamants*)

The Boy of Figures (*Le Garçon des Figues*)
The Witch (*La Sorcière*)
The Coat of the Old Woman (*Le Manteau de la Vieille Dame*)
The Cruel Queen and the Showman of Story (*La Reine Cruelle et le Montreur de Fabulo*)
Prince et Princesse
Kirikou and the Wild Beasts (*Kirikou et les bêtes sauvages*, 2006)
Azur et Asmar (2007)

George Pal (1908–1980)

Sleeping Beauty (1935)
Aladdin and the Magic Lamp (1936)
Sinbad (1936)
Tulips Shall Grow (1942)
The Sky Princess (1942)
Jasper and the Beanstalk (1945)
Tom Thumb (1958)
The Wonderful World of the Brothers Grimm (1962)

Alexandr Ptushko (1900–1973)

The Golden Key (1938)
The Stone Flower (1946)
Sadko (1953), also known as *The Magic Voyage of Sinbad*
Sampo (1959)
A Tale of Time Lost (1964)
A Tale of Tsar Saltan (1966)

Lotte Reiniger (1899–1981)

The Flying Suitcase (*Der Fliegende Koffer*, 1921)
Cinderella (*Aschenputtel*, 1922)
The Stolen Heart (*Das gestohlene Herz*, 1934)
The Little Chimney Sweep (*Der kleine Schornsteinfeger*, 1934/1953)
Puss in Boots (*Der Graf von Carabas/Der gestiefelte Kater*, 1934/1935)
The Golden Goose (*Die goldene Gans*, 1944–1947)
Puss in Boots (1953/1954)
Cinderella (1953/1954)
Thumbelina (1953/1954)
Sleeping Beauty (1953/1954)
The Three Wishes (1953/1954)
The Frog Prince (1953/1954)
Hansel and Gretel (1953/1954)
Caliph Stork (1953/1954)
Snow White and Rose Red (1953/1954)
The Gallant Little Tailor (1953/1954)
Aladdin and the Magic Lamp (1954)
Jack and the Beanstalk (1955)
The Frog Prince (1961)

Michael Sporn (1946–)

The Dancing Frog (1989)
The Little Match Girl (1999)
Mike Mulligan and his Steam Shovel (1990)
Nightingale (1999)
The Red Shoes (1990)

Ladislav Starewicz (1882–1965)

The City Mouse and the Country Mouse (*Le rat de ville et le rat des champs*, 1926)
The Lion Who Became Old (*Le lion devenu vieux*, 1932)

Kurt Stordel (Dates Unknown)

Hansel and Gretel (*Hänsel und Gretel*, 1935–1938)
The Bremen Town Musicians (*Die Bremer Stadtmusikanten*, 1935–1938)
Sleeping Beauty (*Dornröschen*, 1935–1938)
Puss in Boots (*Der gestiefelte Kater*, 1935–1938)
Red Riding Hood and the Wolf (*Rotkäppchen und der Wolf*, 1945)

Jan Svankmajer (1934–)

Alice (1989)
Little Otik (*Otesek*, 2000)

Guillermo del Toro (1964–)

Pan's Labyinth (*El labertino del fauno*, 2006)

Jiří Trnka (1912–1970)

Granpa Planted a Beet (*Zasadil dedek repu*, 1945)
The Animals and the People of Petrov (*Zviratka a petrovsti*, 1946)
The Spring-Man and the SS (*Perak a SS*, 1946)
A Treasury of Fairy Tales (*Spalicek*, 1947)
The Emperor's Nightingale (*Cirasuv Slavik*, 1948)
Director: Jirí Trnka, Jiri Brdecka (animation)
Director: Milos Makovec (live-action scenes)

The Devil's Mill (*Certuv mlyn*, 1949)
Prince Bajaja (*Bajaja*, 1950)
The Golden Fish (*O ziate rybce*, 1951)
The Cybernetic Grandmother (*Kyberneticka babicka*, 1962)

Mikhail Tsekhanovsky (1889–1965) and Vera Tsekhanovskaia (1902–1977)

The Flower with Seven Colors (*Cvetik-Semicvetik*, 1948)
The Tale about the Fisherman and the Fish (*Skazka o Rybake i Rybke*, 1950)
The Frog Princess (*Carevna-Lyagushka*, 1954)
A Girl in the Jungle (*Devochka v Dzhunglyah*, 1956)
The Tale about Chapayev (*Skaz o Chapaeve*, 1958)
The Wild Swans (*Dikie Lebedi*, 1962)

Václav Vorlícek (1930–)

Saxana—The Maiden on the Broomstick (*Dívka na kostéti*, 1971)
Three Wishes for Cinderella (*Tri Orísky Pro Poelku*, 1973)
Waking Sleeping Beauty (*Jak se budi Princezny*, 1977)
The Prince and the Evening Star (*Princ a Vecernice*, 1978)
Arabela (1979)
Arabela Returns (*Arabela se vraci*, 1993)
The Magic Book (*Das Zauberbuch/Kouzelný mesec*, 1996)
The Firebird (*Ptak ohnivak/Der Feuervogel*, 1997)
The Sea Queen (*Jezerní Královna/Die Seekönigin*, 1998)
Tomas and the Falcon King (*Král sokulu/Tomas und der Falkenkönig*, 2000)

Taiji Yabushita (1903–1986)

The Tale of the White Serpent (*Hakujaden*, 1958)
Director: Taiji Yabushita, Kazuhiko Okabe

Magic Boy (*Shônen Sarutobi Sasuke*, 1959)
Director: Taiji Yabushita, Akira Daikubara

Alakazam the Great (*Saiyu-ki*, 1960)
Director: Taiji Yabushita, Daisaku Shirakawa, Osamu Tezuka

The Littlest Warrior (*Anju to zushio-maru*, 1961)
Director: Taiji Yabushita, Yugo Serikawa

The Arabian Nights: The Adventures of Sinbad (*Arabian naito: Shindobaddo no bôken*, 1962)
Director: Taiji Yabushita, Yoshio Kuroda

Young Jack and the Witch (*Shônen Jakku to Mahô-tsukai*, 1967)

Borivoj Zeman (1912–1991)

The Proud Princess (*Pysná Princenza*, 1952)
Once Upon a Time, There Was a King (*Byl jednou jeden král . . .*, 1955)
The Incredibly Sad Princess (*Sílene Smutná Princezná*, 1968)

Karel Zeman (1910–1989)

The Fabulous Baron Munchausen (*Baron Prásil*, 1961)
The Sorcerer's Apprentice (*Carodejuv ucen*, 1978), also known as *Krabat*
A Thousand and One Nights (*Pohádky tisíce a jedné noci*, 1974)

Canonical Fairy-Tale Films

Alice in Wonderland

Alice in Wonderland (1903)
Director: Cecil Hepworth, Percy Stow

Alice in Wonderland (1915)
Director: W. W. Young

Alice in Wonderland (1931)
Director: Bud Pollard

Alice in Wonderland (1933)
Director: Norman Z. McLeod

Alice in Wonderland (1937)
Director: George More O'Ferrall

Alice in Wonderland (1949)
Director: Dallas Bower

Alice in Wonderland (1951)
Director: Clyde Geronimi, Hamilton Luske, Wilfred Jackson

Alice in Wonderland (1955)
Director: George Schaefer

Alice in Wonderland (1966)
Director: Jonathan Miller

Alice in Wonderland, or What's a Nice Kid Like You Doing in this Place? (1966)
Director: Alex Lovy

Alice (*Alicja*, 1982)
Director: Jacek Bromski, Jerzy Gruza

Alice in Wonderland (1985)
Director: Harry Harris

Alice in Wonderland (1986)
Director: Barry Letts

Alice in Wonderland (1988)
Screenplay: Paul Leadon

Alice (*Neco z Alenky*, 1988)
Director: Jan Svankmajer

Alice in Wonderland (1995)
Director: Toshiyuki Hiruma, Takashi Masunaga

Alice in Wonderland (1999)
Director: Nick Willing

Alice in Wonderland (2005)
Director: Sibi Malayil

Alice in Wonderland (2010)
Director: Tim Burton

Arabian Nights

Aladdin

Aladdin, or The Marvelous Lamp (*Aladin ou la lampe merveilleuse*, 1906)
Director: Albert Capellani and Segundo de Chomon

A-lad-in Bagdad (1938)
Director: Cal Dalton and Cal Howard

The Adventures of Aladdin (*Les Aventures d'Aladin*, 1959)
Director: Jack Kinney

Aladdin and his Magic Lamp (*Volshebnaya lampa Aladdina*, 1966)
Director: Boris Rytsarev

Aladdin and his Marvelous Lamp (*Aladin et la lampe merveilleuse*, 1970)
Director: Jean Image

Aladdin and the Magic Lamp (*Aladin et la lampe merveilleuse*, 1971)
Director: Sidney A. Franklin, Chester M. Franklin

Aladdin (1992)
Director: John Musker, Ron Clements

Ali Baba

Ali Baba and the Forty Thieves (*Ali Baba et les 40 voleurs*, 1902)
Director: Ferdinand Zecca

Ali Baba and the Forty Thieves (*Ali Baba et les quarantes voleurs*, 1905)
Director: Segundo de Chomón

Ali Baba and the Forty Thieves (*Ali Baba wa al arbain harame*, 1942)
Director: Togo Mizrahi

Ali Baba and the Forty Thieves (1944)
Director: Arthur Lubin

Son of Ali Baba (1952)
Kurt Neumann

Ali Baba and the Forty Thieves (*Ali Baba et les 40 voleurs*, 1954)
Director: Jacques Becker

The New Adventures of Ali Baba (*Les Nouvelles Aventures d'Ali Baba*, 1962)
Director: Emimmo Salvi

Ali Baba and the Sacred Crown (*Le sette fatiche di Alì Babà*, 1962)
Director: Emimmo Salvi

Ali Baba and the Seven Saracens (Sindbad contro i sette saraceni, 1963)
Director: Emimmo Salvi

Arabian Nights

The Palace of the Thousand One Nights (Le Palais des Mille et Une Nuits, 1905)
Director: Georges Méliès

One Arabian Night (Sumurun, 1920)
Director: Ernst Lubitsch

The Tales of the Thousand and One Nights (Les Contes des Mille nuits et nuit, 1921)
Director: Viktor Tourjansky

Two Arabian Nights (1927)
Director: Lewis Milestone

The Thousand and One Nights (Alf layla wa-layla, 1941)
Director: Togo Mizrahi

The Arabian Nights (1942)
Director: John Rawlins

The Thousand and One Nights (Las mil y una noches, 1958)
Director: Fernando Cortés

1001 Arabian Nights (1959)
Director: Jack Kinney

The Thousand and One Nights (Alf layla wa-layla, 1964)
Director: Hasan al-Imam

The Thousand and One Nights (Les Mille et Une Nuits, 1961)
Director: Mario Bava and Henry Levin

Arabian Nights: The Adventures of Sinbad (Arabian naito: Shindobaddo no boken, 1962)
Director: Kuroda and Taiji Yabushita

The Arabian Knights (1968, TV series)
Director: William Hanna and Joseph Barbera

The Thousand and One Nights (Senya ichiya monogatari, 1969)
Director: Eiichi Yamamoto

Arabian Nights (1972)
Director: Jules Bass and Arthur Rankin, Jr.

The Flower of the Arabian Nights (Il Fiore delle mille e una notte, 1974)
Director: Pier Paolo Pasolini

The Thousand and One Nights (Pohádky tisíce a jedné noci 1974)
Director: Karel Zeman

Arabian Nights (Arabian naitsu: Shinbaddo no boken, 1975, TV series)
Director: Fumio Kurokawa and Kunihiko Okazaki

Arabian Nights (Arabische Nächte, 1979)
Director: Klaus Lemke

Arabian Adventure (1979)
Director: Kevin Connor

The Thousand and One Nights (Les Mille et Une Nuits, 1990)
Director: Philippe de Broca

In Search of the Thousand and One Nights (À la recherché des Mille et Une Nuits, 1991, documentary)
Director: Nacer Khémir

Arabian Nights (1994)
Director: Jun Falkenstein and Joanna Romersa

Pages Taken from the Thousand and One Nights (Pages arrachées aux Mille et Une Nuits, 1996)
Director: Jean-François Jung

The Thousand and One Nights (Les Mille et Une Nuits, 1999)
Director: Hady Zaccak

1001 Nights (1999)
Director: Mike Smith

Arabian Nights (2000)
Director: Steve Barron

Kismet

Kismet (1916)
Director: Martin Berger

Kismet (1920)
Director: Louis Gasnier

Kismet (1930)
Director: John Francies Dillon

Kismet (1930)
Director: William Dieterle

Kismet (1932)
Director: Baburao Patel

Kismet (1944)
Director: William Dieterle

Kismet (1955)
Director: Vincent Minnelli

Kismet (1967)
Director: Luther Davis

Marouf the Cobbler

The Cobbler and the Caliph (1909)
Director: J. Stuart Blackton

Ma'ruf the Cobbler (Ma 'ruf al-iskafi, 1947)
Director: Fu'ad al-Jaza 'irly

Marouf, the Cairo Cobbler (1947)
Director: Jean Mauran

Nur al-Din

Nur al-Din and the Three Sailors (Nur al-Din wa-l-bahara el-talata, 1944)
Director: Togo Mizrahi

Qamar al-Zaman

Kamar-al-Zaman (1922)
Director: J. J. Madan

Kamar-al-Zaman (1931)
Director: Shah G. Agha

Qamar el-Zaman (1976)
Director: Hasan al-Imam

Scheherazade

Shahrazad (1946)
Director: Fu'ad al-Jaza'irly

Song of Scheherazade (1947)
Director: Walter Reisch

Schéhérazade (1963)
Director: Pierre Gaspard-Huit

The Beautiful Days of Scheherazade (Layali Shahrazad al-jamila, 1982)
Director: Mustapha Derkaoui

Scheherazade's Nights (Layali Shahrazad, 1991)
Director: Wadi' Yusuf

Schéhérazade (1995)
Director: Florence Miailhe

Once Upon a Time Donyazad (Il était une fois Donyazad, 1996)
Director: Marzak Allouache

Sindbad

Sindbad the Sailor (1947)
Director: Richard Wallace

Simbad el Mareado (1950)
Director: Gilberto Martínez Solares

Sadko, or The Magic Voyage of Sinbad (1952)
Director: Alexsandr Ptushko

Son of Sinbad (1955)
Director: Ted Tetzlaff

Son of Sinbad (1958)
Director: Nanabhai Bhatt

The 7th Voyage of Sinbad (1958)
Director: Nathan Juran

Captain Sinbad (1963)
Director: Byron Haskin

Sindbad, Ali Baba and Aladdin (1963)
Director: Prem Narayan Arora

Sindbad versus the Seven Saracens (Sinbad contro i sette saraceni, 1964)
Director: Emimmo Salvi

The Golden Voyage of Sinbad (1973)
Director: Gordon Hessler

Simbad Calife de Bagdad (1973)
Diretor: Pietro Francisci

Sinbad and the Eye of the Tiger (1977)
Director: Sam Wanamaker

Sinbad of the Seven Seas (1989)
Director: Enzo G. Catellari

Sinbad, Legend of the Seven Seas (2003)
Director: Patrick Gilmore and Tim Johnson

Thief of Baghdad

The Thief of Bagdad (1924)
Director: Raoul Walsh

The Thief of Bagdad (1940)
Director: Ludwig Berger, Michael Powell, Tim Whelan

Ali, Caliph of Bagdad (Ali califfo di Bagdad e ditorni, 1948)
Director: Paolo Campani

Bagdad (1949)
Director: Charles Lamont

The Thief of Baghdad (Die Diebin von Bagdad, 1952)
Director: Carl Lamac

The Thief of Damascus (1952)
Director: Will Jason

Siren of Bagdad (1953)
Director: Richard Quine

Hallaq Baghdad (1954)
Director: Husayn Fawzi

The Thief of Bagdad (Il Ladro di Bagdad, 1961)
Director: Arthur Lubin and Bruno Vailati

The Thief of Tibidabo (Le Voleur de Tibidabo, 1964)
Director: Maurice Ronet

The Pink of Bagdad (1978)
Director: Arthur Davis

The Thief of Bagdad (2003)
Director: Diane Nerwen

Miscellaneous

The Carpet from Bagdad (1915)
Director: Colin Campbell

A Caliph of the New Bagdad (1916)
Director: Van Dyke Brooke

The Princess of Bagdad (La principessa de Bagdad, 1918)
Director: Baldassarre Negroni

The Sheik (1921)
Director: George Melford

The Son of the Sheik (1926)
Director: George Fitzmaurice

Bagdad Daddy (1941)
Director: Larry Ceballos

Little Miss Devil (Afrita Hanem, 1949)
Director: Henry Barakat

Bagdad (1949)
Director: Charles Lamont

The Singing Princess (La rosa di Bagdad, 1949)
Director: Anton Gino Domenighini

Bowery to Bagdad (1955)
Director: Edward Bernds

The Magic Lamp (al-Fanus al-sihri, 1960)
Director: Fatin 'Abd al-Wahhab

Nights (Layalin, 1982)
Director: Hasan al-Imam

Sir 'Ali Mazhar and the 40 Thieves ('Ali Beh Mazhar wa-l-arba'in harami, 1985)
Director: Ahmad Yasin

Baron Münchhausen

The Wonderful Adventures of Herr Munchausen (Monsieur de Crac, 1910)
Director: Émile Cohl

The Adventures of Baron von Münchausen (Les aventures du Baron de Munchhausen, 1911)
Director: Georges Méliès

The Adventures of Baron von Munchausen (*Le avventure del Barone di Münchausen*, 1914)
Director: Paolo Azzurri

Baron Münchausen (*Baron Prásil*, 1961)
Director: Karel Zeman

The Fabulous Adventures of the Legendary Baron Munchausen (*Les fabuleuses aventures du légendaire Baron de Munchausen*, 1979)
Director: Jean Image

The Adventures of Baron Münchausen (1987/88)
Director: Terry Gilliam

Bearskin

Bearskin, or The Man Who Didn't Wash for Seven Years (1984)
Director: Tom Davenport

Bearkskin (*Bärenhäuter*, 1986)
Director: Walter Beck

Bearskin: An Urban Fairy Tale (*Na Pele do Urso*, 1989)
Director: Ann Guedes, Eduwardo Guedes

Beauty and the Beast

Beauty and the Beast (*La Belle et la Bête*, 1899)
Studio: Pathé Frères

Beauty and the Beast (1903)

Beauty and the Beast (1905)
Director: Percy Stow

Beauty and the Beast (*La Belle et la Bête*, 1908)
Director: Albert Capellani

Beauty and the Beast (1912)
Studio: Rex Motion Picture Company

Beauty and the Beast (1913)
Director: R. H. C. Matthews

Beauty and the Beast (1922)
Director: Guy Newall

Beauty and the Beast (1924)
Director: Herbert Dawley

Beauty and the Beast (1934)
Director: Friz Freleng

Beauty and the Beast (*La Belle et la Bête*, 1946)
Director: Jean Cocteau

The Scarlet Flower (*Alenki zwetotschek*, 1952)
Director: Lev Atamanov

Beauty and the Beast (1960)
Director: Gerard Baldwin, Frank Braxton, Pete Burness, Sal Faillace, Paul Harvey, Jim Hiltz

Beauty and her Beast (1960)
Director: Gerard Baldwin, Frank Braxton, Pete Burness, Sal Faillace, Paul Harvey, Jim Hiltz, Bill Hurtz, Lew Keller, Ted Parmelee, Gerry Ray, Dun Roman, Bob Schleh, George Singer, Ernie Terrazas, John Walker, Rudy Zamora

Son of Beauty and the Beast (1961)
Director: Gerard Baldwin, Frank Braxton, Pete Burness, Sal Faillace, Paul Harvey, Jim Hiltz

Beauty and the Beast (1961)
Director: Edward Cahn

Beauty and the Beast (1969)
Director: Seymour Robbie

Finist, the Bright Falcon (*Finist, jasni sokol,* 1975)
Director: Gennady Vassiliev

Beauty and the Beast (*Die Schöne und das Tier,* 1976)
Director: Katja Georgi

The Scarlet Flower (*Alenki zwetotschek,* 1978)
Director: Irina Povolotskaya

Beauty and the Beast (*Panna a netvor,* 1978)
Director: Juraj Herz

Beauty and the Beast (1982)
Director: John Woods

Beauty and the Beast (1983)
Director: Rudy Larriva

Beauty and the Beast (1983)
Director: Roger Vadim

Beauty and the Beast (1986)
Director: Eugene Marner

King Kong Lives (1986)
Director: John Guillerman

Beauty and the Beast (1987–1990)
Creator: Ron Koslow
Director: Victor Lobl (16 episodes), Gus Trikonis (12 episodes), Thomas Wright (9 episodes)

Beauty and the Beast (1991)
Director: Gary Trousdale, Kirk Wise

The Polar Bear King (*Kvitebjørn Kong Valemon,* 1991)
Director: Ola Solum

Beauty and the Beast (1992)
Director: Timothy Forder

Beauty and the Beast (1992)
Director: Lisa Hammer

Beauty and the Beast (1993)
Director: Masakazu Higuchi, Chinami Nama

Beauty and Beast: The Enchanted Christmas (1997)
Director: Andy Knight

Belle's Magical World (1998)
Director: Cullen Blaine, Daniel de la Vega, Barbara Dourmashkin, Dale Kase, Bob Kline, Burt Medall, Mitch Rochon

No Such Thing (2001)
Director: Hal Hartley

Blood of Beasts (2003)
Director: David Lister

Beauty and the Beast: A Latter-Day Tale (2007)
Director: Brian Brough

Belle and the Beast: A Christian Romance (2007)
Director: B. J. Alexander

Bluebeard

Bluebeard (1901)
Director: Georges Méliès

Bluebeard (1902)
UK, black and white, silent

Bluebeard (1909)
Director: J. Searle Dawley

Monsieur Bluebeard (1914)
Director: Charles Giblyn

Bluebeard, Jr. (1922)
Director: Scott R. Dunlap

Landru, the Bluebeard of Paris (*Landru, der Blaubart von Paris*, 1922)
Director: Hans Otto

Bluebeard's Brother (1932)
Director: Paul Terry, Frank Moser

Blue Beard (*Barbe-Bleue*, 1936–1938)
Director: René Bertrand

Love from a Stranger (1937)
Director: Rowland V. Lee

Bluebeard's Eighth Wife (1938)
Director: Ernst Lubitsch

Gaslight (1940)
Director: Thorold Dickinson

Gaslight (1944)
Director: George Cukor

Bluebeard (1944)
Director: Edgar G. Ulmer

The Modern Blue Beard (*El moderno Barba Azu*, 1946)
Director: Jaime Salvador

Monsieur Verdoux (1947)
Director: Charlie Chaplin

Secret Beyond the Door (1948)
Director: Fritz Lang

Bye, Bye Bluebeard (1949)
Director: Arthur Davis

Bluebeard (*Blaubart*, 1951)
Director: Christian-Jaque

The Confusions of Bluebeard (*Los lios de Barba Azul*, 1955)
Director: Gilberto Martinez Solares

Bluebeard's Ten Honeymoons (1960)
Director: W. Lee Wilder

Bluebeard's Treasure (1962)
Director: Hal Seeger

Landrou (*Bluebeard*, 1963)
Director: Claude Chabrol

Bluebeard (1972)
Director: Edward Dmytryk

Landru (1973)
Director: Juan José Gurrola

Black Day for Bluebeard (1974)
Director: David Friedkin

Very Blue Beard (1979)
Director: Vladimir Samsonov

Bluebeard (*Blaubart*, 1984)
Director: Krzyszlof Zanussi

Bluebeard, Bluebeard (*Barbablú, Barbablú*, 1987)
Director: Fabio Carpi

Bluebeard (*Aotti Ge*, 1988)
Studio: Nippon Animation

The Last Wife of Bluebeard (*La dernière femme de barbe bleue*, 1996)
Director: Alexander Bubnov

Bluebeard's Crate (2004)
Screenplay: Michelle Lamoreaux, Robert Lamoreaux, Kat Likkel, Michael Maler, Joseph Purdy, Ford Riley, Tom Sheppard, William Forrest Cluveri

Désiré Landru (2005)
Director: Pierre Boutron

Bluebeard (2008)
Director: Jessica Fox

Bluebeard (2009)
Director: J. J. Harting

Bluebeard (*La Barbe Bleue*, 2009)
Director: Catherine Breillat

Cinderella

Cinderella (1898)
Director: George Albert Smith

Cinderella (*Cendrillon, ou La petite pantouffe de verre*, 1899)
Director: Georges Méliès

Cinderella (Cendrillon, 1907)
Director: Albert Capellani

Cinderella (1907)
Director: Lewis Fitzhannon

A Modern Cinderella (1908)
Director: Percy Stowe

A Modern Cinderella (1910)
Director: J. Stuart Blackton

A Modern Cinderella (1911)
Director: J. Searle Dawley

Cinderella (1911)
Director: George Nichols

A Cowgirl Cinderella (1912)
Producer: David Horsely

Cinderella (*Cendrillon, ou La petite pantouffe de verre*, 1912)
Director: Georges Méliès

Cinderella (1912)
Director: Colin Campbell

Cinderella (1912)
Director: Arthur Melbourne Cooper

Cinderella (1912)
Director: Arthur Cooper

Lord Browning and Cinderella (1912)
Director: Van Dyke Brooke

A Modern Cinderella (*Cenerentola*, 1913)
Director: Eleuterio Rodolfi

Cinderella's Gloves (1913)
A Southern Cinderella (1913)
Director: Burton King

Cinderella and the Boob (1913)
Director: Dell Henderson

A Reluctant Cinderella (1913)
Director: C. J. Williams

An Awkward Cinderella (1914)
Director: Otis Turner

Mr. Cinderella (1914)
Director: Eugene Moore

Cinderella (1914)
Director: James Kirkwood

Cinderella (*Aschenbrödel*, 1916)
Director: Urban Gad

A Cripple Creek Cinderella (1916)
Director: Ulysses Davis

The Cinderella Man (1917)
Director: George Sloan Tucker

A Modern Cinderella (1917)
Director: John Adolfi

A Kentucky Cinderella (1917)
Director: Rupert Julian

A Studio Cinderella (1917)
Director: Matt Moore

Cinderella and the Magic Slipper (1917)
Director: Guy McDonell

Daddy Long Legs (1919)
Director: Marshall Neilan

Cinderella Cinders (1920)
Director: Frederick Ireland

A Kitchen Cinderella (1920)
Director: Malcolm St. Clair

The Irish Cinderella (*c*.1920)
Cinderella's Twin (1921)
Director: Dallas Fitzgerald

A Rural Cinderella (1921)
Director: Erle Kenton

Cinderella of the Hills (1921)
Director: Howard Mitchell

A Lowland Cinderella (1922)
Director: Sidney Morgan

Cinderella (1922)
Director: Walt Disney

Cinderella (*Aschenputtel*, 1922)
Director: Lotte Reininger

The Lost Shoe (*Der verlorene Schuh*, 1923)
Director: Ludwig Berger

Cinderella (1924)
Director: Herbert Dawley

A Kick for Cinderella (1924)
Director: Bud Fisher

The Comediennes (1924)
A Kiss for Cinderella (1925)
Cinderella (1925)
Director: Walter Lantz

Ella Cinders (1926)
Director: Alfred E. Green

Mr. Cinderella (1926)
Director: Norman Taurog

A Bowwery Cinderella (1927)
Director: Burton King

The Patsy (1928)
Director: King Vidor

The Bush Cinderella (1928)
Director: Rudall Hayward

Cinderella (1930)
Director: Manny Gould, Ben Harrison

Cinderella Blues (1931)
Director: John Foster, Harry Bailey

The Jazz Cinderella (1930)
Director: Scott Pembroke

Cinderella Blues (1931)
Director: Harry Bailey, John Foster

A Modern Cinderella (1932)
Director: Roy Mack

Cinderella (1933)
Director: Frank Moser

Naughty Cinderella (1933)
Director: John Daumery

Cinderella's Fella (1933)
Director: Raol Walsh

Poor Cinderella (1934)
Director: Dave Fleischer

Hollywood Here We Come (1934)
Director: Archie Gottler

Mister Cinderella (1936)
Director: Edward Sedgwick

A Coach for Cinderella (1936)
Animation: Frank Goldman

Cinderella (*Cendrillon*, 1937)
Director: Pierre Caron

Steve Cinderella (1937)
Director: Roland Davies

A Ride for Cinderella (1937)
Director: Max Fleischer

Farewell to Cinderella (1937)
Director: Maclean Rogers

Cinderella Meets Fella (1938)
Director: Tex Avery

Campus Cinderella (1938)
Director: Noel Smith

The Glass Slipper (1938)
Director: Mannie Davis

Vassalisa the Beautiful (1939)
Director: Aleksandr Rou

Midnight (1939)
Director: Mitchell Leisen

Princess Cinderella (*Cenerontola e il signor Bonaventura*, 1941)
Director: Sergio Tofano

Cinderella Goes to a Party (1942)
Director: Frank Tashlin, Bob Wickersham

Swing Shift Cinderella (1945)
Director: Tex Avery

Cinderella Jones (1946)
Director: Busby Berkeley

Clun Brown (1946)
Director: Ernst Lubitsch

Cinderella (*Zolushka*, 1947)
Director: Nadezhda Koshevrova, Mikhail Shapiro

Sepia Cinderella (1947)
Director: Arthur Leonard

Cinderella (*Cenerentola*, 1948)
Director: Fernando Cerchio

Cinderella (1950)
Director: Wilfred Jackson, Hamilton Luske, Clyde Geronimi

April in Paris (1952)
Director: David Butler

Sabrina (1954)
Director: Billy Wilder

Cinderella (*Aschenputtel*, 1955)
Director: Fritz Genschow

Glass Slipper (1955)
Director: Charles Walters

Cinderella (1957)
Director: Ralph Nelson, Roland Vance, Clark Jones

Cinderefella (1960)
Director: Frank Tashlin

Cinderella (*Khrustalnyy bashmachok Zolushki*, 1960)
Director: Aleksandr Rou, Rostislav Zakharov

Cinderella (1960)
Director: Gerard Baldwin, Frank Braxton, Pete Burness, Sal Faillace, Paul Harvey, Jim Hiltz, Bill Hurtz, Lew Keller, Ted Parmelee, Gerry Ray, Dun Roman, Bob Schleh, George Singer, Ernie Terrazas, John Walker, Rudy Zamora

Cinderella Returns (1960)
Director: Gerard Baldwin, Frank Braxton, Pete Burness, Sal Faillace, Paul Harvey, Jim Hiltz, Bill Hurtz, Lew Keller, Ted Parmelee, Gerry Ray, Dun Roman, Bob Schleh, George Singer, Ernie Terrazas, John Walker, Rudy Zamora

No Biz Like Show Biz (1960)
Director: William Hanna, Joseph Barbera

Cinderella (1961)
Bolshoi Ballet
Score by Sergei Prokoviev

Slippery Slippers (1962)
Director: William Hanna, Joseph Barbera

Cinderella on the Left (1962)
Director: Donald Brittain

Señorella and the Glass Huarache (1964)
Director: Hawley Pratt

The New Cinderella (*La nueva Cenicienta*, 1964)
Director: George Sherman

Cinderella (1964)
Rodgers & Hammerstein musical
Director: Charles Dubin

Sinderella and the Golden Bra (1964)
Director: Loel Minardi, Lowell Terry

How Now Cinderella (1965)
Director: William Hanna, Joseph Barbera

Hey Cinderella! (1969)
Director: Jim Henson

Cinderella (1969)
Director: John Vernon

Cinderella (1972)
Director: Arthur Rankin, Jr., Jules Bass

Three Wishes for Cinderella (*Tri Orísky Pro Popelku*, 1974)
Director: Václav Vorlícek

Chickenrella (1975)
Director: William Hanna, Joseph Barbera

The Slipper and the Rose (1976)
Director: Bryan Forbes

Cinderella 2000 (1977)
Director: Al Adamson

Cinderella (1977)
Director: Michael Pataki

Cindy (1978)
Director: William Graham

Cinderella (1979)
Director: Mark Hall

Cinderella (1979)
Director: Ivan Aksenchuk

The Cinderella Wearing Sabots (*Kigutsu No Cinderella*, 1979)
Director: Yuji Endo

The Tender Tale of Cinderella Penguin (1981)
Director: Janet Perlman

Cinderella '87 (*Cenerentola '87*, 1983)
Director: Ricardo Malenotti

Cinderella (*La Cenerentola*, 1983)
Director: John Cox

Cinderella (1985)
Director: Mark Cullingham

Girl with the Diamond Slipper (*Mo deng xian lu qi yuan*, 1985)
Director: Jing Wong

Cinderella? Cinderella! (1986)
Director: Charles Nichols

Cinderella (1986)
Director: Ericka Beckman

Pretty in Pink (1986)
Director: Howard Deutsch

Maid to Order (1987)
Director: Amy Jones

Working Girl (1988)
Director: Mike Nichols

Ashpet (1988)
Director: Tom Davenport

Cinderella (*Aschenputtel*, 1989)
Director: Karen Brandauer

Pretty Woman (1990)
Director: Gary Marshall

The Magic Riddle (1991)
Director: Yoram Gross

Prince Cinders (1993)
Director: Derek Hayes

Cinderella (1994)
Producer: Ken Cayre, Stan Cayre

Cinderella Frozen in Time (1994)
Director: Sterling Johnson

A Tale of Cinderella (1996)
Director: Patricia di Benedetto Snyder and Tom Gliserman

Cinderella (1997)
Director: Robert Iscove

The Shoe (*Kurde*, 1998)
Director: Laila Pakalnina

Tale of Cinderella (1998)
Ever After (1998)
Director: Andy Tennant

Cinderelmo (1999)
Director: Bruce Leddy

Cinderella: Single Again (2000)
Director: Kellie Ann Benz

Are You Cinderella? (2000)
Director: Charles Hall

Cinderella (2000)
Director: Beeban Kidron

Cinderella (*Aschenputtel*, 2000)
Director: Gary Blatchford, Jody Gannon, David Incorvaia

The Adventures of Cinderella's Daughter (2000)
Director: Scott Zakarin

I Was a Rat (2001)
Director: Laurie Lynd

Mr. Cinderella (2002)
Director: Ahmad Idham

Cinderella II: Dreams Come True (2002)
Directors: John Kafka, Darrell Rooney

Confessions of an Ugly Stepsister (2002)
Director: Gavin Millar

Ella Enchanted (2004)
Director: Tommy O'Haver

A Cinderella Story (2004)
Director: Mark Rosman

Cinderella (2006)
Director: Man-dae Bong

Cinderella III: A Twist in Time (2007)
Director: Frank Nissen

A No Fairy Fairytale: The Cinderella Nightmare (2008)
Director: Annika Pampel

Another Cinderella Story (2008)
Director: Damon Santostefano

A Scrooge Meets Cinderella Story (2009)
Director: Andrea Litto

Donkey Skin

Donkey Skin (*Peau d'âne*, 1908)
Director: Albert Capellani

Tattercoats (1924)
Director: Herbert M. Dawley

Donkey Skin (*Peau d' âne*, 1970)
Director: Jacques Demy

Donkey Skin (*Oslinaja Schkura*, 1982)
Director: Nadeshda Koscheverova

Sapsorrow (1987)
Director: Steve Barron

The Frog Prince/King

The Frog and the Princess (1944)
Director: Eddie Donnelly

The Frog Prince (1954)
Director: Vivian Milroy

The Prince Frog (1957)
Director: Gene Deitch

The Frog Prince (1960)
Director: Gerard Baldwin, Frank Braxton, Pete Burness, Sal Faillace, Paul Harvey, Jim Hiltz, Bill Hurtz, Lew Keller, Ted Parmelee, Gerry Ray, Dun Roman, Bob Schleh, George Singer, Ernie Terrazas, John Walker, Rudy Zamora

The Enchanted Frog (1961)
Director: Gerard Baldwin, Frank Braxton, Pete Burness, Sal Faillace, Paul Harvey, Jim Hiltz, Bill Hurtz, Lew Keller, Ted Parmelee, Gerry Ray, Dun Roman, Bob Schleh, George Singer, Ernie Terrazas, John Walker, Rudy Zamora

The Tale of a Frog (1962)
Director: Gerard Baldwin, Frank Braxton, Pete Burness, Sal Faillace, Paul Harvey, Jim Hiltz, Bill Hurtz, Lew Keller, Ted Parmelee, Gerry Ray, Dun Roman, Bob Schleh, George Singer, Ernie Terrazas, John Walker, Rudy Zamora

The Frog Prince (1966)
Director: Joy Batchelor

Tales from Muppetland: The Frog Prince (1971)
Director: Jim Henson

The Frog King (1981)
Director: Tom Davenport

The Tale of the Frog Prince (1982)
Director: Eric Idle

The Frog Prince (1984), also known as *The French Lesson*
Director: Brian Gilbert

The Frog Prince (1987)
Director: Jackson Hunsicker

The Frog King (*Froschkönig*, 1987)
Director: Walter Beck

The Frog Prince (*Zabí král*, 1991)
Director: Juraj Herz

The Frog King (1994)
Director: David Kaplan

Frog Prince (1995)
Director: Simon Bor, Sara Bor

Prince Charming (2001)
Director: Allan Arkush

The Frog Prince (2008)
Director: Seth MacFarlane

The Princess and the Frog (2009)
Director: Ron Clements, John Musker

Hansel and Gretel

Hansel and Gretel (1909)
Director: J. Searle Dawley

The Babes in the Woods (1917)
Director: Chester M. Franklin, Sidney Franklin

Hansel and Gretel (1923)
Director: Alfred J. Goulding

Babes in the Woods (1932)
Director: Burt Gillett

Hansel and Gretel (1933)
Director: Frank Moser, Paul Terry

The Story of Hansel and Gretel (1951)
Director: Ray Harryhausen

Hansel and Gretel (1952)
Director: Connie Rasinski

Hänsel und Gretel (1954)
Director: Fritz Genschow

Hansel and Gretel (1954)
Director: Walter Janssen

Hansel and Gretel (1954)
An opera fantasy. Electric puppet version of the Humperdinck opera.
Directors: Michael Myerberger/John Paul

Hansel and Gretel (1955)
Director: Vivian Milroy

Hansel and Gretel (1960)
Director: Gerard Baldwin, Frank Braxton, Pete Burness, Sal Faillace, Paul Harvey, Jim Hiltz, Bill Hurtz, Lew Keller, Ted Parmelee, Gerry Ray, Dun Roman, Bob Schleh, George Singer, Ernie Terrazas, John Walker, Rudy Zamora

Creepy Time Pal (1960)
Director: William Hanna, Joseph Barbera

Hansel and Gretel (1963)
Director: Allan Wargon, Martin Andrews

The Hansel and Gretel Case (1965)
Director: William Hanna, Joseph Barbera

Hansel and Gretel (1966)
Director: Joy Batchelor

Hansel and Gretel Got Lost in the Woods (Hänsel und Gretel verliefen sich im Walde, 1970)
Director: Franz Josef Gottlieb

Whoever Slew Auntie Roo? (1972)
Director: Curtis Harrington

Hansel and Gretel (1975)
Director: Tom Davenport

Hänsel und Gretel (1976)
Director: Klaus Georgi

Hansel and Gretel (1982)
Director: Tim Burton

Hansel and Gretel (1982)
Director: James Frawley

Hansel and Gretel (1982)
Director: Nathaniel Merrill
Opera at the Metropolitan. Engelbert Humperdinck

Hansel and Gretel (1987)
Director: Hiroshi Saito, Takayoshi Suzuki, Shigeru Omachi

Hansel and Gretel (1987)
Director: Len Talan

Hansel and Gretel (1989)
Director: David Feiss

Hansel and Garfield (1989)
Director: Steve Clark, John Walker

Hansel and Gretel (1995)
Director: Simon Bor, Sara Bor

Hansel and Gretel (1999)
Producer: Melinda Rediger

Hänsel und Gretel (1999)
Director: Gary Blatchford, Jody Gannon

The Wacky Adventures of Hansel and Gretel (1999)
Director: Tom Galt, Mark Galt

Freeway 2 (1999)
Director: Matthew Bright

Master Hansel and Miss Gretel (2001)
Director: Tony Collingwood

Criminal Lovers (Les Amants Criminels, 2001)
Director: François Ozon

Hansel and Gretel (2002)
Director: Gary Tunncliffe

The Hansel and Gretel Witch Project (2002)
Director: Robert Alvarez, Kent Butterworth, Russell Calabrese, Butch Hartman, John McIntyre, Van Partible, Rumen Petkov, Kirk Tingblad

Grimm (2003)
Director: Alex van Warmerdam

Hansel and Gretel (2003)
Director: David Germain

Milchwald: Ein Märchen in Angst und Farbe (This Very Moment, 2003)
Director: Christoph Hochhäusler

Hansel and Gretel (2005)
Director: David Alexovich

Hansel and Gretel (2007)
Director: Yim Pil-Sung

Jack and the Beanstalk

Jack and the Beanstalk (1902)
Director: George Fleming, Edwin Porter

Jack and the Beanstalk (1912)
Director: J. Searle Dawley

Jack and the Beanstalk (1913)
Writer: Lloyd Lonergan

Jack the Giant Killer (1916)
Director: W. L. Glacken

Jack and the Beanstalk (1917)
Director: Chester Franklin, Sydney Franklin

Jack and the Beanstalk (1922)
Director: Walt Disney

Jack and the Beanstalk (1924)
Director: Alfred Goulding

Jack and the Beanstalk (1924)
Director: Herbert Dawley

The Giant Killer (1924)
Director: Walter Lantz

Jack the Giant Killer (1925)
Director: Herbert Dawley

Jack and the Beanstalk (1931)
Director: Dave Fleischer

Jack the Giant Killer (1933)
Director: Briant Fryer

Jack Wabit and the Beanstalk (1943)
Director Friz Feleng

Woody the Giant Killer (1947)
Director: Dick Lundy

Jack and the Beanstalk (1952)
Director: Jean Yarbrough

Jack and the Beanstalk (1955)
Director: Lotte Reiniger

Popye and the Spinach Stalk (1960)
Director: Seymour Kneitel

Jack the Giant Killer (1962)
Director: Nathan Juran

Jack and the Beanstalk (1965)
Director: Nick Havinga

Jack and the Beanstalk (1967)
Director: Gene Kelly

Jack and the Witch (*Shonen Jakku to Maho-tsukai*, 1967)
Director: Taiji Yabushita

Jack and the Beanstalk (1970)
Director: Barry Mahon

Jack and the Beanstalk (1974)
Director: Gisaburo Sugii

Jack and the Beanstalk (1983)
Director Lamont Johnson

Jack and the Beanstalk (1991)
Director: James Simon

Jack and the Beanstalk (1998)
Director: John Henderson

Jack and the Beanstalk (2000)
Director: Martin Gates

Jack and the Beanstalk: The Real Story (2001)
Director: Brian Henson

Jack and the Beanstalk (2010)
Director: Gary Tunnicliffe

The Juniper Tree

The Juniper Tree (1990)
Director: Nietzschka Keene

Peter Pan

Peter Pan (1924)
Director: Herbert Brenon

Peter Pan (1953)
Directors: Hamilton Luske, Clyde Geronimo, Wilfred Jackson

Peter Pan (1960)
Director: Vincent J. Donehue

Peter Pan (1988)
Screenplay: Paul Leadon

Peter Pan and the Pirates (1990)
Director: John Wilson

Hook (1991)
Director: Steven Spielberg

Peter Pan (2000)
Director: Glenn Casale, Gary Halvorson

Return to Never Land (2002)
Director: Robin Budd, Donovan Cook

Neverland (2003)
Director: Damion Dietz

Peter Pan (2003)
Director: P. J. Hogan

The Pied Piper

The Pied Piper (1907)
Director: Percy Snow

The Pied Piper of Hamelin (1911)
Director: Theodore Marston

Sammy Opheus, or The Pied Piper of the Jungle (1912)
Director: Colin Campbell

The Pied Piper of Hamelin (1913)
Director: George Lessey

The Ratcatcher of Hamelin (*Der Rattenfänger von Hameln*, 1918)
Director: Paul Wegener

Alice the Piper (1924)
Director: Walt Disney

The Pied Piper (1924)
Director: Walter Lantz

http://www.bcdb.com/cartoon_characters/23055-Pied_Piper.html *Pied Piper Malone* (1924)
Director: Alfred Green

The Pied Piper of Hamelin (1926)
Director: Frank Tilley

The Pied Piper (1933)
Director: Wilfred Jackson

Pied Piper Porky (1939)
Director: Robert Clampett

Playing the Pied Piper (1941)
Director: Lou Lilly

The Pied Piper (1942)
Director: Irving Pichel

Pied Piper of Basin Street (1945)
Director: James Culhane

The Hep Cat (1946)
Director: Mannie Davis

Svengali's Cat (1946)
Director: Eddie Donnelly

Paying the Piper (1949)
Director: Robert McKimson

The Last Mouse of Hamelin (1955)
Director: Connie Rasinski

Too Hop to Handle (1956)
Director: Robert McKimson

The Pied Piper of Hamelin (1957)
Director: Bretaigne Windlust

The Pied Piper (1960)
Director: Gerard Baldwin, Frank Braxton, Pete Burness, Sal Faillace, Paul Harvey, Jim Hiltz, Bill Hurtz, Lew Keller, Ted Parmelee, Gerry Ray, Dun Roman, Bob Schleh, George Singer, Ernie Terrazas, John Walker, Rudy Zamora

The Pied Piper Pipe (1960)
Director: William Hanna, Joseph Barbera

The Pied Piper of Guadalupe (1961)
Director: Friz Freleng, Hawley Pratt

The Clown and the Kids (1967)
Director: Mende Brown

The Pied Piper of Hamelin (1970)
Director: Bernard Queenman

Land of the Giants: Pay the Piper (1970)
Director: Henry Harris

Simon and the Pied Piper (1971)
Director: Ivor Wood

The Pied Piper (1972)
Director: Jacques Demy

The Pied Piper from Space (1978)
Director: Ray Patterson, Carl Urbano

Pied Piper Puss (1980)
Director: Don Christensen

The Pied Piper of Hamelin (1981)
Director: Mark Hall

The Pied Piper of New York Town (1981)
Screenplay: Jeffrey Scott

The Pied Piper of Hamelin (1985)
Director: Nicholas Meyer

Krysar (*The Ratcatcher*, 1985)
Director: Jirí Barta

The Pied Piper Power Play (1990)
Director: John Kimball, Bob Zamboni

The Pied Piper of Hamlin (1992)
Screenplay: Peter Jennings, Leonard Lee

The Pied Piper of Taz-Mania (1992)
Director: Art Vitello, Keith Baxter

Piped Piper of Gorpdale (1993)
Director: Paul Field, David Johnson

The Sweet Hereafter (1997)
Director: Atom Egoyan

Pied Piper of Manhattan (1997)
Director: Chris Berkeley, Alan Caldwell, Vic Dalchele, Chris Dozois, Tim Eldred, Bob Fuentes III, Gloria Jenkins, Sam Liu, Audu Paden, Rafael Rosado, Frank Squillace, Scott Wood

It's the Pied Piper, Charlie Brown (2000)
Director: Bill Melendenz, Kristy Mendelson

The Pied Piper (2003)
Director: Louis Piche

The Piper (2005)
Director: Abbe Robinson

Pied Pussycat Piper (2006)
Director: Scott Jeralds

Pinocchio

Pinocchio (1911)
Director: Giulio Antamoro

The Golden Key (*Zolotoy klyuchik*, 1939)
Director: Alexsandr Ptushko

Pinocchio (1940)
Director: Ben Sharpstein and Hamilton Laske

Pinocchio (1957)
Director: Hanya Holm

Pinocchio in Outer Space (1965)
Director: Roy Goosens

Pinocchio's Adventures (*Turlis Abenteuer*, 1967)
Director: Walter Beck, Ron Merk

Pinocchio (1968)
Director: Sid Smith

Erotic Adventures of Pinocchio (1970)
Director: Corey Allen

The Adventures of Pinocchio (*Le avventure di Pinocchio*, 1972)
Director: Luigi Comencini

The Adventures of of Pinocchio (*Un burattino di nome Pinocchio*, 1972)
Director: Giuliano Cenci

Pinocchio (1976)
Director: Ron Field, Sid Smith

The Adventures of Pinocchio (*Pikorîo no bôken*, 1976)
Director: Shigeo Koshi, Hiroshi Saitô

Pinocchio's Christmas (1980)
Director: Arthur Rankin, Jr., Jules Bass

Pinocchio (1984)
Director: Peter Medak

Pinocchio and the Emperor of the Night (1987)
Director: Hal Sutherland

Pinocchio 964 (1991)
Director: Shozin Fukui

Pinocchio (1993)
Director: Masakazu Higuchi, Chinami Namba

The Adventures of Pinocchio (1996)
Director: Steve Barron

Pinocchio's Revenge (1996)
Director: Kevin Tenney

The New Adventures of Pinocchio (1999)
Director: Michael Anderson

Pinocchio (1999)
Director: Gianluigi Toccafondo

Gepetto (2000)
Director: Tom Moore

Artifical Intelligence: A.I. (2001)
Director: Steven Spielberg

Pinocchio (2002)
Director: Roberto Begnigni

Pinocchio 3000 (2004)
Director: Daniel Robichaud

Pinocchio (2008)
Director: Alberto Sironi

Puss in Boots

Puss in Boots (*Le chat botté*, 1903)
Director: Lucien Nonguet, Ferdinand Zecca

Puss in Boots (*Le chat botté*, 1908)
Director: Albert Capellani

Puss in Boots (1917)
Studio: Peter Pan Company

Puss in Boots (1922)
Director: Walt Disney

Puss in Boots (1934)
Director: Ub Iwerks

Puss in Boots (1936)
Director: Lotte Reiniger

Puss in Boots (1954)
Director: Lotte Reiniger

Puss in Boots (1982) (TV)
Director: John Clark Donahue, John Driver

Puss in Boots (1988)
Director: Eugene Marner

Puss in Boots (1993)
Director: Leonard Lee, Rodney Lee

Puss in Boots (*Kotvsapogakh*, 1995)
Director: Garri Bardin

Puss in Boots (1999)
Director: Phil Nibbelink

The True Story of Puss in Boots (*La véritable histoire du Chat Botté*, 2009)
Director: Jérome Deschamps, Pascal Hérold, Macha Makeleff

Rapunzel

The Story of Rapunzel (1951)
Director: Ray Harryhausen

Rapunzel, Rapunzel (1979)
Director: Tom Davenport

Rapunzel (1983)
Director: Gilbert Cates

Rapunzel, or The Magic of Tears (*Rapunzel oder der Zauber der Tränen*, 1988)
Director: Ursula Schmanger

Classic Stories for Children (1990)
Director: Peter Babakitis
Contains: *Rapunzel, Frog Prince*, and *Jack and the Beanstalk*

Barbie as Rapunzel (2001)
Director: Owen Hurley

Rapunzel: The Blonde Years (2008)
Director: Fiona Ashe

Rapunzel (2009)
Director: Bodo Fürneisen

Red Riding Hood

Little Red Riding Hood (1901)
Director: Georges Méliès

Little Red Riding Hood (1911)
Director: James Kirkwood, George Loane Tucker

Little Red Riding Hood (1911)
Director: A. E. Coleby

When Lillian Was Little Red Riding Hood (1913)
Director Colin Campbell

Little Red Riding Hood (1918)
Director: Otis Thayer

Little Red Riding Hood (1922)
Director: Walt Disney

Little Red Riding Hood (1922)
Director: Alfred J. Goulding, Al Herman

Little Red Riding Hood (1922)
Director: Anson Dyer

Little Red Riding Hood (*Cervená Karkulla*, 1922)
Director: Svatopluk Innemann

Big Red Riding Hood (1925)
Director: LeoMcCarey

Little Red Riding Hood (1925)
Director: Walter Lantz

Little Red Riding Hood (1930)
Director: Alberto Calvacanti

Dizzy Red Riding Hood (1931)
Director: Dave Fleischer

Red Riding Hood (1931)
Director: Harry Bailey, John Foster

The Big Bad Wolf (1934)
Director: Burt Gillett

A Modern Red Riding Hood (1935)
Director: Frank Moser, Paul Terry

Little Red Walking Hood (1937)
Director: Tex Avery

The Bear's Tale (1940)
Director: Tex Avery

Red Riding Hood Rides Again (1941)
Director: Sid Marcus

The Trial of Mr. Wolf (1941)
Director: Friz Freleng

Red Hot Riding Hood (1943)
Director: Tex Avery

Little Red Riding Rabbit (1944)
Director: Friz Freleng

The Shooting of Dan McGoo (1945)
Director: Tex Avery

Wild and Woolfy (1945)
Director: Tex Avery

Uncle Tom's Cabana (1947)
Director: Tex Avery

Little Rural Riding Hood (1949)
Director: Tex Avery

The Story of Little Red Riding Hood (1949)
Director: Ray Harryhausen

A Girl Good Enough to Eat (*Une fille à croquer*, 1951)
Director: Raoul André

Little Red Rodent Hood (1952)
Director: Friz Freleng

Little Red Riding Hood (*Rotkäppchen*, 1953)
Director: Fritz Genschow

Little Red Riding Hood (*Rotkäppchen*, 1954)
Director: Walter Janssen

Red Riding Hoodwinked (1955)
Director: Friz Freleng

Red Riding Hoodlum (1957)
Director: Paul J. Smith

Little Red Riding Hood (*La Caperucita Roja*, 1960)
Director: Roberto Rodriguez

Riding Hood Magoo (1961)
Director: Grant Simmons

Little Red Riding Hood and her Friends (*La Caperucita y sus Tres Amigos*, 1961)
Director: Roberto Rodriguez

Little Red Riding Hood (*Rotkäppchen*, 1962)
Director: Götz Friedrich

Little Red Riding Hood and the Monsters (*Caperucita Y Pulgarcito Contra Los Monstruos*, 1962)
Director: Roberto Rodriguez

The Dangerous Christmas of Red Riding Hood (1965)
Director: Sid Smith

Red Riding Richochet (1965)
Director: Joseph Barbera, William Hanna

Rough Riding Hood (1966)
Director: Sid Marcus

The Stuck-Up Wolf (1967)
Director: Al Eugster

Little Red Riding Hood and the Timebomb (1968)
Director: Guido Henderickx

Little Red Riding Hood (1969)
Director: Rhoda Leyer

Take Care, Red Riding Hood (*Akazukinchan kiotsukete*, 1970)
Director: Shirô Moritani

Little Red Riding Hood (*Pro Krasnuyu Shapochku*, 1977)
Director: Leonid Mechayev

Little Red Riding Hood (1983)
Director: Graeme Clifford

The Company of Wolves (1984)
Director: Neil Jordan

Red Riding Hood (1989)
Director: Adam Brooks

Bye Bye Red Riding Hood (*Bye bye Chaperon rouge*, 1989)
Director: Márta Mészáros

Grey Wolf and Little Red Riding Hood (*Seryy Volk end Krasnaya Shapochka*, 1990)
Director: Garry Bardin

In the Deep Woods (1992)
Director: Charles Cornell

The Trial of Red Riding Hood (1992)
Director: Eric Till

Little Red Riding Hood (1995)
Director: Toshiyuki Hiruma, Takashi Masunaga

Little Red Riding Hood (1995)
Rhino Home Video

Little Red Riding Hood (1995)
Happily Ever Fairy Tales for Every Child
Narrated by Robert Guillaume

The Last Red Riding Hood (*Le Dernier Chaperon Rouge* (1996)
Director: Jan Kouren

Freeway (1996)
Director: Matthew Bright

Little Red Riding Hood (1997)
Director: David Kaplan

Redux Riding Hood (1997)
Director: Steve Moore

The Wolves of Kromer (1998)
Director: Will Gould

Black XXX-mas (2000)
Director: Pieter Van Hees

Deep in the Woods (*Promenons-nous dans les bois*, 2000)
Director: Lionel Delplanque

Red Riding Hood (2003)
Director: Giacomo Cimini

Little Erin Merryweather (2003)
Director: David Morwick

Red Riding Hood (2004)
Director: Randal Kleiser

Hard Candy (2005)
Director: David Slade

Hoodwinked (2005)
Directors: Cory Edwards and Todd Edwards

A Wicked Tale (2005)
Director Tzang Merwyn Tong

Big Bad Wolves (2006)
Director: Rajneel Singh

Little Red Riding Hood (2006)
Director: S.J. Chiro

Teeth (2007)
Director: Mitchell Lichtenstein

Rotkappchen: The Blood of Red Riding Hood (2009)
Director: Harry Sparks

The Red Riding Trilogy (2009)
TV films include:

1974   Director: Julian Jarrold
1980   Director: James Marsh
1983   Director: Anand Tucker

Rumpelstiltskin

Rumpelstiltskin (1915)
Director: Raymond West

Rumpelstilzchen (1955)
Director: Herbert B. Fredersdorf

Mischief in Wonderland (1957)
Director: Otto Meyer

Rumpelstiltskin and the Golden Secret (*Das Zaubermännchen*, 1960)
Director: Christoph Engel

The Porcupine—Rumpelstiltskin (*Das Stacheltier—Rumpelstilzchen*, 1961)
Director: Hans-Dieter Mäde

Rumpeltstiltskin (*Rumpelstilzchen*, 1962)
Director: Fritz Genschow

Rumpelstiltskin (*Repelsteeltje*, 1973)
Director: Harry Kümel

Rumpelstiltskin (1982)
Director: Emil Ardolin

Rumpelstiltskin (1985)
Director: Pino Van Lamsweerde

Rumpelstiltskin (1987)
Director: David Irving

Rumpelstiltskin (1995)
Director: Mark Jones

Rumpelstilzchen (2007)
Director: Andi Niessner

Rumpelstilzchen (2009)
Director: Ulrich König

Sleeping Beauty

Sleeping Beauty (*La Belle au bois dormant*, 1902)
Director: Lucien Nonguet, Ferdinand Zecca

Sleeping Beauty (*La Belle au bois dormant*, 1908)
Director: Albert Capellani, Lucien Nonguet

Sleeping Beauty (*Dornröschen*, 1922)
Director: Lotte Reiniger

Sleeping Beauty (1924)
Director: Herbert Dawley

Sleeping Beauty (*La Belle au bois dormant*, 1935)
Director: Alexander Alexeieff

Sleeping Beauty (*La Bella adormentata*, 1935)
Director: Luigi Chiarini

Sleeping Beauty (1953/1954)
Director: Lotte Reiniger

Sleeping Beauty (*Dornröschen*, 1955)
Director: Fritz Genschow

Sleeping Beauty (1959)
Director: Clyde Geronimi

Sleeping Beauty (*Shui mei ren*, 1960)
Director: Huang Tang

Sleeping Beauty (*Dornröschen*, 1971)
Director: Walter Beck

Sleeping Beauty (1987)
Director: David Irving

Sleeping Beauty (1987)
Director: Nicholas Clay

Sleeping Beauty (*Sipová Ruzenka*, 1990)
Director: Stanislav Parnícky

Sleeping Beauty (1991)
Director: James Simon

Sleeping Beauty (1992)
Director: Joan Sugerman

Sleeping Beauty (1995)
Director: Toshiyuki Hiruma, Takashi Masunaga

Teen Sorcery (1999)
Director: Victoria Muspratt

Sleeping Betty (2007)
Director: Claude Cloutier

Granny O'Smith's Sleeping Beauty (2008)
Director: Nicky Phelan

Snow White

Little Snow White (*La Petite Blanche-Neige*, 1910)
The Legend of Snow White (1914)
Screenplay: T. O. Eltonhead

Snow White (1916)
Director: J. Searle Dawley

Snow White (1916)
Director: Charles Weston

Snow White (1933)
Director: Dave Fleischer

Snow White and the Seven Dwarfs (1937)
Director: David Hand

Snow White and the Seven Dwarfs (*Schneewittchen und die sieben Zwerge*, 1939)
Director: Karlheinz Wolff

Ball of Fire (1941)
Director: Howard Hawks

Coal Black and de Sebben Dwarfs (1943)
Director: Robert Clampett

Snow White and the Seven Thieves (*Biancaneve e i sette ladri*, 1949)
Director: Giacomo Gentilomo

The Seven Dwarfs to the Rescue (*I Sette Nanni alla Riscossa*, 1951)
Director: Paolo William Tamburella

Snow White (*Schneewittchen*, 1955)
Director: Erich Kobler

Snow White and the Three Stooges (1961)
Director: Walter Lang

Prince Charming Magoo (1961)
Director: Brad Case

Snow White (*Schneewittchen*, 1961)
Director: Gottfried Kolditz

Snow White and the Seven Circus Performers (*Schneewittchen und die sieben Gaukler*, 1962)
Director: Kurt Hoffmann

Snow White and the Seven Dwarfs (*Pamuk Prenses ve 7 Cüceler*, 1970)
Director: Ertem Görec

Snow White and the Seven Perverts (1973)
Director: Marcus Parker-Rhodes

Stories Our Nannies Don't Tell (*Histórias Que Nossas Bab"as Não Contavam*, 1979)
Director: Oswaldo de Oliveira

Snow White and her Seven Lovers (*Blanca Nieves y sus 7 amantes*, 1980)
Director: Ismael Rodriguez

Snow White & Co. (*Biancaneve & Co.*, 1982)
Director: Mario Bianchi

Snow White and the Seven Dwarfs (1984)
Director: Peter Medak

Snow White and the Seven Muppets (1985)
Director: Jeffrey Scott

Snow White (1987)
Director: Michael Berz

Snow White and the Secret of the Dwarfs (*Schneewittchen und das Geheimnis der Zwerge*, 1992)
Director: Ludvik Ráza

Snow White (1995)
Director: Toshiyuki Hruma, Takashi Masunaga

Snow White: A Tale of Terror (1996)
Director: Michael Cohn

Willa: An American Snow White (1996)
Director: Tom Davenport

Snow White . . . Ten Years Later (*Biancaneve . . . dieci anni dopo*, 1999)
Director: Franco Lo Cascio (Luca Damiano)

Snow White: The Fairest of Them All (2002)
Director: Caroline Thompson

Snow White (*Branca de Neve*, 2000)
Director: João César Morteiro

Rugrats: Tales from the Crib: Snow White (2005)
Director: Ron Noble, Michael Deadelus Kenny, Andrei Sviskotski
Creator: Arlene Klasky, Gabor Csupo, Paul Germain

Snow White: The Sequel (*Blanche Neige: La Suite*, 2007)
Director: Jean-Paul "Picha" Walravens

Sydney White (2007)
Director: Joe Nussbaum

The Snow White Syndrome (*Syndromo tis Hionatis, To*, 2008)
Director: Angelos Spartalis

Happily N'ever After 2: Snow White: Another Bite at the Apple (2009)
Director: Steven Gordon, Boyd Kirkland

Tom Thumb

Tom Thumb (*Le petit Poucet*, 1909)
Director: Segundo de Chomón

Tom Thumb (*Le petit Poucet*, 1912)
Director: Louis Feuillade

Tom Thumb (*Le petit Poucet*, 1920)
Director: Robert Boudrioz

Tom Thumb (1934)
Director: Manny Gould, Ben Harrison

Tom Thumb (1936)
Director: Ub Iwerks

The Adventures of Tom Thumb, Jr. (1940)
Director: Burt Gillett

Tom Thumb in Trouble (1940)
Director: Chuck Jones

Tom Thumb's Brother (1941)
Director: Sid Marcus

The Mite Makes Right (1948)
Director: Bill Tytla

Tom Thumb (*Pulgarcito*, 1957)
Director: René Cardona

Tom Thumb (1958)
Director: George Pal

Tom Thumb (1960)
Director: Gerard Baldwin, Frank Braxton, Pete Burness, Sal Faillace, Paul Harvey, Jim Hiltz, Bill Hurtz, Lew Keller, Ted Parmelee, Gerry Ray, Dun Roman, Bob Schleh, George Singer, Ernie Terrazas, John Walker, Rudy Zamora

Tom Thumb #2 (1960)
Director: Gerard Baldwin, Frank Braxton, Pete Burness, Sal Faillace, Paul Harvey, Jim Hiltz, Bill Hurtz, Lew Keller, Ted Parmelee, Gerry Ray, Dun Roman, Bob Schleh, George Singer, Ernie Terrazas, John Walker, Rudy Zamora

I Was a Teenage Thumb (1963)
Director: Chuck Jones

Little Tom Thumb (1966)
Director: Joy Batchelor

Tom Thumb (*Le petit Poucet*, 1972)
Director: Michel Boisrond

Crossing to Freedom (1990)
Director: Norman Stone

The Secret Adventures of Tom Thumb (1993)
Director: Dave Borthwick

Tom Thumb (1995)
Director: Simon Bor, Sara Bor

The Adventures of Tom Thumb & Thumbelina (2000)
Director: Glenn Chaika

Tom Thumb (*Le petit Poucet*, 2001)
Director: Olivier Dahan

Wonderful Wizard of Oz

The Wonderful Wizard of Oz (1910)
Director: Otis Turner

His Majesty, the Scarecrow of Oz (1914)
Director: L. Frank Baum

The Patchwork Girl of Oz (1914)
Director: J. Farrell MacDonald

The Magic Cloak of Oz (1914)
Director: J. Farrell MacDonald

The Wizard of Oz (1925)
Director: Larry Semon

The Land of Oz (1932)
Director: Ethel Meglin

The Wizard of Oz (1933)
Director: Ted Eshbaugh

The Wizard of Oz (1939)
Director: Victor Fleming

Shirley Temple's Storybook: The Land of Oz (1960)
Director: William Corrigan

The Wonderful Land of Oz (1969)
Director: Barry Mahon

The Wizard of the Emerald City (*Volshebnik izumrudnogo goroda*, 1974)
Director: Valentin Popov, L. Smironov

Journey Back to Oz (1974)
Director: Hal Sutherland

20th Century Oz (1976)
Director: Chris Löfvén

The Wiz (1978)
Director: Sidney Lumet

Dorothy in the Land of Oz (1981)
Director: Charles Swenson, Fred Wolf

The Wizard of Oz (*Ozu No* Mahotsukai, 1983)
Director: Fumihiko Takayama, John Danylkiw

Return to Oz (1985)
Director: Walter Murch

The Wonderful Wizard of Oz (1987)
Director: Gerald Potterton

The Wizard of Oz (1991)
Director: James Simon

The Lion of Oz (2000)
Director: Time Deacon

The Muppets' Wizard of Oz (2005)
Director: Kirk Thatcher

Tin Man (2007)
Director: Nick Willing

Studios, Series, Selected Countries

Hans Christian Andersen Films

General Andersen Films
Two series of animated films were produced in 2004 and 2005 to commemorate the 200th birthday of Andersen.

The Fairytayler (2004–2005)
Director: Jørgen Lerdam

A series of cel animated fairy tales
Lille Idas blomster Little Ida's Flowers
Prinsessen på ærten The Princess on the Pea
Kejserens nye klæder The Emperor's New Clothes
Den lille havfrue The Little Mermaid
Nattergalen The Nightingale
Fyrtøjet The Tinder Box
Loppen og professoren The Flea and the Professor
Den grimme ælling The Ugly Duckling
Snemanden The Snowman
De vilde svaner The Wild Swans
Gartneren og herskabet The Gardner and the Noble Family
Tommelise Thumbelina
Rejsekammeraten The Traveling Companion
Kjærestefolkene The Sweethearts
Svinedrengen The Swineherd
Skarnbassen The Dung Beetle
Hvad fatter gør What the Old Man Does is Always Right
Ole Lukøje
Lykkens galocher The Galoshes of Fortune
Klodshans Clumsy Hans
Grantræet The Spruce Tree

Hans Christian Andersen's Fairy Tales (2005)
Director and Writer: Jorgen Bing

A series of 20 short marionette films
Den grimme ælling The Ugly Duckling
Den lille pige med svovlstikkerne The Little Match Girl
Den standhaftige tinsoldat The Steadfast Tin Soldier
Den uartige dreng The Naughty Boy
Det er ganske vist It's Quite True!
Fyrtøjet The Tinder Box
Hjertesorg Heartache
Hvad fatter gør What the Old Man Does is Always Right
Hyrdinden og skorstensfejeren The Shepherdess and the Chimneysweep
Kejserens nye klæder The Emperor's New Clothes
Kjærestefolkene The Sweethearts
Klodshans Clumsy Hans
H.C. Andersens eventyrlige verden: Konen med æggene The Woman with the Eggs
Lille Claus og Store Claus Little Claus and Big Claus
Marionetspilleren The Puppet-Show Man
Nattergalen The Nightingale
Prinsessen på ærten The Princess on the Pea
Rejsekammeraten The Traveling Companion
Svinedrengen The Swineherd
Tommelise Thumbelina

Hans Christian Andersen (1954)
Director: Charles Vidor

The Blue Light (*Das blaue Licht*, 1976)
Director: Iris Gusner

The Daydreamer (1986)
Director: Jules Bass

The Princess and the Swineherd (*Die Prinzessin und der Schweinehirt*, 1953)
Director: Herbert B. Fredersdorf

La Bergère et le Ramoneur (*The Curious Adventures of Mr. Wonderbird*, 1952)
Director: Paul Grimault

The King and Mr. Bird (*Le Roi et l'Oiseau*, 1979)
Director: Paul Grimault

The Tinderbox (*Das Feuerzeug*, 1959)
Director: Siegfried Hartmann

The Traveling Companion (*Vandronik/Der Reisekamerad*, 1990)
Director: Ludvík Ráza

H. C. Andersen's The Long Shadow (*H. C. Andersen og den skæve skygge*, 1998)
Director: Jannik Hastrup

The Twelve Dancing Princesses (1999)
Happily Ever Fairy Tales for Every Child
Director: Ted Bell

The Emperor's New Clothes

The Emperor's New Clothes (*Novoye platye korolya*, 1919)
Director: Yuri Zhelyabuzhsky

The Emperor's New Clothes (1953)
Director: Ted Parmelee

The Emperor's New Clothes (1972)
Director: Arthur Rankin and Jules Bass

The Emperor's New Clothes (1985)
Director: Peter Medak

The Emperor's New Clothes (1987)
Director: David Irving

The Emperor's New Clothes (1991)
Director: Michael Sporn

The Emperor's New Clothes (*Cisarovy saty/Des Kaisers neue Kleider*, 1994)
Director: Juraj Herz

The Emperor's New Clothes (1995)
Director: Bruce Smith and Edward Bell

The Emperor's New Clothes (1997)
Director: Robert Van Nutt

The Emperor's New Clothes (2007)
Director: Tang-Minh Nguyen

The Little Match Girl

The Little Matchgirl (*La Petite Marchande d'Alumettes*, 1928)
Director: Jean Renoir

The Little Match Girl (1999)
Director: Michael Sporn

The Little Mermaid

Hans Christian Andersen's The Little Mermaid (1975)
Director: Tomoharu Katsumata and Tim Redi

The Little Mermaid (*Malá morská víla*, 1975)
Director: Karel Kachyna

The Little Mermaid (*Rusalochka*, 1976)
Director: Vladimir Bychkov

La Petite Sirène (*The Mermaid*, 1980)
Director: Roger Andrieux

The Little Mermaid (1984)
Director: Robert Iscove

The Little Mermaid (1989)
Director: Ron Clements and John Musker

The Little Mermaid (1992–1994)
Director: Jamie Mitchel

The Little Mermaid II: Return to the Sea (2000)
Director: Jim Kammerud and Brian Smith

The Little Mermaid III: Ariel's Beginning (2008)
Director: Peggy Holmes

The Nightingale

The Emperor's Nightingale (*Cirasuv Slavik*, 1948)
Director: Jirí Trnka, Jirí Brdecka (for the animation)
Director: Milos Makovec (live-action scenes)

The Nightingale (1983)
Director: Ivan Passer

Nightingale (1999)
Director: Michael Sporn

The Princess on the Pea

The Princess on the Pea (*Die Prinzessin auf der Erbse*, 1953)
Director: Alf Zengerling

The Princess and the Pea (1976)
Director: Boris Rytsarev

The Princess and the Pea (1983)
Director: Tony Bill

Once Upon a Mattress (2005)
Director: Kathleen Marshall

The Red Shoes

The Red Shoes (1948)
Director: Michael Powell and Emeric Pressburger

The Red Shoes (1983)
Director: John Clark Donahue and John Driver

The Red Shoes (1990)
Director: Michael Sporn

The Snow Queen

The Snow Queen (*Snezhnaya Koroleva*, 1957)
Director: Lev Atamanov

The Snow Queen (*Snezhnaya Koroleva*, 1966)
Director: Gennadi Kazansky

The Snow Queen (1976)
Director: Andrew Gosling

The Snow Queen (1985)
Director: Peter Medak

The Snow Queen (*Lumikuningatar*, 1986)
Director: Päivi Hartzell

The Snow Queen (1992)
Director: Marke Buchwald, Vadlen Barbe

The Snow Queen (1995)
Director: Martin Gates

The Snow Queen (*Snedonnigen*, 2000)
Director: Jacob Jørgensen and Kristof Kuncewicz

The Snow Queen (2002)
Director: David Wu

The Snow Queen (2005)
Director: Julian Gibbs

Snow Queen (*Snezhnaya Koroleva*, 2007)
Director: Yelena Raiskaya

The Ugly Duckling

Stanley the Ugly Duckling (1982)
Director: John Wilson

The Ugly Duckling and Me! (*Grimme ælling og mig*, 2006)
Directors: Michael Hegner and Karsten Kilerjen

Cannon Fairy-Tale Films

Beauty and the Beast (1986)
Director: Eugene Marner

Snow White (1987)
Director: Michael Berz

The Frog Prince (1987)
Director: Jackson Hunsicker

Puss in Boots (1987)
Director: Eugene Marner

Hansel and Gretel (1987)
Director: Len Talan

The Emperor's New Clothes (1987)
Director: David Irving

Red Riding Hood (1988)
Director: Adam Brooks

Czech Fairy-Tale Films

The Emperor's Nightingale (*Cirasuv Slavik*, 1948)
Director: Jirí Trnka, Jirí Brdecka (animation)
Director: Milos Makovec (live-action scenes)

The Proud Princess (*Pysná Princenza*, 1952)
Director: Borivoj Zeman

Once Upon a Time, There Was a King (*Byl jednou jeden král
. . .*, 1955)
Director: Borivoj Zeman

Stick, Start Beating (*Obusku z pytle ven!*, 1956)
Director: Jaromir Pleskot

The Incredibly Sad Princess (*Sílene Smutná Princezná*, 1968)
Director: Borivoj Zeman

Saxana—The Maiden on the Broomstick (*Dívka na kostéti*,
1971)
Director: Václav Vorlícek

Prince Bajaja (*Princ Bajaja*, 1971)
Director: Antonín Kachlík

Six Bears and a Clown (*Sest medvedue a cibulkou*, 1972)
Director: Oldrich Lipský

Three Wishes for Cinderella (*Tri Orísky Pro Popelku*, 1974)
Director: Václav Vorlicek

The Little Mermaid (*Malá morská víla*, 1976)
Director: Karel Kachyna

Waking Sleeping Beauty (*Jak se budi Princezny*, 1977)
Director: Václav Vorlícek

The Prince and the Evening Star (*Princ a Vecernice*, 1978)
Director: Václav Vorlícek

Arabela (1979)
Director: Václav Vorlícek

The Brave Blacksmith (*O Statecném Kovári*, 1983)
Director: Petr Svéda

Three Veterans (*Tri veterani*, 1983)
Director: Oldrich Lipský

King Thrushbeard (*Král Drozdia Brada*, 1984)
Director: Miloslova Luther

The Feather Fairy (*Perinbaba*, 1985)
Director: Ludvík Ráza

The False Prince (*Falosny princ*, 1985)
Director: Dusan Rapos

The Magic Galoshes (*Galose Stastia*, 1986)
Director: Juraj Herz

Mahuliena, Golden Maiden (*Mahuliena, zlatá panna*, 1986)
Director: Miloslav Luther

Big and Little Claus (*Der große und der kleine Klaus*, 1987)
Director: Dusan Trancík

The Princess and the Flying Shoemaker (1987)
Director: Zdenek Troska

The Water of Life (*Das Wasser des Lebens*, 1987)
Director: Ivan Balada

The Traveling Companion (*Vandronik/Der Reisekamerad*,
1990)
Director: Ludvík Ráza

The Frog Prince (*Zabí král*, 1991)
Director: Juraj Herz

The Dumb Augustine (*Die Dumme Augustine*, 1991)
Director: Juraj Herz

Arabela Returns (*Arabela se vraci*, 1993)
Director: Václav Vorlícek

The Emperor's New Clothes (*Císarovy nové Saty*, 1994)
Director: Juraj Herz

The Magic Book (*Das Zauberbuch/Kouzelný mesec*, 1996)
Director: Václav Vorlícek

The Firebird (*Ptak ohnivak/Der Feuervogel*, 1997)
Director: Václav Vorlícek

The Queen of the Lake (*Jezerní Královna/Die Seekönigin*,
1998)
Director: Václav Vorlícek

Tomas and the Falcon King (*Král sokulu/Tomas und der
Falkenkönig*, 2000)
Director: Václav Vorlícek

Little Otik (*Otes ek*, 2000)
Director: Jan Svankmajer

Faerie Tale Theatre

The Tale of the Frog Prince (1982)
Director: Eric Idle

Rumpelstiltskin (1982)
Director: Emil Ardolin

Rapunzel (1983)
Director: Gilbert Gates

The Nightingale (1983)
Director: Ivan Passer

Sleeping Beauty (1983)
Director: Jeremy Kagan

Jack and the Beanstalk (1983)
Director: Lamont Johnson

Little Red Riding Hood (1983)
Director: Graeme Clifford

Hansel and Gretel (1983)
Director: James Frawley

Goldilocks and the Three Bears (1984)
Director: Gilbert Cates

The Princess and the Pea (1983)
Director: Tony Bill

Pinocchio (1984)
Director: Peter Medak

Thumbelina (1984)
Director: Michael Lindsay-Hogg

Snow White and the Seven Dwarfs (1984)
Director: Peter Medak

Beauty and the Beast (1984)
Director: Roger Vadim

The Boy Who Left Home to Find Out About the Shivers (1984)
Director: Graeme Clifford

The Three Little Pigs (1985)
Director: Howard Storm

The Snow Queen (1985)
Director: Peter Medak

The Pied Piper of Hamelin (1985)
Director: Nicholas Meyer

Cinderella (1985)
Director: Mark Cullingham

Puss in Boots (1985)
Director: Robert Iscove

The Emperor's New Clothes (1985)
Director: Peter Medak

Aladdin and His Wonderful Lamp (1986)
Director: Tim Burton

The Princess Who Had Never Laughed (1986)
Director: Mark Cullingham

Rip Van Winkle (1987)
Director: Francis Ford Coppola

The Little Mermaid (1984)
Director: Robert Iscove

The Dancing Princesses (1987)
Director: Peter Medak

German Films

Post-1945 Films

East Germany—DEFA Fairy-Tale Films

The Cold Heart (*Das kalte Herz*, 1950)
Director: Paul Verhoeven

The Story of Little Mook (*Die Geschichte vom kleinen Muck*, 1953)
Director: Wolfgang Staudte

The Devil from Mill Mountain (*Der Teufel vom Mühlenberg*, 1955)
Director: Herbert Ballmann

The Brave Little Tailor (*Das tapfere Schneiderlein*, 1956)
Director: Helmut Spieß

The Singing, Ringing Tree (*Das singende, klingende Bäumchen*, 1957)
Director: Francesco Stefani

The Story of Poor Hassan (*Die Geschichte vom armen Hassan*, 1958)
Director: Gerhard Klein

The Tinderbox (*Das Feuerzeug*, 1959)
Director: Siegfried Hartmann

Little Red Riding Hood (*Rotkäppchen*, 1959)
Director: Götz Friedrich

Rumpelstiltskin (*Das Zauber-Männchen*, 1960)
Director: Christoph Engel

Cinderella (*Aschenbrödl*, 1960)
Director: Erika Just

The Golden Tent (*Die goldene Jurte*, 1961)
Director: Gottfried Kolditz, Rabschaa Dordschpalam

Snow White (*Schneewittchen*, 1961)
Director: Gottfried Kolditz

Mother Holle (*Frau Holle*, 1963)
Director: Gottfried Kolditz

The Golden Goose (*Die goldene Gans*, 1964)
Director: Siegfried Hartmann

King Thrushbeard (*König Drosselbart*, 1965)
Director: Walter Beck

How to Marry a King (*Wie heiratet man einen König*, 1969)
Director: Rainer Simon

Sleeping Beauty (*Dornröschen*, 1971)
Director: Walter Beck

Six Make their Way through the World (*Sechse kommen durch die Welt*, 1972)
Director: Rainer Simon

Hans Roeckle and the Devil (*Hans Röckle und der Teufel*, 1974)
Director: Hans Kratzert

The Blue Light (*Das blaue Licht*, 1976)
Director: Iris Gusner

Who's Afraid of the Devil? (*Wer reisst denn gleich vor'm Teufel aus*, 1977)
Director: Egon Schlegel

Snow White and Rose Red (*Schneewittchen und Rosenrot*, 1979)
Director: Siegfried Hartmann

Gritta von Rattenhaus (*Gritta von Rattenzuhausebeiuns*, 1985)
Director: Jürgen Brauer

Bearskin (*Der Bärenhäuter*, 1986)
Director: Walter Beck

The Frog Prince (*Froschkönig*, 1988)
Director: Walter Beck

Iron Jack (*Eisenhans*, 1988)
Director: Karl Heinz Lotz

The Story of the Goose Princess and her Faithful Horse Falada (*Die Geschichte von der Gänseprincessin und ihrem treuen Pferd Falada*, 1989)
Director: Konrad Petzold

West Germany

Hans Makes His Fortune (*Hans macht sein Glück*, 1936/1952)
Director: Robert Herlth, Walter Röhrig

The Princess on the Pea (*Die Prinzessin auf der Erbse*, 1953)
Director: Alf Zengerling

The Princess and the Swineherd (*Die Prinzessin und der Schweinehirt*, 1953)
Director: Herbert B. Fredersdorf

Hansel and Gretel (*Hänsel und Gretel*, 1954)
Director: Fritz Genschow

Mother Holly (*Frau Holle*, 1954)
Director: Fritz Genschow

Cinderella (*Aschenputtel*, 1955)
Director: Fritz Genschow

Rumpelstiltskin (*Rumpelstilzchen*, 1955)
Director: Herbert B. Fredersdorf

Sleeping Beauty (*Dornröschen*, 1955)
Director: Fritz Genschow

Table Be Covered (*Tischlein deck dich*, 1956)
Director: Fritz Genschow

Rübezahl (1957)
Director: Erich Kobler

The Goose Girl (*Die Gänsemagd*, 1957)
Director: Fritz Genschow

Mischief in Wonderland (*Aufruhr im Schlaraffendland*, 1957)
Director: Otto Meyer

The Wolf and the Seven Kids (*Der Wolf und die sieben jungen Geisslein*, 1957)
Director: Peter Podehl

Mother Holly (*Frau Holle*, 1961)
Peter Podehl

The Golden Goose (*Die goldene Gans*, 1964)
Director: Siegfried Harmann

Cinderella (*Aschenputtel*, 1989)
Director: Karen Brandauer

Jim Henson The Storyteller

The Soldier Death (1988)
Director: Jim Henson

Fearnot (1988)
Director: Steve Barron

The Luck Child (1988)
Director: Jon Amiel

A Story (1988)
Director: Charles Sturridge

Hans My Hedgehog (1988)
Director: Steve Barron

The Three Ravens (1988)
Director: Paul Weiland

Sapsorrow (1988)
Director: Steve Barron

The Heartless Giant (1988)
Director: Jim Henson

The True Bride (1988)
Director Peter Smith

Russian Fairy-Tale Films

Vassalisa the Beautiful (1939)
Director: Alexander Rou

The Stone Flower (*Kamennyy tsvetok*, 1946)
Director: Alexandr Ptushko

Cinderella (*Zolushka*, 1947)
Director: Nadezhda Koshevrova, Mikhail Shapiro

Sadko (1952)
Director: Alexandr Ptuschko

Puss in Boots (*Novyje Pochoshdenija Kota Sapogach*, 1957)
Director: Alexander Rou

Kingdom of the Crooked Mirrors (*Korolevstvo krivykh zerkal*, 1963)
Director: Alexander Rou

Father Frost (*Morozko*, 1964)
Director: Alexander Rou

The Tale of Time Lost (*Skaska o poterjannom wremeni*, 1964)
Director: Alexandr Ptushko

Aladdin's Magic Lamp (*Volschebnaja lampa Aladdina*, 1966)
Director: Boris Ryzarjev

Viy or Spirit of Evil (*Buǐ*, 1967)
Director: Konstantin Yershov, Georgy Kropachyov

The Czar Saltan and the Wonder Island (*Skaska o Zare Saltane*, 1968)
Director: Ivan Ivanov-Vano, Lev Miltschin

Through Fire, Water and Brass Pipes (*Ogon, voda i . . . mednye truby*, 1968)
Director: Alexander Rou

Barbara the Fair with the Silken Hair (*Varvara-krasa, dlinnaya kosa*, 1969)
Director: Alexander Rou

The Snow Maiden (*Snegurochka*, 1969)
Director: Pavel Kadochnikov

Warwara the Beautiful (*Warwara—krasa dlinnaja kosa*, 1970)
Director: Alexander Rou

The Secret of the Iron Door (*Tayna zheleznoy dveri*, 1970)
Director: Mikhail Yuzovsky

The Golden Horns (*Zolotye roga*, 1972)
Director: Alexander Rou

Finist, the Bright Falcon (*Finist, jasni sokol*, 1975)
Director: Gennady Vassiliev

The Humpbacked Little Horse (*Konjok Gorbunok*, 1975)
Director: Ivan Ivanov-Vano

The Little Mermaid (*Rusalochka*, 1976)
Director: Vladimir Bychkov

The Princess on the Pea (*Printsessa na goroshine*, 1976)
Director: Boris Rytsarev

The Little Mermaid (*Rusalochka*, 1976)
Director: Vladimir Bychkov

How Ivanushka the Fool Traveled in Search of Wonder (*Kak Ivanushka-durachok za chudom khodil*, 1976)
Director: Nadeschda Koscheverova

The Scarlet Flower (*Alenki zwetotschek*, 1978)
Director: Irina Povolotskaya

The Rider on the Golden Horse (*Vsadnik nasolotom konje*, 1980)
Director: Vasili Zhuravlyov

The Donkey's Hide (*Oslinaja Schkura*, 1982), also known as *The Princess with the Donkey Skin*
Director: Nadezhda Kosheverova

The Story of the Voyages (*Skaska stranstvij*, 1982)
Director: Alexander Mitta

Index

Note 1: only films that receive ample discussion are included in the index. A comprehensive list of films mentioned throughout the book can be found in the Filmography on pages 388–425.

Note 2: *italic* page numbers denote references to figures.

eBooks – at www.eBookstore.tandf.co.uk

A library at your fingertips!

eBooks are electronic versions of printed books. You can store them on your PC/laptop or browse them online.

They have advantages for anyone needing rapid access to a wide variety of published, copyright information.

eBooks can help your research by enabling you to bookmark chapters, annotate text and use instant searches to find specific words or phrases. Several eBook files would fit on even a small laptop or PDA.

NEW: Save money by eSubscribing: cheap, online access to any eBook for as long as you need it.

Annual subscription packages

We now offer special low-cost bulk subscriptions to packages of eBooks in certain subject areas. These are available to libraries or to individuals.

For more information please contact webmaster.ebooks@tandf.co.uk

We're continually developing the eBook concept, so keep up to date by visiting the website.

www.eBookstore.tandf.co.uk